10651343

READER'S DIGEST

FAMILY TREASURY OF GREAT BIOGRAPHIES

Reader's Digest

FAMILY TREASURY OF GREAT BIOGRAPHIES

selected and condensed by the editors of The Reader's Digest

VOLUME III

The Reader's Digest Association
Pleasantville, New York

920.02
R286
v.3

The condensations in this volume have been created
by The Reader's Digest Association, Inc.

Life of Christ,
copyright 1923 by Harcourt, Brace & World, Inc.,
copyright 1951 by Dorothy Canfield Fisher,
is published in the United States by Harcourt, Brace & World, Inc.

The Needle's Eye
is a condensation of part of *The Thread That Runs So True,*
copyright 1949 by Jesse Stuart, and published in the United States
by Charles Scribner's Sons.

The House of Exile,
copyright 1933 by Little, Brown & Co., Inc.,
© 1961 by Nora Waln, is an Atlantic Monthly Press book
published in the United States in association with Little, Brown & Co.
and in Great Britain by the Cresset Press.

Good Night, Sweet Prince,
copyright 1943, 1944 by Gene Fowler,
is published in the United States by The Viking Press, Inc.,
and in Great Britain by Hammond, Hammond & Co., Ltd.

Queen Victoria,
copyright 1921 by Harcourt, Brace & World, Inc.,
copyright 1949 by James Strachey,
is published in the United States by Harcourt, Brace & World, Inc.

© 1970 by The Reader's Digest Association, Inc.
© 1970 by The Reader's Digest Association (Canada) Ltd.

FIRST EDITION

All rights reserved, including the right to
reproduce this book or parts thereof in any form.

Library of Congress Catalog Card Number: 76–86526
Printed in the United States of America

Contents

076804

METHODIST COLLEGE LIBRARY
Fayetteville, N. C.

A CONDENSATION OF

LIFE OF CHRIST

by

GIOVANNI PAPINI

TRANSLATED FROM THE ITALIAN BY

DOROTHY CANFIELD FISHER

When this life of Jesus Christ was published in the United States
a Protestant minister wrote in *The Living Church*, a magazine
of the Episcopal Church, "It is vivid, powerful, close to the earth,
and so fascinatingly interesting . . . that it surpasses most
of the jaded thrillers of melodramatic literature."

Although Giovanni Papini was one of the foremost Italian men
of letters, the publication of this book in 1921 came as a stunning
surprise to many of his friends and admirers. For Papini had
been an atheist, a vocal enemy of the Church and a self-appointed
debunker of any form of mysticism. A more unlikely source
for a reverent portrait of Jesus could hardly be imagined.

What brought about his sudden conversion—so reminiscent
of Saul's on the road to Damascus? Like many cynics he was,
under the surface, a tormented soul, disgusted with a humanity
that could accept the first World War, unable to see hope for
better things unless, somehow, the hearts of men could be changed.
And he craved, as he later said, "a crumb of certitude."

During that war he took his family to live in a mountain
village. There, living with the peasants, observing their devotions,
something began to happen to him. Sometimes, in the evenings,
he was asked to read aloud stories from the New Testament.
This rediscovery of the Bible, against the background of his own
uncertainties, became a revelation to him, and soon he determined
to write his own version of the life of Christ. Before long he
became convinced that the only power that could change the
hearts of men was the teachings of Jesus.

This conviction pervades the *Life of Christ*, a book which,
in the words of a distinguished critic, "will stand for many years
as a rallying sign for thousands making their way painfully
to a less inhuman, because a more Christlike, world."

INTRODUCTION

FOR FIVE HUNDRED YEARS those who call themselves free spirits have been trying desperately to kill Jesus a second time—to kill Him in the hearts of men.

Jesus, some have said, was a myth developed in the time of Augustus and of Tiberius, and all the Gospels can be reduced to a clumsy mosaic of prophetic texts. Others conceived of Jesus as a good, well-meaning man, but too high-flown and fantastic, who went to school to the Greeks, the Buddhists, and the Essenes and patched together His plagiarisms as best He could to support His claim to be the Messiah of Israel. Others made Him out to be an unbalanced humanitarian, precursor of Rousseau and of divine democracy; an excellent man for his time but who today would be put under the care of an alienist.

But who could have taken the place of the man they were trying to dispose of? The grave they dug was deeper every day, and still they could not bury Him from sight. On the walls of the churches and schools, on the tops of bell towers and mountains, in street shrines, at the heads of beds and over tombs, thousands of crosses recall the death of the Crucified One. Take away the frescoes from the churches, carry off the pictures from the altars and from the houses, and the life of Christ fills museums and picture galleries. You find His name and His words in all the books of literature. Even oaths are an involuntary remembrance of His presence.

Christ is an abyss of divine mystery between two divisions of human history. Our civilization begins with the birth of Christ. What comes before Christ no longer moves our passions; it may be beautiful, but it is dead. Caesar was more talked about in his time than Jesus, and Plato taught more science than Christ; but who nowadays is hotly for Caesar or against him, and where now are the Platonists and the anti-Platonists?

Christ, on the contrary, is still living among us. There is a passion for the love of Christ and a passion for His destruction.

We live in the Christian era, and it is not yet finished. If we are to understand the world, our life, ourselves, we must refer to Christ. No life of Christ could be more beautiful and perfect than the Gospels. But who reads the Gospels nowadays?

Every generation has its preoccupations and its thoughts, and its own insanities. The old Gospels must be retranslated if Christ is to remain alive in the life of men.

The world is full of such bookish resuscitations of Christ, learned or literary. But which of them seeks, instead of learned discussions, to give food fit for the soul, for the needs of men of our time? The book we need is a living book to set Christ the Ever Living with loving vividness before the eyes of living men, to make us feel Him as actually and eternally present in our lives. The author of this book does not pretend to have written such a book; but at least he has tried to draw near to that ideal.

This book is not a "scientific history." It is based on the Gospels; on "the Logia and the Agrapha," which seemed to have the most evangelical flavor; on some apocryphal texts used with judgment; and finally, on nine or ten modern books. The author has approached Jesus with the simple-heartedness of longing and of love, just as during His lifetime He was approached by the fishermen of Capernaum.

THE BIRTH OF CHRIST

JESUS WAS BORN in a stable, a real stable, not the modern Christmas Eve "Holy Stable," made of plaster of paris, with little candylike statuettes, prettily painted, with a neat, tidy manger, an ecstatic ass, a contrite ox, and angels fluttering their wreaths on the roof.

A real stable is the prison of the animals who work for man. The poor, old stable of Christ's old, poor country is only four rough walls, a dirty pavement, a roof of beams and slate. It is dark, reeking. The only clean thing in it is the manger where the owner piles the hay and fodder.

Fresh in the clear morning, waving in the wind, sunny, lush, sweet-scented, the spring meadow was mown. The green grass, the long, slim blades were cut down by the scythe; and with the grass the beautiful flowers in full bloom—white, red, yellow, blue. They withered and dried and took on the one dull color of hay. Oxen dragged back to the barn the dead plunder of May and June. And now that grass has become dry hay and those flowers, still smelling sweet, are there in the manger. The animals take it slowly with their great black lips, and later the flowering fields, changed into moist dung, return to light on the litter which serves as bedding.

This is the real stable where Jesus was born. The Son of man had as His cradle the manger where the animals chewed the cud of the miraculous flowers of spring. There Jesus appeared one night, born of a stainless Virgin armed only with innocence.

First to worship Jesus were animals, not men. Among men He sought out the simplehearted; and among the simplehearted He sought out children. Simpler than children, and milder, the beasts of burden welcomed Him.

Up to that time the kings of the earth and the populace craving material things had bowed before oxen and asses. Christ's own people, the chosen people whom Jehovah had freed from Egyptian slavery, when their leader left them alone in the desert to go up and talk with the Eternal, did they not force Aaron to make them a golden calf to worship? In Greece the ass was sacred to Ares, to Dionysius, to Hyperborean Apollo.

But Jesus was to bring to an end the bowing down before beasts. In the meantime the beasts of Bethlehem warm Him with their breath.

After the animals came those who care for animals. Shepherds live almost always alone and far away. They are moved by whatever happens near to them. Even if the Angel had not announced the great birth, they would have gone to the stable to see the son of the stranger woman.

But as they were watching their flocks in the long winter night, they were shaken by the light and by the words of the Angel. "Fear not, for behold, I bring you good tidings of great joy. . . . Glory to God in the highest, and on earth peace to men of good will." In the dim light of the stable they saw a beautiful young woman gazing silently at her son. And they saw the baby with His eyes just open, His delicate rosy flesh, His mouth which had not yet eaten. For the shepherds forewarned, this newborn child was not just a baby, but He for whom their suffering race had been waiting for a thousand years.

The shepherds offered what little they had, that little which is so great when offered with love. They carried the white offerings of their craft, milk, cheese, wool, the lamb. Even today in our mountains, where one finds the last dying traces of hospitality and fraternal feeling, as soon as a wife is delivered of a

child, the sisters, wives and daughters of the shepherds come hurrying to her; and not one of them empty-handed. One has three or four eggs still warm from the nest, another a cup of freshly drawn milk, another a little cheese, another a pullet to make broth for the new mother.

Themselves poor, the old-time shepherds did not look down on the poor. Their first kings had been shepherds—Saul and David—shepherds of herds before being shepherds of tribes. These shepherds of Bethlehem knew that this boy, born of poor people in poverty, was to be the redeemer of the humble, of those men of good will, on whom the Angel had called down peace.

Some days after this, three wise men came and knelt before Jesus. They came perhaps from Chaldea, perhaps from the shores of the Caspian Sea. Mounted on their camels with their full-stuffed saddlebags, they had forded the Tigris and the Euphrates, crossed the great desert of the nomad tribes, followed along the Dead Sea. They were guided to Judea by a new star like the comet which appears every so often in the sky to announce the birth of a prophet or the death of a Caesar. They had come to adore a king.

The wise men found no king; they found a nursing baby, poorly swaddled, hidden within a stable, a tiny boy who could neither ask nor answer questions.

They were not kings, these wise men; but in Media and Persia the wise men directed the kings. They alone could communicate with Alma Mazda, the good God. They alone knew the future. Except from their hands God accepted no sacrifices. No king began a war without consulting them. In the midst of a people sunk in material things they represented the spirit.

After the animals which are nature, after the shepherds which are the common people, this third power which is knowledge knelt at the manger in Bethlehem. The old priestly caste of the Orient made its act of submission, the learned men knelt before Him who was to set above the learning of words and numbers the new wisdom of love.

Scarcely had the wise men gone when persecutions were begun by those who were to hate Him to the day of His death.

WHEN CHRIST APPEARED upon the earth, He was born subject to two sovereigns. One lucky adventurer after wholesale slaughter had seized the Roman empire, another had murdered his way to the throne of David and Solomon in Judea. They were, as a matter of fact, friends and accomplices.

Son of the usurer of Velletri, Octavius Augustus showed himself cowardly in war, vindictive in victory, false to his friends, cruel in reprisals. To a condemned man who begged only for burial he answered, "That is the business of the vultures." To the Perugians begging for mercy during the massacre he cried, *"Moriendum esse!"* [To die!] Now, possessed of the empire, with his enemies crushed and scattered, he put on a mask of mildness and of his youthful vices kept only his lust. He amused himself with the wives of his friends, and with posing as the restorer of morality.

This man, sovereign of the western world when Jesus was born, never knew that One had been born who would bring the dissolution of the empire he had founded. The philosophy of Horace was enough for him, "Today let us enjoy wine and love: hopeless death awaits us: there is not a day to be lost!"

But his vassal of Judea may have had a presentiment of the birth of Jesus, of the true King.

Herod was not a Jew, nor a Greek, nor a Roman. He was an Idumaean, a barbarian who prostrated himself before Rome and aped the Greeks, the better to secure his dominion over the Jews. Son of a traitor, he had usurped the kingdom of his sovereign from the last unfortunate Hasmonaeans. To legalize his treachery he married their niece. Afterwards, he had her killed. Her mother, her brothers (last of the conquered dynasty), even the sons he had had by her, were also put to death.

Voluptuous, impious, greedy of gold and of glory, Herod humiliated himself before Augustus to make him the accomplice of his infamies and, meanwhile, attempted to conciliate the Greeks and the Jews. In Athens they put up a statue to him, but to the Jews he was always the heathen and the usurper. It did him no good, in their eyes, to build up Samaria and restore the Temple of Jerusalem.

Apprehensive like all aging evildoers, and credulous of soothsayers, he readily believed the three wise men when they said that, led by a star, they had come from the interior of Chaldea, and when he knew from the wise men that a King of Judea was born, his uneasy barbarian's heart gave a great leap of fear. Seeing that the astrologers did not come back to tell him the place where the new nephew of David had appeared, he ordered that all the boy babies of Bethlehem should be killed.

Nobody ever knew how many children were sacrificed to the terror of Herod, but if we can believe Macrobius we know that among them was a little son of Herod who was at nurse in Bethlehem. For the old king, wife killer and son killer, who knows but that he suffered when they brought him news of the mistake? A short time after this, suffering from loathsome disease, burnt up with fevers, gasping, disgusting to himself, he tried to kill himself with a knife at table, and finally died.

A CHRISTIAN POET, an Italian, sang this lullaby to the newborn Jesus:

> *"Sleep, baby, do not weep,*
> *Sleep, heavenly babe. . . .*
> *Over your head, the tempests shall not dare to rage!"*

But how can the Son of Mary sleep when the shuffling steps of Herod's assassins draw near?

And Mary cannot sleep. In the evening as soon as the houses of Bethlehem disappear in the darkness and the first lamps are lighted, the mother steals away like a fugitive. She is snatching a life away from the king as she presses upon her breast her man-child, her hope, her sorrow.

She goes toward the west, she crosses the old land of Canaan and comes by easy stages—the days are short—to the Nile, to that country which had cost so many tears to her ancestors fourteen centuries before.

The people of Jesus left Chaldea with Abraham and came with Joseph into Egypt. When the Jews were under the whip of the Egyptian slaves, Moses, the Shepherd of Median, made himself the Shepherd of Israel, and led his people across the desert till they were in sight of the Jordan and of the miraculous vineyards. Jesus, who carried on the work of Moses and at the same time demolished the work of Moses, now in danger of his life, went back to the banks of that river where the first Saviour had been saved from the water and had saved his brothers.

Death was the obsession of Egypt. The rich, portly Egyptian, adorer of the sacred bull and the dogheaded god, would not accept death. He manufactured for his second life immense necropolises full of bandaged and perfumed mummies, of images of wood and marble, and raised up pyramids over his corpses, as if stone and mortar might save them from decay.

When Jesus could speak, He was to pronounce the verdict against Egypt with its kings, its sparrow hawks, its serpents, and its wealth which came from the rich snake-breeding mud that the Nile rolled out each year upon the desert. Christ was to condemn the wealth which comes from mud and returns to mud, and He was to conquer death by teaching that sin is greedier than worms and that spiritual purity is the only aromatic which preserves from decay.

BUT THE EXILE in Egypt was short. Jesus was brought back, held in His mother's arms, rocked throughout the long journey by the patient step of the ass, to His father Joseph's humble house and shop in Nazareth, where the hammer pounded and the rasp scraped until the setting of the sun.

The canonical gospels say nothing of these years: the Apocrypha give many details but are unworthy of belief. Luke, the wise doctor, is content to set down that the boy grew and was strong. He was healthy, a bearer of health, as was fitting in one who was to restore health to others by the touch of His hand.

Every year, says Luke, the parents of Jesus went to Jerusalem for the feast of unleavened bread in memory of the escape from Egypt. They went with a crowd of neighbors, friends, and acquaintances: for the Passover had become at Jerusalem a great feast day, when all the Jews scattered about the empire came together.

On the twelfth Passover after the birth of Jesus, as the group from Nazareth was returning from the holy city, Mary found that her son was not with them. All day long she sought for

Him, asking every acquaintance, but in vain. The next morning the mother turned back, retraced her steps over the road and went up and down the streets and open places of Jerusalem, fixing her dark eyes on every boy she met, asking the mothers standing in the open doors, begging her countrymen not yet gone, to help her find her lost son. A mother who has lost her son does not rest until she has found him; she thinks no more of herself, she does not feel weariness, effort, hunger. She does not shake the dust from her clothes nor arrange her hair. Her distracted eyes see nothing but the image of him who is no longer beside her.

Finally on the third day she came to the Temple, looked about in the courts, and saw at last in the shadow of a portico a group of old men talking. She came up timidly, for those men with long cloaks and long beards seemed people of importance, who would pay no attention to a plain woman from Galilee, and discovered in the center of the circle the shining eyes, the tanned face of her Jesus. Those old men were talking with her son of the Law and the Prophets. They were asking Him questions and He was answering; He put questions to them in His turn and they marveled at Him, astonished that a boy should know the words of the Lord so well. But His memory had retained every syllable of the books which He had heard read out in the little synagogue of Nazareth.

Mary remained for a few moments gazing at Him, hardly believing her eyes. But she could not restrain herself anymore and suddenly in a loud voice called Him by name. The old men took themselves off and the mother snatched her son to her breast and clasped Him to her, the tears which she had kept back till then raining down.

"Son, why hast thou thus dealt with us? behold, thy father and I have sought thee sorrowing."

"How is it that ye sought me? wist ye not that I must be about my Father's business?"

Weighty words when said by a twelve-year-old boy to a mother who had sought Him for three long days.

The Evangelist goes on, "And they understood not the saying which he spake unto them." But after so many centuries of

Christian experience we can understand those words, which seemed at first sight to be hard and proud.

"Who is this father of whom you speak to me? He is the human father. But my real Father is in heaven. If I am to do what He has commanded me, I must be busy about what is truly His. What is a temporal tie confronted with a mystic, spiritual and eternal bond?"

But the hour for really leaving His home had not come for Jesus. The voice of John the Baptist, last of the Prophets, had not yet been heard. With His father and mother Jesus once more went along the road to Nazareth and returned to Joseph's shop to help him in his trade.

Jesus did not go to school to the scribes nor to the Greeks. But He did not lack for teachers. He had three teachers greater than all the learned: work, nature and the Book.

It must never be forgotten that Jesus was born poor, among people who worked with their hands. The adopted son of a workingman, before He gave out His gospel, He earned His daily bread. Those hands which blessed the simplehearted, which cured the lepers, which gave light to the blind, which brought the dead to life, those hands which were pierced with nails upon the cross, were hands which had known the numbness of work, hands which were calloused with work, hands which had held tools, the hands of a workingman.

Jesus, descendant of kings, lived in a woodworker's shop: Son of God, He was born in a stable. He did not belong to the caste of the aristocracy of warriors, to the Sanhedrin of the priests. When He became no longer a manual worker, He went down lower yet in the eyes of respectable folk, and sought His friends in that miserable huddle which is even below the common people: the vagabonds, the beggars, the fugitives, the slaves, the criminals, the prostitutes.

Jesus' trade is one of the four oldest and most sacred of man's occupations. The peasant breaks the clod and takes from it the bread eaten by the saint in his grotto and the murderer in his prison; the mason squares the stone and builds up the house of the poor man, the house of the king, the house of God. The smith heats and fashions the iron to give a sword to the soldier, a plowshare to the peasant, a hammer to the carpenter. Jesus, the carpenter, made the table around which it is so sweet to sit in the evening with one's friends, the chest where the country wife keeps her handkerchiefs for festivals and the starched white shirts for great days. He made the kneading trough where the flour is put, and the leaven raises it until it is ready for the oven.

While the thin, light shavings curled up under His plane and the sawdust rained down on the ground, Jesus thought of the prophecies of old time, of what He was to create, not with boards and rules, but with spirit and truth. His trade taught Him that just as a child's crib or a wife's bed can be made out of a log of olive wood, gnarled, knotty and earthy, so the money changer and the prostitute can be transformed into true citizens of the Kingdom of Heaven.

IN NATURE, where wheat ripens and grows golden to give bread to Jew and heathen, where the stars shine on the shepherd's cabin and the murderer's prison; where grape clusters turn purple and swell to give wine to the wedding banquet; where the birds of the air freely singing find their food without fatigue, where thieving foxes have their refuge and the lilies of the field are clad in more splendor than kings, Jesus found the earthly confirmation of His eternal certainty that God is not a Master who punishes one day of enjoyment by a thousand years of reproach, nor a fierce warlike Jehovah who commands the extermination of enemies, nor a kind of grand sultan who delights in being served by satraps of high lineage.

As a Son, Christ knew that God is Father of all mankind and not only of the people of Abraham. This idea of God as Father, which is one of the great new ideas of the gospel of Christ, this profoundly renovating idea that God loves us as a father loves his children, and gives daily bread to all his children and has a loving welcome even for those who sin if only they return to lean their heads upon his breast: this idea Jesus found in nature. Sharing all human experience He was to use the most beautiful images of the natural world to transmit to men the first of His joyful messages.

Jesus, like all great souls, loved the country. His talk blossoms with colors, is perfumed by odors of field and of orchard, is peopled by the figures of familiar animals. He saw in His Galilee the figs swelling and ripening under the great, dark leaves: He saw the dry tendrils of the vine greened over with leaves: and from the trellises the white and purple clusters hanging down for the joy of the vintage; He saw from the invisible seed, the mustard raise itself up with its rich light branches, He heard in the night the mournful rustle of the reeds shaken by the wind along the ditches: He saw the seed of grain buried in the earth and its resurrection in the form of a full ear; when the air first began to be warm, He saw the beautiful red, yellow and purple lilies in the midst of the tender green of the wheat: He saw the fresh tufts of grass, luxuriant today and tomorrow dried and cast into the oven; He saw the peaceful animals and the harmful animals, the dove a little vain of its brilliant neck, cooing of love on the roof, the eagle swooping down with widespread wings upon its prey; the swallows of the air; the crows tearing flesh from carrion with their beaks; the loving mother hen calling the chickens under her wings when the sky darkens and thunders; the fox slinking back into its lair; and the dogs under the table of their masters begging for scraps that fall to the ground. He saw the serpent writhing through the grass and the viper hiding among the scattered stones of the tombs.

Born among the shepherds, He who was to become shepherd of men knew and loved the flocks; the ewes searching for the lost lamb, the lambs bleating weakly, and sucking, almost hidden under their mothers' woolly bodies, the flocks sweltering on the thin hot pastures of their hills; He loved with equal love the ancient fig tree, casting its shade over the poor man's house; the fish silvering the meshes of the nets to feed His faithful; and raising His eyes in the sultry evenings, He saw the lightning flashing out of the east and shattering the darkness of the night.

But Jesus did not read only in the many-colored book of the world. Jesus read the books where His ancestors had set down the story of His people, the will of the Lord, the vision of the Prophets. He knew that God spoke to men through angels, patriarchs and prophets, and His words, His laws, His victories are written in the Book.

THE OLD COVENANT

AMONG ALL PEOPLES the Jew was the most happy and the most unhappy. His story is a mystery which begins with the idyl in the Garden of Eden. His first parents were molded by the luminous hands of God, were made masters of Paradise, the country of eternal, fertile summer, set in the midst of rivers, where the rich Oriental fruits hung down ready to their hand, heavy with pulp in the shade of the new young leaves. The new-created sky watched over the first two with all its stars.

The first couple had as their duty to love God and to love each other. This was the First Covenant. Weariness unknown, grief unknown, unknown death and its terror! The first disobedience brought the first exile; the man was condemned to work, the woman to bring forth her young in pain. Work is painful, but it brings the reward of harvests; to give birth means suffering, but it brings the consolation of children. And yet even these inferior and imperfect felicities passed away. For the first time brother killed brother: human blood gave forth an exhalation of sin: from the daughters of men were born fierce hunters and slayers of men, who turned the world into a bloody hell.

Then God sent His second punishment: to purify the world He drowned in the waters of the flood all men and their crimes. One only, a righteous man, was saved and with him God signed the Second Covenant.

With Noah there began the happy days of antiquity, the epoch of the patriarchs, nomad shepherds, centenarians who wandered between Chaldea and Egypt searching for grazing lands, for wells, and for peace. They brought along in caravans, numerous as armies, their fruitful wives, their loving sons, their docile daughters-in-law, their innumerable descendants, obedient manservants and maidservants, goring, bellowing bulls, cows with hanging udders, playful calves, rams and strong-smelling he-goats, mild sheep laden with wool, great earth-colored camels, mares with round cruppers, she-goats holding their heads high and stamping impatiently; and hidden in the saddlebags, vases of gold and silver, domestic idols of stone and metal.

Arrived at their destination, they spread their tents near a cistern, and the patriarch sat out under the shade of the oaks and sycamores contemplating the great camp from which rose up the smoke of the fires, the bustling of the herdsmen, the moo-ings, the brayings, the bleating of the animals. And the patri-arch's heart was filled with content to see all this progeny issued from his seed, all these, his herds, the human increase and the animal increase multiplying year by year.

In the evening, he raised his eyes to greet the first punctual star which shone like white fire on the summit of the hill; and sometimes his curled white beard shone in the white light of the moon, which for more than a century he was wont to see in the sky at night.

Sometimes an angel of the Lord came to visit him, and before giving the message with which he was charged, ate at his table. Or, in the heat of the day, the Lord Himself, in the garb of a pilgrim, came and sat down with the old man in the shadow of the tent where they talked with each other, face-to-face, like two old friends who come together to discuss their affairs. And between Jehovah and Abraham was signed the Third Covenant, more solemn than the other two.

The son of a patriarch, sold by his brothers as a slave, rises to power in Egypt, and calls his race to him. The Jews think that they have found a fatherland and grow great in numbers and riches. But they allow themselves to be seduced by the gods of Egypt, and Jehovah prepares the third punishment. The envi-ous Egyptians reduce them to abject slavery. That the punish-ment may be longer, Jehovah hardens the heart of Pharaoh, but finally raises up the second Saviour, who leads them forth from their sufferings and from the mud of Egypt.

Their trials are not yet finished: for forty years they wander in the desert. A pillar of cloud guides them by day and a pillar of fire by night. God has assured them a Land of Promise, with rich grazing lands, well watered, shaded by grapevines and olives. But in the meantime they have neither water to drink nor bread to eat, and they yearn for the fleshpots of Egypt. God brings water gushing from a rock; and manna and quails fall from heaven; but tired and uneasy, the Jews betray their God, make a calf of gold and worship it.

Moses, saddened like all prophets, misunderstood like all saviours, followed unwillingly like all discoverers of new lands, falls back of the restive and rebellious crowd and begs God to let him lie down forever. But at any cost, Jehovah desires to sign the Fourth Covenant with His people. Moses goes down from the smoke-capped thundering mountain, with the two tables of stone whereon the very finger of God has written the Ten Commandments.

Moses is not to see the Promised Land, but the divine pledge is kept: Joshua and the other heroes cross the Jordan, enter into the land of Canaan, and conquer the people; the cities fall at the breath of their trumpets; Deborah can sing her song of triumph. The people carry with them the God of battles, hidden behind the tents, on a cart drawn by oxen. But the enemies are numerous and have no mind to give way to the newcomers. The Jews wander here and there, shepherds and brigands, victorious when they maintain the covenants of the Law, defeated when they forget them.

A giant with unshorn hair kills, single-handed, thousands of Philistines and Amalekites, but a woman betrays him; enemies blind him and set him to turn a mill. Heroes alone are not enough. Kings are needed. A young man of the tribe of Benjamin, tall and well-grown, while looking for his father's strayed asses, is met by a Prophet who anoints him with the sacred oil, and makes him king of all the people. Saul becomes a powerful warrior, overcomes the Ammonites and Amalekites and founds a military kingdom, dreaded by neighboring tribes. But the same Prophet who made him king, now aroused against him, raises up a rival. David, the boy shepherd, kills the king's giant foe, tempers with his harp the black rages of the king, is loved by the king's oldest son, marries the daughter of the king, is among the king's captains. But Saul, suspicious and unbalanced, wishes to kill him.

David hides himself in the caves of the mountains, becomes a robber chief. He goes into the service of the Philistines, and when they conquer and kill Saul on the hills of Gilboa, he becomes in his turn king of all Israel. The bold sheep-tender, great as poet and as king, founds his house in Jerusalem and subjugates the surrounding kingdoms. For the first time, the Jew is feared: for centuries after this he was to hope for a descendant of David to save him from his abject subjugation.

David is the king of the sword and of song. Solomon is the king of gold and of wisdom. Gold is brought to him as a tribute: he decks with gold the first sumptuous house of Jehovah. He sends ships to faraway Ophir in search of gold; the Queen of Sheba lays down sacks of gold at his feet. He takes strange women to wife and worships strange gods. The Lord pardons his old age, in memory of his youth, but at his death the kingdom is divided and the dark and shameful centuries of the decadence begin. Plots in the palace, murders of kings, revolts of chiefs, wretched civil wars, periods of idol worship, fill the period of the separation. Prophets appear and admonish, but the kings turn a deaf ear or drive them away.

The enemies of Israel grow more powerful. The Phoenicians, the Egyptians, the Assyrians, the Babylonians, one after another, invade the two kingdoms, extort tribute and finally, about six hundred years before the birth of Jesus, Jerusalem is destroyed, the Temple of Jehovah is demolished and the Jews are led as slaves to the rivers of Babylon. The same God who liberated them from the slavery of the Egyptians gives them over as slaves to the Babylonians.

This is the fourth punishment and the most terrible. From that time on, the Jews were always to be dispersed among strangers and subject to foreigners. Some of them were to return to reconstruct Jerusalem and its temple, but the country, invaded by the Scythians, tributary to the Persians, conquered by the Greeks, was after the last attempt of the Maccabeans finally given over to the hands of a dynasty of Arab barbarians, subject to the Romans. This race, which believed itself, under the protection of its God, the first people of the earth, was now dreadfully chastised, the Job among peoples.

FINALLY FROM THIS RACE was born He who had been awaited by all the Prophets.

India has its ascetics, who hide themselves in the wilderness to conquer the body and drown the soul in the infinite. China had its familiar sages, peaceful grandfathers who taught civic morality to working people and emperors. Greece had her philosophers, who in their shady porticos contrived harmonious systems and dialectic pitfalls. Rome had its lawgivers who recorded on bronze for the centuries the rules of the highest justice attainable to those who command and possess. The Jewish people had the Prophets.

The Jewish Prophet is not a priest, for he has never been anointed in the Temple. But he is a voice speaking in the name of God, or a hand writing at God's dictation, a voice speaking in the palace of the king or in the caves of the mountains, on the steps of the Temple. His mouth is full of bitterness, his arm is raised, pointing out punishment to come; because he loves his people, he vituperates them: and after massacres and flames, he teaches the resurrection and the life, the reign of the new David and the Covenant not to be broken.

The Prophet leads the idolater back to the true God, recalls charity to the oppressor, purity to the corrupt, mercy to the fierce, obedience to rebels, humbleness to the proud. He goes before the king and reproaches him, he greets priests with blame; and brings the rich to confusion. He announces consolation to the poor, health to the sick. A troublesome importunate voice, hated by the great, out of favor with the crowd, not always understood even by his disciples, the Prophet goes up and down the streets of Israel followed by suspicion and malediction, avoided like a leper, persecuted like an enemy.

Elijah is forced to flee before the wrath of Jezebel; Amos is banished beyond Israel by Amaziah, priest of Bethel; Isaiah is killed by the order of Manasseh; Uriah cut down by King Jehoiakim; Zacharias stoned between the temple and the altar; Jonah thrown into the sea; the sword is prepared for the neck of John; and the cross is ready from which Jesus will hang.

The Prophet is an announcer, but the deaf do not hear his promises. He is a saviour, but men refuse to be cured.

HE WHO WILL COME

IN THE HOUSE at Nazareth Jesus recognizes in the fiery laments of the Prophets His destiny. When, at the beginning of His thirtieth year, He presents Himself to men as the Son of man, He knows what awaits Him. His life to come is already set down day by day in pages written before His earthly birth.

He knows that God promised Moses: "I will raise them up a Prophet from among their brethren, like unto thee, and will put my words in his mouth; and he shall speak unto them all that I shall command him." God will make a new covenant with His people. "Not according to the covenant that I made with their fathers . . . but I will put my law in their inward parts, and write it in their hearts. . . . I will forgive their iniquity, and I will remember their sin no more."

The Messiah will have a precursor to announce Him. "Behold, I will send my messenger, and he shall prepare the way before me."

"For unto us a child is born, unto us a son is given: and the government shall be upon his shoulder: and his name shall be called Wonderful, Counsellor, the mighty God, the everlasting Father, the Prince of Peace."

He will not come in proud triumph: "Rejoice greatly, O daughter of Zion; shout, O daughter of Jerusalem: behold, thy King cometh unto thee: he is just, and having salvation; lowly, and riding upon an ass, and upon a colt the foal of an ass."

He will bring justice and will lift up the unhappy: ". . . because the Lord hath anointed me to preach good tidings unto the meek; he hath sent me to bind up the brokenhearted, to proclaim liberty to the captives, and the opening of the prison to them that are bound; . . . to comfort all that mourn."

But He will be vilified and tortured by the very people He comes to save: "he hath no form nor comeliness; and when we shall see him, there is no beauty that we should desire him. He is . . . rejected of men; a man of sorrows, and acquainted with grief: and we hid as it were our faces from him; he was despised, and we esteemed him not."

Too late they will understand what they have done and will repent.

". . . and they shall look upon me whom they have pierced, and they shall mourn for him, as one mourneth for his only son, and shall be in bitterness for him, as one that is in bitterness for his firstborn."

"Yea, all kings shall bow down before him: all nations shall serve him."

These and other words are remembered by Jesus in the vigil before His departure. He knows that the Jews are not awaiting a poor, gentle, despised Messiah. They are dreaming of a terrestrial Messiah, a second David, a warrior who will rebuild more splendidly than ever the palace of Solomon and the Temple.

He knows He cannot give them what they seek, that His kingdom is not of this earth. But He knows that the seed of His word thrown into the earth among thistles and thorns, trampled underfoot, will start into life when spring comes. Little by little it will grow, until finally it becomes a tree stretching its branches up to the sky, covering the earth with the boughs. And all men can sit round about it, remembering the death of Him who planted it.

WHILE JESUS, in the poor little workshop at Nazareth, was handling the axe and the square, a voice was raised in the desert toward Jordan and the Dead Sea. Last of the Prophets, John the Baptist called the Jews to repent, announced the approach of the Kingdom of Heaven, predicted the coming of the Messiah, reproved the sinners who came to him, and plunged them into the water of the river, that this outer washing might be the beginning of an inner purification.

John's figure was one to conquer the imagination. A child sprung by a miracle from parents of great age, he was set apart from his birth to be *nazir*—pure. He had never cut his hair, had never tasted wine or cider, had never touched a woman nor

known any love except that for God. While he was still young, he had left his parents' home and buried himself in the desert. There he lived for many years alone, without a tent, wrapped in his camel's skin, his flanks girt by a leather belt, tall, bony, his chest hairy, his hair hanging long on his shoulders, his long beard almost covering his face. His piercing eyes flashed like lightning from under his bushy eyebrows when from his mouth hidden by his beard burst out the tremendous words of his maledictions.

This hypnotic wild man, solitary as a Yogi, despising pleasure like a stoic, seemed to those whom he baptized the last hope of a despairing people.

The desert sun burned John's body and he was a foreteller of fire who saw in the Messiah, soon to appear, the master of flame. He will gather His wheat into the garner, but He will burn up the chaff with unquenchable fire; and every tree which bringeth not forth good fruit will be hewn down and cast into the fire. He will be a baptizer who will baptize with fire.

Rigid, wrathful, harsh, shaggy, quick to insult, impatient and impetuous, John was not gentle with those who came to him. When Pharisees and Sadducees, notable men, learned in the Scriptures, esteemed by the crowd, of authority in the Temple, came to be baptized, he shamed them more than the others. "O generation of vipers, who hath warned you to flee from the wrath to come? Bring forth therefore fruits meet for repentance."

It is not enough to bathe in the Jordan. Change your life. "And the people asked him, saying, What shall we do then? He answereth and saith unto them, He that hath two coats, let him impart to him that hath none; and he that hath meat, let him do likewise.

"Then came also publicans to be baptized, and said unto him, Master, what shall we do? And he said unto them, Exact no more than that which is appointed you.

"And the soldiers likewise demanded of him, saying, And what shall we do? And he said unto them, Do violence to no man, neither accuse any falsely; and be content with your wages."

Almost superhuman when he announced the terrible separation of the good from the bad, John becomes commonplace when he descends to particulars. This is nothing more or less than the Mosaic Law. Long before him, Amos and Isaiah had gone further.

Perhaps the fierceness of John is justified by his consciousness of being an ambassador, a consciousness which leaves a tinge of sadness, even in his humility. They came from Jerusalem to ask him who he was, "What then? Art thou Elias?"

"No. I am not."

"Art thou the Christ?"

"No. . . . I am the voice of one crying in the wilderness. . . . He it is, who coming after me is preferred before me, whose shoe's latchet I am not worthy to unloose."

At Nazareth, meantime, an unknown workingman was lacing up His shoes with His own hands to go out to the wilderness. Jesus had heard the people talk of those "washed ones" who returned from Jordan and He understood that His day grew near. He was now in His thirtieth year, the destined age.

JESUS PRESENTED Himself to John to be baptized. Did He then acknowledge Himself a sinner? The prophet preached the baptism of repentance in remission of sins. He who goes to wash feels himself polluted.

The fact that we know nothing of the life of Jesus from His twelfth to His thirtieth year, exactly the years of fallible adolescence, of hot-blooded youth, has given rise to the idea that He held Himself to have been a sinner like other men. The three remaining years of His life are the most brightly lighted by the words of the four Gospels. Nothing of what we know of those three years gives any indication of this supposed existence of sin in Christ's life between the innocence of its beginning and the glory of its ending.

And yet Jesus came in the midst of a crowd of sinners to immerse Himself in the Jordan. The problem is not mysterious; He went to John that the prophecy of the precursor might be fulfilled. Jesus, about to begin His true life, did not go down to the Jordan to cleanse Himself, but to show that His second life was beginning.

AS SOON AS Jesus emerged from the water He went into the desert. He went up on the rocky mountains whence no springs arise, where the only living creatures are snakes.

For those rich in soul, solitude is a prize and not an expiation. The people who cannot endure solitude are afraid of their own emptiness. Jesus loved men. But in the years to come He often hid Himself, to be alone, far even from His disciples. To love your brothers, you need from time to time to depart from them: far from them, you draw near to them.

For Jesus these forty days of solitude are the last of His preparation. For forty years the Jewish people wandered in the desert before entering into the kingdom promised by God. For forty days Moses remained close to God to hear His laws; for forty days Elijah wandered, fleeing the vengeance of the wicked queen. So also the time allotted to the new liberator before announcing the promised kingdom, the Kingdom of Heaven which is in ourselves, was forty days of close communion with God to receive the supreme inspiration. About Him in His vigil will be animals and angels; beings all matter, beings all spirit.

Man is matter changing by slow transmutation into spirit. If the animal gets the upper hand, man descends below the level of the beasts because he puts the remnants of his intelligence at the service of bestiality: if the angel conquers, man partakes of divinity itself. But the fallen angel, Satan, condemned to wear the form of a beast, is the enemy of all men who wish to climb that height from which he was cast down. Satan seduced the innocence of the first two created beings, he suborned David the strong, corrupted Solomon the wise, accused Job the righteous before the throne of God. Satan tempts and always will tempt all those who love God.

Therefore at the end of the forty days, Satan came into the desert to tempt Jesus.

Whenever Jesus shared human lives, He consented to eat and drink, because it is right to give to the flesh that which belongs to the flesh. But our slavery to matter is branded on our lives by the daily need of our bodies for food, so His first act after His baptism had been a fast. After forty days He was hungry. Satan, tenacious and invisible, was waiting for this moment of material need, and spoke: "If thou be the Son of God, command this stone that it be made bread."

The reproof was prompt: "It is written that man shall not live by bread alone, but by every word of God."

Satan, from the top of a mountain, showed Him all the kingdoms of the earth: "All this power will I give thee, and the glory of them: for that is delivered unto me; and to whomsoever I will I give it. If thou therefore wilt adore me, all shall be thine."

And Jesus answered, "Get thee behind me, Satan: for it is written thou shalt worship the Lord thy God, and him only shalt thou serve."

Then Satan took Him to Jerusalem and set Him on the pinnacle of the Temple: "If thou be the Son of God, cast thyself down from hence."

But Jesus answered quickly: "It is written; thou shalt not tempt the Lord thy God."

"And when the Devil had ended all the temptation," Luke goes on, "he departed from him for a season."

Satan asks material bread and a material miracle of Jesus and promises Him material power. Jesus refuses what is offered.

He is not the material Messiah. He did not come to bring food to bodies but food to souls—truth, that living food. Man does not live by bread alone, but by love, fervor, and truth. Jesus conquers Satan in Himself and now comes out of the desert to conquer him among men. He is ready to transform the kingdom of earth into the Kingdom of Heaven.

THE RETURN

As soon as Jesus came again among men, He learned that the tetrarch Antipas (son of Herod the Great and second husband of Herodias) had imprisoned John in the fortress of Machaerus. The voice crying in the wilderness was stilled and was now to give way to a more powerful voice. John waited in the blackness of the prison until his bloody head was carried on a golden platter to the banquet—almost the last dish served to Salome, that evil woman, betrayer of men.

Now Jesus understands that His day is at hand, and crossing Samaria He returns into Galilee to announce at once the coming of the Kingdom. There He is to find His first listeners, His first converts, His first disciples.

He does not wish to begin His message in Jerusalem. If He should go to that capital city of the great king now, He would be taken prisoner at once and would not be able to sow His word on less stony soil. At Jerusalem live the powerful of the world: the Romans, masters of the world and of Judea, with their soldiers in arms; the high priests, the old custodians of the Temple; the Pharisees, Sadducees, scribes, the Levites and their guards, the petrifiers of the Law.

He wishes to arrive at Jerusalem later with a following behind Him, when already the Kingdom of Heaven has begun slowly to lay siege to the city. The conquest of Jerusalem will be the last test, the supreme trial.

A man from the provinces, He goes back to His province. He arrives in Galilee, and begins to teach. He wishes to carry the tidings of good news to the poor and the humble because the tidings are especially for them, because they have long been waiting for them.

THE FIRST WORDS of Jesus are few and simple, very much like those of John, "The time is fulfilled, and the Kingdom of God is at hand: repent ye, and believe the Gospel."

Words incomprehensible to moderns by their very sobriety. To understand them and to understand the difference between the message of John and the message of Jesus, they need to be translated into our language, filled again with their eternally living meaning. John said that a King would come ready to found the new Kingdom, the Kingdom of Heaven. Now the King has come and announces that the doors of the Kingdom are open. He is the guide, the path, the hand.

When Jesus says "The time is fulfilled," he does not refer to the fact that it was the fifteenth year of the reign of Tiberius.

The time of Jesus is now and always is eternity. The Kingdom is not the worn-out fancy of a poor Jew nearly twenty centuries ago. The Kingdom is of today, tomorrow, of always. There is no chronology in eternity. Jesus threw the seed into the earth, but the seed has scarcely germinated in two thousand years passed like a stormy winter, in the space of sixty human generations. Begin at once: it is our work. The Kingdom of God will be founded among men. The spirit is the dominion of goodness.

Jesus added "repent," but the old word has been distorted from its true and magnificent meaning. *Metanoia*—a changing of the spirit—ought rather to be translated "conversion," that is, the renewing of the inner life of man.

As one of the conditions of the arrival of the Kingdom and at the same time as the very substance of the new order, Jesus demands complete conversion, a revolution of the common values of life, a transmutation of feelings, of intentions. Little by little He was to explain in what way this total transformation, this "second birth" of the ordinary human soul, is to be effected. But in the meantime, He contented Himself with adding one conclusion, "Believe in the Gospel."

By "Gospel" men nowadays mean usually the book where the quadruple story of Jesus is printed; but Jesus neither wrote books nor thought of volumes. By "Gospel" He meant, according to the plain and sweet meaning of the word, "good tidings." Jesus is a messenger (in Greek "angel") who brings good tidings: the cheerful message that the sick will be cured, that the blind will see, the poor will be enriched with imperishable riches, that the sad will rejoice, that sinners will be pardoned, the unclean purified, that the imperfect can become perfect.

With those few words Jesus began His teaching. He taught His Galileans on the thresholds of their shabby little white houses, on the small shady open places of their cities or the shore of the lake, leaning against a beached boat, His feet on the stones, toward evening when the sun sank red in the west.

Many listened to Him and followed Him because, says Luke: "His word was with authority." Here was a prophet living like a man among other men, friendly to the unfriended, searching out His brothers where they work in the houses, in the busy streets, eating their bread and drinking wine at their tables, lending a hand with the fisherman's nets, with a word for the sad, for the sick, for the beggar.

If He returned to Nazareth, He stayed there but a short time. He was to go back later, accompanied by the Twelve and preceded by the renown of His miracles, and they were to treat Him as all the cities of the world—even the most renowned for amenity, Athens and Florence—have treated those of their citizens who made them great above others. After ridiculing Him they tried to cast Him down from the precipice.

Jesus spent His time with them walking from one region to another. He was such a man as is called a vagabond. His life is an eternal journey. He is the true Wandering Jew. He was born on a journey. Still a baby at the breast, He was carried along the sun-parched road to Egypt; from Egypt He came back to the waters and greenness of Galilee. The voice of John called Him to the Jordan: an inner voice drove Him out into the desert; and after the forty days of hunger and the temptation, He began His restless vagabond life from city to city, from village to village, from mountain to mountain, across Palestine.

We find Him in Galilee, in Chorazin, in Cana, in Magdala, in Tiberias, but often He crosses Samaria to sit down near the well of Sychar. We find Him from time to time in the tetrarchy of Philip at Bethsaida, at Gadara, at Caesarea, also at Gerasa in the Perea of Herod Antipas. In Judah He often stops at Bethany, a few miles away from Jerusalem, or at Jericho, but He did not shrink from journeying outside the limits of the old kingdom and from going down among the Gentiles. We find Him in Phoenicia, in the regions of Tyre and Sidon, and in Syria. His bed is the furrow in a field, the bench of a boat, the shadow of an olive tree. Sometimes He sleeps in the houses of those who love Him, but only for short periods.

IN THE EARLY DAYS we find Him most often at Capernaum. His journeys began there and ended there. Matthew calls it "His city." Situated on the caravan route which from Damascus crosses Ituraea and goes toward the sea, Capernaum had become a commercial center of some importance. Artisans, bargainers,

brokers, and shopkeepers had come there to stay; publicans, excise men and other fiscal tools. The little settlement, half rustic, half a fishing village, had become a mixed and composite city where the society of the times—even to soldiers and prostitutes—was fully represented. And yet Capernaum, lying along the lake, freshened by the air from the nearby hills and by the breeze from the water, was not a prey to stagnation and decay like the Syrian cities and Jerusalem. There were still peasants who went out to their fields every day, and fishermen who every day went forth to their boats. Good, poor, simple, warm-hearted people who talked of other matters than money. Among them a man could draw his breath freely.

In Capernaum there is nothing to do on Sabbaths except go to the synagogue, where everybody has the right to enter, to read aloud, and to expound what has been read. The gardener who no longer turns his waterwheel to irrigate the green rows, and the country smith, whose face is scrubbed and rinsed in many waters like his hands, and whose beard is anointed with a cheap ointment (but still perfumed like a rich man's beard), come to the synagogue to hear the ancient word of the God of their fathers. Family, friends, neighbors—they find them all together.

The mason comes, he who has worked on this house and made it small because the Elders did not wish to spend too much. The mason still feels his arms a little numb and lame from his six days' labor. The fishermen have turned over their boats on the sand, have spread the nets on the roof and have come too, with faces tanned by the sun and with eyes half shut from the constant glare of sunlight reflected by the water. They are not used to being within walls and perhaps continue to hear a confused murmur of water lapping about the bow.

The peasants of the neighboring countryside are here, prosperous farmers who have put on a tunic as good as anybody's, who are satisfied with the harvest almost ready for the scythe. There are shepherds in town that morning, with the smell of their flocks still on them, shepherds who live all the week in the mountain pastures, alone with their quiet animals. The gentry of Capernaum all have come, the smaller property owners, the small-business men. They stand in the front row, their eyes cast down, the line of their well-clad backs bowed but broad and masterful—employers' backs, backs full of authority and of religion. There are also transient foreigners, merchants going toward Syria or returning to Tiberias.

At the back of the room (for the synagogue is only a long whitewashed room a little larger than a school) the poor of the countryside are huddled together like dogs near a door, like those who always stand in fear of being sent away: old widows, young orphans, humpbacked old men, those who are incurably sick, those whose wits no longer rightly serve them. Those who pick up what others throw away, the pieces of dry bread, fish heads, fruit cores and skins; those who suffer from the winter cold and every year wait for summer, paradise of the poor, for then there are fruits to be plucked along the roads. Every Sabbath the poverty-stricken throng at the back of the synagogue waits for somebody to read a chapter from Amos or from Isaiah because the Prophets take the part of the poor, and announce the punishment and the new world.

ON THAT SABBATH there was One who had come back from the desert to announce good tidings. He stood up, had someone give Him one of the scrolls of the Scriptures (more likely the Prophets than the Law) and recited in a tranquil voice two, three, four or more verses. Then He commenced to speak with a bold eloquence which put the Pharisees to confusion, touched sinners, won the poor, and enchanted women.

Suddenly the old text was transfigured, became transparent, belonged to their own times; the words, dried up by repetition, were fresh words coined at that moment, shining before their eyes like an unexpected revelation.

Nobody in Capernaum could remember having heard such a Rabbi. No one had ever spoken of the poor and the sick as He did, no one had shown so much love for them. Like the old Prophets, He had for them a special affection which offended more fortunate men, but which filled their hearts with comfort and hope.

When Jesus had finished speaking, the elders, lords, and Pharisees shook their heads forebodingly and got up, making wry faces among themselves, half contemptuous, half scandalized, and grumbling disapprobation. The merchants followed them, erect, already thinking of the next day.

There remained behind the shepherds, the peasants, the gardeners, the smiths, the fishermen, and the herd of beggars, the diseased, the maimed. When He came out from the synagogue all those stood waiting in the street. They followed Him timidly as if in a dream; then, grown more bold, they accosted Him and went along together beside the shores of the lake, and now one and now another (they were braver under the open sky) began asking questions. And Jesus paused and answered this obscure crowd with words never to be forgotten.

AMONG THE FISHERMEN of Capernaum, Jesus found His first disciples. Almost every day He was on the beach of the lake; sometimes the boats were going out, sometimes they were coming in, the sails swelling in the breeze; and from the barks the barefooted men climbed down, wading knee-deep in water, carrying the baskets filled with the wet silver of dead fish, and with the old dripping nets.

They put out sometimes at nightfall when there was a moon, and came back early in the morning just after the setting of the moon and before sunrise. Often Jesus was waiting for them on the strand. But sometimes they came back empty-handed, tired and depressed. Jesus greeted them with words which cheered them, and the disappointed men, although they had not slept, listened to Him willingly.

One morning two boats came back toward Capernaum while Jesus standing by the lake was talking to the people who had gathered around Him. The fishermen disembarked and began to arrange the nets; then Jesus entered into one of the boats and asked them to put it out a little from the land so that He might not be pressed upon by the crowd. Upright near the rudder He taught those who had remained on the land, and when He had left speaking He said to Simon, called Peter, "Launch out into the deep, and let down your nets for a draught."

Simon, son of Jona, owner of the boat, answered, "Master,

we have toiled all the night, and have taken nothing: nevertheless at thy word I will let down the net."

When they were only a short distance from the bank, Simon and Andrew, his brother, threw out into the water a large net. And when they drew it back it was so full of fish that the meshes were almost breaking. Then the two brothers called their partners in the other boat, that they should come to help them, and they threw out the net again and drew it up again full. Simon, Andrew and the others cried out "a miracle!" and thanked Jesus. Simon, impulsive by nature, threw himself at the knees of their guest crying, "Depart from me; for I am a sinful man, O Lord."

But Jesus, smiling, said, "Follow me, and I will make you fishers of men."

When they went back to the shore they pulled the boat up on the land, and leaving their nets, the two brothers followed Him. And a few days after this, Jesus saw the other two brothers, James and John, sons of Zebedee, who were partners of Simon and Andrew, and he called them, while they were mending the broken nets; and they too said farewell to their father, who was in the boat with the sailors, and leaving the broken nets half mended, followed Him.

Four poor men of the lake, men who did not know how to read, nor indeed how to speak correctly, were called by Jesus to found with Him a kingdom which was to occupy all the earth. Who among us today, among all those now living, would be capable of imitating those four poor men of Capernaum? "Give away all your goods, for you will acquire with me an inestimable treasure."

Not by chance did Jesus select His first companions from among fishermen. The fisherman who lives a great part of his days in the pure solitude of the water is the patient, unhurried man who lets down his nets and leaves the rest to God, who sends abundance and famine. He washes his hands in water and his spirit in solitude.

Jesus made saints whom men even today remember and invoke. A great man creates great men.

When David appears he finds at once his *gibborim*—his bodyguard; an Agamemnon finds his heroes, an Arthur his knights, Charlemagne his paladins, Napoleon his marshals. Jesus found among the men of the people of Galilee His apostles. They were to speak in His name in places where He could not go, and in His name to carry on His work after His death.

THE MOUNT

THE SERMON ON THE MOUNT is the greatest proof of the right of men to exist in the infinite universe. It is the patent of our soul's worthiness, the pledge that we can lift ourselves above ourselves, the hope of our rising above the beast. And if men were called before a superhuman tribunal and had to give an account to the judges of all our inexplicable mistakes, our perfidy, our hardness of heart, the bloodshed between brothers, and the ancient infamies every day renewed, the one attenuation of all those accusations is the Sermon on the Mount. Who has read it and has not felt, at least in that brief moment while he read, a passion of love and remorse, a confused but urgent longing to act?

From the Mount on which Jesus sat the day of the sermon you could see only the plain, calm under the sunset light; on one side the silver-green oval of the lake, and on the other the long crest of Carmel where Elijah overcame the scullions of Baal. From this little rocky hill scarcely rising above the level earth, Jesus disclosed the song of the new man.

He sat in the midst of the first apostles and someone asked Him to whom would be allotted this Kingdom of Heaven, of which He so often spoke. Jesus answered with the nine Beatitudes.

The Beatitudes, so often spelled out even nowadays by people who have lost their meaning, are almost always misunderstood, mutilated, deformed, cheapened, distorted. And yet they epitomize the first day of Christ's teaching.

"Blessed are the poor in spirit: for theirs is the kingdom of heaven." Luke leaves out the words "in spirit," seeming to mean the "poor" and nothing else; and many people after him have understood him to mean the simpleminded. They see in the words only a choice between the bankrupt and the imbecile.

When He spoke, Jesus was not thinking either of the first or the second. For Him supreme intelligence consisted in realizing that the intelligence alone is not enough. Poor in spirit are those who are fully and painfully aware of their own spiritual poverty, of the smallness of the good that is in us all. The poor who realize that they are really poor suffer from their poverty, and try to escape from it. Those therefore who confess themselves poor and undergo suffering to acquire that veritable wealth named perfection, will become holy as God is holy, and theirs shall be the Kingdom of Heaven.

"Blessed are the meek: for they shall inherit the earth." The earth here promised is not monarchies with built-up cities. In the language of the Messiah, "to inherit the earth" means to partake of the New Kingdom. He who fights within himself for the conquest of the new earth and the new heaven does not break out into rage when things go badly. The meek are like water which seems to give way before other substances, but silently attacks, and calmly consumes, with the patience of the years, the hardest granites.

"Blessed are they that mourn: for they shall be comforted." Those who feel disgust for themselves; who weep over the wrong they have done and over the good they might have done and did not; hasten with their tears the day of grace, and it is right that they shall some day be comforted.

"Blessed are they that hunger and thirst after justice: for they shall be filled." The justice which Jesus means is not the justice of men, obedience to human law. The just man is he who lives according to the one simple Law which Jesus reduces to one commandment, "Love all men near and far, your fellow countrymen and foreigners, strangers and enemies." Those who hunger and thirst after this justice shall be filled in the Kingdom of Heaven.

"Blessed are the merciful: for they shall obtain mercy." We constantly commit sins against the spirit and those sins will be forgiven us only as we forgive those committed against us. Christ is in all men and what we do to others will be done to us. "Inasmuch as ye have done it unto one of the least of these my brethren, ye have done it unto me."

"Blessed are the pure in heart: for they shall see God." The pure of heart are those who have no other joy than victory over evil. He who has his heart crammed with furious desires, with the earthly ambitions which convulse this ant heap of the earth, can never see God face-to-face.

"Blessed are the peacemakers: for they shall be called the children of God." When Jesus said He had come to bring war and not peace, He meant, in short, war against war. The peacemakers are those who bring about concord. When every man loves his brothers more than himself, the peacemakers will have conquered the earth and they will be called the true children of God, and they will enter among the first into His Kingdom.

"Blessed are they who have been persecuted for justice' sake: for theirs is the kingdom of heaven." I send you out to found the Kingdom of Heaven, of that higher justice which is love. You will be tortured in body, crucified in soul, deprived of liberty and perhaps of life; but if you accept this suffering cheerfully to carry to others that justice which makes you suffer, this persecution will be for you an incontestable title to enter into the Kingdom which you have founded as far as was in your power.

"Blessed are ye, when men shall revile you, and persecute you, and say all manner of evil against you falsely, for my sake. Rejoice, and be exceeding glad: for great is your reward in heaven: for so persecuted they the prophets which were before you." The persecutors can take away your bread, and the clear light of the sun; they may break your bones. You must expect insult and calumny. But you must always rejoice because the mud thrown at you by evil men is the consecration of your own goodness. This is, as St. Francis says, "the perfect joy." All the prophets who have ever spoken upon the earth were insulted by men, and men will insult those who are to come. We can recognize prophets by this: that smeared with mud and covered with shame, they pass among men, bright-faced, speaking out what is in their hearts. Even if the obstinate prophet is killed, they cannot silence him. His voice multiplied by the echoes of his death will be heard in all languages and through all the centuries.

This promise brings the beatitudes to their end.

THE FIRST PROPHETS, the earliest legislators, the leaders of young nations, the saints, began the domination of the beast. The old law that is found with only a few variations in the Manava Dharmasastra, in the Pentateuch, in the Ta-Hio, in the Avesta, in the traditions of Solon and of Numa, in the sententious maxims of Hesiod and the Seven Wise Men, is the first attempt, rough and inadequate, to mold animality into a sketch of humanity.

This law reduced itself to a few elementary rules necessary for a common life, useful to all: not to steal, not to kill, not to perjure, not to fornicate, not to tyrannize over the weak, not to mistreat strangers and slaves any more than was necessary.

Men of ancient times, lusty, sanguine, ravishers, cattle stealers, warriors who, having dragged by the feet their slaughtered antagonists, refreshed themselves with haunches of oxen, emptying enormous cups of wine; such as we see them in the Mahabharata, and in the Iliad, in the poem of Izdubar, and in the book of wars of Jehovah; such men without the fear of punishment and of God would have been still more unrestrained and ferocious. In times when a head was asked for an eye, an arm for a finger, and a hundred lives for a life, a law of retaliation which asked only an eye for an eye and a life for a life was a notable victory of generosity, appalling though it seems after the teaching of Jesus.

They had come to this point when Jesus spoke on the Mount.

With Jesus therefore begins the new law: the old is abrogated and declared insufficient.

He begins at every example with the words: "Ye have heard it said . . ." and at once He substitutes for the old command, "But I say unto you . . ." With these "buts" a new phase of the human education begins.

"Ye have heard that it was said by them of old time, Thou shalt not kill; . . . But I say unto you, That whosoever is angry with his brother . . . shall be in danger of the judgment: and whosoever shall say to his brother, Raca [vain fellow], shall be in danger of the council: but whosoever shall say, Thou fool, shall be in danger of hell fire." A single moment of anger, a single abusive word, a single offensive phrase, are for Jesus the equivalent of assassination. Murder is only the final carrying out of a feeling.

Anger is like fire: it can be smothered only at the first spark. Jesus goes straight to the extreme and utters the profoundest truth when He decrees the same penalty for the first hot words as for murder.

"Ye have heard that it was said by them of old time, Thou shalt not commit adultery: But I say unto you, That whosoever looketh on a woman to lust after her hath committed adultery with her already in his heart."

Even here Jesus soars from the body to the soul, from flesh to will. What counts is the intention, the feeling; to imagine, to desire a betrayal is already a betrayal.

Jesus advises expressly to pluck out the eye and cast it away if evil comes from the eye, and to cut off the hand and throw it away if evil comes from the hand—advice which dismays the cowardly and even the strong. Yet even the most cowardly, when threatened by cancer, are ready to have their bodies cut open to save their lives. Men are concerned to save the body, but grudge any sacrifice to keep in health the soul.

"Let the dead bury their dead." In the old law there were hundreds of minute, tiresome, complicated precepts for the purification of the body, without any true earthly or heavenly foundation. The Pharisees made the best part of religion consist in their observance of these traditions because it is much less trouble to wash a cup than your own soul.

"Not that which goeth into the mouth defileth a man; but that which cometh out of the mouth, this defileth a man. . . . those things which proceed out of the mouth come forth from the heart; . . . out of the heart proceed evil thoughts, murders, adulteries, fornications, thefts, false witness, blasphemies: These are the things which defile a man: but to eat with unwashen hands defileth not a man."

Jesus does not believe in the perfection of the natural soul.

He believes in its future perfection, only to be reached by a complete overturning of its present nature.

Nothing is more common among men than the thirst for riches. But poverty is the first requisite for the citizenship of the Kingdom. He who wishes to come with me, said Jesus, must go and sell that which he has and give it to the poor and he shall have treasures in Heaven.

Men are always afraid lest there may not be enough bread to last to the next harvest. They fear that they will not have clothes to cover their bodies and the bodies of their children. But Jesus teaches us, "Take therefore no thought for the morrow: . . . Sufficient unto the day is the evil thereof."

The whole history of men is only the terror of standing second; but Jesus teaches us, "And whosoever of you will be the chiefest, shall be servant to all."

Vanity is another universal curse of men. Jesus commands us: "But when thou doest alms, let not thy left hand know what thy right hand doeth: . . . And when thou prayest, thou shalt not be as the hypocrites are: for they love to pray standing in the synagogues and in the corners of the streets, that they may be seen of men. . . . But thou, when thou prayest, enter into thy closet. . . ."

The instinct of self-preservation is the strongest of all those which dominate us. But Jesus tells us: "For whosoever will save his life shall lose it; but whosoever shall lose his life for my sake, . . . the same shall save it." Jesus says, "Judge not, that ye be not judged: condemn not, and ye shall not be condemned: forgive, and ye shall be forgiven."

The Pharisee avoids if possible the company of sinners, but Jesus tirelessly announces that He has come to seek for sinners, and sits down to dinner in the house of the publican, where a prostitute anoints his feet. The truly pure man does not feel that for fear of soiling his garments he needs must leave the corrupt to die in their own vileness.

The avarice of men is so great that everyone tries to take as much as he can from others and to give back as little; but Jesus affirms, "It is more blessed to give than to receive."

But Jesus had not yet arrived at the most stupefying of His

revolutionary teachings. "Ye have heard that it hath been said, An eye for an eye, and a tooth for a tooth: But I say unto you, That ye resist not evil: but whosoever shall smite thee on thy right cheek, turn to him the other also. And if any man will sue thee at the law, and take away thy coat, let him have thy cloak also. And whosoever shall compel thee to go a mile, go with him twain."

There could be no more definite repudiation of the old law of retaliation. "Not to resent offenses," says Aristotle, the disciple of Plato, to Nichomachus in the *Ethics*, "is the mark of a base and slavish man." For the greater part of those who call themselves Christians this principle of not resisting evil has been the unendurable scandal of Christianity.

Literally to follow this command of Jesus demands a mastery possessed by few, of the blood, of the nerves, and of all the instincts of the baser part of our being. But Jesus never said it would be possible to obey Him without harsh renunciations, without stern and continuous inner battles.

These are acts of heroic excellence, supine though they may appear. Only the saints can charm wolves to mildness. Only he who has transformed his own soul can transform the souls of his brothers, and transform the world into a less grievous place for all.

Love for ourselves is the origin of our hatred for others. He who conquers self-love is already entirely transformed. The greatest victory over the fierce, blind, brutal man of antiquity is this and nothing else.

"YE HAVE HEARD that it hath been said, Thou shalt love thy neighbour, and hate thine enemy. But I say unto you, Love your enemies, bless them that curse you, do good to them that hate you, and pray for them which despitefully use you and persecute you; That ye may be the children of your Father which is in heaven: for he maketh his sun to rise on the evil and on the good, and sendeth rain on the just and on the unjust. For if ye love them which love you, what reward have ye? do not even the publicans the same? And if ye salute your brethren only, what do ye more than others? do not even the publicans so?

Be ye therefore perfect, even as your Father which is in heaven is perfect."

People who refuse Christ have many easily understandable reasons: they are afraid of losing the dusty rubbish which seems magnificence to them. As an excuse for not following His teachings they claim that He said nothing new.

These experts in the genealogy of ideas do not look carefully to see whether there is a real identity of sense and of spirit between the ideas of Jesus and those other older ideas.

After the promulgation of the old Law there was amity between blood kin; and the citizens of the same city bore with each other; but for strangers there was only hatred and extermination. Centuries later voices were heard which asked for a little justice even for strangers, for enemies. These voices were not heeded.

Four centuries before Christ, a wise man of China, Mo Ti, wrote a whole book to say that men should love each other. "The wise man who wants to improve the world can improve it only if he knows with certainty the origin of disorders. Whence come disorders? They spring up because men do not love each other."

For Mo Ti, love is the mortar to hold citizens and the state more closely united, a social panacea.

"Answer insults with courtesy," suggests timidly the mysterious Lao-tse; but courtesy is prudence, not love. Confucius taught a doctrine which consisted in loving one's neighbor as oneself, but he did not dream of condemning hate. In the oldest Confucian text, the Ta-Hio, we find these words: "Only the just and human man is capable of justly loving and hating men."

His contemporary, Buddha, sees no other way to suppress suffering than to drown personal souls in Nirvana—in nothingness. The Buddhist loves his brother to avoid suffering, to approach absorption in the stream of life. His universal love is a form of indifference, stoical in grief as in joy.

In Egypt every dead body took with it into the tomb a copy of the book of the dead, an anticipatory apology of the soul before the tribunal of Osiris. The dead praises himself: "I have

starved no one! I have made no one weep! I have not killed! I have not commanded treacherous murder! I have defrauded no one! I have given bread to the hungry, water to the thirsty, clothes to the naked, a boat to the traveler halted on his journey, sacrifices to the gods, funeral banquets to the dead." This is righteousness, but we find no love here.

Zarathustra also leaves a law for the Iranians. This law commands the faithful of Ahura Mazda to give clothes to the naked and they are not to refuse bread to the hungry workingman. There is no talk of love.

It is written in Exodus: "Also thou shalt not oppress a stranger: for ye know the heart of a stranger, seeing ye were strangers in the land of Egypt." This is a beginning; we have reached Love, but not for an enemy. The Psalms resound at every step with violent demands to the Lord to destroy enemies. "As for the head of those that compass me about, let the mischief of their own lips cover them. Let burning coals fall upon them: let them be cast into the fire; into deep pits, that they rise not up again. And my soul shall be joyful in the Lord!"

In such a world it is natural that Saul should be astounded that he was not killed by his enemy David, and that Job should boast of not having exulted in the misfortunes of an enemy. Only in the later proverbs does the anonymous moralist of the Old Testament come finally to charity, "If thine enemy be hungry, give him bread to eat; and if he be thirsty, give him water to drink."

This, too, is progress: but the marvels of love of the Sermon on the Mount cannot have sprung from these timid maxims hidden away in a corner of the Scriptures.

The world of antiquity did not know love. It knew passion for a woman, friendship for a friend, justice for the citizen, hospitality for the foreigner. Zeus protected pilgrims and strangers; he who knocked at the Grecian door was not denied meat, a cup of wine, and a bed. The poor were to be covered, the weak helped; but the men of antiquity did not know love that shares another's sorrow.

Jesus was the first to speak of such love in the Sermon on the Mount. Of all His teachings, this is the greatest and the most original of Jesus' conceptions; this is still his greatest innovation. Even to us it is new because it is not understood, not imitated, not obeyed; infinitely eternal like truth.

JESUS ON THE MOUNT taught for the first time the Paternoster, the only prayer which He ever taught. The apostles had asked Jesus for a prayer. It is one of the simplest prayers in the world, but it is not always understood.

"Our Father"—for we have sprung from Thee and love Thee as sons; from Thee we shall receive no wrong.

"Which art in heaven"—in that which is opposed to the earth, in the opposite sphere from matter, in spirit and in that small but eternal part of the spirit which is our soul.

"Hallowed be thy name." Let us not only adore Thee with words but be worthy of Thee, drawing nearer to Thee with greater love, because Thou art no longer the avenger, the Lord of Battles, but the Father who teaches the joyfulness of peace.

"Thy kingdom come"—the Kingdom of Heaven, of the spirit of love, that of the Gospel.

"Thy will be done, in earth as it is in heaven." May Thy law of goodness and perfection rule both spirit and matter, both the visible and invisible universe.

"Give us this day our daily bread." We do not ask of Thee riches, dangerous burden, but only that small amount which permits us to live, to become more worthy of the promised life.

"Forgive us our debts, as we forgive our debtors." Pardon us because we pardon others. It is more effort for us to forgive a single debt of our debtors than for Thee to sweep away the record of all we owe Thee.

"Lead us not into temptation." Help us that our struggling transformation may not be too difficult, and that our entry into the Kingdom may not be too long delayed.

"Deliver us from evil"— Thou who art spirit, who hast power over evil, over stubborn and hostile matter which surrounds us everywhere, and from which it is hard to free ourselves, Thou negation of matter, help us!

In the Lord's Prayer the only word of praise is the word "Father"; and that praise is a pledge, a testimony of love.

POWERFUL DEEDS

AFTER HE HAD given out the new law of the imitation of God, Jesus came down from the Mount. He knew that these exalted words would not be enough to spread the good news, His Gospel, to all.

But the rustic, coarse, humble people who followed Jesus were men who could not understand a spiritual truth without evidence stated in the terms of the everyday world. An illustrative fable can lead men to moral revelation, so Jesus spoke in parables. A prodigy is to them confirmation of a new truth, so Jesus had recourse to miracles.

For many moderns it is out of the question that Jesus can ever have raised the dead: therefore, the miracles recounted by the Evangelists are a compelling reason for turning away from His words.

The people who reason in this way give to miracles a weight and a meaning much greater than that which Jesus gave them. He does not feel that this divine power of His is of supreme importance. Often, as soon as the healing was complete, He asked the ones He had healed to keep it secret. "See thou tell no man; but go thy way."

Every time that He finds a fair reason for refusing, He refuses; if He yields, it is to reward the faith of the sorrowing man or woman who calls on Him; but the Gospels show that He performs no miracles at Nazareth when they wish to kill Him, none at Gethsemane when they come to arrest Him, nor on the cross when they challenge Him to save Himself.

Jesus never held that miracles were His exclusive privilege. This power was not denied to the Disciples. "Heal the sick, cleanse the lepers, raise the dead, cast out devils: freely ye have received, freely give."

But miracles are not enough to enter into the Kingdom. Even charlatanical wizards could perform prodigies which seemed miracles. In His time a certain Simon was doing miracles in Samaria; even the disciples of the Pharisees performed miracles. And hardened hearts, locked shut against truth, are not converted even by the greatest miracles. "If they hear not Moses and the Prophets, neither will they be persuaded, though one rose from the dead."

Jesus heals the sick, but He is in no way like a wizard or an exorcist. His will is enough, and the faith of the petitioner. To them all He puts the question, "Dost thou believe I can do this?" and when the cure is accomplished, "Go, thy faith hath made thee whole."

For Jesus the miracle is the union of two wills for good, the living contact between the faith of the healer and the faith of the one healed. "Verily I say unto you, If ye have faith as a grain of mustard seed, ye shall say unto this mountain, Remove hence to yonder place; and it shall remove; and nothing shall be impossible unto you."

In the Gospels the miracles are called by three names: *dunameis*—forces; *terata*—marvels; *semeis*—signs. They are signs for those who remember the prophecies of the Messiah; they are marvels for those who look for proofs that Christ is the Messiah; but in Jesus there are only dunameis, victorious lightning flashes from a superhuman power. The healings of Jesus are healings not only of bodies but of souls.

Jesus cured the maimed, the fevered, a man with the dropsy, a woman with an issue of blood. He healed also a sword wound (Malchus' ear struck off by Peter on the night of Gethsemane); this only in order that His law—"do good to those who wrong you"—might be observed to the very last. But Jesus healed more often the paralytics, the lepers, the blind, the deaf-mutes, those possessed by devils.

The old name for mental diseases is possession by devils; even Aristotle believed in possession by devils. It was thought that lunatics, epileptics, hysterical patients, were invaded by malign spirits.

This learned and popular explanation lent itself admirably to that allegorical and figurative teaching of which Jesus was so fond. There is a likeness between the maniac and the epileptic, between the paralytic and the slothful, the vile and the leprous, the blind and he who cannot see the truth, the deaf and he who will not listen to the truth.

"THE DEAD shall arise!" The Evangelists know three resurrections, historical events narrated with a sober but explicit statement of the evidence. Jesus raised up three who were dead: a young lad, a little girl, and a friend.

He was entering Nain, "the beautiful," set on a little hill some miles from Nazareth, and met a funeral procession. They were carrying to the grave the young son of a widow. She had lost her husband a short time before. He saw the mother walking among the women, weeping with the amazed and smothered grief of mothers which is so profoundly moving.

Jesus had compassion on this mother; her grief was like an accusation. "Weep not," He said.

He went to the side of the cataleptic and touched him. The boy was lying there stretched out, wrapped in his shroud, but with his face uncovered, set in the stern paleness of the dead. The bearers halted; all were silent; even the mother, startled, was quiet.

"Young man, I say unto thee, Arise." And he that was dead sat up, and began to speak. And He delivered him to his mother.

Another day as he was returning from Gadara, a father fell at His feet. His only little daughter lay at the point of death. The man's name was Jairus, and although he was a leader at the synagogue he believed in Jesus. They went along together. When they were halfway, a servant met them, saying, "Thy daughter is dead; trouble not the Master." But when Jesus heard it, He answered him, saying, "Fear not: believe only, and she shall be made whole." When He came into the house, He suffered no man to go in, save Peter, and James, and John, and the father and the mother of the maiden. All wept, and bewailed her: but He said, "Weep not; she is not dead, but sleepeth." And they laughed, knowing that she was dead. He put them all out, and took her by the hand, and called, saying, "Maid, arise." And her spirit came again, and she arose straightway, a living body.

Lazarus and Jesus loved each other. More than once Jesus had eaten in his house at Bethany with him and his sisters. Now one day Lazarus fell ill, and sent word of it to Jesus. And Jesus answered, "This sickness is not unto death." Two days went by. But on the third day He said to His disciples, "Our friend Lazarus sleepeth; but I go, that I may awake him out of sleep." He was near to Bethany when Martha came to meet Him as if to reproach Him.

"Lord, if thou hadst been here, my brother had not died." And a little later Mary too said, "Lord, if thou hadst been here, my brother had not died." Their repeated reproach touched Jesus, not because He feared He had come too late, but because He was always saddened by the lack of faith even of those dearest to Him.

"And He said, Where have ye laid him? They said unto Him, Lord, come and see. . . . Jesus therefore again groaning in himself cometh to the grave. It was a cave, and a stone lay upon it. Jesus said, Take ye away the stone."

Martha, the housekeeper, the practical, concrete character, interrupted, "Lord, by this time he stinketh: for he hath been dead four days." But Jesus did not heed her, "Take away the stone." And the stone was rolled away. Jesus made a short prayer, His face lifted towards the sky, drew near to the hole and called His friend in a loud voice, "Lazarus, come forth."

And Lazarus came forth, stumbling, for his hands and feet were shrouded and his face covered with a napkin.

"Loose him, and let him go."

And all four, followed by the Twelve and by a throng of thunderstruck Jews, returned to the house. Lazarus's eyes grew used to the light again. He walked on his feet, although with pain, and used his hands. Martha, moving rapidly, got together the best dinner she could in the confusion after four days of demoralizing sorrow—and the man come back to life after death ate with his sister and his friends. Mary could scarcely swallow a mouthful of food, nor take her eyes from the conqueror of death, who, having wiped the tears from His eyes, broke His bread and drank His wine as if this day were like any other day.

These are the resurrections narrated by the Evangelists. In all

His life Jesus raised from the dead only three persons, and in all these three cases Jesus spoke to the dead person as if he were not dead but asleep. Death for Him was only a deeper sleep than the common sleep of everyday, a sleep to be broken by a superhuman love.

JESUS LIKED to go to weddings. In the old days, the workingman, the countryman, the Oriental who lived all the year round on barley bread, dried figs and a few fish and eggs, and only on great days killed a lamb or a kid, saw in weddings the truest and greatest festival of his life. The festivals of the people and those of the church were the same for everybody, and they are repeated every twelfth month; but a wedding was his very own and only came once for him in all the cycle of his years.

Marriage is the supreme effort of the youth of man to conquer Fate with love. All the delights and splendors of the world were centered around the bride and groom, to make the day unforgettable for them. Torches went at night to meet the groom with singers, dancers and musicians. The house was filled with all sorts of meats cooked in all sorts of ways; wine-skins of wine leaning against the walls, vases of unguents for the friends; nothing was lacking for the gratification of the senses.

On that one day all the things which are the daily privilege of princes and rich men triumphed in the poor man's house.

Jesus was touched by the exultation of those simple souls, snatched for those few hours from the gloomy, niggardly poverty of their everyday life. It is not surprising therefore that He should have accepted the invitation to the wedding at Cana. Everyone knows the miracle He wrought that day. Six jars of water were changed by Jesus into wine, and into wine better than that which had been drunk. Old rationalists say that this was a present of wine kept hidden until then, a surprise from Jesus at the end of the meal, in honor of the bride and groom. And six hundred quarts of wine, they add, are a fine present, showing the liberality of the Master.

They have not noticed that only John, the man of allegories, tells of the marriage at Cana. It was not a sleight-of-hand trick,

but a true transmutation, performed with the power of Spirit over matter, and at the same time it is one of those parables told by actual deeds.

ON ANOTHER OCCASION there was a multiplication of bread, similar in its spiritual meaning.

Thousands of poor people had followed Jesus into a place in the wilderness, far from any settlements. For three days they had not eaten, so hungry were they for the bread of life which is His word. But on the third day, Jesus took pity on them—there were women and children among them—and ordered His Disciples to feed the multitude. But they had only a little bread and a few fishes, and there were thousands of mouths. Then Jesus had them all sit down on the ground on the green grass, in circles of fifty to a hundred. He blessed the small amount of food they had; all were satisfied, and baskets of the broken pieces were left.

The less there is of the bread of truth, the more it satisfies. One Word alone will fill the soul; the multitudes will be satisfied and there will be enough to eat also for those who were not present on that day. A loaf of wheat bread is only enough for a very few, and when they have finished it, there is no more for anyone! But the bread of truth, spiritual bread, can never be finished.

The miracle of the loaves is the foundation of all the others. Every parable spoken in poetic words or expressed with visible prodigies was as bread prepared in different manners, so that His own followers should understand the one needful truth that the man who is nourished on the Spirit is master of the world. And yet the Twelve, the chosen, the blessed, the faithful, do not sufficiently believe.

In the boat, the night of the tempest, Jesus was obliged to reprove them. The Master had gone to sleep in the stern, His head on the pillow of one of the rowers. Suddenly the wind rose, a storm came down on the lake, the waves beat against the boat and it seemed from one moment to the next that they would be wrecked. The Disciples, alarmed, awakened Jesus, "Master, carest thou not that we perish?" And He arose, and rebuked the wind, and said unto the sea, "Peace, be still." And the wind ceased, and there was a great calm. And He said unto them, "Why are ye so fearful? how is it that ye have no faith?" And they feared exceedingly, and said one to another, "What manner of man is this, that even the wind and the sea obey him?" But there is one, Simon Peter, who has no fear. Great is his faith, great his love. Everyone can partake of this power.

A few years before Christ, a great captain in many wars was on a real sea, in a boat with a few rowers, in search of an army which had not come up in time to win the victory for him. The wind began to blow, the tempest bore down on the boat and the pilot wished to turn back to the harbor. But Caesar, taking the hand of the pilot, said to him, "Go forward, fear not, Caesar is with thee and his fortune sails with you." These words heartened the crew; every one, as if a little of Caesar's strength had entered into his soul, did his best to overcome the opposition of the sea. But notwithstanding the efforts of the seamen the ship was nearly sunk and was obliged to turn back.

Caesar's faith was only faith in himself: Christ's faith was love for the Father.

With this love He could walk to meet the boat of the Disciples tacking against a contrary wind, and could step upon the water as on the grass of a meadow. They thought in the darkness that it was a specter, and once again He was obliged to reassure them, "Be of good cheer; it is I; be not afraid." As soon as He was in the boat, the wind fell and in a few minutes they reached the shore. Once again they were astounded, says the honest Mark in a revealing comparison, "For they considered not the miracle of the loaves: for their heart was hardened."

CITY LADIES do not make their own bread, but old countrywomen and housewives know what leaven is. A handful of dough from the last baking, as big as a child's hand, wet with warm water and put into the new dough, raises even as much as three measures of flour.

The grain of wheat is not large, the farmer throws it into the ground and then goes on about his other affairs; he sleeps, he goes away from home and comes back. Days pass and nights pass, no thought is given to the seed, but underneath there in

76804
METHODIST COLLEGE LIBRARY
Fayetteville, N. C.

the moist, plowed field the seed has germinated. There comes out a blade of green and at the top of this blade an ear, at first green and graceful, then becoming golden grain. Now the field is ready and the farmer can commence his harvesting.

Likewise with the Kingdom of Heaven and the first news of it. A word seems nothing. What is a word? And yet the word of the Kingdom is like yeast; it ferments and grows. It is like the seed of the fields, patient as the earth which hides it, which, when spring comes, grows green and strong and with the beginning of summer, lo, the harvest is ready!

The Gospel is made up of few words, "The Kingdom is at hand, change your souls!" Only a few men of those living about Christ believed in the Kingdom and prepared themselves for the great day. Only a few, insignificant men, scattered like tiny particles of yeast in the midst of the divided nations and the immense empires, but these few dozen insignificant men gathered together in the midst of a predestined people were to become, through the contagion of their example, thousands upon thousands, and only three hundred years after them, in the place of Tiberius, ruled a man who bowed the knee before the heirs of the Apostles.

THE PARABLES

WEDDINGS AND BANQUETS serve as subjects for many of Christ's parables.

The Kingdom is an eternal feast. There was a king who celebrated his son's wedding, and those whom he invited did not come. One had bought a piece of ground, another five yoke of oxen, a third had taken a wife that day. They were all deep in their affairs, and did not even trouble to send an excuse. Then the king sent his servants to pick up out of the streets the blind, the poor, the maimed and the halt, the lowest of the rabble.

The invitation to the banquet of the Kingdom is a promise of spiritual happiness, absolute, perpetual. And yet the men whom Jesus called first of all to the divine feast of the reborn did not respond. They made wry faces, complained, slipped away and continued their habitual actions. Then all the others were called in their place: beggars instead of the rich, sinners instead of Pharisees, women of the streets instead of fine ladies, the sick and sorrowing instead of the strong and happy.

Even the latest arrivals if they come in time will be admitted to the feast. The master of the vineyard saw in the marketplace certain laborers who were waiting for work and agreed on their wages. Later at noonday he sent others. They all worked, some at pruning and some at hoeing, and when the evening came the master gave the same pay to all. But those who had begun in the morning murmured, "Why do those who have worked less than we receive the same payment?" But the master answered one of them, "If it is my pleasure to give the same to the workingmen of the last hour, is that robbing you others?"

The apparent injustice of the master is only a more generous justice. He who arrived last but works with equal hope has the same right to enjoy that Kingdom for which he has labored.

The master has gone to the wedding and the servants do not know when he will come back. Fortunate are those whom he will find awake. The master himself will seat them at the table and will serve them. But if he finds in the house no lamp lighted, no water warmed, he will drive the servants out without pity.

Everyone should be ready because the Son of man is like a thief in the night who sends no word beforehand. Or like a bridegroom who has been detained by someone in the street.

In the house of the bride there are ten virgins who are to meet him with the light of the procession. Five wise virgins take oil for their lamps, and wait to hear the approaching voices. The foolish five do not think of the oil, and fall asleep. Suddenly there is the sound of the nuptial procession. The five wise virgins light their lamps and run joyfully to welcome the bridegroom. The other five wake up with a start and run from one house to another to get a little oil; but everybody is asleep, the shops are closed and the roaming dogs bark at their heels. They go back to the house of the wedding. The five wise virgins are already there and feasting with the bridegroom. The five foolish virgins knock and cry out, but no one comes to open for them. Through the cracks in the window casings they see the glowing lights of the supper. They hear the clatter of the dishes, the clinking of the cups, the songs of the young men, but they cannot enter; they stay there until morning, in the dark, and the wind.

"ASK, AND IT SHALL be given you; seek, and ye shall find; knock, and it shall be opened unto you." Even hard, slothful, obstinate men give way to persistent entreaty.

There was in a certain city a judge who cared for no one, a morose and scornful man who wanted to do everything as it suited him best. A widow went every day before him and asked for justice, and although her cause was just the judge would not do what she wished. But the widow patiently endured all his repulses and did not weary. And finally the judge, to get rid of this woman who wore him out with her supplications, pleadings, and prayers, gave the sentence and sent her in peace. If even men are not always insensible to pleadings, how much surer will be the response from a Father who loves us?

To listen to the word of the Kingdom is not enough. The only thing which counts is the actual doing. "Whosoever cometh to me, and heareth my sayings, and doeth them, I will show you to whom he is like: He is like a man which built an house, and digged deep, and laid the foundation on a rock: and when the flood arose, the stream beat vehemently upon that house, and could not shake it: for it was founded upon a rock. But he that heareth, and doeth not, is like a man that without a foundation built an house upon the earth; against which the stream did beat vehemently, and immediately it fell; and the ruin of that house was great."

The same teaching is in the parable of the sowing: "A sower went out to sow his seed: and as he sowed, some fell by the wayside; and it was trodden down, and the fowls of the air devoured it. And some fell upon a rock; and as soon as it was sprung up, it withered away, because it lacked moisture. And some fell among thorns; and the thorns sprang up with it, and choked it. And other fell on good ground, and sprang up, and bare fruit an hundredfold." This is the parable which the Twelve were incapable of understanding. Jesus was obliged to explain it Himself. The seed is the Word of God. But it is not enough to hear it merely, to understand it, to practice it. He who has received it should not keep it to himself. Who is the man who having a lamp hides it under the bed or covers it with a vessel?

A Lord traveling into a far country left to each of his servants ten talents with the understanding that they should use the money to good purpose. And when he came back he reckoned with them. And the first delivered to him twenty talents, because with the first ten he had earned ten other talents. And the Lord made him steward over all his goods. And the second delivered him fifteen talents, for he had not been able to earn more than five more. But the third presented himself timorously and showed him, wrapped up in a napkin, the ten talents which he had received. "Lord, I knew thee that thou art an hard man, reaping where thou hast not sown, and gathering where thou hast not strawed: And I was afraid, and went and hid thy talents in the earth." And the Lord answered, "Thou wicked and slothful servant, I will judge thee by thine own words. Take the talents and give them to him who has twenty. For unto every one that hath shall be given, and he shall have abundance: but from him that hath not shall be taken away even that which he hath." And the unprofitable servant was cast into outer darkness. He who has received the Word ought to double his wealth. Those who do not use the treasure of the Word are faithless husbandmen, to whom was entrusted the most fruitful field in all the universe.

A MAN HAD TWO SONS. His wife was dead. He loved his sons like his two eyes and his two hands, equally dear, and he saw to it that both lacked for nothing.

The older was a serious-minded young man, the head of a family. He respected his father as master, without any impulsive show of affection. He worked faithfully, but he was hard and captious with the servants; he went through all the religious forms, but did not let the poor come about him. He pretended to love his brother, but his heart was full of the poison of envy. For brothers rarely love each other. Jewish history, not to speak of any other, begins with Cain, goes on with Jacob's cheating Esau, with Joseph sold by his brothers, with Absalom, who killed Amnon, with Solomon who had Adonijah killed; a long bloody road of jealousy.

The second son splashed about and made merry in his youth as in a warm lake. He was fitful with his father. He was capable of not saying a word for weeks together and then suddenly throwing himself on his father's neck in the highest spirits. He refused no invitations to drink, stared at women and dressed better than other people.

But he was warmhearted; he gave money to the needy, was charitable without boasting of it. He was seldom seen at the synagogue, wanted to spend more than his father's resources allowed him, talked recklessly. He said it was better to look for adventure in rich countries, beyond the mountains and the sea, where the big, luxurious cities are, with marble buildings and the best wines and shops full of silk and silver, and women dressed in fine clothes like queens, fresh from aromatic baths, who lightly give themselves for a piece of gold.

His father, although he was rich, measured out the drachmas as if they were talents. His brother was vexed if he bought a new tunic or came home a little tipsy; in the family all they knew was the field, the furrow, the pasture, the stock; a life that was one long effort.

And one day (he had thought of it many times before, but had never had the courage to say it) he hardened his heart and his face and said to his father, "Father, give me the portion of goods that falleth to me, and I will ask nothing more of thee."

When the old man heard this, he was deeply hurt, and for a while neither of them spoke any more of this matter. But the son suffered, was sullen, and lost all his ardor and animation, even to the fresh color of his face. And the father, seeing his son suffer, suffered himself. Finally paternal love conquered self-love. The estimations and valuations of the property were made, and the father gave to both his sons their rightful part and kept the rest for himself.

The young man lost no time, he sold what he could not carry away, gathered together a goodly sum, and one evening, without saying anything to anyone, mounted his fine horse and went away. The older brother was rather pleased by his departure; now he was the only son, first in command.

But the father secretly wept. Every line of his old face was washed with tears, his aged cheeks were soaked with his grieving.

In the meantime the young man drew rapidly near to the rich city of revels where he meant to live. At every turning of the road he felt of the moneybags which hung at either side of his saddle. It seemed to him that those thousands of coins would last forever. He rented a fine house, bought five or six slaves, dressed like a prince, and soon had many friends who were guests at his table, and who drank his wine till their stomachs could hold no more.

He did not economize with women and chose the most beautiful the city contained, those who knew how to dance and sing and dress with magnificence, and undress with grace. The little provincial lord from the dull country, repressed in the most sensual period of his life, now vented his voluptuousness, his love of luxury, in this dangerous life.

But the moneybags of the prodigal son were not bottomless. There came a day when there were only empty bags of canvas and leather lying limp and flabby on the brick floor of his room. His friends disappeared, the women disappeared, slaves, beds and dining tables were sold. A famine came on the country and the prodigal son found himself hungering in the midst of a famine-stricken people.

The unfortunate man, destitute, left the city, traveling with a lord who was going to the country where he had a fine estate. The lord hired him as swineherd because he was young and strong and hardly anyone was willing to be a swineherd. For a Jew nothing could be a greater affliction than this. Even in Egypt, although animals were adored there, the only people forbidden to enter the temples were swineherds.

The prodigal son was given no pay and very little to eat, because there was only a little for anyone; but there was no famine for the hogs, because they could eat anything. There were plenty of carob beans and they gorged themselves. Their hungry attendant watched the pink and black animals rooting in the earth and longed to fill his stomach with the same stuff and wept, remembering the abundance of his own home. Sometimes, overcome with hunger, he took one of the black bean husks from under the grunting snouts of the pigs, tempering the bitterness of his suffering with that insipid and woody food.

His dress was a dirty slave's smock which smelled of manure, his footgear a pair of worn-out sandals scarcely held together with rushes; on his head a faded hood. His fair young face, tanned by the sun of the hills, was thin and long, and had taken a sickly color.

Who was wearing now the spotless homespun clothes, which he had left in his brother's chests? His father's hired servants were better dressed than he.

Returned to his senses, he said to himself, "How many servants of my father's have bread enough and to spare, and I perish with hunger!"

But how could he return without a garment, unshod, without a penny, without the ring—the sign of liberty—stinking and contaminated by this abominable trade, to show that his serious-minded brother was right, to bow himself at the knee of the old man whom he had left without a greeting!

No, there was something of his always in his home, his father! He was his creation, made of his flesh, issued from his seed in a moment of love. "I will arise and go to my father, and will say unto him, Father, I have sinned against heaven, and before thee, and am no more worthy to be called thy son: make me as one of thy hired servants."

And the young man gave back the hogs to his master, and went towards his own land. He begged a piece of bread from the countrypeople, and wept as he ate this bread of pity in the shadow of the sycamores. His sore and blistered feet could scarcely carry him, but his faith in forgiveness led him homeward step by step.

And finally one day at noon he arrived in sight of his father's house; but he did not dare to knock, nor to call anyone, nor to go in. He hung around outside to see if anyone would come out.

And behold, his father appeared on the threshold. His son was changed, but the eyes of a father even dimmed by weeping could not fail to recognize him. He ran towards him and caught him to his breast, and kissed him, and could not stop from pressing his pale, old lips on that ravaged face, on those eyes whose expression was altered but still beautiful, on that hair, dusty but still waving and soft, on that flesh that was his own.

The son, covered with confusion and deeply moved, did not know how to respond to these kisses, and as soon as he could free himself from his father's arms he threw himself on the ground and repeated tremulously the speech he had prepared. "Father, I have sinned against heaven, and before thee, And am no more worthy to be called thy son."

The old man never felt himself more father than at this moment; he seemed to become a father for a second time, and without even answering, with his eyes still clouded and soft, but with the ringing voice of his best days, he called to the servants:

"Bring forth the best robe, and put it on him; and put a ring on his hand, and shoes on his feet:

"And bring hither the fatted calf, and kill it; and let us eat, and be merry: For this my son was dead, and is alive again; he was lost, and is found."

The servants obeyed him and the calf was killed, skinned, cut up and put to cook. The oldest wine was taken from the wine cellar, and the finest room was prepared for the dinner in celebration of the return. Servants went to call his father's friends and others went to summon musicians, that there should be music.

The older son was in the field, working, and in the evening when he came back and was near to the house he heard shouts and stampings and clapping of hands, and the footsteps of dancers. And he could not understand. "Whatever can have happened? Perhaps a wedding procession has arrived unexpectedly at our house."

Disliking noise and new faces, he would not enter and see for himself what it was. But he called to a boy coming out of the house and asked him what all that clatter was.

"Thy brother is come; and thy father hath killed the fatted

calf, because he hath received him safe and sound." These words were like a thrust at his heart. He turned pale, not with pleasure, but with rage and jealousy. And he would not go into the house.

Then his father went out and entreated him: "Come, for your brother has come back and has asked after you, and will be glad to see you, and we will feast together."

But the serious-minded young man could not contain himself, and for the first time in his life ventured to reprove his father to his face.

"Lo, these many years do I serve thee, neither transgressed I at any time thy commandment: and yet thou never gavest me a kid, that I might make merry with my friends: But as soon as this thy son was come, which hath devoured thy living with harlots, thou hast killed for him the fatted calf."

With these few words he discloses all the ignominy of his soul hidden until then under the Pharisaical cloak of good behavior. "This thy son." He does not say "brother."

But his father pardoned this son, as he did the other son. "Son, thou art ever with me, and all that I have is thine. It was meet that we should make merry, and be glad: for this thy brother was dead, and is alive again; and was lost, and is found."

No story—after that of Joseph—that came from human lips ever touched more deeply the hearts of men. Interpreters are free to explain the story of the prodigal son, but Jesus Himself says expressly that the meaning is this: "More joy shall be in heaven over one sinner who repents than over all the righteous."

"What man of you, having an hundred sheep, if he lose one of them, doth not leave the ninety and nine in the wilderness, and go after that which is lost, until he find it? And when he hath found it, he layeth it on his shoulders, rejoicing. And when he cometh home, he calleth together his friends and neighbors, saying unto them, Rejoice with me; for I have found my sheep which was lost."

BUT FORGIVENESS CREATES an obligation for which there are no exceptions allowed. He who has received must give; it is better to give much, but it is essential to give a part at least.

A king one day wanted a reckoning with his servants and one by one he called them before him. Among the first was one who owed him ten thousand talents, but as he had not anything to pay this, the king commanded that he should be sold and his wife and his children and all that he had, in payment of a part of the debt.

The servant in despair threw himself at the feet of the king. He seemed a mere bundle of garments crying out sobs and promises. "Have patience with me, wait a little longer and I will pay you all, but do not have my wife and my children separated from me, sent away like cattle, no one knows where."

The king was moved with compassion—he also had little children—and he sent him away free and forgave him that great debt. The servant went out and he met one of his fellow servants who owed him a hundred pence, a small thing compared with ten thousand talents, and he sprang on him. "Pay me what thou owest and at once, or I will have thee bound by the guards." The unlucky man fell down at his feet and besought him and wept and swore that he would pay him in a few days and kissed the hem of his garment, and recalled to him their old comradeship and begged him to wait in the name of the children who were waiting for him in his home.

But the servant took his debtor by the arm and had him cast into prison. The news spread quickly to the ears of the king, who called that pitiless man and delivered him to the tormentors: "I forgave you that great debt, shouldst thou not have had compassion on thy brother, for his debt was so much smaller? I had pity on thee, oughtest thou not to have had pity on him?"

TWO MEN went up into the temple to pray; the one a Pharisee, and the other a publican. The Pharisee, with his phylacteries hanging upon his forehead and on his left arm, with the long, glittering fringes on his cloak, erect like a man who feels himself in his own house, prayed thus: "God, I thank thee, that I am not as other men are, extortioners, unjust, adulterers, or even as this publican. I fast twice in the week, I give tithes of all that I possess."

But the publican did not have the courage even to lift his

eyes and seemed ashamed to appear before his Lord. He sighed and smote on his breast and said only these words: "God be merciful to me, a sinner."

"I tell you, this man went down to his house justified rather than the other: for every one that exalteth himself shall be abased; and he that humbleth himself shall be exalted."

A LAWYER asked Jesus who is one's neighbor, and Jesus told this story: "A man, a Jew, went down from Jerusalem to Jericho through the mountain passes. Thieves fell upon him, and after they had wounded him and taken away his clothes, they left him upon the road half dead.

"A priest passed that way and saw the unfortunate man stretched out, but he passed by on the other side of the road. A little after came a Levite. He also knew every detail of all the holy ceremonies, and seemed more than a sacristan, seemed one of the masters of the Temple. He looked at the bloody body and went on his way.

"And finally came a Samaritan. To the Jews the Samaritans were only slightly less detestable than the Gentiles, because they would not sacrifice at Jerusalem and accept the reform of Nehemiah. The Samaritan, however, did not wait to see if the unfortunate man thrown among the stones of the street was circumcised or uncircumcised, was a Jew or a Samaritan. He was quickly moved to pity, took down his flasks from his saddle and poured upon the man's wounds a little oil, a little wine, bound them up as well as he could with a handkerchief, put the stranger across his ass and brought him to an inn, had him put to bed, tried to restore him, giving him something hot to drink, and did not leave him until he saw him come to himself and able to speak and eat.

"The next day he called the host apart and gave him two pence: 'Take care of him, do the best thou canst and whatsoever thou spendest more, when I come again, I will repay thee.'

"The neighbor, then, is he who suffers, he who needs help, whoever he is, of whatever nation or religion he may be. Even thine enemy, if he needs thee, even if he does not ask help, is the first of 'thy neighbors.' "

THE TWELVE

FATE KNOWS no better way to punish the great for their greatness than by sending them disciples. Every disciple, just because he is a disciple, cannot understand all that his master says, but at very best only half, and that according to the kind of mind he has. Thus without wishing to falsify the teaching of his master, he deforms it, vulgarizes it, belittles it, corrupts it.

Or else, sometimes, he twists and turns the master's thought to make it seem that he has a thought of his own, different and original, and teaches exactly the opposite of what he was taught.

And yet no one has been able to dispense with these pupils and followers, nor even to wish to. For the great man cannot teach without the illusion that someone understands his words, receives his ideas, transmits them to others far away before his death and after his death.

Christ accepted with the other trials of earthly life the burden of disciples. We know who His Apostles were. A Galilean, He chose them from among the Galileans. A poor man, He chose them from among the poor; a simple man, He called simple men.

He knew that these souls were rough but had integrity, were ignorant but ardent, and that He could in the end mold them like clay from the river, which is only mud, and yet when modeled and baked in the kiln, becomes eternal beauty.

But their imperfect nature had too often the upper hand. Our hearts ache if we look at them closely in the Gospels: those men who were so inestimably fortunate as to live with Christ, to walk, to eat with Him, to sleep in the same room, to look into His face, to touch His hand, to kiss Him, to hear His words from His very mouth; those twelve fortunate men, whom throughout the centuries millions of souls have secretly envied.

We see them, hard of head and of heart; not always capable of understanding, even after His death, who Jesus had been and what sort of a new Kingdom was proclaimed by Him; often lacking in faith, in love, in brotherly affection; envying each other; impatient for the revenge which would repay them for their long wait; intolerant of those who were not one with them; vindictive toward those who would not receive them, materialistic, avaricious, cowardly.

One of them denies Him three times; one of them delays giving Him due reverence until He is in the sepulcher; one does not believe in His mission because He comes from Nazareth; one is not willing to admit His resurrection; one sells Him to His enemies, and gives Him over with His last kiss to those who come to arrest Him. Others, when Christ's teachings were on a too lofty level, "went back, and walked no more with Him." Like the common people they constantly feel that Jesus should be the worldly Messiah, political, warlike, come to restore the temporal throne of David. Even when He is about to ascend into Heaven they continue to ask Him: "Lord, wilt thou at this time restore again the kingdom to Israel?"

PETER BEFORE THE RESURRECTION is like a body beside a spirit. He is the earth which believes in Heaven but remains earthy.

When Jesus pronounced the famous words: "It is easier for a camel to go through the eye of a needle, than for a rich man to enter into the kingdom of God," Peter thought this sweeping condemnation of wealth very harsh. "Then answered Peter and said unto him, Behold, we have forsaken all, and followed thee; what shall we have therefore?" Jesus promises him that everyone shall have a hundred times what he has given up.

Again Peter does not understand what Christ means when He asserts that only what comes from man himself can defile men. "Then answered Peter, and said unto him, Declare unto us this parable. And Jesus said, Are ye also yet without understanding? Do not ye yet understand?"

Peter was not an alert spirit. He fell asleep on the Mount of the Transfiguration. He fell asleep on the night at Gethsemane, after the Last Supper, where Jesus had uttered the saying which would have kept even a scribe everlastingly from sleep.

When Jesus that last evening announced that He was to suffer and die, Peter burst out: "Lord, I am ready to go with thee, both into prison, and to death. Although all shall be offended, yet will not I. If I should die with thee, I will not deny Thee in any wise."

Jesus answered him: "Verily I say unto thee, That this night, before the cock crow, thou shalt deny me thrice." Jesus knew him better than Peter knew himself.

Peter had, like all crude personalities, a tendency to see the material in spiritual manifestations. On the Mount of the Transfiguration, when he was awakened and saw Jesus refulgent with white light, speaking with two others, with two spirits, with two prophets, the first thought which came to him, instead of worshipping and keeping silence, was to build a tabernacle for these great personages.

"Master, it is good for us to be here: and let us make three tabernacles; one for thee, and one for Moses, and one for Elias." Luke, the wise man, adds to excuse him, "not knowing what he said."

When he saw Jesus walking in all security on the lake, the idea came to him to do the same thing. "And when Peter was come down out of the ship, he walked on the water, to go to Jesus. But when he saw the wind boisterous, he was afraid; and beginning to sink, he cried, saying, Lord, save me. And immediately Jesus stretched forth His hand, and caught him, and said unto him, O thou of little faith, wherefore didst thou doubt?"

His great love for Christ, which makes up for all his weakness, led him one day almost to rebuke Him. Jesus had told His disciples how He must suffer and be killed. "Then Peter took him, and began to rebuke him, saying, Be it far from thee, Lord: this shall not be unto thee. But he turned, and said unto Peter, Get thee behind me, Satan: thou art an offense unto me: for thou savorest not the things that be of God, but those that be of men."

Peter's mind was still occupied with the vulgar idea of the triumphant Messiah; he *thought as men do*. And yet he was the first to recognize Jesus as the Christ; and this primacy is so great that nothing has been able to cancel it.

THE TWO FISHERMEN, the brothers James and John, who had left their boat and their nets on the shore at Capernaum in order to go with Jesus, form together with Peter a sort of favorite triumvirate. They are the only ones who accompany Jesus into the house of Jairus, and on the Mount of the Transfiguration, and they are the ones whom He takes with Him on the night of Gethsemane. But in spite of their long intimacy with the Master, they never acquired sufficient humility. Jesus gave them the surname of "Boanerges—Sons of Thunder," an ironic surname, alluding perhaps to their fiery, irascible character.

When they all started together towards Jerusalem, they were crossing Samaria and were badly received in a village. "And they did not receive him, because his face was as though he would go to Jerusalem. And when his disciples James and John saw this, they said, Lord, wilt thou that we command fire to come down from heaven, and consume them? But he turned, and rebuked them." For them, Galileans, faithful to Jerusalem, the Samaritans were always enemies. In vain had they heard the Sermon on the Mount: "Do good to them that hate you, and pray for them which despitefully use you, and persecute you." Angry at an affront to Jesus, it seemed to them a work of righteous justice to reduce the inhospitable village to ashes. Yet far as they were from a loving rebirth of the soul, these men wanted to claim the first places on the day of triumph.

James and John, the sons of Zebedee, came unto him, saying: "Master, grant unto us that we may sit one on thy right hand and one on thy left hand in thy glory." But Jesus said unto them: "Ye know not what ye ask." And when the ten heard it they began to be much displeased with James and John. But Jesus called them to Him and saith unto them: "Whosoever will be great among you let him be your servant, for even the Son of man came not to be ministered unto but to minister."

This miraculous paradox is the proof of the fire of genius. He who cannot or will not serve shows that he has nothing to give. But the genius is no true genius if he does not exuberantly benefit his inferiors. There is nothing servile in serving.

James and John understood this stimulating saying of Jesus. We find one of them, John, among the nearest and most loving of the Disciples. At the Last Supper he leans his head on Jesus' breast; and from the height of the cross Jesus, crucified, confides the Virgin to him, that he should be a son to her.

THOMAS OWES his popularity to the quality which should be his shame. Thomas, the twin, is the guardian of modernity, as Thomas Aquinas is the oracle of medieval life. He is the true patron saint of Spinoza and of all the other deniers of the Resurrection, the man who is not satisfied even with the testimony of his eyes, but wishes that of his hands as well. And yet his love for Jesus makes him pardonable. When they came to the Master to say that Lazarus was dead, and the Disciples hesitated before going into Judea among their enemies, it was Thomas alone who said: "Let us also go, that we may die with him." The martyrdom which he did not find then came to him in India, after Christ's death.

Matthew is the dearest of all the Twelve. He was a tax gatherer, a sort of under-publican, and probably had more education than his companions. He followed Jesus as readily as the fishermen. "And after these things he went forth, and saw a publican, named Levi, sitting at the receipt of custom: and he said unto him, Follow me. And he left all, rose up, and followed him. And Levi made him a great feast in his own house." It was not a heap of torn nets which Matthew left, but a position, secure and increasing earnings. Of no other Disciple is it told that he could offer a great feast. Giving up riches is easy for a man who has almost nothing. Among the Twelve, Matthew was certainly the richest before his conversion.

Matthew and Judas were perhaps the only ones of the Disciples who knew how to write, and to Matthew we owe the first collection of Logia or memorable sayings of Jesus. In the Gospel which is called by his name, we find the most complete text of the Sermon on the Mount. Our debt to him is heavy; without him many words of Jesus, and the most beautiful, might have been lost.

Philip of Bethsaida also knew how to reckon. When the famished multitude pressed about Him, Jesus turned to him to ask what it would cost to buy bread for all those people. Philip answered Him: "Two hundred pennyworth of bread is not sufficient for them." It was to him that the Greeks of Jerusalem turned when they wished to speak to the new prophet, and he it was who announced to Nathanael the coming of Jesus.

Nathanael answered Philip's announcement with sarcasm: "Can there any good thing come out of Nazareth?" But Philip succeeded in bringing him to Jesus, who as soon as He saw him, exclaimed, "Behold an Israelite indeed, in whom is no guile! Nathanael saith unto him, Whence knowest thou me? Jesus answered and said unto him, Before that Philip called thee, when thou wast under the fig tree, I saw thee. Nathanael answered and saith unto him, Rabbi, thou art the Son of God; thou art the King of Israel. Jesus answered and said unto him, Because I said unto thee, I saw thee under the fig tree, believest thou? thou shalt see greater things than these."

Less enthusiastic and inflammable was Nicodemus, who, as a matter of fact, never wished to be known as a disciple of Jesus. Nicodemus was old, had been to school to the Rabbis, but the stories of the miracles had shaken him, and he went by night to Jesus to tell Him that he believed that He was sent by God. Jesus answered him, "Verily, verily, I say unto thee, Except a man be born again, he cannot see the kingdom of God." Nicodemus did not understand these words, or perhaps they startled him. He had come to see a miracle worker and had found a sibyl, and with the homely good sense of the man who wishes to avoid being taken in by a fraud he said, "How can a man be born when he is old? can he enter the second time into his mother's womb, and be born?"

Jesus answers with words of profound meaning, "Except a man be born of water and of the Spirit, he cannot enter into the kingdom of God." But Nicodemus still did not understand. "How can these things be?"

Nicodemus always respected the young Galilean, but his sympathy was as circumspect as his visit. Once when the leaders of the priests and the Pharisees were meditating how to capture Jesus, Nicodemus ventured a defense: "Doth our law judge any man, before it hear him, and know what he doeth?" A few words of reproof were enough to silence him. "They answered and said unto him, Art thou also of Galilee? Search, and look: for out of Galilee ariseth no prophet!" He belonged by right to the Sanhedrin, but there is no record that he raised his voice in favor of the accused when He was arrested. The trial was at night and probably to avoid his own remorse for the legal assassination, Nicodemus remained in his bed. When he awoke Jesus was dead, and then, forgetting his avarice, he bought a hundred pounds of myrrh and aloes to embalm the body.

Nicodemus is the eternal type of the lukewarm. He is the halfway soul.

But the Church to reward his posthumous piety has chosen him to become one of her saints. And there is an old tradition that he was baptized by Peter and put to death for having believed, too late, in Him whom he did not save from death.

THOSE WHOM Jesus sent out to the conquest of souls were rustic countrymen, but they could be mild as sheep, wary as serpents, simple as doves.

The Disciples destined to preach the beauty of poverty to both poor and rich were to set an example of happy poverty to every man in every house on every day. They were to carry nothing with them except the clothes on their backs and the sandals on their feet. They were to accept nothing; only the small piece of daily bread which they would find on the tables of their hosts. The wandering priests of the goddess Siria and of other Oriental divinities carried with them, along with the sacred images, the wallet for offerings, the bag for alms, because common people do not value things which cost them nothing. The Apostles of Jesus, on the contrary, were to refuse any gift or payment: "Freely ye have received, freely give."

They were to enter into the houses, open to all in a country where the locks and bolts of fear were not yet known, and which preserved some remembrance of nomad hospitality—they were to speak to the men and the women who lived there. Their duty was to announce that the Kingdom of Heaven was at hand, to explain in what way the kingdom of earth could become the Kingdom of Heaven, and to explain the one condition for this happy fulfilling of all the prophecies—repentance, conversion, transformation of the soul. Pilgrims without purses or bundles, they carried with them truth and life—peace.

"And when ye come into an house salute it," and this was the salutation, "Peace be with you."

OTHER TEACHINGS

JESUS IS THE POOR MAN, infinitely and rigorously poor. The prince of poverty. Richness is a curse. The rich man does not belong to himself, but to inanimate things. Outside of himself man can possess nothing. The absolute secret of owning other things is to renounce them. But he who wishes to grasp for himself alone a part of the world's goods loses both what he has acquired and everything else.

"For what shall it profit a man, if he shall gain the whole world, and lose his own soul?" This question of Christ's, simple like all revelations, expresses the exact meaning of the prophetic threat. The rich man not only loses eternity, but, pulled down by his wealth, loses his life here below, his present soul, the happiness of his present earthly life.

"Ye cannot serve God and mammon." He who desires gold puts an end to the spirit and renounces all the benefits of the spirit: peace, holiness, love, perfect joy. When the mystery of wealth is deeply probed, it is easy to see that the most precious thing is exchanged for the most worthless. For poverty, voluntarily accepted, joyfully desired, is the only poverty which gives spiritual wealth. Absolute poverty frees men for the conquest of the absolute. The Kingdom of Heaven does not promise poor people that they shall become rich, it promises rich people that they shall enter into it when they become freely poor.

"Sell whatsoever thou hast, and give to the poor, and thou shalt have treasure in heaven where neither moth nor rust doth corrupt and where thieves do not break through nor steal; for where your treasure is, there will your heart be also. Give to him that asketh thee, and from him that would borrow from thee, turn not thou away, for it is more blessed to give than to receive."

Jesus was not the first to find in poverty one of the steps to perfection. Buddha exhorted his disciples to a similar renunciation. The Cynics stripped themselves of all material goods to be independent of work and of men, and to be able to consecrate their freed souls to truth. Crates, the Theban nobleman, disciple of Diogenes, distributed his wealth to his fellow citizens and turned beggar. Plato wished the warriors in his Republic to have no possessions as a measure of political prudence. The first republics conquered and flourished as long as the citizens contented themselves, as in old Sparta and old Rome, with strict poverty, and they fell as soon as they valued gold more than sober and modest living.

But in Jesus the love of poverty is not an ascetic rule. In the Gospel, poverty of the body is a preliminary requisite, like humility of the spirit. The poor man who glories in his poverty instead of tormenting himself to convert it into wealth is nearer to moral perfection than the rich man. But the rich man who has despoiled himself in favor of the poor and has chosen to live side by side with his new brothers is still nearer perfection than the man who was born and reared in poverty. That he has been touched by a grace so rare and prodigious gives him the right to hope for the greatest blessedness.

EVERY TIME that the powerful have desired to sanctify violence and make Christ surety for Genghis Khan or for Bonaparte or even the outrider of Mohammed, you will see them quote the celebrated Gospel text, which everybody knows by heart and very few have ever understood.

"Think not that I am come to send peace on earth: I came not to send peace, but a sword." Some more learned add, "I am come to send fire on the earth." Others rush forward to present the decisive verse, "The kingdom of heaven suffereth violence, and the violent take it by force."

These hardened quoters do not look at the words which come

before and after; they pay no attention to the occasion on which they were spoken. They do not imagine for a moment that they can have another meaning from the common one.

When Jesus says that He has come to bring a sword—or as it is written in the parallel passage of Luke, "Discord," He is speaking to His Disciples who are on the point of departing to announce the coming of the Kingdom. And immediately after, He explains with familiar examples what He meant to say: "For I am come to set a man at variance against his father, and the daughter against her mother, and the daughter-in-law against her mother-in-law. And a man's foes shall be they of his own household. For from henceforth there shall be five in one house divided, three against two and two against three." The sword therefore is a figure of speech which signifies division; the preaching of the Gospel shall divide men of the same family; those who are slow and those who are quick, those who deny and those who believe. Until all are converted and "brothers in the Word," discord will reign on earth.

When Jesus proclaims that He comes to bring fire, only the literal-minded can think of destructive fire, auxiliary of human warfare. The fire desired by the Son of man is the fire of purification, of enthusiasm, the ardor of sacrifice, the flame of love, which Jesus came to kindle in our hearts.

Jesus can say, "The kingdom of heaven suffereth violence, and the violent take it by force." The word "violent" has as a matter of fact in the text the evident meaning of "strong," of men who know how to take doors by assault without hesitating or trembling. "Sword," "fire," "violence," are figurative words which we are forced to use to reach the imagination of the crowds. The sword is the symbol of the divisions between those first persuaded and those last to believe; fire is purifying love; violence is the strength necessary to make oneself over and to arrive on the threshold of the Kingdom.

Jesus is the Man of Peace. He has come to bring Peace. The Gospels are nothing but proclamations and instructions for Peace. The very night of His birth celestial voices sang in the sky: "Peace on Earth to men of good will." On the Mount one of the first promises is that directed to the peacemakers, "Blessed

are the peacemakers: for they shall be called the children of God." To the disciples, to His friends, He counsels, "Have peace one with another." On that terrible night on the Mount of Olives, while the mercenaries armed with swords are binding Him, He pronounces the supreme condemnation of violence, "For all they that take the sword shall perish with the sword." He understands the evils of discord, "Every kingdom divided against itself is brought to desolation; and every city or house divided against itself shall not stand." And in His talk on the last things, in the grand apocalyptic prophecy, He announces among the terrible signs of the end together with famine, earthquakes and tribulation, also wars. "And ye shall hear of wars and rumors of wars. . . . For nation shall rise against nation, and kingdom against kingdom."

But when hate is abolished in every heart, then at last will arrive the day longed for by Isaiah when, "they shall beat their swords into plowshares, and their spears into pruning hooks: nation shall not lift up sword against nation, neither shall they learn war any more."

That day announced by Isaiah is the day on which the Sermon on the Mount shall become the only law recognized on earth.

In the Kingdom of Heaven men will not hate each other and will no longer desire riches; every reason and need for government will disappear immediately after these two great changes. The name of the path which conducts to perfect liberty is not Destruction but Holiness.

JESUS SANCTIONS the union of man and woman even in the flesh. In marriage Jesus sees first of all the joining of two bodies. On this point He ratifies the metaphor of the Old Law, "So then they are no more twain, but one flesh." Husband and wife are one body, inseparable.

This man shall never have another woman; this woman shall never know another man until death divides them. The mating has an almost mystic character which nothing can cancel. The two have been fused into one, their two souls become one soul, and from this communion will be born a new creature formed of the essence of both, which will be the visible form of their union. Love makes them like God, creators of a new and miraculous creation.

But this duality of the flesh and of the spirit—the most perfect among imperfect human relations—should never be disturbed or interrupted. Jesus always condemns adultery and divorce in the most absolute manner. His whole nature holds unfaithfulness in horror. There will come a day, he warns people, in speaking of heavenly life, in which men and women will not marry; but up to that day marriage should have at least all the perfections possible to its imperfection. In the new organization of salvation, spiritual affiliations will surpass the simple relationships of the flesh.

Jesus was speaking in a house, perhaps at Capernaum, and men and women, all hungering for life and justice, all needing comfort and consolation, had filled the house, had pressed close around Him.

There came a stir and voices were heard at the door. One of those present told Jesus, "Behold, thy mother and thy brethren without seek for thee." But Jesus did not stir. "Who is my mother, or my brethren?" And he looked round about on them which sat about him, and said, "Behold my mother and my brethren! For whosoever shall do the will of God, the same is my brother, and my sister, and mother."

He who wishes to serve the universe with a broad spirit must give up, and if that is not enough, deny the common affections. "If any man come to me, and hate not his father, and mother, and wife, and children, and brethren, and sisters, yea, and his own life also, he cannot be my disciple."

The family will disappear when men shall be better than men. "And call no man your father upon the earth: for one is your Father, which is in heaven." He who leaves his family shall be infinitely rewarded. "And he said unto them, Verily I say unto you, There is no man that hath left house, or parents, or brethren, or wife, or children, for the kingdom of God's sake, Who shall not receive manifold more in this present time, and in the world to come life everlasting."

According to Jesus, fathers have more duties towards their sons than sons towards their fathers. "Honor thy father and thy mother," said Moses. But from Jesus' point of view, fathers are debtors. "Or what man is there of you, whom if his son ask bread, will he give him a stone? Or if he ask a fish, will he give him a serpent?"

JESUS, WHOM no one called Father, was drawn to children as to sinners. Lover of the absolute, He loved only extremes. Complete innocence and complete downfall were for Him pledges of salvation. Innocence because it does not need to be cleansed; abject degradation because it feels more keenly the need to be cleansed.

Mothers brought their children to Him to have Him touch them. The Disciples, with their habitual roughness, cried out on them—and Jesus once more was obliged to reprove them, "Suffer little children, and forbid them not, to come unto me: for of such is the kingdom of heaven."

The bearded men, proud of their authority as lieutenants of their future Lord, could not understand why their Master consented to waste time with children who could not yet speak plainly and could not understand the meaning of grown people's words. But Jesus set in their midst one of these children and said: "Verily I say unto you, Except ye be converted, and become as little children, ye shall not enter into the kingdom of heaven. Whosoever therefore shall humble himself as this little child, the same is greatest in the kingdom of heaven. And whoso shall receive one such little child in my name receiveth me. But whoso shall offend one of these little ones which believe in me, it were better for him that a millstone were hanged about his neck, and that he were drowned in the depth of the sea."

Here, too, Jesus reversed the Old Law. Perfection was supposed to lie in years of maturity, or, better yet, in old age. Jesus loves children as the actual mediums of truth. "I thank thee, O Father, Lord of heaven and earth, because thou hast hid these things from the wise and prudent, and hast revealed them unto babes."

Only the simple can understand simplicity; the innocent, innocence; the loving, love.

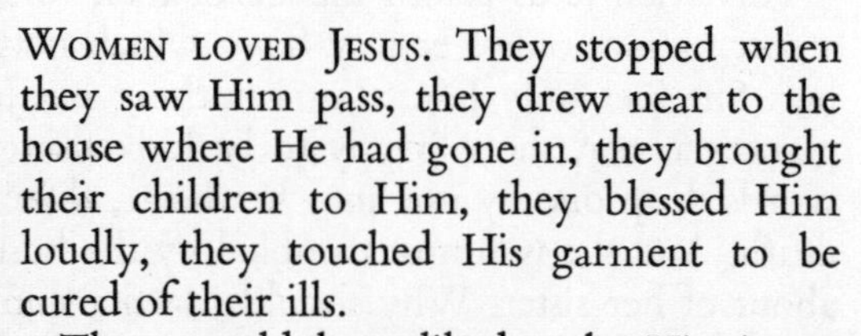

MARTHA AND MARY

WOMEN LOVED JESUS. They stopped when they saw Him pass, they drew near to the house where He had gone in, they brought their children to Him, they blessed Him loudly, they touched His garment to be cured of their ills.

They would have liked to be His sisters, His servants, His slaves; to serve Him, to set bread before Him, to pour Him wine, to wash His garments, to anoint His tired feet and His flowing hair. Some of them were fortunate enough to be allowed to follow Him, and knew the still greater good fortune of helping Him with their money. ". . . and the twelve were with Him, And certain women, which had been healed of evil spirits and infirmities, Mary called Magdalene, out of whom went seven devils, And Joanna the wife of Chuza, Herod's steward, and Susanna, and many others, which ministered unto him of their substance."

Many followed Him to death. Salome, mother of James and John, the Sons of Thunder; Mary, mother of James the less; Martha and Mary of Bethany.

When He appears in the house of Lazarus, the man brought back from death, the two sisters seem distracted with joy. Martha rushes towards Him, leads Him to the couch that He may lie down, puts over Him a blanket lest He be cold, and runs with a pitcher to get fresh cool water. Then she sets to work to prepare for the Pilgrim a fine meal. With all haste she lights a great fire, goes to get fresh fish, new-laid eggs, figs and olives; she borrows from one neighbor a piece of new-killed lamb, from another a costly perfume, from another richer than she, a flowered dish. She pulls out from the linen chest the newest tablecloth, and brings up from the wine cellar the oldest wine. And while the wood snaps and sparkles in the fire and the water in the kettle begins to simmer, poor Martha, bustling, flushed, hurrying, sets the table, runs between the kneading trough and the fire, glances at the waiting Master, at the street to see if her brother is coming home, and at her sister, who is doing nothing at all.

For when Jesus passed the sill of their house, Mary fell into a sort of motionless ecstasy from which nothing could arouse her. She sees only Jesus, hears nothing but Jesus' voice. If He glances at her, she is happy to be looked at; if He speaks, His words drop one by one into her heart, there to remain to her death. And she is almost troubled by the bustling and stepping about of her sister. Why should Martha think that Jesus needs an elaborate dinner? Mary is seated at His feet and does not move even if Martha or Lazarus calls her. She is at the service of Jesus, but in another way. She is a contemplative soul, an adorer. She will take action only to cover the dead body of her God with perfumes.

Women loved Him and no woman who turned to Him was sent away disconsolate. The unknown woman which had a "spirit of infirmity" eighteen years, and was bowed together and could in no wise lift herself, was cured, although it was on the Sabbath day and the rulers of the synagogue cried, "Sacrilege!" In the first part of His wanderings He cured Peter's wife's mother of fever. He cured that unknown woman who had suffered for twelve years from a bloody flux.

"The words of the Law," says a rabbinical proverb of that time, "rather than teach them to a woman, burn them up!" Jesus on the other hand did not hesitate to speak to them of the highest mysteries. When He went alone to the well of Sichar, and the Samaritan woman who had had five husbands came there, He did not hesitate to proclaim His message to her, although she was a woman and an enemy of His people. "But the hour cometh, and now is, when the true worshippers shall worship the Father in spirit and in truth: for the Father seeketh such to worship him. God is a Spirit: and they that worship him must worship him in spirit and in truth." His Disciples came up, "And marveled that he talked with the woman." They did not yet know that the Church of Christ would make the Virgin Mother the link between the sons and the Son.

On another occasion, at Jerusalem, Jesus found Himself before a woman. A hooting crowd pushed her forward. The woman, hiding her face with her hands and with her hair, stood before Him, without speaking. Jesus detested adultery. But He detested still more the cowardice of talebearers, the hounding by the merciless. And He stooped down and with His finger wrote upon the ground. It is the first and last time that we see Jesus lower Himself to this trivial operation. No one has ever known what he wrote at that moment. He chose the sand on which to write expressly that the wind might carry away the words, which would perhaps frighten men if they could read them. But the persecutors insisted that the woman should be stoned. Then Jesus lifted Himself up, looked deep into their eyes, one by one: "He that is without sin among you, let him first cast a stone at her."

On this earth there are no innocents, and even if there were, their mercy would be stronger than justice itself.

Such thoughts had never occurred to those angry spies; Christ's words troubled them. Every one of them thought of his own secret sins of the flesh. The old men were the first to go. Then, little by little, all the others, avoiding each other's eyes, scattered and dispersed. Jesus had again stooped down to write upon the ground. The woman had heard the shuffling of the departing feet, and heard no longer any voice crying for her death, but she did not dare to raise her eyes. Jesus for the second time lifted Himself up and saw the open place was empty.

"Woman, where are those thine accusers? hath no man condemned thee?"

"No man, Lord."

"Neither do I condemn thee: go, and sin no more."

And for the first time the woman dared to look in His face. But Jesus had begun again to write on the ground of the court, His head lowered, and she saw only His finger moving slowly over the sunlit earth.

BUT NO WOMAN loved Him so much as the woman who anointed Him with nard and bathed Him with her tears in the house of Simon the Pharisee. Every one of us has seen that picture in imagination; and yet the true meaning of the episode is understood by very few, so greatly has it been disfigured by both the ordinary and the literary interpretations.

This woman who silently entered the house of Simon with her box of alabaster had heard the voice of Jesus; His voice had troubled her, His words had shaken her. When she came to the house of Simon the sinning woman wished to reward her Saviour with a token of her gratitude. She took one of the most costly things left to her, a sealed box full of nard. Hers was an act of public gratitude. The woman wished to thank Him who had brought her heart to life.

She went in silently with her little box of perfume, raising her eyes for only a moment to see at a glance where Jesus was reclining. She went up to the couch, her knees trembling under her, her hands shaking, because she felt all those men's eyes were fixed on her beautiful swaying body, wondering what she was about to do.

She broke the seal of the little alabaster flask, and poured half the oil on the head of Jesus. The whole room was filled with the fragrance; every eye was fixed on her with astonishment.

The woman, still silent, took up the opened box and knelt by the feet of the Peace-bringer. She poured the remaining oil into her hand and gently, gently rubbed the right foot and the left with loving care. Then she could restrain no longer the burst of tenderness which filled her heart, made her throat ache and brought tears to her eyes. She would have liked to speak, to say that this was her thanks for the great help she had received. But in such a moment, with all those men there, how could she find words worthy of the wonderful grace? And besides, her lips trembled so that she could not pronounce two words together. Her tears fell down one by one, swift and hot on the feet of Jesus, like so many silent thank offerings.

Yet it was not alone for her own sorrow and joy she wept. The tears that bathed His feet were also shed for Jesus. The unknown woman had anointed His head as the high priests had anointed the kings of Judea; she had anointed His feet as the lords and guests anointed themselves on festal days. But at the same time the weeping woman had prepared Him for death and burial. Jesus, about to enter Jerusalem, knew that those were the last days of His life in the flesh. He said to His disciples, "For in that she hath poured this ointment on my body, she did it for my burial."

Now the feet of the Saviour, the feet of the condemned one, are bathed with tears. The poor woman does not know how to dry those feet. She has no white cloth with her. Then she thinks of her long hair which has been so much admired for its fine silkiness. She loosens the braids. The blue-black tresses fall over her face, and taking these flowing curls in her hands, she dries the feet which have brought her King into that house.

Among the men who were present at this dinner there was no one except Jesus who understood the loving service of the nameless woman, but all respected obscurely the solemnity of the enigmatic ceremony, except two who wished to interpret the woman's action as an offense to the guest. These two were the Pharisee and Judas Iscariot. The first said nothing, but his expression spoke more clearly than words.

Simon the Pharisee thought to himself, "This man, if he were a prophet, would have known who and what manner of woman this is that toucheth Him: for she is a sinner."

There were still ringing in his ears the execrations of the Law against prostitutes. "Thou shalt not bring the hire of a whore, or the price of a dog, into the house of the Lord thy God for any vow: for even both these are abomination unto the Lord thy God." Jesus had read in the heart of Simon, and answered the Pharisee with the parable of the two debtors. "There was a certain creditor which had two debtors: the one owed five hundred pence, and the other fifty. And when they had nothing to pay, he frankly forgave them both. Tell me therefore, which of them will love him most? Simon answered and said, I suppose that he, to whom he forgave most. And he said unto him, Thou hast rightly judged.

"And he turned to the woman, and said unto Simon, Seest thou this woman? I entered into thine house, thou gavest me no water for my feet: but she hath washed my feet with tears, and wiped them with the hairs of her head.

"Thou gavest me no kiss: but this woman since the time I came in hath not ceased to kiss my feet.

"My head with oil thou didst not anoint: but this woman hath anointed my feet with ointment.

"Wherefore I say unto thee, Her sins, which are many, are forgiven; for she loved much: but to whom little is forgiven, the same loveth little.

"And he said unto her, Thy sins are forgiven. . . . Thy faith hath saved thee; go in peace."

Simon could think of no answer; but from the side of the Disciples a rough, angry voice was raised, well known to Jesus. It was the voice of Judas, who held the purse: "Why was this waste of the ointment made, why was not this ointment sold for three hundred pence and given to the poor?" And the other Disciples, so the Evangelists say, approved the words of Judas, and murmured against the woman.

But Jesus answered the words of Judas as He answered the silence of Simon. "Let her alone; why trouble ye her? she hath wrought a good work on me. For ye have the poor with you always, and whensoever ye will ye may do them good: but me ye have not always. She hath done what she could: she is come aforehand to anoint my body to the burying. Verily I say unto you, Wheresoever this gospel shall be preached throughout the whole world, this also that she hath done shall be spoken of for a memorial of her."

The woman listened. Then with her face hidden in her loosened hair, she went away as silently as she had come.

The Disciples were abashed. To hide his chagrin Simon filled the guest's cup with better wine, but in the yellow light of the lamps the silent table seemed a banquet of ghosts among whom had passed the shadow of death.

THOSE WORDS OF DEATH were not the first they had heard from Jesus' lips. They should have remembered that day, not long before, when on a solitary road near Caesarea, Jesus had asked His Disciples what people said of Him. "Who am I?"

"Some say that thou art John the Baptist: some, Elias; and others, Jeremias, or one of the prophets."

"But whom say ye that I am?" They should have remembered the impetuous outcry of belief from Peter's heart. "Thou art the Christ, the Son of the living God. Thou hast the words of eternal life. And we believe and are sure that thou art that Christ, the Son of the living God."

From Peter the Rock sprang forth this wellspring which from that day to this has quenched the thirst of sixty generations of men. Peter had been the first to follow Christ in the divine wanderings: it was for him to be the first to recognize in the wanderer the Messiah whom all men had been awaiting in the desert of the centuries, who had finally come and was there Himself, clothed in flesh, standing before their eyes, with His feet in the dust of the road.

"Blessed art thou, Simon Bar-jona: for flesh and blood hath not revealed it unto thee, but my Father which is in heaven.

"Thou art Peter, and upon this rock I will build my church; and the gates of hell shall not prevail against it. And I will give unto thee the keys of the kingdom of heaven: and whatsoever thou shalt bind on earth shall be bound in heaven: and whatsoever thou shalt loose on earth shall be loosed in heaven."

For these words many men suffered, many were tortured. To deny or uphold, to interpret or cancel these words, thousands of men have been killed in city squares and in battles; kingdoms have been divided, societies have been shaken and rent.

Their meaning in Christ's mouth is plain and simple. He means to say, "Thou, Peter, shalt be hard and staunch as a rock, and upon the staunchness of thy faith in me, which thou wast the first to profess, is founded the first Christian society, the humble seed of the Kingdom."

THE THREE-PEAKED MOUNTAIN of Hermon is covered with snow even in the hot season, the highest mountain of Palestine, higher than Mount Tabor. Jesus became incarnate light on this mountain.

Three Disciples alone were with Him: he who was called Peter, and the Sons of Thunder—the man with the rugged, mountainous character, and the stormy men—fitting company for the place and hour. He prayed alone, higher than all of them, perhaps kneeling in the snow. We have seen in winter how the snow on a mountain makes any other whiteness seem dull and drab. A pale face seems strangely dark, white linen seems dingy, paper looks like dry clay. The contrary of all this was seen on that day up in the gleaming, deserted height.

Jesus prayed by Himself apart from the others. Suddenly His face shone like the sun and His raiment became white "as no fuller on earth can white them." Over the whiteness of the snow a more brilliant whiteness, a splendor more powerful than all known splendors, outshone all earthly light.

The Transfiguration is the feast and the victory of light. Jesus' body, awaiting its liberation, became the most subtle, the lightest and most spiritual aspect of matter. His soul transfigured in prayer shone out through the flesh, pierced the screen of His body and His garments, like a flame consuming the walls and flashing through them.

But Jesus, all light, His face gleaming with quiet refulgence, was not alone. Two great figures, returned from death, gleaming like Him, stood by Him, and spoke with Him—the Prophets Moses and Elias. All those who have spoken with God remain radiant with light. The face of Moses when he came down from Mount Sinai had become so resplendent that he covered it with a veil, lest he dazzle the others. And Elias was caught up to Heaven in a chariot of fire drawn by fiery steeds. But on Hermon there was One whose face shone more than Moses' and whose ascension was to be more splendid than that of Elias. A luminous cloud hid the glorious three from the eyes of the obscure three, and from the cloud came out a voice: "This is my beloved Son: hear him."

The column of smoke which guided the fleeing Hebrews in the desert toward Jordan, the black cloud which hid the ark in the day of desolation and fear, had finally become a cloud of light so brilliant that it hid even the sunlike splendor of the face which was soon to be buffeted in the dark days, close at hand.

When the cloud disappeared, Jesus was once more alone. His face had taken on its natural color. His garments had their everyday aspect. Christ, once more a loving brother, turned back to His swooning companions. "Arise, and be not afraid. . . . Tell the vision to no man, until the Son of man be risen again from the dead."

MARANATHA
(OUR LORD, COME!)

JESUS HAD KNOWN that He must soon die a shameful death. The Disciples were troubled at this revelation and unwilling to believe. But Jesus, foreseeing those terrible last days of His life, could go on His way to Jerusalem in order that His words should be fulfilled. And yet for one day at least He was to be like that King awaited by the poor every morning on the thresholds of the holy city.

Passover draws near. It was the beginning of the last week which even now had not yet ended—since the new Sabbath has not yet dawned. But this time Jesus does not come to Jerusalem as in other years, an obscure wanderer mingled with the crowd of pilgrims, into the evil-smelling metropolis huddled with its houses, white as sepulchers, under the towering vainglory of the Temple destined to the flames. This time, which is the last time, Jesus does not come alone; He is accompanied by His faithful friends, by the women who were later to weep, by the Twelve who were to hide themselves, by His fellow Galileans, peasants who come in memory of an ancient miracle, but with the hope of seeing a new miracle. This time He does not come unknown; the cry of the Resurrection has preceded Him.

This time He does not come on foot into the city which was to be His tomb. When He had come to Bethpage, He sent two Disciples to look for an ass, "Go into the village over against you, and straightway ye shall find an ass tied, and a colt with her: loose them, and bring them unto me. And if any man say ought unto you, ye shall say, The Lord hath need of them."

Even up to our days it has been said that Jesus wished to ride on an ass as a sign of humble meekness, as if He wished to signify symbolically that He approached His people as the Prince of Peace. It has been forgotten that in the robust early periods of history the ass was a fiery and warlike animal; handsome and bold as a horse, fit to be sacrificed to divinities; rebellious to the end of time.

The ass's back is hard, and Christ's friends throw their cloaks over it. Stony is the slope which leads from the Mount of Olives and the triumphant crowds throw their mantles over the rough stones.

Then began the descent in the heat of the sun and of glory. It was at the beginning of breezy April and of spring. The golden hour of noon lay about the city with its green vineyards, fields and orchards. The sky, immense, deep blue, miraculously calm, clear and joyful, stretched away into the infinite. A warm breeze, still scented with the freshness of heaven, gently swayed the tender treetops and set the young, growing leaves aflutter.

Those who accompanied Christ in that descent were swept away by the rapture of the world and of the moment. Never before had they felt themselves so bursting with hope and adoration. The cry of Peter became the cry of the fervent little army winding its way down the slope towards the queen city. "Hosanna to the Son of David!" said the impetuous, exultant voices of the young men and of the women. Even the Disciples almost began to hope, although they had been warned that this would be the last sun, that they were accompanying a man about to die.

The procession approached the mysterious, hostile city with the roaring tumult of a torrent that has burst its banks. These countrymen, these people from the provinces, came forward flanked as by a moving forest, as if they had wished to carry a little country freshness into the noisome alleyways. The boldest had cut palm branches along the road, boughs of myrtle, clusters of olives, willow leaves, and they waved them on high, shouting out the impassioned words of the Psalmist.

Now the first Christian legion had arrived before the gates of Jerusalem and the voices did not still their homage: "Blessed be the King that cometh in the name of the Lord: peace in heaven, and glory in the highest!"

Their shouting reached the ears of the Pharisees, who arrived, haughty and severe. The seditious cries scandalized those learned ears and suspicious hearts; and some of them, well wrapped up in their doctoral cloaks, called from among the crowd to Jesus:

"Master, rebuke thy disciples."

And then He, without halting, "I tell you that, if these should hold their peace, the stones would immediately cry out!"

With this answer, Jesus had asserted His right to be called "the Christ." It was a declaration of war at the very moment of His entrance into His city.

HE WENT up to the Temple; there on the hilltop the sacred fortress sunned its new whiteness in the magnificence of the day. The old Ark of the nomads, drawn by oxen through sweltering deserts and over battlefields, had halted on that height, petrified as a defense for the royal city. The movable cart of the fugitives had become a pompous citadel of stone and marble, palaces and stairways, enclosed by walls, sheer above the valley. It was not only the precinct of the Holy of Holies, and the sacrificial altar, it was no longer only the Temple, the mystic sanctuary of the people. With its great towers, its guardrooms, its warehouses for offerings, its strongboxes for deposits, its open piazzas for trade and covered galleries for meetings and amusement, it was a stronghold in case of assault, a bank vault, a marketplace in time of pilgrimage and feast days, a bazaar on all days, a forum for the disputes of politicians, the wranglings of doctors and the gossip of idlers; a thoroughfare, a rendezvous, a business center. Built by a faithless king to win over the favor of a captious and seditious people, to satisfy the pride and avarice of the priestly caste, it must have seemed to the eyes of Jesus the natural focus for all the enemies of His truth.

Jesus goes up to the Temple to destroy the Temple. He will leave to the Romans of Titus the task of literally dismantling the walls, of stealing the bronze and gold, of reducing to a smoky and accursed ruin the great stronghold of Herod; but He will destroy the values which the proud Temple upheld with its piled-up blocks of ordered stone and its golden doors. Jesus goes up toward the Temple, among the songs of His fervent band.

Well does He know the street. How many times He had gone over it as a child led along by the hand in the crowd of Galilean pilgrims, longing to arrive at the summit, the sacred precincts!

But today everything is transformed. He is not led along. He leads along. He does not come to adore, but to punish.

He enters into the Court of the Gentiles, the most spacious and most densely crowded of all. From the great, sunny, well-paved terrace rises up an immense, roaring din. There are herdsmen with their oxen and their flocks of sheep; vendors of pigeons and turtledoves, standing by the long lines of their coops; bird sellers with cages of chirping sparrows; benches for money changers, a coin hung at their ears as a mark of their trade, with bowls overflowing with copper and silver. Merchants, their feet in the fresh-dropped dung, handle the flanks of the animals destined for sacrifice; or call with monotonous iteration women who have come there after childbirth, pilgrims who have come to offer a rich sacrifice, lepers who offer living birds for their cure. Wary provincials hold excited conferences before loosening their purse strings for a votive offering, and from time to time a restless ox drowns out with his deep bellow the thin bleating of the lambs, and shrill voices of the women, the clinking of drachma and shekels.

Christ was familiar with the spectacle. He knew that the house of God, instead of silently invoking the Spirit, had been turned into the house of Mammon. But this time He did not restrain His scorn and His repugnance.

He had in His hand a length of rope, which He knotted together like a whip, and with it He opened a passageway through the astonished people. The benches of the money changers crashed down at the first shock. The coins were scattered on the ground amid yells of astonishment and wrath; the seats of the bird sellers were overturned beside their scattered pigeons. The herdsmen began to urge towards the doors the oxen and the sheep. The sparrow sellers took their cages under their arms and disappeared. Cries rose to Heaven, some scandalized, some approving; from the other courtyards other people came running towards the disturbance. Jesus, surrounded by the boldest of His friends, was brandishing His whip on high, and driving the money changers towards the door. And He repeated in a loud voice, "My house shall be called the house of prayer; but ye have made it a den of thieves!"

With that violent action, Jesus antagonized all the commercial middle class of Jerusalem. The men He had driven away demanded that their patrons should punish Him, and they found ready hearing. Jesus in disturbing the business of the Temple had condemned and harmed the priests themselves. The most successful bazaars were the property of the sons of Annas, that is, close relations of the High Priest Caiaphas. And the money changers, who should not have been allowed to stay in the Temple, paid the great Sadducee families of the priestly aristocracy a goodly tithe on their profitable exchange of foreign money into Hebrew money. Had not the Temple itself perhaps become a national bank?

If Jesus had His way, He would ruin them all: the twenty thousand priests of Jerusalem and their associates, the merchants. The two threatened castes drew together to do away with the dangerous intruder. It was perhaps that very evening that they agreed on the purchase of a betrayer and a cross. The bourgeoisie were to give the small amount of money necessary; the clergy to find the religious pretext; the foreign government, naturally desiring to be on good terms with clergy and bourgeoisie, would lend its soldiers.

But Jesus, having left the Temple, went His way towards Bethany, passing by the Mount of Olives.

THE NEXT morning when He went back, the herdsmen and merchants had squatted down outside, near the doors, but the courts were humming with crowds of excited people.

The sentence pronounced and executed by Jesus had awakened the poor to joyous hope. Early in the morning, they had gone up there from the dark alleys, from the workshops and from the public squares, leaving their affairs, with the restless anxiety of those who hope for miracles, or revenge. The day laborers had come, the weavers, the dyers, the cobblers, the woodworkers, all those who detested the shearers of poverty. Among the first had come the lamentable vermin-ridden scum of the city, with leprous scabs, with their sores uncared for, with their bones showing beneath the skin to testify to their hunger. There had also come pilgrims from outside, those of Galilee, who had accompanied Jesus in His festal entrance; and with them Jews from the Syrian and Egyptian colonies.

But there came up also, in groups of four or five, the scribes and the Pharisees, the puritans of the Law. Nearly all the scribes were Pharisees, many Pharisees were scribes.

These men went up to the Temple proudly wrapped in their long cloaks, with their fringes fluttering, with sneering mouths and quivering nostrils, with a step which announced the indignation felt by them, God's privileged sheriffs.

Jesus, in the midst of all these eyes turned on Him, waited for them. It was not the first time that they had come about Him. How many discussions between Him and the provincial Pharisees had taken place in the country! They were Pharisees who had demanded a sign from Heaven that He was the Messiah—because the Pharisees, unlike the skeptical Sadducees, believed in the imminent arrival of the Saviour.

But the Pharisees expected to see this Saviour as a Jew, strictly observing all laws as they did. The Messiah, the son of David, would save only those who had avoided all contact with foreigners and with heathens, who had observed the smallest detail of legal purification, who had paid all the tithes of the Temple. In their eyes Jesus could not possibly be the Divine Redeemer. They had seen Him dining with publicans and sinners, and had heard with horror that His disciples did not always wash their hands before sitting down to the table. But the unendurable scandal had been that Jesus had not hesitated to cure the sick, even on the Sabbath, claiming blasphemously that the Sabbath was made for man, rather than man for the Sabbath.

As long as Jesus went about in the provinces drawing after Him a few dozen peasants, the Pharisees had let Him alone, sure that some day or other the last beggar, disillusioned, would leave Him. But, accompanied by a band of excitable countrymen, He had gone so far as to enter into the Temple as though it belonged to Him, and had seduced some unfortunates to call Him the Messiah. More than that, usurping the place of the priests, and almost giving Himself the airs of a king, He had roughly driven out the honest merchants, pious people who admired the Pharisees. The public challenge called for condemnation and punishment. The false Christ must be disposed of at once.

Jesus was waiting for just those men. He wanted to say to them publicly what He thought of them. The day before, with His whip, He had condemned the animal sellers and money changers. Now He was dealing with the merchants of the Word, the swindlers of Truth.

"Woe unto you, scribes and Pharisees, hypocrites!"

And so the indestructible race of Pharisees was created for all centuries, for all peoples. With every generation such men spring up again, innumerable, with new names. Everything in them is pretense: their dress and their talk, their teaching and their practice. What they say is contradicted by what they do. The Pharisees are those who wish to appear saints, and who hate the real saints. They are those who are not visibly sinners, but who are the incarnation of the ugliest of all sins, the betrayal of Truth. Whoever they are, wherever they are born, their faces are stamped forever by the condemnation of that day.

Jesus, while He spoke to them in the great open courtyard crowded with witnesses, knew that He spoke to His judges, and to those who would be, through intermediate persons, the real authors of His death. By speaking out on this day, He justified His later silence before Caiaphas and Pilate. For He had judged them first and had nothing more to add when they wished to judge Him.

THE THIRTEEN went down from the Temple to make their daily ascent to the Mount of Olives. One of the Disciples (who could it have been?—perhaps John, son of Salome, still rather childish and naively full of wonder at what he saw? Or Judas Iscariot, with his respect for wealth?) said to Jesus, "Master, see what manner of stones and what buildings are here!"

The Master turned to look at the high walls faced with marble which the ostentatious calculation of Herod had built up on the hill and said, "Seest thou these great buildings? there shall not be left one stone upon another, that shall not be thrown down."

The admiring exclamation suddenly died. Perplexed and surprised, each of them continued to turn over in his mind these words. He whom they loved had said in these last days many other hard words, hard to understand, hard to believe. But those ambitious provincials did not remember any other words so hard as these. They knew that He was the Christ and that He was to suffer and die, but they hoped that He would rise again at once in the glorious victory of the new David, to give abundance to all Israel and to award the greatest prizes and power to them, faithful to Him in the dangerous wanderings of His poor days. But if the world was to be commanded by Judea, Judea was to be commanded by Jerusalem, and the seats of command were to be in the Temple of the great King. Christ was to drive away the faithless Sadducees, the hypocritical Pharisees, the traitorous scribes, to give their places to His Apostles. How then could the Temple be destroyed, splendid memorial of the kingdom in the past; hoped-for rock of the new Kingdom?

They would not understand that those great massive stones, quarried out patiently from the mountains, drawn from afar by oxen, squared and prepared by chisels and mallets, put one upon another by masters of the art to make the most marvelous Temple of the universe; that these stones, warm and brilliant in the sun, should be pulverized into ruins.

They had scarcely arrived at the Mount of Olives, and Christ had only had time to sit down opposite to the Temple, when their curiosity burst out:

"Tell us, when shall these things be? and what shall be the sign when all these things shall be fulfilled?"

The answer was the discourse on the last things. This discourse, read all in one piece in the Gospels, is not, as is generally believed, the answer to one question only. The Disciples had put two questions, "When shall these things be?"—that is, the ruin of the Temple; and "What shall be the signs of Thy coming?"

Jesus first describes the events which will precede the destruction of Jerusalem, a prophecy that was fulfilled before the end of His generation.

His Disciples, He warns, cannot escape persecution: "Then shall they deliver you up to be afflicted, and shall kill you: and ye shall be hated of all nations for my name's sake. . . . take heed to yourselves: . . . in the synagogues ye shall be beaten: and ye shall be brought before rulers and kings for my sake, for a testimony against them. . . . Now the brother shall betray the brother to death, and the father the son; and children shall rise up against their parents, and shall cause them to be put to death. . . . And because iniquity shall abound, the love of many shall wax cold. But he that shall endure unto the end, the same shall be saved.

"And . . . ye shall hear of wars and rumors of wars. . . . For nation shall rise against nation, and kingdom against kingdom: and there shall be earthquakes in divers places, and there shall be famines and troubles. And when ye shall see Jerusalem compassed with armies, then know that the desolation thereof is nigh. . . . But when ye shall see the abomination of desolation, spoken of by Daniel the prophet . . . then let them that be in Judea flee to the mountains: And let him that is on the housetop not go down into the house, neither enter therein, to take any thing out of his house: And let him that is in the field not turn back again for to take up his garment. But woe to them that are with child, and to them that give suck in those days! And pray ye that your flight be not in the winter. . . . They shall fall by the edge of the sword, and shall be led away captive into all nations: and Jerusalem shall be trodden down of the Gentiles, until the times of the Gentiles be fulfilled."

This is the end of the first prophecy. Jerusalem shall be taken and destroyed and of the Temple there shall remain not one stone upon another.

But until now Jesus has not spoken of His Second Coming.

The Second Coming of Christ from Heaven, the Parousia, will be the end of this world and the beginning of the true world, the eternal Kingdom. This end will be preceded by signs divine and celestial. ". . . the sun shall be darkened, and the moon shall not give her light, And the stars of heaven shall fall. . . . and upon the earth distress of nations, with perplexity; the sea and the waves roaring; . . . And then shall appear the sign of the Son of man in heaven: and then shall all the tribes of the earth mourn, and they shall see the Son of man coming in the clouds of heaven with power and great glory."

It is the day of God's wrath described in their times by Ezekiel, Jeremiah, Isaiah and Joel. But the day of the Son follows immediately after.

"When the Son of man shall come in his glory, and all the holy angels with him, then shall he sit upon the throne of his glory:

"And before him shall be gathered all nations: and he shall separate them one from another, as a shepherd divideth his sheep from the goats:

"And he shall set the sheep on his right hand, but the goats on the left.

"Then shall the King say unto them on his right hand, Come, ye blessed of my Father, inherit the kingdom prepared for you from the foundation of the world:

"For I was an hungered, and ye gave me meat: I was thirsty, and ye gave me drink: I was a stranger, and ye took me in:

"Naked, and ye clothed me: I was sick, and ye visited me: I was in prison, and ye came unto me.

"Then shall the righteous answer him, saying, Lord, when saw we thee an hungered, and fed thee? or thirsty, and gave thee drink?

"When saw we thee a stranger, and took thee in? or naked, and clothed thee?

"Or when saw we thee sick, or in prison, and came unto thee?

"And the King shall answer and say unto them, Verily I say unto you, Inasmuch as ye have done it unto one of the least of these my brethren, ye have done it unto me.

"Then shall he say also unto them on the left hand, Depart from me, ye cursed, into everlasting fire, prepared for the devil and his angels:

"For I was an hungered, and ye gave me no meat: I was thirsty, and ye gave me no drink;

"I was a stranger, and ye took me not in: naked, and ye clothed me not: sick, and in prison, and ye visited me not.

"Then shall they also answer him, saying, Lord, when saw we thee an hungered, or athirst, or a stranger, or naked, or sick, or in prison, and did not minister unto thee?

"Then shall he answer them, saying, Verily I say unto you,

Inasmuch as ye did it not to one of the least of these, ye did it not to me.

"And these shall go away into everlasting punishment: but the righteous into life eternal."

On that great day of final judgment, the code of this dividing of good from evil men will be based on one idea only: compassion—charity. During all the time which lies between His first and second coming He has gone on living under the appearance of the poor and the pilgrims, of the sick and persecuted, of wanderers and slaves. And on the last day He pays His debts. Only those who did not receive Him when He appeared in the innumerable bodies of the poverty-stricken will be condemned to eternal punishment, because when they drove away the unfortunate they drove away God.

BUT WHEN shall these things come to pass? The first prophecy of Jesus announces the destruction of the Temple as close at hand. It was fulfilled to the letter, detail by detail, about forty years after the Crucifixion.

A few years after Jesus' death the signs of the first prophecy began to be seen. The persecutions arrived promptly. The Disciples had scarcely begun to preach the Gospel in Jerusalem when Peter and John were thrown into prison; freed, they were captured again, and beaten and commanded to speak no more in the name of Jesus. Stephen, one of the most ardent of the neophytes, was taken by the priests outside the city and stoned.

Then the war against Christian converts began in the capital of the empire. In 64 the burning of Rome, desired and executed by Nero, was the pretext for the first great persecution. An innumerable multitude of Christians obtained their martyrdom in Rome and in the provinces. Many were crucified; others wrapped in the *tunica molesta* lighted up the nocturnal amusement of the Caesar: others wrapped in animal skins were given as food to dogs: many, enforced actors in cruel comedies, made a spectacle for amphitheaters and were devoured by lions. Peter died on the cross, nailed head downward. Paul ended under the axe a life which since his conversion had been one long torment.

Most of the other Disciples met with similar fates. Thomas

met a martyr's death in India, Andrew was crucified at Patras, Bartholomew was crucified in Armenia. Simon the Zealot and Matthew, like their Master, ended their lives on the cross.

Nor were there lacking wars and rumors of wars. When Jesus was killed, the "peace" of Augustus still existed, but very soon nations rise against nations and kingdoms against kingdoms. Under Nero the Britons rebel and massacre the Romans, the Parthians revolt and force the legions to pass under the yoke; Armenia and Syria murmur against foreign government; Gaul rises with Julius Vindex.

In 69, insurrection breaks out in the north, with the Batavians led by Claudius Civilus; and in Palestine the insurrection of the Jews is fomented by the Zealots, who claim that the Romans and all the heathen should be driven out in order that God might return to triumph with His own people. In less than two years Italy is invaded twice, Rome taken twice, two emperors kill themselves; two are killed.

The other afflictions announced by Jesus accompany these upheavals. In the time of Claudius a series of poor crops brought famine even to Rome. Under Nero pestilence was added to the famine. In 61 and 62 earthquakes shook Asia, Achaia and Macedonia. In 63 it was Italy's turn: at Naples, Nocera and Pompeii the earth shook. All the signs were fulfilled: now had come the fullness of time for the punishment of Judea.

For forty years the country had had no peace, not even the peace of defeat and slavery. Under the Roman procurators the disorders knew no truce; the flames of the revolt flared ever more boldly. The holy place, during the great rebellion, had become a refuge for assassins; and the Zealots took possession of the Temple.

Then Vespasian, going to Rome to become emperor, gave the command to his son Titus, who on Easter Day in the year 70 came up before Jerusalem and laid siege to it. Horrible days began. The Zealots, carried away by wild frenzy, quarreled among themselves and split up into factions, who fought for the control of the city and cut the throats of those whom the Romans had not yet killed. To the horror of fratricidal massacre and of the siege was added that of hunger. The famine was so great that mothers were seen, so says Josephus, to kill their children and eat them.

On the tenth of August the Temple was taken by Titus and burned; the Zealots succeeded in shutting themselves up into the upper city, but conquered by hunger they were obliged to surrender on the seventh of September.

The prophecies of Jesus had been fulfilled: by Titus' order the city was laid waste: and of the Temple, already swept by fire, there remained not one stone upon another. The Jews who had survived hunger and sword were massacred by the victorious soldiery. Those who still remained were deported into Egypt to work in mines, and many were killed for the amusement of the crowd in the amphitheaters of Caesarea and Berytus.

"Verily I say unto you, This generation shall not pass, till all these things be fulfilled." It was the seventieth year of the Christian era and His generation had not yet gone down into the tomb when these things happened. One at least of those who heard Him on the Mount of Olives, John, was witness of the destruction of Jerusalem and of the ruin of the Temple.

Now nothing remains of the Temple, three times built and three times destroyed, but a piece of a wall, barely enough so that a line of mourners may lean their heads against it to hide their tears.

THE SECOND COMING, the triumphal Parousia, is still awaited by those who believe what Jesus said that day on the Mount of Olives: "Heaven and earth shall pass away, but my words shall not pass away."

If the words of the second prophecy are true, as the words of the first prophecy were shown to be true, the Second Coming cannot be far distant. Once again in these years nations have risen against nations, the earth has quaked, destroying many lives, and pestilences, famines and seditions have decimated nations.

For more than a century the words of Christ have been translated and preached in all languages. And still men do not think of Jesus and His promise.

They live as if the world were always going to continue as it has been, and they work only for their earthly interests. They hurry about without rest, occupied by possessions. They never look up to Heaven—they fear only their brothers. No one thinks of the Divine Thief who will come suddenly in the night, no one waits for the Real Master, who will return unexpectedly.

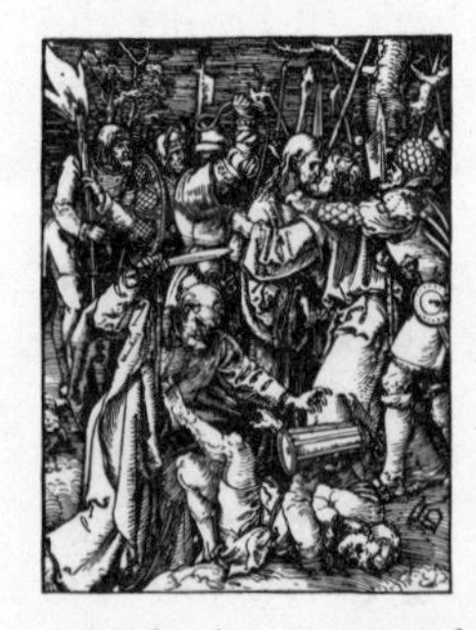

THE HIGH PRIEST AND JUDAS ISCARIOT

WHILE JESUS was condemning the Temple and Jerusalem, those maintained by the Temple and the lords of Jerusalem were preparing His condemnation. They believed that they would save themselves by putting Him to death. To have an idea of the hatred which the upper classes of Jerusalem felt towards Jesus, priestly hatred, scholastic hatred and commercial hatred, we must remember that the Holy City apparently lived by faith, but in reality on the faithful. Only in the capital could valid and acceptable offerings be made to the old God, and therefore every year, especially on great feast days, streams of Israelites poured in from all the provinces. Josephus says that at Jerusalem on special occasions there were gathered together as many as three million pilgrims.

The priestly caste, which numbered in Christ's lifetime twenty thousand descendants of Aaron, got their living from the taxes of the Temple, from the payments for the firstborn—five shekels a head!—and got their food from the flesh of the sacrificial animals, of which only the fat was burned. They were the ones who had the pick of herds and crops; even their bread was given them by the people, for the head of every Jewish family was obliged to hand over to the priests the twenty-fourth part of the bread which was baked in his house. It is not impossible that some of them were really bankers, because people readily deposited their savings in the strongboxes of the Temple.

Religion was thus the greatest and perhaps the only business in Jerusalem, and the Gospel of Jesus threatened directly the positions and fees of the prosperous. If all the prescriptions of the

Law were to be reduced to the practice of love, there would be no place for the scribes and doctors of the Law who made their living out of their teachings. If God did not wish animal sacrifices and asked only for purity of soul and secret prayer, those who did business in oxen and calves and sheep and lambs and kids and doves and sparrows would have seen their business slacken and perhaps disappear. If to be loved by God you needed to transform your life, if it were not enough to wash your drinking cups and punctually pay your tithes, the doctrine and the authority of the Pharisees would be reduced to nothing.

Thus, as a matter of course, Jesus, who preferred fishermen, if they were pure and loving, to members of the Sanhedrin; who took the part of the poor against the rich, who valued ignorant children more than scribes, drew down on His head the hatred of the priests, the merchants and the doctors.

When He came back to Jerusalem, the attack with the whips on the animal sellers and money changers, the loud invectives against the scribes and Pharisees, the allusion to the ruin of the Temple, made the cup run over. The high priests, the Pharisees and the scribes, uneasy and embittered, set on His track spies, destined to become false witnesses in a few days. If we are to believe John, the order was given to certain guards to capture Him, but they were afraid to lay their hands upon Him. Time pressed; Jerusalem was full of foreigners and many were listening to Him. An uprising of the provincial crowds who were less attached to the privileges and interests of the metropolis might easily spring up. A meeting of the Sanhedrin to reconcile law with assassination was arranged.

THE SANHEDRIN was the supreme council of the aristocracy which ruled the capital. It was composed of the priests jealous of the clientele of the Temple which gave them their power and their stipends; of the scribes responsible for preserving the purity of the law and of tradition; of the elders who represented the interests of the moderate, moneyed middle class.

They were all in accord that it was essential to take Jesus on false pretenses and to have Him killed as a blasphemer against the Sabbath and the Lord. Only Nicodemus attempted a defense, but they were able quickly to silence him. "What do we? for this man doeth many miracles. If we let him thus alone, all men will believe on him: and the Romans shall come and take away both our place and nation."

Caiaphas, who that year was high priest, settled their doubts with the maxim which has always justified in the eyes of the world the immolation of the innocent. "Ye know nothing at all, Nor consider that it is expedient for us, that one man should die for the people, and that the whole nation perish not." This maxim, transposed into a higher meaning and transferred into the Absolute, changing nation into humanity, was a principle which Jesus Himself had accepted and which has become under another form the crucial mystery of Christianity. Caiaphas did not know—he who had to enter alone into the Holy of Holies to offer up to Jehovah the sins of the people—how much his words, cynical in sentiment as they were, were in accord with his victim's thought. Caiaphas who, together with the crown of thorns and the sponge of vinegar, was to be one of the instruments of the Passion, did not imagine in that moment that he was bearing witness solemnly, though involuntarily, to the divine tragedy about to begin.

And yet the principle that the innocent can pay for the guilty, that the death of one man can be salvation for all, was not foreign to the consciousness of ancient peoples. The heroic myths of the pagans recognize and celebrate voluntary sacrifices of the innocent. They record the example of Pylades, who offered himself to be punished in place of the guilty Orestes; Macaria of the blood of Hercules, who saved her brother's life with her own; Alcestis, who died that she might avert from her Admetus the vengeance of Artemis; and Iphigenia, who offered her throat to the knife that Agamemnon's fleet might sail safely towards Troy.

But such sacrifices were for the salvation of one being alone, or of a restricted group of men. No man had yet taken upon his head all the sins of men, a God who would imprison Himself in the wretchedness of flesh to save all the human race.

The perfect man, who takes upon himself all imperfections, the pure man who burdens himself with all infamies, the righteous man who shoulders the unrighteousness of all men, had now appeared under the aspect of a poor Galilean workingman. He who was to die for all was disquieting the rich and the priests of Jerusalem, was there on the Mount of Olives only a short distance from the Sanhedrin.

The Seventy, who knew not what they did, who did not know that they were obeying the will of the very man they were persecuting, decided to have Him captured before the Passover; but one thing restrained them, the fear of the people who loved Jesus. They consulted that they might take Jesus by subtlety and kill Him. But they said, "Not on the feast day, lest there be an uproar among the people." To solve their difficulty, by good fortune, there came to them the day after one of the Twelve, he who held the purse, Judas Iscariot.

ONLY TWO CREATURES in the world knew the secret of Judas: Christ and the traitor.

Sixty generations of Christians have racked their brains over it, but the man of Iscariot remains stubbornly incomprehensible. His is the only human mystery that we encounter in the Gospels. We can understand without difficulty the depravity of Herod Antipas, the rancor of the Pharisees, the revengeful anger of Annas and Caiaphas, the cowardly laxity of Pilate. But the four Gospels tell us too little of Judas and of the reasons which induced him to sell his King.

"Then entered Satan into Judas." But these words are only the definition of his crime. Evil took possession of his heart, therefore it came suddenly. Before that day Judas was not in the power of the Adversary. But why did Satan enter into him and not into one of the others?

Thirty pieces of silver are a very small sum, especially for an avaricious man. In modern coinage it would amount to about twenty dollars, and, granting that, as the economists say, its buying power was in those days ten times greater, two hundred dollars seems hardly a sufficient price to induce even a man whom his companions describe as grasping to commit the basest perfidy recorded by history. It has been said that thirty pieces of silver was the price of a slave, but the text of Exodus states that thirty shekels was the compensation to be paid by the owner of an ox which had injured a slave. The cases are too far apart for the doctors of the Sanhedrin to have had this early precedent in mind.

The most significant indication is the office which Judas held among the Twelve. Among them was Matthew, a former tax collector, and it would have seemed almost his right to handle the small amount of money necessary for the expenses of the brotherhood. In place of Matthew, we see the man of Iscariot as the depository of the offerings. Money is insidious and saturated with danger.

John said of Judas the thief, that he, "having the bag, took away what was put therein." If he had needed those miserable thirty pieces of silver, could he not have procured them by running away with the purse, without needing to propose the betrayal of Jesus to the high priests?

These common-sense reflections about a crime so extraordinary have induced many to seek other motives for the infamous transaction.

A sect of heretics, the Cainites, had a legend that Judas sorrowfully accepted eternal infamy, knowing that Jesus through His will and the will of the Father was to be betrayed to His death. A necessary and voluntary instrument of the Redemption, Judas was according to them a hero and a martyr to be revered and not reviled.

According to others, Iscariot, loving his people and hoping for their deliverance, perhaps sharing the sentiments of the Zealots, had joined with Jesus, hoping that He was the Messiah such as the common people then imagined Him: the King of the revenge and restoration of Israel. When little by little it dawned on him from the words of Jesus that he had fallen in with a Messiah of quite another kind, he delivered Him over to His enemies to make up for the bitterness of his disappointment.

Others have said that Judas, mingling with the people to find out the temper of the day, had perhaps heard a rumor as to the decisions of the meeting of the elders and feared that the Sanhedrin would not be satisfied with one victim alone, but would condemn all those who had long followed Jesus. Overcome by fear, he thought he could ward off the danger and save his life by treachery.

Others give revenge as the reason. Why did Judas hate Jesus? They remember the dinner in the house of Simon and the nard of the weeping woman. The reproof for his stinginess and hypocrisy must have exasperated the Disciple who perhaps had been reproved for these faults on other occasions. And as soon as he could revenge himself without danger, he went to the palace of Caiaphas.

But did he really think that his denunciation would bring Jesus to His death or did he rather suppose that they would content themselves with flogging Him and forbidding Him to speak to the people? The rest of the story seems to show that the condemnation of Jesus unnerved him as a terrible and unexpected result of his kiss. Matthew describes his despair in a way to show that he was horrified by what had happened through his fault. The money which he had pocketed became like fire to him: and when the priests refused to take it back he threw it down in the Temple. Even after this restitution he had no peace and hastened to kill himself. He died on the same day as his victim.

In spite of all the unraveling of unsatisfied minds, mysteries are still tangled about the mystery of Judas. But we have not yet invoked the testimony of Him who knew better than all men, even better than Judas, the true secret of the betrayal. Jesus alone could give us the key to the mystery; Jesus who saw into the heart of Judas as into the hearts of all men, and who knew what Judas was to do before he had done it.

Jesus chose Judas to be one of the Twelve and to carry the Gospel to the world along with the others. Would He have chosen him, kept him with Him, beside Him, at His table, for so long a time if He had believed him to be an incurable criminal?

Up to the last days, up to that last evening, Jesus treated Judas exactly like the others. To him He gave His body, symbolized by bread, His soul, symbolized by wine. He washed and wiped, with His own hands, the feet of Judas, those feet which had carried him to the house of Caiaphas—with those hands which, through Judas' fault, were to be nailed to the cross on the following day. And when, in the red light of the flickering lanterns and the flashing of swords, Judas, under the dark shadow of the olive trees, came and kissed that face still wet with bloody sweat, Jesus did not repel him, but said, "Friend, wherefore art thou come?"

Friend! It was the last time that Jesus spoke to Judas, and even in that moment He would use none other than that word. Jesus had said at the Last Supper, "Woe unto that man by whom the Son of man is betrayed! it had been good for that man if he had not been born." These words might have been, rather than a condemnation, an exclamation of pity at the thought of a fate which could not be escaped. He knew that Judas must needs do what he did and He did not curse him, as He did not curse the people who wished His death, or the hammer which drove the nails into the cross. One prayer alone broke from him, to beg Judas to shorten the dreadful agony, "That thou doest, do quickly."

Thus the testimony of Him who was betrayed increases our bewilderment instead of raising the veil of the dreadful secret. The mystery of Judas is doubly tied to the mystery of the Redemption and we lesser ones shall never solve it.

THE BARGAIN was struck, the price paid, the buyers were impatient to finish the transaction. They had said "not on the feast day." The great feast day of the Passover fell on a Saturday and this was Thursday.

Jesus had but one more day of freedom, the last day.

Before leaving His friends, those who were to abandon Him that night, He wished once more to dip His bread in the same platter with them. This last evening before His death was to be like an anticipation of the banquet of the Kingdom.

On the evening of Thursday, the Disciples asked Him, "Where wilt thou that we go and prepare that thou mayest eat the passover?"

The Son of man, poorer than the foxes, had no home of His own. He had left His home in Nazareth forever. The home of Simon of Capernaum, which had been in the early days like His own, was far away; and the home of Mary and Martha in Bethany, where He was almost Master, was far outside the city.

He had only enemies in Jerusalem or shamefaced friends: Joseph of Arimathea was to receive Him as his guest only the next evening, in the dark cave, the banquet hall of worms.

But a condemned man on his last day has a right to any favor he might ask. The Father would give Him the house best suited to shelter His last joy. He sent two Disciples with this mysterious command, "Go ye into the city, and there shall meet you a man bearing a pitcher of water: follow him. And wheresoever he shall go in, say ye to the goodman of the house, The Master saith, My time is at hand; where is the guestchamber, where I shall eat the passover with my disciples? And he will shew you a large upper room furnished and prepared: there make ready for us."

The Disciples set out, found the man with the pitcher, entered the house, talked with his master, prepared there what was necessary for the supper: lamb cooked on the spit, round loaves without leaven, bitter herbs, red sauce, the wine of thanksgiving, and warm water. They set the couches and pillows about the table and spread over it the white cloth. On the cloth they set the few dishes, the candelabra, the pitcher full of wine, and one cup—one cup only to which all were to set their lips. Both were experienced in this preparation. From childhood up, in their home beside the lake, they had watched, wide-eyed, the preparations for the most heartwarming feast of the year. And it was not the first time since they had been with Him whom they loved, that they had thus eaten all together of the feast of the Passover.

But for this last supper—and perhaps their dull minds had finally understood the dreadful truth that it was really the last —which all the thirteen were to have together, the Disciples performed those humble menial tasks with a new tenderness, with that pensive joy that almost brings tears.

With the setting of the sun, the other ten came with Jesus and placed themselves around the table, now in readiness. All were silent, as if heavyhearted with a presentiment which they were afraid to see reflected in their companions' eyes. They remembered the repeated warnings of ignominy and of the end; the signs of hatred increasing about them, and the indications, now very plain, of the conspiracy, which with all its torches was about to come out from the darkness.

Judas had finished his bargain, he had the thirty pieces of silver on his person wrapped tightly so that they would not clink. But he knew no peace. To see Him still at liberty in the company of those who loved Him—and yet the affair was arranged for that very night—those bargainers who had paid the price were only waiting for Judas to act.

All these thoughts darkened his somber face, more and more blackly, and he looked furtively at the eyes of Jesus. Jesus broke the silence:

"With desire I have desired to eat this passover with you before I suffer: For I say unto you, I will not any more eat thereof, until it be fulfilled in the kingdom of God."

Such great love had not up to that moment been expressed by any words of Christ to His friends: such a longing for the day of perfect union. He had eaten with them thousands of other times, seated in boats, in their friends' houses, in strangers' houses, in rich men's houses, or seated beside the road, in mountain pastures, in the shadow of bushes on the shore. The blue skies of happy Galilee, the soft winds of the spring just passed, the sun of the last Passover, the waving branches of His triumphant entry, did He think of them now? Now He saw only His first friends and His last friends, the little group destined to be diminished by treachery and dispersed by cowardice. For a time they were still there about Him in the same room, and at the same table.

Now that He was on the point of being snatched from those whom He loved, He wished to give them a supreme proof of this love.

For raw, untrained minds, action has more meaning than words. Jesus prepared Himself to repeat, with the symbolic aspect of a humiliating service, one of His most important instructions.

John tells us, "He riseth from supper, and laid aside his garments; and took a towel, and girded himself. After that he poureth water into a basin, and began to wash the disciples' feet, and to wipe them with the towel wherewith he was girded."

Only a mother or a slave would have done what Jesus did that evening. And yet He was willing to wash and wipe those twenty-four calloused and sweaty feet.

After He had finished and taken His garments, He sat down again and said unto them, "Know ye what I have done to you? Ye call me Master and Lord: and ye say well; for so I am. If I then, your Lord and Master, have washed your feet; ye also ought to wash one another's feet. For I have given you an example, that ye should do as I have done to you. Verily, verily, I say unto you, The servant is not greater than his lord; neither he that is sent greater than he that sent him. If ye know these things, happy are ye if ye do them."

Jesus had not only given them a memory of complete humility, but an example of perfect love. "A new commandment I give unto you, That ye love one another; as I have loved you, that ye also love one another. Greater love hath no man than this, that a man lay down his life for his friends."

THESE THIRTEEN men seemed to be thirteen devout men of the people, come together to perform the old social rite in memory of the liberation of their people from Egyptian slavery. In reality it was a vigil of leave-taking and separation. Two of these thirteen, He into whom God had entered and he into whom Satan had entered, were to die terrible deaths before the next nightfall. The very next day the others were to be dispersed, like reapers at the first downfall of hail.

But this supper which was an ending, was also a wonderful beginning. In the midst of these thirteen Jews the observance of the Passover was about to be transfigured into something more universal, into something unequaled; into the great Christian mystery. The simple eating of bread was to become actual communion with God.

For the Jews, Passover commemorates their victorious flight from Egypt, accompanied by so many prodigies, so manifestly under God's protection. Exodus prescribed an annual festivity which took the name of the Passover; Pasch, the paschal feast. It was intended to bring to mind the hastily prepared food of the fugitives.

A lamb or a goat should be roasted over the fire, that is, cooked in the simplest and quickest way; bread without leaven, because there was no time to let yeast rise. And they were to eat of it with their loins girded, their staves in their hands, eating in haste, like people about to set out upon a journey. The bitter herbs were the poor wild grasses snatched up by the fugitives as they went along, to dull the hunger of their interminable wanderings. The red sauce, where the bread was dipped, was in memory of the bricks which the Jewish slaves were obliged to bake for the Pharaohs. The wine was something added: the joy of escape, the hope of the land of promise, the exaltation of thanksgiving to the Eternal.

Jesus changed nothing in the order of this ancient feast. After the prayer He had them pass from hand to hand the cup of wine, calling on God's name. Then He gave the bitter herbs to each one and filled a second time the cup which was to be passed around the table for each to sip.

Jesus in that deep silence pronounced those words of longing and hope: Take this and divide it among yourselves, "But I say unto you, I will not drink henceforth of this fruit of the vine, until that day when I drink it new with you in my Father's kingdom."

A sad farewell; but comforted by the certainty of an early and glorious reunion, they chanted together, as the custom was, the Psalm of the first Thanksgiving.

Then Jesus, who saw how insufficiently they understood, took the loaves, blessed them, broke them and, as He gave them each a piece, set the dreadful truth before their eyes. "Take, eat; This is my body which is given for you: this do in remembrance of me."

So He was not to return as quickly as they thought! After His brief stay during the Resurrection, His Second Coming was to be delayed, so long that it might be possible to forget Him and His death.

"This do in remembrance of me." Eat this unleavened bread, these loaves which have felt the heat of the oven and which my hands, not yet cold in death, have divided amongst you—and which my love has changed into my flesh so that it may be your everlasting food. You know how many efforts, how much anxiety, are contained in a piece of bread; how the great oxen cultivated the earth, how the countrymen threw great handfuls of the grain into the fallow land in winter, how the first blade softly penetrated the damp darkness of the earth, how the reapers all day long cut down the ripened stalks, and then the sheaves were bound, and carried to the threshing floor and beaten so that the ears let fall the grain. The workers must wait for a little wind, neither too gentle nor too violent, to winnow out the good grain from the chaff. Then they grind it, sift out the bran from it, make a dough with warm water, heat the oven with dry grass or twigs.

All this must be done with love and patience before the father may break a piece with his children, the friend with his friends, the host with strangers; before the golden wheat can be transformed into well-baked golden bread for our table.

Remember the prayer which I taught you: "Give us this day our daily bread—" For today and for always your bread is this bread, my Body.

AS SOON as they had eaten the lamb with the bread and the bitter herb, Jesus filled the common cup for the third time and gave it to the Apostle nearest Him, "Drink ye all of it; For this is my blood of the new testament, which is shed for many."

If bread is the body, blood is in a certain sense the soul. When Moses had received the Law, he had sacrificed oxen, took half of the blood and put it in basins, and half of the blood he sprinkled on the altar:

"And Moses took the blood, and sprinkled it on the people, and said, Behold the blood of the covenant, which the Lord hath made with you concerning all these words."

The blood of oxen, the impure blood of earthly animals, involuntary and inferior victims, is no longer sufficient. The New Covenant was established that night with the words of Christ. "This cup is the new testament in my blood, which is shed for you."

The bread given by Christ does not strengthen the flesh, but the soul, and His wine gives that divine intoxication which is

Love, that Love which the Apostle was to call in his Epistle to the Corinthians, "the foolishness of God."

Judas also ate that bread and swallowed that wine, partook of that body, in which he had trafficked, drank that blood which he was to help shed, but he had not the courage to confess his infamy, to throw himself at the feet of Him who would have wept with him. Then the only friend remaining to Judas warned him, "Verily I say unto you, that one of you shall betray me."

The eleven were capable of leaving Him alone in the midst of Caiaphas' guards, but they never could have brought themselves to sell Him for money, and at this they shuddered. Everyone looked in his neighbor's face, almost dreading to see in his companion the look of guilt, and all, one after the other, said, "Lord, is it I?"

Even Judas was able to force his voice to say, "Lord, is it I?" But Jesus, who the next day would not defend Himself, would not even bring an accusation and only repeated the sad prophecy in more definite words, "He that dippeth his hand with me in the dish, the same shall betray me." And while they all still gazed at Him in painful doubt, for the third time He insisted ". . . the hand of him that betrayeth me is with me on the table." He added no more, but to follow the old customs up to the last, He filled the cup for the fourth time and gave it to them to drink. And once more the thirteen voices rang out in the old hymn, the "great Hallel" which ended the liturgy of the Passover. Jesus repeated the vigorous words of the Psalmist which were like a prophetic funeral oration for Him, pronounced before His death.

"The Lord is on my side; I will not fear: what can man do unto me? . . . They compassed me about like bees; they are quenched as the fire of thorns: . . . I shall not die, but live. . . . The Lord hath chastened me sore: but he hath not given me over unto death."

When the hymn was ended they left the room and the house, at once. As soon as they had emerged from the house Judas disappeared into the night. The remaining eleven silently followed Jesus, who, as was His wont, made His way to the Mount of Olives.

ABBA, FATHER

ON THE MOUNT there was a garden, and a place where olives were crushed, which gave it its name, Gethsemane. Jesus and His friends had been spending the nights there, either to avoid the odors and noise of the great city, distasteful to them, country-bred as they were, or because they were afraid of being treacherously captured in the midst of their enemies' houses.

And when He was at the place, He said to His Disciples, "Sit ye here, while I go and pray yonder."

But He was so heavyhearted that He dreaded being alone. He took with Him the three whom He loved the best, Simon Peter, James and John. And when they had gone a little way from the others, He began to be sorrowful and very heavy. "My soul is exceeding sorrowful, even unto death: tarry ye here, and watch with me."

He withdrew Himself from them. He was alone now in the night, before God, and He could show His weakness without shame. He fell on the ground on His face and prayed, saying, "Abba, Father, all things are possible unto thee; O my Father, if it be possible, let this cup pass from me."

This was the second temptation. Jesus knew that He had to confirm by His death that greater life which He announced. The Cross is the rigorously necessary consequence of the Sermon on the Mount. He who brings love is given over to hatred, and He can conquer hatred only by accepting condemnation. The greatest good, which is love, must be paid for by the greatest evil in men's power, assassination.

But if the torture and the end of His body had really terrified Him, was there not yet time to save Himself? Even on that night there were ways of escaping. He would have been safe if, either alone or with His most faithful friends, He had taken the road back to the Jordan, and thence by hidden paths have passed across Perea into the tetrarchy of Philip, where He had already taken

refuge to escape the ill will of Herod Antipas. The Jewish police were so few and primitive that they could scarcely have found Him.

The fact that He did not flee shows that He did not try to escape death and the horrors that were to accompany it. From the point of view of our coarse human logic His death was a suicide—not unlike that of the heroes of antiquity who fell upon the sword of a slave. But what sort of a life would He have had after such a flight? To grow old obscurely, the timorous master of a hidden sect, to die at the last, worn out, like any other man! Better, infinitely better to finish the sowing of the Gospel on the Cross.

If the cup that Jesus wished to pass from Him was not fear of death, what else could it have been? Had He in the darkness of this last vigil glimpsed the fate which would befall His children later on, the bewilderment of the first saints, the martyrdoms, the massacres? Was He asking from His Father not His own safety from death, but safety from the evils which were to overwhelm those who believed in Him?

No one will ever know the true meaning of the words cried out by the Son to the Father, in the black loneliness of the Olives. A great French Christian called the story of this night the "Mystery of Jesus." The mystery of Judas is the only human mystery in the Gospels; the prayer of Gethsemane is the inscrutable, divine mystery of the story of Christ.

AND WHEN He had prayed, He turned back to find the Disciples, who were to wait for Him to return. But crouching on the ground, wrapped as best they could in their cloaks, Peter, James and John, the faithful, the specially chosen, had allowed themselves to be overcome with sleep. The voice of the Master called them: "What, could ye not watch with me one hour? . . . the spirit indeed is willing, but the flesh is weak." Did they hear these words in their sleep? Did they answer, shamefaced, putting their hands to their confused eyes?

Jesus went away again, more heavyhearted than ever. He was once more alone, utterly alone as men are alone who raise themselves above other men. Every hero is always the only one awake in a world of sleepers, like the pilot watching over his ship in the solitude of the ocean and of the night.

Of all these eternally solitary souls, Jesus was the most solitary. Everything slept about Him. The city slept, its white, shadow-checkered mass sprawling beyond the Kidron; and in all the houses the blind race of ephemeral men were sleeping. The only ones awake at that hour were His enemies and their guards. Caiaphas was not asleep and the only Disciple awake was Judas.

Until the arrival of Judas, He was alone, and that He might feel less alone He began to pray to His Father; once more those imploring words rushed to His lips. The effort to keep them back, the conflict which convulsed Him, the tension of the terrible struggle did such violence that the sweat stood out on Him, not merely the natural sweat which runs down the face of the man working in the fields. Great drops of blood mixed with sweat fell on the earth as a first offering of His conquered flesh. It was the beginning of liberation, almost a relief to that humanity which was the greatest burden of His expiation.

Then from His lips arose a new prayer: "O my Father, if this cup may not pass away from me, except I drink it, thy will be done . . . not my will, but thine, be done."

From that moment His victory over death is assured, because he who gives himself wholly to the Eternal cannot die. "For whosoever will save his life shall lose it: and whosoever will lose his life for my sake shall find it."

He stood up calmed, and turned back toward His Disciples. His sad reproof had been vain; worn out and exhausted, the three were again sleeping. But this time Jesus did not call them.

Now He can listen almost longingly for the footsteps of Judas.

For a time He hears only the beating of His own heart, so much calmer than at first, now that the horror is nearer. But after some moments, He hears approaching the sound of cautious shuffling, and there among the bushes which border the road, red flickerings of light appear and disappear in the darkness. They are the servants of the assassins who are following Iscariot along the path.

Jesus turns to the Disciples, still asleep, "Behold, the hour is come; Rise up, let us go; lo, he that betrayeth me is at hand."

The eight other Disciples, sleeping farther away, are already aroused by the noise, but have no time to answer the Master because while He is still speaking the crowd comes up and stops.

IT WAS THE RABBLE who swarmed around the Temple, bunglingly made over for the time being into warriors; sweepers and doorkeepers who had taken up swords; a great multitude, so the Evangelists say, although they knew they were going out against only twelve men, who had only two swords. It is not credible that there were Roman soldiers among them. Caiaphas wished to make Christ a prisoner before he presented Him to the procurator, and the few forces at his disposition (the last vestiges of David's army) with the addition of some clients and relatives were enough to carry out the far-from-dangerous capture.

This haphazard mob had come with torches and lanterns almost as if out for an evening celebration. The face of Judas seemed to waver in the torchlight. Christ offered His face, more luminous than the lights, to Judas' kiss. "Betrayest thou the Son of man with a kiss?" He knew what Judas came to do, and He knew that this kiss was the first of His tortures and the most unendurable. This kiss was the signal for the guards who did not know the delinquent by sight. "Whomsoever I shall kiss, that same is He; take Him, and lead Him away safely," Judas had told the rough crowd who followed him as they came along the road.

As soon as the sign was given the boldest came up to their enemy.

"Whom seek ye?"

"Jesus of Nazareth."

"I am he." Even at such a moment Jesus took thought of His friends. "I have told you that I am he: if therefore ye seek me, let these go their way."

At the moment, profiting by the confusion of the guards, Peter, coming suddenly to himself from his sleep and from his panic, laid his hand to a sword and cut off the ear of Malchus, a servant of Caiaphas. Peter on that night was full of contradictory impulses; after the supper he had sworn that no matter what happened he would never leave Jesus; then in the garden he could not keep himself awake; after that, tardily he set himself up as a militant defender; and a little later he was to deny that he had ever known his Master. Peter's untimely and futile action was at once repudiated by Christ: "Put up thy sword into the sheath: for all they that take the sword shall perish with the sword. . . . the cup which my Father hath given me, shall I not drink it?" And He offered His hands to be tied with the rope which they had brought.

While they were busy tying Him, the prisoner accused them of cowardice. "Are ye come out, as against a thief, with swords and with staves to take me? When I was daily with you in the temple, ye stretched forth no hands against me: but this is your hour, and the power of darkness."

The guards, eager to return triumphantly and to receive their fees, did not trouble to answer; they dragged Him by the rope towards the road to Jerusalem. Then, confesses Matthew, ". . . all the disciples forsook him, and fled." Only two followed the procession, and they from a safe distance. We shall see them later in the courtyard of Caiaphas' house.

All this bustle awakened a young man who had been sleeping in the house in the grove of olives. Inquisitive like all young men, he did not take the time to dress, but wrapping a sheet about him, stepped out to see what was happening. The guards thought him a disciple who had not had time to escape, and laid hands on him, but the young man, casting off the sheet, left it in their hands and fled from them naked.

No one has ever known the identity of this mysterious man who appeared suddenly in the night, and as suddenly disappeared. Perhaps he was the youthful Mark, the only one of the Evangelists who tells this story. If it were Mark, it is possible that on that night the involuntary witness of the beginning of the Passion conceived the impulse to become, as Mark did, its first historian.

IN A SHORT TIME the criminal was taken to the house which Annas shared with his son-in-law, the high priest Caiaphas. Although the night was now well advanced, and although the assembly had been warned the day before that Caiaphas hoped to capture the blasphemer early in the morning, many of the Sanhedrin were still in bed and the prosecution could not begin at once. In order that the common people might not have time to rise in rebellion, nor Pilate to take thought, Annas was in haste to finish the affair that very morning. Some of the guards who returned from the Mount of Olives were sent to awake the more important scribes and elders, and in the meantime old Annas, who had not slept all that night, set himself on his own account to question this false prophet.

Annas had been for seven years high priest, and though deposed in the year 14 under Tiberius, he was still the real primate of the Jewish church. A Sadducee, head of one of the most aggressive and wealthy families of the ecclesiastical patriarchate, he was still, through his son-in-law, leader of his caste. Five of his sons were afterwards high priests, and one of them, also called Annas, later caused James, the brother of the Lord, to be stoned to death.

Jesus was led before him. It was the first time that the woodworker of Nazareth found Himself face-to-face with the religious head of His people. Up till then He had met only the subalterns in the Temple, the common soldiers, the scribes and Pharisees; now He was before the head, and He was no longer the accuser but the accused. This was the first questioning of that day. In the space of a few hours, four authorities examined Him: two rulers from the Temple, Annas and Caiaphas; and two temporal rulers, Antipas and Pilate.

The first question Annas put to Jesus was to ask Him who His disciples were. The old political priest wished to know who were the followers of the new prophet, and from what rank of society He had picked them up. But Jesus looked at him without answering.

Then Annas asked about His doctrine. Jesus answered that it was not for Him to explain: "I spake openly to the world; . . . in secret have I said nothing. Why askest thou me? ask them which heard me, what I have said unto them: behold, they know what I said."

Annas must have made a wry face at an answer which presupposed an honest trial, for one of the officers standing by struck Jesus with the palm of his hand, saying, "Answerest thou the high priest so?"

This blow was the beginning of the insults which were henceforth rained upon Christ up to the cross. But He who had been struck, with His cheek reddened by the boor, turned towards the man who had struck Him. "If I have spoken evil, bear witness of the evil: but if well, why smitest thou me?"

Annas, seeing that he was not succeeding in extracting anything from Him, sent Him bound to Caiaphas, the high priest, so that the fiction of a legal prosecution might begin at once.

ONLY TWO of the fleeing Disciples repented of their cowardice, and trembling in the shadow of the walls, followed from afar the swaying lanterns which accompanied Christ: Simon Peter, son of Jonas, and John, son of Zebedee.

John, who was known in the household of Caiaphas, went into the courtyard of the building with Jesus; then after a few moments, not seeing his companion, and wishing to have him at hand for sympathy or defense, went out and persuaded the suspicious doorkeeper to let Peter also come in. But as Peter stepped through the door, the woman recognized him: "Art not thou also one of his disciples?"

But Peter took on an offended air. "I know not, neither understand I what thou sayest. I know him not."

And he sat down with John near the brazier which the servants had kindled in the courtyard because, although it was in April, the night was cold. But the woman would not give up her idea, and coming to the fire and looking at him earnestly, said, "Thou also wast with Jesus of Nazareth," and he denied again with curses, "Woman, I know him not!"

The gatekeeper, shaking her head, turned back to her gate, but the men aroused by these heated denials looked at him more closely and said, "Surely thou art one of them: for thou art a Galilean, and thy speech agreeth thereto."

Then Peter began to curse and to swear, but another, a kinsman of Malchus whose ear Peter had cut off, broke into his testimony: "Did I not see thee in the garden with him?"

But Peter, now hopelessly involved in lies, began again to protest that they had mistaken him for another and that he was not one of the friends of the Man.

At this very moment Jesus, bound among the guards, crossed the courtyard after His colloquy with Annas, passing to the other part of the palace, where Caiaphas lived: and He heard the words of Simon Peter and looked at Him, with eyes whose gentleness was more unendurable than any contempt. And this look pierced the pitiable, distracted heart of the fisherman. To the day of his death he could never forget those sad, mild eyes fixed on him in that terrible night; those eyes which in one flash expressed more and moved him more than a thousand words.

Under the weight of his look, Simon hung his head and his heart beat furiously in his breast. Torn by an unbearable tumult of passion and of remorse, he was scarcely able to drag himself to his feet and to stumble to the door. As he went out into the street in the silent, solitary darkness a distant cock crew. This gay, bold note was for Peter like the cry which awakens a sleeper from his nightmare. Then in the dim light of dawn the last stars saw a man staggering along like a drunkard, his head hidden in his cloak, his shoulders shaken by the sobs of a despairing lament.

CAIAPHAS' REAL NAME was Joseph. Caiaphas is a surname and is the same word as Cephas, Simon's surname, that is to say, Rock. On that Friday morning's dawn, between the denial of Simon Peter and the hatred of Joseph, between those two rocks Jesus was like wheat between the millstones.

The Sanhedrin had already come together and was awaiting Him. Together with Annas and Caiaphas who presided, the Sanhedrin was composed of twenty-three priests, twenty-three scribes, twenty-three elders, and two presidents, in all, seventy-one. But on this occasion some were absent, those who had more fear of an uprising of the people than hatred for the blasphemer, and those few who would not lift a finger to condemn Him, but would not defend Him openly: among these last was certainly Nicodemus, the nocturnal disciple, and Joseph of Arimathea, who was devoutly to lay Jesus in His tomb.

The great room of the council was already full of people. The new day showed itself hesitatingly: the orange-colored tongues of the torches were scarcely visible in the dim light of dawn. In this sinister half shadow the Sanhedrin waited: aged, portly, harsh, wrapped in their white cloaks, their heads covered, seated in a half circle. The rest of the hall was occupied by the clients of the seated assembly, by guards with staves in their hands, by the domestic servants of the house. The air was heavy and dense.

Jesus, His wrists still tied with ropes, was thrust into their midst. Annas had gathered in all haste from among the rabble some false witnesses to make an end of any discussion or defense. The pretense of a trial began with calling these perjurers. Two of them came forward and swore that they had heard these words: "I will destroy this temple that is made with hands, and within three days I will build another made without hands."

At the time and for those hearers this accusation was a very grave one, meaning nothing less than sacrilege and blasphemy. For in the minds of its upholders the Temple of Jerusalem was the one intangible home of the Lord. And to threaten the Temple was to threaten the Master of all the Jews. But Jesus had never said these words or at least not in this form, nor with this meaning. It is true that He had announced that of the Temple not one stone would remain upon another, but not through any action of His. And the reference to the Temple not made with hands, built up in three days, was part of another discourse in which He had spoken figuratively of His resurrection.

The false witnesses could not even agree about these words, confusedly and maliciously repeated, and one statement from Jesus would have been enough to confound them utterly. But Jesus held His peace.

The high priest could not endure this silence, and standing up, cried out, "Answerest thou nothing? what is it which these witness against thee?"

Jesus answered nothing, but looked about Him with His great calm eyes, at the troubled faces of His judges.

These silences of Jesus were weighty with magnetic eloquence, and enraged his judges. Caiaphas, exasperated by this disrespectful taciturnity, finally hit on a way to make him speak. "I adjure thee by the living God, that thou tell us whether thou be the Christ, the Son of God."

The priest's invocation of the living God was irresistible. Jesus could not deny Himself to the living God, to the God who will live eternally, and who lives in all of us. And yet He hesitated a moment with the splendor of His formidable secret.

"If I tell you, ye will not believe: And if I also ask you, ye will not answer me."

Now Caiaphas was not alone in putting the question; all of them, excited, sprang to their feet and cried out, "Art thou then the Son of God?"

Jesus could not, like Peter, deny the irrefutable certainty which was the reason for His life and for His death. But, as at Caesarea, He wished others to be the ones to pronounce His real name, and when they had said it He did not refuse it, even though death were the penalty. "Ye say that I am. I say unto you, Hereafter shall ye see the Son of man sitting on the right hand of power, and coming in the clouds of heaven."

He had condemned Himself out of His own mouth. He had proclaimed what He had secretly admitted to His most loving friends. Although they might betray Him, He had not betrayed Himself or His Father. Now He was ready for the last degradation.

Caiaphas was triumphant. Pretending a shocked horror which he did not feel—because like all the Sadducees he had no faith whatever in the apocalyptic writers and cared about nothing but the fees and honors of the Temple—he rent his priestly garments, crying out, "He hath spoken blasphemy; what further need have we of witnesses? behold, now ye have heard his blasphemy. What think ye?" And without any further examination they condemned Him to death as a blasphemer and false prophet.

The comedy of legal pretense was played to an end.

WHILE THE high officials went apart to take counsel on the manner of securing the ratification from the procurator and executing the death sentence with all speed, Jesus was thrown to the rabble in the palace.

The captors of Christ had been awake all night long, and the night had been cold; they had made the march up to the Mount of Olives, fearing resistance, a well-grounded fear, since one of them had had his ear stricken off. It was a very tiring business especially on those festal days when the city and the Temple were full of foreigners. They felt that they really deserved some amusement.

But they did not know how to begin. He was tied and his friends had disappeared. This man, bound, exhausted, condemned to death by the highest and holiest tribunal of the Jewish people, this human rubbish destined to the cross of slaves and thieves, this man who did not speak nor complain nor weep, but who looked on them as if He had compassion on them, inspired a mysterious reverence.

But one of the scribes or the elders gave the example, and spat at Jesus as he passed by Him. Then the guards who were nearest Him struck Him in the face; those who could not strike His face rained down blows and threats. Then one of the mob, more quick-witted than the others, had an idea: he took a dirty cloth and with it covered the bleeding, buffeted face, tying the corners behind. And he said: "Let us play blind-man's buff. This man boasts of being a prophet; let us see if he can guess which of us is striking him."

Was that look of suffering love really unendurable to them? With childish cruelty, they arranged themselves in a circle about Him and first one and then another twitched a fold of His garment, gave Him a blow on the shoulder, struck Him with a staff over the head: "Prophesy, who it it that smote thee?"

Luke adds, "And many other things blasphemously spake they against him."

But Caiaphas and the others were in haste. The false king must be taken to Pilate that his sentence be confirmed: the Sanhedrin could pronounce judgment, but since Judea was under Roman rule, it had no longer, unfortunately, the *Jus Gladii* [the right of the sword]. And the high priests, scribes and elders, set out for the palace of the procurator, followed by the guards leading Jesus with ropes, and by the yelling horde which grew larger as they went.

PONTIUS PILATE

SINCE A. D. 26, Pontius Pilate had been procurator in the name of Tiberius Caesar. Historians know nothing of him before his arrival in Judea. If the name comes from Pileatus it may be supposed that he was a freedman or descendant of freedmen, since the *pileus*, or skull cap, was the headgear of freed slaves. He had been in Judea only a few years, but long enough to draw upon himself the bitterest hate of those over whom he ruled. It is true that all our information about him comes from Jews and Christians, who were, of course, his declared enemies.

In the first place the hatred of the Jews came from the profound scorn which he showed from the start for this stiff-necked, indocile people, who must have seemed to him, brought up in Roman ideas, a low crowd. To have an idea of Pilate's personality, make a mental picture of an English viceroy of India, a subscriber to the *Times*, a reader of John Stuart Mill and Shaw—with Byron and Swinburne on his bookshelves—destined to administer the government over a ragged, captious, hungry and turbulent people, wrangling among themselves over a confusion of castes and mythologies for which their ruler feels in his heart the deepest aversion. Pilate was one of those skeptics of the Roman decadence, a devotee of Epicurus, an encyclopedist of Hellenism without any belief in the gods of his country, nor any belief that any real God existed at all.

The idea certainly can never have occurred to Pilate that the true God could be found in this superstitious mob, in the midst of this factious and jealous clergy, in this religion which must have seemed to him like a barbarous mixture of Syrian and Chaldean oracles. The only faith remaining to him, or which he needed to pretend to hold because of his office, was the new Roman religion, civic and political, concentrated on the cult of the emperor. The first conflict with the Jews arose in fact from this religion. When he had changed the guard of Jerusalem, he ordered the soldiers to enter the city by night, without taking off from their ensigns the silver images of Caesar. In the morning, as soon as the Jews were aware of this, great was the horror. It was the first time that the Romans had lacked in external respect for the religion of their subjects in Palestine. These figures of the deified Caesar planted near the Temple were for them an idolatrous provocation. All the country was in an uproar. A deputation was sent to Caesarea to have Pilate take them away. Pilate refused; for five days and nights they stormed about him. Finally the procurator convoked them in the amphitheater and treacherously had them surrounded with soldiers with naked swords, assuring them that no one would escape if they did not make an end of their clamor. But the Jews, instead of asking for mercy, offered their throats to the swords, and Pilate, conquered by this heroic stubbornness, ordered that the insignia be carried back to Caesarea.

A little while after this, he introduced into Herod Antipas' palace, where he lived when he stayed at Jerusalem, votive tablets dedicated to the emperor. But the priests heard of it and once more the people were aroused to outraged anger. He was asked to take away the idolatrous objects at once. Pilate this time also did not yield. The Jews then appealed to Tiberius, who decreed that the tablets should be sent back to Caesarea.

Twice Pilate had had the worst of a dispute. But the third time he was triumphant. Coming from the city of public baths and aqueducts, he noticed that Jerusalem lacked water and he planned to have a fine large reservoir constructed and an aqueduct several miles long. But the undertaking was expensive and to pay for it he used a goodly sum taken from the treasury of the Temple. The priests cried out on the sacrilege, and the people incited by them made such a commotion that when Pilate came for the Feast of the Passover to Jerusalem, thousands of men gathered in a tumultuous crowd in front of his palace. But this time he sent among the multitude a large number of disguised soldiers who at a given signal began to lay about them so vigorously that they all fled, and Pilate could enjoy in peace the water of the reservoir paid for with the Jews' money.

Only a short time had passed since this last encounter and now these very priests who three times had risen against his authority were forced to have recourse to him. Only hard necessity drove them to it, because death sentences could not be carried out if they were not confirmed by Caesar's representative.

That Friday, at dawn, Pontius Pilate, wrapped in his toga, still sleepy and yawning, was waiting for them in Herod's palace, very ill-disposed towards those tiresome troublemakers.

THE CROWD of the accusers and of the rough populace finally came before Herod's palace, but they stopped outside, because if they went into a house where there was leaven and bread baked with leaven, they would be contaminated all day long and could not eat the Passover.

Pilate, warned of their coming, went out on the doorsill and asked abruptly: "What accusation bring ye against this man?"

Instinctively Pilate took the part of their enemy.

Caiaphas answered at once as if offended: "If he were not a malefactor, we would not have delivered him up unto thee."

Then Pilate, who wished to lose no time with ecclesiastical squabbles and did not think that there was any question of a capital crime, answered dryly: "Take ye him, and judge him according to your law."

Already in these words appears his wish to save the man without being forced to take sides openly, because the Sanhedrin could inflict only light sentences. They answered: "It is not lawful for us to put any man to death."

Pilate suddenly understood what sentence they wished passed on the wretched man who stood before him, and he wished to find out what crime He had committed.

The foxes of the Temple had thought of this difficulty before taking action. They were prepared to lie. They knew very well that Pilate would not be satisfied if they told him that Jesus was a false Messiah. Pilate would smile. But if they said that He was trying to rouse the common people against Rome, Pilate could not do less than put Him to death.

"We found this fellow perverting the nation, and forbidding to give tribute to Caesar, saying that he himself is Christ, a

King. . . . He stirreth up all the people, teaching throughout all Jewry, beginning from Galilee to this place."

Every word was a lie. Jesus had commanded men to render unto Caesar that which was Caesar's. He said that He was Christ but not in the political meaning of a King of the Jews. These accusations increased Pilate's suspicions of the priests. Was it probable that they, whose one dream was to sweep away the governing pagans, should suddenly be kindled with so much zeal to denounce a rebel of their own nation?

Pilate wished to find out for himself, by questioning the accused man in private. He went back into the palace and commanded that Jesus be brought to him. Disregarding the less important accusations, he went at once to the essential: "Art thou the King of the Jews?"

But Jesus did not answer. How could He ever make this Roman understand! This Roman whose only religion was the artificial cult of a living man—and of what a man—the Emperor Tiberius!—how could He ever explain to this pupil of the lawyers and rhetoricians of decadent Rome that He was the King of a spiritual Kingdom which would abolish all human kingdoms?

Jesus made no answer, as He had kept silent at first before Annas and before Caiaphas.

The procurator could not understand this silence on the part of a man over whom hung the threat of death. "Hearest thou not how many things they witness against thee?"

Pilate, who wished to triumph over those who hated him as much as they hated this man, insisted, hoping to extract a denial which would permit him to set Him at liberty: "Art thou the King of the Jews?"

Jesus had said to His disciples and to the Jews that He was Christ. The better to sound the Roman's mind He answered him, as was his wont, with another question: "Sayest thou this thing of thyself, or did others tell it thee of me?"

Pilate answered, as if offended, "Am I a Jew? Thine own nation and the chief priests have delivered thee unto me. Art thou the King of the Jews?"

Jesus determined to try to shed more light on this pagan.

"My kingdom is not of this world: if my kingdom were of

this world, then would my servants fight, that I should not be delivered to the Jews: but now is my kingdom not from hence."

The difference between "of this world" and "my kingdom is not from hence" was obscure to Pilate. And once more he asked: "Art thou a king then?"

"Thou sayest that I am a king. To this end was I born, and for this cause came I into the world, that I should bear witness unto the truth. Every one that is of the truth heareth my voice."

Then Pilate, annoyed by what seemed to him truculent mystification, answered with the celebrated question: "What is truth?"

And without waiting for an answer, he rose to go out.

JUST AS Pilate was preparing to go out and give his answer to the Jews, who were muttering restlessly and impatiently before the door, a servant sent by his wife came up to him, giving him this message:

"Have thou nothing to do with that just man: for I have suffered many things this day in a dream because of him."

No one in the four Gospels tells us what impression was made on the procurator by this unexpected intercession. We know nothing of his wife except her name. According to the Apocryphal Gospel of Nicodemus her name was Claudia Procula, and if this name was really hers she may have belonged to the *gens* Claudia, distinguished and powerful at Rome. We may thus suppose that she was by birth and connections of a higher social rank than her husband, and that Pilate, a mere freedman, may have owed to her influence in Rome his post in Judea.

If all this was true, certainly the request of Claudia Procula must have made some impression on Pilate, especially if he loved her; and that he loved her seems proved by the fact that he had asked to take her with him into Asia. The *Lex Oppia* usually forbade the proconsuls to take their wives with them, and Pontius Pilate had a special permit from Tiberius allowing Claudia Procula to accompany him.

The motives for this intercession, so briefly stated, are mysterious. The words of Matthew refer to a dream in which she had suffered because of Jesus: it is probable that she had heard people talking for some time of the new Prophet; perhaps she had seen Him, and Jesus' words had been pleasing to the imagination of a fanciful Roman woman. She did not understand the language spoken in Jerusalem, but some interpreter of the law courts might have accompanied her.

In those days the Romans, especially Roman women, were beginning to feel the attraction of Oriental cults, which gave more satisfaction to the longing for personal immortality than the old Latin religion, a cold, legal, businesslike exchange of sacrifices to obtain utilitarian ends. Patrician women had been initiated into the mysteries of Mithra and Osiris, and of Isis, the Great Mother, and in that very reign of Tiberius many Jews living in Rome were exiled from the capital because, according to Josephus, some of them had converted to Judaism a matron, Fulvia; and Fulvia, as we see from a reference of Suetonius, was not the only one.

Together with the centurion of Capernaum and with the Canaanite woman, Claudia Procula is the first pagan who believed in Christ, and the Greek Church has good reason to revere her as a saint.

This message from his wife strengthened Pilate's reluctance. Claudia Procula had not said, "Save Him"—but: "Have thou nothing to do with that just man." This was Pilate's idea, also. A way to evade the responsibility occurred to him. He went back to Jesus and asked whether He were a Galilean.

The procurator had found a legitimate subterfuge. Jesus did not belong to his jurisdiction, but to that of Herod Antipas. By good luck Antipas was there at Jerusalem, come for the Passover. Losing no time, he ordered the soldiers to take Jesus before Antipas.

THE THIRD JUDGE before whom Jesus was led was a son of that bloody-minded Herod the Great, by one of his five wives. Antipas was the true son of his father because he wronged his brothers as his father had wronged his sons. When his half brother, Archelaus, was accused by his subjects, he managed to have him exiled. At seventeen years of age he began to reign as tetrarch over Galilee and over Berea.

To ingratiate himself with Tiberius, he offered himself as a secret talebearer of the sayings and doings of his brothers and of the Roman officials in Judea. On a voyage to Rome he fell in love with Herodias, who was both his niece and his sister-in-law, since she was the daughter of his brother Aristobulus, and wife of his brother Herod, and not shrinking from the double incest, he persuaded her to follow him, together with Salome, her daughter. His first wife, daughter of Aretas, king of the Nabatei, went back to her father, who declared war on Antipas and defeated him.

This happened while John the Baptist was beginning to be talked about among the people. That Prophet let slip some words of condemnation against these two adulterers, and this was enough for Herodias to persuade her new husband to have him taken and shut up in the fortress of Machaerus. Everyone knows how the tetrarch, inflamed by cruel Salome and perhaps meditating a new incest, was forced to offer her the bearded head of the Prophet of Fire on a golden platter.

But even after his decapitation John's shade disturbed Herod Antipas, and when he began to hear talk of Jesus and of His miracles he said to his courtiers, "This is John the Baptist; he is risen from the dead."

Deciding that he would have no more to do with prophets, he saw that the best way was to force Jesus to leave his tetrarchy. One day some Pharisees, very probably acting on Herod Antipas' instructions, went to say to Jesus: "Get thee out, and depart hence: for Herod will kill thee."

"And he said unto them, Go ye, and tell that fox . . . I must walk today, and tomorrow, and the day following: for it cannot be that a prophet perish out of Jerusalem."

And now at Jerusalem near His death, He appeared before that fox. Jesus had named him well: he was more fox than tiger, and he shrank from being a substitute for Pilate.

Antipas began to put many questions, to which Jesus made no answer. But the high priests and the scribes had followed their victim there, and their furious accusations as well as the silence of the accused man deepened the hidden rancor of Antipas. He threw over Jesus' shoulders a gorgeous mantle, shining with whiteness, which was, so Josephus says, the garment of the Jewish kings, and sent Him again to Pilate.

Antipas wished to ridicule the pretensions of Jesus by ironically making him a present of the regal robe; but when he covered Him with that whiteness, which is the symbol of innocence and of sovereignty, he sent to Pilate a symbolical message which involuntarily confirmed the message of Claudia Procula, the accusation of Caiaphas, and what Christ Himself had said.

PILATE SAW Jesus wrapped in that regal white garment and understood that he must get the matter settled. He had decided to save Jesus.

Perhaps while Jesus was with the tetrarch, Pilate had learned from one of His followers more about the pretended King. Jesus taught love for enemies, and in Judea the Romans were considered enemies; He called the poor blessed, hence He exhorted them to resignation and not to revolt; He advised men to render unto Caesar that which was Caesar's, that is, to pay tribute to the emperor; He was opposed to the Pharisaical formalism which made the relations of the Romans with their subjects so difficult; He did not respect the Sabbath; He ate with publicans and with Gentiles. If Pilate knew these things, he must have said to himself that it would be good for Rome if many Jews followed Jesus, rather than fomented rebellion in the councils of the Zealots.

Therefore, causing Jesus to be led out, Pilate went to the door and said to the high priests and the others who crowded about, their faces thrust forward to hear the sentence given at last, "Ye have brought this man unto me, as one that perverteth the people: and, behold, I, having examined him before you, have found no fault in this man touching those things whereof ye accuse him: No, nor yet Herod: for I sent you to him; and, lo, nothing worthy of death is done unto him. I will therefore chastise him, and release him."

This was not the answer awaited by the horde yelling in the square before the procurator's house. A bestial cry burst out, "Kill Him!"

As soon as this uproar was a little quieted, Pilate asked, "What will ye then that I shall do unto him whom ye call King of the Jews?"

And they all answered, "Crucify him!"

But the procurator resisted. "Why, what evil hath he done?"

And they cried out the more exceedingly, "Crucify him!"

Jesus, pale and calm in the whiteness of the mocking, regal cloak, looked quietly at the crowd, which desired to give Him what in His heart He had been seeking.

But obstinate Pilate at any cost wanted to win his point. He had not succeeded in transferring to Antipas the disagreeable responsibility of a death sentence; he had not succeeded in persuading the people of the innocence of their wretched king. The mob wanted to see a little blood; on these festival days they wanted to enjoy the spectacle of a crucifixion. He would satisfy them with a bargain, giving them the carcass of a murderer in exchange for the body of an innocent man.

"I find in him no fault at all. But ye have a custom, that I should release unto you one at the passover. Whom will ye that I release unto you? Barabbas, or Jesus which is called Christ?" Taken by surprise, the people did not know what to answer. Until then there had been but one name, one victim, one punishment asked for; everything was as clear as the sky on that mid-April morning.

But the elders, scribes and priests were still there and they had no intention of letting Jesus escape. When Pilate asked them a second time which of the two they wished him to free, they answered with one voice, "Away with this man, and release unto us Barabbas!"

The common tradition has preserved Barabbas' memory as a street ruffian, a criminal by profession. Mark and Luke say expressly that he was accused of having committed murder during a sedition, hence a political assassin. Barabbas, a student in the school of the scribes, lamenting the loss of the Jewish kingdom, hating Judea's pagan masters, was probably a Zealot and had been captured in one of the unsuccessful revolts, so common at that time. Was it likely that such an absurd bargain would satisfy the Sadducee and Pharisee assembly which shared the sentiments of the Zealots, even if for reasons of state they hid them?

Barabbas, precisely because he was an assassin, was a patriot, a martyr, persecuted by the foreigners. On the other hand, Jesus, although He had never killed anyone, had wished to overturn the law of Moses, and to ruin the Temple. "Free Barabbas! Let this man die!"

Once more Pontius Pilate had failed to save Christ or himself.

Pontius Pilate was cowardly. He was afraid of displeasing his wife; he was afraid of giving satisfaction to his enemies; but at the same time he was afraid to have his soldiers disperse that sullen, arrogant crowd. A Roman of the true Roman stock would not have wasted a moment in defending an obscure visionary; or would at once have decreed that this man was innocent and was under the august protection of the empire. The fact that Pilate had not decided the question with a yes or no had increased the insolence of the high priests and the excitement of the people.

Now there were only two alternatives: either to give in shamefully after resisting so long, or to risk starting a tumult which in those days, when Jerusalem included almost a third of the population of Judea, might become a perilous uprising.

Undone by his own wavering, deafened by the yells, the only thing that came into his mind was to ask once more the advice of men to whom he should have issued orders.

"What shall I do then with Jesus which is called Christ?"

"Crucify him, let him be crucified!"

"Why, what evil hath he done?"

"Crucify him! Crucify him!"

"Take ye him and crucify him," cried Pilate, "for I find no fault in him."

"We have a law, and by our law he ought to die, because he made himself the Son of God."

But Pontius Pilate still would not yield the point. He would restore Barabbas to his accomplices, but he would not give up Jesus. The crowd was still shrieking, "Let him be crucified!" But Pilate gave Jesus over to the Roman soldiers to be flogged. Perhaps when the people saw the bruises and the blood dripping from His back they would be satisfied with that punishment.

THE MERCENARIES, WHO (in the provinces) were the majority in the Roman legions, were to have their turn at amusing themselves. All the company was ordered into the courtyard of the palace, and the white cloak given by Antipas was taken from Jesus' back—the first spoils of the enterprise—together with part of His other clothes. The lictors chose the rods, and the strongest among the soldiers snatched at them.

Jesus, half of His body bared, tied to a pillar that He might not lessen the force of the blows by bending forward, silently prayed. "Love those who hate you, do good to those who persecute you, offer the left cheek to him who has struck the right." They knew not whom they were flogging with such innocent heartiness. They themselves had been flogged sometimes for small breaches of discipline.

Finally, the number of blows prescribed had been duly administered, but the legionaries wished to have some further entertainment. This man pretended to be a king. Let us give Him His wish.

A soldier took off his scarlet cloak, the chlamys of the legionaries, and threw it over those red, torn shoulders; another took up a handful of dry thorns, kindling for the brazier of the night watch, twisted a couple of them together like a crown and put it on His head; a third had a slave give Him a reed and forced it into the fingers of His right hand; then, roaring with laughter, they pushed Him upon a seat. One by one, passing before Him, they bent their knees awkwardly, crying: "Hail, King of the Jews!"

But some were not satisfied with this burlesque homage, and one of them, snatching the reed out of His hand, gave Him a blow on the head, so that the thorns of His crown pierced the skin and made about His forehead a border of red drops.

The procurator appeared and smiled. He ordered them to lead the scourged King outside. This fitted in well with Pilate's sarcastic intention. Taking Jesus by the hand, he presented Him to the crowd.

"Behold the man!"

And he turned Christ's shoulders so that they might see the welts left by the rods, oozing blood. It was as if he said: Was it

His blood you desired? It is shed as a favor to you—to satisfy you. And now be off from here, for you have troubled me long enough!

But the crowd was not quieted by that spectacle. Pilate thought that he could make mock of them, but he would realize that this was no time for feeble jokes. They had had the best of him twice already and they would again. And their hoarse voices shouted all together, "Let him be crucified! Let him be crucified!"

Too late Pilate realized that they had driven him into a tangle from which he could not disengage himself.

By a flash of inspiration he had pronounced the great words, "Behold the man!" But he himself did not understand that he had found the truth he was seeking. Jesus is the Man of Sorrows announced by Isaiah, the man without form or comeliness, despised and rejected of men, who was to be killed for all men; He is God's only Son who had taken on man's flesh. But to the eyes of Pilate, He was wretched, insignificant flesh for rods.

And yet, standing beside that silent man, the Roman felt his heart heavy with an oppression he had never known before. Who could this man be whom all the people wished to kill, and whom he could neither save nor sacrifice? He turned once more to Jesus. "Whence art thou?"

But Jesus gave him no answer.

"Speakest thou not unto me? knowest thou not that I have power to crucify thee, and have power to release thee?"

Then the insulted King raised His head. "Thou couldest have no power at all against me, except it were given thee from above: therefore he that delivered me unto thee hath the greater sin."

The procurator in his perplexity found no new expedient to free himself from the net about him, and returned to his fixed idea. "Behold your King!"

The Jews, infuriated by this repeated insult, burst out, enraged, "If thou let this man go, thou art not Caesar's friend: whosoever maketh himself a king speaketh against Caesar."

At last they had hit on the right words to bring pressure on weak, cowardly Pilate. Every Roman magistrate depended on Caesar's favor.

Pilate surrendered. All his maneuvers had failed, and he certainly did not wish the whole province to rise on account of that unfortunate prophet; and even less was he willing that on His account they should accuse him before Tiberius and have him deposed.

In order that they might all have a visible representation which they would not forget, Pilate had a basin of water brought to him and washed his hands there before them all, saying, "I am innocent of the blood of this just person: see ye to it.

"Then answered all the people, and said, His blood be on us, and on our children.

"Then released he Barabbas unto them: and when he had scourged Jesus, he delivered him to be crucified."

Little did his shift avail him; for the fate he now sought to avert by giving Jesus over into the hands of his adversaries fell upon him a few years later. The Jews and the Samaritans accused him; the governor of Syria deposed him in A.D. 36, sending him to Rome to justify himself before the emperor. And Caligula banished him to Gaul. But he was followed by the shade of that great, silent man; exiled into Gaul, he killed himself.

FORGIVE THEM

THE SUN rose higher in the clear April sky and now it was near noon. The contest had wasted most of the morning, and there was no time to lose. According to Mosaic law, the bodies of executed criminals could not remain after sunset on the place of punishment. Moreover, Caiaphas remembered how, a few days before, Jesus had entered the city surrounded with waving branches and joyful hymns. Those Galileans who had followed Him until now, who loved Him, might make some effort at resistance and put off, even if they did not actually prevent, the real votive offering of that day.

Pilate, too, was in haste. He hoped to forget his own corroding uneasiness, so painfully like remorse. To vent his uneasiness on those who really caused it, he dictated the wording of the *titulus*, or superscription, which the condemned man was to wear about His neck until it was fastened above His head at the top of the cross, as follows: "Jesus of Nazareth the King of the Jews." The scribe wrote these words three times in three languages—Latin, Greek and Hebrew—in clear, red letters on the white wood.

The leaders of the Jews, who had remained there to hasten the preparations, read this sarcastic inscription and protested. They said to Pilate, "Write not, The King of the Jews; but that he said, I am King of the Jews."

But the procurator cut them short with a dry brevity: "What I have written I have written."

In the meantime the soldiers had put back on the King His poor-man's garments and had tied the notice about His neck. Others had brought out three massive crosses of pine, the nails, the hammer and the pincers. Pilate pronounced the usual formula: *"Io lictor, expedi crucem"* [Ho, Lictor, make ready the cross]— And the sinister procession moved forward.

The centurion rode at the head, he whom Tacitus calls with terrible brevity, *exactor mortis* [collector of the dead]. Immediately after him came, in the midst of the armed legionaries, Jesus and the two thieves who were to be crucified with Him. Each of them carried a cross on his shoulders, according to the Roman rule. And behind them, the uproar of the excited crowd, increased at every step by idle sightseers.

It was Parasceve, the day of preparations, the last night before the Passover. Thousands of lambs' skins were stretched out on the sunlit roofs; and from every house rose a column of smoke, delicate as a flower bud, which opened out in the air and then was lost in the clear, festal sky. Old women emerged from the dark alleyways; bearded men carried on their shoulders a kid or a cask of wine; children stared at the foreigners. In every home the housemother was busy, preparing everything needful for the next day, because with the setting of the sun everyone was exempt for twenty-four hours from the curse of Adam.

The lambs, skinned and quartered, were all ready for the fire; the loaves of unleavened bread were piled up fresh from the oven; men were decanting the wine, and the children to lend a hand somewhere were cleaning the bitter herbs.

Everywhere there was that good-natured tumult, that joyous bustle which goes before a great, popular feast day. And the great eastern sun sent down a flood of light upon the four hills.

SLOW as a funeral procession, the column of the bearers of the cross made its way. About them everything spoke of life, and they were going to burning thirst and to death; cold in death, they would be thrown into the cold earth.

At the sound of the centurion's horse, people stepped to one side and stopped to look at the wretched men toiling under their dreadful burden. The two thieves seemed more sturdy, but the first seemed scarcely able to take another step. Worn out by the endless night, by His four questionings, by the buffetings, by the flogging; disfigured with blood, sweat, saliva, and by the terrible effort of this last task set Him, He did not seem like the fearless young man who a few days before had scourged the money changers out of the Temple. His face was drawn and contracted by the convulsions of pain; His eyes, red with suppressed tears, were sunken in their sockets; His clothes clung to the wounds on His shoulders, His legs bent under His weight and under that of the cross.

Some women, their heads wrapped in their cloaks, came behind all the rest, weeping, but trying to hide this seditious grief.

They were almost to the Gate of Gardens when Jesus fell to the ground and lay there stretched under His cross. The reddened eyelids were dropped over His eyes; He would have seemed dead if it had not been for the painful breath coming and going through His half-open mouth.

They all stopped, and a dense circle of jeering men stretched out their faces and hands towards the fallen man.

"He is only pretending," they cried. "He ought to carry the cross to the last! That is the law! Give Him a kick, and let Him get along!"

But the centurion saw clearly that the unfortunate Jesus

would never be able to drag the cross all the way to Golgotha. He cast his eyes about to find someone to carry that weight. Just at that moment a Cyrenian called Simon had stepped into the crowd and was looking with an astonished and pitying expression at the body prostrate under the two beams. He was strongly built, and the centurion called to him, saying, "Take this cross and come after us."

Without a word the Cyrenian obeyed.

We know nothing more of the merciful-hearted man who lent his broad countryman's shoulders to lighten Jesus' load, but we know that his sons, Alexander and Rufus, were Christians. It is probable that they were converted by their father's telling them of the death of which he was an enforced witness.

Two soldiers helped the fallen man up on His feet, and urged Him forward. The procession took up its way again under the noonday sun.

THE CENTURION halted outside the old walled city, in the midst of the young green of the suburban gardens. The city of Caiaphas did not allow capital punishment within its walls.

They had stopped on the summit of a mound of limestone resembling a skull. This resemblance might seem to be the reason for choosing this place for executions, but the reason was rather because the two great roads from Jaffa and Damascus crossed each other close at hand, and it was well that the cross should show its terrible warning to the traveling multitude.

The sun, the high noonday sun, shone on the white mound and on the mattocks ringing sonorously in the rock. In the nearby gardens singing birds filled the sky with the silver arrows of their warblings; doves flew about in pairs in the warm, pastoral peace. It would be sweet to live there in some well-watered garden, in the perfume of the earth awakening and clothing itself, awaiting the harvest moon, in company with loving friends! Days of Galilee, days of sunshine among the vineyards, beside the lake, days of wandering with friends who listened understandingly, days drawing to a close with the well-earned cheerfulness of supper, days which seemed eternal, although they were so short!

Now Thou hast no one with Thee, Jesus, called the Christ. These soldiers preparing that appalling bed are only shadows, cast by the great shadow of God. God's human face is wet with cold sweat. The blows of the mattocks ring in His head; His whole body aches with weariness, trembles in a yearning for rest. At the same time it seems to Him that He loves with a more intimate tenderness those whom He is leaving, even those who are working for His death.

From the depths of His soul, like a song of victory over the torn flesh, rise up the words, never to be forgotten: "Father, forgive them; for they know not what they do."

It is not the prayer of a man, but of a God to a God.

Wrongs consciously wrought cannot be absolved without assurance of repentance. But the ignorance of men is so appallingly great that only a few really know what they do. The Pharisees, fearful of losing their preeminence; the doctors, fearful of losing their privileges; the rich, fearful of losing their money; Pilate, fearful of losing his office; and most ignorant of all were the people, misled by their leaders, and the soldiers obedient to orders; none of them knew who Christ was and what He came to do.

Now, at the point of death, He had confirmed His most difficult and divine teaching, "Love for enemies."

The crosses had been raised; they were piling stones about them to steady them under the weight, and were filling the holes with earth, stamping it down with their feet.

ON THE TOP of the Hill of the Skull the three crosses, tall, dark, with outspread beams like giants with outstretched arms, stood against the great sweep of the sweet spring sky, outlined by brilliant reflections from the sun. The beauty of the world on that day in that hour was so great that tortures were unthinkable; could they not, those wooden branches, blossom out with field flowers, and be wreathed with garlands of tender green, hiding the scaffold with verdure, in the shade of which reconciled and friendly brothers might sit down?

But the priests, the scribes, the Pharisees were stamping with impatience, and hastening on the Romans.

The centurion gave an order. Two soldiers approached Jesus and with rough gestures removed all His clothes. The criminal condemned to crucifixion must be entirely naked.

They passed two ropes under His armpits, and hoisted Him on the cross. Halfway up on the upright was a rough wooden peg like a seat where the body was to find a precarious and painful support. Another soldier leaned the ladder against one of the arms of the cross, climbed up on it, hammer in hand, seized the hand which had cured lepers, spread it out on the wood and drove a nail into the middle of the palm. The nails were long, and with a wide head so that they could be easily hammered. The soldier struck a vigorous blow, which pierced the flesh at once, and then another and a third so that the nail would hold firmly and so that only the head would remain outside. Then the diligent workman came down the ladder; and did the same to the other hand.

All the spectators had fallen silent, hoping to hear screams from the condemned man. But Jesus made no sound.

Now they turned their attention to the feet. This was work which could be done standing on the ground, for the Roman crosses were set low.

The soldier who was nailing Christ on the cross now lifted up His knees so that the soles of His feet should be flat against the wood, and taking the measure so that the iron nail should be long enough to go through the instep, he pierced the first foot, and drove the nail home. He did the same to the other foot, and at the end glanced up, still with his hammer in his hand, to see if anything was lacking. He remembered the scroll which they had taken from Jesus' neck and flung to the ground. He picked it up, climbed again on the ladder, and with two nails fastened it on the upright of the cross, above the thorn-crowned head.

Then he came down for the last time, threw away his hammer, and looked to see if his companions had finished their work. The thieves, too, were now in place. The four soldiers could divide the garments. These came to them by law. This left Jesus' tunic, which was without seam, woven all in one piece. It would be a sin to cut it; one of them took out his dice, threw them, and the tunic was awarded by luck.

All was done: the drops of blood fell slowly from His hands on the ground and the blood from His feet reddened the cross.

The throne of the King was a hard wooden peg; the Master with so many disciples now had as companions only two thieves.

Some of the priests, shaking their heads, said: "Thou that destroyest the temple, and buildest it in three days, save thyself. If thou be the Son of God, come down from the cross." Now their consciences were perfectly at rest. If any miracle were possible, He would no longer be crucified there to agonize; but the sky was empty and the sun, God's light, shone clearly that all men might see the contractions of His face and the painful heaving of His chest.

THE THIEVES who had been crucified with Jesus had begun to be hostile to Him in the street when He was liberated from the weight of His cross. No one seemed to think of them; it was for Him that the women were weeping and that even the centurion was moved to pity.

But one of them, when he heard the great words, "Forgive them; for they know not what they do," suddenly fell silent. This prayer of Jesus' found an unexpected echo in his own thought, which now seemed to him luminous in the darkness of his fate. Had he really known what he was doing? If he had had a little more bread and love, a friendly word when suddenly temptations laid siege to his lonely and dissatisfied soul, would he have committed the actions which had brought him to Golgotha?

These thoughts went through his distracted heart while he waited to be fastened to the cross.

When they were all on the cross, the other thief, suffering terribly from his pierced hands and feet, began to insult Jesus. "If thou be Christ, save thyself and us."

But the good thief, listening to the voices shrieking down below, now turned to his companion. "Dost not thou fear God, seeing thou art in the same condemnation? And we indeed justly; for we receive the due reward of our deeds: but this man hath done nothing amiss." And he cried out these words, "Lord, remember me when thou comest into thy kingdom."

Jesus, who had answered no man, turned His head as well as He could toward the pitying thief and answered, "Verily I say unto thee, Today shalt thou be with me in paradise."

The good thief was Jesus' last convert, the last disciple. We know nothing more of him; only his name preserved in an apocryphal manuscript. The Church has received him among her saints because of this promise of Christ, with the name of Dismas.

AS ANCIENT WRITERS admitted, crucifixion was the cruelest of punishments. It gave the greatest torture for the longest time. If tetanus set in, a merciful torpor hastened death; but there were men who held out until the second day after crucifixion, and even longer. The thirst of their fever, the congestion of their hearts, the rigidity of their veins, their cramped muscles, the dizziness and terrible pains in the head, the ever greater agony —all these were not enough to make an end of them. But most men died at the end of twelve hours.

The blood from the four wounds of Jesus had clotted about the nailheads. His head drooped on His neck; His eyes, those mortal eyes from which God had looked out upon the earth, were glazing over in the death stupor.

A king of barbarians pronounced the most vigorous words ever spoken by Christian lips about that agony. They were reading to Clovis the story of the Passion, and the fierce king was sighing and weeping when suddenly, no longer able to contain himself, clapping his hand to the hilt of his sword, he cried out, "Oh, that I had been there with my Franks!" Words of a soldier and of a violent man, but words beautiful with all the naïve beauty of a candid and virile love.

Now Nature itself seemed to wish to hide the horror of that sight: a thick cloud rose above the hills and little by little spread to every corner of the horizon. Black clouds gathered about the sweet, clear April sun, encircled it, laid siege to it . . . "and there was a darkness over all the earth until the ninth hour."

Many, alarmed by the falling of that mysterious darkness, fled away from the Hill of the Skull, and went home, silenced. But not all; the air was calm; no rain fell as yet, and in the obscurity, the three pallid bodies shone out whitely.

The women had not deserted Him. On one side at some distance from the cross, through fear of the howling men, Mary, His mother, Mary Magdalene, Mary of Cleophas, Salome, mother of James and John—and perhaps also Joanna of Cusa, and Martha—were present, terrified witnesses. He still had the strength to confide to John's care the Virgin of Sorrows. But after this, through the veil of His suffering, He saw no one and believed Himself alone. Even the Father seemed remote, inexplicably absent. And then there was heard in the silence of the darkness, these words, *"Eli, Eli, lama sabachthani?"* that is to say, "My God, my God, why hast thou forsaken me?"

This was the first verse of a psalm which He had repeated to Himself many times because He had found there so many presages of His life and His death; but He no longer had the strength to cry it all aloud as He had in the desert.

"My God, my God, why hast thou forsaken me? why art thou so far from helping me? . . . Our fathers trusted in thee: they trusted, and thou didst deliver them. They cried unto thee, and were delivered: . . . But I am a worm, and no man; a reproach of men, and despised of the people. All they that see me laugh me to scorn: . . . they shake the head, saying, He trusted on the Lord that he would deliver him: let him deliver him, seeing he delighted in him. . . . Be not far from me; for trouble is near; for there is none to help. . . . I am poured out like water, and all my bones are out of joint: my heart is like wax; it is melted in the midst of my bowels. . . . my tongue cleaveth to my jaws; and thou hast brought me into the dust of death. . . . the assembly of the wicked have inclosed me: they pierced my hands and my feet. . . . they look and stare upon me. They part my garments among them, and cast lots upon my vesture. But be not thou far from me, O Lord: O my strength, haste thee to help me."

The supplications of this prophetic psalm rose as the last expression of His dying humanity.

One of the soldiers now took a sponge, soaked it in vinegar, put it on a reed and held it to the lips of Christ. But certain of the Jews nearest to the cross thought that He was calling Elias, the Prophet, who in the popular imagination was to appear with

Christ, and said, "Let alone; let us see whether Elias will come to take him down."

The legionary, not wishing to make trouble, laid down the reed. But after a little Christ's voice came down as if from a great distance, "I thirst."

The soldier took up the sponge again, dipped it once more in the vessel full of the mixture of water and vinegar and once more held it to the parched mouth. And Jesus when He had taken the vinegar said, "It is finished."

With His last strength He cried with a loud voice in the darkness: "Father, into thy hands I commend my spirit!"

And Jesus bowed His head and gave up the spirit. That cry, so powerful that it freed the soul from the flesh, rang out of the darkness and lost itself in the furthermost ends of the earth.

More than nineteen hundred years have passed and men have intensified the tumult of their lives that they may drown out that cry. But in the fog and smoke of our cities, in the darkness ever more profound where men light the fires of their wretchedness, that prodigious cry of joy and of liberation still summons every one of us.

WATER AND BLOOD

CHRIST WAS DEAD. Some people, says Luke, went away smiting their breasts. Some did not speak, they hurried home to their supper—perhaps it was terror which they were feeling. But a foreigner, the centurion, Petronius, who had been the silent witness of the execution, was moved, and from his pagan mouth came the words of Claudia Procula, "Certainly this was a righteous man."

The leaders of His people had no thought of recantations. Evening was close at hand and with the setting of the sun the great Sabbath began. The Passover would be spoiled if the bloody corpses were not carried away at once. Therefore they sent word to Pilate to have the condemned men's legs broken at once and to have them buried. The breaking of the legs was to shorten the sufferings of crucified men. The soldiers, when they had received the order, came up to the bad thief, who, more robust than his companions, was still alive, and they broke his legs with a club.

They had seen Jesus die, but John says that one of them, to make quite sure, pierced His side with a spear, and saw with astonishment that water and blood came out from the wound. The name of this soldier according to an old tradition was Longinus, and it is said that some drops of that blood fell upon his eyes which had been infected, and immediately cured them. The history of martyrs tells of him that Longinus believed in Christ from that day on, and was a monk for twenty-eight years at Caesarea until he was murdered because of his faith.

Now that He was a silent, harmless, quiet corpse, His friends of the twenty-fifth hour, the tepid followers, the secret disciples, the anonymous admirers, came out from the houses where they had shut themselves in. To His sorrow in life Christ had many friends of this sort. Two of them stepped forward in that Good Friday twilight. They were notables of Jerusalem, rich lords; in short, two members of the Sanhedrin—Joseph of Arimathea and Nicodemus—who had hidden themselves in their houses. But in the evening when they ran no risk of offending their colleagues, when the elders had left Golgotha, the two nocturnal disciples thought that they would diminish their remorse by providing for the burial of the executed man.

The bolder of the two, Joseph, "... went in ... unto Pilate" (Mark noted the fact as remarkable) and asked for the body of Jesus. Pilate was astonished that He should already be dead, since crucified men often lived for two days; he called in Petronius, who had been charged with the execution.

After Pilate had heard his report, he "gave" the body to Joseph. The procurator was generous on that day because as a rule the Roman officers forced the families of condemned men to pay for the corpses.

When Joseph had received permission he took a fine white winding-sheet and linen bands, and went toward the Hill of the

Skull. On the way there he met Nicodemus, who may have been his friend, and who had come with the same thought. Nicodemus also had not spared expense, and had brought with him on the shoulders of a servant a hundred pounds of a mixture of myrrh and aloes.

And when they came to the crosses, while the soldiers were taking down the two thieves to throw them into the common grave of condemned men, they prepared themselves to take down the body of Jesus.

NIGHT WAS shutting down on the world which had lost the only Being which could give it light. Against the scarcely visible whiteness of the Hill of the Skull, the naked corpses glimmered dimly. The soldiers were obliged to work by the light of torches, flaming without smoke in that windless air.

Joseph, aided by Nicodemus and by a third helper, was scarcely able to draw out the deep-driven nails which held the feet. The ladder was still there. One of them, climbing up on it, took out the nails from the hands, supporting the loosened body with his shoulder. The others helped him to lower the corpse, and the body was placed on the knees of the Virgin of Sorrows who had borne Him. Then they all made their way towards a garden nearby belonging to the rich Joseph, who had had a sepulcher hewn out of the stone for himself and his family. In those days every well-to-do Jew had a family sepulcher.

As soon as they had arrived at the garden, the two bearers of the dead had water brought from the well, and washed the body. Now the women, the three Marys—the Virgin Mary, the contemplative Mary, the liberated Mary—more skillful than men, began to help in order that this burial, performed thus at night and in haste, would not be unworthy of Him. They lifted from His head the crown of Pilate's legionaries, and plucked out the thorns which had penetrated the skin. Many loving tears fell upon that face where in the calm paleness of death the old sweetness shone once more.

When the washing was finished, the corpse was sprinkled abundantly with Nicodemus' spices. Then, when the hundred pounds had covered Jesus with a fragrant pall, the winding-sheet was tied about the body with long linen bands, the head was wrapped in a napkin and another white cloth was spread over the face, after they had all kissed Him on the forehead.

Recently made, the open sepulcher had never been used. According to the ritual the two members of the Sanhedrin recited aloud the mortuary psalm, and finally, after they had placed the white-wrapped body in the cave, they closed the opening with a great stone and went away silently.

But the women did not follow them. They could not bring themselves to leave that rock which separated them forever from Him whom they loved. They whispered prayers, and recalled to each other memories of Him. Sometimes they called Him by name as they leaned against the rock, and spoke to Him.

Then, chilled and terrified by the night's blackness, they too went away, stumbling amid the bushes and the stones, promising one another to return there as soon as the feast day had passed.

THE SUN had not yet risen on the day which for us is Sunday, when four women once more drew near to the garden; but over the eastern hills a white hope rose slowly in the midst of the throbbing constellations. The clear air seemed stirred as by a recent stir of angels' wings.

In the half-light, the women advanced, lost in their sadness, under the spell of an emotion they could not have explained. Were they returning to weep upon the rock? Or to see Him once more, He who had captured their hearts without laying them waste? And speaking among themselves, they said, "Who shall roll us away the stone from the door of the sepulcher?"

There were four of them; Joanna of Cusa and Salome had joined Mary of Magdala and Mary of Cleophas.

But when they came to the rock they stood astounded. The opening into the sepulcher showed black against the darkness. Not believing her eyes, the boldest of them touched the sill with her trembling hands. In the daylight, brightening now with every moment, they saw the stone there beside them, leaning against the rocks.

The women, struck into silence by their fright, turned around as if expecting someone to come tell them what had happened in those two nights which had passed. Mary of Magdala feared at once that the body had been stolen by those unwilling to have the honorable Jewish sepulcher used by a heretic; perhaps they had thrown Him into the shameful common grave for men stoned and crucified.

But perhaps Jesus was still lying inside in His perfumed wrappings. As the sun, climbing at last above the summit of the hills, shone into the opening of the sepulcher, they took courage and entered.

At first they saw nothing, but they were shaken by a new fear. At their right, seated, was a young man clothed in a long white garment, showing in that darkness like snow. He seemed to be awaiting them.

"Be not affrighted: he is not here: for he is risen. Why seek ye the living among the dead? Remember how he spake unto you when he was yet in Galilee, saying, the Son of man must be delivered into the hands of sinful men, and be crucified, and the third day rise again."

The women listened, terrified, not able to answer, but the youth went on, "Go quickly, and tell his disciples that he is risen from the dead; and, behold, he goeth before you into Galilee; there shall ye see him."

All four of them, quivering with terror and joy, left the grotto. But after a few steps, when they were almost outside the garden, Mary of Magdala stopped, and the others went along the road towards the city without waiting for her. She herself did not know why she had remained behind. Perhaps she remembered that they had not even made sure that the sepulcher was really empty; perhaps the youth in white was an accomplice of the priests who wished to deceive them?

Suddenly she turned and saw a man near her, outlined against the green of the garden; but she did not recognize Him even when He spoke. "Woman, why weepest thou? whom seekest thou?"

Mary thought that it might be Joseph's gardener come early to his work. "Because they have taken away my Lord, and I know not where they have laid him. Sir, if thou have borne him hence, tell me where thou hast laid him, and I will take him away."

The unknown man, touched by this impassioned childlike simplicity, answered only one word, her name: "Mary!"

At this, as if awakened with a start, the despairing woman found her lost Master: "*Rabboni*, Master!" And she fell at His feet in the grass and clasped in her hands those bare feet still showing the two red marks of the nails.

But Jesus said to her, "Touch me not; for I am not yet ascended to my Father: but go to my brethren, and say unto them, I ascend unto my Father, and your Father; and to my God, and your God."

And at once, He withdrew from the kneeling woman, and moved away. Mary lifted herself up from the grass, her face convulsed, wild, blind with joy, and ran after her companions.

They had but just come to the house where the Disciples were in hiding and they had told breathlessly the incredible news: the sepulcher opened, the youth clad in white, the things which he had said, the Master risen, the message to His brothers.

But the men, still stunned by the catastrophe, were not willing to believe this wildly improbable news. Hallucinations, hysterical women's dreams, they said. How could He be risen from the dead after only two days?

They believed in the resurrection of the Master, but not before the day when all the dead would rise again, and He would come in glory to rule His kingdom.

But in the meantime, Mary of Magdala rushed in, all haste. She herself had seen Him with her own eyes, and He had spoken to her: she had touched His feet with her hands, had seen the wounds on His feet; and He had told her to go to His brethren, so that they should know that He had risen from the dead as He had promised.

Simon, called Peter, and John, finally aroused, rushed out of the house and began to run towards Joseph's garden. John, who was younger, outran Peter and came first to the sepulcher. He looked through the door but did not go in. Peter came up panting and rushed into the grotto. The linen cloths were lying on the ground, but the napkin which had been about the head of the corpse was folded together in a place by itself. John also went in, saw, and believed.

And without another word they returned towards the house, still running, as if they expected to find the Risen One in the midst of the others whom they had left.

But Jesus, after He had left Mary, withdrew from Jerusalem.

EMMAUS

AFTER THE solemn interval of the Passover, plain everyday life began again for all men. Two friends of Jesus, among those who were in the house with the Disciples, were to go that morning on an errand to Emmaus, a hamlet about two hours' journey from Jerusalem. They left as soon as Simon and John had returned from the sepulcher. All these amazing tales had shaken them, but had not really convinced them.

Cleopas and his companion were good Jews, men burdened with many material cares who left a place for the ideal in their minds. Like almost all the Disciples, they had expected the coming of a Messiah who should be the son of David, a warrior on horseback, a Liberator who would liberate Israel first of all. The words of Christ had almost given them a glimpse of higher truths, but the Crucifixion disheartened them. His death—what a death, on a scaffold of murderers and parricides!—looked to their narrow, practical minds sadly like a failure.

They were reasoning together of all these things as they went along under the warm noonday sun. Then suddenly they caught a glimpse of a shadow on the ground near them. They turned around. The shadow was that of a man who was following as if he wished to hear what they were saying. They stopped, as was the custom, to greet him, and the traveler joined them. His did not seem an unknown face to the two men, but they could not think who it was. The newcomer asked them, "What manner of communications are these that ye have one to another, as ye walk?"

Cleopas, who must have been the older, answered with a wondering gesture, "Art thou only a stranger in Jerusalem, and hast not known the things which are come to pass there in these days?"

"What things?" asked the unknown man.

"Concerning Jesus of Nazareth, which was a prophet mighty in deed and word before God and all the people: And how the chief priests and our rulers delivered him to be condemned to death, and have crucified him. But we trusted that it had been he which should have redeemed Israel: and beside all this, today is the third day since these things were done. Yea, and certain women also of our company made us astonished, which were early at the sepulcher; And when they found not his body, they came, saying, that they had also seen a vision of angels, which said that he was alive. And certain of them which were with us went to the sepulcher and found it even so as the women had said: but him they saw not."

"O fools, and slow of heart to believe all that the prophets have spoken," exclaimed the stranger. "Ought not Christ to have suffered these things, and to enter into his glory?" And almost indignantly He recited the old words and the prophecies of Ezekiel and Daniel, recalled the description of the Man of Sorrows given by Isaiah. The two listened, docile and attentive, without answering, because the newcomer spoke with so much heat, and the old admonitions in His mouth took on a meaning so clear that it seemed almost impossible that they had not understood them before.

In the meantime they had arrived at the entrance of Emmaus, and the sun was going down. Now the two friends were not willing to part with their mysterious companion, and they begged Him to stay with them.

"Abide with us," they said, "for it is towards evening, and the day is far spent." And they took Him by the hand and made Him come into the house.

When they were at table, the guest who sat between them took bread, and broke it and gave a little to one of His friends.

At this action, the eyes of Cleopas and the other man were opened. They had recognized His blessed and wounded hands, and they found themselves face-to-face with the splendor of Christ risen from the dead. Both of them sprang to their feet, pale, amazed.

But they had no time even to run to kiss Him, for Jesus vanished out of their sight.

Tired and fasting as they were, they went back over the road which they had come, and after nightfall arrived at Jerusalem.

The Disciples were still awake. Without drawing breath the newcomers told of their encounter and how they had recognized Him only at the moment when He broke the bread. And in answer to this new confirmation, three or four voices cried out together, "The Lord is risen indeed!"

In the excitement of the day no one had eaten. The women had prepared supper, and now all sat down to the table. Simon, called Peter, remembered the Last Thursday: "This do in remembrance of me."

And tears dimmed his eyes while he broke the bread and gave it to his friends.

THEY HAD scarcely eaten the last mouthfuls when Jesus appeared in the doorway, tall and pale. He looked at them, and in His melodious voice greeted them: "Peace be unto you."

No one answered. Their astonishment overcame their joy, even for those who had already seen Him since His death. On their faces He read the doubt which He knew they all felt. "Art Thou really Thyself a living man, or a spirit which comes from the caverns of the dead to tempt us?"

"Why are ye troubled? and why do thoughts arise in your hearts? Behold my hands and my feet, that it is I myself: handle me, and see; for a spirit hath not flesh and bones, as ye see me have."

And He stretched out His hands towards them, showed them the marks still bloody left by the nails, opened His garment over His breast so that they could see the mark of the lance in His side. Some of them, rising from their couches, knelt down and saw on His bare feet the two deep wounds, each with its livid ring around it. But they could not bring themselves to touch Him.

To make an end of their last doubts, Jesus asked, "Have ye here any meat?"

A piece of broiled fish was left in a dish. Simon put it before the Master, who sat down at the table and ate the fish with a piece of bread while they all stared at Him.

And when He had finished, He raised His eyes towards them. "When I was with you, did I not tell you that all things which were written and which I announced must be fulfilled; that it behooved Christ to suffer and to rise from the dead on the third day, and that repentance and remission of sins should be preached in His name among all nations, beginning at Jerusalem? . . . Go ye into all the world, and preach the gospel to every creature. All power is given unto me in heaven and in earth, and as the Father sent me, I send you. He that believeth and is baptized shall be saved; but he that believeth not shall be damned. I am with you alway, even unto the end of the world."

Little by little as He spoke, His Disciples' faces lighted up with a forgotten hope, and their eyes shone with exaltation. Their enemies, apparently victorious, were conquered; the visible truth bore out all the prophecies. If the Master was risen from the dead, they themselves could not die; if He could leave the sepulcher, His promises were the promises of a God and He would fulfill them to the uttermost.

THOMAS, CALLED DIDYMUS, was not present when Jesus appeared, but the day after, his friends ran to seek him, still agitated by what Jesus had told them. "We have seen the Lord!" they said. "It was really He. He talked with us. He ate with us like a living man."

Thomas was one of those who had been profoundly shaken by the shame of Golgotha. He had said once that he was ready to die with his Master, but he had fled away with the others when the lanterns of the guard had appeared on the Mount of Olives. He hoped for the Kingdom—not a spiritual Kingdom but a kingdom where living, warm-blooded men might govern with new laws a fairer earth assigned to them by God.

After the scandal of the Crucifixion, Thomas was not at all disposed to believe a hearsay report of the Resurrection. He answered to those who joyfully brought him the news, "Except I shall see in his hands the print of the nails, and put my finger into the print of the nails, and thrust my hand into his side, I will not believe."

This answer of Thomas has made him one of the most famous men in the world: for it is Christ's eternal characteristic to immortalize even those men who affronted Him.

A week later, the Disciples were in the same house as on the first occasion and Thomas was with them. Suddenly Jesus entered at the door, his eyes seeking out Thomas, and He called him by name and came up to him so that he could see Him clearly, face-to-face. "Reach hither thy finger, and behold my hands; and reach hither thy hand, and thrust it into my side: and be not faithless, but believing."

But Thomas did not obey Him. He dared not put his finger in the nail print nor his hand in the wound. He only said to him: "My Lord and my God."

Then Jesus, who could not forget Thomas' doubt, answered, "Thomas, because thou hast seen me, thou hast believed: blessed are they that have not seen, and yet have believed."

This is the last of the Beatitudes and the greatest.

Thomas is one of the saints and yet he was not one of those blessed by that Beatitude.

CHRIST'S FIRST COMPANIONS were at last convinced that His second and eternal life had begun. But how long it took them to admit the reality of His return!

And yet the enemies of Christ have accused those very astonished, perplexed Disciples with having willingly or unwillingly invented the myth of the Resurrection. The Disciples, they say, hoped so vividly to see Jesus rise from the dead as He had promised, and the Resurrection was so urgently needed to counteract the disgrace of the Crucifixion, that in that atmosphere of superstitious suspense, the visions of hysterical women, the delusions of unbalanced men sufficed to spread the news of the appearance of Christ about the little circle of desolate survivors.

But those who try to undermine the certainty of the first Christian generation forget the testimony of Paul.

Saul the Pharisee had been to school in Gamaliel, and might have been present, even though at a distance and as an enemy, at Christ's death, and certainly knew all the theories of his early teachers, the Jews, about the pretended Resurrection. But Paul, who received the first Gospel from the lips of James, called the brother of the Lord, and from Simon, Paul famous in all the churches of the Jews and the Gentiles, wrote thus in his first letter to the Corinthians: "Christ died for our sins according to the scriptures; And that he was buried, and that he rose again the third day according to the scriptures: And that he was seen of Cephas, then of the twelve: After that, he was seen of above five hundred brethren at once; of whom the greater part remain unto this present. . . ." The first letter to the Corinthians is generally recognized as authentic. It cannot have been written later than the spring of the year 58, and hence it is older than the oldest Gospel. Many of those who had known the living Christ were still living at that time. If Paul could have thought a valid confutation possible, he never would have dared write those words.

It is extremely probable that the appearance of Christ to the five hundred happened in Galilee on the mountain spoken of by Matthew, and that the Apostle had known one of those who had been present at that memorable meeting.

WHEN THE TRAGEDY of the Crufixion had drawn to a close with its greatest sorrow, its greatest joy, everyone turned again to his own destination, the Son to the Father, the King to His Kingdom, the high priest to his basins of blood, the fishermen to their nets.

These water-soaked nets, with broken meshes, torn by the unaccustomed weight of the great draughts, so many times knotted together again, which had been left by the first fishers of men without one backward look, on the shores of Capernaum, had been laid on one side, by someone with the prudence of the stay-at-home who knows that dreams are soon over and hunger lasts for all one's lifetime. The wife of Simon, the father of James and John, the brother of Thomas, had saved their casting nets and their dragnets as tools which might be useful, in memory of the exiles.

And for a time the wisdom of the stay-at-homes, taken root in their native countryside like moss on a stone, was vindicated. The fishers of men appeared again in Galilee and once more took the old nets into their hands. Christ on His return had said, "We will meet again in Galilee." And they had gone away away from ill-omened Judea and they had trod once more the road back to their sweet, calm fatherland.

The old houses had a mellow beauty, with the white banners of newly washed linen, and the young grass greening along the old walls, and the tables cleaned by humble old hands, and the oven, which every week spat out sparks from its flaming mouth. And the quiet fishing town had beauty, too; with its tanned, naked boys, the sun high over the level marketplace, the bags and baskets in the shadow of the inns, and the smell of fish which at dawn was wafted over it, with the morning breeze. But more beautiful than all was the lake: a gray-blue and slate-colored expanse on cloudy afternoons; a milky basin of opal with lines and patches of jacinth on warm evenings; a dark shadow flecked with white on starry nights; a silvery heaving shadow in the moonlight.

On this lake which seemed the very spirit of the quiet, happy countryside, the boat with its slanting sails, its worn seats, the high red rudder, had from their childhood been dearer to them than that other home which awaited them, stationary, whitened, foursquare on the bank. Those infinitely long hours of tedium and of hope as they gazed at the brilliant water, the swaying of the nets, the darkening of the sky, had filled the greater part of their poor and homely lives.

Before beginning the work which He had commanded, they were waiting to see Him whom they loved in the place which He had loved. They were different men from the men who had gone away, more restless, sadder, almost estranged. But the nets were there, hung up on the walls, and the boats at anchor rode up and down. Once more the fishers of men, perhaps out of material need, began to be lake·fishermen.

SEVEN DISCIPLES of Christ were together one evening in the harbor of Capernaum, Simon called Peter, Thomas called Didymus, Nathaniel of Cana, James, John and two others. Simon said, "I go afishing."

His friends answered, "We also go with thee."

They went into the boat and put off, but all that night they caught nothing. When day broke, a little depressed because of the wasted night, they came back towards the shore. And when they were near they saw in the faint light of the dawn a man standing on the shore, who seemed to be waiting for them. "But the disciples knew not that it was Jesus."

"Children, have ye any meat?" called the unknown man.

And they answered, "No."

"Cast the net on the right side of the ship, and ye shall find."

They obeyed and in a moment the net was so full that they were scarcely able to draw it in. And they all began to tremble because they had guessed who it was awaiting them.

"It is the Lord," said John to Simon.

Peter answered nothing, but hastily drew on his fisher's coat (for he was naked), and cast himself into the sea that he might be first on shore. The boat was scarcely two hundred cubits from the land and in a few moments the seven Disciples were about their Lord. And no one asked Him, "Who art thou?"

On the shore there was bread and a lighted brazier with fishes broiling on it, and Jesus said, "Bring of the fish which ye have now caught."

And for the last time He broke the bread and gave to them and the fish likewise. After they had finished eating Jesus turned to Simon and under His look the unhappy man, silent till then, turned pale: "Simon, son of Jona, lovest thou me more than these?"

The man who had denied Him, when he heard this question full of tenderness, but for him so cruel, felt himself carried back to another place beside another brazier with other questions put to him, and he remembered the answer he had made then, and the look from Christ about to die and his own great lamentation in the night. "Yes" in his mouth would have been shamelessness: "No" would have been a lie.

"Yea, Lord; thou knowest that I love thee."

He had not the courage to add "more than these" in the presence of the others, who knew what he had done.

Christ said to him, "Feed my lambs."

And for the second time He asked him: "Simon, son of Jona, lovest thou me?"

And Peter in his trouble found no other answer than, "Yea, Lord; thou knowest that I love thee."

Then Jesus said, "Feed my sheep."

And for the third time He insisted, "Simon, son of Jona, lovest thou me?"

He was drawing from Peter three affirmations, three new promises to cancel his three denials at Jerusalem. But Peter could not endure this repeated suffering. Almost weeping, he cried out, "Lord, thou knowest all things; thou knowest that I love thee!"

The terrible ordeal was over, and Jesus went on, "Feed my sheep. Verily, verily, I say unto thee, When thou wast young, thou girdest thyself, and walkedst whither thou wouldest: but when thou shalt be old, thou shalt stretch forth thy hands, and another shall gird thee, and carry thee whither thou wouldest not."

You must answer for all the lambs which I leave in your care and as reward at the end of your labors you will have two crossed beams, and four nails as I had, and life eternal. Choose: it is the last time that you can choose and it is a choice for all time—irrevocable.

"Follow me!"

Peter obeyed, but turning about saw John coming after him and said, "Lord, and what shall this man do?"

Jesus said to him, "If I will that he tarry till I come, what is that to thee? follow thou me!"

For Simon the primacy and martyrdom. John, who bore the same name as the precursor of Christ's first coming, was to prophesy His second coming. The historian of the end was to be persecuted, a solitary prisoner, but he was to live longer than all the others and to see with his own eyes the crumbling of the stones, not one left upon another, of the ill-omened hill of Jerusalem. Peter followed Christ, was crucified for Christ and left behind him the eternal dynasty of the Vicars of Christ: but John was not permitted to find rest in death: he waits with us, the contemporary of every generation, eternal as hope.

THE CLOUD

ONCE MORE they returned to Jerusalem, leaving their nets, this time forever, travelers setting out upon a journey, the stages of which were to be marked by blood. In the same place where He had gone down to the city glorified by men, He was to rise again after the interval of His dishonor and His Resurrection, in the glory of Heaven. He remained in the midst of men, for forty days after the Resurrection, for as long a time as He had remained in the desert after His baptism—His symbolic death by water. He did not, as before, lead a life in common with the Disciples, because He was separated now from the life of living men; but he reappeared to them more than once to confirm His great promises.

The last time they saw Him was on the Mount of Olives, where before His death He had prophesied the ruin of the Temple and of the city and the signs of His return.

It was one of the last evenings of May and the clouds in that golden hour, like celestial islands in the gold of the setting sun, seemed to rise from the warm earth towards nearby heaven. In the fields of grain, the birds began to call back the fledglings to the nests, and the cool breeze lightly shook the branches and their drooping, unripened fruit. From the distant city, still intact, from the pinnacles, the towers and the white squares of the Temple rose a smoky cloud of dust.

And once more the Disciples asked Jesus the question they had put to Him on the evening of the two prophecies. "Lord, wilt thou at this time restore again the kingdom to Israel?"

They may have meant the Kingdom of God, which in their minds, as in the minds of the Prophets, was one with the Kingdom of Israel, since the divine restoration of the earth was to begin with Judea.

Christ answered: "It is not for you to know the times or the seasons, which the Father hath put in his own power. But ye shall receive power, after that the Holy Ghost is come upon you: and ye shall be witnesses unto me both in Jerusalem, and in all Judea, and in Samaria, and unto the uttermost part of the earth."

And having said this, He lifted up His hands and blessed them. And while they beheld, He was taken up from the earth and suddenly a shining cloud as on the morning of the Transfiguration wrapped Him about and hid Him from their sight. But they could not look away from the sky and continued to gaze steadfastly up in their astonishment, when two men in white apparel spoke to them: "Ye men of Galilee, why stand ye gazing up into heaven? this same Jesus, which is taken up from you into heaven, shall so come in like manner as ye have seen him go into heaven."

Then having prayed in silence, they entered Jerusalem, but heaven was no longer merely the barren dome where swift, tumultuous storm clouds appear and disappear; where the stars shine out silently.

He is still with us, the Son of man, who was light made manifest. He is still present in the world which He meant to free. He is still attentive to our words and to our tears, if they truly come from the depths of our hearts. He is with us, an invisible, benignant guest, never more to leave us, because by His wish our earthly life is an anticipation of the Kingdom of Heaven, and is a part of Heaven from this day on.

THE NEEDLE'S EYE

THE NEEDLE'S EYE

A CONDENSATION FROM THE BOOK
"THE THREAD THAT RUNS SO TRUE"

by
JESSE
STUART

WOODCUTS BY WALTER FERRO

Lonesome Valley! The very name evokes the misty stretch of Kentucky hill country where Jesse Stuart spent six of the most critical months of his life. Here, in the 1920's, cut off from the rest of a booming America by rugged mountains, children trudged to their one-room schoolhouse through sweltering July heat because in winter the trails were impassable. And here, when he was just seventeen, Jesse Stuart came to his time of trial as a teacher.

Like his pupils, he was Kentucky born and bred. He too had stayed home from school when needed as a hand on his father's farm. But he was also a dreamer who had scribbled poems on old tobacco sacks, on poplar leaves, on anything that came to hand, and he believed he could sow learning and love where ignorance and bitter feuding flourished.

"The Needle's Eye" is the opening section of *The Thread That Runs So True*, Stuart's autobiographical account of his stormy but effective career as an educator. An inspiration to teachers and a delight to all who read it, it is a fragment of pure Americana written in the lyrical, picturesque language of the Kentucky hills.

MONDAY MORNING when I started on my way to school, I had with me Don Conway, a pupil twenty years of age, who had never planned to enter school again. I was the new teacher here at Lonesome Valley and I didn't know what kind of brains he had. He had left school when he was in the fourth grade. But I did know that he had two good fists and that he would be on my side. All day Sunday while I had worked at the schoolhouse, I was trying to think of a plan so I could stay at Lonesome Valley School. I knew I had to stay. I knew if one had to go it would be Guy Hawkins. I might have to use my head a little but that was why I had it.

It had taken a lot of persuasion to get Don Conway to return to school. He had planned to get married after his tobacco crop was sold. But I explained the value of an education to him in dollars and cents. I told him I would teach him how to measure a field and figure the number of acres, how to figure the number of bushels in a wagon bed, corn bin, and how many cubic yards of dirt one would have to remove to dig a cellar or a well. Don Conway was interested in this type of knowledge. I told him no man should be married and live on a farm unless he knew these simple things, for he could easily be cheated the rest of his days. I was interested in his learning these things all right, but I was interested in something else.

Don, his two small brothers, and his sister Vaida, were all going to school together. I congratulated John Conway for sending them. I told him he should set the example for other farmers on the creek. It would have been hard on John to try to worm and sucker his ten acres of tobacco and care for his other crops if Flossie, his eighteen-year-old daughter, had not volunteered to stay home and help him. And Bertha, his wife,

assured him she would divide her time between the house-work and work in the field.

I had begged Don Conway to return to school when he and I were sitting on the porch late one Sunday afternoon and Ova Salyers and Guy Hawkins rode past on their horses. They glanced toward the porch for their first look at the new teacher, but never spoke.

Don Conway looked at Guy and Ova and then he looked at me. He didn't ask me how old I was. I didn't tell him I was not yet seventeen. One had to be eighteen before he could teach school. Don knew the fate of my sister when she was employed to teach the Lonesome Valley School. He knew how Guy Hawkins had blacked her eyes with his fists, had whipped her before the other pupils. She was a fair-haired, beautiful blue-eyed girl of nineteen when she had come to Lonesome Valley.

She went home a nervous wreck, long before her school was finished. After I'd seen the way my sister was beaten up, I begged to go to Lonesome Valley. My parents would have none of it. They thought if I went hunting trouble I would get more than my share.

Then one day at Landsburgh High School I walked into our American-literature room and found the Greenwood County rural teachers were having "teacher's examination" there. When Superintendent Harley Staggers mistook me for a rural teacher an idea came to me. I knew the school I wanted if I passed the examination.

I made a second-class certificate. Then I had John Hampton, a rural teacher and friend, contact John Conway, Lonesome Valley District School trustee, and get the school for me. Superintendent Staggers didn't want me to go to Lonesome Valley. But there wasn't anything he could do about it after that. That was why I was here.

When Don and I reached the schoolhouse, at least thirty-five pupils were waiting outside. Guy Hawkins and Ova Salyers were standing together near the coal house. They looked out of place with the other pupils. They were larger than either Don or me. They were older too. They looked at me when I said "Good morning" to them. Many of the pupils turned shyly away and did not speak. Each had his dinner basket or bucket in his hand. Most of them carried tattered-edged and backless books.

It wasn't eight o'clock yet and school didn't start until eight thirty. The July sun hadn't dried the dew from parts of the valley and dew was ascending in white formless clouds from the tobacco, cane, and corn patches. But the people in Lonesome Valley went to bed early and got up early. All of my pupils came from farms.

The girls wore pigtails down their backs tied with all colors of ribbons. They wore clean print dresses and they were barefooted. Not one pupil in my school, large or small, boy or girl, wore shoes.

"Well, I'm opening the door," I said, to break the silence.

When I opened the door my pupils laughed, screamed, and

raced for the schoolhouse. Their shyness was gone now. There was a mad scramble to get inside for seats. Then there was some discussion among them as to who would sit by whom. There were a few controversies and a few hurt feelings. Guy and Ova walked inside reluctantly and sat down in a seat on the boys' side farthest from my desk.

"Now let me make an announcement to you," I said, after walking up to my desk. "There will not any longer be a girls' side and a boys' side. Sit anyplace you want to."

They looked strangely at one another. Not one boy crossed to the girls' side. Not one girl crossed to the boys' side. In Lonesome Valley it was hard to break a teaching tradition more than a century old. But after I had been to high school, where there were no such things as a girls' side and a boys' side in a schoolroom, I didn't see why it wouldn't work here. Little did I dream that what I had said would be talked about by everybody in Lonesome Valley, and that many would criticize me and call my school "a courting school." Boys and girls sitting together? Who had ever heard tell of it?

Each rural teacher had to make his own schedule. And I had done that before I left home. I knew what I had to teach and I went to work, making out my schedule and dividing my time as accurately as possible for my six hours of actual work. I had to conduct fifty-four classes in this time, for I had pupils up to and including the eighth grade.

When I walked down the broad center aisle and pulled on the bell rope, the soft tones sounded over the tobacco, corn, and cane fields and the lush green valley; with the ringing of this bell, my school had begun. I knew that not half the pupils in the school census were here. The census showed a hundred and four of school age, for whom the state sent per capita money. I had thirty-five. I thought the soft tones of this bell through the rising mists and over fields where parents and their children were trying to eke out a bare subsistence might bring back warm memories of happy school days. For I remembered the tones of the Plum Grove school bell, and how I had longed to be back in school after I had quit at the age of nine to work to help support my family. I would have returned to school, if

I could have, when I heard the Plum Grove bell. So I rang the bell and called the Lonesome Valley pupils back to school—back to books and play. For going to school had never been work to me. It had been recreation. And I hoped it would be the same for my pupils.

During my first day I enrolled my pupils in their classes, called them up front to the recitation seat and gave them assignments in the few textbooks they possessed. At that time, each pupil had to furnish his own textbooks. A meager allotment of cash was set aside by the Greenwood County School Board to buy books for those whose parents were not able to buy them. I knew that many would not buy books until after the tobacco crops had been sold or the cane had been made into sorghum and sold.

I also made some temporary changes in seating arrangements. I often put a pupil without books beside a pupil with books, if they were in the same grade. I tried to familiarize myself with each name and get acquainted with my pupils. I found them very shy. I had grown up under circumstances much like theirs. Only about thirty miles separated their Lonesome Valley from my W-Hollow. But I was a stranger here.

When I dismissed my pupils for the fifteen-minute morning recess, they all jumped up from their seats and raced out of the house. I had a few minutes' work to do before I could join them on the playground. As I worked, I heard them singing these familiar words:

"The needle's eye that does supply,
The thread that runs so true,
Many a beau, have I let go,
Because I wanted you.

"Many a dark and stormy night,
When I went home with you,
I stumped my toe and down I go,
Because I wanted you."

I walked to the door and watched them. They had formed a circle, hand in hand, and around and around they walked and sang these words while two pupils held their locked hands high for the circle to pass under. Suddenly the two standing—one inside the circle and one outside—let their arms drop down around a pupil in the line. Then the circle continued to march and sing while the two took the pupil aside and asked him whether he would rather be a train or an automobile. If the pupil said he'd rather be an automobile, he stood on one side; if a train, he stood on the other side of the two who held hands. And when they had finished taking everybody from the circle, the two groups faced each other, lined up behind their captains. Each put his arms around the pupil in front of him and locked his hands. The first line to break apart or to be pulled forward lost the game.

It had been a long time since I had played this game at Plum Grove. The words brought back pleasant memories. And my Lonesome Valley pupils played this game with all the enthusiasm and spirit they had! Because they were having the time of their lives, I hated to ring the bell for "books," so I let recess extend five minutes.

Then I lined them up, smaller pupils in front and larger ones behind, and had them march in orderly fashion back into the schoolroom.

Guy Hawkins and Ova Salyers were the last on the line. When they came inside, Guy asked permission for them to go after a bucket of water. We didn't have a well or a cistern at the schoolhouse. We had to get water from some home in the district. I told them they could go but not to be gone too long, for the pupils, after running and playing, were thirsty. The sun beat down on the galvanized tin roof. This made the pine boards so hot inside they oozed resin. We raised all the windows but still the place was hot as the room in which I slept at Conways'. My little upstairs room there with a high unscreened window of only one sash didn't cool off until about midnight. Then, I could go to sleep.

All the rural schools had to begin in July, though the farmers had objected because they needed their children at home to help with farm work. Rural schools began early because coal was an added expense for winter months. The county schools all over the state had barely enough funds to keep them going, and if they could have school during the hot months it kept down their budgets. But it was hard on the children and the teachers.

The first bucket of water Guy and Ova brought didn't last five minutes. Most of the pupils were still thirsty, so I sent Guy and Ova back for more, telling them to borrow another bucket. I sent them in a hurry. And I knew I had to do something about the dipper problem. At Plum Grove, too, we had all drunk from the same dipper, but when I went to Landsburgh High School I was taught something different.

So I told my pupils that each had to bring his own drinking cup the next day. It could be a glass, teacup, gourd, dipper, just so it was his own and no one else drank from it. My pupils laughed as if my announcement was funny. But I had seen sweat run from their faces into the dipper, and the next in line put his mouth where the sweat had run or where the other pupil had put his lips. I noticed, too, several pupils had put the rim up near the handle to their mouths, so I knew they didn't like to drink after the others.

On Tuesday they brought their dippers, tin cups, and glasses. Only a few had forgotten, and I showed them how to take a clean sheet of paper from a tablet and fold it to make a paper cup. I gave them a lecture about drinking water. I told them never to drink from a stream. I told them how I had gotten typhoid fever twice: once from drinking cool water from a little stream, and once from drinking in a river. I had my pupils use the dipper to dip water from the bucket into their cups. They accepted my suggestion gladly.

I also borrowed another water bucket from Bertha Conway and brought it to school. The one bucket allowed me for thirty-five pupils (and there would be more as soon as the farmers were through with their summer work on the tobacco and cane crops) was not enough. They played hard at recess and noon, and in the "time of books" sat in a schoolroom almost as hot as an oven.

Tuesday I stood beside Guy Hawkins and showed him how to hold his book when he read. I was trying to teach Guy to read as he stumbled over the simple words in the *First Grade Reader*. My pupils laughed until I had to stop them because Guy was taller by two inches than I was and heavier. He had a bull neck and a prominent jaw. His beard was so heavy that he had to shave every day.

Guy had big hands too. His right hand covered the back of his *First Reader*. And he had powerful arms. The muscles rippled under his clean blue-faded shirt. I measured him as I stood beside him. I knew that if I ever had to fight him, it would be a fight. And I knew that I wasn't going to fight him unless he forced me. He was more powerful physically than I was. And the outcome of our fight might depend on the one who successfully landed the first haymaker to the other's jaw.

If it were not for Guy and Ova, I wouldn't have had any trouble disciplining my school. All the other pupils were obedient. They would have been good in their classwork if they had had the proper training. I had ten-year-old pupils just starting to school. Nineteen-year-olds in the first grade. Fourteen-year-olds in the second grade. I had one twelve-year-old girl in the eighth grade.

They had not been promoted because they had never attended a full school term. They had taken the same grade over and over until they could stand and recite some of the beginning lessons from memory.

"Guy, how long have you been in the first grade?" I asked.

"Oh, about eight years." He laughed.

"Well, I'm going to promote you," I said. "Tomorrow you start in the second grade."

Then I had Ova Salyers read. He had also been in the first grade eight years. I promoted him.

When these young men sat down again I saw them look at each other and laugh as if they thought my promoting them was funny. I knew they accepted school as a joke, a place to come and see people. A place where they could play "the needle's eye" with smaller children. I knew I couldn't reason with either one. And I had a feeling that Guy was waiting his chance for me.

I had doubted that my second-class certificate and my three years in high school qualified me to teach. But now, when I measured my knowledge with my pupils', I knew that I was an educated man. I had never known that youth could be so poorly trained as were my Lonesome Valley pupils. But unless I was chased out of the school, as my sister had been, I was determined to give them my best.

JUST ACROSS Lonesome Creek, at the other end of the footlog bridge, was a small country store, not more than ten feet long and six feet wide. All the merchandise in the store would not have filled a wagon bed. But Nancy Cochran, a slender, blue-eyed, fair-complexioned girl with charcoal-black hair, ran the store. She sold pencils, paper, ink, pens and pen points, crackers, cakes, and candy to my pupils.

From my desk I could look through the window during school hours. Nancy was about eighteen, and she would be sitting on the small store porch, playing her guitar and singing "Red River Valley," "Listen to the Mockingbird," "Down by the Old Mill Stream," "Barbara Allen," and "The Needle's Eye." When she played and sang "The Needle's Eye," I always had to stop my pupils from tapping their feet. They did it unconsciously. They didn't tap their feet for any other tune, but when she played "The Needle's Eye" their dirty bare feet all over the room marked time to the music.

I loved to hear music, especially a guitar, but not when I was trying to teach school. Nancy's singing distracted my thoughts.

Every time I looked from my window toward her, she was looking toward my school, playing and singing. I rarely saw a customer except my pupils go inside her store. I didn't want to say anything but I knew I was going to have to. Monday through Friday of the first week she played during school hours.

So on Friday after school was out, I dropped into the store to see Nancy Cochran. She was sitting in a comfortable armchair with her guitar across her lap. When I entered she arose, laid her guitar upon the small candy showcase, and asked me

very politely if there was anything I wanted. She spoke with soft words and she was beautiful to see. Immediately I was sorry for the hard looks I had given her from my window. I hoped she hadn't seen me frowning at her.

"I'd like to have a bottle of ink," I said.

I bought the bottle of ink, some paper, and a pencil. I decided that my trustee could help me here. It was not my duty to tell her that she was disturbing my school. I would tell John Conway and he could ease a suggestion to her that would not disturb her. For I knew she felt very kindly toward me. John Conway was the man to do it. Then there wouldn't be any talk.

THE FOLLOWING MONDAY I had stayed at the schoolhouse to do some work on my school records. All my pupils had gone and the room was very silent. I was busy working when I heard soft footsteps walking around the building. I looked through the window on my left and saw Guy Hawkins' uncombed, tousled head. I wondered why he was coming back. Had he forgotten something?

Then I realized this was the first time he had been able to catch me by myself. And I remembered a few other incidents in Greenwood County's rural schools where a pupil had come back to the school when the teacher was there alone, and had beaten hell out of him.

Guy came in the door with his cap in his hand. I didn't want him to see me looking up at him, but I did see him coming down the broad middle aisle, taking long steps and swinging his big arms. He walked up to my desk and stood silently there before me.

"Did you forget something, Guy?" I asked.

"Naw, I've never forgot nothin'," he replied.

"Then what do you want?" I asked.

"Whip you," he said.

"Why do you want to whip me?" I asked him.

"I didn't like your sister," he said. "You know what I done to her."

"Yes, I know what you did to her," I said.

"I'm a-goin' to do the same thing to you," he threatened.

"Why do you want to fight me?" I asked him. I dropped my pencil and stood up facing him.

"I don't like you," he said. "I don't like teachers. I said never another person with your name would teach this school. Not as long as I'm here."

"It's too bad you don't like me or my name," I said, my temper rising. "Can you go to another school? The Valley School is not too far from where you live."

"Naw, naw," he shouted, "if anybody leaves, you'll leave. I was in Lonesome Valley first. And I ain't a-goin' to another school because of you!"

"Then there's nothing left for us to do but fight," I said. "I've come to teach this school and I'm going to teach it!"

"Maybe you will," he snarled. "I have you penned in this schoolhouse. And I aim to whip you right where you stand!"

His face was red as a sliced beet. Fire danced in his pale blue, elongated eyes. I knew Guy Hawkins meant every word he said. I knew I had to face him and to fight. There was no other way around. I had to think quickly.

"Will you let me take my necktie off?" I said, remembering I'd once been choked by a fellow pulling my necktie in a fight.

"Yep, take off that purty tie," he said. "You might get it dirty by the time I'm through with you."

I slowly took off my tie.

"Roll up the sleeves of your white shirt too," he said. "But they'll be dirty by the time I sweep this floor up with you."

"Sweep the floor up with me," I said.

He shot out his long arm but I ducked. I felt the wind from his thrust against my ear.

I mustn't let him clinch me, I thought.

Then he came back with another right and I ducked his second lick. I came around with my first lick—a right—and planted it on his jaw, not a good lick but just enough to jar him and make him madder. When he rushed at me, I sidestepped. He missed. By the time he had turned around, I caught him a haymaker on the chin that reeled him. Then I followed up with another lick as hard as I had ever hit a man. Yet I didn't bring him down.

He came back for more. But he didn't reach me this time. He was right. I did get my shirt dirty. I dove through the air with a flying football tackle. I hit him beneath the knees. Guy's feet went from under him, and he went down so fast he couldn't catch himself with his hands. His face hit the floor and his nose was flattened. The blood spurted as he started to get up.

I let him get to his feet, and then I waded into him. I hit fast and I hit hard. He swung wild. His fingernail took a streak of hide from my neck and left a red mark that smarted and the blood oozed through. I pounded his chin. I caught him on the beardy jaw. I reeled him back and gave him a left to the short ribs while my right in a split second caught his mouth. Blood spurted again.

"Had enough?" I panted.

He didn't answer. I didn't ask him a second time. I hit him hard enough to knock two men down, and he reeled back against a seat. I followed up. I caught him with a haymaker under the chin and laid him across the desk. Then he rolled to the floor, with blood running from his nose and mouth. I was nearly out of breath. My hands ached. My heart pounded. If this is teaching school! I thought. If this goes with it! Then I remembered vaguely I had asked for it. I'd asked for this school and would take no other.

Guy Hawkins lay there sprawled on the unswept floor. I went back and got the water bucket. With a clean handkerchief, I washed blood from his mouth and nose. I couldn't wash it from his shirt. I put cool water to his forehead.

I worked over a pupil—trying to bring him back to his senses—who only a few hours before I had stood beside and tried to teach how to pronounce words when he read. I had promoted him. I had known a time of reckoning would eventually come, but I had wanted to put it off. Now I had whipped him and I wondered how I'd done it.

When Guy Hawkins came to his senses, he looked up at me. I was applying the wet cool handkerchief to his head. When he started to get up, I helped him to his feet.

"Mr. Stuart, I really got it poured on me," he admitted. "You're some fighter."

This was the first time he had ever called me "Mr. Stuart." I had heard, but had pretended not to hear, him call me "Old Jess" every time my back was turned. He had never before, when he had spoken directly to me, called me anything.

"I'm not much of a fighter until I have to fight, Guy," I said. "But I had to fight you."

"I know it," he said. "I've had in mind to whip you ever since I heard you's a-goin' to teach this school. But you win. You winned fair too," he honestly admitted. "I didn't think you could hit like that."

Guy was still weak. His nose and mouth kept bleeding. He didn't have a handkerchief and I gave him a clean one.

"Think you can make it home all right, Guy?"

"I think so," he said.

He walked slowly from the schoolhouse. I was too upset to do any more work. I stood by the window and watched him walk across the schoolyard, then across the footlog and down the Lonesome Creek Road until he went around the bend and was out of sight.

I felt better now that the fight was over, and I got the broom and swept the floor. Sweeping was easy, but it was difficult to clean bloodstains from the floor.

I carried a coal bucket of sand and poured it on the blood and then shoveled up the sand and carried it out. Then I scrubbed the place but the stain was there. I could not get it from the oily, soft pine wood. It would always be there, this reminder, as long as I taught school at Lonesome Valley.

NEWS TRAVELED FAST in Lonesome Valley. When I reached Conways' they had gathered in the living room waiting to see if I would be disfigured. They were surprised to see me in one piece after my fight with Guy Hawkins.

Everybody knew Guy was going to fight me. And no one had ever seen him beaten up before. Before sundown the news of our fight had reached the Valley. Mort Hackless knew about it and he was surprised. Mort had seen Guy have many a fight. Guy went to the Valley on Saturdays and Sundays and if anybody wanted to fight him he was always ready. Often when one didn't want to fight him, he insisted. He was always the winner.

Guy Hawkins was respected by a certain group of people who believed that might made right, by people who loved a dog fight, chicken fight, man fight, any sort of a fight. If Guy didn't have "trouble" at the Valley, he sat around the store and told his fighting stories to young boys looking for a hero and traded his fighting stories with the old men who told fighting stories of their dead ancestors, that grew and grew with the years. This was one fighting story Guy Hawkins would be slow to tell.

Nothing I could do for my pupils at Lonesome Valley would give me the reputation this fight gave me. I didn't know, until after Guy and I tangled, that the people talked behind my back and had said I would be a good teacher as long as I lasted but my days were numbered. They thought when Guy Hawkins got through with me that I would be catching the Old Line Special in a hurry back to Landsburgh. And since there was not much excitement in Lonesome Valley, many of them craved the excitement of a good fight. They loved to talk about it. And they loved the suspense. For Guy had told everybody he knew in Lonesome Valley, the Valley, Chicken Creek, and Unknown what he was going to do.

Never was any teacher more respected in his community

than I was now. Men that had shyly spoken to me or had not spoken at all stopped me on the road and introduced themselves and thanked me for "doing the job." And nearly everyone said that he needed his children at home to help strip cane and cut cane wood and cut tobacco, but he was going to try to do the work himself so he could send his children to school to me. And these words, coming from tall, lean, beardy-faced figures of the earth, men who when they liked and respected you would die for you, men who when they hated and despised you would kill you, made me feel good.

Narrow-gauged Lonesome Valley had made men like these. This was their small world. They had been born here. They had married here. Their children had been born here. The only ones who had seen any of the world were those who had fought in World War I. And when these men became vitally interested in sending their children to school to me instead of having them help with the work at home, I knew that I would give all to have a good school for their children, whose schooling would end with Lonesome Valley.

I DIDN'T EXPECT Guy Hawkins to return to Lonesome Valley School. I thought his schooling was ended. But when he left the schoolhouse he didn't take his books. I wondered if he would come back to get them, and would he bring his father or one of his married brothers with him? Would he start another fight? The same thoughts must have troubled John Conway too. When I went to school on Tuesday morning, John went with me.

When we got there, big Guy with his black eyes, swollen lips, was in a circle with the other pupils, going around, and singing "The Needle's Eye." Guy greeted me: "Good morning, Mr. Stuart."

Then John Conway smiled and turned to go. I watched him cross the footlog and go into Nancy Cochran's little store. I joined in the game with my pupils. Guy and I were captains. I was the hard-boiled egg and he was the soft-boiled egg. When we took pupils from the line and asked them whether they would rather be a soft-boiled or a hard-boiled egg, the majority chose the soft-boiled egg. And when we formed our tug-of-war lines to pull against each other, his side toppled my side and everybody laughed, especially Guy. It was great fun. And never did Guy or a pupil ask me about the fight. If they talked about it, I didn't know. I did notice them observing the bloodstain on the floor. If Guy ever said anything against me to a fellow pupil again, I never heard of it. He had, for the first time, become a pupil like the rest.

THAT VERY DAY another thing happened. During the noon hour a big ruddy-complexioned man of perhaps fifty drove down Lonesome Valley with a mule team hitched to a wagonload of coal. He stopped his team in the shade of a giant sycamore and climbed down from his wagon. He walked over to where I was standing. I had seen this same man go down on this coal wagon toward the Valley every day I had taught at Lonesome. This was the first time he had stopped.

"Are you Mr. Stuart? My name is Burt Eastham," he introduced himself.

"Yes, I am," I said, shaking his coal-dusty hand. "I'm glad to know you."

"You wouldn't have any drinking water, would you?" he asked.

"Yes, we have water in the schoolhouse," I said. "It might be a little warm."

"Warm water will wet the throat," he said.

"Then let's go get it."

He followed me into the school. He started to lift the dipper to drink from the water bucket.

"Don't drink from that dipper," I snapped.

"Is it pizened?" he asked, startled.

"No," I said. "But no one drinks from a dipper here."

He looked curiously at me. "What do you use it for, then?"

"To dip water from the bucket into drinking cups," I said. "Wait a minute and I'll make you a cup."

I tore a sheet of paper from a tablet and made him a cup. He dipped the water from the bucket and poured it into the cup.

"People don't drink one another's slobbers this way, do they?" he laughed, after he had finished drinking. "But I wasn't exactly thirsty. I wanted to see the man that whipped Guy

Hawkins. That boy came to Upper Lonesome Church one night, and he nearly beat my boy to death without any reason. Whipped Les Brown's boy and Booten Tolliver's boy, too. I wanted to see the first man to whip him. Say," he continued, as he looked me over admiringly, "you're not so big. I'd a-thought you had to be a giant to whip 'im."

We walked out of the schoolhouse and back toward his wagon. He stood for a minute and looked at Guy who was now enjoying himself playing games. I was looking at the wagonload of coal.

"How many bushels do you have on this wagon?" I asked.

"Twenty-five bushels," he said.

"You weigh your coal?" I asked.

"Nope," he said.

"Then how do you know how many bushels you have?"

In the meantime Don Conway walked over where we were standing.

"Guess at it," Burt Eastham said.

"I believe you've got more than twenty-five bushels."

"You got any way finding out?" he asked.

"Do you know the length, width, and depth of your wagon bed?"

"Nope," he answered.

"Don, go and fetch the yardstick from my desk," I said.

Don brought the yardstick and did the measuring and I put the figures on paper.

"According to my figures you have thirty-nine and a fraction bushels," I said to Burt Eastham. "Since your coal is stacked a little higher than the bed, you may have over forty bushels!"

"What?" he exclaimed. "I've been selling this wagon bed of coal for twenty-five bushels for the past seven years! How can I really find out how much coal I have?"

"Have it weighed down at the Valley," I said. "They have scales there."

Burt Eastham, greatly excited, climbed onto his coal wagon and drove off. That afternoon, just before school let out, there was a knock on the wall beside our open schoolhouse door. I went to the door. There stood Burt. His face was so dirty with coal dust that his not-too-white teeth looked white as dogwood blossoms in April. His smile was so broad he was showing nearly all his teeth.

"Thank you a hundred times, young man," were his first words. "I don't know how I can ever repay you! I had forty-three bushels of coal on my wagon. Here!" He excitedly showed me the weigh bill.

I called Don Conway to the door and let him see it.

"Something told me to stop and take a look at you," Burt Eastham said. "I'm glad I stopped. I've been swindled for seven years."

"Well, you can be sure you've given good measure," I said. "Your conscience won't bother you. You've not cheated anyone."

"But I won't be cheated from now on," he said. "Gee, I wish I'd gone to school. Can't write my name."

"You can come here if you want to," I invited him.

"Too late to start at fifty," he admitted sadly. "Too late when a man is married and has nine children."

His words were worth more to Don than any teacher's words. Don now realized the value of a simple education.

"I've just been thinking, Mr. Stuart, whether you were married or not," Burt Eastham said. "When you're old enough to teach school you're old enough to be married."

"No, I'm not married," I laughed. "Haven't any prospects!"

"Then I have a prospect for you," he said rejoicingly. "See, I want to do something for you. May Woods, the teacher at Upper Lonesome, is pretty as a speckled pup. If I's a young single man, I'd go for her myself!"

At Burt Eastham's words, my pupils laughed until I had to pound on the wall for order. Guy Hawkins and Ova Salyers shook all over and whispered to each other. For they had listened to every word Burt Eastham had said to me. Before he left he assured me that he would "fix up everything with May Woods" for me.

MR. EASTHAM worked fast. The very next day he stopped and told me he had everything "fixed." He said, "You know, I told May Woods last night about you. I went over to Oscar

Pennix's place, where she boards, and I told her you'd straightened that school out down where they's run off every teacher. And I told her you figured how many bushels of coal on my wagon bed. Oh, she was excited about it," he continued. "I was very frank with her. I put the cards on the table. I told her that she needed to go with a man like you and you needed a woman like her. I'm not a matchmaker but I think you'd make the best married pair that ever lived in these parts. Now I've made the date for you to go see her tomorrow evening. It's not more than two miles up there and you won't have any trouble finding

the house. It's the first house on your right after you pass the schoolhouse."

"I'll be there," I said. There was nothing left for me to say. I had never had a blind date before. I had not had many dates in my life. This was a long shot in the dark. I didn't know May Woods. But if she is a schoolteacher, I thought, and is as beautiful as he says she is, she must be all right.

At about seven that evening I was on my way to Upper Lonesome. I had waited for the dew to settle the dust before I started, because I wore white shoes and I didn't want to get them brown with dust. And I didn't want to get any dust on my white suit. I wanted to show May Woods that I was everything Burt Eastham had told her I was and more. This was a blind date, but I knew that blind dates had often developed into marriage. These thoughts raced through my mind as I walked swiftly along the brown winding road, always careful not to step too hard to stir the dust beneath the thin gossamer of dew dampness.

I passed the Faith Healing Holiness Church. Little crowds had already begun to gather. The men carried unlit lanterns and the women carried babies. They would need their lanterns for they would stay until the moon was down. Just a few steps beyond, on the opposite side of the road, was the Free Will Baptist Church, which John Conway attended. And I met the Free Will Baptists on their way to church. The men carried unlit lanterns and the women carried babies.

I had learned from the people of Lonesome Valley that on the same night a meeting was held at one church, a meeting was held at the other. These churches were great rivals. In Lonesome Valley there were no other churches, no people of any other religious faith. And, according to the conversations of these "religious people," there were two heavens. There was a Faith Healing Holiness heaven and a Free Will Baptist heaven. The two churches fought it out like two rival stores, across the street from each other, selling the same kind of merchandise, each merchant giving a slightly different sales talk to the people ready to buy. This religious feeling divided the people more than politics.

Lonesome Valley in reality was one little world to itself, but, in thought of the hereafter, it was two separate worlds. One was high-pressured to take sides, to believe in one of these worlds. I had steered clear of both, though I was accused of leaning toward the Free Will Baptists because I lived with John Conway, one of their members.

I chuckled to myself after I passed the Free Will Baptist Church, about what John Conway said to me after he had gone to see Nancy Cochran: "She is one of them Sanctifiers," he said, "but I told her plainly we didn't want Lonesome Valley School disturbed by her guitar playing and singing during book hours. First time I'd ever been in her store and she was skeered to death of me. I was skeered of her too."

The jolt-wagon wheel of yellow moon was rolling not too high above the green hills under heaven. It was soft and bright and beautiful. And its mellow shafts of light flooded Lonesome Valley with tainted moonlight-gold. This was the kind of night to have a date. It was the kind of night to be young and dressed in white and to be hatless with crow-wing black hair slicked back over the head. It was the kind of night for a young man to go see a beautiful girl he had never seen before. The whip-poorwills, nightingales, and insects were inspired to sing. I sang too. And the distance seemed shorter.

The road crossed Lonesome Creek. And when I leaped the stream to keep from soiling my white shoes, I leaped a golden stream. The moonlight had changed it to the color of the moon. What a night! What a beautiful journey! Dreams of May Woods raced through my mind as I came into shadows that cut away the moonlight.

Lonesome Creek and the Lonesome Creek Road parted here like two lovers. Lonesome Creek went into the dark forest, heavy with aromatic leaf and blossom. At this point the forest closed in on both sides of the road. I followed, feeling my way with my feet, a road that was as dark and strange as time. I looked to my left and to my right for an opening of light; of golden moonlight upon the open fields, upon the patches of ripening wheat and oats, broad-leafed, lusty, green-growing tobacco, and the dark clouds of stalwart corn. I was thinking just a few yards beyond I would reach the light, and then I would be there, when a barrage of something came through the trees like a flushed covey of birds flying for their lives. One of the objects caught me square on the jaw and the juice spattered my lips. I knew by the taste and the smell it was a rotten tomato.

I stopped in the road. I couldn't think fast enough. My white suit was the same kind of target to my attackers as a white chicken roosting in a winter-leafless tree at night is to a hoot owl. They could see me but I couldn't see them. And how many there were throwing at me, I could only guess by the way the tomatoes, rotten eggs, good eggs, apples, squashes, pumpkins, and melons hit me like hailstones. A rotten egg yellowed my hair. A squash, melon, or pumpkin caught me on the leg above the knee, and broke into fragments. I put my hands over my eyes to protect them, and ran forward. Then I heard laughter and screams back in the darkness under the trees.

In the middle of the road I did an about-face and started back, laying my feet down on the dusty road like a running horse. The missiles kept coming, and the wild crowd—there must have been fifty boys and men laughing and giving war whoops—came from the dark shadows in hot pursuit. Pistols were fired and bullets went high over my head. I could hear them spatting the leaves and hitting the branches and singing off into space.

When I came back into the light, Lonesome Creek that had been golden when I crossed it going up, was lead-colored to me. I sailed over it like a bird. Dust on my shoes meant nothing to me now. For I was running as I had never run before, with the pack on my trail; and the eggs and tomatoes were flying. Just before I reached the Free Will Baptist Church, a rotten egg exploded on top of my head. I thought of running inside the church but something urged me on. I pushed my tired body with every ounce of energy I had. I knew if they followed much farther, I would dive into the second church. But for some reason they didn't.

When I passed the Faith Healing Holiness Church, I was barely walking. I was wet with egg goo mixed with rotten tomato, melon, squash, pumpkin, and sweat. My white suit was so wet it stuck to my body and encased it like long underwear. The front door of the church was wide open on this hot night, and the house was packed with people. They were using all sorts of fans, from cardboard backs of tablets to short, leafy poplar limbs. I saw Nancy Cochran standing up front playing her guitar and singing a special number, "I'm Naturalized for Heaven." Amens were going up from all parts of the room.

I didn't linger before the church. I moved down the road that was not as beautiful as it had been. When I reached Conways' I couldn't go inside with the clothes I was wearing. I found a bar of soap in the soapbox on the back porch. I found a hole of water in Lonesome Creek surrounded by willows. It was the only place where the moon's rays could come through. I pulled off my clothes and shoes. I soaped and washed my body from head to toe. I washed my clothes and spread them on the brush for tomorrow's sun. Then I hurried to the house to beat the Conways home from church.

THE NEWS of my going to see May Woods spread like wildfire up and down Lonesome Valley. When I ate my breakfast the next morning, everybody at Conways' breakfast table wanted to laugh. John Conway would break out laughing and then he would tell a joke. He tried to make me think he was laughing at something else. Bertha Conway smiled as she poured my coffee. Don would look across the table at me and grin like a possum. Everybody puffed like frogs trying to hold their laughter. But not one mentioned what had happened to me. I didn't mention it either.

When I went to school my pupils whispered and smiled at one another. They wanted to laugh, too, because they had heard Burt Eastham make the date for me. But not one mentioned the affair where I could hear him.

In the afternoon Burt Eastham drove his mule team under the sycamore shade and stopped. He jumped off the wagon and ran stiff-legged toward the schoolhouse. I met him at the door, and we walked out to the coal wagon together to get away from my pupils' hearing.

"I'm sorry about what happened last night," he apologized. "I never heard about it until this morning. They say this fellow, Bill Coffee, Miss Woods has been a-sparkin', rounded back unexpectedly from the Auckland Steel Mills. He found out she had a date with you and he went wild when she wouldn't break the date with you for him. He said he'd break it."

"He broke it all right," I said, "but you didn't tell me she dated anybody else!"

"Yep, she's sparked Bill for a couple of years now," Burt spoke softly, "but I thought you had a good chance a-beatin' his time! He went around there among the Upper Lonesome boys, and you know they don't have much use for the Lower Lonesome boys, let alone a stranger, and they got ready for you. See, Bill Coffee is an Upper Lonesome boy hisself."

"Bill can have May as far as I'm concerned," I said. "I've never seen her or him and I don't care to see them."

"I'm sorry it all happened the way it did," he said. "Did they hurt you?"

"Not exactly," I said.

"Did they run you a fur piece?"

"Just to the Faith Healing Holiness Church," I said.

" 'Pon my word," he said, "ain't it awful."

I HAD JUST RETURNED from school that day and sat down on the porch where the Conway family was sitting, fanning themselves with long fronds of a creek willow, shooing the flies, and stirring the stuffy air, when I saw a big green convertible coming down the Lonesome Creek Road. The top was down and the young man behind the steering wheel was wearing a striped silk shirt and a high collar and flashy tie. He had a long cigar in his mouth, and a thin stream of smoke trailed behind the car and thinned to nothingness on the wind. He was driving with one hand and he had his right arm around a beautiful girl. Her black hair was blown back by the wind.

"Who in the world is that?" I asked.

Then everybody on Conways' porch started laughing. The pent-up laughter they had been wanting to turn loose, burst forth like water from a swimming hole when the mud dam gives way to pressure. They laughed until the car turned the bend and was out of sight.

"That's Bill Coffee and May Woods," Don finally said.

I felt a warm glow spread over my face. "He must own the Auckland Steel Mills," I said.

"No, he just works there," Don replied. "He's a welder."

"You know," John said, "people around here never thought old Bill would amount to a hill o' beans. He got to the *First Reader*. Then he quit school and tried to farm. He couldn't do that. Then he went to the Auckland Steel Mills and now he makes over three hundred dollars a month so I've heard."

"He's not been at the Auckland mills but a couple of years," Don continued. "First year he came back here with a new car and he was wearing ten-dollar shirts and fifteen-dollar shoes.

Every girl on Lonesome was a-tryin' to go with 'im, but May Woods beat all their times. She makes him awful jealous by having a date with somebody else now and then."

What a fool I've been! I thought. I knew I would never be able to live this event down in Lonesome Valley.

FRIDAY AT NOON of my third week, I dismissed school. I had to fetch much-needed supplies from Landsburgh.

It took me one hour to walk through the sweltering August heat and clouds of dust to the Valley. There I caught the afternoon Old Line Special, and as I rode toward Landsburgh, the thoughts I had had about teaching while riding this train three weeks before came back to me.

I had heard many teachers say that schoolteaching was dull and uninteresting. It was the most interesting thing I had ever done. I was trying to impart my scant knowledge to youth with even lesser knowledge, but I had learned more from my pupils than I had ever learned in three weeks before. When the train reached Landsburgh, I hurried home.

Next morning, bright and early, I went to see John Hampton to find out if his old car still climbed hills in reverse instead of low. But he had had it overhauled, and he promised to take me back to Lonesome Valley on Sunday. Since he had to get supplies for his school, we went together to Landsburgh in his car. Then we went to Superintendent Staggers's office.

"Well, how are you getting along, Mr. Stuart?" the Superintendent asked me. "You haven't come in to give the school up, have you?"

"Oh, no," I said. "I've just come for supplies."

"What do you want?" he asked. "Coal bucket, erasers, chalk, windowpanes?"

"All of that and more too," I said. "I want two bags of lime, a water cooler, enough paint to paint my schoolhouse, paintbrushes, hatchet, hammer, nails, hoe, rake, axe, and shovel."

"Just a minute," Mr. Staggers broke in, "who's goin' to paint the house?"

"I am," I said. "I'm going to clean that place up!"

"And the lime?" he asked. "First call I've ever had for lime."

"Use it as an antiseptic in the outdoor privies," I said. "Flies won't mess around lime."

After we had discussed the use of each item, he agreed to let me have all the supplies—although I was far beyond my allowance—because I said I'd paint the house free of cost. He wrote an order for my supplies at the Lawson Hardware.

Sunday at noon, John Hampton and I started for Lonesome Valley. As he drove along he told me of his many experiences teaching. He said I might think that I would turn the world over to see what was on the underside while I was young, but

later I would slow down and be well contented to accept what was on top the world.

I let him do the talking and I listened. By six o'clock we were at the Conways'. We had made approximately seven and a half miles an hour, and I heard the death bells ringing in my ears after all the clatter his car engine had made climbing the steep hills.

John Hampton went back to Landsburgh, and after supper Don Conway helped me carry the lime over to the schoolhouse. We took a sack to the boys' privy, and, when we went inside, I got a surprise. On Friday, when I had left, there was not a mark on the walls. Now they were marked all over. And I was depicted in all sorts of vulgar caricatures. May Woods's name was written beside my name. And there were vulgar caricatures of her. And Flossie Conway's name was printed all over the walls beside mine. She was also portrayed in obscene pictures.

"Who on earth did a thing like that?" I asked Don. "Suppose one of the pupils?"

"I don't think so," he said. "I think it's somebody that doesn't go to school."

We went back to Conways', where we got a bucket of water, soap, and broom, and returned and cleaned the walls.

Monday I told my pupils that somebody had drawn obscene pictures on the walls of the boys' toilet and that, since I couldn't

believe I had a pupil in my school that would do such a thing, I hoped each pupil would cooperate with me to protect our school property and help keep it clean. I told them that we planned to paint the house. I told them that this building was our home, that we were a unit same as a family and we had to work together. I believed that the schoolhouse should be made prettier and cleaner than any of the homes the pupils came from so they would love the house and the surroundings, and would think of it as a place of beauty and would want to keep it that way.

Then I explained to them we wouldn't need another dipper. And the only need we had for a water bucket was to carry water. For now we had a water cooler with a faucet. I showed them this new gadget, the first one they had ever seen, and they were pleased.

That afternoon John Conway brought our supplies to the schoolhouse, including ladders he had made for us. When school was over, Don and I started painting. Instead of taking off soon as school was out, many of the pupils stayed to watch us work, among them Guy Hawkins and Ova Salyers.

"Mr. Stuart, I can paint," Guy Hawkins said. "I'll help."

"I can paint too," Ova Salyers said.

Guy and I scraped off the old paint while Ova and Don started putting on the first coat. The summer days were long, and we worked until it was late. We made a considerable showing our first day. And while Guy and I removed the old paint we found a brown stain on the paint-scaled walls up about four feet from the ground. It was in blotches, big and brown as autumn oak leaves. Guy laughed while I took my knife and scraped on one of these spots.

"Don't you know what that is?" Guy asked me.

"I'm not sure," I said.

"It's ambeer spittle." Guy laughed. "Somebody has been spittin' on the walls!"

We found ambeer (tobacco juice) spittle all around the back of the schoolhouse. I knew this was something that had to stop before we got the house painted with our new white paint.

THE WRITING in the boys' privy and the spitting of ambeer on the schoolhouse walls worried me, but I had another problem that worried me more. In Landsburgh Graded School they had a teacher for each grade from the beginners to the junior high school. The pupils in each room were almost on the same age level. Here, I had from the beginners to the eighth grade, all in one room. Their ages ran from five to twenty.

The beginners were the most difficult to teach. I would bring them up and teach them ABC's on the dilapidated chart, used years and years before I came to Lonesome Valley. My eighth-grade pupils had been taught on this same chart. After I had gone over their ABC's with the beginners, they went back to their seats and had nothing to do. Many of them fell asleep in the hot schoolroom.

I had once been a beginner in this same type of school. I

had been taught to read on this kind of chart. Once after I had awakened from a nap, I had wandered from my seat and found a dead wasp and carried it up to the teacher while he was busy with a recitation. All the pupils laughed. I was given a sound spanking and put back in my seat. Thereafter, I was afraid of my teacher.

When one of these little fellows went to sleep, I never thought of spanking him. I let him sleep. What else could I do when I was trying to hear fifty-four classes recite in six hours, give them new assignments, grade their papers? What else could I do when I had to do janitorial work, paint my house, keep the toilets sanitary, the yard cleaned of splintered glass and rubbish?

One evening I told John Conway about my problem with beginners, but he didn't understand. He said a child should never be allowed to sleep in school. Then, I argued, the teacher should have something for the child to do interesting enough to keep him awake. I told John that if Upper Lonesome, Lonesome Valley, Unknown, and Chicken Creek Rural Schools were moved to the Valley—the approximate center of all these surrounding school districts—it could be worked out as it was in Landsburgh. It would take fewer teachers and each teacher would have pupils of the same age. Then one teacher could handle all the beginners.

His face reddened when he asked me how the pupils could get to school as faraway as the Valley. Haul them by bus or by jolt-wagon, I told him. He said I didn't know about the Lonesome Creek Road in winter. I told him the time would come when we would get gravel on the roads and then we could have this type of school. He said he hoped when this time came—when they took Lonesome Valley School from the people, where his children, himself, his father, and his grandfather had gone to school—he would be dead and know nothing about it. He went into as much of a tirade against this idea as if someone had walked into a field of his green-growing tobacco and started chopping it down with a hoe. He said my thought was dangerous, and, if I wanted to stay healthy, I better stop such crazy talk.

I was in his house. I taught his children. I couldn't tell him what I thought. But I thought if I ever got to a position high enough in education, if I was ever elected any kind of legislator, so help me God, I would abolish the abominable trustee system. If I couldn't do it singlehanded, I would help others do it. Why should I, a teacher, be at the mercy of John Conway?

John Conway hadn't gone any further than the third grade. He could see that coal was properly placed in the coal house, make ladders for us to use in painting, tell Nancy Cochran to stop playing a guitar while school was going on! But he had never persuaded the Greenwood County School Board to have a well dug for his school. He hadn't been able to get the schoolhouse painted. He hadn't offered to dig the well or paint the house himself. I finished my supper, left the table, and went outside to think about what I would do with my beginners. It was a problem.

LATER THAT NIGHT, I lay on my bed and thought. My room was hot as an oven and I heard the clock downstairs strike twelve, but I didn't have the solution.

Next morning I started early for school and walked slowly along trying to think of a way. As I walked along beneath the willows in the morning sun, I watched the pencil stripes of shifting shadows on the sand the sun made when it found little open spaces between the quivering fronds. Above my head the jeweled dewdrops were evaporating into thin white clouds and ascending toward the sun. It was the kind of morning that made me want to breathe deeply of the cool fresh wind. The kind of morning that made me want to be alive. Why should I worry about the school problem that had troubled me all night? Maybe it would come to me sometime. Why not walk along on this bright August morning and whistle "The Needle's Eye"?

The needle's eye that does supply,
The thread that runs so true . . .

What was the needle's eye? What was the thread that ran so true? The needle's eye, I finally concluded, was the schoolteacher. And the thread that ran so true could only be play. The needle's eye that does supply the thread that runs so true.

The teacher that supplied the play that ran so true? Play that ran so true among little children, little foxes, little lambs! My beginners should play. Their work should be play. I should make them think they were playing while they learned to read, while they learned to count! That was it! I had it. Play. As long as my beginners could play they wouldn't want to sleep, not during the school day.

On my father's farm I had seen the lambs play in the springtime on the green fields. I had seen the young foxes play among the monster rocks where they denned. I'd seen them chase each other's tails, around and around on top of a sunlit rock. I'd seen the young, pretty ring-tailed coons play when they washed their food—a good lesson in sanitation—in an unpolluted mountain stream. I'd seen young groundhogs slide on their tummies over the slick-worn banks on the cool summer earth. I'd seen young rabbits play in the wheat. I'd seen young squirrels play in the green canopy of the gray-barked beeches. That was it. Play. Play.

The word was magic to my brain. I'd never thought of it in this light before. Play. Play. Learn to work by play. All work should be play. Actually, teaching to me was a game. Maybe this was the reason I loved teaching.

WHEN TIME CAME for my first beginners' class, I tore the big sheet from the Lawson Hardware calendar. I took the scissors from my drawer and sat in a semicircle with the class. Every eye was upon me. I cut the numbers apart, told or asked what they were and handed them to the children. Then I cut the stiff backs of tablets into squares of approximate size. Taking a jar of paste, I pasted one number to one cardboard. Then I told the class to paste all the numbers and cardboard squares together.

While I went on with my other classes these children were busy. When recess came they wanted more to do—rather than go out to play. Some numbers were pasted sideways, but what did that matter? They had done well.

I drew objects on the board with which they were familiar—apples, cups, balls, and stick figures of boys and girls—in groups of one, two, three, and four. When time came for my next beginners' class, I asked the children to identify the objects, first by name, which I wrote above the object, then by number, which I wrote beneath it. They were so excited they sat on the edge of the recitation bench, their bare feet tapping nervously on the floor. Then I reached for the stack of number cards and held them up asking the class to name the number. I was surprised they recognized so many.

The room was so quiet you could hear a pin fall. Every pupil in the room was interested. This was something they had never done—had never seen done—but they recognized it as an

interesting way to learn. This was play. This was the thread that ran so true.

One idea led to another. There were dozens of ways to use the number cards. The few minutes I had to spend with each class were not nearly long enough. As days passed, the children learned to draw objects to represent a number on a card chosen by someone. They learned to add and subtract numbers and objects. They learned the names of the pictures drawn. We varied this by erasing the picture and number and reading the word. We placed a row of number cards along the board in the chalk ledge, and let the children draw pictures to represent the number on the card. There were no more little sleepy heads on desks now.

With the problem of my beginners solved, something happened to mar my happiness. That morning I had let Don, Guy, and Ova use their free periods to paint the house. After I had finished my lunch, I walked behind the house to see how the paint was drying. My face must have flushed red as a turkey's snout. There were twelve big brown blotches of ambeer spittle on the last coat of our snow-white paint.

When the noon hour was over, I told my pupils that if I caught anybody chewing tobacco on the school ground, I would punish that pupil. If I caught one spitting on the paint, I would spank, and spank hard. I knew it was one of my pupils. There hadn't been anybody else in the schoolyard. That afternoon, after school was dismissed, Don and I took a bucket of soapy water and a broom and scrubbed off this ambeer spittle. Then we went ahead with our painting. We worked late and finished the job.

THE NEXT DAY I took my lunch, and walked outside and around in back of the schoolhouse. My pupils were sitting under the shade of the tall sycamores, eating their lunch. All but one. She was making the ambeer spittle fly against the newly painted boards. A girl! And Vaida Conway, the beautiful fourteen-year-old daughter of my trustee.

"Vaida," I said, before she saw me, "what do you have in your mouth? What are you doing?"

"Nothing," she said.

"Don't you spit it out," I warned her. "Let me see it."

She took the quid from her mouth and showed it to me. Then she looked down at her bare feet.

"Why did you do this?" I asked.

"Mr. Stuart, I worked in the green tobacco," Vaida said. "It was hot and smelly and after I quit working in it I craved a chaw."

"You mean you got the tobacco habit by working in green tobacco and smelling it?" I asked her.

"Yes," she answered.

"I've worked in it all my life and I never got the habit by smelling green-growing tobacco," I told her.

If she had ever chewed tobacco at her home, I had never seen her do so. I had actually thought Ova Salyers and Guy Hawkins were the guilty ones. If I had picked over my students, trying to select the pupil that had spit on this white wall, Vaida Conway would have been one of the last I would have picked.

"Vaida, why did you spit on this white wall?" I asked her.

"Because I liked to spit on it," she admitted. "I like to see brown against white."

"When I dismiss school this afternoon, I want you to remain," I told her.

That afternoon when I dismissed school, Vaida remained. I waited until the schoolyard was cleared of pupils. Then I had to back up what I had said. I laid big and beautiful Vaida Conway across my lap and I applied the geography book to her in stinging spanks. Not enough to make her whimper, though. She was durable, and a little spanking didn't hurt her. It only wounded her pride.

Two problems were solved. I had one more. I had to find the guilty person or persons drawing the obscene pictures in the boys' toilet.

AFTER I HAD SPANKED Vaida, she stopped on her way out of the schoolhouse. She stood there for a minute and glared at me. "I'll go straight home and tell my Daddy on you," she said. "He'll fix you. He doesn't like you nohow. Not after you talked about moving our school down to the Valley."

Then she ran out the door. I finished making my monthly report so I could get my much-needed pay. This was the only rule for the Greenwood County rural teachers that Superintendent Staggers enforced. The monthly attendance report must be in his office before the teacher's check was sent to him.

When I got to Conways', I found that Vaida had made her threat good. A cold silence greeted me. John Conway had little to say. And the few words he was forced to say to me were sharp and cold as long icicles hanging from a winter cliff. Bertha didn't even speak to me. I knew they regarded Vaida as a woman grown. In four more years, when she became as old as Flossie, they would regard her as old enough to marry. If she weren't married, or about to get married, they would start worrying about her.

I sat down and ate my supper. I was paying for my board and their cold silence couldn't keep me from eating. Then I walked to the Valley and mailed my attendance report. I didn't hurry back. I gave my room plenty of time to get cool.

When I returned to Conways', the place was silent. They had to get up early and go to the tobacco patch on Saturday morning. John Conway would plan a big day's work, since he had all of his children home from school. Vaida would smell the green-growing tobacco, and she would perhaps not require a chew. Her system would absorb enough of the intoxication of this magic plant while she pulled the big, long, green worms from under the broad leaves, and pulled them apart with her shapely fingers or laid them on the hot ground and quashed them with her brown bare feet.

IN THE MORNING I got up late and ate my breakfast after John Conway and all his children had gone to work. Bertha was the only one there and she was silent. Then I took a volume of Kentucky School Laws and went to the Lonesome Valley School and sat down on the brace root of a giant sycamore in the shade. The hot August sun had begun to climb up the sky and the formless clouds of mist rose from the tobacco and corn up and down the valley. I began reading the school laws while Nancy Cochran came out on her store porch and picked her guitar and sang.

The only time she stopped singing and playing for me was when she had a customer. These times were few and far between. While Nancy entertained me I found some interesting items in Kentucky School Laws—a document I had never bothered to read before. I discovered that the use of tobacco was not only prohibited to pupils but to patrons, and that visitors were not allowed to use this fragrant weed on school property at any time, at any school, in the state. This was the law. I was also trying to find out whether a teacher had to board in the school district where he was teaching. I failed to find such a provision.

Sometime in the afternoon I was getting ready to go back to Conways' when I saw a tall young man walk down the Lonesome Creek Road. He looked first to his left, then to his right.

He looked toward the little store where Nancy sat playing her guitar and singing. He slowed down when he reached the schoolhouse. He turned and looked in every direction, even toward where I was sitting, but the sycamore tree partially blocked his view. Then he headed for the boy's privy. When he didn't come out I walked cautiously down to the privy and eased the door open. I found him smearing the walls with vulgar pictures of me, Flossie Conway, and May Woods.

"So you're the man doin' this!" I shouted.

He threw his piece of chalk down and dashed for the door.

I was standing in the right position to catch him square on the chin with an uppercut. I know it sounds unbelievable, but I flipped him completely over in the air and he hit on his feet running. He didn't run toward the store but he leaped the rusted strands of barbed wire toward the cornfield. I couldn't clear the fence. I had to go between the wires. And when I got through the fence he was nearly to the tall, green-growing corn. I had never seen a man who could run like this fellow. He had a long pair of "rabbit legs," and he used them. He was off and I trailed until I lost his footprints under the tall corn.

Nancy Cochran had seen the chase. When I passed her store on my way back to Conways', she said: "What were you tryin' to do to Alvin Purdy?"

"Who is this Alvin Purdy?" I asked her.

"Oh, he's a boy from Upper Lonesome, and he nearly

worries me to death," she said proudly. "He tries to have dates with me. I won't have anything to do with him, though."

I didn't tell her what he had been doing. I had never seen him before, but I later learned he was jealous of me. He was in love with Nancy Cochran. Nancy and Flossie Conway were old rivals. Each tried to take the other's beaus. And this was the reason for the ugly pictures in the school privy. Again, the secret thoughts I had harbored about Guy Hawkins and Ova Salyers proved false.

MONDAY I GOT my check for my first month's teaching, exactly sixty-eight dollars. I knew then it was better that my going to see May Woods had turned out the way it had. If I had had a date with her and had fallen in love with her, I could never have shown her a "good time."

For Bill Coffee, even if he did have only a third-grade education, was four times as successful as I was, if success was measured in dollars and cents. And, believe me, it was measured that way among the young people in Lonesome Valley. I could understand why May Woods dated Bill Coffee. Why shouldn't she date someone who could drive her around in a big green convertible? What could I show her on sixty-eight dollars a month? I was young, too, and wanted to date girls and show them a good time. But I was also fascinated by schoolteaching.

There had been months, when I lived at home and went to Landsburgh High School, that I made more than fifty dollars a month by hunting and trapping. After I had paid my board, how much would I have left now that I was teaching school? I didn't have long to wait to know how much. Bertha Conway charged me twenty-five dollars for a month's room and board, and I knew this was reasonable in these times when America was booming. But it was not reasonable compared with my salary. I had only, not counting the little things I had bought for my pupils and my school, forty-three dollars left.

MY HAVING TO PAY Bertha Conway twenty-five dollars a month was not the reason I was leaving Conways'. There were other reasons. It was all right as long as I corrected Guy Hawkins, but when I disciplined Vaida it wasn't. Also, my trustee was peeved at me for suggesting consolidation of rural schools.

"I'm not tryin' to keep you here," John Conway said, when I was packed to go, "but you do have to stay in this district."

"Mr. Conway," I said, "I'm leaving here a copy of the Kentucky School Laws. I've marked only one place for you to read."

Then I was off down Lonesome Creek Road to the Valley. For I was going to stay with Uncle Amos Batson, who ran the store and post office there. I would be five miles from my school and have to walk ten miles each day. But I would be away from the two factions that made up my school district. The score was evened in the minds of both groups, for I had disciplined Guy Hawkins, whose father belonged to one faction, and Vaida Conway, whose father belonged to the other. Each group knew now I didn't show partiality. I was there to teach the school. That was all. I was determined to stay until my school year was finished. But I could do it better by not living with either faction. I had learned, in my brief experience, that a teacher must keep himself above the petty bickering of prejudiced groups.

There were twelve rooms in Uncle Amos Batson's two-story, white frame house. Uncle Amos and Aunt Effie had the downstairs and I had all of the upstairs I wanted. There were six large rooms upstairs, with screened windows and feather beds. The house didn't have a bathroom, but it did have running water downstairs. It was the best house in this section of Greenwood County. I could raise my windows. My room was cool enough so I had to sleep under cover and not naked on top of the covers. I didn't have to fight insects all night. And the food was delicious. I had never eaten better hot biscuits, hickory-smoked ham, and wild honey in my life!

And Uncle Amos, though sixty-seven years old, could draw a fiddle bow the smoothest I'd ever heard. He could make his fiddle talk, laugh, or cry. He could play music that made Aunt Effie put her long-stemmed pipe aside, and dance. Though she was sixty-seven, too, the mother of eleven children all married and moved away, she was as agile as a sparrow. She danced the old reels, her small feet nimbly tapping the tunes that Uncle

Amos played on his magic fiddle, fast as snow-melted water poured over the cliffs in an early mountain spring.

My five-mile walk to school up Lonesome Valley was a pleasant one. The morning sun was like a golden sunflower in a deep, upturned bowl of blue. In the afternoons, the Lonesome Valley sun was a wilted sunflower in a shallow, upturned plate of blue.

The first week I lived at Batsons', Uncle Amos' hired man, Bill Strickland, left to work in the Auckland Steel Mills. Uncle Amos, though he could play the fiddle, couldn't milk a cow. Aunt Effie said she hadn't milked a cow in the forty-nine years she had been married and she didn't plan to start it now. Then I volunteered to go after the cows and to milk them.

Uncle Amos knew I would have to hurry if I did all this and got to school on time. He went to the barn lot and saddled and bridled Sundance, his large white pony, and I climbed into the saddle. I was off to get the cows up a twisting cow path that led to the mountaintop. There were hundreds of acres of grassy slope, dotted here and there in the deep hollows and ravines with tracts of giant trees. There were four hundred acres in this pasture, and below it lay the Valley. I could see the winding stream, like a silver ribbon in the early morning sun, flowing gently past the farmhouses, through the fertile level land where grew corn, cane, and tobacco. The dew was rising up in shapeless forms between the green valley and the sun. I sat for a moment in the soft saddle looking at this miracle of beauty while Sundance pranced, pawed, champed at the bridle bits. He was restless to go after the cows.

This large, intelligent, and beautiful pony, the color of an early morning sunbeam dancing on the Valley Creek waters below, knew what his mission was. He had been after the cows before. I gave him the rein and he found the cows. When the cows saw Sundance, they were ready to be led home to be milked.

It didn't take me too long to milk the seven cows. Then I strained the milk and separated the cream for Aunt Effie to put in cans to ship on the Old Line Special. When I was through with my work, I didn't have time to walk five miles to school.

I would be late and I knew there would be talk—since I had left the Lonesome Valley District—if I were late once.

"Ride Sundance to school," Uncle Amos said. "Put him in Charlie Abraham's barn durin' the day."

And that is what I did. After that Uncle Amos didn't try to get another man to do the milking and going after the cows. I loved Sundance. I loved to ride him up the Lonesome Valley Road in the morning when the corn tassels and morning glories vining up the corn were so alive with pink, blue, purple and white horn-shaped blossoms. The world was beautiful and I

was a schoolteacher with a big white pony to ride. In the afternoon when I mounted the saddle for home, Sundance was anxious to return to his barn in the Valley and wanted to run like a fox. It was only a matter of minutes for us from school to the Valley.

MY SECOND MONTH at the Lonesome Valley School, I enjoyed the cooperation of the two factions. Living in a home that didn't belong to either faction worked satisfactorily. And my pupils understood. They went home and told their parents how fair I was with everybody.

Don Conway held no malice toward me. And even Vaida soon forgot what I had done to her. She didn't chew any more tobacco, not after her father had read the section of Kentucky School Laws I had marked for him. And he didn't say anything about my leaving Lonesome Valley School District. There wasn't much he could say, anyway. For I became too popular with the patrons of my school district for one man to do much against me.

During that second month we started applying arithmetic to problems in the community. Burt Eastham had told almost every man in Lonesome Valley about my figuring up the bushels of coal on his wagon bed. Now they came for me to figure wagonloads of coal, bushels of corn in the bins, sizes of coal houses, how much dirt to remove from a cellar or a well. And I never refused a request.

If it was a small job, we did it after school; if it was a large one, we did it on Saturday. I took with me as many boys and girls as wanted to go along. Don Conway was always with me. Guy Hawkins became very much interested in figures and what could be done with them. When he got interested, his friend Ova Salyers did too.

One of my pupils, a large twelve-year-old boy, Denver Lykins, who was in the first grade and could count in his head with figures fast as I could, always went along. He couldn't write figures because he hadn't gone to school more than three months in his life. I gave him special attention because he was so interested. I held his hand at the blackboard and helped him make figures, and he went with us everywhere to figure land, corn bins, coal houses.

One Saturday we figured the number of acres in Tim Conley's farm. Denver Lykins carried the rod pole while Don Conway kept tally of the number of rods. Guy and Ova blazed a trail along the line fences so we could measure on the line and measure correctly. We figured the small farm to have 48.6 acres. When the county surveyor, Don Shackleford, ran a survey two weeks later, he figured the farm to have 48.7 acres. We had come that close.

But one of the funniest things to happen was when a small man named Silas Higgins came to the school to ask me to figure a pasture field where he had cut the sprouts. He said he was to receive six dollars per acre cutting the sprouts, and the fellow he'd cut the sprouts for, Willis Hager, had measured the land and he had measured it. He said that he had measured it for twelve and one-half acres and Willis had measured it for six. He spoke loudly so all the pupils could hear.

Guy Hawkins said somebody must be wrong, that was too much difference. Don said he would like for all of us to measure it. We told Silas Higgins we'd be there at four o'clock that afternoon.

When we got there—Don, Guy, Ova, Denver, and I—the two men were waiting and arguing. Willis Hager must have been seven feet tall. Silas was not much over five feet. Willis would look down at Silas and laugh sarcastically and threaten to pick him up by the neck and seat of the pants and throw him from the field if he didn't accept his measurement. They had stepped the distances around the field, counting each step for three feet.

My pupils began laughing. Willis was so tall he could step six feet at a step and Silas so short he couldn't step three. We didn't do any stepping. We measured the land and Don figured it while Ova, Guy, and Denver looked on. He figured the field for 9.6 acres. Willis wasn't satisfied at all. He threatened Silas physically and with the law. Then I went over the figures. They were correct.

"You see, Mr. Higgins, your legs are short," Ova Salyers said, "and your steps are not long enough. Mr. Hager"—Ova laughed as he looked up at the tall man—"your steps are too long. That's why you measured this field for only six acres."

Willis Hager was going to hit me with a sassafras stick when I told him if he went to law that he would lose and our measurement was approximately what a surveyor's measurement would be. But he didn't get very far with the stick. Four of my pupils stepped forward and little Silas Higgins picked up a rock. Willis knew the odds were against him, and he settled down and listened to reason. Before we had left, we had the dispute settled and both parties were satisfied. They shook hands and made friends. I have often thought if a little simple learning and arithmetic hadn't been applied here, one of these men would have killed the other before a lawsuit was filed in court.

My pupils were seeing the practical appliance of simple learning to everyday problems. Don Conway became so interested in school that he decided not to get married but to go through the Lonesome Valley School, then on to high school, and to college. His brain and his heart were fired with enthusiasm for more education. His enthusiasm caught on with the other boys, who had once thought of running the teachers off. Now they were the most loyal and finely behaved pupils I had in the school. Instead of wanting to tear down everything, and leave a path of destruction behind them, they were con-

structive and wanted to build and help shape their own lives differently and to help their community.

Near the end of my second school month something happened that made the pupils take more interest in schoolwork than ever. Burt Eastham had again contacted May Woods and told her that our school was much better than hers. This infuriated her and she challenged me to bring my pupils to her school for an arithmetic match.

Challenge was all we wanted. On that Friday, we all set out at noon, on foot, for Upper Lonesome.

And for the first time, I came face-to-face with one of the most beautiful teachers I had ever seen. She had crow-wing black hair, big, soft brown eyes shaded with heavy lashes, pretty white teeth, and lovely lips. Her schoolhouse was immaculately clean. Her pupils were well disciplined. They were all on one side of the big center aisle, and the other side was reserved for my pupils. The two long recitation seats were moved to the back of the schoolroom for visitors. They were filled and people were standing. Among the visitors was Burt Eastham.

Before we began, Miss Woods and I agreed on a few simple rules. One was that she, Burt Eastham, and I would be the judges. We agreed that if a pupil could work the problem in his head and call out the correct answer, he didn't have to write the figures on the blackboard. And we agreed that the pupil called from his seat to the board to work against the one still standing, had his choice in addition, multiplication, subtraction, common or decimal fractions, long or short division.

We started with the beginners. She called one and I called one. We matched them at the blackboard in front so all could see. They were about evenly matched for speed and accuracy. But she had twice as many beginners so each of my pupils had to turn down two of hers before we had an even break. Then I called Denver Lykins to the blackboard—my big first-grader. He stood there calling out the answers until he had eliminated all her beginners. Someone shouted, "Eighth-grader!" But I showed Miss Woods my record book. Finally one of Miss Woods's pupils asked for four columns of figures to add. Denver couldn't add four columns in his head, though he could add three. This girl turned down Denver, who couldn't make figures on the blackboard, but the match left him with a determination to learn how.

Denver had turned down seven pupils. Then Guy turned down five. Ova turned down three. When we got to the fourth grade, I called big Don Conway. He turned down ten—all of Miss Woods's fourth-grade pupils and six of her fifth grade. Don was pleased with himself, for many of them were as large as he was.

In the upper grades Miss Woods had three pupils to my one. But I had one girl, Margaret Prater, who was excellent in decimal and common fractions. She was the best pupil in my school. I held her for the last. The match went on, with shouts from our side if we turned down one of theirs. Shouts came from the other side when they turned down one of ours. Also, the visitors in the back of the room applauded for Upper Lonesome, for they were from this school vicinity.

I had only Margaret Prater left when Miss Woods had seven eighth-graders. Margaret beat Miss Woods's pupils one by one, in addition, subtraction, short division, long division, multiplication of common fractions, and decimal fractions. We had won against odds. Then we had to hurry home. Everybody had his evening chores to do. And I had to ride to the Valley, and fetch my cows from the pasture.

THIS ARITHMETIC MATCH made news the entire length of Lonesome Valley and beyond. Burt Eastham reported it to anyone willing to listen. It created a school spirit at Lonesome Valley. Though it was late in the summer, we organized a baseball team. Good clean play, good clean fun, in the form of competition, was the thing.

The last week in August my pupils met pupils of the Chicken Creek School in an arithmetic match and defeated them. The first week in September we met the Unknown School and defeated them. We had only the Valley, largest of all the rural schools, left.

When this match came off we had visitors that had to stand in the yard and look through the windows. People could hardly believe it when Guy Hawkins turned down fifteen. This was a new kind of fighting for Guy, and he liked it. We had spelling matches against these same schools, and we lost two and won two. They organized ball teams, too, and we played them. We lost two and won seven games.

Play for my pupils! Play for myself! I was the needle's eye! Play was the thread that ran so true! Teaching was not work as it had been. Teaching was play! I had never in my life enjoyed myself more.

Perhaps John Conway thought we were doing too much play. I will never know for sure who reported my school to the county superintendent. But John Conway made a trip to Landsburgh to pay his taxes and get winter supplies; and it was shortly afterward that Superintendent Staggers "slipped in" to my schoolhouse and sat down. It was the first time he had ever been to Lonesome Valley in his five years as superintendent. But his presence didn't bother me. I went ahead teaching. I let Margaret Prater teach my numbers game to the beginners outside the schoolhouse. Superintendent Staggers followed her outside and listened. My school was not too noisy but it did have a working noise, as I explained to Superintendent Staggers later. Bees made noise in the hive when they made honey.

"You're doin' a wonderful job," the superintendent admitted. "One of the most wide-awake schools I have seen in this county."

Then I told him about the substitute of play for work in my school. I told him about the spirit of competitive play in our arithmetic matches, spelling bees, ball games; and how people were interested enough to come and watch these matches, and how the school spirit had stimulated the parents and pupils alike. I told him how we had applied arithmetic in the community, and then I answered every question he asked me. He knew, after he had questioned me, that my school and its community was as alive as a beehive when the bees are gathering their summer sweets from the blossoms.

When I drew my second check and started to pay Uncle Amos and Aunt Effie, they would take only twelve dollars because I had milked their cows. This left me fifty-six dollars clear money from teaching. In addition to getting my expenses cut to less than half for this excellent place to live, I got the use of the most intelligent and one of the prettiest ponies that ever carried a saddle.

SELDOM IF EVER did one of my pupils stay out of school because he wanted to. He stayed out usually for one of three reasons: he was sick; he had to help harvest the crops; he didn't have sufficient clothes, shoes, or books. In September the tobacco ripened and many of my pupils had to stay home and help with tobacco cutting and hauling to the barn. The cane ripened in September, too, and it had to be stripped, topped, cut, hauled to the mill, and the juice pressed from it and boiled into sorghum molasses. Potatoes had to be dug. Corn had to be cut. September was a busy time in Lonesome Valley, where the men of this rugged American earth eked a bare subsistence for themselves and their families.

Although my pupils' attendance was down considerably in September, there wasn't an attendance officer to see why they didn't come to school. If they went, it was all right. If they didn't, it was all right too. But we had made our school so attractive that the pupils loved the place. They had helped to make it beautiful—to make their school their home during school days, their workshop, their beehive. It was the liveliest spot in our community, and these were their happy days.

Beyond these days, for most of them, it was eternal work, work, work, and the sameness of life. It was marriage, children, death, and burial in Lonesome Valley.

I thought of these things when I taught my pupils all the practical things I could teach them. How to write letters, measure land, be clean with drinking water, about personal sanitation, screens for their windows, and so many things aside from the dry-as-powder textbooks I had to teach because they were standard. When I gave them assignments to write themes, I never gave them the topics listed in their books. I told them to write about the things they knew about: people, places, things, and adventures in Lonesome Valley.

In October my attendance grew. Many of my pupils came thinly clad and barefooted, after the white frosts had blanketed the frozen land. For the farmers didn't sell their tobacco, which was their "money crop," till about Christmastime. Many times I saw the red spots on the white frost from the bleeding little bare feet of those who came to school regardless of shoes. I couldn't buy shoes for them—not on my salary and in my circumstances.

But for one little boy and girl, whose father was in the federal penitentiary for converting his corn into moonshine whiskey, I did buy shoes. No one knew I bought them. Their mother, with another child on the way, was fighting a brave battle to keep her home together. I had lived all my life in a community where these things happened. When I saw blood on the snow from this moonshiner's children coming to my school, it did something to me. I wanted to fight for them harder than I had ever fought Guy Hawkins.

THE SEA OF multicolored leaves was whipped from the trees by the raw November winds. The two great furrows, turned in opposite directions by some great mythical plow in the beginning of time to make Lonesome Valley, were naked, grotesque, and ugly now. Great, gray scaly rocks showed high on the rugged slopes. The valley had lost the beauty of summer bloom, bud, and leaf that had clothed its scars with many shades of green. Autumn had passed. Winter was on us.

We crowded close to the potbellied stove. We fired it until it was red-hot. The heat from it hurt our eyes. And now we wished for the evenness of the July heat. We knew we could bear that more easily than we could the fury of the icy wind. The corners of our schoolroom were cold even when our stove was dangerously overheated. Seats had to be pulled up and placed in circles around the stove like an amphitheater. But my pupils were free of home labors, and my attendance grew.

Suddenly sunshine would thaw the frozen earth, and Lonesome Valley would be a sea of mud. Sundance would sink to his knees in mud as he carried me to school on these short winter days. Birds would fly hither and thither, looking for weed seeds, chirruping their mournful winter notes. The wind lifted old leaves from the bottom of this funnel-like valley and swept them away to unknown places.

And when I saw this desolate land, where there was not food for beast or fowl in winter, I knew why everybody worked in the fields while the season was here. It was the fable of the ant and the grasshopper. And the Lonesome Valley people were ants. They were not the idle dancing grasshoppers. They worked while the season for growth was with them. And they laid away, but not too much, for the horrible, monstrous winter weather we now knew.

December came. We had a Christmas tree and my pupils drew numbers from a hat and exchanged gifts. We had a Christmas program and I bought candy, apples, oranges, and bananas. We lost only one day for Christmas holiday. My pupils hardly knew the meaning of letting out school a week for Christmas. For these were the days when they could go to school. These were the days when they couldn't plow and till the earth and harvest the crops. These were the days to get an education. Our six months' school couldn't go too far into the late winter. For the children had to start burning tobacco beds and getting ready for another crop year.

January came. The number of pupils leaped to sixty, though I had never seen more snow, more icy winds, more unbearable weather. But this was our last month of school. Time was running out for them. Time to get their education, time for their play, the fun of association, was coming to a close.

OUR GOOD SCHOOL YEAR, our good time together, ended on February 4th. And now was the time for the pupils to get their promotions. Guy Hawkins had received the highest number. He had gone from the first to the fifth grade. Ova Salyers was promoted to the fourth. Don Conway leaped to the seventh. No one had failed. Six eighth-graders had finished school. Their "good years" had ended.

Last day of school, we had a program. Members of the community were invited. They packed the house. We had readings, and then Guy and Don "chose up" and we had an arithmetic match. Finally I shook hands with my pupils, their mothers and fathers, and thanked them for sending me such rugged, fine young Americans. I told them that I would soon be a pupil again, and expressed my heartfelt joy for this chance to teach their children. I made them laugh when I told them I had learned more in six months of teaching than I had learned in my three years of high school.

That afternoon I was in the saddle for the last time. My pupils watched me ride away, around the bend and out of sight. They waved to me and shouted their good-bys and I waved to them and shouted my good-bys. The ground was frozen and I made good time, giving Sundance the rein. I looked to my right and to my left, for the last time, at Lonesome Valley.

EDITORS' NOTE

JESSE STUART's school days—both as a teacher and a student—did not end when he left Lonesome Valley. He went back for his final year of high school and then, at eighteen, succumbed to the glamour of a traveling carnival and ran off to join it. Eleven months in a Birmingham steel mill followed, but by now his hunger for further education could not be stilled, and he enrolled at Lincoln Memorial University in Tennessee. Here, as he remembers, he wrote "about five hundred poems," edited the school newspaper, and crushed limestone for the State Highway Department to earn money to support himself.

Returning to his native Greenup County (the Greenwood County of the book), he became the entire faculty of a rural high school, at night poring over subjects he had never mastered as a student so he could teach them to *his* students the next day. In 1930, at the age of twenty-three, he was chosen principal of the high school where he himself had been a pupil, and at twenty-five he was superintendent of the county schools. A salary of one hundred dollars a month and battles with the school board soon made him wonder if the job was quite the opportunity he had thought.

By now, however, he had certain other interests. One was a local girl named Naomi Deane Norris; another was the writing he had always pursued. His poems and short stories were beginning to be published and his reputation as an author grew. In 1937 he received a Guggenheim Fellowship to write and travel abroad. The next year saw the publication of an autobiography, *Beyond Dark Hills*, and in 1939 he married Naomi. For four more years he continued his career as a schoolteacher and administrator until at last, eager to devote full time to his writing, he took his slender savings and bought the farm in W-Hollow where he had lived as a child with his parents.

But his ties to schools and to students were not over. The success of his novel *Taps for Private Tussie*, of new poems and stories, brought him invitations as a teacher and lecturer in schools far beyond those native Kentucky hills. Although hardships had kept him from gaining his M.A. degree as a young man, his later writings won him several honorary doctorates.

Today, Jesse Stuart continues to live on his farm near Riverton, Kentucky, in the valley where he was born.

THE HOUSE OF EXILE

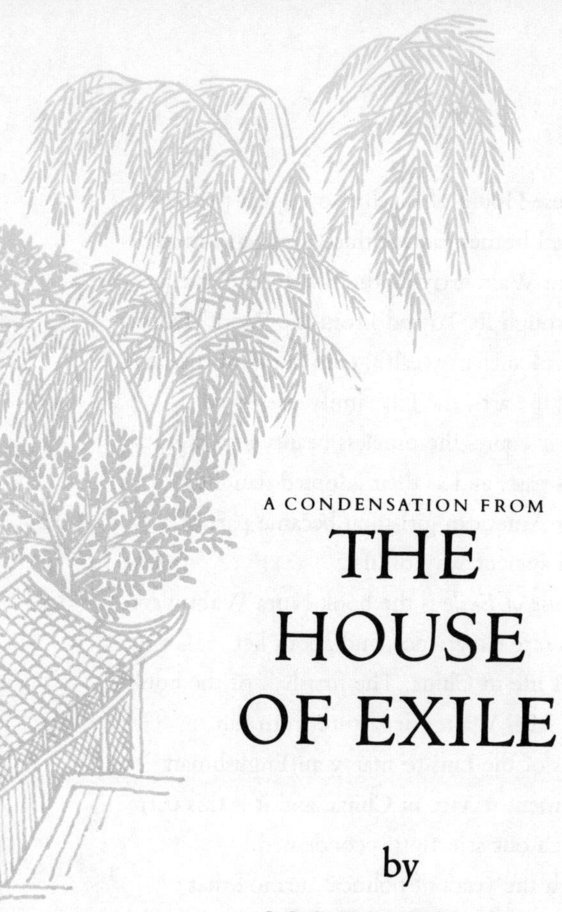

A CONDENSATION FROM

THE HOUSE OF EXILE

by

NORA WALN

The Chinese House of Lin had occupied the same walled homestead for thirty-six generations when Nora Waln arrived, the first foreigner ever to pass through its To and From the World Door. Possessors of ancient wealth, cultivators of the land, patrons of the arts, the Lin family preserved within their courts the timeless beauty and dignity of China's past; and as their adopted daughter the young American girl soon became part of a subtle and ancient way of life.

The House of Exile is the book Nora Waln wrote about this rare experience, and about her subsequent life in China. The first half of the book ends with Miss Waln's departure from the courtyards of the Lins to marry an Englishman in government service in China, and it is this part from which our selection is condensed.

Through the years of political turmoil that followed, the House of Exile stood fast, and Nora Waln's bonds with the Lins remained close. But the great revolution that took place in 1948 destroyed the traditional fabric of Chinese life forever, and it is doubtful that the graceful, civilized, intensely private world she has fixed on paper any longer exists.

PROLOGUE

The House of Exile
Hopei Province, China

LATE IN THE EIGHTEENTH and early in the nineteenth century, Lin Yan-ken selected merchandise for J. S. Waln. Amber, alum-root, beeswax and cassia lignea. Cinnabar, chinaware, chessmen carved from ivory tusks, and an elbow chair of rosewood. Embroidered fans, grass cloth, ginger in earthen pots. Hemp and indigo. Musk, nankeens, orpiment, a miniature pagoda of silver, and medicinal rhubarb. Packets of seeds of the melon and of the apricot. Teas, both green and black. Umbrellas, vases, wall-papers with scenes from Chinese life.

These are some of the items neatly entered in a time-yellowed account book, as sent by the Confucian merchant from Canton in the ancient empire of China to the Quaker merchant in Philadelphia, U.S.A.

It is recorded at the ancestral hall of the Lin homestead that Lin Yan-ken went to Canton and joined the business of his uncle, one of thirteen men appointed by the Emperor of China to trade with foreigners. He served there, by Western calendar, from May 1779 to June 1822.

Then Lin Yan-ken returned to his birth home to enjoy fifteen years of family life. In this time his descendants came to number five sons and two daughters. The last ten years of his life he was Elder of the House of Exile. Axioms given by him still echo in the homestead, as it is the custom in Chinese courtyards to pass from generation to generation the truths that have been garnered from life by those who have lived.

Lin Wei-sung is now Elder of the House of Exile. It is his habit on summer afternoons to gather us into the cool shade under the interlacing branches of two trees that form a leafy canopy over the library courtyard, and in winter to draw us into the library, where the sun shining through the rice-paper windows lays a warm gold carpet on the floor. The trees that make the courtyard canopy are called "Yan-ken's trees." He planted the one near the east wall on the morning of his departure from home, the one near the west wall forty-three years later on the evening of his return.

The Elder reads from the classics or recounts incidents from his experience. Always he encourages others to contribute. Even the littlest child is accustomed to entertain without self-consciousness. Once the Elder sent a servant to fetch an ivory box from the green lacquer cabinet. When he had it, he withdrew a yellowed envelope, from which he took two sheets of paper. One of the sheets was in English. The other was its translation into Chinese. The English page was dated "Philadelphia, Sixth Month 10, 1804," and signed "J. S. Waln."

The letter, addressed to Lin Yan-ken, expressed satisfaction that any packet with his seal did not need examination to assure that its contents were of the promised quality. The writer regretted that conditions of the era did not permit the exchange of other than material goods, and ended with the hope that in later generations, "when suspicion between peoples disappears," the Lins and the Walns might exchange visits.

We were each permitted to hold the letter a few seconds. Then the Elder put it in the ivory box and had it returned to the cabinet. Said he, "We Chinese have a longer history than any other people in the world: forty-six centuries. We keep to ourselves. Our experience with Westerners has seldom been such as to give us confidence in Western friendship. Too often we trusted and were betrayed.

"Of these experiences I shall tell you three:

"*Firstly:* In the zenith of the Ming dynasty, a flock of white-sailed ships came up the Canton River. Their commander gave his name as Fernão Peres de Andrade and his birthplace as Portugal. He asked for the privilege of trade. His manners were charming. The Canton viceroy was impressed and reported favorably to the throne.

"Wu Tsung, the Emperor, used the vermilion pencil to reply, permitting trade and inviting the stranger to Peking. The ships were filled with silks, embroideries, porcelain, ivories, teas, and dispatched to Portugal. Then, with royal escort, Andrade journeyed to the court, where he was welcomed and resided as an honored guest.

"The white-winged ships returned with the tidings that the Emperor of Portugal was delighted with the Chinese things. Portugal paid generously for the first shiploads. To facilitate the business, Andrade secured permission for several hundred of his countrymen to settle in our beautiful southern cities, Ningpo and Foochow.

"Then Andrade's brother arrived with an enormous fleet

manned by armed men. Our smooth-voiced visitors no longer bothered to be polite. They pirated our warehouses and temples. To rid ourselves of our guests, we had to rise up and massacre them.

"*Secondly:* Through history we traded amiably with the Filipinos. When Western ships sailed into Manila, the major population was Chinese. The commander of these ships said his birthplace was Spain. His conduct was gentle on arrival.

There was advantageous business for all. But when the Westerners got a foothold, they declared that we Chinese were too numerous. They slaughtered thousands of us as though we were wild beasts.

"*Thirdly:* Near the end of the Ming dynasty when the decadent imperial family were occupied with base pleasures, Western ships again sailed up the Canton River. They induced China to establish a trading post outside the walls of Canton. They had with them a charter from Charles I of England, dated 1635. This trading station was viewed with anxiety. But we had no gunboats with which to drive the bold intruders away. All our precepts were against military power. Then, as now, the soldier ranked lowest in society.

"The vermilion pencil was used to protect us. An edict forbidding any man, woman, or child to leave our homeland, under threat of death on return, was posted at each magistrate's office. Thirteen merchants of prudent character were appointed to the Western trade. They and their staffs were the only Chinese permitted to have contact with the intruders.

"There was fortune in the Western trade. Merchants vied for appointment. Each family tried to hold the seal from generation to generation. The situation was delicate because each merchant had to give the Emperor bond for the Westerners. If a Western trader disobeyed a regulation, the Chinese merchant bonded for him not only lost his seal of appointment, but he and all his family were ruined—their fortune forfeit to the throne.

"The vermilion pencil forbade Westerners to approach China at any place except outside the Canton city wall. They were forbidden to ride in riverboats, rickshaws, or sedan chairs, or attempt to stare in through the city gate.

"But in the reign of the fourth Emperor, the powerful merchant sponsors drew the Emperor's attention to the fact that in coming to China the traders were confined on their small vessels for four or five months and had a similarly long return journey. So on four days of four moons each year, under the guardianship of their sponsor, they were permitted an excursion to the Fati flower gardens.

"On those days the gardens were closed to Chinese. Our

Emperor did not want us near Westerners, who were judged uncultured savages.

"It was some decades before Westerners discovered that we had no military power behind our edicts and that they could force their religions and merchandise upon us."

After a long silence the Elder said, before he dismissed us: "The letter I showed you is kept and shown to each generation, not only as evidence of Yan-ken's integrity, but as proof that all Westerners are not savages."

MY INTEREST IN China began in April 1904. I was nine then and the guest of my paternal grandparents on their farm in Pennsylvania. The day was rainy. As I had torn a hole in one of my rubber boots, I had been told by Grandmother to go to my room. I went on into the attic. There, in a chest under the eaves, in use to keep the moths from the wedding dress of a slim-waisted Quaker bride, I found copies of the *Gazette of the United States*.

Later, Grandmother gave the *Gazettes* to me; they are on my table before me as I write this prelude to the selections from my Chinese journals which form the body of this book.

Each *Gazette* has a column of marine notices announcing vessels berthed at Philadelphia with lists of merchandise in them. In my childhood it was only the goods consigned to Waln that captured my imagination; only the movements of brigs, sloops, schooners, frigates, or ships identified as at some time serving Waln that concerned me. I accepted all cargoes consigned to J. S. Waln as my own. And Canton, in southern China, immediately became my favorite port of purchase.

My elders spoke with satisfaction of the quietness in which I sat during the hour of silent worship at our meetinghouse; I was troubled by this praise, because I did not always seek the company of God in my quietness, but was planting "lily flowers" or "seeds of the melon and the apricot" that had come from Canton.

Years passed. I came to possess a row of Chinese histories and dictionaries, volumes of verse, and old letters collected from relatives. And I wrote a sad ballad (which was printed in a magazine) about the little boy Emperor of China, Pu-yi, the last Son of Heaven.

Then one golden morning when I was an undergraduate at Swarthmore College, I was called to the telephone. A lady explained that she and her husband, of the Lin family of China, were on a tour of the Western world and, desiring to meet one of the Waln family, had looked through the catalogues listing scholars at the Society of Friends schools, and found my name.

Scarce able to believe that it was not a dream, I arranged to go to her at Philadelphia by the next train. I had never seen a Chinese other than those of my mind's creation. I saw Shun-ko and her husband, Lin Yang-peng, standing in Philadelphia's Broad Street Station, before I passed through the exit gate. They were two exquisitely neat slim figures, with faces of smooth ivory, dressed in high-collared, heel-length gowns of dark silk, with short sleeveless jackets of brocade. Yang-peng wore a round brimless cap on his close-cropped head. Shun-ko had no hat. Her glossy black hair was brushed tidily from a center parting. As she turned to look at the station clock, I saw a tiny bouquet of chrysanthemums in her nape knot. Their detailed perfection of dress and their self-possession amid the staring crowd made me timid.

But when Shun-ko's dark eyes met mine, I was at peace. From that instant there have been no barriers between us. Strong, wise, and true, despite our difference in race she took me into her heart. She had never had a daughter. I had lost my mother four years previously.

We had a week together—seven magic days in which we found ourselves uncannily akin in seriousness and in humor. Too soon her husband reminded her that she must travel on, and an anxious dean reminded me of college routine I had forgotten. When she was on the train, Shun-ko leaned from her compartment window and said: "You must come to me."

Through five years Shun-ko and I wrote to each other frequently. I meant to go, but there are so many entrancing things to capture one's attention. Time passed, and I did not get off.

Then, in the summer of 1920, when my brothers and sisters were all still at boarding school and college, we seven decided to summer where we had not been before. We took an advertised isolated cottage on Lake Erie, near enough to Cleveland to make a journey there and back in one day. I had a desire to see Cleveland.

"I wouldn't think of it," each of my brothers and sisters replied when I suggested the trip.

So I went alone. I lunched at a drugstore counter, reading the third volume of Mr. Giles's *Chinese Dictionary*, which I had taken along for company.

A lady in brown tapped me on the shoulder. When I looked up she smiled and we fell to talking of the readability of dictionaries. I found that she also read them.

Her name was Grace Coppock, and she lived in China. I told her about Shun-ko. She said, "You must come to China." I answered that I hoped to go, but that it was an expensive trip and not possible just now.

She studied me for a bit. Then she said: "It must be made possible. China needs girls like you. I am General Secretary of the YWCA in China. I invite you to come."

I drew back at this and assured her that I had no desire to go anywhere to do people good. She laughed and said no more about it.

We spent the remainder of the day looking at Cleveland together, and she visited the cottage several times that summer. We all enjoyed her, and she declared that she enjoyed us. Through the autumn she wrote to me, and each time she told me that the way was open if I wanted to return with her. She had read and liked all she had been able to collect of my printed verse and stories. Certainly she did not urge me to write anything in China, unless inspired, but she liked to think of me in China, as she thought I belonged there.

I did not go with her. But I went out two months after she sailed—every step of the journey, ticket, passport, and people to look after me at each change en route, arranged by her. She was on the jetty at Shanghai to meet me. After three days of visit there, she put me on the train for Peking in the care of a YWCA secretary traveling north.

So I came to China.

I. ARRIVAL

It was in December 1920, when the waterways of North China were ice-sealed, that I came to the homestead of the Lins on the Grand Canal. Accompanied by her husband, her husband's brother and his wife and daughter, and three serving matrons, Shun-ko journeyed to Peking to welcome and escort me to her dwelling place.

Of the serving matrons—who are called Bald-the-third, Sweet Rain, and Faithful Duck—she presented the first to me, saying, "This is your woman."

We were carried an hour by train and then boarded the Lin family boat with five baskets of provisions. "Enough for two weeks," Shun-ko explained, "because, although this journey usually occupies only one day, it is wisest when traveling to provide so as not to be fretted if there is delay."

The boat was fitted with sledge runners and a sail. But there was no wind, so the sail was folded. There were two compartments. The men took the fore, we women the aft. Snug red mattresses, fur rugs, backrests padded with camel's wool, silk quilts of duck down, and charcoal foot braziers made travel comfortable.

The craft was manned by three boatmen. Each timed his duty by setting an incense stick alight at the boat's stern, and continuing until it burned down. We were propelled forward with a long metal-tipped staff. We left the canal side and turned south on the ice. In a nest of soft furs and gay quilts I was cozy between Shun-ko and her niece, Mai-da.

We kept to the right on the frozen highway. On our left passed a continuous line of boat sledges piled high with country

produce. Crates of chickens, white geese, brown ducks. Demure gray pigeons in wicker hampers. Rabbits contentedly nibbling at greens. Squealing black pigs protesting rancorously. Broad-tailed fat sheep. Heaps of eggs. Bushels of hulled rice. Red corn. Golden millet. Trays of candied red fruit neatly terraced. Pickled mushrooms in salt-crusted tubs.

Packed amid their produce were farmers and their families, en route to town for market day, all dressed in long blue gowns over wadded coats and trousers, their cheeks like hard rosy pippins, their dark eyes sparkling, and their jolly faces quick to smile.

Boys and girls darted through the traffic on small sledge boats, miraculously escaping accident by fractions of an inch. Skaters pursuing earnest errands glided swiftly up and down the frozen highway. With care not to endanger the double-track sledge path, men cut ice, stacked it in flat baskets of twigs, and hung each basket by its handle from a carrying pole. A man at each end of the pole carried the ice to the canal side, where they buried it away for summer use, exactly as explained in the annals of Wei, written thirty centuries ago. All along the frozen road fishermen made round holes and squatted over them with nets.

We slid under frequent stone bridges, some humped so that the name, camelback, by which they are called, is apt. A few were perfect half circles that cast a shadow, when the sun was just right, so that travelers passed through a "good-luck ring."

In passing, the Lins noted the ice level against each bridge. Mai-da's father recorded his findings in a notebook. Shun-ko explained: "Engineers constructed the Grand Canal system. In previous centuries the best engineers of each generation were detailed by the throne to tend it. It is a dragon of enormous strength sprawling through the provinces. So long as we keep it in good health we ride on it peacefully. But when neglected it sweeps out, in time of melting snow or summer rain, devastating fields and cities, taking heavy tribute of human life.

"The canal has been dangerously ignored. Each year of the Republic, our family has reported that there were weakened dikes in our neighborhood. My husband and Mai-da's father have just interviewed the President. They were received politely, but their conclusion is that nothing will be done. According to what they heard in the guildhalls and teahouses, representatives from canal districts in other provinces and from the Yangtze and Yellow River valleys are of the same conclusion."

There was little snow. The country was beige-colored and appeared barren. At intervals there were patches of sparse winter wheat on which cattle pastured. I saw no isolated farmsteads. Worn paths radiated from the fields to walled villages, and connected village with village. The people had built their homes well away from the water. "Because it is wiser to carry water up and to take washing down than to dwell where all sorts of people pass."

The village gates were closed to travelers, Shun-ko explained. For the accommodation of strangers there were inns on the canal side. These served meals, provided sleeping quarters, mangers for beasts, and usually a craftsman to do repairs. The rooms in the two at which we stopped to buy hot water for tea were alive with insects and putrid with the sour sweat of centuries of travelers.

Men and women rode over the paths, straddling wooden saddles perched on the backs of little donkeys. Other folk reclined in comfortable-looking litters swung between shaggy ponies. A few traveled in gaudy sedan chairs carried by four bearers, who cleared lesser folk out of the way shouting: "Lend light! Lend light! An important person would pass!" All lesser folk moved aside. They appeared to enjoy the pageantry as much as I did.

A number of riders sat in mule carts. These had high wooden wheels thickly studded with polished brass nails, and axles that protruded far beyond the cart on each side. Each cart had a cloth-covered cabin, in which the occupants sat crosslegged on a sheepskin-padded floor.

Pedestrians peopled the paths, carrying sometimes a rooster, sometimes a paper image to burn at a family grave; most had shoulder poles loaded with looped-up clouds of threadlike spaghetti or tissue-thin moon cakes of gelatine. Shun-ko told me spaghetti and gelatine were the two staples of the district. The bearers were en route to the town, which has as its chief industry the packing of these products in bright paper containers for sale in the cities.

At a bend in the canal the Weary Pagoda graced our journey. We loitered there to enjoy the music of the wind bells swaying under the pagoda's five-storied eaves. Shun-ko's husband told the pretty legend of the pagoda's trek from beyond a mountain three thousand miles away. The pagoda meant to go to Peking,

but stopped to rest. And, when it saw how the country people were made peaceful at heart by its beauty, it decided to stay, reasoning that the Emperor at the capital had plenty of other pagodas.

As Shun-ko's husband spoke, he leaned forward and by accident brushed two oranges from a basket. The fruit rolled across the path of a tall skater dressed in a claret silk gown and a marten-skin cap. The stranger bent gracefully, picked up the oranges, and returned them with a polite bow. Then he skated on.

Shun-ko murmured something in a stern manner to Mai-da in Chinese—then said in the same tone to me: "Girls of marriageable age are as dangerous to family peace as smuggled salt. Never again, while under my chaperonage, look *at* a man. Direct your gaze modestly to the ground when one is in front of you."

Just before midday we sighted the painted ruby, emerald, and sapphire gate towers of the City of Noonday Rest. At great speed we circled the wall around to the South Gate wharf, where broad stone steps went down under the ice.

We disembarked and climbed the steps to the sunny area between the wharf and the wall, where a merry throng was gathered. Here idle sedan-chair bearers and boatmen loafed. Young girls, carrying kettles of steaming water, soap, soft towels, and blue basins, cried, "Wash your face for a penny!" Barbers trimmed the cropped heads of republicans, or combed the queues of the old-fashioned, or jerked out with tweezers the stray hairs that marred the faces of their beardless countrymen, or cleaned ears with spoon tools. Two letter writers and a fortune-teller, each with an oilpaper umbrella to shade his worktable, brushed letters for "those who have no leisure to write for themselves" and gave advice to the anxious.

Here, too, itinerant cooks had wheeled their portable stoves. The caldrons gave off a delicious steam which whetted my hunger. Thick meat and vegetable soup, piping hot! Crusty golden doughnut twists! Sweet steamed yams! Flaky white rice! Roasted chestnuts! Pork dumplings! Candied apples! Nougat-stuffed dates! Bean curd of rich brownness! As they worked, the cooks advertised the quality of their food with songs and gestures which brought laughter and retorts from the crowd. As each purchaser received his filled bowl, with chopsticks laid across the top, he carried it to the communal stone tables under an ancient evergreen.

Bald-the-third motioned me into the fifth of nine sedan chairs, in which the men led and the serving women came last. The chairs for Shun-ko, her sister-in-law, niece, and me were closed so that we "need not be stared at." Level with my eyes there was an oblong slit covered with brown gauze. Through this I saw that we were carried inside the town, up a steep narrow street along which shop signs swung, and then into a narrow passage between high gray brick walls broken at intervals by tightly closed vermilion gates. One of these was clankingly unchained to Yang-peng's order, and we were put down in the inner courtyard of a quiet posada.

A man in a rich dark blue silk gown met us. He bowed us into a small room, to stools placed around a square rosewood table. We did not give a special order, but had the restaurant's usual "five dishes," which cost one dollar per person. Chicken and walnuts with sour-sweet gravy. Shrimps, mushrooms, and green onions. Cabbage, pork, and bean curd. Noodles, celery, and pigeon eggs. Fish and bamboo soup. Warm rice wine, served in thimble cups to aid digestion. And dishes of salted radishes and red fruit jelly set in the center of the table.

While we ate a soldier came in. He leaned over Shun-ko's husband and examined our food. He stared at me for what seemed a long time. The others took no notice of him but continued intent on their chopsticks and bowls. I tried to do the same.

Finally he laid his gun across the only other table in the room. The soldier had a stupid face and wore ill-fitting garments of coarse cotton, but our elegantly gowned inn host carried food to him with his own delicate hands. The servants who waited on us were called away to help please him, and he was even given our dish of jelly without the Lins seeming to notice his insolence.

He fed quickly, sucking and hiccuping. Having finished, he rose and slapped down a twenty-dollar paper note (which Shun-ko later told me was worthless because printed by a governor who had since gone out of office). Our inn host bowed so that his skirt swept the floor, and told the soldier with soft cadence that he had been the guest of the house for his meal.

The soldier did not return the bow. In a harsh rumble he replied that he did not accept bribes of food, and wanted his change in silver. Then he thrust the note in the host's face.

Our host took the worthless money, deducted one dollar and gave the soldier nineteen silver dollars. The soldier rang each dollar against his bayonet to test the purity of the coin. All rang true. He dropped them into his purse. Then, picking his teeth as he went, he walked out. As he passed, I saw that his cloth shoes were badly torn. He had put newspapers in them to keep his feet warm.

A brazier heated the room. When the noise of the soldier's departure had died away, the innkeeper dropped the twenty-dollar bill and the chopsticks that the soldier had used into the fire. Our meal closed with clean bowls of steaming rice and fragrant tea made in a squat brown pot. Shun-ko explained that all good restaurants and careful homes have teapots for different needs. Our inn host, who had never seen a Western girl before, had asked about me. When he learned that I was to visit in the Lin homestead, he suggested tea from "the pot which prevents misunderstanding."

We were carried back to the boat. For a time fields and frozen highway were occupied as before. Then we crossed paths with a sledge boat overcrowded with soldiers and propelled by a frightened boatman.

Farther on we saw another boat commandeered by half a dozen young boys and an officer. They pushed an old farmer and his "lily foot" wife about ruthlessly, scattering their produce over the ice. One lad speared the old lady's brown rooster with his bayonet and held him high while the others applauded. When she struggled to help the dying bird, the officer clouted her on the head. Half a mile on, we heard a shot and saw a child fall—she had been reluctant to give up the donkey hitched to the mill where she was grinding flour. The soldier who shot her led the donkey down to the canal for sledge transport to "the war."

The Lins conferred in low voices with their boatmen and we turned down a branch of the canal to detour trouble. The fields we now passed were deserted. We met no one on the way to the hamlet where the uncle of one of the Lin boatmen lived. The boatman went in to borrow a cart to take us overland to the Lin homestead. He returned weeping. Five boys from the hamlet, one of them his uncle's only son, had been taken to be made soldiers. All were between the ages of twelve and fourteen.

It was impossible here, or at four further villages, to secure assistance. The people were occupied with their own affairs. There had been no soldiers in the district for five months. This foraging raid had come as a surprise, when the gates were open and folk scattered. They had lost carts, animals, food, winter clothing, and all their sons between the ages of twelve and sixteen—excepting those who had been quickly hidden. One village elder had parleyed with the soldiers while three boys had been dropped in a bucket to a niche in the well wall prepared for such emergencies, and the bucket left to swing empty.

"The soldiers passed too quickly," villagers said. "This was but a survey and they will return in larger numbers." So they were busy tightening walls and gates, taking their saddles, sedan chairs, and carts apart to hide the pieces separately, driving their cattle in, and sharpening knives and tools as weapons.

Our party agreed that we were safest to keep off the main canal. We could not walk, as Shun-ko, Mai-da's mother, and the serving matrons had lily feet. We sledged devious ways. I saw plentiful supplies of hot food set in caldrons before each barred village gate. Twice we saw soldiers feeding on this "peace rice."

It was night when we came to the Lin homestead city. The gates are sealed at sunset. The city wall, thick enough for nine horses to trot abreast on it, rises from the canal. A boatman beat against the heavy gate. Finally the gateman was roused, but he refused to open the gates before sunrise. He acknowledged that he knew all the persons who had gone to Peking to meet the foreigner. And the voices were like the voices of these Lins. Yet he could not open until the appointed time.

After much parley, the gateman's son was dispatched to the Lin homestead. We waited a weary while until at last someone hailed us from within the gate. The eldest among us replied. There was another call. The next eldest replied. So on, through all our number. Lastly Shun-ko told me to shout my name. The gate creaked open. We walked in. The man from the homestead who had identified us by voice closed the gate again. He secured its locks and pasted a fresh strip of paper over the paper he had broken, across the crevice where the two halves of the gate meet. On the fresh paper he brushed his name with black ink.

He had brought sedan chairs. In them, we followed him up steep narrow streets and then down a broader street to a scarlet gate in which a peephole was slid open at the sound of our coming. Camel-back, the gateman, opened the To and From the World Gate, bowing and smiling his joy in the family's safe return from the perils of travel. Massed behind him were Lins, young and old. I stood forgotten as my escorts were welcomed home. *"Chia ho fu tzu shêng,"* they said again and again, a sentence which I now know means, "Happiness springs up of itself in a united family."

Thus I entered the Lin homestead, on the Grand Canal, in Hopei Province, North China—which was once named in derision, and is now called in affection, the House of Exile.

II. THE HOUSE OF EXILE

FROM THE MOMENT of my arrival in China it was as though, like Alice, I had stepped through a looking glass into another world. The world I left behind became a dim, fantastic dream. Only this into which I entered seemed real.

"Glazed brick, white mortar, and blue roof tiles do not make a house beautiful; carved rosewood, gold cloth, and clear green jade do not furnish a house with grace; a man of cultivated mind makes a house of mud and wattle beautiful; a woman, even with a pockmarked face, if refined of heart, fills a house with grace," is a literal translation of the carving on the first stone laid in the building of the Lin homestead.

The Lins dwell in single-room houses, built about a square paved courtyard. The roofs extend over the pillared verandas, so that one can get into a sedan chair in rainy weather without exposure to wet; and, after their utilitarian duty is done, tilt upward in easy curves, displaying fairy scenes and fabulous creatures painted gayly under the eaves.

To go from one room to another in the homestead one must always cross a courtyard. The houses have doors and windows only on the side opening into the court to which they belong. The homestead is composed of sufficient courts to house comfortably the family, who are eighty-three men, women, and children at the time of this writing.

The courtyards are connected by gateways in the walls, each cut in the shape of a flower, a fan, a vase, or a full moon. The courts cluster around the Hall of Ancestors, which shelters the life tablets of twenty-nine generations of Lins and their wives who have "plucked the flower of life."

A protective wall, six feet thick and four times a man's height, surrounds the homestead. The homestead neither overlooks nor is overlooked by its neighbors. From the many times higher city wall above it, only the flamboyant roofs can be seen through the trees; or occasionally, before the poplars come into leaf, the flutter of a bright silk gown as someone walks along the path to the summerhouse by the lotus pond. The Gate of Compassion, a small window cut in the north wall, where charity is given to the needy, and the To and From the World Gate, large enough for a horse and carriage to be driven into the entrance court, are the only openings connecting with the outside world.

The view in through the Gate of Compassion is closed by a shrine which holds a portrait of the Goddess of Mercy. The view in at the To and From the World Gate is closed by a screen of porcelain tiles twice as wide as the gate and as high as the homestead wall. On it a gorgeous green dragon writhes over a blue sea after a scarlet ball of life.

The people of Hopei speak of the Lin family as the Kwangtung Lins. The Lins in Canton speak of the Lins in the House of Exile as "temporarily from home." But Lin Fu-yi, founder of the House of Exile, came from Canton, of Kwangtung province, six and a half centuries ago. He was eighteen when the command came for him to extend the Imperial Grand Canal northward for the Mongol Emperor. He had made a name for himself by building a new kind of lock in a local waterway. Since he was the only son of a father who had "plucked the flower of life," his departure was delayed, by the Emperor's permission, to permit the consummation of his betrothal, and extended until it was certain that his bride had conceived.

Then he traveled up to the Imperial Grand Canal to find Sun Hung-shen, the engineer under whom he was to work. He fell in love at sight with Sun's daughter. Sun Li-la, at fourteen, should have been safely hidden in the Springtime Bower of her parents' homestead. But she was only three when her father, drafted north, had taken her along to soften his exile. The years had enlarged his affection for her; so he evaded his wife's written demands that he should send their daughter home.

When Lin Fu-yi's bride delivered a girl, a request submitted to the governor of Canton by the Lin family resulted in an order dispatching Lin Fu-yi to his parental homestead. Twice in six years he made this journey, siring a second daughter and a son.

The country was prosperous. Over the Imperial Grand Canal passed the riches of the empire en route to the capital. In addition to sending his homestead elders sufficient to satisfy them, Fu-yi built his dwelling, the Three Eastern Courtyards, and put aside a small fortune by the time Li-la was twenty. Then, although Fu-yi could not make her his wife, she climbed over the wall of her father's dwelling and entered the courts that her lover had made for her as a green-skirt mate, or concubine. Fu-yi never went south again. Sixty years later his clan claimed his body after death.

Fu-yi has two life tablets. The one in the Lin homestead at

Canton records an unfilial son. The one in Hopei stands in the shrine Li-la designed for it at the place of first honor in the Hall of Ancestors of the House of Exile.

"Man and woman in perfect harmony are like the music of the harp and lute" is what Shun-ko, who told me the story of the founding of the House of Exile, said.

Li-la's union with Lin Fu-yi was blessed with a son, a daughter, and a son. When the son born to Fu-yi's wife died, his aged grandfather made the difficult journey north and pleaded with his grandson to come home once more. Fu-yi turned the old man away with the gruff answer that he would sire no more children except with Li-la. Li-la, in compassion, quieted the old grandfather's sorrow by giving him her firstborn son, then her only son, to complete the line of succession. The daughter married a Wong, of the next-door neighbors. The passage through the division wall, still in daily use between the two households, was cut so that she could visit her parents without ceremony of departure by the To and From the World Gate. It is called Mai-lin's Walk.

On completion of the system of canals uniting the kingdom, Fu-yi was appointed supervisor of the transportation of tribute rice. When he retired, his second son (who had brought the joy of seven grandsons to the House of Exile and for whom the Sons' Courtyards were built) slid into his place. When he retired, *his* son came into his place. The phrase "in control of canal improvements" was added to the original title with the vermilion pencil before the post was passed to *his* son. Thus, in four generations, the House of Exile was firmly established.

The records in the ancestral hall show that the loyalty of the descendants of Li-la and Fu-yi has always been to the Imperial Grand Canal. Each new emperor accepted this inland waterway as the most valuable of China's assets. The records of the Lins show them not only intelligent in canal improvement and management but also astute in adapting themselves to conditions in national government. The Lins received grants for the use of land, tax free, as early as the Yuan dynasty, and they have tilled the same fields through the centuries. As they have need for more dwelling space, they add to the original

Three Eastern Courtyards. The library was built, and the collection of ancient manuscripts begun, by the fifth son of Fu-yi's second son. He won distinction for the House by securing first place at the imperial examinations when, in 1315, the Emperor restored the system of appointing the nation's governors from the nation's scholars.

"Better establish a branch than cut off a line" was chiseled over the front gate by his brother's grandson. He did not come into power as Elder of the household until he was eighty years of age. Yet he established the custom of consultation in family matters by journeying to Canton to confer with the Elder of the southern homestead. He brought back a four-year-old Cantonese bride for his favorite great-grandson, who was then a child of five.

This couple are remembered as ideally happy. It is now the custom when a Lin daughter marries to say, "May you be as happy as the maid from Canton." The azalea terraces in the Springtime Bower were planted by a Lin who was a magistrate. The schoolroom court was added by Lin Shih-mo, who disliked children at lessons in the library. The Garden of Children, with its shallow sand pool, was designed by his son, who was a merchant.

The main garden was begun by Lin Wu-lin. He collected rocks, made pools, built pavilions, and planted bamboos to give his mother pleasure. It was then enlarged by his great-nephew so that his wife, a poetess, could have a private place for meditation. The Poet's Retreat is separated from the rest of the garden by a hedge of dwarf pines. Although it is encompassed within a surprisingly small space, he so carved the land that the perspective is seemingly one of many miles, as the winding path goes by a tumbling waterfall, climbs through mountain foliage, penetrates a forest, comes out at a teahouse by a lake where lilies blow, follows a lazy river through a grassy field, and ends at a rustic cottage where all his wife's verses are treasured in a pretty inlaid chest.

The courtyard named the Place of the Meeting of Winged Friends was constructed by a Lin wife who loved birds. She carved the feeding boards where rice is scattered, made the baskets which hold suet in zero weather and stuffs for nest-making in mating season, and designed the lovely sand-and-water baths.

In such ways the homestead has grown, and so it continues to grow. The high gray wall is stretched out to surround whatever land can be secured as more space is needed.

And as in homes in all parts of the world where a family have

dwelled for many generations, legends and beliefs have collected about the House of Exile. When two gray doves perch silently on the roof of the Hall of Ancestors, the Lins expect the immediate death of a family member. When two gray doves moan in the maidenhair tree in the Three Eastern Courtyards, they abandon any marriage contemplated for a son or a daughter, even if the daughter has already left the homestead in her bridal chair, or the son's betrothed has been welcomed over the "apple of peace."

III. INSIDE THE ORCHID DOOR

THE NIGHT OF MY ARRIVAL at the House of Exile, Bald-the-third set up a screen and pushed me behind it to undress. She took each garment as I removed it, examined it, then passed it on to Faithful Duck for examination, and thence to Mai-da, who was undressing behind a similar screen.

Mai-da pantomimed my death from cold and cuddled down in a nest of quilts on the brick bed. Bald-the-third and Faithful Duck brought an earthen jar of a size that I could sit in. They filled it with hot water and pushed it behind my screen. Bald came and poured in hotter water until the bunch of herbs that she had added floated just under my chin.

I was terribly sleepy, but she kept me soaking until Faithful Duck brought supper. Then I dried on warm towels and was folded up in quilts on one side of the brick bed. A six-inch-legged table was set between Mai-da's nest and mine. Our supper was served on it.

First two lovely robin's-egg blue bowls and two pairs of ivory chopsticks with silver handles were laid; then three steaming covered dishes. These contained breasts of chicken, red cabbage and green pepper, and tenderloin of pork with chestnuts—each cooked in a delicious sauce. When we had eaten, I managing as best I could with my chopsticks, Bald-the-third took the dishes away.

Faithful Duck then brought a covered tureen of fish soup. We ladled the soup into bowls and ate it with porcelain spoons. It was good, and, having a spoon, I got more of it than of the previous dishes.

The soup was taken away and steamed rice brought in transparent white bowls. We had chopsticks to eat with. I did not manage to convey much to my mouth. Mai-da and the serving matrons laughed merrily at my attempts. We finished with hard white winter pears and cups of jasmine tea served without milk or sugar.

After the meal we were given hot towels to wipe our faces and hands. Bald-the-third thrust more cornstalks into the fire in the stomach of the bed and snuffed the candles. On the merry music of crackling flames I went to sleep.

I woke to the homely sound of cocks' crowing. The sun shone on my face. Mai-da was asleep. Bald-the-third came in with cups of hot rice water. She wakened Mai-da. We drank, then washed and dressed.

My clothes were gone. Two lacquer chests stood side by side against the wall under the windows. Mai-da, who then spoke no English and has always stubbornly refused to learn any since, made me understand by gesture that one was hers and one mine. The serving matrons took identical outfits from the chests for us to put on.

Following Mai-da's lead, I wound myself from armpits to hip joints with flesh-colored silk, then put on pajamas of peach silk. These had trousers that wrapped over in pleats in back and front. Over the pajamas, I put on a second suit of heliotrope satin lined with white rabbit fur.

Next I pulled on white socks, tucked the legs of the two pairs of trousers neatly into them, and wrapped my ankles in puttees of apple-green satin. After this I had a third pajama suit fashioned exactly as the first two, of wine-red brocade, warmed with a lining of gray squirrel fur. I felt so stiff in all my garments that I was glad to let Bald-the-third put on my black velvet boots lined with red fox.

Shun-ko came. She explained that my clothes were put away because they were not suitable in the House of Exile. She pulled out my hairpins, saying that my hair had best be dressed like Mai-da's. Otherwise it would cause comment, since a girl does not pin up her hair in China until she is married. It was gummed smooth, parted in the middle, pulled back behind my ears, braided into a pigtail that swung to my knees. Bald-the-third wanted to dye my hair black, as it is the color of the yellow gentian of misfortune. But Shun-ko reminded her that yellow is also the color of the innermost petals of the sacred lotus. So Bald was content, and took satisfaction in my hands, which she discovered measure exactly as Shun-ko's. But when she found that my ears had not been pierced and I could not wear the sapphire earrings provided to match Mai-da's, her depression was pitiful.

Mai-da handed me a sleeveless blue jacket lined with beaver and I put it on. We took leave of Mai-da and went to Shun-ko's dwelling, which is in the Court of the White Jade Rabbit—so called because the legend of the jade rabbit is told on the eaves of the four houses that open into the court.

En route, Shun-ko stopped to explain a long burning spiral:

"This is the Time Stick.* Camel-back, our gateman, makes it each day of sawdust and clay and lights it. His fathers for eleven generations have measured time for the Lins. His young grandson proved last spring, when the old man was sick, that he has inherited the gift. They take the time from the sky and their own intuition. We regulate our Western-made watches by our Time Stick, and we amuse ourselves by setting them when we

---

* The carved divisions on the Time Stick represent the hours: twelve in one day. Two hours of foreign time correspond to one of Chinese time. The hours are named: rat, ox, tiger, hare, dragon, snake, horse, sheep, monkey, cock, dog, and pig. Usually candle dips are extinguished and we sleep (all but Camel-back, who carries his lantern through the courts sounding his "I am here, robbers!" rattle during the hours of the night) from the Hour of the Pig to the rising Hour of the Dragon. Then, after rice water and sweet cakes, the children go to their studies, women to the household tasks, and men to their duties, until a gong announces the morning meal in the Hour of the Snake. The afternoons pass according to age, necessity, and inclination until the evening meal in the Hour of the Cock.

start to Peking so that we can compare them with the big Western clock there. We have never found it more than a quarter of an hour wrong!"

As in Mai-da's house, Shun-ko's dwelling has a brick bed which is built across the back of the room and touches three walls. It is used as a sofa in the daytime, when the folded quilts are stacked at one side in bright layers of scarlet, gold, leaf green, lavender, and sapphire.

We removed our shoes and outer jackets before sitting, with our feet tucked under us, on Shun-ko's bed. She gave me a small mortar and pestle and set me to pounding paint for her to use on the charts she was preparing. This is an annual record kept as a help with garden and farm work. Shun-ko drew a plum tree. She gave it nine branches and each of the branches nine twigs. Then she mixed the pigments on her palette with a thin, round knife, selected her brushes, and shaded the trunk and the branches realistically. She compounded color for leaf buds of brown, green, and silver, and added a generous number to the sketch. After the winter solstice she would paint one blossom each day, according to the weather.

A pair of cabinets carved with garden and farm scenes stood against the wall. Shun-ko opened one and took out fifty silk scrolls. A plum tree with eighty-one blossoms was painted on each of the scrolls. But no two trees were alike.

Shun-ko taught me how to read these pictures, so as to know whether a day had been cold or mild, cloudy or fair, windy or still, rainy or snowy, by the way the paint had been put on the petals of a blossom. It is the custom for the wife resident in the Second House of the White Rabbit to keep these records, started twenty-two generations ago by the wife for whom this house was designed.

While we cleaned the brushes with evil-smelling kerosene, Shun-ko told me how my place in the House of Exile had been decided.

"Each dwelling place here is inherited by a person entering the family by birth or marriage in accord with customs that have grown into the family regulations with the generations. There is no precedent in our knowledge for the entrance of an unmarried woman, without the chaperonage of her mother, as a guest in a Chinese homestead. You are the first foreigner to enter our To and From the World Gate.

"I am responsible both for your conduct and safety. I prefer to be a mother to you than a friend. As my daughter, your place is in the most carefully guarded court of the homestead—the Springtime Bower. This is the only safe place, in a Chinese

homestead, for a maiden of marriageable age. But the Springtime Bower in this house is inadequate for a family of this size. It has only three houses. The twins, Ching-mei and La-mei, share the first. The second belongs to Su-ling. She is studying in France, but her room could not even be borrowed. The rule in the House of Exile is that each daughter's house is absolutely hers until she acquires, by marriage, a house in another homestead. The third house is Mai-da's, although, but for the slackness of the Elder, she would have been married last Lotus Moon. So we puzzled for two moons about where to put you.

"You had given me the year, month, day, and hour of your birth in a letter, so that I could have a horoscope cast for you, and they were identical with Mai-da's. As Mai-da was willing to have the test made, the Elder wrote your name and hers on a slip of red paper and put it on the altar in the Circle of Ancestors. It lay there for three days, during which tranquil weather and fortune in the repayment of a loan were taken as omens of a peaceful double domicile. Mai-da prepared to share her house with you."

Next, Shun-ko drew for my guidance a list of the living generations of the family. She wrote in the names according to English sound, and left space below each for me to add phrases to aid me in remembering who was who.

After this she drew a map of the homestead to aid me to find my way about. As she worked, she explained, "The general plan of all Chinese homes is the same as this, whether of one court or one hundred. This is sensible. One knows on entering a homestead which way to go to find the books, the garden, the abode of the Oven God, or the residence of the family Elder."

Mai-da's mother joined us. We lunched together, waited on by her Swift Needle, Shun-ko's Sweet Rain, and my Bald-the-third. When the meal ended, the women fussed nervously over my appearance. They added cuffs to my coat, re-combed my hair, plucked my eyebrows to a high thin arch, rouged my mouth and the lobes of my ears, and perfumed the palms of my hands.

Shun-ko put on ceremonial garments. She adorned herself with pearl earrings, pearl hair ornaments, pearl coat buttons. She rubbed her polished nails to a high pink gloss. Then she turned her attention to my appearance again, worrying, until at last Mai-da's mother teasingly placed my hand in Shun-ko's and pushed us out to the round of visits which Shun-ko dreaded.

We went first to the Garden of Children. There nine little boys and girls received us. Shun-yi, who was ten and had an intelligent face, rose from a game of chess which he was playing with his sister. He took her left hand and the right hand of their half brother, Wen-wu, and all bowed together. A chubby lad, Tsai-fu, thrust a shuttlecock into the pocket of his long turquoise gown and bent so that his forehead tapped the playroom floor. Nan-wei, slim and graceful, assisted by her cousin Mai-lei—a maid of five summers—gave us jasmine tea and saw to it that the boys passed the salted watermelon seeds frequently.

Next we went to the court adjoining the Springtime Bower and called on capable Shou-su and shy Li-niang. In the bower the lovely twins, Ching-mei and La-mei, and my house partner Mai-da, greeted us with formal ceremony. Following Shun-ko's example, I soon learned that when a hostess lifts her teacup to her lips the polite moment to say farewell has arrived, and that one should then go, no matter how much the hostess begs one to stay.

Li-la, the first mother of the House of Exile, was a green-skirt mate. So in the courtyards of the mates of Lin sons, Shun-ko was careful to stay as long in the dwellings of green skirts as in the houses of wives. We visited first with the fourth generation, who live in courts called the Favorite Eaves of Nesting Swallows.

Young Sung-li fulfilled the rites of courtesy in the first house, but made me feel uncomfortable. She is antiforeign, with bitter memories of the invasion of her father's house by Western soldiers in 1900, when she saw her mother raped.

Ah-chiao, a bride of a year, and Sou-mai, a bride of a month, both asked Shun-ko to tell me I must not be troubled by whatever reception Sung-li had given me. They wanted me to excuse her because she cannot forget what her parents suffered and so thinks it dangerous to have invited me into the homestead.

We called next on the women of the third generation. Mai-da's mother, who shares the court with Shun-ko and Fu-erh, is a student and needs a study, so has two houses. Fu-erh has made her house into a comfortable, homey dwelling place. She is a timid wife, afraid to live away from the family homestead, and chose the daughter of a neighbor to accompany her husband to Malay, where he is the manager of the family interests.

In the Court of the Goldfish the lake was frozen over. Yu-lin and Chu-kang showed me the fish moving sluggishly about in wooden tubs in a heated paper house, where they rest all winter. They all had descriptive names. Looking up to Heaven was a variety with large eyes in the top of the head. Gray Chiffon Veil had a filmy fin. Silver Arrow was slim-bodied, with a broad head. There were seventy-two pairs in all.

The visits to this generation were completed with calls in the Court of the Ginkgo Trees—one on Mei-lui, the first Wong mother who did not break her daughter's feet to the golden-lily fashion.

We went then to the mates of the second generation. In the dower court, Within the Orchid Door, the widows of the Elder's first son gave us tea, seasoned by wrapping it in lotus petals, and tiny doughnuts stuffed with chestnuts.

In the Court of the Son's Wife, the only mate of the financial head of the family showed me snapshots of the school she runs for the village poor.

In the Court of the Meeting Place of Winged Friends, I exchanged smiles with Fan-li, the woman versed in folklore; with Mi-ying, whose mating with the Elder's fourth son gave the family a wizard in money accumulation and in growing chrysanthemums; and with Kang-nen, the widow of the Elder's fifth son, who is deeply concerned over the stabilization of the Chinese Republic, for which cause her husband gave his life on the battlefield in 1911.

Shun-ko explained the Elder's sixth son to me as we walked to the courts of his mates, which are called the New Courts. In babyhood Wen-lieh selected military toys from the peddlers, and demanded that the candymakers make warriors. He was educated at home and in the School for Military Officers in Japan, from which he graduated with distinction. Since then he has been occupied with a war to end war in China. He is wise in politics and gentle to women. He has married seven times.

When the Elder said that he should be careful not to take up more space in the homestead than rightfully belonged to a sixth son, he received the hint with good nature. He bought land which touched on the boundary wall of the House of Exile, which was built out to embrace it. Then it was divided into seven spacious courts. A poetic name was set in colored pebbles over each court gate. As the winter violets came into bloom, he asked Hua-li to make him seven bouquets. He put one of the seven court names in each of the bouquets and asked his mother to give each of his mates one. Thus there was no favoritism in deciding who should have a particular court. This done, he gave each woman the same generous purse to build whatever house she desired and went off to his army.

In the New Courts, each of Wen-lieh's seven mates received me kindly in her house. But even on that first day I knew that Nuan, whom her husband had rescued from the Manchu massacre at Nanking, was drawn to me, as I was to her, by that mutual esteem which is called friendship.

"The first generation will not receive you in their residences in the Three Eastern Courtyards, but in the guest hall of the Court of Dignity," Shun-ko said, and took me back to her house.

There she anxiously retidied me, and rehearsed me for this audience. When she was satisfied that I could bow "like a bamboo sapling swept by the wind," that I understood how to take the cup of tea that would be offered to me in both hands and to offer it back as though I felt myself unworthy to drink in such company, then when the tea had been pressed upon me three times to walk backward, in "flowerlike modesty," and seat myself in the most lowly place, "the chair by the table nearest the door," she made me warm myself by the charcoal brazier and we started out again.

The Court of Dignity had slippery ice frozen over the paving stones. We had to walk with care and help each other. As we approached the guest hall, blue-clad serving women opened the velvet door. The front of this hall is of carved openwork rosewood picturing historical legends, just as in the West it is the custom to picture Biblical stories in stained glass in churches. The carvings are set off by gold paper placed between the two surfaces of the wood, which are identical whether viewed from the court or from inside the hall.

The hall occupies one entire side of the court and its depth takes the space of an additional court. It is beamed with dark rafters, on the sides of which brilliantly colored scenes from the lives of Lin men and women are painted. A portrait of Confucius hangs on the north wall, and on either side of it are gilt scrolls on which are written two of his analects. Portraits of the founders of the house, and of other ancestors dressed in rich silk robes, decorate the east and west walls. The floor is of gray tile.

The furniture is of heavy black polished wood. There are small tables, straight-back chairs, and stiff settees, so arranged that Chinese people know exactly which seat is in what grade of honor.

The only heat to combat the winter chill of the hall came from one small brazier in the center of the floor. Each of the First Ladies of the homestead had a tiny charcoal-filled hand warmer, but it would not have been polite for Shun-ko and me to have so warmed our hands.

The three ladies sat stiffly erect, not touching the backs of their chairs. Kuei-tzu, the wife of the Elder, was directly under the portrait of the first mother of the homestead. She is small and delicately made. Her face is marked by surprisingly few wrinkles. Her eyes are two bright black crystals. Her hands taper and are very white. She wore a black brocade gown with hairpin, earrings, and dress buttons set with large diamonds.

The Elder's second mate sat to the left. She is five feet nine inches. She has a dry yellow skin stretched over her gaunt frame. She drops her black hair in waxed wings over her ears in defiance of fashion. She heightens her high cheekbones with carmine, paints her thin lips, and plucks her eyebrows out and draws in thick eyebrows with a black pencil. That afternoon she was

in green taffeta and had scarlet shoes. She scared me in our first exchange of glances. I stayed scared for many years.

The widow of the Elder's brother sat in a chair to the right. She wore a gray cotton gown and the white cord of mourning in her hair. Her wrinkled face is sweet and sad. She is blind to earthly things, but gifted with sight into the future.

I made my three bamboo-sapling bows to each lady. I took the cup of tea and then refused it. When it had been pressed upon me three times, I did my best to walk modestly backward to the chair nearest the door.

This over, the First Lady spoke to me, and Shun-ko changed her sounds into English. I replied in English. The First Lady then made sounds like ice tinkling in a glass. Shun-ko told me to bow my head and withdraw. I was dismissed. Kuei-tzu, Lady of First Authority in the House of Exile, had commanded that I was not to be presented again until I was sufficiently civilized to hear and speak for myself, and that no member of the family was ever to speak with me in any language except Chinese.

Shun-ko took me back to Mai-da's house. Mai-da dropped the lid of her chest as we entered and busied herself with the embroidery of a shoe. Shun-ko left us.

Mai-da barred our door on her departure. With pretty grimaces and signs she dramatized herself and me against all others. Then she put her embroidery away and took out the work she had thrust into her chest on hearing our footsteps. While I entered the day's activities in my journal, she finished an excellent likeness of the tall skater who had picked up our oranges on the way from Peking.

Originally it had been arranged that the announcement of my arrival in the House of Exile would be made to the ancestors on the evening of the same day as my introduction to the family. But the First Lady's dismissal postponed this for a considerable time.

Eventually my ear and tongue were sufficiently well trained for Shun-ko to present me for examination. Then the Hall of Ancestors was swept. Laurel incense was bought. The family gathered under the "lamp of continuous life" within the circle of tablets of the Lin generations who have gathered the flower of life. The Elder announced my arrival and explained how I had been invited. As instructed, I lit three tapers before the tablets of the founders, three tapers before the tablets of each of the men and women whose earthly lives are woven into the homestead pattern, nine candles to the memory of Lin Yan-ken, and nine candles before a tablet to the memory of J. S. Waln.

IV. THE FARMER'S CALENDAR

TIME IN CHINA has no immediacy as in America. Here I find the swift passage of our few earthly years accepted as naturally as the fall of a leaf. This philosophical acceptance of the individual life as just a part of the life of the race, which goes on as the life of the tree goes on, makes time limitless. A century past or a century in the future is not considered far off.

I hear and speak a language in which grammar has no tense. Both scholars and illiterates in daily speech tell an event of centuries ago as casually as an incident of the hour. Only as my knowledge has accumulated have I been able to know whether something related happened just then or in some past dynasty. Even now I often do not know.

"Events," a ricksha runner explained as he pulled me to market one day, "are not put away in books. That would not be fair. Only a few have leisure to read, and history belongs to everyone. It becomes a part of everyone's experience to use when needed. That which happened is not past. It is all a part of our now."

I have always had difficulty in keeping any schedule. Consequently I slipped more unconsciously into time's easy flow in China than one of different temperament might have. Weeks and months glided smoothly by in the cycle of seasons, from which serenity we were occasionally summoned by the special festivals.

With the three-day fast of Li Chun, men prepare to welcome the spring. On the last day of the fast, Kuei-tzu, Lady of First Authority, summoned all the maidens, including me, to the Court of Sunrise. We found her seated in a wicker chair with her back to a sun-warmed wall. And we promptly knelt as "flowers bent by the nourishing rain," which is the name of the salute due from daughters to the home mother. She had called us to make the things ready for the Welcome to Spring Procession.

The procession torches are by tradition lit with fire drawn from the sun with a concave mirror. Seeds of each crop the House intends to plant have to be carried in the procession. At the proper time in the ceremony this seed would be watered with dew. The family Elder had set metallic plates on pedestals in the center of the court. These had already drawn a plentiful supply of dew, which was now transferred to a white jade bottle.

A craftsman brought a life-sized papier-mâché water buffalo and driver. Camel-back wheeled in a barrow filled with willow whips. Each farmer in the procession must have a whip to beat the buffalo in the chase that drives winter away.

I had to dust the drum used to call the patrons of the soil. One beat calls the spirits from the water. They come easily. It takes three loud raps to waken the sluggish spirits that dwell on the seashore. The spirits of the field, who are busy folk, will not come for less than four. The spirits that live in the sky are proud: they wait until they have been called by six beats. The spirits of the mountain—the most important—are given seven beats. They make harmony between man and nature. When they are stubborn, farming is not successful.

Kuei-tzu does not trust maidens under her protection to join in any procession which includes men—except that procession which goes direct to the bridegroom's door. So on the holiday morning, when the wives and girl children went to join in the Welcome to Spring Procession, we maids of marriageable age were left inside the homestead. Kuei-tzu locked the To and From the World Gate with the special key she uses for such occasions.

Folk go to meet the spring in their winter clothes. They change to the pastel silks worn during spring when they return home. It is the maidens' duty to take them from the chests; also to finish the preparation of the feast.

The other girls had all ridden in the procession each year until puberty. As we sat on top of the Wall of Heaven, with our arms about each other's waists, Mai-da said that I must hurry to marry so that I might have a wife's right to ride in it.

When the family returned, the young wives made me envious, chatting elatedly about how they had joined the tenant-farmer families at the Temple of Agriculture, watched the Elder draw fire from the sun, admired the young farmers who whipped the buffalo into the chase, watched the seed poured on the earth altar and moistened with dew from the white jade bottle, clapped hands to the drumbeats that summoned the patrons of the soil, joined in the glad chorus when the singers announced that spring had arrived, and enjoyed the Elder's oration, a combination of welcome to spring and prudent advice to the farmers.

When we had all changed into spring dress, Camel-back played a flute through the courts, calling the family to feast together in the Hall of Family Gathering. The Lady of First Authority presided. The Elder left to preside over a feast in the Cantonese guildhall. By their invitations to the spring feast at the guildhall, the House of Exile signify that they are content to continue a farmer's lease. By breaking his fast at this table, the tenant signifies that he is content to continue to farm the land he farmed last year.

DURING THIS SEASON the Elder explained land to the homestead children and the brides of the year in the library court. I was told to attend.

From the beginning of history—that is, for about forty-six

centuries—there has been no freehold ownership of land. The government in power holds the earth in trusteeship for the populace. There is no historic mention of the granting of large tracts in return for feudal services; but there is frequent mention of idle families, even emperors, forced to give up for cultivation arable soil that they have walled in as private parks.

Since a country is indeed weak which cannot produce its own

food, agriculture in China has been accorded first place among the branches of labor since time immemorial. The government must give a lease, or "red card," to one who is willing to cultivate any idle piece of land. The holder of a red card can sell his lease to another farmer, but the land still belongs to the government. It does not matter how many times the red card has changed hands or whether the government that issued it went out of office centuries ago. If the government in power decides, for the general good of the populace, to put up a building, cut a canal, make a broad highway, or change the course of a river, they have the right to call for the land. They can sweep homesteads and crops out of the way. The deed holder has no right to indemnity.

Yet such disaster does not descend on one family in every thousand twice in a hundred generations. Land in China produces the major revenue which makes it possible for governments to function. So land is dealt with carefully. Governments have always been cautious about committing acts which would frighten folk away from land. Instead they have so fostered land that if a family makes some profit in trade or office, land is always considered the wisest investment; even though under the most careful husbandry it brings in only an average of from three to four percent interest.

Since property in China is almost always held by a family and not by an individual, the title to possession is not disturbed by the death of an individual. A change in the family does not concern the government so long as the House continues to pay taxes at the time of demand.

Unoccupied land, whether originally waste, or abandoned through famine, war, or neglect—even graves become wasteland if not swept annually—may be acquired by planting a crop in it and making application to the government for a red card. They can see by the planted seed that the applicant is a farmer and not a land speculator. The government must then issue a call to the last cultivators to come and do the work of the season. If they do not respond, the new applicant must be given a red card. He in turn must produce a harvest. If he fails to grow crops, then he can be ousted by another farmer who can.

The holder of every red card pays the government a tax on his harvests. This amount varies with fertility of the soil, and the ease with which it can be tilled, and the custom that has maintained in that field. When rough or poor land is first brought into cultivation, it is usual for governments to allow the farmer time for a return on capital expended before assessment, as it is to the interest of the government to induce people to till the soil.

Wasteland which no one can be induced to farm belongs to the inhabitants of the nearest village, in common, until such time as someone will bring it into cultivation. There can be no private possession without annual sowing and reaping. Anyone can pasture goats, trap or hunt rabbits, pheasants, geese, and duck, or cut firewood on any unplowed land. The selling of game and firewood from such common land is the only livelihood of some poor people in every settlement.

When a flood washes away land under cultivation, the farmer is entitled to follow his soil. When more than one farm has been moved, the new formation must be divided among the claimants in a ratio proportional to their loss. If there are no claimants for such land, which is often carried hundreds of miles, the first person to plant a crop in it has the right to a red card.

The House of Exile is the second largest landowner of its district. It possesses title to 1,543 acres, made up of small holdings, some as small as one-sixth of an acre, scattered over an area which is dotted by the holdings of others.

The Lins farm ten acres, called the Home Farm. The rest is divided among six hundred tenant farmers. The largest lessee farms three acres; the smallest one-eighth of an acre. The tenant rights are for no settled time, but "at will"—meaning the will of both parties. The longest lease in the Lins' possession has been renewed with one family for thirty generations. The tenants do not dwell on the farms. They live in the same city as the Lin family or in one of the two villages farther up the canal.

Under Lin management the tenant provides the farm implements and the animal or man power—also the seeds, except in special cases where they prefer to control the seed. The House of Exile pays all government taxes, provides the material for extension or repair of the irrigation system, and names the principal crop to be grown, as the family is concerned with producing that for which there is a good market and in keeping up the fertility of the soil.

In addition to the principal crop, most tenants can and do produce subsidiary crops, which belong entirely to the tenant, but they must not encroach upon the principal crop.

The rent is a proportion of the principal crop only. If the

agreed crop is fruit or vegetables, it is gathered by the tenant and divided in the village marketplace. If it is grain, it is threshed on the village threshing floor by the labor of the tenant, in the presence of a Lin who superintends the work and measures the grain. The crop is divided when the flailing is finished. Thus a year's rent is settled at the harvest. The tenant is never in arrears. Landlord and tenant share fortune in good and bad seasons.

THE FARMER'S CALENDAR is a sun calendar. It traces the sun's path across the heavens by twelve stars. It divides the sun's journey into four sections. These are the seasons. And the seasons are further divided into periods, each with an indicative name.

In Rain Water we had gray weather at sunrise each day, a south wind each morning, and a fine drizzle all day. The family were pleased. We all went about in thatched-straw raincoats and peaked thatch hats. Stable dung was hauled and spread around the walnut trees that beautify the fields, and around the giant chestnut tree, in which the Lins have only a half interest, as it is on the boundary line dividing their land from the Wongs's.

On Get-up Insects Eve we unfurled pennants on the roofs to greet the bees. Unless the bees assist by carrying the pollen, a harvest is impossible. It is the rule in the House of Exile to sterilize the water jars and fumigate the sleeping rooms on the first day of Get-up Insects. We were busy with these tasks until long after sunset, as might be expected where there are no modern conveniences.

In midafternoon there was a rainbow in the east. Camel-back came through the courts playing a roundelay on his flute. His grandson ran beside him singing that the heavens announced clear, bright weather. Had the rainbow appeared in the west, he caroled, the future would have been wet.

The fortnight of gentle rain had broken the ice in the canal and thawed the frost from the earth. A radiant sun now dried the earth, clearing up mud and dirty mounds of honeycombed snow. The hibernating creatures came out. Frogs croaked a chorus from the ponds. Beetles came up through the crevices of the court paving stones and warmed themselves. The goldfish were suddenly restless and fed greedily when food was offered to them. Wild geese flew over the House of Exile, going north. Wild duck followed them. The swallows came back and fluttered in graceful swoops in and out of the Favorite Eaves.

During this season I heard much concerning the danger of flood. Wei-sung, Elder of the House of Exile, wrote a petition reporting weaknesses in the canal and advising that repairs be completed before the summer rains. This petition was circulated until it held the signature of one thousand family elders.

In company with representatives from eighteen other clans,

Shun-ko's husband took the petition to the President of the Republic. On his return he reported in family council that it was as futile as ever to expect government attention.

The family decided that the canal must be mended. Ho-min was sent out to collect what funds he could from the signers of the petition. Uncle Shao-chun called for farmer volunteers to do the repairs under his direction. In the courts beyond the Orchid Door I heard that this was the way that the canal had been kept under control for more than a dozen years.

"It is our duty to prevent flood if we can," Shun-ko said. "Should our efforts fail it is always our duty, as a big House, to feed and reestablish the survivors. Big Houses, with wealth placed where the water cannot carry it away, must do all they can for the little Houses."

After his canal-mending was done for the season, Uncle Shao-chun continued to go to the farms each day on errands relating to the spring planting. He took lunch with him. He was accompanied by Camel-back's grandson, who drove the gray donkey hitched to the basket cart.

By our diligence in cutting seed potatoes, Mai-da and I won permission to drive with Uncle Shao-chun one day. He managed his itinerary so that we picnicked beside the natural spring in the walnut grove. We were ambitious about the food. We had fried pasties of chicken minced with celery, which we had made at home; then broiled mushrooms, steamed noodles with dried-apricot sauce, and cabbage sauced with vinegar, cloves, and paprika. We rounded the picnic with dates stuffed with almonds. Uncle Shao-chun said that after feasting on our cooking he felt more like a comfortable sleep than an afternoon of mental activity.

At the vernal equinox—the first day of Spring Divided in the Middle—the Elder put on the ceremonial plowing coat and opened the plowing season by cutting three furrows across the eastern fields. Then in succession according to birth, each son of the House of Exile plowed three furrows. Next, in precedence determined by length of service to the family, each laborer opened three furrows.

Day by day, until all the land was turned up in brown waves, the plowmen went out of the city gate when it was unlocked at dawn and down to the fields—small squares among other similar squares to which plowmen from other families hastened. Each carried a light plow on his shoulder and had a teapot with a packet of lunch tied to it swinging from his left hand.

The five oxen went; the three brown donkeys; the white mule; also the dappled goat. Each beast with his lunch on his

back. The men did not ride on the animals. To ride would take some of the creature's strength needed for work. But there were not sufficient beasts to draw all the plows. Many rich furrows were turned up to the sun by men hitched in the yokes. After the land was plowed, it was crushed and smoothed by harrows and rollers.

The House of Exile does not rest one day in seven. Although many of the family can read and all know that the official calendar of the Republic is the Gregorian calendar, they have not yet adopted it. In public they give it lip service. They explain their not using it by saying that each dynasty must have a calendar—but that no matter how many dynasties come and go, farming must continue serenely. On the evening of the Time of Clear and Bright Air all the people of the House of Exile were called to the Court of Dignity. The Elder read to us from the farmer's calendar:

"All the plowing, harrowing, and rolling that has tortured the earth since the vernal equinox shall now stop for three days, that the earth may be rested by undisturbed enjoyment of the sun's caresses. All the beasts shall have three days to relax their muscles and no person shall even hitch an animal to a light pleasure cart. For three days tools must be laid down; shops shuttered; offices closed. Men, women, and children must lift their spirits above mundane concerns and make merry in appreciation of all that the gods give them."

The winter wheat was a lusty green and high as an ox's hoof. Tender grass had broken through last year's stubble. Wild wisteria hung from every rocky ledge. The hawthorn and the wild cherry mingled their perfume by every gentle breeze with the fragrance of orchard blossoms.

On the first day of the festival, we all went out in gowns and shoes of springtime silk in blossom colors. We swept the graves of the ancestors while musicians of the family piped on reed flutes for the pleasure of the souls. The family kowtowed at each grave to show their respect for their forbears, to whom they are grateful for the establishment and continuance of the family. The family sat on cushions and picnicked of the food that had been ceremoniously offered at the graves. There was no mourning. The descendants had come in happiness. They spoke of the places where they hoped their bodies would be placed. They talked calmly of their descendants a hundred years in the future.

We brought home branches of sweet pine and decorated the courtyards. Shun-ko brought baskets filled with pigeon, hen, duck, and turkey eggs: a gift from the wives to the children. We of the Springtime Bower gave packets of bright dye. Assisted by their nurses, the children colored the eggs, and when they were cool, they polished them with perfumed oil, arranged them in woven nests, and presented some to each adult.

The men's courts gave the children gay-hued feather shuttles. Children and adults played a graceful game of keeping the toy in the air as long as possible, kicking it up with their heels.

A green pillar ten feet high was planted in the center of the garden. A huge purple wheel was fastened to the top and twelve silk ropes of different colors, one for each star on the sun's road, were hung as swings from the stout spokes.

The Elder said we were like shimmering butterflies in our festival gowns as we whirled round and round on the wheel. This sport is called the sport of the immortals because it gives the sensation of flying.

After the festival, work began again. The House of Exile sows in accord with a system of crop rotation which will keep the soil ever enriched. Shun-ko was kept busy verifying what had grown in each plot last year according to her charts. Uncle Shao-chun diligently inspected the seeding to make certain that the tenants planted what should go into the soil.

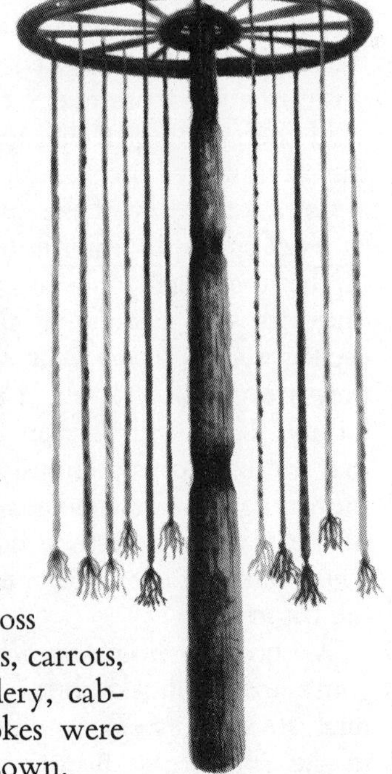

At Come Summer, the rice plants, now five inches tall, were transplanted into terraced fields prepared for flooding. Peanuts were hoed in. Sweet-potato tubers were cut into small pieces and planted in sandy soil. Cucumbers and melons were set in groups of four, and covered with bamboo frames that had coarse cotton cloth stretched across to keep out the bugs. Turnips, leeks, carrots, onions, parsnips, chili peppers, celery, cabbage, lettuce, ginger, and artichokes were thinned. Beets and eggplant were sown.

Mai-da's brother, Peng-wen, came home from the Nanking School of Agriculture with new theories about thinning the tiny green peaches. He was enthusiastic about Sun Yat-sen's ideas, ardent in his belief that government by the people was possible in China, and convinced that Nanking should be the capital of the Republic.

Everyone agreed that Nanking was a central location, and that one capital for the country was more economical than one at Peking, one at Canton, and the people in every province left to the mercy of whatever man seized power. The family also agreed that the only reason, ever, that any government exists is "for the benefit of the people."

But the courtyards rang with argument each time Peng-wen attempted to make converts to "by the people." That, they considered, was absurd. Since time immemorial people were entirely occupied with their own affairs, and paid willingly, or even gave one or two sons to the service of the government, to be relieved of such responsibility.

Sun Yat-sen was called a donkey so repeatedly that the Elder forbade the use of the word, as it upset Peng-wen and took his thoughts away from the care of the fruit orchards. Sun Yat-sen was called a donkey because, after appointment to the presidency of the newborn Republic ten years earlier, he resigned in favor of his bitter enemy, Yüan Shih-k'ai, hoping to make peace in the land, "when even the barbers knew that Shih-k'ai was a reptile."

The Springtime Bower found all this occupation with politics tiresome. But the maids all encouraged Peng-wen when he told of serious, pretty Mrs. Sun Yat-sen, the daughter of the Shanghai House of Soong. No one was tired when he described her dresses on the different occasions he had seen her. He had found them intriguingly individual in design—sometimes of Western pattern, sometimes of the simplicity of the early Ming period, often combining the best features of many fashions.

The family liked especially to hear about her house in the French Concession at Shanghai. I had told them of homes where one does not have to draw water from a well, carry it across courtyards in buckets, heat it in caldrons—but where one just turns a tap with thumb and finger, and it gushes out hot or cold. But they never believed me until Peng-wen told us that Mrs. Sun Yat-sen had such taps.

All the family encouraged Peng-wen to tell about the handsome, intelligent young man whom he had met at Fenghwa. He had dined at the homestead of this young man, who was named Chiang Kai-shek and had been secretary to Sun Yat-sen. Maida's mother asked her son if, since he found this young man so admirable, he had remembered that a suitable marriage had yet to be arranged for his sister. He murmured that an acquaintance could not mention such a matter to Chiang Kai-shek. His mother reminded him that the Lins, as well as her own House of Tong, were equal to any in the hundred names. Peng-wen said that younger Republicans disapproved of family-arranged marriages.

She retorted, "Ah! Then when this Republic gets established, girls will have to go out and hunt for their mates? If their families cannot help them get married, then they will have to become bold and deceitful, preying on any man they can get, yet pretending that they are not wanting one. Only the most artful will mate! Shy, plain, good maids will wither into a fruitless age!"

IN SMALL FULLNESS, men's backs were bent to weeding. Soil was loosened around each stalk of the winter wheat, now heavy with swelling grain. The red-cherry crop was so abundant that few could be sold in the local marketplace. The profit in cherries was decidedly too small to warrant taking them to Peking by hired boat, and the homestead boatmen were already occupied hoeing the more important winter wheat. So what could not be eaten were made into vinegar, compotes, and jellies.

Each afternoon the homestead mother dispatched Camelback's grandson to the Home Farm, driving the gray donkey hitched to the basket cart; he carried refreshments to the men toiling in the dusty fields—tender pickled lotus roots and refreshing green tea.

In Sprouting Plants, the tutors voluntarily picked strawberries, enjoying the days in the meadows as much as the children, whom the family Elder released from lessons to help gather the fruit when it ripened faster than the men, even though ably assisted by the women, could harvest it.

Packed in leaf-lined trays, nine boatloads of strawberries were dispatched to Peking. Many foreigners resided in Peking, "and foreigners like strawberries," but they were brought home next day and sold in the village at less than half the expected price.

It had been impossible to get to either Peking or Tientsin, as a war of unprecedented fierceness was raging between Wu P'ei-fu and Chang Tso-lin, to settle which of them had the right to appoint the President of the Republic.

In Summer Divided in the Middle, straw was heaped under the tiger-apple trees and the fruit left to drop off of its own ripeness and lie for a few hours in the sun. The vibrating *thu-ing* of whetstone on scythe echoed as the winter wheat was cut. Tied in sheaves, it was then carted to stacks safe inside the city wall.

The tenants to the northeast, where the crop is always later in ripening, had just begun to harvest when a contingent of Chang Tso-lin's army came across country foraging from the farm crops, commandeering men and beasts to carry them and their loot to Manchuria.

As soon as the alarm spread, farmers ran to their villages. Gates were quickly barred. Only five men of the district were taken. Camel-back's grandson, with the pet gray donkey, was among them. The crops were not tended again until three sunrises after the soldiers had passed.

In Big Heat, although there were rumors of terrible famine to the east, south, and west, there was a welcome but heavy downpour which damaged the summer pears; but it left sufficient pears for the home table, and pears are of no value compared with grain. The rain increased the height of the summer wheat, rye, oats, millet, buckwheat, alfalfa, soybeans, and corn so rapidly that Uncle Shao-chun said he could hear them grow.

Come Autumn arrived the first week in August. Young Shao-yi, fifth-generation heir to eldership, told me that the white tiger is monarch of the agricultural year from autumn until winter. He is the hardest master of all. If men do not harvest industriously enough to please him, he reaps for them with white frost. He is to be feared because he comes so quietly that it seems summer is going on forever.

Black beans were gathered; rosy-cheeked apricots carefully picked so as not to bruise them; ripe chili peppers and capsicums were pulled, dried, roasted, and ground to fine spice. The men brought tender ears of yellow and red corn home to boil for each evening meal.

In Go Heat, fleecy white clouds drifted lazily across the sky. The sun continued to coax the crops and set the crickets singing.

Chang Tso-lin had followed his men home to Manchuria. After considerable delay, President Li Yüan-hung, who had been residing in Tientsin since his resignation in 1917, had returned to Peking and reassumed the presidency. The road to the capital was decided safe. Peng-wen went up with boatloads of grain, vegetables, and fruit. He found the produce in much demand because of the shortage in other districts, and sold it for a high price.

In White Dew, the sound of the flail hummed through the daylight hours. Harvest called home every available Lin man. Daily they visited the village threshing floors to measure the harvests of the tenant farmers. The Lin women supervised the crop division where tenants were reputed to be cunning, as women are most capable in material matters.

New tax collectors came through the district assessing farms. The House of Exile had paid taxes one year in advance. But the departed officials of the Republic had taken away the treasury, and the new officials must have finances to be able to serve the people. The collectors were feasted at the Cantonese guildhall. The first course was melon and when each guest opened his fruit he found one hundred dollars inside. The taxes had to be paid—but just half what had been demanded.

As a reward for committing to memory the first book of Confucius, young Tsai-fu was taken to Peking. He attended ceremonies at which China accepted an airplane from the French, and on returning home he resolved to be an aviator. He was not depressed by the fact that the School of Aviation was not functioning just then, nor that all the American, French, Italian, and British instructors had gone home. He had faith that when he was of age to start his career the time would be propitious for flying mail, passengers, and goods over the old trade routes of China.

At Autumn Divided in the Middle, the farmer's calendar devotes three days to Thank the Harvest. All work stopped. The storehouses were already well filled, and field and orchard still held the promise of further abundance. Goldenrod and gentian were in bloom. Larks sang above the meadows.

At dawn on the first morning of the festival, the men, women, and children of the House of Exile met the tenant farmers at the Temple of Agriculture and went together to the eastern fields. While music was played for the Earth Mother's delight, they offered a part from each crop and burned yellow scrolls on which they had written prayers of gratitude.

They returned along the detour—worn smooth by processions through the centuries—by way of the hillside spring, where

they knelt in a circle of thanks to Water for nourishing their seed.

Then came three days of pleasuring, on the last of which the House of Exile gave a great banquet to their tenant farmers in the Cantonese guildhall. After the feast the Elder gave each tenant's little boy a packet of seeds. Every absent member of the homestead who could returned to help thank the harvest. There were games, feasts, plates of juicy white walnut meats—the special midautumn delicacy—and gifts for everyone.

But the young wives, maids, and girl children were sulky. The village was in carnival but the Lady of First Authority forbade them to go outside the Orchid Door. She said that the men of the village were rowdy with too much barley wine.

The men, youths, and boys of the homestead—over whom she had no control—joined the village gaiety. The young women of the adjoining House of Wong went out at will. It was they who told us of the theatricals arranged by the village elders, also of the troupes of lion dancers that the festival attracted. Each troupe of four mountebanks manipulated their blue-and-yellow lion, made of cloth and wire, in an agile dance after a scarlet ball bounced by a fifth mountebank. The beast's tongue, jaw, ears, and tail wiggled as the lion pursued the ball through doorways, pushed a pedestrian forward, or peered under a fat man's skirts in search of it—indulging in capers that made everyone laugh except the person who happened to be the butt of the joke.

There were stilt walkers, who wore humorous makeup and exaggerated dress; they pranced, minced, strode, and anticked in a parody of life and manners—as a fashionable lady, a hunchback pawnbroker, an ugly wife and her husband, a pious priest—for the amusement of the crowd, who rewarded them with coin when pleased.

In Cold Dew, all crops were lifted from the soil. Then plows, harrows, and tiny stone rollers were busy again breaking the land to pulverized fineness. Soon men swayed back and forth, sowing the winter grains in the plots where the summer crops had grown.

Winter pears were packed in sawdust to keep until the New Year festivities. Grapes were sent to Peking markets. Threshing was finished. Stone mills in every homestead creaked out the song of flour as women ground the grain that had been spread out on their roofs to dry in golden sheets.

In Frost's Descent, plump speckled pheasants were disturbed while the red persimmons were gathered from the hillside orchards. Chestnuts were harvested in competition with industrious squirrels. Nuts in excess of homestead needs were sold to the dealers who came through the district. Ripe walnuts, picked from the shell, brought a good price from an export merchant who trades with America.

Frost turned shrub and tree, lichen and grass, to burgundy and crimson, russet and amber. The shortening days were filled with the plaintive melody of the sparrow and the blithe call of the katydid. The wild geese passed over, going south. Lastly the black dates ripened. Then folk said that winter was near. Tools were brought in. The homestead shrubs were wrapped in straw. The House of Exile was tightened against blizzard.

At Come Winter the homestead gave up hope of ever seeing Camel-back's grandson again on earth. They had sent scouts to follow every clue. Now they ceased their search and said: "The somber black tortoise has got him." The black tortoise is king from the arrival of winter until the coming of spring, Shao-yi said.

When the Milky Way drooped, summer clothes were packed in cedar and everyone dressed in fur-lined garments. Windows were sealed and fires lit in the beds.

Small Snow and Big Snow passed. Then came Winter Divided in the Middle. We had Little Cold and Big Cold to pass before the weather would grow slowly warmer, and it would be time to welcome spring again.

V. THREE BIRTHDAYS

From the time I left America, kind relatives and friends sent me frequent letters, current magazines, and books to keep me in touch with home. But I was too entranced with China to read these. I found their contents too faraway to hold my attention.

While resident in China, I had no intention of insulting my own countrymen, but when I met them I was sometimes unconsciously rude. My nature is slow. In each new experience, my thought must germinate before I can share it. I resent having others, even those closely associated with me, probe into my mind. I avoided both contact and correspondence. I could not answer the kindhearted attempts made for my "good" to warn me against "going native."

It was not that China charmed me more than America. I am devoted to the land of my birth. But I find the earth so entrancing that I can never stretch myself to encompass more than the part that has captured my attention at the time.

As my stay in China lengthened, many people seemed anxious about my future. Especially when Grace Coppock, who had sponsored me, died. Urgent letters, then cables, advised me to return.

My answers only created more alarm. I was made unhappy by the concern for me. Yet I was charmed by the spell I could not break. So I did not go.

If I could have told people that I was writing verse or story, it might have given comfort. But I have always been evasive and shy about writing. Writing is something that I am ever driven to do, and concerning which I am never satisfied.

In my childhood I hid my verse and story in a box buried under a tree in my grandfather's woodlot. The urge to put down what flowed through my imagination stayed with me as I grew older. But I never mentioned it to parent, school friend, or teacher. I am one of seven brothers and sisters. We all wrote, and shared what we had written, although we kept it carefully concealed from our elders.

When we were pressed for funds, in my teens, I sent things out to be printed. I felt no elation that they were accepted; only an unexplainable shame because of their inadequacy. But they brought me friendship with John Burroughs and the welcome at Slabsides, where I was privileged to listen to his other guests, Henry Ford, Thomas Edison, and Theodore Roosevelt among them.

One of my sisters also sacrificed some secret things to our monetary need. Among them *Conquests of Peace*, a pageant we had enacted in our wood. Meg was dissatisfied with it when she posted it in answer to the widely published Chautauqua quest for a pageant. It won first place and was enacted all over the United States. When the letter came announcing that it was chosen, she wanted to get it back so that she could do it all over. She was kept from demanding it only by the cash prize, which happened to be the exact amount needed for our youngest sister's fee at George School.

But our writing not only supplied needed money. As we matured, it gave satisfaction to our relatives. We are bred of generations of Quakers—serious, gentle, loving people, who educate their young to listen to the voice of God and apply themselves to practical usefulness in life.

In my verse and story my relatives and elder friends found sensible excuse for my childhood truancy from schoolroom lessons. It was the same about China.

A group of my Chinese poems appeared in *Scribner's*. The Woman's Press of the YWCA published my novel, *The Street of Precious Pearls*, and put it in the bookshops at Christmas. The *Pictorial Review* announced my story "Beyond the Orchid Door" on their January cover. Then cables and letters came from relatives and friends assuring me that all who had been troubled about me were now at peace.

"WE KNOW NOT the beginning nor the end of life." So Sou-mai's mother spoke on the day it was known that her daughter carried a new life under her heart. "We do not know what is helpful to the soul about to be born, so it is best to use all advised methods to safeguard a child's entry into the world."

Then she took from a basket she had brought all the things that had safeguarded her when she carried Sou-mai. She placed a long sharp knife under Sou-mai's bed and pinned two pairs of scissors, cut from red paper, on the bed curtains, and stretched a tiger skin in her mattress. Pictures of wild animals were pasted on the surrounding walls and above the courtyard gate. She purchased two sets of charms against evil, one prepared by the Buddhist and the other by the Taoist priests, and hung them under the eaves of Sou-mai's dwelling.

During the time of waiting, each mother in the House of Lin went to the Temple of Motherhood and prayed for Sou-mai's child. Sou-mai made sweetmeats of honey, white rice flour, and jasmine petals for the God of One Hundred Happy Children, whose image has always a great knapsack on its back from which adorable children are peeping. She stitched a pair of baby shoes of bright satin and laid them on the lap of the Goddess of Mercy.

The child entered the world at dawn on the Birthday of the Sun, after distress, alarm, and delay so prolonged that the family elders met to consider the wisdom of sending to Peking for a Western-educated doctor to assist.

For a day and a night of Sou-mai's pain, her husband waited before her door. As Mai-da and I were dispatched on errands for the women who attended Sou-mai, we were awed by his stillness. He stood hour after hour, refusing to sit or to take refreshment. Then when Sou-mai's mother came to the door just as the sun rose and announced, "A man is born," he disappeared. He returned some time later dressed in his ceremonial robes. After another long wait at the door *his* mother opened it and told him to come in.

Sou-mai was wrapped in her marriage-bed nightdress. She held the child against her breast and smiled as her husband came near. Before he took the child she offered, he put on her pillow a gold hairpin such as each mother of a son wears in her nape knot.

Then he took the child in its warm wrappings of rosy satin. He knelt to his mother and to his wife's mother. He carried his son through every court in the homestead, making the new Lin's arrival known to all the family and to the God of the Hearth. Standing under the lamp of continuous life, he told the glad tidings in the Hall of the Ancestors. Then he gave his son back to his wife for the "three days of quietness," when her mother and her serving woman were the only persons permitted to enter her court.

When the sun was high overhead, the family Elder dispatched couriers to relatives and friends with small boxes of fruit, announcing without words the arrival of a son in the House of Lin. The relatives and friends responded with gifts of millet, eggs, brown sugar, and walnut meats, which are the only foods a mother in the Lin clan is permitted to eat during the days that a carpet of sawdust stills the sound of footfalls on the stone-paved courts.

On the morning of the fourth day, Little Tiger brought me an invitation on a red card brushed with gold characters to attend the "bath in the Hour of the Sheep." She explained how difficult it had been for Sou-mai to make selection of a "good-fortune eight" from her host of loved relatives and friends. We eight were the baby's two grandmothers, the family Elder's wife, three little cousins, a maternal aunt, and I.

As gifts we took white eggs, symbols of long life; red eggs, symbols of happiness; bunches of acacia incense, symbols of health; bowls of uncooked rice, symbols of prosperity; and flower seeds, symbols of lovely children. Sou-mai sat propped up on silk cushions and was dressed in a pale pink gown embroidered with plum blossoms. Her only jewelry was the gold pin in her nape knot. The dimples danced in her flushed cheeks as she unfolded the quilt to show us the little son at her side.

We placed our eggs in a basket which stood ready to receive them. We laid our flower seeds on the little boy's bed, asking his mother to plant a garden for him. We thrust our acacia incense into our bowls of rice and brought them to the child. Sou-mai took the torch that Little Tiger had ready, guided the baby's hand to light it, bid us carry our gifts to the Hall of Ancestors and leave them on the altar.

The maternal grandmother boiled water for the bath, putting locust leaves in as a disinfectant and artemisia flowers to give a pleasant perfume. Little Tiger poured the water into the copper basin, which had been turned upside down and used as a table for Sou-mai and her husband's marriage-night supper, and Sou-mai let the little children help to undress the baby.

He kicked his fat legs and wrinkled his face, but did not cry. His mother bade each of us put a handful of water over his chubby pink body. The bath was but a ceremony, quickly finished. After it, Little Tiger rubbed him with sweet-smelling oil, and we helped to wrap him in a quilted robe of scarlet silk. Then he was put to sleep at the back of the great bed, on his own mattress, with a tiny screen placed around him to shut out the light.

Outside Sou-mai's door we arranged a life-size papier-mâché sedan chair, with eight bearers and attendant phoenix, unicorn, tortoise, and tiger, so that she could see the Mother of Heaven go back into the sky. Little Tiger took the portrait of the Mother of Heaven from the wall niche whence it had watched over the child during the months of germination and the ordeal of separation, and placed it in the chair.

Sou-mai said, "Thank you, Heavenly Mother, for much kindness."

We each lit a fuse and the papier-mâché procession started slowly, gaining momentum as the fire spread its wings.

THE PEAR TREES were in ivory flower. It was Mai-da's quarter-moon of kitchen service, but before she went to help prepare the evening meal she had rolled up our bamboo-paper windows. Tired, I stretched out on our bed to rest for a few minutes before bathing and changing. With three wives and four serving women, I had been down by the lotus pond helping to rub and bleach the family wash since sunup, with only a brief interval for lunch at midday.

Three courts away Sou-mai was singing to her baby. The contralto lullaby drifted on the perfumed air.

It was the eve of the eightieth birthday of Wei-sung, the family Elder. Invitations had not been sent out, as it would be bad taste to ask folk to come with congratulations, but the homestead had hummed with activity since the new moon.

Wei-sung was an official of the government during the Ch'ing dynasty. But his posts were always minor ones, in places far distant from the capital, to which he was appointed with flowery words of sham honor—as the House of Lin, of Canton origin, was continuously under suspicion of disloyalty to the throne. He succeeded to the eldership of the family when his father plucked the flower of life; but he had to wait three years before he was permitted to resign his government appointment.

He was sixty when he came home. He settled into the routine of the House of Exile in quiet contentment, and he told me he planned never to go out until his body was carried to its final resting place in the eastern fields. Once when his wife urged him to travel, I heard him say: "Go and see the world if you like. You will soon come home. I was abroad for forty-two years, and I know that the best of the world is inside our homestead wall."

It is Mai-da's duty to distribute and dispatch the letters which come and go by government post. So I know he receives fat letters frequently from the places where daughters have gone in marriage or where members of the family are staying for study or work; and that he always sends a fat letter in prompt return.

In the weeks preceding his birthday, letters with the same postmarks as those he usually receives came addressed to his wife, who seldom has letters. Mai-da lingered with each to learn its secret contents: that Su-ling had decided not to accept the scholarship for further study at the Sorbonne, but was returning in time for the Elder's birthday; that the husband of Fu-erh and the companion she had chosen to accompany him to Malaya were coming, bringing two sons who had not yet bowed to the ancestors; that a great-grandnephew would come from San Francisco, leaving a cousin in charge of his business; that Wen-lieh had been granted leave from his army command to honor his Elder; that Wei-chun was arriving from Canton by airplane; and so on with each day's mail.

Orders were given to clean the homestead, to make lunch baskets for those who went to meet the voyagers, to ask Hua-li for "welcome" flowers from the hothouses, and to launder all the family linen. As members of the family arrived, they joined in the preparations. The courts echoed with the swish of brooms, the beat of flays on dusty shutters, the tap of hammers. By the birthday eve, every dwelling house had reached perfection. Pillars and eaves shone with new paint. The sand-scoured court paving stones reflected a white radiance. Even the goldfish in the cleaned pools seemed brighter. The hothouses were filled with plants to distribute at sunrise the next morning. The carpenters had built a stage opposite the Hall of Ancestors.

The birthday dawned bright and clear. The children, dressed in lovely new birthday clothes, accompanied the Elder's breakfast tray caroling greetings, each dragging a red carpet piled high with birthday cards. When he had breakfasted, the Elder opened his gifts in the Court of Sunrise, where the maidens of the Springtime Bower helped him to arrange them on satin-covered tables.

Usually in the House of Exile we dined in small groups, each in our own court. But on the Elder's birthday the meal in the Hour of the Snake was a joint family meal. As the weather was unusually mild, the table was set not in the hall, but in the court, where pear trees were in flower and orioles were making a silken nest. We could all sit down, because the Elder had thoughtfully arranged for a restaurant to take charge of the homestead kitchens, as he wanted the women to be free that day from domestic concern.

Shortly after this meal, guests began to arrive. The eldest grandson, as proxy for the Elder, received all callers in the Hall of Dignity, saving the honored one much fatigue, as the ceremony of congratulation includes the exchange of three kowtows. The guests then passed on to the Three Eastern Courtyards, where they talked with the Elder as though they had already greeted him.

Before long the Elder, who always keeps the children of the family clustered about him, asked, "Where is my daughter Sou-mai? Is the baby Shao-jo's birth month not yet full?"

His favorite, Mai-lei, answered, "Today is the day of his full month, but his mother says that it is a day short because she does not want anyone to consider anything except the fullness of your eighty years."

"I am the firstborn in the House of Exile. Shao-jo, five generations below me, is the lastborn," the Elder responded. "What more perfect arrangement could Heaven make than that we be congratulated together?"

He dispatched Mai-lei to bring Sou-mai and her son. When

they came, he kept them beside him until all the guests had praised the mother and admired the child.

Family and guests wore elegant gowns of springtime silk, as delicate in color as the springtime blossoms. They wandered at will through the courts. Some lingered in conversation by the pool. Others renewed friendships in quiet corners, or listened to

the minstrel who sang in the Poet's Retreat. All accepted refreshments and gave attention to the theatricals on the stage opposite the Hall of Ancestors.

The players were from Peking. They filled the women's parts with such skill that I did not know until long afterward that they were all men. The plays were given without scenery, but so vivid was the acting that it created the impression of background. As soon as one play was finished another began.

The theatricals charmed me. The actors did not speak their parts. They gave them in poetic beaten measure to which an orchestra kept time. The principal guests were requested to name a play which they would like the actors to perform. The guests were politely considerate. If they saw that a play had just started, they said that it was their favorite play, as they knew that the day was too short for the actors to perform a tragedy or a comedy for every guest.

There was never any hesitation from the players. They seemed to have all the plays in their heads and all the necessary costumes in their boxes. With slight intervals for refreshment, the players went on until after sunset, when the stage was lit by flaming pine knots. A table was arranged in the Court of Sunrise, covered with a vermilion altar cloth which fell to the paving stones, and the portrait* of the God of Longevity was put on it. Six plates of apples, symbols of peace, and six candles, symbols of the six generations it was hoped the Elder would remain on earth to count, were placed before the portrait. A satin kneeling cushion was laid before the table. The Elder knelt first and gave thanks for eighty years of life. Then each member of his family knelt and thanked Heaven for permitting the homestead the blessing of his eldership, and petitioned that it should continue for another decade. Then the guests prayed, and departed.

When the last guest had gone, and the To and From the World Gate had been closed, the Elder examined his gifts. Three long

* This portrait is one of the homestead treasures. It was painted four hundred years ago by an artist who knocked at the Gate of Compassion in a bitter blizzard. When the news of his call was brought to the wife of the family Elder of that time, she had him welcomed through the To and From the World Gate, and ordered that fur garments, food, and shelter be given him. He painted the picture in return. The god is riding a stag. A purple bat is flying over his head. He has a ripe peach in one hand, a staff in the other, and a gourd and a scroll attached to his golden girdle.

tables were loaded with presents. Each had an attached card on which was written the donor's name and an appropriate greeting. From among the jewelry, scrolls, pictures, books, lengths of silk, silver plates, and such, he was attracted by a huge peach made of satin and painted in realistic colors.

" 'Prince Erh-sung,' " he read aloud, from its card. "It is a Manchu name. There was one of that name stationed with me at my first government post. But we were not friends. Surely he would not have sent me a Peach of Long Life."

He pressed the fruit and it sprang open. A frightened bird nested inside on a heap of fluffy silk. The bird was one whose name is the same as Mai-da's pet name. As he thoughtfully let it fly away over the homestead wall, the Elder said: "Ah—now I understand. This gift is perhaps more a request than a symbol of long life."

And Shun-ko, who stood near him, said: "It is years past the time at which Mai-da should have married. In my father's house daughters are arranged for at eighteen."

IN THE HOUSE OF EXILE the birthdays of childhood are the Fullness of the Month, the Rounding of the Year, and the Cycle of Ten. After these the only birthday celebrated, until the half century is past, is the bride's first birthday after marriage. The birthdays of childhood and the bride's day are family affairs.

The twins Shao-yi and Ching-o and the cousins Nan-wei and Ming-chi all completed the Cycle of Ten in the autumn of the same year as the Elder filled his eighth decade. So when the moon was round in Chrysanthemums, the birthday awnings were spread over the Garden of Children and their courts decorated with lanterns, happiness banners, and crimson joy characters. Their houses were filled with flowers, and model ships were set afloat on the shallow pool with all flags flying.

The relatives sent gifts. The birthday children were dressed in festival gowns and received congratulations from all the family. The family elders permitted each birthday child to choose an entertainment for the combined party.

Shao-yi asked for the marionette players. A tiny stage was put up for them, and the troupe responded to every request.

Shao-yi's favorite, *The Battle of the Red Cliff*, had to be repeated three times for his special benefit.

Shao's twin asked for the juggler. He threw plates above his head and caught them on a twirling stick balanced on his nose, turned handsprings while he tossed eggs, and finally took a live rabbit out of Ching-o's pocket and gave it to her as a present.

Nan-wei asked for the candymaker, who was one of the most popular features of the birthday. He made three-sailed fishing craft, prancing horses, a cat with kittens, the God of Happiness, a monkey eating an orange, and whatever was asked for, from syrup which he boiled—on a little charcoal stove that he carried with him—and then blew deftly into shape through a hollow reed.

Ming-chi asked for the fortune-teller. He found good signs in the palms of all the children, and foretold marvelous adventures to come to them all in the future.

At evening the feast, for which the birthday children chose the menu, was served on a long table in the open courtyard. The table was lighted by forty candles arranged in groups of ten each, held in bronze holders made in the likeness of the tortoise. After dark, old Camel-back set off a bevy of skyrocketing stars—one for each child to wish on.

VI. HOMESTEAD HERITAGE

My life in China was broken by a brief visit to America. I traveled home on the *Empress of Asia* with Mr. and Mrs. Arthur Scribner. They had an Englishman, then seventeen years in the Chinese government service, to sit at the same table. He had just been stationed at Peking.

After introducing us, Mrs. Scribner told him that I had been resident for some time in North China. When he turned his fierce attention down on me, from his more than six feet height, and said, "It is strange that if you have been in North China I have not known it," I knew that if he next said that I had not been there, I should not be certain that I had.

This was my first encounter with the type that England educates for foreign service—that is, the class to whom she teaches endurance on playing fields, whom she drills to quiet command of self and others, and impregnates with a tender love for England; then dispatches abroad to positions of responsibility and authority—posts where for years they must live far from their kind, and where they must make their decisions alone, affecting not only the future of the service but the lives of others of different race.

The majority of these men are abroad from twenty to about sixty, with home leave about once every five years. They do not take on any of the native ways of the countries to which they go. Their food, dress, habit, and speech is of home. When one of them says home he means England, the place to which he will retire when his life's work is done. To those unacquainted with this kind of Englishman, as I was then, the manner, when met for the first time, seems alarmingly self-assured.

I had a premonition, from the first moment I saw this one, that he would marry me. I accepted the fact that one would eventually marry, but I had always prayed that I should marry a mild man. This man was disturbing. He never raised his voice, yet when he spoke people listened. He seemed to win at games without effort. When asked, he sat at a piano and played or sang what was requested, just as though that was an accomplishment which everyone had. Also, he was too handsome. I distrusted handsome men, even if they acted unconscious of their looks.

I avoided him with diligence. But I could not avoid meals. I did get my place moved so that I did not have to meet his eyes every time I took a spoonful of soup. I just had to be careful never to get left alone with him. He was very polite. He did not pursue me in any way. It was just that the more information he gathered about me, the more he treated me as one who should have a keeper.

I went first to Swarthmore, where I received a brief letter from him. It hoped that I had arrived safely, trusted that I would not go to China again, and assured me that my going had been more dangerous than I had worldly knowledge to realize.

I spent the month of August with my six brothers and sisters at camp in the Pocono Mountains. I woke on the morning of the eighth remembering that I had heard the disturbing Englishman say his birthday was that day and ashamed that I had not answered his kind letter. I found my youngest brother already up and saddling a horse for a morning canter. I told him that I wanted to cable a birthday greeting. Jim said that he would go with me. We had a fine ride through wooded trails to the nearest telegraph, twelve miles away.

My brother eased the saddles and rubbed the horses while I went in to wire my message. When I had the telegraph blank before me, I realized that sending a birthday greeting to a stranger was a foolish idea. I could not disappoint the telegraph man, so I sent love to one of my aunts.

Some months after I had returned to China, I received another letter from England, addressed care of *Scribner's* magazine. The writer presumed that the first had failed to reach me. He had accepted an invitation to visit in the States on his way back to China and trusted that he would again see me at the house where he was to stay. It closed by setting me right regarding a conclusion on China that he had read in one of my recently published stories. I am not a competent letter writer, and I did not accomplish a reply. Neither did I ever mention him to anyone in China or America.

WHEN PERSIMMONS WERE RIPE, Shun-ko sent me through Mai-lin's Walk, which tunnels the wall between the houses of Lin and Wong, with a basket of gold fruit, and the request to borrow a set of drying racks. I found the women of the Wong homestead in tearful agitation because their Elder had given the order for his burial clothes to be stitched. While I waited for the racks, he came in through the Orchid Door, followed by a merchant with materials from the big shop in the Street of the Sound of Thunder.

On the approach of the Elder, his wife motioned the two young women of the family who were pregnant to leave the court, as women concerned with the beginning of life must not loiter where consideration is given to the end of life's pilgrimage.

The merchant and the elder wives exchanged greetings. Tea was brought. Two lads, close on the merchant's heels, set down the bamboo pole over which they carried his pack and spread it out as a carpet on the flat stones. The merchant then gave attention to the display of his silks.

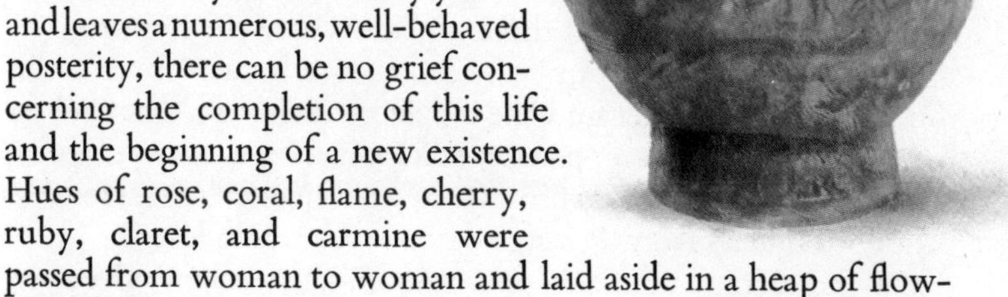

Squatting on satin-clad feet, his long cashmere gown folded neatly under his knees, the merchant undid the gold wrapper around each bale. Reds for the coffin-bed curtains came first. Red is the color of joy. When a man has conscientiously filled seventy years and leaves a numerous, well-behaved posterity, there can be no grief concerning the completion of this life and the beginning of a new existence. Hues of rose, coral, flame, cherry, ruby, claret, and carmine were passed from woman to woman and laid aside in a heap of flowing color.

For the inner trousers and short jacket of his heavenly costume the Elder indicated a length called Sky in the Late Summer from a heap of blue silks. Then the yellow silks for the winding sheet were opened. When I left, Wong Mai-su politely walked back with me to the gate in the dividing wall, discussing the cut of sleeves in the Ming period. When I asked why the garments would be fashioned as in the Ming dynasty, she answered, "Because we always enter Heaven dressed that way."

In a dream two days earlier the Elder of Wong had seen his soul stand beside him, dressed in traveling clothes and carrying a scroll. So he knew that his earthly scroll was filled. Through a circle of seasons, in which he continued in robust health, he made ready.

Of clothes he had five complete changes, as he desired to be suitably garbed for whatever occasion he must meet. His wife took the pearls from her dowry earrings and sewed them into the lining of his money pocket, should his cash be insufficient to satisfy the gatemen on the toll road through Hell. His eldest daughter embroidered and filled a tobacco pouch, and her husband sent an amber-stemmed pipe.

In the House of Lin we made a quilt on which we stitched appropriate sentiments. The House of Chow sent a jade-green quilt filled with thistledown. Other houses sent Warmth of Affection coverlets until there were sufficient for the coffin bed. The sons prepared the coffin. When it was made, priests came to bless it. Then it stood ready in the Hall of Ancestors. The Houses of Lin and Wong believe that Li-hua, the blind widow of Lin, is more gifted than any other seer of their knowledge. She chose the soil under the red bean tree, on the Wongs's farm, as the place where the Elder of Wong should give his body to the earth. He labored to build there a place where the members of his family would be happy to spend leisure hours. "I want the music of their laughter and the ripple of their talk," he said to me. He planted three poplars, a scarlet maple, a walnut, and a cutting our Elder gave him from the maidenhair tree. He brought builders from Peking to construct a pavilion.

On the second of the Pepper Moon, thirteen months after the Elder of Wong's dream, we had a fall of snow. Mai-da and I were in Yu-lin's dwelling, learning to do seed-stitch embroidery, when the Elder Wong's green skirt came to ask if she might look down the road through the telescope which Su-ling brought home when she returned from the Sorbonne. She was anxious because he had set out at dawn and had not yet returned. But the telescope had no power to open a road of light through falling snow. When the Elder's green skirt had tried in vain to find her man, she put her head down on the table and sobbed.

Bald-the-third came to us with umbrellas. She took us to my dwelling place, where she made the woman drink tea laced with corn spirit, and then escorted her home. She told us that the Elder of Wong had arrived some time before and gone to his bed, where he lay alternating between chill and fever. He did not get up again. The daughters of the homestead knelt in a circle of prayer, asking that Heaven's gate be unlatched for the earth-departing soul. But the soul did not leave until the light of a new day illuminated the sky.

The instant the soul of the Elder became unconscious of earthly details, the next heir in line became the Elder of Wong and took control of proceedings. He climbed to the roof of the late Elder's dwelling and begged the departing soul to tarry a little longer. The family, gathered in the courtyard below, echoed his pleas. When all efforts failed to bring the soul back, the new Elder ordered the males of the homestead to unravel their queues, the females to twist white cotton in their hair, and candles to be lit before the God of the Hearth.

The body was washed and placed on the coffin bed, with the changes of clothes, the pipe and tobacco pouch, a book, and the necessary passports and money conveniently near to the hands. Warmth of Affection quilts were tucked around. The curtain of joy, on which the wives had stitched wishes for a long and prosperous life in the western sky, was hung in the Court of Dignity, where the coffin stood.

The new Elder set a table at the coffin head. On it he put a tablet carved with the late Elder of Wong's name in gold lettering. This is the life tablet now cherished in the Wong Hall of Ancestors as the symbol of the spirit in Heaven. He replenished the sesame oil in the basin of the pagoda-shaped lantern of Heaven. In the street a red pole was set, to announce that a man in a coffin lay within.

These details attended to, the males of the House of Wong dressed in gowns of coarse white cloth and walked to the Temple of Agriculture to announce to the Lord of the Soil that their ancestor now had need of a place in the earth.

The scribes of the Wong family brought large sheets of yellow paper into the Lin library, which the Elder of Lin offered as a quiet place to write the funeral invitations. The invitations recorded briefly the life of the late Elder of Wong, listed the honors he had won, and stated the days appointed for the reception of guests.

The Lin twins and I worked much of the day helping the children of Wong fold yellow envelopes to hold the invitations. On each we pasted stripes of blue and red. Mai-da attended to the posting, carefully accounting the cost of the stamps, and moderately tipping the green-coated postman.

On guest days, a young priest beat a drum in the entrance court to let the family know of each arrival. But the visitors did not address them until after honoring the departed man by kowtowing three times to his coffin. Each time the family bowed with them, and the courts were filled with music and the chanting of priests. Serving folk then conducted the guests to the banqueting room, and set food before them. Men and women of the House thanked the guests for honoring their ancestor, and for the gift that each brought. In this exchange of greeting no word of sorrow or consolation was spoken, as such would be a slur on the departed one's chances of preferment in Heaven.

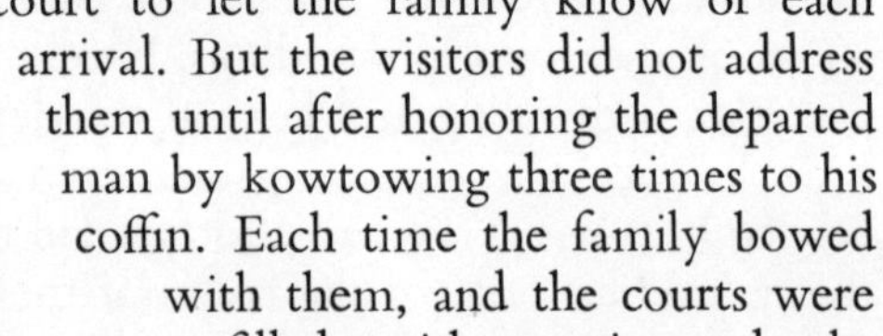

The funeral catafalque was covered with a heavy white satin cloth, and was carried by seventy-two bearers dressed in green embroidered with red characters, meaning long life in the western sky. The order of the procession was: the deceased's sedan chair; his portrait on an easel; chanting priests—eighteen of them Taoists, eighteen Buddhists; one hundred and eight bearers carrying heavenly gifts; twenty-one bearers of white paper brooms to sweep the road to the western sky; the sons on foot, the eldest carrying the spirit tablet; the time-beater with his wooden clappers; the catafalque; the wives and married daughters riding in carts drawn by mules; friends in their own conveyances; more bearers with gifts; more chanting priests; and at the rear a band of musicians.

When the procession reached the grave, the beater called relatives and friends to a circle. Then, to the throb of eerie music, each of us threw earth on the coffin. When it was covered, the priests sent the heavenly gifts to the sky by fire. Some of the gifts were life-size papier-mâché servants, horses, carriages, and grooms, and a motor car with uniformed chauffeur; pots of cypress bent to animal shapes; a chest of books; a table lute; a set of chess; a three-sailed boat; and a basket of ripe peaches.

Then the House of Wong took home their spirit tablet, symbol of the ancestor who had plucked the flower of life, and set it in their ancestral hall. Never in the House of Lin or of Wong have I heard anyone speak of any ancestor as dead. On all days the late Elder of Wong is very much alive on the lips of his family, who speak of him as having a keen interest in their affairs.

During the first sixty days following his departure they wore coarse cotton gowns, white shoes, and white knots in their hair. In this time no one went abroad, except by necessity, when the dress was changed to black. The women used no ornaments until one hundred days were passed. Until three years had gone they did not wear either silk or satin.

In thirty years the late Elder of Wong accumulated more money than is recorded of any other of their family, but his decease gave no member of the House concern about his wealth. The power of bequeathing a will does not exist in China. No member of a House, on plucking the flower of life, can make disposal of any material thing which he has accumulated. The family, as a unit, is heir to all the credits and liabilities of each member.

When a person leaves the homestead, arrangement must be made as to whether he will be held as "separately established." If so, his earnings do not fall into the common fund, nor will his fortune ever be enhanced by any inheritance from the homestead. He goes forth to brave fortune with an empty pocket, and he has neither voice nor liability concerning the family. One separately established has made a life decision, and may not return.

If he decides to continue "of the homestead," his dwelling is kept ready to welcome him, even if he is absent until old age. Intention of separate domicile must be told in the Hall of Ancestors, with the family gathered, and published abroad for all the world to know, so that no one deals with the separately established under false pretenses. Should a man go abroad without making such an announcement, it is understood that he continues of the homestead.

The late Elder of Wong elected to remain of his House, so his fortune was a part of the common fortune of the homestead. His second son found family membership irksome, and chose to be separately established. So he received nothing from his father's prudent industry, nor from the fortune of the thirty-four earlier generations. Property cannot go to an heir, except the House dissolve by mutual consent of its members.

On the day following the Star Festival, Chu Lu-mai came to stay in the House of Exile, as the House of Chu was dissolving by mutual consent. She is Su-ling's cousin. Graceful as a willow, with skin soft as the petals of the peony, brows arched like the butterfly's wings, she is gentle, unselfish, skilled with needle and lute, quick at hedged-in chess, and gifted in cookery.

Our courts were filled with gossip of the partition of the House of Chu's worldly goods. I heard the Lin Elder say, "Sons are heirs to material wealth in equality, whether born of wives or green-skirt mates; but on the firstborn falls the responsibility of the care of his father's ancestral tablets."

The family eldership descends from the homestead founder through the eldest son. A man may be Elder in a household where he has uncles belonging to an earlier generation. But he is a priest, not a civil ruler. He leads the ceremonies in the ancestral hall, but in family council each member has voice according to generation, beginning with the generation nearest the founder, and decreasing in descent.

Chu Lu-mai told me one day, as we sat shelling beans: "Each daughter of a homestead has the right of maintenance until marriage, and power to demand that the family arrange a suitable marriage. She cannot be kept at home unmated even to care for ill or aged parents, nor can she be forced to work to support her birth home. She has the right to exchange her father's household for the homestead she is to 'complete' as a bride; she has the right to a wedding ceremony with music and a procession. Her dowry should contain clothes for four seasons and adequate household furniture. Whether or not her equipment includes jewels depends upon the wealth of her home, and the love of its members for her."

Chu Lu-mai lived in the House of Exile under the care of

Shun-ko, who was made her patron on her first birthday. The other unmarried daughters of Chu lived in other homesteads until marriage. The inheritance money for Chu Lu-mai's living, dowry, and wedding was sufficient to provide her more lavishly than any daughter of Lin who had been married in my time. Yet the House of Lin did not propose marriage for either son to her.

Wei-sung, Lin Family Elder, said quietly, " 'You cannot take ivory from the mouth of a rat.' She is a charming, lovable girl, but she is of the House of Chu, and the House of Chu has dissolved twice in three hundred years."

While Chu Lu-mai was still with us, Mai-da, Su-ling, and I were working under Hua-li's direction. We had unwrapped the winter coat of straw from the roses, and were sweeping the blanket of leaves from the violet beds, when we heard the voice of the hot-cake vendor, and sent Camel-back to purchase refreshment.

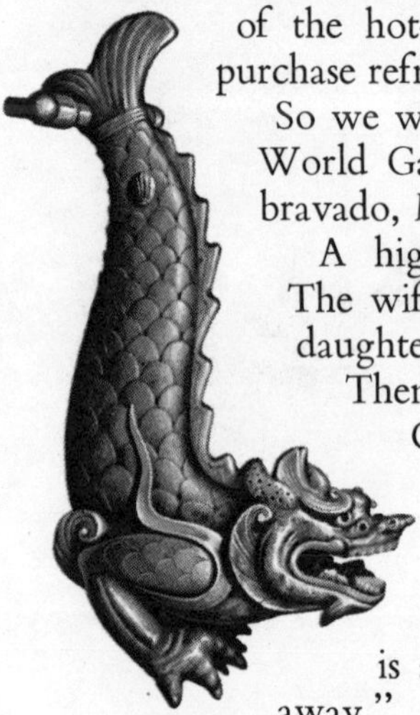

So we were his deputies at the To and From the World Gate when the brass knocker clanged. In bravado, Mai-da called, "Who knocks there?"

A high feminine voice answered, "It is I. The wife of Lin Chien-lu, with his son and his daughter on either hand."

Then Su-ling took charge. "The wife of Lin Chien-lu is within and sitting now by the window in her dwelling in the Court of the Ginkgo Trees. The daughter of Lin Chien-lu is married and lives in Peking. The son of Lin Chien-lu is a grown man. Fly away, evil spirit. Fly away."

"Call the Elder of our House," the voice continued. "Tell him I am the woman Lin Chien-lu mated at Shanghai. I have the clothes he wore on leaving the homestead and his likeness in the faces of our children."

When Camel-back returned with the cakes he was consulted. He recognized the garments of Lin Chien-lu and the Lin brow and nose. So the woman came into the Hall of Ancestors where the family were assembled in council, and convinced the House of her rights.

Although Lin Chien-lu had not communicated with his homestead since the day, nine years previously, when he departed for Canton; although the woman had not known his whereabouts for seven years, she was entitled to shelter, food, and raiment for life; to a funeral; to have her spirit table set in the Circle of Ancestors. She must do her share of cooking, cleaning, and sewing, but she cannot be forced to earn for the common fund, and she must be nursed in sickness.

His first wife, married with music and ceremony twenty-two years before his departure, had to give the newcomer living space. The children he sired in Shanghai have inheritance equal to the rights of his children born here. In the event of the death of the first wife, the newcomer would speak with the authority of Lin Chien-lu in his absence in matters concerning property and *all* his children. Even if a woman's husband has deserted her, as Chien-lu appears to have done, the homestead cannot frown upon her as an extra rice bowl. Even though her husband be expelled from the homestead for misdemeanor, she can continue in her full rights.

If a woman mates twice, it must be by her own choice. A woman need not ever be anxious about material things so long as the fortune of the homestead with which she mates is good. A mother is never subject to the child to whom she gave life. Public opinion is such that no purchaser would venture to take transfer of property which a son offered for sale without his mother's approval.

One day, in the midst of the turmoil about the admittance of the woman and the two children, Shun-ko said, "On my world tour I heard much concerning woman's rights. I even heard folk, in comparing their condition with ours, pity us Chinese women. But I have returned home to the customs in force in China for centuries, well content with my rights as a daughter of the House of Ho and a wife of the House of Lin. And I trust that civil war will so occupy the country during my lifetime that there will be no time for a new code of law modernizing our privileges."

THE FAMILY KNEW that Ko-nen was with child. She had failed to conceive on her marriage bed, and her husband had since been away at Canton, where he had mated and bred three sons.

A wife may be returned to her father's house for insubordination, as harmony is the keynote of courtyard life. But if a bride goes forth from her father's care as a virgin, then unchastity is her husband's fault, and it is his duty to inflict punishment.

The Elder of the House of Exile sent for Ko-nen's husband. He came, and astonished the homestead by calling a council and declaring that he was willing to accept the child in Ko-nen's womb as his own. But this the homestead refused to permit.

A woman may not be punished in China while she carries new life in her body. From the day of his speech in council, her husband, who could not leave the homestead until after the birth, refused to take part in family life and took no food except rice water.

Suspicion pointed to her husband's cousin, a youth of twenty-two years, whose marriage had been arranged with a daughter of Ho, Shun-ko's niece. The House of Ho immediately withdrew their red card of agreement and returned the betrothal bracelets. Sin can rot the foundation of a homestead and bring a family to corruption. The most insidious of sins is trespass beyond the Orchid Door.

Ko-nen had been married at seventeen. She was now twenty-two. I had always considered her exceedingly plain. But now her dull eyes brightened and her hair had gloss. Her sallowness cleared to rose-petal creaminess. Her breasts swelled in lovely curves under gowns that had once hung slack.

Despite ostracism, she was in radiant beauty, and in the fullness of time she delivered a boy. At breakfast call next day, when her serving woman took her gruel, Ko-nen had swallowed gold and given gold to her child. Beautiful, as all love children seem to be, he rested in the curve of his mother's arm.

He who was suspected of knowing the wife of his cousin was brought to audience with his assembled kindred, including three from the Lin clan at Canton. He was denounced by his nearest of kin—his own mother. He had been a well-loved lad. One dissenting voice could have saved him. That, or the appearance of two gray doves. But among all the Lins there was not one from man, woman, or child.

Disinherited, he was sent from the homestead, doomed forever to use only the name "outcast," with no place to set his spirit tablet—and no rights in the patrimony beyond the cotton gown and straw sandals in which he was dressed and the packet of rice tied to his shoulder.

VII. MARRIAGE

IT WAS THE AFTERNOON of Feast of Lanterns Eve, in 1922. "You are," said Su-ling, as Mai-da cut another bias ruffle from the shell-pink velvet, "about to cause us all to be reminded in council that marriage is not a relation for personal pleasure, but a contract involving ancestors, descendants, and property. A contract not to be emotionally entered into, in our land, where we pride ourselves on a continuous procession of prudent generations."

"It might also," added Ching-mei as she bit off a thread, "be wise to remember that while negligent farming brings temporary poverty, a mistake in marriage brings poverty for life."

Immediately after the meal in the Hour of the Snake, the wives of the homestead had gone out to burn incense at the Temple of Eternal Greenness. They would not return until after dusk. Their chair bearers would loiter so that the women might enjoy the ice lanterns, chiseled in the image of trees, frogs, tigers, dragons, sprites, and such, in accord with the fancy of the ice men. On every Feast of Lanterns Eve they are set up on each side of the avenues leading to the pond. They are lit at dusk. Then the village elders present prizes to the three best.

Above her sewing table Mai-da had tacked a sketch of the Pearl Fairy holding open her oyster-shell home, as a pattern from which to create her costume for the Lanterns Eve masque. She had shaped an oyster shell of whalebone, in size to close comfortably about herself, covered it with gray cotton touched up realistically with white and green paint, and lined it with fine pink gauze. It lay finished on her bed. She had fringed the pale chiffon veil that makes the fairy invisible, cleaned her best satin slippers, and completed the waist of the shell-pink velvet dress. It awaited the attachment of a wide ruffled skirt. But the task of hemming and attaching the tiny ruffles was more than she was equal to in the time remaining before the masque. This circumstance had forced her to trust her cousins concerning her intent to dance in the street masquerade.

She told of the note she had received from Erh-sung, the Manchu prince, asking her to come as the Pearl Fairy to meet him, who would be disguised as the Fisherman's Son. Also how she had put her consenting answer under the loose stone behind the shrine of the Old Man in the Moon, in the Street of the Purple Bamboo Forest, which had been her letter box for communication with him for many months.

So, as the wives were all safely out, Su-ling and Ching-mei lectured Mai-da wisely on marriage while they sewed with diligence. I polished the jade earrings Mai-da had promised to give her servant Faithful Duck if she helped her get safely out through the Gate of Compassion and in again. Mai-da cut ruffles from the roll of exquisite fragile tissue velvet which her great-aunt had given her for her bridal gown.

When the stitching was finished, she donned the costume. She held the shell in her hands and mischievously closed its dullness around her dainty beauty.

We had tidied the room before the pat-pat of the chair bearers' feet sounded at the Orchid Door. The wives found Mai-da in the kitchen, assisting at the preparation of the evening meal.

Clouds covered the moon in the early night. Mai-da squeezed her slim loveliness through the Gate of Compassion and handed one earring to Faithful Duck. A Fisherman's Son kept tryst with her at the homestead wall. He flirted in a dance down the lantern-decorated streets, returning her frolic. She was puzzled, thrilled, and half frightened.

She knew that he was not Erh-sung. Yet he enchanted her with his charm. They dined with other masqueraders at the Abode of Orchids. He brought her safely back to the Gate of Compassion just before dawn.

Faithful Duck awaited her. When Mai-da was again under the shadow of the Goddess of Mercy and had lit a tall taper of thanksgiving, her escort recalled her to the door with a low whistle. Then he lifted his mask—the gay companion of her escapade was her favorite uncle, Keng-lin.

Next day, when Mai-da was polishing brasses in the Hall of Ancestors, Uncle Keng-lin told her how her letter had come into his possession. An itinerant priest had seen her put it under the shrine in the Street of the Purple Bamboo Forest; secured it; followed her home; and sat down at the To and From the World Gate to sell it to the first man of the family who came out. He had demanded five hundred dollars. Keng-lin had got the letter for three hundred, and sealed the priest's lips against gossiping Mai-da's name all along his holy pilgrimage.

Two days after the Feast of Lanterns, Wei-sung, the family Elder, called Mai-da to the library. Five cards offering suitable proposals of marriage were laid face down on his writing table. He told her to take one. Thus she, who for many years had managed to avoid betrothal, selected her husband.

Mai-da is bred of centuries of folk who accept marriage as a duty; she accepted her fate with philosophy, and seemingly without curiosity concerning her future husband. Uncle Keng-lin carried a red card containing the record of her year, month, day, and hour of birth to the man's homestead, which is but three streets away.

"Marriage," Shun-ko told me, "is a contract between two families. A maid is wed in accord with the wisdom of her clan. We are careful to have our descendants mate well. The name of Mai-da's proposed husband will lie with hers for three days on our family altar, and on his homestead altar. Only if there is peace in both households during this time will the alliance go further. If criticism of the union be spoken in either homestead, the matter will be dropped. But no person will speak without real concern."

Late on the third day, Mai-da and I were in the central room of the Three Eastern Courtyards where especially honored callers are received. We were searching for a volume of poems when the Elder's servant came in and put down a wicker tea basket. We realized that a visitor had been announced. To avoid being met in the courtyard, we stayed behind a lacquer screen. The doors were flung open. The Elder entered, pulling his ceremonial robe about him. From our peep-crack we recognized the visitor's sedan chair. It was from the House of Mai-da's proposed husband.

An uncle of that House descended from it dressed in a richly ornamented gown. He knelt before the Elder of Lin, despite the latter's polite attempt to stop him, and presented a betrothal contract signed by his family Elder and the four heirs-in-succession.

"I am the voice of our homestead," he announced, "who are united in eagerness to welcome the daughter of Lin."

The men drank tea. They talked of crops, weather, political conditions. We grew weary and cramped. When the call had stretched to proper politeness, the visitor asked to pay his respects to the First Lady of the homestead. They left to go to Kuei-tzu's apartment. We slipped back to the Springtime Bower.

After the caller had gone, Kuei-tzu sent for Mai-da. She gave her the betrothal gift from the Lady of First Authority in her future husband's homestead—a gold bracelet set with rubies.

Next morning Uncle Keng-lin rode out in the Elder's chair with a contract signed by the Elder of Lin and four heirs-in-succession, also a gift of jade coat buttons for the betrothed bridegroom.

In the afternoon, the Elder of the groom's homestead came to the House of Lin to ask for the wedding date. The nineteenth day of the Peony Moon, the birthday of the Protectress of Blossoms, was chosen. This is Mai-da's favorite day.

As soon as they could be baked, and while they were still

warm from the oven, the groom's mother sent sweet cookies, called phoenix-and-dragon cakes, to Mai-da. Two servants garbed in wedding coats of green and red carried them in a basket on a red pole by way of the principal streets of the village. So it was made public that the betrothal was complete and the wedding day named.

Mai-da then had to present to Kuei-tzu a list of the homesteads which she wished to have help with preparations for her marriage. Each phoenix-and-dragon cake had the wedding date stamped into it with red sugar. Packets of five cakes were wrapped in wedding paper, then sealed in lacquer wedding-cake boxes, and dispatched by messenger or by post to each household on the list.

These homesteads responded with gifts: trousseau garments, furniture, bedding, crockery, silverware, kitchen utensils, and jewelry. Seamstresses helped sew gowns of flowered silk for all the family, as well as wedding garments for the bride. Luckily Mai-da received three rolls of shell-pink tissue velvet. In the confusion of the preparations no one appeared to remember that she should now have four rolls.

Mai-da was teased about her husband. She was laughingly told that he had flat feet, a terrible temper, a pockmarked face, untidy habits, a finicky appetite, the body of a giant, and the mind of a simpleton. She met this jesting with admirable self-control, but she bartered away her birthday camera to her cousin, Tsai-fu, in return for snapshots of her betrothed. She satisfied herself that he was a man whom she had once seen worshipping the God of Knowledge at the city temple.

Hua-li was busy in court and garden coaxing the peonies with liquid fertilizers. The showing of flowers and buds was perfect. In varieties of every size, they gave dignity and fragrance to the House of Exile. They rose, on terraces facing the pond, in a luxurious hill of color shading through dark plum, wine red, sunrise pink, apple bloom, and cloud white. Beyond the arbor, pale yellow peonies unfurled their beauty. In the library court, the plant called Maiden Asleep in the Moonlight, brought by a bride from the city of Loyang one hundred years ago, proudly lifted purple buds beyond counting.

Awnings were put up to shade the courts, crimson carpets laid on the tiles. Rosy banners floated on the spring breezes over the courtyard. The house pillars were wrapped in bindings of silk. All the decorative treasures of ivory, porcelain, bronze, and jade were brought from chests and set where their antiquity showed best. Scrolls of red and gold were pasted on the To and From the World Gate, announcing that Mai-da would go to

complete the House of Tseng, as wife of Tseng Huai-ching, on the birthday of the Protectress of Blossoms.

Friends and relatives who desired to assist in the preparation began to arrive four days before the wedding. Courtesy demands that feast food be ready to welcome these guests, so there was continuous bustle in the kitchens a week before the wedding.

With thoughtful consideration, the groom's household sent gifts of wine, cakes, roast geese, braised duck, pickled pork, spiced mutton, sugared nuts, candied fruit, and sweetmeats prepared by their recipes. With equally thoughtful consideration, the bride's family, realizing that early guests would be arriving at the groom's house too, sent wine, cakes, geese, duck, pork, mutton, sugared nuts, candied fruits, and sweetmeats made by *their* recipes. There was a delightful confusion of servants carrying baskets between the two households—in itself a source of happiness, as carriers are tipped each time they deliver a parcel in Chinese homes.

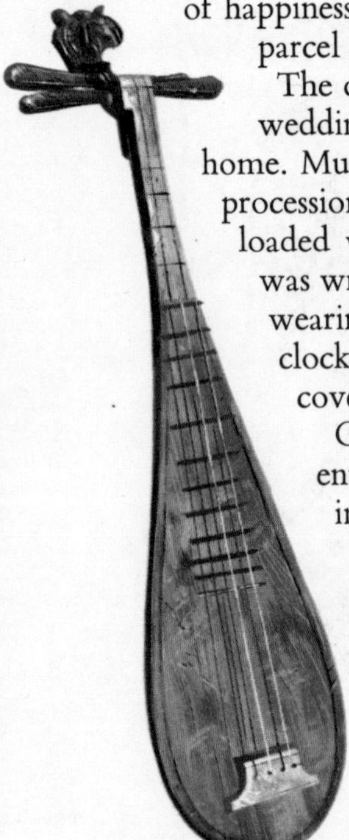

The day before the bride was sent, bearers in brilliant wedding garments carried Mai-da's dowry to her new home. Musicians played at the front and at the rear of this procession. It was ninety-one carrying poles long, each loaded with what two men could carry. The furniture was wrapped in red covers. The smaller articles and the wearing apparel were packed in chests. But a Swiss clock with a bird that sang the hour was carried uncovered so that the village might enjoy it.

Camel-back walked behind the procession. He was entrusted with Mai-da's jewel box and with the inventory of her possessions.

On the marriage eve, the Maid's Feast was held. The Hall of Hospitality was decorated with the symbols of happiness and illuminated with scarlet candles. Mai-da's mother presided. Mai-da came to the hall when the first course had been served and poured wine into each guest's cup. She was dressed, for the last time, in the costume of girlhood. Her hair had been brushed to a blue-black gloss and hung in a thick plait far below her waist. Her eyes were bright with excitement. She was exquisite in the straight bamboo-green dress made for the occasion.

On the evening before she leaves home, each girl of the House of Exile dines alone with the Lady of First Authority. Mai-da dined with Kuei-tzu. Then she burned incense of farewell in the Hall of Ancestors, and was sent to bed.

The pad-pad of cloth shoes on the dusty road heralded the

approach of the bridal chair at sunrise. The flutes played the Call for the Bride and the To and From the World Gate creaked open.

Faithful Duck hurried to our room to say that the groom's musicians numbered thirty-two. That the bridal chair had eight bearers, all in new wedding coats of scarlet satin. That there were two green chairs, one which had held the groom's aunt, who had the bridal cloak and red handkerchief, and who had gone to drink tea with Mai-da's mother; the other to carry herself, Faithful Duck. Also more bannermen than she had been able to count, as they moved about so much.

Shun-ko ordered Faithful Duck to stop her chatter and fetch bath water for her mistress. She laid out Mai-da's lotus-perfumed wedding garments. She hid her emotion by scolding Mai-da for being too lenient with her servant. Another aunt came and painted Mai-da's alarming pallor with a lotion. Then Ching-mei used lip rouge on the bride's mouth, saying that it was absolutely proof against coming off on the nuptial cup.

A cousin came to say that the bridegroom had arrived, and was kneeling before the Elders, making formal request for their daughter to "complete himself," and would soon return to his homestead to await Mai-da.

The wedding dress was slipped over Mai-da's head and admired by all the women and children who were now clustered in the room. Mai-da had been a quiet doll to paint and dress, but suddenly she began to laugh with shrill hysteria. No one could stop her. The Elder's wife sent word that everyone—excepting Shun-ko, who "has sense," and Faithful Duck—was to leave the Springtime Bower. Uncle Keng-lin came with his lute and played lullabies to quiet Mai-da's nerves.

It was noon when Mai-da came to the Hall of Dignity. She bowed to the guests. She knelt in farewell to the Elders and her parents. Her father fastened the groom's cloak about her shoulders. Her mother dropped his handkerchief as a veil over her face. The family cried, "May you be as happy as the maid from Canton!" Crackers were fired in loud explosion. Mai-da was lifted into the bride's chair. The chair was closed and the sealing papers were fastened.

Kuei-tzu put her name on the seals. Drums rapped the call to start. The cymbals clanged assent. Flutes gave the Wail of Departure. The groom's aunt and Faithful Duck got into the two green chairs. Lifting poles creaked. The bride's procession passed out of the house of her girlhood. The To and From the World Gate was locked behind her.

The clan of Lin, gathered from far and near, feasting and playing games to pass time, waited until the invitation should come from the Tseng clan inviting the bride's mother to the "after-the-rites-of-the-marriage-bed breakfast," which is assurance that the groom's family are satisfied.

Thus Mai-da went to her husband.

IT WAS THE LAST DAY of the Dragon Moon, several weeks after Mai-da had gone. The weather was uncomfortably warm and the Elder's wife had told La-mei and me to put jasmine tea on the shelf of the Gate of Compassion, that the poor might refresh themselves and not be tempted to drink canal water. Ching-mei came running into the kitchen where we were boiling water.

"Whatever has happened?" La-mei demanded of her twin.

"Chao-li has just told her son that she intends to marry the proprietor of the Abode of Orchids Restaurant," Ching-mei answered. "And he has retorted that 'She who has been wife to one man does not go to eat the rice of another.' "

"Hot boiled sweet potato!" La-mei exclaimed.

Chao-li was then thirty-six and had been a widow for three years. The Elder's wife showed her disapproval by hiring craftsmen to regild the Memorial Arch to Virtuous Widows, which records the widows who have chastely refused to "drink the tea of two families." The Elder reminded Chao-li that a widow who goes out through the gate to marry again loses all rights and voice in the family. Her daughters may accompany her, but they also lose all rights in their birth home. Sons and whatever property the woman brought to the homestead belong to her husband's family.

Chao-li continued in her desire to marry Kwong Ching-lei. A widow can demand that her husband's family negotiate her marriage. The Lin family Elders had to receive the jolly proprietor of the Abode of Orchids with all the courtesy which custom demands shall be accorded an honorable suitor for a bride. The House had to accept his proffered wedding gifts, and give Chao-li to him.

A woman may not ride twice in a bride's chair or have the music of union played a second time. She takes only what she wears, and servants may not make a procession for her through the streets. Chao-li walked out of the House of Exile with her second husband on the tenth day of the Lotus Moon. Two hours later, the serving woman who had been Chao-li's childhood nurse and had come to the House of Exile in her wedding procession followed her out of the gate, accompanied by ten coolies hired to carry what appeared to me an enormous amount of luggage for a servant to possess. But no one of the Lin household took any interest in this.

"MARRIAGE," SO I HEAR OFTEN in China, "is the most important act in life. It is the seed of all future existence. If the seed is unhealthy the harvest will be misery." And just as often I hear, "Marriage involves rights and duties, both for the parties wed and for the children born of their union. But the rights of the child stand first, as the purpose of marriage is creation. No matter how blessed with happiness the man and woman are, the marriage is a failure if it is childless. This misfortune is to be remedied by adoption, or by taking a handmaiden into the marriage to make it fruitful."

From girlhood Mai-da's mother had been interested in the history of marriage in China. She had a notebook in which she wrote the customs and regulations that govern the present-day wedding. From her notebook, I learned that if a man and a woman are incompatible they may be divorced, with the mutual consent of their two homesteads, and the woman return to her father's house. In such cases there is no need to refer the matter to the civil authorities. It is a family affair, arranged by mutual goodwill on the part of the parties concerned.

But, as a woman's ancestors are responsible for her breeding and her education, her husband's family can force her birth home to take her back for any of the "seven rights"—i.e.,

barrenness, wanton conduct, discourtesy, gossip, theft, envy, or an infirmity misrepresented in the betrothal contract. Even if a man dearly and passionately loves his mate, his family may return her. Marriage is a family, not a personal, affair in which the happiness of the group is paramount and not the happiness of the individual.

Three compensatory rights prevent a woman from being divorced: i.e., if she has kept three years of mourning for either of her husband's parents, if her husband's homestead is more wealthy than when she entered it, or if her birth home has been broken up since her marriage and she has no place to go. In case of adultery, however, they are inoperative.

Mai-da's mother has further noted that adultery is only a feminine vice. Copulation on the man's part is not his wife's concern, unless he sires a child. Then she must accept the child as one of her household. All a man's offspring inherit equal rights in his homestead. It is his wife's duty to have all his children fed, clothed, and educated in accord with his property. In the event of his death or his absence, she must assume custody of all his children's shares in the property and speak as his voice to defend their rights. No child in China can ever suffer bastardy, as no man's offspring is an illegitimate child.

TAI-CHUN WAS MARRIED in the Chrysanthemum Moon, when he was eighteen. The present Elder of Lin is industrious in keeping the admonition of the sages: "Marry your sons as soon as they are grown." By the marriage of a son he can bring into his homestead another charming young woman, and fill the homestead courtyards with more beautiful Lin children.

The messenger delivering the announcements of the birth of Lin Tai-chun, great-grandnephew of the Lin family Elder, had crossed paths with the messenger delivering announcements of the birth of Pien Wei-ling, great-granddaughter of the Pien family Elder. Stopping to gossip, the messengers had agreed that the newborn boy and girl would certainly marry. This supposition was also voiced in every house which received the announcements.

Before the Rounding of the Year, Tai-chun's mother had

accepted an invitation to spend a moon in the Pien courtyards, during which the babies shared the same cradle. The children sat in a double pushcart and each had a handstring to the kite that old Camel-back made and flew for them.

From then until the Cycle of Ten they were together a month or two every year in the Garden of Children of the Lin or the Pien homestead. The year that they were twelve, Tai-chun wove Wei-ling a sewing basket of rice straw (the one she still uses). And Wei-ling, helped by her younger brother, made Tai-chun a boat to sail on the shallow pond.

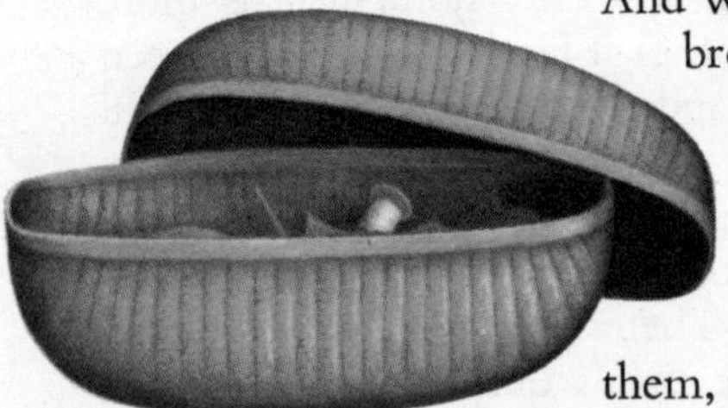

After that, of course, Tai-chun was too old to play with girls. He had a tutor who, if he even so much as mentioned them, punished such idleness by obliging him to commit to memory pages from Confucius's books, to cleanse his mind.

Naturally Wei-ling also was no longer permitted the license of a child. Promoted to the Springtime Bower, she was chaperoned in maidenly seclusion. As marriage was to be her career, her educators seldom permitted her thoughts to stray away from man or the arts by which to please him.

The clans of Lin and Pien are both exceedingly cautious. Both received invitations to betrothal from other clans as the years passed. Neither entirely rebuffed any of these. Then, at New Year 1919, the House of Lin included a pair of embroidered pockets in the gifts to the House of Pien. One pocket held a red card on which Tai-chun's name, birth hour, day, moon, and year were brushed in gold. The other was empty. The House of Pien returned the empty pocket filled with a red card on which was brushed Wei-ling's name, birth hour, day, moon, and year.

At certain festivals for three years after this, the House of Lin sent sweetmeats to Wei-ling. On the third Dragon Festival they included pink flowered silk of the shade used only by a bride, indicating that they but waited for her to name the day. She announced it by sending the wife of the Lin family Elder a square of the bride's silk on which she had painted seven chrysanthemums, thus indicating the seventh day of the Chrysanthemum Moon.

Phoenix-and-dragon cookies, in addition to those sent to the promised bride, were baked for the betrothed groom. Accompanied by Camel-back to carry the red kneeling mat, he called at each homestead within visiting distance and gave his wedding invitation to the Elder and his wife. Others were sent by post.

Moon lanterns (symbolic of marriage, because each month the pale moon throws herself into the embrace of her lover, the sun, leaving him only when he has kindled new light in her) were hung outside the To and From the World Gate. Red and gold scrolls announced that the great-granddaughter of Pien was soon coming to complete the House of Exile by union with the great-grandnephew of Lin.

The family portraits, even the most ancient and fragile, were unrolled and hung in the halls. Silk banners and candelabra were arranged with even more elaborateness than for Mai-da's marriage. A daughter's marriage holds the sadness of departure, but a son's marriage holds only the joy of arrival.

Guests began to arrive ten days before the date. Food in abundance was ready for them, and they also brought hampers of cooked meats, cakes, and fruit. Gifts were displayed at one end of the Hall of Family Gathering. There were fans, furs, lengths of brocade and heavy silk, and jeweled coat buttons; books, furniture, bed quilts, pillows, tapestries, rugs, porcelain, mirrors; gold and silver bars; ducks, geese, turkeys, and goats (which were taken to the stable); rice, barley, wheat, millet, corn, rose trees, and a canoe.

The magnificent Lin bride's chair, whose tapestry occupied the wives of Lin ten years, is of such workmanship that two centuries of use have but enriched its elegance. At dawn on the marriage eve, the groom knelt before his elders. He said that he intended to take the bride's chair to a worthy maid. Firecrackers were set off as he departed, attended by musicians, banner bearers, and his aunt who carried the cloak and veil. The House of Pien is three villages up the canal.

The bride's house in the Lin homestead was ready when the

Pien servants came with her dowry at midday. The Lin Elder's wife, as Lady of First Authority, superintended the placing of her bed. The rosewood chest, carved with one hundred laughing chubby babies, which contains the bedding the bride uses on her marriage night, was opened and unpacked. Pink silk bed curtains were hung under the four-posted canopy. Coverlets of peach blossom, primrose, and heliotrope were put in place.

The groom returned next day, an hour before the arrival of his bride. The family Elder welcomed her at the To and From the World Gate. The Lin women lifted the bride's chair in. The seals were broken and she descended. She placed an apple, pledge of peace, beside the string of cash, pledge of fortune, that lay in the center of the court.

Her husband welcomed her by offering her refreshment after her journey. Then he led her to kneel with him in the Hall of Ancestors before his elders; which observance is a symbol that henceforth they are one in rights and responsibilities, as though she had been born in his clan.

The women's feast was served that evening in the Court of Favorite Eaves of Nesting Swallows; the men's feast in the Court of the Happy Waterfall. Little girl children sat at table with the women, and little boys with the men. The courtesy to them was identical to that shown their elders. When the wedding couple had accomplished "wine and food politeness" (pouring wine and pressing some special dish on each guest), they went to the bride's house, where their supper had been placed on the upturned copper basin. While they ate, the family Elder and his wife sat together outside the bride's window and sang the Mating Song, which may be sung only by a man and a woman who have loved each other for more than five decades.

The bride's mother came to breakfast. The sulky chrysanthemums had refused to bloom earlier but they opened their silken petals that morning to welcome the young wife. She was dressed in bell-legged trousers and a graceful short coat embroidered with flowers in threads so fine that they appeared to be painted on. Her husband's gift, a sapphire like a bit of the China sky at night, sparkled as she patted her anxious parent reassuringly before she sat down.

CHING-MEI, ONE OF THE LIN TWINS, betrothed at birth, was married to Kui Wen-chow at the end of Chrysanthemums. She had been ill with typhoid when he won the scholarship which took him to America for five years, so could not be wed before he sailed. Both she and her twin La-mei accepted marriage as an inevitable event.

Yet they were heartbroken at the thought of separation, as they had never been apart for an hour in their lives. La-mei had learned some English from me and was keenly interested in foreign thought. Ching-mei believes Chinese the only medium for self-expression. She has her mind shut against all other civilizations. She was dumb with fear concerning the occidentalisms that her husband might have acquired. Yet the contract had to be completed. So La-mei went with her. Of course La-mei could not ride in a bride's chair, nor bow to the Kui ancestors. But all children born to her have equal rights with those of her sister, and the two trousseaus were similar in every detail.

Three weddings in a year, one of them requiring a double dowry, had strained the resources of the House of Exile. Su-ling suggested in family council that the consummation of her betrothal be put forward a year. As reward for her thoughtfulness, she went to visit the clan at Canton for six months.

Two weeks after her arrival, she slipped over the wall of the house one night and married a young Chinese lawyer named Lui whom she had met when they were students in Paris. Their marriage was in the way advocated by the radicals of the rising Nationalist Party who repudiated the marriages contracted for them by their family elders. They mated together, then announced their act in the newspapers the next morning.

Su-ling had dishonored her House, but wayward, independent, winsome Su-ling has never been long in disgrace. Seven months after her mating, she was heavy with child. She knocked at the To and From the World Gate of the House of Lin at Canton. It was the birthday of the gentle, gracious god Ti Tang, the Redeemer who descends into Hell to secure release for all in trouble. Su-ling saw the Lady of First Authority. Thereafter she wore that lady's famous pearls in public token of her favor. Su-ling's husband was received by the Elder of Lin, who wrote a letter to the Elder of the House of Exile. I heard no further criticism of Su-ling. Nor was it long before she was acknowledged by her husband's family.

THE ENGLISHMAN whom I met on the *Empress of Asia* was given my China address during his stay in America. In the Peony Moon, he returned to China and sent his sister-in-law to call upon me. I liked her at first meeting.

The second time she came to see me, he came with her. He said that he had been appointed to Nanking. Mai-da had accompanied her husband to Nanking three months previously. Their residence was just five minutes' walk from that of the Englishman. Aside from giving me this information, the rest of the call was taken up with telling me gravely that I made a mistake in staying on in China. He came to see me twice in the Dragon Moon and three times in the Lotus Moon. On the fifth day of the Harvest Moon he asked me in marriage.

I was most confusedly in love. From the first meeting he had distracted my mind. His face would keep appearing between me and a book I tried to read, or his voice would suddenly sound instead of the words I tried to write. This still happens even now. I found love annoying and uncomfortable until I got used to it.

I wanted to keep my American citizenship. My people have had it a long time. So my husband-to-be made arrangements and I signed a paper declaring my intent to remain a citizen of the United States despite my marriage with a British subject. A British subject in China is not legally married unless there is a civil service in a British consulate. This ceremony was brief. When it was done, I found that England does not recognize a woman's right to remain a citizen of her country after marriage with a British subject. Regardless of my protests, my name was written under my husband's in the count of British subjects in China.

During the weeks that my betrothed's intent to marry me was publicly posted at his country's consulate, it was also read out each Sunday morning in the Church of England: "If any of you know cause or just impediment why these two persons should not be joined together in holy matrimony, ye are to

GOOD NIGHT,
SWEET PRINCE

A CONDENSATION OF

GOOD NIGHT, SWEET PRINCE

The Life and Times of John Barrymore

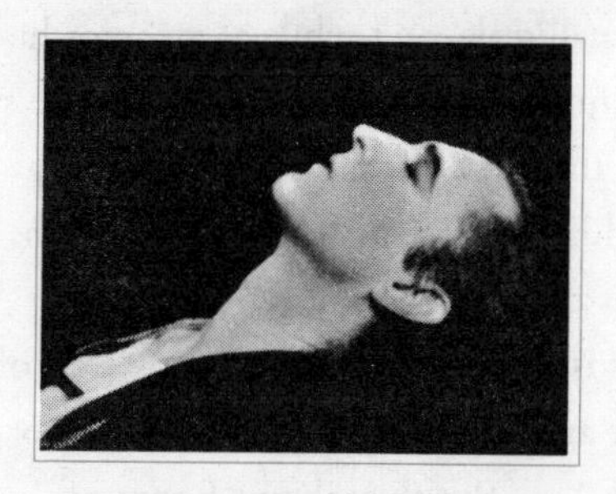

by

GENE FOWLER

John Barrymore has been described as the greatest actor of this century, and Gene Fowler's story of his life has been called "the best biography of an actor ever written." The two were close friends; yet the newspaperman's affection for his subject never gets in the way of a clear-eyed account of his foibles.

For Barrymore offstage was a flamboyant and unpredictable figure, a great wit who consorted with wits, a spendthrift playboy, a prey to immoderate passions. Nothing he did was done on a small scale, and while as an actor he reached the summit of achievement both on the stage and in the most glittering era of films, as an individual he often touched tragic depths of self-torture and humiliation.

This is a very entertaining book, full of humor and anecdote and the exotic color of the Gilded Age. But the vibrant figure of John Barrymore always holds center stage, as was his wont, and at the end we have come to know an appealing and memorable man.

PROLOGUE

I WAS A REPORTER for the New York *American* when I first met my friend John Barrymore. A sports writer on temporary loan to the theatrical department, I had been sent to get an interview with the actor who was then starring in the Tolstoy play *Redemption*.

I found him in his dressing room at the Plymouth Theatre after a matinee performance. He was perspiring and swearing eloquently, while molting a false beard. I never had seen him before, on or off stage, and when he rose to put on his somewhat seedy coat, I noticed that he was athletic, had an extraordinary sense of balance, and moved on the balls of his feet like a boxer.

He was on his way to see the Baron. "The Baron," he explained, "is my only true friend."

The star of *Redemption* now put on a fedora, a vintage number in every respect. It might once have been forest green. But as he adjusted the crown, giving it certain deft tugs and pats, it suddenly took on a quality of magnificence.

"The only reason why a man should pay the least attention to a hat," he said, as we went outside the theater, "is that it is something one tips to a lady."

It was twilight as we walked into the West Forties, and the last of the matineegoers, stragglers from other playhouses, were turning to look at the eminent actor. In that decent era, shortly after the end of World War I, autograph seekers had not yet begun to pounce like gadflies upon their celebrities. Barrymore caught the attention of the Broadway pedestrians but did not take much notice of them. Vanity was not among his vices.

"You'll love the Baron," he said. "He is a savant, a philosopher, the seventh son of a seventh son, and one of the greatest alchemists since Trismegistus. The Baron is seeking the philosophers' stone."

The Baron, I discovered in due time, was making gin.

Soon after we arrived at the Baron's boardinghouse lodgings, where we were greeted warmly by our host and his elderly pug dog, I found myself standing with Barrymore in the dark hall outside a tiny bathroom, watching the celebrated alchemist at his labors over an ancient zinc bathtub.

"Prohibition enforcement will not find me napping," announced the Baron, a small balding fellow of perhaps seventy. He was busy diluting some alcohol with juniper essence.

Barrymore and I, meanwhile, were speaking of pug dogs. The affection the Baron's dog had displayed for the actor was evidently mutual. And I was interested because this was the first pug I had seen since my own had gone mad and been chloroformed when I was a child.

"I don't think you'll find many pug dogs left in this whole world," Barrymore said.

"I had one," I replied.

He now looked at me with genuine interest. His bantering manner fell like a bullfighter's cape. "You really owned one? Tell me about him."

"There's not much to tell," I said. "I was living with my grandmother . . ."

"You *were?*" he asked, with such emphasis that I hesitated a moment.

"Is there anything remarkable about having lived with one's grandmother?"

"Yes," he said quietly. "Yes, there is." There was no mistaking his sincerity. "The only bringing up I ever had was by my grandmother, Mrs. Drew. . . ."

He seemed to catch himself being sentimental. He called to the Baron, "Are you dissolving a pearl?"

"All in good time," the Baron replied gently.

I found Barrymore studying me in the half-light from the bathroom door. "I interrupted you," he said. "The pug dog?"

"He went mad," I replied. "I couldn't understand why they had put him under a wooden washtub, then placed a rag soaked with something beneath the tub, and my uncle standing there like an elephant hunter being photographed after the kill."

"What did you do?" he asked slowly.

"I yelled my head off. And told my grandmother I'd never forgive my uncle. She was a religious woman. She told me what a sin it was not to forgive—anything. She said that Jesus always had forgiven everybody. I remember how terribly shocked she was when I blurted out, 'Yes, but He never had a dog.' "

Until now we had not shaken hands, nor had Barrymore even asked my name. He put out his hand, and said, "Hello!"

The Baron, carrying a filled jug, emerged from the bathroom, an aura of ecclesiastical peace upon him.

We followed him back to his quarters and sampled his experimental nectar, drinking from cracked china cups with no handles. Then we helped ourselves to another portion.

Suddenly Barrymore remembered he was due at the theater.

"Good God!" he said. "Time to smear on the paint and pretend I'm somebody else."

It wasn't until we were on our way back to the theater that I remembered I had been sent to get an interview.

CHAPTER I

A GLASSED-IN CARRIAGE with an Irish coachman drew up at the entrance of the old Chestnut Street wharf in Philadelphia on a cold, rainy Saint Valentine's Day, 1882. Sitting upright in this smart brougham, looking rather like the Queen Victoria of calendar chromos, was a smallish lady, caped with a dolman of embossed black velvet, who did not seem her sixty-two years. There was authority in the way she sat on the broadcloth cushions, a regal fire in the large, bright blue eyes. Even the dullest beer guzzler among the passing rivermen could sense that she was a personage.

This was Louisa Lane Drew, manager of the Arch Street Theatre; widow of John Drew, a fine actor who had died young; and herself in her fifty-seventh season of footlights and grease-paint, having recently returned home after thirteen weeks as the famous Mrs. Malaprop in Sheridan's *The Rivals*. Mrs. Drew was presently awaiting the arrival of one Dr. J. Nicholas Mitchell on the steamboat from Wilmington. She had summoned the family doctor home from his emergency labors in Delaware, fighting cholera, because her actress daughter, Georgianna Drew, wife of actor Maurice Barrymore, was momentarily expecting a third child.

She *was* history, this woman. Born the same year in which King George III had died, 1820, her parents, players of provincial reputation, had brought her at the age of seven from England to Philadelphia. Here, at nine, when she had played all five roles in *Twelve Precisely*, a Revolutionary War veteran had come backstage to hold her on his knee. She had listened to the Liberty Bell tolling in 1834 for the death of Lafayette; and a year afterward heard its last note, as the great bell cracked while sounding the requiem for Chief Justice John Marshall. A block to the east of her Arch Street Theatre lay the wise bones of Benjamin Franklin, and a square beyond his grave the Betsy Ross house.

Now a whistle sounded. "She's a-dockin'!" the coachman announced. Soon the doctor came ashore, carrying a battered clinical valise and an umbrella, and he and the expectant grandmother were at once driven through the rain to a three-story brick house at Number 2008 Columbia Avenue.

This was not so fine a home as might have been expected of the successful manager of a famous theater, one who maintained a coachman and brougham, a cook and maids; still, it was not commonplace. Mrs. Drew was prospering at this time. An adroit actress-manager, she had persuaded Edwin Booth, Joseph Jefferson, and others of public favor to appear before her footlights, and her own achievements as an actress enlarged her personal income. Yet, underneath the armor plate of her dignity was a warm generosity. Always she shared her purse and herself; her several successive homes sheltered her children and theirs, and an assortment of poor relations. Perhaps she regarded the saving of money too lightly, a quirk that became manifest in her talented descendants.

As she and the doctor entered the hallway, a maid helped her remove the dolman, and informed her that an actor who was appearing at the theater in a new comedy that night was in the parlor. "He's excited," the maid reported.

Mrs. Drew removed her plumed turban. "Never mind him. How's Georgie?"

"She's havin' pains."

Mrs. Drew turned to the doctor, gesturing toward the stairs with a long hatpin. "I think you know the way, Doctor," she said, and followed him up, ignoring the distraught actor who emerged from the parlor to call after them, "It's about the scenery. My cliff has been lost." But Mrs. Drew had disappeared.

As the actor turned to go back to the parlor, Mrs. Drew's favorite son, Sidney Drew, appeared in the hallway carrying his sister Georgianna's three-year-old Ethel, and followed by four-year-old Lionel, burbling happily.

"I've lost my cliff," said the actor, solemnly eyeing the Barrymore children while addressing himself to Sidney. "Your mother pays no attention whatsoever."

In her daughter's bedroom, Mrs. Drew was paying attention to the new baby boy she held in her arms. "He looks like a pretty little lad in a storybook," said his grandmother.

John Sidney Blythe Barrymore had arrived.

JOHN BARRYMORE'S FATHER, Maurice, a much-loved, sometimes envied man of wit, charm, and outstanding physical endowments, had first come to America some seven years before the birth of his younger son, having crossed to New York from Liverpool in the spring of 1875. At that time, Maurice Barrymore's fellow passengers, mostly of English stock themselves, had accounted their twenty-eight-year-old shipmate an amiable dandy, and were uncritical of the tall silk hat and monocle he wore. But when he went ashore he attracted considerable attention.

As soon as he had cleared the customs at Castle Garden, Maurice, deciding not to ride the horsecar, started walking confidently up Broadway as if on a familiar round. Soon he entered the famed Hoffman House Bar, where he ordered a whiskey and soda, without ice, his speech as neatly clipped as the hedges of Oxford University. The bartender pretended not to notice the eyeglass, the silk hat, or the un-American request for no ice, but not the guests in this best of all possible bars. They stared, nudged their companions, and several were not satisfied to let Mr. Barrymore mind his own thirst.

Their leader, a locally renowned social light and all-around athlete, placed a silver dollar in his eye, leaned toward Mr. Barrymore, and drawled, "I say, Percy, I suppose this is the *English* way? Wot?"

"Oh, no," replied the actor, removing his monocle and settling the silk hat to his head. "Allow me to show you." His fist traveled a short, jolting arc. "*This* is the English way!"

The spectators sucked in their breaths. Their leader lay like a dissected frog on the tiles, while the Barrymore hat remained as solidly on his head as a cornice. Lifted to his feet and informed where he was, the vanquished sportsman blinked, then put out his hand to Barrymore. He was delighted to learn, in the friendly conversation that ensued, that his conqueror, during student days at Oxford, had been amateur lightweight champion of England.

During this and other evenings at the Hoffman House, Maurice Barrymore's new friends learned many other things about him. He had been born in India, in 1847, as Herbert Blythe, son of an army officer. Sent to England for his formal education, he finally matriculated at Lincoln College, Oxford, where he occupied the rooms of John Wesley. Upon leaving there, his family had decided that he should read for the law, which he proceeded to do.

Yet Herbert Blythe really wished to be an actor, an ambition that horrified his elders. When he obtained his first acting role, therefore, he had assumed the stage name Maurice Barrymore,

Maurice Barrymore, and, at right, his wife, Georgianna Drew with Ethel, Lionel and John.

Above, Maurice and Georgie together; at left, Maurice's mother, Mrs. John Drew.

a name he had once seen on an old playbill hanging in the foyer of London's Haymarket Theatre. Then, forsaking the law forever, he had toured the provinces until, after a series of family harangues against theatricals, he had finally left for America.

During those first several months in New York, Maurice Barrymore lived rather scantily. But, in the autumn of 1875, he became a member of the famous stock company founded by Augustin Daly. There he met the twenty-two-year-old John Drew, Jr., himself destined to become one of the most accomplished actors on the American stage, but now only a short time away from Louisa Lane Drew's apron strings, having made his debut in a minor role in his mother's Philadelphia theater. Together Drew and Maurice appeared in support of Edwin Booth's eighty-fourth appearance as Hamlet. Maurice was Laertes, and Drew was Rosencrantz.

At the close of the *Hamlet* engagement, John Drew said to Maurice, "I'm going home for the weekend. Like to come along?" Barrymore accompanied his friend to Philadelphia, there to meet John's younger sister, Georgianna, herself a talented actress, and, after a swift courtship, to marry her.

Mrs. Drew did not bless the merger. She not only had little respect for any actor whose family, unlike her own, had not been professionals for at least fifty years, but she also believed no one good enough for her daughter, particularly an irresponsible dreamer like this new son-in-law. She consistently addressed him as "you," nor did he feel safe to address her as other than "Ma'am." He may have been amateur lightweight champion of England, but in her house *she* was the champion.

CHAPTER 2

GEORGIANNA, after her marriage to Maurice Barrymore, appeared with her husband and her brother as well as far better known players like Edwin Booth and Mme. Helena Modjeska. She also became a Catholic, for Mme. Modjeska converted her from the Episcopal faith of her upbringing. Mrs. Drew was well pleased by her daughter's choice of career, and, being a believer in freedom of religion, neither opposed nor approved her change of creed. As for Maurice, it made no difference to him so long as Georgie was satisfied.

Georgianna won the favor of critics and public, and was best known as a skilled comedienne. Her daughter, Ethel Barrymore, later said of her: "My mother was blond, fair, and gay. She was a natural actress, so restrained in word and action that many persons could not appreciate her. She was twenty-five years ahead of her time."

The Drew household in Philadelphia readily expanded to include Maurice and Georgie Barrymore, whenever they were not on tour, and, eventually, their children too. Mrs. Drew was a burden bearer. No matter how many relatives thronged her home, she never complained. Whenever the increase strained domestic comfort, she would promptly move to more commodious quarters. Of these successive residences which they shared with their grandmother, Lionel, Ethel, and John remembered best the house at Number 140 North Twelfth Street, near the Arch Street Theatre. It was a three-story building with cavernous halls, a nursery known as "The Annex," and two attics. The boys slept in one of the attics. Across the street was a tombstone carver, samples of whose handiwork occupied the sidewalk in front of his establishment, and Georgie named their house the "Tomb of the Capulets."

Some overnight actor guests thought the place well named, for the faint tinklings of a little bell could be heard at all hours of the night, like something from the Great Beyond. Not daring to ask—people of the theater have an absorbing respect for the supernatural—the guests seldom learned that the ghostly sound came from the bedroom of the aged, bedridden Eliza Lane Kinloch, Mrs. Drew's mother and great-grandmother to the Barrymore children, who had been a sweet singer of ballads in England, where she was born in 1799. She would tinkle a little bell, like that used by Punch in the old puppet shows, whenever she needed attention or was lonesome—which was often, and could be anytime, for Great-grandmother Kinloch kept later hours even than Maurice Barrymore.

Whenever Lionel and little Jack sought a pretext for staying up beyond their prescribed curfew, they would visit Great-grandmother's room and, after the customary good-night kiss, begin questioning her about her memories of performers of the past. "Isn't it time to say your little prayers?" the dear old lady would say. She was, however, easily sidetracked, and would happily lapse into reminiscences of Joseph Grimaldi, greatest of the clowns, and others long gone.

Then, at last, when further delay was impossible, the Barrymore boys would kneel to say the prayer their father had been at solemn pains to teach them.

"God bless Mother, and Papa, and Grandmother, and Great-grandmother, and Uncle Sidney; and please, God, make Uncle Jack a good actor."

The Twelfth Street house has long since been razed. So has the Arch Street Theatre with which it was, for the Barrymore children, linked in memory. But one can vicariously relive the days when Charles Dickens visited the theater during his second American tour, and, in imagination, see Walt Whitman, who often crossed over from Camden as a welcome though non-paying patron of the storied playhouse. President Lincoln, too, had visited the theater.

The Barrymore children's uncle, John Drew, used to tell them of the day he ran home from the Episcopal Academy where he attended school to inform his mother of the death of Abraham Lincoln. Mrs. Drew was greatly shocked. For a long time she sat wordlessly at her desk. Then she took from a drawer a letter Lincoln had written in 1862, thanking her for providing the presidential party with seats at the Arch Street Theatre.

"Who did such a monstrously wicked thing?" she said, still gazing at the letter.

"Mr. Booth's brother," said John.

"No!" she exclaimed. The gentle, talented kinsman of the slayer had been a star at her playhouse and often a guest in her home. "It is unthinkable! . . . Will our profession ever atone?"

WHENEVER MAURICE PLAYED the Arch Street Theatre the three little Barrymores behaved as if their grandmother had done them a personal favor. Although the iron-encased businesswoman was really only booking the best available attractions, and if such an attraction happened to be Modjeska, and Maurice Barrymore tagged along as her leading man, well, we must take the bitter with the sweet. But to the children their father's Philadelphia engagements meant that Papa had come home for a season.

What a gay companion he was! If not otherwise occupied after the night performance, he would pay surreptitious visits to the attic, smuggling food for late suppers in violation of Mrs. Drew's strictest orders against waking the children. Recalling his own boyhood, he would tell them stories of India, or act out the Sepoy Mutiny, playing the parts of both armies. It was perhaps the only military action in all history to be dramatized on tiptoe and in whispers.

And Papa was never grouchy, even when the boys came shouting into his room of a morning. He refused to wear nightshirts, but reposed in a kind of rowing-club jersey. As he rose from tousled sleep, he would gulp some water, shudder, snort, as if returning to mortality, then stride up and down the room like a Roman senator in half a toga. Pointing a long finger at his sons, he would recite excerpts from the Bard.

All three children inherited his theatrical presence and charm, and also partook in varying degrees of his offstage attributes and deficits. In appearance, Ethel and Lionel resembled their mother, while Jack possessed his father's physique, quicksilver humor, and voice, along with many of his epic frailties—such as moods of self-centered arrogance, deafness to others' opinions, and a constant tragic restlessness.

Maurice loved his wife and family in his own will-o'-the-wisp fashion. When among his children, he seemed a doting and contented parent, elaborately suggesting what he and his young ones would do on a tomorrow that was to find him gone. If his waywardness seemed inexcusable to the Broadway moralists, his family (other than the stern Mrs. Drew) conceded that Papa was not a homing pigeon. His wife, as beautiful as any of his admirers, seemed serenely confident that no matter how far or for how long he might wander, he would always come back to her.

On one of these belated homecomings, a Sunday morning, Maurice approached the Tomb of the Capulets as Georgie and the little ones were descending the marble steps.

"Why, hello, darling!" he called, with the overdone cordiality of the two-faced male. "I was delayed getting in from New York. Up all night with Wilton Lackaye."

"Until now," said Georgie, "I had always thought Wilton Lackaye to be a *man*."

Maurice sought to change the subject. "Where are you going, darling?"

"I'm going to Mass," said Georgie, leading the children away, "and you can go to hell!"

BY NOW Maurice was an acknowledged figure in the theater, although not eulogized by everyone. American critics deplored his English accent. In London, when he returned for an engagement, they scoffed at his Yankee nasalities.

"Great God!" he groaned. "Must I be condemned for the rest of my life to giving recitations on ocean liners?"

Maurice also had difficulty in learning and remembering a part—a trait that offered an odd contrast to the retentiveness of other members of the family. His children became remarkably quick studies, as all the Drews had been.

Such flaws as could be found in his portrayals did not lessen the ardor of his partisans, however. Maurice Barrymore had an arresting personality, and the foremost actresses of that day, notably Olga Nethersole and Minnie Maddern Fiske, as well as Mme. Modjeska, regarded him as first choice among their leading men.

One weekend Maurice appeared at the Drew home in Philadelphia to announce that he would take his wife and ten-year-old Lionel on a tour with Mme. Modjeska, during which he would present a play he had written especially for the Polish star. The work was named *Nadjezda*, and it incorporated much coquetry, terror, and some retributory bloodletting to parade her talents. In fact, Maurice went on, he might become a playwright exclusively. He had grown a little tired of taking orders—as if he ever had!

The children rejoiced over Papa's becoming a playwright. They saw in him a magnificent success. But their grandmother continued to sit complacently at her desk, her back turned. "Mme. Modjeska," she said over her shoulder, "is deserving, after all she has suffered, of the cream of the gentleman's efforts in her behalf."

Perhaps Mrs. Drew was remembering how Modjeska, even though she regarded Maurice as a splendid necessity in her company, still complained about his failure to memorize his lines, and his occasional amazing excursions from the text. Indeed, one evening, after he had slipped away from the scene at hand into an entirely different play, Mme. Modjeska had rebuked him. "Now look, Mr. Barrymore, you must not be so careless. Please remember who made it possible for you to rise to such fame as you may think you own."

This was no way to address a Barrymore. "Madam, I was quite well known to the American public at a time when they thought Modjeska the name of a toothwash."

ON THE NIGHT they went to Philadelphia's Reading Station to see their parents and Lionel off on the train for the great American tour which, Papa had now revealed, would extend all the way to San Francisco, little Jack and Ethel Barrymore huddled in the background watching their older brother's actions with wide appraising eyes. They marveled as he moved about like a world traveler, conferring with the man at the ticket gate, advising the porter about the luggage. A windfall of grandeur blessed him.

Then came the call of "All aboard!" There was a last embrace by Mamma, then Ethel and Jack watched the lucky ones disappear through the ticket gate. Outside, Mrs. Drew's coachman was waiting to drive them home.

Ethel took Jack's hand and they walked slowly, like Hansel and Gretel, to the brougham. The coachman helped Ethel into the carriage where she sat upright and regal, as her grandmother always did. Jack climbed onto the box beside the driver and from time to time, when the roadway became clear of traffic, held the reins.

CHAPTER 3

When, in 1889, shortly after returning from the successful western tour, Papa decided to move Georgie and the children to New York, their grandmother showed no tears. Mrs. Drew knew the family had outgrown the Tomb of the Capulets. Her home already had lost some of its familiar members. The tinkle of Great-grandmother Kinloch's bell was heard no longer, and both of the children's uncles, Sidney, now married, and John Drew, had become residents of New York.

And, too, Mrs. Drew's Philadelphia fortunes had begun to fade, for the city was moving away from the Arch Street Theatre. Yet the courageous little manager would not leave the historic neighborhood, and the older actors still answered her calls when rheumatism and ague permitted. On occasional weekends, after the move, Mrs. Drew would travel to New York, however, to see her grandchildren.

Lionel was then eleven years old, Ethel ten, and Jack seven, and New York a city of almost one million four hundred thousand population. It was the Horatio Alger time of luck and pluck, of rags and riches, and there was so much to be seen and heard in this Manhattan of adventurous growth!

Each afternoon a parade of great names moved along Broadway, where the Barrymore children often strolled, for their first Manhattan home was a brownstone house at 1564 Broadway, afterward the site of the Palace Theatre, shrine of vaudevillians. Papa would sometimes introduce them to his friends, such as John L. Sullivan, the heavyweight champion, but the Barrymore children were timid with strangers.

Indeed, an inward shyness possessed them during their subsequent private lives, notwithstanding their ease on the stage. To protect his mental privacy, each child set up his own kind of barrier. Lionel might either punch a well-meaning dullard in the nose, or retreat into an ossified cocoon. Ethel could become a bundle of claws when approached clumsily. Jack, after adolescence, concealed from the world his sensitivity by cock-o'-the-walk mannerisms and prussic-acid humor, too often closing the door on those who otherwise might have come to know his surpassing inner decencies, his starlit charm.

On Indian summer days Papa took the children to the Central Park Zoo. He knew a great deal about animals because of his experiences in India. His lectures enchanted other zoo visitors, and a crowd would soon be following them from cage to cage. "The llama," he would explain, "is a domesticated variety of guanaco, and spits in your eye if he doesn't like you. The first dramatic critic was a llama. Llama meat is not good for the dinner table. Tastes like a forgotten sponge."

In Philadelphia the children had attended Catholic day schools, but now the elder Barrymores, because of their frequent theatrical tours, decided to send Ethel to a convent school and to place the boys in Catholic boarding schools. Jack went to Georgetown's elementary school near Washington, and Lionel to Seton Hall at South Orange, New Jersey.

Jack did not stay long at Georgetown. His preceptors soon notified Papa that Jack had been cast out for a "serious breach of conduct," a circumstance which caused Maurice to inquire of the lad, "What did they catch you doing? Selling French postcards to congressmen?"

It was agreed that Jack should join Lionel at Seton Hall. Maurice accompanied his younger son to South Orange. There they toured the campus with the head of the school, Father Marshall, and Lionel.

Father Marshall had a serene personality, and the face of an ascetic Spanish nobleman. In the gymnasium he indicated the parallel bars. "Have you ever exercised on the horizontal bars, my son?"

"Yes, Father," Jack replied.

"Then get up on the bars and try the giant swing, my son."

While Father Marshall, Papa, and Lionel looked on, Jack stood on his hands on the bars. Suddenly from his pockets there showered a razor, a pistol, a pack of playing cards, and a pair of dice.

Father Marshall picked up the contraband, saying matter-of-factly, "I don't think you will need these articles *here*, my son."

THE YOUNG STUDENTS OF SETON HALL found the locker room of the gymnasium a comparatively safe place for their smoking exercises. One afternoon after baseball practice they opened a box of Sweet Caporals, a brand of lung-foggers that had as a premium in every package a colored picture of some famous athlete or actor.

To the astonishment of the Barrymore boys, the card in today's cigarette box contained a bright miniature portrait of Georgie Drew in an evening gown.

"It's Mamma!" Jack shouted. "Look, everybody!"

"It's Mamma, all right," Lionel said. "What an honor!"

One of the baseball players, a boy of such severe moral restraints as never to countenance the locker-room vice, said, "I think it's disgusting."

Lionel stared incredulously. Then he knocked the boy down. The lad lay quite still. "Even if he dies," Lionel blurted out, "he never should have said my mother was disgusting."

On another occasion an assistant instructor at the seminary reprimanded Jack for reading *Buffalo Bill's Adventures* behind an opened textbook. During this rebuke he placed a hand on Barrymore's head.

That night Jack composed a letter to his grandmother in Philadelphia:

> I was attacked by this huge fellow and without cause. I tried to placate him; but he struck me, and as I reeled beneath the cruel blow the world went black before my eyes. . . .

When Mrs. Drew read this curdling document, she hastened to New York. She displayed the letter to Sidney, commanding him to find Maurice. "Here's something, for once, that he can take care of."

Sidney commissioned his brother-in-law, in Mrs. Drew's name, to punish the brute of Seton Hall. When Jack got wind of his father's coming visit, he ballyhooed the event to his schoolmates: "My father's on his way to beat seven kinds of hell out of the entire faculty. Blood will flow from here to Newark."

Jack and a gallery of expectant fellows waited in the shrubbery to witness the arrival of the fierce avenger. Finally a carriage drew up and a sturdy yet seemingly carefree Mr. Barrymore entered the building where Father Marshall had an office.

The boys listened for the beginning of the battle. "It's mighty quiet in there," said one of them. "Mighty quiet."

"Just wait," Jack advised. "My father is studying the situation. In a minute priests will sail out of doors and windows, their ears torn loose."

But silence, except for laughter, continued over this scene. Peering through a window, Jack saw his father seated opposite Father Marshall, engaged in amiable discussion. After their talk, Mr. Barrymore and the head of the school walked arm in arm out of the building, past the group of gaping schoolboys to Maurice's carriage.

Papa was so delighted by his visit with Father Marshall, of whom he afterward said: "A priest so honest that Diogenes would have put away his lantern," that he failed to see Jack and his friends. And Jack was so let down by the collapse of his own advertisement of the decimation of the faculty that he had no voice left to call out to his father as he drove off.

IN 1892, WHEN JACK WAS TEN, his mother went to Philadelphia to keep an engagement at the Arch Street Theatre. She caught cold, but insisted on taking her place at the opening performance, and became quite ill. Back in New York, Georgie's health faded rapidly, and physicians decided she must take a rest. But when she returned from a long cruise to the Bahamas, the doctors diagnosed her condition as advanced tuberculosis. They then advised sending her to California.

Since the family was now widely scattered—Mrs. Drew, having at last given up the Arch Street Theatre, was playing an engagement in Boston, Uncle John Drew was abroad, and Papa was with a stock company out West—the theatrical tradition of never missing a curtain left no one but Ethel, barely fourteen, available to accompany her mother on the eight-day train trip, and to stay with her in Santa Barbara. It was a shock for a girl to exchange the cloistered serenity of the convent for the shove-about rudeness of railway stations, but Ethel managed everything.

"All my children," said Georgie, "have Drew eyes and Drew hair—" then she added, as if to herself "—and Drew courage."

The Barrymores' old friend, Mme. Modjeska, between Shakespearean tours with Edwin Booth, was now residing in California at Anaheim, not far from Santa Barbara. Sometimes she visited her friend Georgie at the sanitarium, and saw that she undoubtedly was gravely ill. The great actress tried gently to prepare Ethel for the coming shock. Death came to Georgie Barrymore one morning in July 1893, just as Ethel was returning from Mass. Now the young girl was faced with the responsibility for returning her mother's body to Philadelphia. Papa had not been heard from for weeks, and his young daughter spent almost her last dollar on a telegram to her uncle Sidney. He would know how to break the terrible news to the family. Perhaps he could even find Papa.

Once more Ethel sat for eight days and nights in a day coach, wearing a long black dress to make herself look older. She would never be a child again. And from this time on she would be the successor to Mrs. Drew as family burden bearer, a willing, dependable, uncomplaining refuge for madcap relatives in their hours of bewilderment.

CHAPTER 4

It was at Madame Bourquin's, a theatrical boardinghouse on Staten Island, the summer after their mother's death, that the young Barrymores appeared in their first dramatic effort. Mrs. Drew, now seventy-three years old, had undertaken the temporary care of her grandchildren, pending a tour in *The Rivals* under the management of her son, Sidney. The Barrymore boys had said good-by to Seton Hall, and they, along with Ethel, their grandmother, and their uncle Sidney and his family, were living at Madame Bourquin's, where Barrymore and Drew credit always was good. Their hostess knew she would get her money eventually, with Mrs. Drew at the family helm.

There, one afternoon, for an audience of neighborhood children, relatives, and out-of-work Hamlets, they performed

Camille. Ethel played the name role, coughing most convincingly. Lionel, after much coaxing (he always detested love scenes), undertook the part of Armand, and Jack that of the Count de Varville, with a swirling black mustache. Actually, none of them had a compulsion toward acting, despite the century of stage tradition on the Drew side of their house, and the mimicry bequeathed them by their handsome father.

"We became actors," Ethel once said, "not because we wanted to, but because it was the thing we could do best."

Meanwhile old Mrs. Drew, gallantly preparing once again to lift the plumes and corset stays of Mrs. Malaprop from the mothballs, still regarded her son-in-law Maurice as an untrustworthy guardian. Though he had at first seemed unable to believe his wife had died, he was now often seen in bright spirits at The Lambs bar, or in company of beautiful young women. He could hardly be depended on to look after the children while she was away. So, once more, the family's living arrangements were revised.

Lionel, it was decided, would tour with his grandmother. He made his professional debut in the small part of a coachman in *The Rivals* when they opened in Kansas City, and survived, despite the fact that, at age fifteen, his voice was still changing. Later he recalled that the experience was "like trying to play a French horn while standing on my head." Jack, meanwhile, went to live with his uncle John Drew, who had returned from London and now welcomed his favorite nephew to his rooms at the Marlborough Hotel.

Jack had always drawn pictures. He said he wanted to be an artist and his aunt Dodo, Uncle John's wife, permitted him to sketch on anything other than walls or table linen. His uncle also patronized his passion for the drawing board, yet adroitly sought to keep him on the path of family tradition. Drew now graced the Standard Theatre under the management of Charles Frohman, and before long would move into the newly built Empire Theatre, there to rule the greenroom as the first gentleman of the American stage. He saw himself and his family as a theatrical dynasty, with no allowances made for abdication.

Jack had great respect for his uncle, and would eventually

take on many of his stately mannerisms, but he did not now choose to be reminded of his duty to the profession of acting. At this formative period he was both shy and confused. Lionel might begin to heed the call of tradition. And soon Ethel, too, would make her debut, appearing in a minor role when Louisa Lane Drew and an all-star cast brought *The Rivals* to New York. But their younger brother was still daydreaming, sketching, or strolling about New York, unmindful of the crowds.

JOHN BARRYMORE spent the summer of his fifteenth year with his grandmother at the old Bevan House in Larchmont, New York. The boy seldom left her, for the seventy-seven-year-old actress was afflicted with dropsy, her first and last devastating illness.

"I saw you come into this world," she said to her grandson, "and now you are seeing me out of it. A fair exchange."

It was an early, hot summer, notwithstanding the cool, blue reaches of Long Island Sound. Each afternoon Jack would help his grandmother Drew get settled in her rocking chair on a veranda overlooking the sound. He would sit beside her, sketching seascapes, and listening to her reminiscences when she would sometimes put aside the book she was reading.

"Waves and actors," said the old lady, "are much alike. They come for a little time, rise to separate heights, and travel with varying speed and force—and then they are gone, unremembered. Our good friend Joseph Jefferson has correctly observed, 'Nothing is as dead as a dead actor.' "

The family once again had become widely scattered. Papa was in Kansas City, John Drew was on tour with Maude Adams, Ethel, who had been soaring high by means of both talent and beauty, was in London, where she had appeared in *Secret Service*, a play starring William H. Gillette, one of the great matinee idols of the day. Word reached Larchmont that she had become the most talked of young beauty in England.

Lionel was in New York preparing to play in a new comedy, *Uncle Dick*, and when he came to visit them in Larchmont he was saddened to find his grandmother in constant pain. Her doctor confided to him that she could not live much longer.

After the physician had left, Mrs. Drew said to Lionel, "Whatever that learned calomel merchant has been telling you, pay no attention. I shall appear for rehearsals next season as has been my custom for seventy-two years. And I shall send you a large red apple on your opening night."

The red apple was a traditional gift. Back in the days when John Drew was at boarding school, his schoolmaster used to say: "If you learn your lesson well, you shall have a nice red apple." After he became a star, Drew began to send red apples to his relatives on the first nights of their respective bows as actors, or whenever one of them appeared in a new play. Among the Drews and Barrymores it had become a signal of interfamily regard and a good-luck token as well.

Mrs. Drew now turned to Jack. "We must be sure to send one to Ethel, too. Can one cable an apple?"

That night she fell asleep, never to awaken.

Of his grandmother, Jack said in afteryears, "If such a thing be possible, I know that at Heaven's gate she was given not a red apple but one of purest gold."

AFTER THE PASSING OF his grandmother, Jack entered upon a bouncing behaviorism, together with spontaneous alliances, such as novelists call romantic and physicians diagnose as glandular. It was during his fifteenth year (according to him) that he had his first complete relationship with an ardent and experienced young woman; what is more, a woman currently the loved one of Maurice Barrymore, his father.

Although Jack's was not a nature to harbor feelings of guilt of moral wrongs, it seemed from his own manner of referring to this cyclonic premiere that he felt he had let his father down. And it may well be that his later stage interpretation of Hamlet's problem rested somewhat on the circumstances of this initiation of the adolescent dreamer. In any case, it appeared that the inconstancy of this woman fixed in Jack's mind the idea that all beautiful women might be the same.

When Ethel returned briefly from London to find her younger brother doing nothing with, yet doing everything *to*, his life, she decided to take him back to England with her. Perhaps he would improve himself when meeting some worthwhile per-

Sketch of Dolores Costello, and, below, a fantasy entitled "Fear."

John Barrymore as artist. Above, self-portrait as King Lear; below, a theatrical poster.

sons. No sooner had they arrived than he fell in love with an actress of magnificent face and figure. She had a husband of mellow years, but he suddenly became less mellow and threatened a suit for divorce, until friends pointed out to him how ridiculous it would seem for a man of years to name a "sapling" as corespondent.

Ethel played upon Jack's desire to be a painter, and for a time managed to shunt him from the romantic track and into the Slade School of Fine Art, where he was greatly influenced by the macabre Aubrey Beardsley, although they never met. Perhaps we should discuss John Barrymore's easel abilities now and have done with it. He had an abiding passion for art, a driving imagination, and a compelling sense of color, but he himself once summed up his artistic talents, saying, "I might have been, but wasn't."

When Jack returned to America he still wanted no part of the stage, although his uncle Jack Drew kept reminding him of his "birthright." Newspaper life and newspapermen always enchanted him, and he was now determined to combine his art with journalism.

He obtained a fleeting job on the *Morning Telegraph*, then went to work for Arthur Brisbane, the dome-browed savant who edited Hearst's *Evening Journal*. Mr. Brisbane had such a high regard for Ethel that he waived his usual practicality and assigned Jack to the task of illustrating weekly editorials and occasional court stories.

Jack, however, did not seem to realize that newspapers had to be published on time. He was consistently late with his copy. He also disregarded the text of articles he was supposed to emblazon. Then one day he created a picture that miraculously satisfied Mr. Brisbane. It showed mankind in the chains of dope and liquor habits. But after the first edition reached Park Row newsstands, the picture was found to be published upside down!

Although Jack could in no wise be held accountable for this mishap, Mr. Brisbane's magnificent forehead wrinkled with outrage.

"I believe," he said to Jack, "that all your family were, or are actors?"

"Yes, sir," Jack replied.

"Then shall we allow the Fourth Estate, or anything else, to spoil that splendid record?"

"I AM NOT a constant reader of the calendar," John Barrymore said to Lionel one day, "but Uncle Jack informs me that I am twenty-one years old."

"What do you propose to do about it? Vote?"

"It begins to look as though I'll have to succumb to the family curse, acting," Jack replied sadly.

Lionel was properly sympathetic. "I know how you feel. There is no escape. We are in the cul-de-sac of tradition. Did Uncle Jack finally influence you?"

"Partly, but also my stomach. It abhors a vacuum." They were sitting in the Café Boulevard on Second Avenue, which they patronized for three reasons: Hungarian food, gypsy music, and twin sisters from Budapest, whom they never saw anywhere else. The romance carried over from one visit to the next. It seemed an ideal poetic arrangement.

"Well," Jack went on, "if I do stumble onto the stage, I'll not be any good. Then I'll *have* to come back to painting."

"You'll certainly fail, unless you try. But if you do try—" Lionel paused "—you're hooked forever."

CHAPTER 5

THE FIRST GREAT bell-beat of tragedy sounded for John Barrymore in 1903, the year that saw him at last on the New York stage. The sudden, evil occurrence was the collapse of his father's once brilliant, gay mind. The bleak overtone of this breaking of his parent's reason never quite died away in Jack's thoughts, and toward the end of his own life provoked the only discernible fear in an otherwise exceptionally brave character.

It was Maurice Barrymore's sardonic lot to reach his topmost place in the theater just before the world went dark for him. He had magnificently enacted the part of Rawdon Crawley in support of Mrs. Fiske's Becky Sharp. The irony was that the actor was not entirely simulating the frenzies of this stage role, but giving to it the agonies of his own mental disintegration.

One afternoon in late autumn, as one of John Barrymore's newspaper friends, a police reporter named Jack Francis, was leaving the doorway of the West Thirtieth Street station house, he observed Maurice Barrymore sitting on the cast-iron steps, staring fixedly at a sign across the street advertising a Negro mission. The sign read:

ALL YE THAT ENTER HERE,
LEAVE SIN AND CARE BEHIND.

"May I take you home, Mr. Barrymore?" Francis asked. "You look kind of sick."

Maurice glanced up. "Home?" he asked. "Is there such a place?" He rose slowly, then lurched. Francis caught his arm before he could fall, and hailed a cab.

But when the cab reached the place where Maurice was living, the actor refused to get out, and the worried Francis instructed the cabbie to drive to Bellevue Hospital instead. Barrymore didn't appear to mind. Perhaps he had forgotten where he had wished to be taken. He was for the most part incoherent, but would return abruptly to his usual bright manner for a minute or so. Among other things, he recalled that his friend Wilton Lackaye recently had posted a notice on the bulletin board of The Lambs: LOST: ONE CUFF LINK. WILL BUY OR SELL.

At last the cab arrived at the hospital, where the examining physician told Francis it would be best for the stricken man to remain for observation in the psychopathic ward. It was so arranged, though Ethel and Lionel were out of the city and Francis was unable to locate Jack.

After several days some of Maurice's friends procured his release. Yet they soon conceded that the actor, now in his fifty-sixth year, was deranged. It was recommended that he enter a private sanitarium.

And now the family burden bearer, Ethel, arrived home to take her father to a place in Amityville, Long Island. As in the death of her mother, this, too, became a grievous journey for the beautiful young woman. Yet again she did not shirk her duty. She assumed all the expenses and made all the arrangements for her father's care.

Maurice remained in the sanitarium until his death in 1905, although occasionally when friends visited him, he conversed with such sustained animation that they hoped he might someday be released. But then he would plunge back into the darkness of his malady.

Among these longtime comrades was Frank Case, proprietor of the Hotel Algonquin. On his last visit to the sanitarium he found the actor in comparatively high spirits. Many sheets of manuscript lay on a table in his room.

"I have written a new play," he told Case. He handed the pages to his visitor. "Run your eye over this."

There was but one sentence written on the many pages, repeated again and again: "It was a lovely day in June." Case finally was able to say, "I think it is fine, Barry, perfectly fine."

LONG BEFORE his father's illness had run its course, John Barrymore was on the stage. Yet he had revealed little evidence of the powers locked inside himself. His first appearance (for a single night) had come when he substituted for an absent actor at the Philadelphia tryout of *Captain Jinks of the Horse Marines*. The hastily rehearsed Jack blew up in his lines. His sister Ethel, a principal in *Captain Jinks*, went into a hysterical state which Jack described as "a cross between hilarity and strangulation." As if that were not enough, the mischievous actor took a curtain call by himself.

The play failed to impress Philadelphia. It moved gloomily to New York (with Jack out of the cast!) and stayed on for a triumphant seven months, firmly establishing Ethel Barrymore as a star of the first magnitude.

That summer, while waiting for a second role, Jack enjoyed the hospitality of Frank Case. Members of the Drew-Barrymore family often stayed at the Algonquin. And Uncle John Drew was a resident of that hotel for nineteen winters.

By now Jack had assumed many of the courtly mannerisms of his uncle John, and much of his wardrobe as well, for he was entering upon a "dressy" period. But if his uncle happened to be out of town, Jack levied upon Frank Case for linen. Case was a much larger man, but Barrymore had a talent for pinning up sleeves and making collars fit by adjusting borrowed neckties.

One day a friend asked Jack what kind of man Case was.

"There are no adjectives available. He's . . . he's . . ." Jack resorted to a Broadway phrase: "Why, he's the sort of man who'd give you his . . ." He paused, then pointed to his own bosom and exclaimed, "My God! This *is* his shirt!"

Case became concerned about Jack's drinking, a matter subsequently pondered by a multitude of men and women. Barrymore appeared one morning in the Algonquin restaurant, somewhat earlier than his usual noon, to request, "Waiter, will you create for me an absinthe frappé? On second thought, prepare two."

Case whispered to the waiter to delay the service of absinthe, then invited Barrymore to his own table. "Have a cup of coffee," Case said. "It takes time to mix a real frappé."

Barrymore had three cups of coffee with Case; then, after the absinthe frappé arrived, found his stomach out of humor for wormwood distillations.

"What a great idea, Frank," he said.

"What idea?" Case asked.

"Coffee for breakfast!"

Like numerous other famous Algonquin guests, Barrymore did not pay his bills on the barrelhead. Case was passing through the main dining room one evening when Jack was entertaining an eye-arresting young lady—one of the fabled Floradora show girls—with hearts of artichoke. Case leaned over Barrymore's shoulder to whisper, "Couldn't you have selected something less costly?"

Jack seethed. He insisted that the young lady go with him at once to a restaurant that didn't quibble with guests, and he even went so far as to check out of the Algonquin. No one at the desk brought to his attention a long-standing bill.

It happened that delegates to a political convention had taken all hotel space in the White Light district. Barrymore and his girl drove about mid-Manhattan for hours. Late that night he returned alone to the Algonquin, and, having no money with which to pay the hack driver, matter-of-factly signed Frank Case's name to a tab.

SUCCESSFUL MEN tend to stay silent in regard to benefactors who gave them a leg up, but John Barrymore acknowledged that his career often had been accommodated by timely help. One early monitor of Jack's professional course was the comedian Willie Collier, who had been a friend of the Drews and Barrymores since 1882, the year that he had quit school to enlist as a call boy at Augustin Daly's Theatre, and the year in which Jack had been born.

Collier had left Daly's to become a comedy favorite with Weber and Fields. And by the time Jack began to nibble at his theatrical inheritance, Collier was a star for Charles Frohman. John Drew, Ethel, and Lionel also were Frohman actors, so young Jack's availability was often brought to the attention of the dubious impresario.

Frohman had seen Jack the night he took the curtain call by himself in Philadelphia and admitted that the youngest Barrymore "might" have some hidden talent for comedy. Still, he wasn't too sanguine. So, when Collier was preparing, early in 1904, to open in Richard Harding Davis's new play, *The Dictator*, and suggested Jack for a secondary role, the part of a wireless operator, Frohman hesitated.

"Why overlook a horse of such good bloodlines?" Collier asked.

Then Ethel appeared next day to make a Portian plea, and Mr. Frohman surrendered, becoming one of the first of many theatrical believers in "always taking a chance on a Barrymore."

Collier's new protégé gave him little rest for the better part of the next four years. But for Jack the four years of training under Collier became a solid education as well as a boisterously gay odyssey. It began on the night of *The Dictator*'s out-of-town tryout in New Haven, when Jack met some convivial friends who, later, had to carry him into the theater. Yet, once onstage, Barrymore managed his part well. Fortunately the wireless operator was characterized as a profound bottle man.

But Jack's tardiness and general misbehavior continued through a long season with *The Dictator* in New York and then on the road. His abuse of stage costumes galled Collier. Jack would slip away from the theater in the white tropical pants of the wireless operator, and often would sleep in them. Or he would stand, barefoot, on his makeup towel, then rub his hands on his white trousers instead of the towel. In Bangor, Maine, he didn't materialize for the matinee on Washington's Birthday. When asked if he didn't know that a holiday always meant a matinee, Jack said, "I never knew until this instant that Washington's Birthday was a holiday!"

Such experiences at last caused Collier to telegraph Mr. Frohman that he was about to dismiss Jack from the company.

"Don't fire him, Willie," Frohman wired back. "It would break Ethel's heart."

"If I keep him, it will break mine," Collier replied.

But he never fired Jack. "The trouble," he said, "was that I liked him too much to discipline him. He assimilated direction easily, especially in the art of timing. His memory was wonderful, yet no one ever caught him studying a part. I thought that he would be a fine comedian, which indeed he did become. But I didn't then realize that he was to become a really great actor."

The Dictator proved so popular in America that in 1905 Mr. Frohman sent the company to London. On the opening night, with much at stake for Collier, two of his actors put him in a fine predicament. Jack, of course, was the worse offender.

At the rise of the curtain, Collier, playing the role of a character called Travers, is in desperate need of a new name to cover his identity as a fugitive from the law. Another character enters to sell him his name, Bowie, for twenty-five thousand dollars. That night when Collier asked, "By the way, what is your name, the one I am to purchase?" the actor refused with alcoholic hauteur to tell it. In fact he exited, leaving the first-nighters still ignorant of his identity.

"Of course I know his name," Collier improvised. "Happened to meet his wife. It's 'Bowie.' "

Then Jack, as the wireless operator, arrived onstage. He was to give Collier a dispatch written on two long sheets of paper which the star would read aloud. It was important, for it advised the audience of the why, when, and wherefore of the action. Jack appeared on cue, but in his hand was only a small fragment torn from a menu card. He offered this tiny absurdity to the astounded Collier. "Here, Chief, is the dispatch."

"Where is the longer one?" Collier ad-libbed.

Jack also improvised, "Here it is, sir. Or have your eyes gone back on you again?"

Knowing the long, plot-point speech he was supposed to deliver could hardly be accepted as being read from the menu fragment, Collier said, "Someone is trying to double-cross us. Look again. I'm sure you will find the genuine message."

Jack went offstage, then reappeared with exactly the same bit of paper. "Sir, I have had this authenticated. It was written by the fellow who engraves the Lord's Prayer on the heads of pins." There was no other course for Collier than to take the miserable paper, hurriedly edit down his regular lines, and hope for the best.

CHAPTER 6

THE ONLY LETTER of introduction John Barrymore ever bothered to deliver was handed to drama critic Ashton Stevens, of the San Francisco *Examiner*, late one April night in 1906. Collier had brought *The Dictator* west for a San Francisco season, to be followed by a long Australian tour, and Ethel had written Stevens to keep an eye on her twenty-four-year-old brother, and eventually see that he got aboard ship for Australia.

Mr. Stevens was a brilliant critic who brought a gay creativeness to his job. He never coddled an inferior performance, but he smeared no poison on his critical darts, and thus was celebrated in San Francisco, Chicago, and New York as "the mercy killer." He grew up in friendly intimacy with successive Drews and Barrymores, and he later recalled that, when Jack first visited the *Examiner* office, at one o'clock on an April morning, the young actor was faultlessly attired in evening clothes. How he had managed to acquire this finery is still a mystery.

"The youngest of the Barrymores pulled himself out of a big overcoat," Stevens said, "and sprawled, a picture, in the nearest chair. His supper coat was double-breasted; mine was the same old single; his shirt buttons were three; mine the same old two. And where I wore shoestrings, he wore bows. Even our cigarettes were of different shades. Nevertheless, he treated me as an equal."

Jack sniffed the atmosphere of the newspaper office. Then, Stevens recalled, he smiled and said, "I used to work in a shop like this, drawing cartoons. I liked it—still like it—gives me nostalgia. This acting is a new game. But I don't have to tell a critic that I'm new on the stage."

Stevens told him that under any other name he might fool the best of them.

"Still," Jack said, "don't overlook my good fortune in being the nephew of John Drew and the brother of Ethel and Lionel. It helps, fabulously."

He rose and looked around the room again. "Great, isn't it? I'd like to be back at it. But acting comes easy," he said, "and it pays well. That's the narcotic."

On April 18 and 19, 1906, shortly after this meeting, San Francisco was devastated by its great earthquake and fire. Three days later when Jack finally managed to locate him in the *Examiner's* temporary offices in Oakland, Ashton Stevens said, in reference to that disaster, "When God does such things, He has style."

In early press reports, Barrymore's name was erroneously listed among the missing in the disaster. Regular telegraph facilities were lacking; Jack didn't think his family would worry about him, but Ashton Stevens prevailed upon his editor to permit Jack to tag onto the close of a news-service bulletin to New York a message to Ethel. The actor wrote as dramatically as possible within the space allotted him an imaginative and completely fabricated account of how he had been thrown out of bed, had wandered dazedly to the street, where an army sergeant put a shovel in his hand and made him work for twenty-four hours among the ruins of the city.

When Ethel asked her uncle John whether he believed this, he replied, "Every word. It took an act of God to get him out of bed, and the United States Army to put him to work."

Because of the San Francisco fire, *The Dictator* company sailed for Australia minus scenery, wardrobe, trunks, and prompt-books. Aboard the ship Willie Collier rewrote the play from memory and had Jack draw designs for new sets to be built in Melbourne.

Neither Barrymore nor Collier enjoyed Australia. They found the nights too quiet. One day, after Jack had been late for rehearsal, Collier said to him, "I've been crying wolf long enough. The next time you are late or miss a performance, I'm going to abandon you in Australia. Maybe your sister will send you the boat fare. But I warn you, it will be awful to be marooned among the kangaroos." From then until the close of the Australian tour, Barrymore appeared on time at the theater.

A day or two before the voyage home, Collier pointed out in a "fatherly talk" to Jack that he had been with him for almost four years, but instead of having a dime to show for this he owed the company five hundred dollars.

"I'll write off the debt," Collier continued, "and I'll show you how to make a stake during the five and a half weeks we are at sea. Get some art materials, do some sketches on the ship; then, after you arrive in New York, you can sell them. See?"

Jack promised, and labored over a dozen or so. Weeks afterward, in New York, Collier found him at The Lambs. He said he was broke.

"But what happened to those sketches?" Collier asked.

"Good God!" Jack shouted. "I left them on the ship!"

BARRYMORE SPENT the hot New York summer of 1909 rehearsing a leading part in Winchell Smith's play, *The Fortune Hunter*. And it was during this time that he confided to his sister that he was in love with Nora Bayes, singing star of musical comedies. This time, however, he had fallen in love at long range, a singular departure from his customary behavior.

"But you've never met her," said Ethel.

"Did Dante meet Beatrice?" asked Jack.

"Besides, she's the romantic ideal of W. C. Fields."

"And who is he?"

"Mr. Fields," Ethel informed him, "happens to be the star comedian of the *Ziegfeld Follies*. You should at least know about the *Follies*. They were named after you."

"Will you accompany me to the theater where this trivial mugger is performing? I shall study him for future reference."

After seeing Mr. Fields juggle Indian clubs and otherwise display his remarkable talents, Ethel turned to Jack. "Well, what do you think?"

"Ethel," said Jack, "he's one of the greatest artists of all time. I'm not in love with Miss Bayes now. Hell! I'm in love with W. C. Fields!"

LIONEL RETURNED from Paris in time to witness his brother's debut in *The Fortune Hunter*. He sent a red apple, as did Ethel and Uncle Jack, and that night he saw his brother become a star in a faultless, vital performance. From now on the theater would be enriched by his electric presence, and his fame would endure for as long as his own volatile desires permitted.

Backstage, Lionel found a swarm of first-nighters crowding Jack's dressing room. "Well, Jake," he said, after the room was cleared out, "it looks like you are hooked for good."

"I'm scared stiff. Why didn't I give a stinking performance?"

"Because you couldn't."

"For God's sake!" said Jack. "In all the other arts, poor bastards starve, freeze, and strip their souls year after year. In this stage paradox, so-called success comes overnight. I'll tell you why I'm so scared. I heard thunder in the applause. A sign of storms to come."

CHAPTER 7

ONE NIGHT in 1910, after the curtain had fallen on the final scene of *The Fortune Hunter*, John Barrymore changed to evening clothes and left the Gaiety Theatre to attend a debutante's ball for Katherine Corri Harris, a taffy-haired beauty with blue mirrors for eyes. Her parents occupied a comfortable place in the *Social Register*, and certainly didn't anticipate that a theatrical weasel would spring the golden trap they had baited for ermine, but a few months later the nineteen-year-old girl married the twenty-eight-year-old actor.

"This event," Jack said, "was the first of my four marriages—all of them bus accidents."

The bridegroom announced blandly, after the wedding breakfast, that he had to go on the road with *The Fortune Hunter*. "It will only be for a year," he told his wife. "We'll be seeing each other at propitious moments."

The bride stayed with one of the few family members who cared to receive her as Mrs. Barrymore, and upon Jack's return, the couple moved into an apartment on the east side of Gramercy Park. Kathy tried hard not to quarrel with her husband, but none of his wives could exist happily with him for long. The bottle may have been the chief cause of each domestic furor. But Barrymore always sought the impossible, according to one of his associates, demanding that a mate consist of, all in one, "saint, siren, mother, wife, and friend." Other elements, too, increased the discord of this first marriage. Katherine, young and blossoming, wished to exhibit her husband in public, where everyone might view her handsome prize. Jack wanted no self-display after theater hours.

Between engagements, or on Sundays, in old clothes and with a beard stubble, he would slouch about Gramercy Park feeding the pigeons, or take solitary strolls. He stayed up all night with newspapermen, and sometimes forgot his marriage vows. He failed to advise Katherine as to where he was going or where he had been. He was not a man of explanations, nor a man to be explained. He simply *was*.

Sometimes, however, Katherine would be hopefully gay, as when Jack bought a small automobile, one of the open models then in fashion. One day he parked her and the car outside Tiffany's and went into that Fifth Avenue establishment to buy her a present.

He saw Geraldine Farrar examining some jewels and shyly introduced himself to the Metropolitan Opera beauty.

"If you will do me a favor, Miss Farrar," Jack said, "I'll rear a stained-glass window to you in any cathedral of your choice. Of course you don't know me . . ."

"But I do know you, Mr. Barrymore," Miss Farrar interrupted graciously. "And what is your favor?"

"My wife is outside waiting for me. If you'll only let me introduce you . . . She adores you."

Katherine was indeed impressed. Barrymore got into the car, preened his mustache, then drove off, completely forgetting to buy the present.

Barrymore's first marriage always seemed vague in his own memory, as if he merely had dreamed it. It endured, actually, for seven years. Concerning this and his other alliances, Barrymore once said: "They always ran about seven years, like a certain kind of skin rash."

THE NINE successive roles that Barrymore portrayed following his success in *The Fortune Hunter* found his talents marking time. His popularity increased, largely because of the Villonesque legends that attached themselves to his personality, but he smelled more of alcohol than of fame.

Perhaps it was because of his personal charm that managers put up with his idiosyncrasies. Perhaps it was because the impresarios had loved the Barrymores and the Drews. But during these years Jack survived demerits that, for any other actor, would have meant expulsion from the stage.

When in the spring of 1914, at the age of thirty-two, he undertook a Byronic flight to Italy, certain intimates attributed it to domestic miseries. Others thought his uninspiring roles had become intolerable. Whatever the cause, the effect of that Italian journey, both upon John Barrymore himself and upon the theater, would eventually be expressed in terms of meteors. For it was then that the wise words of a friend combined with the stimulating Italian environment to arouse in his artistic consciousness the powers long hidden beneath superficial charms and headlong actions.

Several years earlier Barrymore had become friends with a young playwright named Edward Brewster Sheldon who was well on his own way to professional eminence. Like Barrymore,

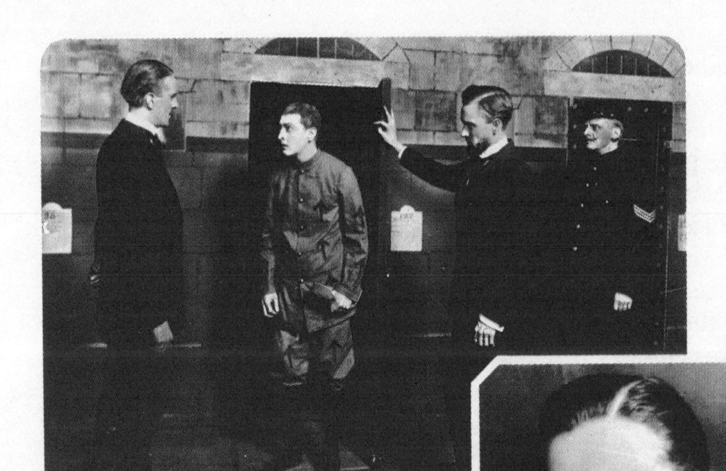

Above, a scene from "Justice"; at right, Barrymore as he looked in 1903, the year of his stage debut.

Above, with Constance Collier in "Peter Ibbetson"; at right, a scene from "The Fortune Hunter."

Sheldon had uncommon physical presence, was courageous and generous; unlike Barrymore, he had consistent professional purpose. *Salvation Nell*, written for Mrs. Fiske while Sheldon was still an undergraduate at Harvard, had brought him immediate recognition. His more recent drama, *Romance*, had achieved equal success, and he was enjoying a holiday in Italy when Barrymore bobbed up at his Venetian quarters that April.

The men were mutually delighted by their reunion. They strolled at night among the deserted squares and across the bridges. They listened to music, and studied architectural classics, sculptures, mosaics, and paintings. They had long serious talks. And some of Jack's confusions of mind began to fall away.

As long ago as *The Fortune Hunter*, Sheldon had advised Barrymore to undertake the playing of serious roles and therewith find recognition comparable to his powers. Now, in Italy, with reminders of man's artistic upsurge to be seen everywhere, this Harvard master of arts judiciously revived his suggestion, and this time Barrymore listened. Though he always blithely ignored friendly counsels regarding matters of the heart, Jack was receptive to artistic recommendations he found valid. They would be pigeonholed in his mind, seemingly forgotten, for he was by birth and by habit a procrastinator, but then they would pop out, vital and fresh. And when creative urgings finally stirred his will to action, he would rise to prodigious labors, undergo drudgeries even, to achieve perfection in his art. Edward Sheldon divined this slumbering quality in his friend, and awakened Barrymore to his mission. He unbound Prometheus.

When Barrymore expressed a desire to see Rome and Florence, the young dramatist didn't hesitate to interrupt his own plans. In Florence, one morning, they watched a sunrise from their hotel roof. They had found a trapdoor and climbed out in their pajamas to negotiate the steep slates seven stories above the ground. They sat there until the sun came up to reveal the Arno, the Ponte Vecchio, Santa Maria del Fiore, the Uffizi Gallery, and Santa Croce, in which was entombed the dust of Michelangelo, Galileo, Machiavelli. . . . Under the blue sky, holy bells and morning songs of peasants began to echo against the surrounding hills.

Barrymore, standing in his pajamas, said, "All this seems highly improbable."

In Rome they visited churches and galleries, the little cemetery where Keats's body and the heart of Shelley are buried, and in the moonlight re-created for themselves the Roman Empire from the shadows of ancient stones.

One night in an outlying village they heard singing, and left their carriage to enter a candle-lighted cellar that proved to be an inn. Mouths of wine caves could be seen dimly in the background, and a hunchback with a great key slung from a chain at his wrist moved about in this medieval scene. Jack *was* medieval. He became a part of the setting as naturally as if, on cue, he had entered into one of his own dreams.

The peasants at the tables were momentarily startled by the advent of the strangers, yet, after Jack had sat with charming familiarity among them, they ate and drank with him as if he were an old, beloved friend. A little girl got up on the table to sing "Tripoli," with what Sheldon recalls as "a voice like a slate pencil." Yet the song seemed entirely right and beautiful.

In a letter to Sheldon, twenty years afterward, Jack wrote:

> Dear Ned:
>
> I spent several days in Rome, where I attempted to make a pious pilgrimage to that marvelous inn where that charming child sang "Tripoli" to us. I found various other *albergi*, but regret to say not that particular one. Perhaps after all it was the walled garden with the little green door that one finds only once. . . .

CHAPTER 8

BARRYMORE RETURNED to America in the early summer of 1914, resolved to find a role that might place him solidly among the serious artists of the theater. Perhaps the gravity of war's announcement in July accentuated his purpose. Such a play was found, Galsworthy's *Justice*, in which Barrymore starred as William Falder, a tragedy-marked bank clerk. The amazement of the critics at his immediate triumph is understandable. They were unprepared for his sudden "size." *Justice* had a memorable season on Broadway, then went on tour.

It was during this time that Katherine Harris Barrymore established residence in Santa Barbara to sue for divorce on the grounds of incompatibility. Jack's unhappiness in this marriage lacked any bitterness, or lasting rancor. And in subsequent marital rifts even the pauperizing drains of alimony brought no martyr's whines.

"A man properly must pay the fiddler," he once said. "In my case it so happened that a whole symphony orchestra often had to be subsidized."

Upon his return to New York after the tour of *Justice*, Jack undertook, somewhat reluctantly, his first straight romantic role. It was only at the urging of Edward Sheldon that he agreed to play the title part in *Peter Ibbetson*, a dramatization of the George du Maurier novel. The English actress Constance Collier was his leading lady, and his brother, Lionel, played the wicked Colonel Ibbetson.

Jack never became convinced he was a romantic figure, nor did he wish to be one and become known as a "pretty boy." In this case, he also had some doubts about the virility of the character he was to play. He interrupted the rehearsal of one love scene with a howl: "This is nauseating! How can I bring myself to say such angel-cake speeches?"

However, the Broadway premiere of *Peter Ibbetson* was a night of excitement. The audience was alive and sympathetic from the moment the curtain rose; even the ushers were affected by the spiritual and emotional appeal of the play. Jack and Constance seemed the greatest lovers since Romeo and Juliet, and the story so poignantly real that even an exasperating mishap failed to spoil the illusion.

At the beginning of the third act a forest is supposed to dissolve before the dripping eyes of the spectators, and a magical opera house is conjured up in response to the romantic pair's wish to hear a song from the opera *Mignon*. Jack and Constance were walking hand in hand toward the opera house when it toppled, enveloping them with canvas and dust. The curtain was lowered, the scene rehung, and the beginning of the act repeated. Despite this intrusion, the audience sat like lotus-eaters, happy and anesthetized.

The play was a great success and it made John Barrymore a legendary romanticist. Love letters and sentimental gifts came in with the tide. But he never read the letters, and each Sunday afternoon consigned the previous week's accumulation to the furnace along with unopened bills and duns. Flowers were sent to city hospitals.

Lionel, with his Colonel Ibbetson role, also took a great step forward in public esteem. The scenes between Jack and Lionel were gritty actorial duels. The brothers often revealed sibling envy of each other's abilities, and with reason. Both men were strikingly honest in private life, but when trying to steal scenes from each other they surpassed the rogueries of purse snatchers.

During the *Peter Ibbetson* run Jack suddenly stopped drinking, his creative urge superseding for a time his self-destructiveness. The period of sobriety lasted two years, his longest dry spell. But as the eventual road tour lengthened, his irritability and restiveness began to increase, possibly because of the lack of alcoholic escape.

Jack began to snarl at those nearest him. He was genuinely fond of Constance Collier, and admired her as an artist, yet he frequently provoked quarrels with her.

He had always detested coughing by an audience during a stage performance. Now he began to do something about it. He would interrupt the play to reprimand the offenders, suggest picturesque clinical procedures, show an ironical concern for the ill health of the stricken ones, or else join in their hackings with thorough sarcasm.

He was tiring of the part. That was his destiny, to tire of parts. To relieve the dullness of one-night stands in the smaller towns, Jack began to collect cookery gadgets purchased at the five-and-ten-cent stores. He set up a portable kitchen in his dressing room, disregarding the fact that the curtain soon would rise on a romantic play, and that fumes of onions, garlic, and sizzling meat would spread over the place. He was entirely serious about his cooking, as he was about anything—for a time.

Then finally, in Chicago, he told Constance that he was physically and mentally tired, and could not continue. It was a blow. *Peter Ibbetson* could have gone on for weeks to capacity business. Yet she understood.

In later years Constance Collier said she considered John Barrymore the greatest of all the actors she had known—and she had known most of the great ones.

IN OCTOBER of 1917 Barrymore found a sanctuary on the attic floor of a century-old house off Washington Square. He began at once to transform it into a studio which he called "the Alchemist's Corner." During his first two years of residence he admitted no women callers, and entertained few men other than his brother Lionel and Edward Sheldon. He embraced this offstage loneliness, it seems, as an opportunity for self-evaluation. That he did possess a deep spiritual consciousness was apparent to those who had access to his confidence.

He was also capable of platonic friendships with women, and one of his deepest friendships of this nature was for his landlady, Mrs. Juliette S. Nicholls. She had been slow to accept him as a tenant, having heard of his bohemian antics. But the agent who had discovered the attic in response to Jack's request for a quiet hideaway "that would please a nun's grandfather" had assured her the actor would behave.

When Barrymore asked her permission to fix up the place, at his expense, she agreed, little knowing the extremes to which he was planning to go. The walls of the bedroom were covered with pink-striped paper; baseboard and moldings were painted black. Square glass mirrors, framed in black, formed the doors. The window drapes were pale mauve taffeta edged with white bead fringe. A French fireplace of white marble faced the foot of a bed which Barrymore specified should be narrow and hard. "A bed that implies celibacy for a change," he said.

He fashioned a bay window on the north side of the studio, stretched saffron chiffon over the wide skylight, from which hung an elaborate lantern. A cover of embroidered gold brocade was flung over the baby grand piano. A tall candlestand, an old Venetian mirror, a large antique globe, and a Lombardian chair completed this music corner. After he had surfaced the walls with Chinese gold, he spent hours smoke-smudging them. It was this "aging" of his retreat that caused him to refer to it as the Alchemist's Corner.

Now he turned his attention to the roof. Mrs. Nicholls was out of the city at the time, so Barrymore wrote to her:

> You have been so lenient in permitting me to exercise my fancy on the studio. Would you mind very much if I did a few ornamental things to the roof, at my own expense, of course? I'd like to build a little stairway to it, and place a few plants there, with perhaps a small pavilion in which I could sit when the locust blossoms come to the courtyards of Greenwich Village. It would be like living in Paris in the twelfth century.
>
> Yours entreatingly,
> Top Floor

Mrs. Nicholls again consented. Barrymore hired a carpenter to build a crooked, steep staircase to the roof, and a small structure near the skylight, which he said was the first penthouse in New York. He put ships' models in the little house, a Franklin stove, and outside it the wheel from a wrecked schooner and a ship's bell.

Now, with customary disregard for consequences to the old beams, or a thought for proper drainage, he had thirty-five tons of topsoil hoisted onto the roof and planted cedars eight feet tall, as a hedge on the street side of the roof. He also installed wisterias, arborvitae, cherry trees, and grapevines, and a fountain, the overflow of which eventually seeped into the bedroom and streaked the Chinese gold walls of the studio.

Mrs. Nicholls returned from a trip to Europe to find a horticultural frenzy atop her house. She was somewhat amazed, but did not complain. She could not, she said, for there was a startling yet weird beauty to Barrymore's creation, and the man himself seemed so childishly content as he fed the birds on his "estate."

Even later, after he had moved away and a subsequent tenant one morning found himself in bed with water from a spring rain pouring down upon him and the ceiling beams sagging dangerously, this remarkably fine woman did not resent what Barrymore had done. It cost fifteen hundred dollars to remove the topsoil and reinforce the beams with steel girders, for which she never billed him. She knew him more objectively than most other women. When asked later what she thought of him, she said: "I think he was a confused child."

IT WAS A SIGNIFICANT MOMENT for me when, during the writing of this book, I sat in Arthur Hopkins's managerial office at the Plymouth Theatre in New York examining old pictures of Jack and inquiring into his promptbooks. Never far from my thoughts was that long-ago afternoon when I had come as a young reporter to a dressing room of this same theater to get an interview with the star of *Redemption*, an actor I had never met or seen.

Now I was seeking the recollections of one who had worked with John Barrymore during that period when he was at his apogee. Arthur Hopkins produced four of the actor's most noteworthy plays, including two by the Bard—*Richard III* and, eventually, *Hamlet*. But that afternoon as we sat talking, Hopkins, too, was remembering *Redemption*. It had been their first venture together, and during rehearsals for that production he came to know Barrymore's deep earnestness about his work.

"He was tireless in preparation," the producer told me, "never burdened by vanity or the need of impressing others. It was less humility than concentration. Rehearsals for him were a ceaseless quest. He created out of his own texture. He borrowed nothing. He copied nothing. His whole search was within himself."

Later Arthur and I went out into the theater, and from the balcony looked down upon the stage where Barrymore had played *Redemption* so many years before. Here, also, he had appeared with his brother Lionel in *The Jest*, another great success. And from this balcony audiences had seen John Barrymore's brilliant playing of *Richard III*.

The pilot light shone small in the down-distance, making the theater seem darkly huge. The stage, the back walls were bare, the seats empty—yet were they? The clear small light, standing like a votive lamp among cathedral shadows, exercised an almost hypnotic power. Illusion was everywhere about the old playhouse. One traveled back to the time when the slim, springing figure of the great young actor dominated this stage, and the voice we knew so well sounded with rhythmic majesty.

Each man carries within his own memory a golden age. Here in the still theater, with the star-gleam of the distant stage light, the halo of dust about it, the smell that is the theater and like no other smell, the slow, chill updraft of air that comes from the great mouth of the proscenium arch, here one dreamed of days that were great with youth and circumstance.

"A man is not old," Barrymore once said, "until regrets take the place of dreams."

CHAPTER 9

A BLITHE AND HANDSOME poetess, whose quill name was Michael Strange, became Barrymore's second wife. She had the face of a Romney portrait and the spirit of a U.S. Marine. Numerous heart experts have written about this striking alliance. The principals themselves, Michael Strange in a memoir, *Who Tells Me True*, and Barrymore in his poppings off to the recording angels of Park Row, alternately evidenced their ardor and their disillusionment.

They dressed alike for a time, a symbol of their unity. Even so they indulged in unreasonable jealousies, trumped-up quarrels, mutual threats of suicide, unpredictable separations and wild reunions, for both were stubborn, egotistical, and intense.

The poetess, born Blanche Oelrichs of Newport's social caste, had first met Barrymore when he was playing in *Justice*. He had already left his first wife and, according to Miss Strange, "looked elfin and forsaken." This courtship—three years of it—leaves confusing echoes, like a voice loosed in a rain barrel. The poetess mentions family opposition to her alliance with the actor, but gives no account of any personality clashes during the wooing period. Barrymore occasionally referred to prenuptial battles, but he was unreliable chronologically and may have had in mind the strife after the wedding aisle had been turned into a warpath.

Movie roles, clockwise: as Svengali; in "The Beloved Rogue"; as Mr. Hyde, the alter ego of Dr. Jekyll; as Louis XV in "Marie Antoinette"; in "Twentieth Century"; as the Duke of Gloucester in "Show of Shows."

Michael Strange, it seems, became the only one of his admirers to breach the walls of his sanctuary, the Alchemist's Corner. Jack maintained that she accomplished this by sending him potted plants instead of cut flowers.

"I never cared to see flowers imprisoned in pots," he said. "It offended my own sense of freedom. Consequently, when potted plants arrived at the house, I would free them, like pigeons, on my roof. I began to notice that Blanche had exquisite taste in flowers, a taste that precisely suited my own predilections. I read into this the existence of other congenial qualities."

She also sent him notes, and he made an exception to his rule against opening mail to read these gracefully worded missives. The barrage of plants and notes had a siegelike quality, and may have stimulated Barrymore's remark, years later: "I never married any of my wives. They married me."

He was in a taut state of nerves before and for a long time after the marriage in August 1920. His theatrical labors taxed him and he also had done a few silent motion pictures, among which was *Dr. Jekyll and Mr. Hyde*. Besides, it was at this time that he was hurling himself with unprecedented intensity into preparations to play the role of Gloucester in *Richard III*.

"We had been planning *Richard* for a year," Arthur Hopkins said. "This was the great challenge. If we could successfully open the door to Shakespeare, then we might someday master *Hamlet*, the crowning dream."

For his role in *Richard*, Barrymore insisted on authenticity of costume, and hired an old armorer who did repair work for museums to fashion actual suits of heavy plate armor, making some forty trips to the armorer's forge in Newark for metallic fittings. This was not the customary tinny plate of wardrobe warehouses. Whenever Barrymore fell encased in it, he suffered skull shocks and body bruises.

In playing the deformed and lamed Gloucester, Barrymore glided across the stage like some unearthly spider. Once he was asked how he managed such a "swift limp," and how he prevented the efforts of contortion from intruding upon his difficult speeches. He replied:

"I merely turned my right foot inward, pointing it toward

the instep of my left foot. Then I forgot all about it. I did not try to walk badly. I walked as *well* as I could. You will find, I think, that a cripple does not try to walk with a worse gait than he has to employ. He endeavors to walk as *well* as he can."

Finally he undertook the task of reforming his voice to meet the classic demands of Shakespearean projection. In spite of the rare quality of his voice, it was of short range and rather furry, due to a complete lack of breath control.

He had met Margaret Carrington, a retired opera singer, who had made a long study of voice production and the relation of words to meaning. She found it difficult to believe that the most popular actor in America was asking her to help him, especially as *Richard III* was announced to open in six weeks. Never before had a voice been "built" in six weeks. With Mrs. Carrington, he now worked incessantly and successfully to gain the control necessary to sustain the long unbroken phrases of Shakespeare's verse, a veritable tour de force in the use of his will.

The production opened on time, but as Arthur Hopkins later said, "With the intensity required by *Richard*, a long run would have been possible only if Jack had saved himself otherwise; but in his frantic pursuit of a new marriage he gave himself completely. The crash occurred. After four weeks he was obliged to close, and thus came an abrupt ending to his great triumph."

It is said that after the evening performance he would take the train to Atlantic City where Michael Strange was temporarily residing, go without sleep, quarrel with his beloved, and get back just in time for the rise of curtain. For him this emotional depletion was catastrophic. As for Miss Strange, being married to Barrymore seemed to have been like setting up light housekeeping inside the crater of Vesuvius.

UNHAPPILY, Jack sublet the Alchemist's Corner, rightly divining that his new wife would not be content in this sequestered, cobwebbed setting. And he went to live with her on Sixty-seventh Street. "It was delightful," Michael Strange said in her memoir, "to have someone in the 'home' at last whom the servants considered more temperamental than myself."

He seemed to have given up the theater during the first year of this marriage. Then when Michael, who was expecting a baby, wrote a play during her pregnancy, her twofold productivity enchanted Jack. He volunteered to appear in it. His producer, Arthur Hopkins, could not share his enthusiasm for the play, *Clair de Lune*, a work suggested by Hugo's novel *The Man Who Laughs*, and its production was undertaken by Alf Hayman of the Frohman offices. Jack played the role of the clown, Gwymplane, and persuaded Ethel to appear as Queen Anne.

The critics set fire to his wife's theatrical monument. As Barrymore's good friend Alexander Woollcott of the New York *Times* later recalled, all the critics "privately thought that the play would scarcely have been produced had it not been for the somewhat irrelevant circumstance of Michael Strange having married Barrymore." One critic elaborated on this conjecture in print, summing up *Clair de Lune* thusly: "For the love of Mike."

In any case, the reviews so irked Barrymore that he went into a three-alarm rage and had to be dissuaded forcibly from making a speech about critics on the second night.

Not long after *Clair de Lune* closed, Michael Strange gave birth to a girl who was christened Joan Strange Barrymore, but afterward officially called Diana. For a time Jack forgot his troubles, private or public. He really had wished for a boy, but said, "I'm glad it's a girl. If she were a boy, she'd inherit all my habits, and I wouldn't know how to combat them: I'd have such sympathy with them."

He had been planning to appear in a dramatization of *Monsieur Beaucaire*, by his friend Booth Tarkington, but now he thought he would postpone it, perhaps retire altogether from the stage. He eventually took Michael abroad, a trip punctuated by the usual quarrels, threats of suicide, noisy accusations of extramarital romance. Barrymore afterward admitted to a major share of the provocations, recalling one of them had been his drinking the alcoholic fuel in Michael's curling-iron heater. Why he should have preferred such a low grade of beverage in Paris, a city of wine, might have perplexed any woman.

One day in June 1922, after months of storms and rages both in Europe and back in New York, Jack appeared at Ethel's home in Mamaroneck. He seemed gaunt and stricken, not because of any specific physical ailment, but from long harassment of mind. "I don't know what the hell to do," he said to his sister. "I feel like a soufflé that has been out of the oven too long. Guess you'd better take me in."

Ethel, of course, "took him in." The next morning she put into his hand a small, inexpensive edition of *Hamlet*. "Jake," she said, "read the two soliloquies. You may enjoy them." He reappeared to announce that he had done so. Then he added slowly: "I think I'll run over to see my friend Margaret Carrington."

"That's the last I saw of him for two months," Ethel said.

CHAPTER 10

HAMLET'S SOLILOQUIES possessed him. His irresolution fled. He would climb the highest of the magic mountains, the last great peak he was to scale in the fabulous domain of the theater.

"Do you really believe," I asked Lionel one day, years later, "that Jack was on the level when he said that Hamlet was the easiest role he ever played?"

"Of course he was," Lionel replied. "You must take into account that when the Bard wrote *Hamlet* he had Jack in mind."

It did not, however, happen quite that simply. Mrs. Carrington agreed to coach Jack only on the condition that there be no date fixed for the *Hamlet* premiere until she felt that he was professionally and psychologically ready for the assignment. Producer Arthur Hopkins readily consented. On the first day Jack appeared at her Connecticut farm, where he was to stay with her, he brought with him an armload of works having to do with the character and the motivations of Hamlet, which she suggested be put away where the silverfish might chew on them. She chose for their only text the small Temple edition of *Hamlet* which sister Ethel had given Jack. It contained not many footnotes, which Jack detested anyway. "Reading footnotes is like having to run downstairs to answer the doorbell during the first night of a honeymoon," he said.

By throwing out all previously conceived Hamlets, Mrs.

Carrington brought immediate response from Barrymore's creative nature. He worked six to eight hours a day, and underwent night sessions of painstaking analysis and evaluation, having agreed not to attempt to memorize the role until he had explored its every shade of meaning.

Wearing tights, as was demanded by the Hamlet role, had always been one of Barrymore's chief antipathies, notwithstanding his superb physique.

"When I first got into these skin-fitting jollities," Barrymore said of his tights, "I felt as if I had put on the intimate wear of Peg Woffington. Good God! What an ass a grown male can become on occasion! Then at last I decided to conquer these counterfeits of nudity or be conquered. I spent at least three hours before a pier glass. True, I had to take a few drinks to brace myself. Then I began to stare at the asinine fellow in the mirror. I sneered at him, I reviled him, I questioned his authenticity in matters of romance. I walked, I turned this way and that, never taking my eyes from him. Finally I got so tired of surveying myself, so sick, so fed up with tights that I no longer gave a damn how they looked on me or anyone else. I had 'em licked."

When the *Hamlet* rehearsals finally began in September, Hopkins followed the directorial plan that had been so rewarding in *Richard*. "Previous interpretations were ignored. We made ourselves servants of the play, untempted by any beckoning to leave our personal imprint on it. The result? The unfolding pattern had the unbelievable authenticity of a witnessed miracle. The unseen and unheard were being communicated. The theater has known few moments so startling as Jack's opening-night reading of his first soliloquy. The new prince was entering his kingdom."

Press and public acclaimed Barrymore as "the first Hamlet of our generation."

Of what did this man himself think during the hour of laurels? With the audience wildly applauding and the curtain lowering, then rising again and again, were we to believe him when he afterward said, "Fear was leaking out of every pore"? Had he again "heard thunder in the applause"?

Whatever his emotions, he allowed no one inside his dressing room following the performance that night, except a few immediate friends and relatives, whom he soon sent away with promises to join them at a supper party in his honor. He picked up the red apple sent by Uncle John Drew.

"I sat there for a long time thinking about Uncle Jack. He was getting old, about seventy, and he had arthritis. His liquor and he were beginning to quarrel with each other. . . . Not long before I had been up with him all night at The Lambs. He was meticulously dressed in evening clothes, but his jaw would drop down, and my job was to tuck it back in place from time to time. He was always so spruce and neat, you know, and would have been shocked to learn that his jaw ever drooped in public. . . ."

Barrymore, now in his street clothes, telephoned his old friend Frank Case at the Algonquin Hotel. "Is the kitchen still open, Frank?" he said. "I'm coming over."

When he arrived, he ordered a glass of milk and some finnan haddie. "We talked until morning," Case said, "and never once, even remotely, did Jack refer to *Hamlet* or to theatrical matters. It was as if the night of his greatest triumph had never been."

ONE THING THAT ENCHANTED Jack with the Hamlet role was the physical leeway it permitted the actor. "You can play it standing, sitting, lying down, or, if you insist, kneeling," he once said. "You can have a hangover. You can be cold sober. You can be hungry, overfed, or have just fought with your wife. It makes no difference as regards your stance or your mood. There are, within the precincts of this great role, a thousand Hamlets, any one of which will keep in step with your whim of the evening."

And yet it wasn't long before Jack was tiring of *Hamlet*, as he invariably wearied of all theatrical iteration, at about the sixtieth performance. He began to talk to Hopkins of "quitting this damned nonsense."

Nevertheless, he played the role of Hamlet on Broadway one hundred and one times, one more than had Edwin Booth. Then he toured as the Dane for a brief season of nine weeks the following year. Concerning this campaign, Hopkins said somewhat sadly: "The largest theaters were inadequate. In Cleveland his last classical appearance in America was made, and there passed from us the theater's richest gift."

It was during this tour, in Boston, that he met the aging portraitist, John Singer Sargent. Sargent had once sketched Ethel, and Jack hoped he might perhaps paint his portrait. Sargent, however, had put away his brushes for all time, but did do a crayon sketch of Barrymore's head and face. "You would be a difficult subject for any artist," Sargent said. "Your features are too regular. There is, you know, a bit of caricature in every great portrait."

The sketch, presented by Sargent to Jack, bears out the artist's contention. Although highly prized by Jack, it lacks distinction, having a pretty-boy aura. A sheriff impounded it many years later in behalf of Barrymore's greathearted persecutors during his dark days, and it now hangs in the San Diego Museum.

AFTER SEVERAL ATTEMPTS to mend his domestic life, Jack went to Europe, where he and Michael Strange were alternately together and apart. He was unhappy with her or away from her.

He finally decided to put on *Hamlet* himself in London. Constance Collier, forever grateful to him for *Peter Ibbetson*, agreed to play Hamlet's mother and offered to try to interest London managers, but it required many months of diplomatic persistence before a six-week lease was signed for the Haymarket Theatre, in the foyer of which, on an old playbill, his father long ago had found the stage name Maurice Barrymore.

Attending Jack's London debut as Hamlet was an old friend and confirmed fan of the Barrymores, Winston Churchill. Also in that critical audience was playwright George Bernard Shaw, who took exception to the shortened version being presented and next day sent Barrymore a letter attacking him not as an actor but as a person who dared to alter Shakespeare's play as written.

Shaw or no Shaw, the production was an incredible success. "Our six weeks were soon over," Constance Collier said afterward, "with standing room only for every performance." Then,

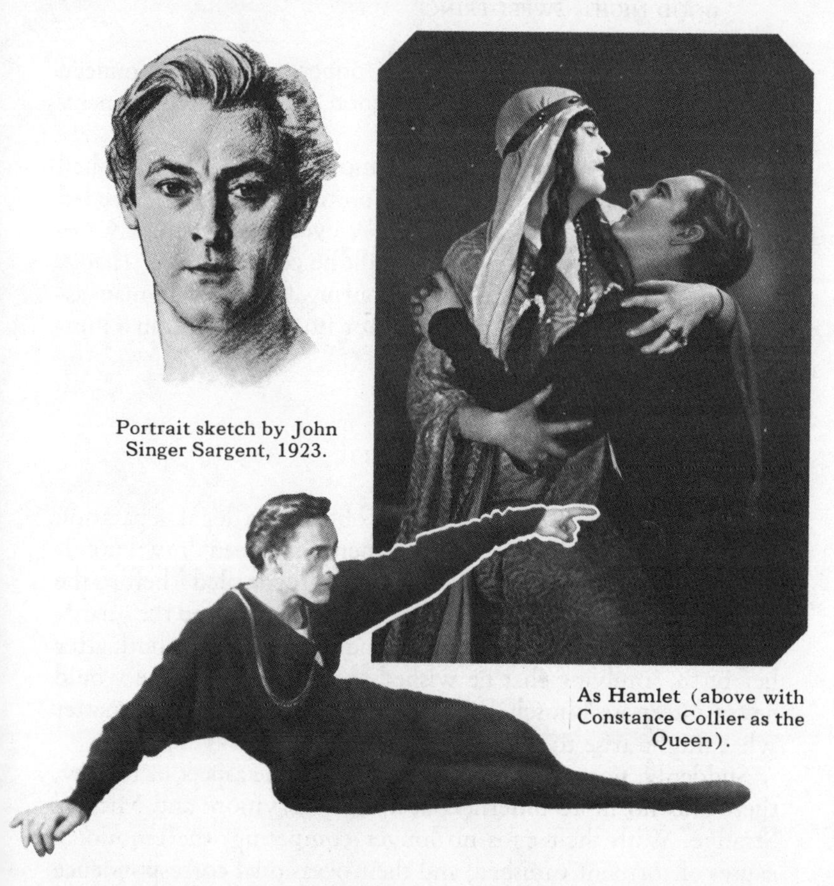

Portrait sketch by John Singer Sargent, 1923.

As Hamlet (above with Constance Collier as the Queen).

to continue for six more weeks, Jack paid the salaries for an entire cast of another play which had been scheduled to open at the Haymarket and was standing by.

At the close of this London run, offers came to Barrymore to take the *Hamlet* company to Berlin and to Paris, but he declined.

"By this time," Miss Collier said, "that strange resentment of any part Jack played too long had overtaken him. He hated the very sight of the stage and the sound of his lines. He gave so much of himself to every performance that each one seemed a chip off his life."

After the London *Hamlet* closed, Jack arrived home in America with a valet, Blaney, a small white-nosed monkey named Clementine, the gift of actress Gladys Cooper, and the announced intention of leaving the theater for good, a decision which many persons deplored.

Alexander Woollcott was not among them. "Why in hell shouldn't he have quit? Must the monstrous demand be heeded that a delicate instrument do *Hamlet* every night, merely because there is a public for it? After all, he couldn't show *Hamlet* to all the population that keeps pouring from the human assembly line if he kept on playing it for fifty years, and in a hundred Yale Bowls at a time."

CHAPTER 11

IN THE SPRING of 1925 Barrymore obtained a legal separation from his second wife. Similar agreements had been drawn previously, but the Barrymores had become "reconciled" before the notarial seals were dry. Jack had, however, renounced the guardianship of his daughter, Diana, in June 1921, a mere month after her birth, implying that he wished to assure his wife he would never interpose himself between mother and child, no matter what might arise to plague the parents.

Suddenly, now that their separation had the aspect of finality, there was no more bitterness between Barrymore and Michael Strange. With their egos no longer competing, the emotional causes of torment vanished, and their occasional correspondence was polite and calm, as if each were more interested in the other's success now than when in wedlock.

The separation agreement provided an annual payment of $18,000 for the maintenance of his wife and daughter, and the premiums on a large life-insurance policy, with Diana as the beneficiary. In regard to alimony—and he paid several hundreds of thousands of dollars of it—Jack once said: "Alimony is the most exorbitant of all stud fees, and the worst feature of it is that you pay it retroactively."

That same spring Jack also signed a contract with Warner Brothers to go to California to appear in three "super" motion pictures. He had made one picture for Warner Brothers, *Beau*

Brummel, the year before his London *Hamlet*. Like his other early cinematic experiments, it had contributed little to his own prosperity or the public's cultural advancement. His new contract, however, was extraordinary. He was to work only seven weeks on each photoplay, and receive $76,250 a picture. Overtime would be $7,625 a week. He was granted the then unusual privilege of approving or disapproving the stories, and of being the only starring actor, unless he himself approved a co-star. Publicity was to be in keeping with his "reputation and prestige." An examination of the first draft of this document discloses that Jack had penciled in numerous shrewd amendments and notations, an indication that he could focus his mind intently and analytically upon matters of moment when he wished to do so.

He was in a high-sky mood all the way to California, accompanied by Blaney and Clementine, perhaps the best loved of the multitude of pets he eventually had. Jack amazed Blaney by holding grave conversations with Clementine, warning her against the pitfalls of Hollywood. Blaney, a short, staid man of much dignity, did not like Clementine at all. His former employer, Sir Herbert Tree, had had several eccentricities, but he never had requested his man to superintend a monkey's business in the WC.

Jack, Blaney, and Clementine took up quarters in a detached bungalow of the Ambassador Hotel. It had a large living room, two bedrooms, and another room which Barrymore used as a combination "museum" and office, and in which he installed a cage for Clementine. During the day she was tied by a long leash to an outdoor balcony.

His initial commitment was *The Sea Beast*, a story based on Herman Melville's *Moby Dick*. Jack himself had chosen that story, although the studio had hoped that he would first make *Don Juan*.

During the formulation of his earlier pictures Barrymore entered into each production with the same great care and industry that had possessed him during his best theatrical days, taking advantage of the terms of his contract to see to it that his stories were superior to the child-mind tales sometimes regarded as proper amusement for motion-picture patrons. He even participated in the supervision of sets and costumes, and refused to have doubles, or stunt actors, take his place in action scenes. He eventually had several deep scars and evidences of old fractures because of this adventurous quirk.

For *The Sea Beast*, Jack was permitted, among other things, to choose his leading lady. There was, to be sure, no lady in the novel *Moby Dick*, not even a woman. However, the studio, somewhat alarmed about the box-office aspects of a picture that had, as its principals, Mr. Barrymore and a whale, devised a scenario that would include a love story. One evening Jack announced to his script writer that he had found a leading lady for *The Sea Beast*.

"She's the most preposterously lovely creature in all the world. She walked into the studio like a charming child. Slender and shy and golden-haired. I shall not eat nor sleep till I see her again." He paused reverently, then said, "But I'll have just one short drink to tide me over till tomorrow."

Barrymore's new star and, as was soon apparent, his new love, was Dolores Costello, the daughter of actor Maurice Costello. She had recently been screen-tested by Warner Brothers and signed to play the part of a maid in another picture. "Maid, hell!" Jack said. "Can you imagine them casting an angel to wear a cap and apron? I suppose they'd hire Lord Nelson to run a coal barge." Thus a little-known girl was about to become a Cinderella because of Barrymore's having chanced to see her. Still, such things did happen in Hollywood.

He looked young, yet Jack was forty-three years old and Dolores in her twenties when they met. She seemed to fill his need for expressing paternal as well as romantic love, and he was incredibly happy with her; but he was annoyed by the fact that he was expected to be secretive about the romance. There was the technical obstacle of Michael Strange, from whom he was legally separated but not divorced, and the studio was on guard against any scandalous implications touching the eminent actor and the young actress.

In the Costello household, to complicate things further, Jack was regarded as an unwelcome suitor. He slyly insisted, therefore, that his on-set love scenes with Dolores be repeated more than was necessary, although he had always maintained that actors in love usually gave unconvincing performances.

"The trouble is," he said, "that their pale faces and throbbing temples can cause an audience to believe that ptomaine poisoning has just set in."

His lovemaking in *The Sea Beast* refuted his own theories. As for Dolores, though her part was a minor one, her actual love for Jack was so like the bright spring that the role seemed important. They won each other, and *The Sea Beast* won the love of the world.

MARY ASTOR had been approved by Jack as leading lady for his second picture, *Don Juan*, before he had met Dolores. Early that October, at Miss Astor's home, he met Mr. and Mrs. Henry Hotchener, two persons who were to become closely associated with him during the ten best years of his Hollywood career.

Mrs. Hotchener had as a girl attracted the attention of the famous Adelina Patti, who recommended she study for the opera. In Europe she sang leading roles, sometimes with composer Puccini conducting the orchestra, then suddenly renounced her operatic career and turned to the study of theosophy and abnormal psychic phenomena. In India she met Annie Besant, president of the Theosophical Society, who called her "Helios," because of her brilliant, sunlike character. Her husband, Henry, was a calm-mannered, experienced businessman whose pleasant exterior, when scratched too rudely, disclosed steel beneath the surface. He would introduce a new word into the Barrymore lexicon, the word "no."

Both Hotcheners had lived much in India, which could explain why Barrymore, upon meeting them at Mary Astor's home, was at once drawn to them. Because his father had been born there, he had always been interested in that land of ancient culture; also, deep within his own nature lay a poetic mysticism. However, on his mind that night besides India—and Dolores—was a materialistic problem. "Hotchener," he said, "do you know anything about the damned income tax?"

Hotchener knew a great deal about the income tax and volunteered to examine Jack's return, which government sleuths had regarded without humor. At lunch next day, at Jack's Ambassador bungalow, Henry found taxes the least garbled of the actor's business affairs. His huge paychecks were sent directly to his New York attorney, who paid alimony and other fixed obligations out of this account, but Barrymore hadn't the slightest idea how much money he had left, for he never kept bank statements. When Hotchener finally had the papers sent to California some weeks later, he discovered that Jack had more than a hundred thousand dollars in his checking account, on which he was receiving no interest.

"Hank, for the love of God," Barrymore cried, "take over! Manage me."

MEANWHILE, JACK WAS FEELING the need to reexamine his life. He wanted to decide how best to ward off the antagonism of Dolores's parents. More than that, though, he sensed that even if he were free to marry Dolores their love might languish. He believed that for him a dark spell lay upon any marriage.

Now, with no Alchemist's Corner in which he might immure himself, he turned to the sea as a place for meditation. He was an excellent sailor. And for the first time in his life he was enjoying financial elbowroom. So he chartered an eighty-foot cabin cruiser, *The Gypsy*, along with its captain and crew, and sailed away upon what he termed "a quest for myself."

His coastwise course to the tip of the Mexican peninsula of Lower California took three weeks, during which he drank no hard liquor. His log, which he subsequently entrusted to Hotchener as his literary executor, expressed the rapture of being alone at sea, and frequently mentioned sleeping well, as if this were a phenomenon. But its overall mood was one of ecstatic yearning, and contained constant references to Dolores, for whom he had various nicknames: "Wink," "Small Cat," "Egg."

He fished, read, lay in the sun, observed with delight herons, curlews, flocks of ducks, and once a school of whales. Remembering his duel with a whale in *The Sea Beast*, he even tried to harpoon one. He went ashore in the little seaside villages of Mexico and made sketches of them. "Perhaps in time," he wrote, "I will again become a human being, the person I *was* fourteen or fifteen years ago."

He returned from his voyage with a dream. He would buy a yacht in which Dolores and he together would sail away from a conventional world. The fact that his grandiose projects hatched out as infrequently as porcelain eggs never occurred to him, nor that until the watchful Mrs. Costello heard the word "marriage" for her daughter she would visa no passports.

Eventually he found a ninety-three-foot schooner, *The Mariner*, sleek and white, and the winner of a San Francisco-to-Tahiti race in record time. Although Jack preferred sail, he wanted the boat both comfortable and safe for Dolores, so he installed a diesel engine.

But, having spent $110,000 on *The Mariner* and her alterations, he had still not asked Mrs. Costello whether Dolores could sail with him to far places, or even near ones. She now informed the pained dreamer that her daughter might not even step aboard without a chaperon: herself, Mrs. Costello.

In early June of 1926, therefore, *The Mariner* left San Pedro harbor and headed for Catalina and adjacent ports, carrying Dolores and her mother. Under full spread of canvas, the yacht heeled over beautifully in a bouncing groundswell which presently caused Mrs. Costello to retire to her cabin.

She became more seasick with each chime of the ship's bell, and after three days, Dolores insisted they put back to San Pedro. Jack said, yielding, "I shall never again celebrate Mother's Day."

CHAPTER 12

SOMETIME EARLIER, attracted by the prestige of United Artists, a company graced by Mary Pickford, Douglas Fairbanks, and Charlie Chaplin, Jack had agreed that upon completion of his Warner Brothers' contract he would make two pictures for them and share in the profits. This was before Henry Hotchener became Barrymore's manager and would, in time, prove why he needed advice in such matters. There was no time clause in this United Artists' contract and it would take two years to complete two pictures. After fixed studio charges and expenses had been subtracted, there would be no profits for Jack other than his original price of $100,000 for each picture. This meant that he would earn less than $2,000 for each workweek, as against the more than $10,000 a workweek he was making at Warner Brothers, who also paid all his hotel and transportation bills, whether he worked or not. When Henry Hotchener officially took over Jack's affairs, however, United Artists signed the actor for a third picture at $150,000, with a time limit and many other concessions.

Meantime, Jack was still under contract to complete another picture for Warner Brothers, a camera version of *Manon Lescaut* entitled *When a Man Loves*. Dolores was again his leading lady.

Between "shots" Jack spent his time (Dolores in a canvas-back chair beside him) designing silverware for *The Mariner*, selecting linens, curtains, and other decorations. Onstage, in his desire to make Dolores an acknowledged actress, he "threw" many scenes to her. Ethel Barrymore, visiting her brother on the set, was amazed at the spectacle of an accomplished artist deliberately "tossing away" his scenes. She expected "a Barrymore to live up to tradition in regard to art."

He was not only immune to her criticism but also wired his future employer, Joseph M. Schenck, the head of United Artists, that he was going to advise Dolores to quit Warner Brothers, and recommended that Schenck help Dolores "jump the league." United Artists handled the message as if it were a bomb, Hollywood having recently appointed Will Hays, former postmaster general, to keep a super-eye on censorship, morals, and the industry's codes of competitive business practice.

When the Hays office telephoned Jack, advising him to confine himself to acting, he could not understand why he was in trouble.

"I simply wanted Dolores to work beside me," he told Hotchener, who vainly tried to explain the sanctity of contracts.

By the end of the year Jack had completed his first picture for United Artists, a scenario based on the life of François Villon called *The Beloved Rogue*. That Christmas he bought jewelry for Dolores, but he himself left aboard *The Mariner* for another

Two Warner Brothers movies. Right, John Barrymore in "The Sea Beast" (with Clementine).

Left, with Dolores Costello in "When a Man Loves."

long cruise in Mexican waters. He was again undergoing emotional conflict over the wisdom of entering for a third time into matrimony. He was also in doubt as to his ability to quit drinking, although he had tried, since meeting Dolores, to do so, not wanting to hurt the one person he said he loved more than he had ever loved anyone else. During these dry intervals he was in excellent health, and would vow never to drink again; then some bottle companion would come along, or some worry arise, and he would lapse into old habits. Each "fall" made him morose and desperate.

Sometimes he was haunted by the fear that his mind was doomed to impairment. Once a visitor to his dressing room had the bad taste to inquire: "Mr. Barrymore, is it true that your father died at an institution for the insane?" Jack rose, his face pale, his eyes turning green. In a slow, agonized tone, he said: "I am now going to kill you, you miserable, stupid son of a bitch!"

The visitor was most fortunate in reaching the door.

On this winter cruise, Jack took along a calendar on which he had asked Helios Hotchener to mark any days of special import to him: she had studied astrology in India and he regarded her as a woman of profound intuition. She circled one date with red crayon, warning him against accidents, and when he returned the Hotcheners asked him if anything of moment had happened that red-crayoned day.

"Happened?" he said. "I damned near lost my life; that's what happened." He then told how, while moored off the Mexican coast, he had reversed his decision to stay in his bunk all day, and had gone ashore alone to hunt game birds. Suddenly he found himself sinking waist-deep in some kind of quagmire. Only with great effort had he managed to draw an overhanging branch within reach of his fingers, and, after five desperate minutes of struggle, free himself.

From that time on Jack would not begin a motion picture, or even an important scene, without first conferring with Helios, who, in turn, consulted the stars. His director would have to accelerate or delay the shooting of various portions of the script, as the heavens might recommend. Barrymore wanted all battle scenes photographed under the sign of Mars, love scenes under the zodiacal influence of Venus.

IN SEPTEMBER 1927 Dolores's parents were divorced, and Barrymore began to visit her more frequently than when her father had been on the premises. Mr. Costello had not regarded him as the village paragon. Dolores also leased a new home which revived his longing for a place of his own, even though it did not resolve his uncertainty about matrimony. One morning he telephoned Hotchener: "Clementine told me last night that she wants a home in the country."

"A bachelor's house?"

"A house for two, meaning myself and Clementine, who has persuaded me that a reconnaissance in Beverly Hills is indicated. All the swells live there."

Hotchener, talking things over at Jack's hotel, suggested that property owners might raise the price when it became known that Barrymore was house hunting. "We'll fix that," the actor said, opening a chest of drawers. Hotchener thought he was looking for a bottle until he wheeled suddenly, to present a horrible face. Fangs protruded from his lips, and talonlike nails curled from his fingers—all part of the makeup he had used in *Dr. Jekyll and Mr. Hyde*. He drew on a wig and a battered hat. "I doubt the real-estate harpies will mistake me for a man of means," he said, tucking Clementine under his arm.

Barrymore eventually bought a hilltop home which had belonged to King Vidor, the Hollywood director. It was a five-room Spanish-type dwelling located on a private drive off Tower Road. "That's the place," he said when he saw it. "Buy it instantly!"

Jack now divided his interests among Dolores, *Tempest* (a film story of the Russian revolution, for United Artists), and his new home, for which he immediately hired a Japanese gardener, who enchanted him with horticultural marvels such as bushes on which red and white roses bloomed simultaneously.

During March of 1928 Dolores and her mother left for a holiday in Havana. Jack was lonesome and still worried about his drinking. He thought that if he could undertake some big theatrical enterprise, such as giving *Hamlet* in the huge open-air Hollywood Bowl, it might help him. With Hotchener he went there very late one evening and, standing in the moonlight on the bare stage, he began the "O, what a rogue and peasant slave am I!" soliloquy.

His voice, clear and resonant in the night air, reached the farthest row of empty seats where Henry sat. The next day he reserved the Bowl for a week in September and said he also intended to do *Hamlet* at the Greek Theatre of the University of California at Berkeley.

After Dolores's return Jack decided to confer with Helios about his romance. He asked her what the stars foretold for Dolores and himself.

"You will marry her," Helios said.

"But Blanche will never divorce me."

"Why not go East to ask her?"

Jack began again to drink, the idea of seeing Michael Strange seeming much on his mind. Finally he went to New York in April and stayed nearly a month. Upon his return he admitted

Away from it all: John Barrymore and the crew of "The Mariner," his 106-ft. racing schooner.

Below, the yacht "Infanta," carrying Barrymore, Dolores Costello and their two children, at anchor in Shoal Bay, British Columbia; inset, the skipper.

that he had not directly broached the matter of a divorce. "Blanche was so friendly that I couldn't," he said. "We had a really happy visit together. How could I tell her I wanted to marry someone else?"

"So you went on a six-thousand-mile errand for nothing," Henry Hotchener said. "I advise you *right now* to telephone and ask her for a divorce."

Jack winced. "I'll wait for a propitious moment."

A few days later a Hollywood gossip column ran an exposé of his romance, which infuriated him.

"It seems the propitious moment has arrived," he said grimly, and was amazed to find that Michael Strange was quite willing to divorce him. This was to take several months, however, because of the legal technicalities.

During this time Jack finished his third and last photoplay for United Artists. He waived all plans for playing *Hamlet* in the Hollywood Bowl and concentrated on the enlargement of his Tower Road estate. He was adding to the original Vidor hacienda a structure of six rooms which he called the "Marriage House." The older house was "Liberty Hall," and the two were connected by a cloisterlike pergola. Jack rose early each day to watch the builders at work.

"This place is beginning to look like Angkor Wat," he said.

But no one foresaw then that this establishment one day would comprise sixteen separate structures, fifty-five rooms, storerooms, dressing rooms, a projection room, a large aviary, a rathskeller, six pools, a bowling green, a skeet range, several fountains, and a totem pole.

Meanwhile plans for the wedding got under way. *The Mariner* was showing signs of dry rot in her hull, but was pronounced safe for a honeymoon cruise. A Unitarian minister agreed to conduct the marriage service, and the prospective groom settled on thirty-seven as the age to put on the license instead of his actual forty-six.

On November 24, 1928, he and Dolores were married in her mother's house on Schuyler Road.

As they set off on their long-delayed voyage without a chaperon, and the weeping Mrs. Costello was saying good-by to her daughter, Jack said, "Don't worry, Mamma. I'll cable you every day, and I'll take good care of Dolores, always."

But the honeymooners' cruise into South American waters was forty-three days old before Barrymore remembered to cable his mother-in-law: DOLORES IS WONDERFUL.

CHAPTER 13

WORK WAS STILL in progress at the Tower Road estate when, in March 1929, its master returned from the wedding cruise. Crews were bringing hundreds of tons of topsoil to the rocky slopes, planting numerous trees and shrubs, among them a dwarf Japanese cedar that cost eleven hundred dollars,. and an olive tree from Palestine, said to be a hundred years old. New water mains were being laid, and power lines brought from considerable distance. Jack was reluctant to turn his thoughts from his unfinished home long enough to confer with producers about *General Crack*, his first talking picture, which he was making under a new contract with Warner Brothers.

He was getting $30,000 a week (including a profit-sharing bonus) for this picture at a time when other stars were quaking in their buskins because voice had come to the screen. Already the thin voice of Douglas Fairbanks, Sr., was disillusioning a public that somehow had associated his athletic virilities with the larynx of a Cossack basso profundo. And the hitherto enormously popular John Gilbert, Greta Garbo's co-star, was suddenly deserted to sit out his fabulous contract, partly because of the chickadee sound recordings of his voice.

"From Garbo to Limbo," Barrymore observed.

"But," a producer inquired, "do you consider your first attempt at the talkies of secondary importance?"

"Not secondary," said Jack. *"Tertiary."*

He had brought back from his cruise a cargo of skins of fishes and reptiles, which now were mounted and placed in the trophy room. He also had become interested in tropical birds. At Balboa, Canal Zone, he had ordered ten pairs of them and had sent a cable costing over a hundred dollars to his business manager in California with detailed instructions as to the immediate construction of an aviary at Tower Road. But this was just the beginning. Now he obtained feathered rarities from many dealers: Australian green parakeets, broadtailed whydahs, red-billed Chinese magpies, bleeding-heart doves, pearl-necked doves, gallinules, black-headed nuns, white-headed nuns, and strawberry, saffron, and fire finches. Six birds of paradise cost him $1,900.

By day he supervised every decorative detail of the aviary, and by night he pored over the available authorities on birdlife. He set artificial as well as stunted live trees inside the aviary, installed birdbaths, and devised cotes for nesting. Instead of gravel, the floor was planted with tough Korean grass, which could be raked without being uprooted.

Ordinarily he was a heavy smoker, but he never smoked when in his aviary, where he often stayed for hours. It was amazing to see his birds yield to whatever power he seemed so definitely to possess over dumb creatures. Perhaps it was his patience with them. Strange dogs singled him out wherever he went. Unlike most persons, he permitted them to lick his face. And now he allowed his birds to peck mealworms from his mouth. He didn't mind when they lime-streaked his clothes or hair.

Strolling near the aviary one day, he heard servants' voices.

"This worm business ain't safe. The way Mr. Barrymore holds them in his mouth for the birds."

"You mean it ain't safe for Mr. Barrymore?"

"Hell no! I mean safe for the birds. It's the booze on Mr. Barrymore's breath. The worms get drunk when he holds them on his lip. Then the birds eat the drunk worms. Get me?"

"By God, you're right! I noticed how some of the birds flies sideways after he feeds 'em off of his lip."

Barrymore promptly went on the wagon—for twenty-four hours.

A king vulture named Maloney occupied an especially high place in Jack's affection. This goose-sized bird would preen Barrymore's mustache lovingly, and even caress his hair and eyebrows with his rapacious beak. This sort of thing drove Lionel out of his wits.

Lionel, Ethel and John Barrymore in the film "Rasputin."

With Katharine Hepburn in "A Bill of Divorcement."

Above, with Mary Astor in "Beau Brummel"; at left, as Captain Ahab in "Moby Dick."

"God Almighty!" Lionel would say. "Get rid of that stinking bird!"

"Vultures are most tidy about their persons," Jack said. "They wash and preen their plumage, and take hours at their toilets!"

"Toilets is right," said Lionel. "They *are* toilets!"

To find enough aged meat to satisfy the ever hungry Maloney, Jack frequently picked up tidbits from trash cans. One evening when the $30,000-a-week actor was strolling in town, dressed rather shabbily, having spent the afternoon in his aviary, he saw a trash can near the curb and began exploring its contents with a stick.

Just then a well-groomed stranger passed by, halted, and reached into his pocket.

"Here, my man," said the generous stranger, gingerly holding out a ten-cent piece. "But be sure to spend it only for food."

Jack looked up, took the dime, and touched the brim of his hat in a kind of salute.

"God bless you, sir!" he said throatily.

THE YEAR 1929 found him with an income of $430,000 and no debts, which seems amazing when one considers that he was putting a quarter of a million dollars into his estate. Furthermore, *The Mariner* had at last succumbed to dry rot, representing a dead loss of more than $110,000.

He should have been happy in his new marriage, and in general he was, although he had quarreled with Dolores as early as May, when she suggested that he do less drinking. His first severe illness also occurred in May, when he was treated for a duodenal ulcer. Then his throat began to bother him. A doctor recommended a tonsillectomy, but another medical man made a sounder diagnosis: "Your throat merely is raw from bad booze," he said. "I advise you to switch to better liquor. No operation necessary."

Ethel arrived in Hollywood in July. Concerned about Jack's drinking, she asked Hotchener, "Why is he doing it so heavily?" to which Barrymore's manager replied, "Is there always a reason?"

For a time Jack became happily occupied in planning a new

yacht, called the *Infanta*, a name suggested by Dolores, who was expecting her first child. The steel diesel cruiser was to be 120 feet in length overall, powered by two engines, and would cost $225,000. Barrymore suggested a mint bed aft the main deckhouse for juleps.

In August he made a Technicolor sequence of *Henry VI* for the Warner Brothers *Show of Shows*—the first time that Shakespeare came to the sound screen. This part of the production was beautifully done and demonstrated that the actor had lost none of his powers.

In September Winston Churchill called at the Warner studio to watch Jack make some scenes for *The Man from Blankley's*. The two men were photographed together and Barrymore sent a copy to his old friend, Max Beerbohm, in London. In an accompanying letter the actor revealed that he had had a recurrence of his ulcer but added that he in no wise blamed Mr. Churchill's visit for this condition.

He went on the bland Sippy diet, and stayed at home for two weeks, occupying himself by painting on navigational charts scenes illustrating his real or fancied adventures, in the style of fifteenth-century cartographers, a hobby he had begun as early as 1913, after a fishing expedition to the Bahamas.

When he returned to the studio he still was not well. His blood pressure was very low. He also began to lose interest in his yacht, partly because he could not associate a shell of metal with the sea. *The Mariner* had been different: born of blue water, descended from a long line of Gloucester boats that made history. A steel hull seems to one who has been under sail as a barnyard hen compared to a bird of paradise.

He did show an interest, however, in one item of the *Infanta*'s equipment, the galley stove. Specifications called for a five-burner range, fueled by diesel oil, but his cook said that he could do better work with an eight-burner.

"Give him eighty burners if he insists," Jack said. "The most important man on a ship, next to the skipper, is the cook. Anyone who thinks that food is merely something to eat is the kind of moron who would make penwipers of the Sistine tapestries or hang a First Folio in an outhouse."

The Honorable Winston Churchill visits John Barrymore on the set of "The Man from Blankley's" in Hollywood (1929); above, a scene from the film, with Loretta Young.

A FEW DAYS AFTER his first wedding anniversary, Jack said to his manager, "Dolores is harping on my drinking, and says I ought to go on the wagon."

"That doesn't seem unreasonable."

"No, but I've noticed it isn't so easy to stop drinking as it used to be."

"Well," his manager replied, "you're getting older, and the habit stronger. The question is, do you really *want* to stop?"

Barrymore looked Hotchener directly in the eye. "I'm not sure that I do. Drinking helps me not to worry too much about the future."

It was the time of his greatest wealth, and of his finest screen portrayals. He was forty-seven, and still vital, but the next five years would be for him a dress rehearsal for personal disaster. The wild winds frequently had blown across his heavens, but soon he would know the gale, and then the hurricane. He hurled himself against these years with fist-shakings and scornful cries. His prodigious follies, quixotic deeds, intense bursts of labor, together with his disregard of repose, would have felled a god.

He strove now, in his own fashion, to keep alive the love that he so gloriously had dreamed. He fleetingly inspired new hopes in Dolores that things again might be as they had been, but soon his good intentions strayed like soap bubbles, bursting to nothingness in the air.

In March of 1930 he began work on *Moby Dick*, the talking-picture version of *The Sea Beast*. By the end of the month the *Infanta* had been launched and taken for a shakedown cruise to Ensenada, but without Jack or Dolores; he was busy, and she expecting their first child. His daughter Dolores Ethel Mae was born the morning of April 8. "I'm sorry for your sake that it's a girl," his wife said.

"Doesn't my whole life prove that I get along better with girls?" he replied.

He was especially restless that autumn and decided to go on a long cruise, taking Dolores and the infant, revisiting the places described with passionate earnestness in his diary nearly five years before when aboard *The Gypsy*. He employed a woman doctor as well as a nurse to look after the baby's health aboard the *Infanta*, and the family sailed from Long Beach bound for Cape San Lucas, Mazatlán. He could not, however, as the voyage progressed, rouse the nodding gods of romance who, in the days of yearning aboard *The Gypsy*, had seemed to promise him a lifelong blessing.

In fact, he was miserable. He had no "freedom," as he interpreted the word. Everywhere he moved about the boat, some shadow of restriction fell: a nurse, a doctor, no sails to hoist in fair winds or shorten when storms might be ridden out adventurously.

About two months after this southward sailing, he suffered a severe gastric hemorrhage. Dolores summoned a doctor in Guatemala. The bleeding was controlled, the doctor given a thousand-dollar fee, then the *Infanta* made for home, her owner stretched out on his bed. When she reached port, Barrymore dressed fully and disembarked to meet reporters and press photographers. Public word of his illness was being withheld. Someone wanted a picture of him holding a sea turtle he had captured, weighing more than a hundred pounds. Dolores started to protest but Barrymore stooped, seized the armature of the turtle, then held it in a pose.

He stayed in bed for the next month. He now suffered headaches on the right side of his head, forerunners of neuralgic attacks that recurred periodically.

IN THE FALL of 1931, since Dolores was expecting a second child the next year, her husband decided to build an addition to the Marriage House, a nursery known as the "Children's Wing." Other additions were undertaken, including a rathskeller with a wine cupboard, the door to which had a combination lock, because he lost keys so often. Then he mislaid the paper with the combination. After a legal safecracker had twice reopened the door, Jack wrote down the numbers on the wall, where anyone might read them—and did.

The rathskeller had in it an old bar which had once been in a Virginia City saloon patronized by Mark Twain. Barrymore decorated this bar with cigarette premium cards and cigar bands of other days, including one which he prized most of all—a John Drew Cigar band with his dapper uncle's picture on it. Often, while sitting in this retreat, Jack would hold his daughter on his lap and improvise stories for her entertainment, fabulous recitals of the deeds of a mysterious people called the "Magoozalums."

From a financial standpoint 1931 had been the best in Barrymore's career, with an income of $460,000, although he spent money almost as rapidly as he made it. The next year also was one of professional activity, beginning with the all-star production *Grand Hotel*, in which he appeared with his brother, Lionel, and Wallace Beery, Joan Crawford, and Greta Garbo.

When he was introduced to Miss Garbo, Jack kissed her hand in the John Drew tradition, then said with Victorian politeness: "My wife and I think you the loveliest woman in the world." He behaved toward this shy, sensitive artist as with a timid bird in his aviary. They became good friends, and once, after completing a particularly difficult scene together, Miss Garbo electrified the director, the camera crew, *and* Barrymore by impulsively kissing him.

In later years she said, "Barrymore was one of the very few

who had that divine madness without which a great artist cannot work or live."

Jack's son was born on the afternoon of June 4, 1932. The expectant father had been pacing the hall in the presence of a considerable audience of nurses and hospital attendants, swearing that if it were a boy he would quit drinking. Yet when he had seen the child who he thought resembled his own father, he said he was going out for a few minutes.

For a few minutes . . .

He stayed away for hours, then returned to the hospital room next to that of Dolores, to sink into a deep sleep with his clothes on. Dolores was heartsick.

"I swore that if God would give me a son, I would never drink again," Jack said some days afterward. "What happens to a man who makes a sacred oath, then breaks it?"

CHAPTER 14

BARRYMORE made five pictures at a fast tempo during 1932. Playing the part of the half-crazed father in *A Bill of Divorcement*, a motion picture that made a star of the dynamic young actress, Katharine Hepburn, he gave a portrayal that was one of the finest of his film career. Indeed, producer David O. Selznick later held it to be the finest all-time performance in the history of the screen.

Immediately after completion of *A Bill of Divorcement*, Jack appeared in *Rasputin and the Empress*, with his brother and sister as co-stars. Playwright Charles MacArthur wrote the *Rasputin* scenario, working on it from hour to hour to tailor it to the measurements of three mighty individualists, and one of his main jobs was assuring the Barrymore brothers that he was not favoring one against the other in the dialogue.

After a summer of hard work in 1933, during which his drinking increased—as did domestic uncertainties, jealousies, and quarrels—Jack began *Counsellor-at-Law* for Universal Studios. This role required the fastest and most sustained delivery of lines of any part he had so far undertaken. He finished it successfully, then completed *Long Lost Father* for RKO. Then he was recalled by Director William Wyler to Universal for the remaking of a single scene opposite actor John Qualen for *Counsellor-at-Law*.

He was tired on that October evening, but definitely not drunk, having had only one or two glasses of beer during recent days. He seemed wearily confident as he began the scene, but suddenly he stumbled over one brief speech. He made a comic face and everyone laughed.

The scene was undertaken again and Barrymore "blew up" in his lines at almost the same place as before. A third take was ordered, and Jack failed at it. He was not making jokes now. He was angry.

He continued to falter during several successive trials, and a recess was ordered to give him an opportunity to consult the scenario. But when the actors at length resumed their places before the camera, Jack again failed to remember the lines he had newly reviewed. Director Wyler and his cameraman exchanged perplexed glances, and Jack's manager, Henry Hotchener, stood in sad amazement on the sidelines as the actor stubbornly persisted and repeatedly flunked out. At the fiftieth attempt he still was fighting gamely to conquer the scene, his face drawn, his jaw set. Finally, at Hotchener's suggestion, the retake was put over until the next morning.

Barrymore looked straight ahead as he walked off the stage. During the drive home he did not speak, and Hotchener left him at about one a.m. with a "get some sleep now; everything will come out all right."

Jack merely nodded. Then he went into his library. What he thought to himself during the next hour, what fears he had of an approaching shadow, we cannot know. But we do know that a knock sounded on his door at two o'clock in the morning, an hour after his manager had left him.

The man who knocked was Noll Gurney, the manager of several of Hollywood's foremost actors, and a trusted friend of Barrymore's neighbor, John Gilbert.

"Jack Gilbert is in a bit of trouble," Gurney explained when Barrymore greeted him at the door in bathrobe and slippers.

Gurney, of course, was unaware at this time of Barrymore's own travail. "Trouble?" asked Jack. "Never heard of the word. What can I do for Gilbert?"

"Would you mind coming over right away?" Gurney said. "He's very depressed. His Filipino servant is keeping an eye on him while I'm here."

"I see," Barrymore said. "Threatens to do away with himself. Is that it? Well, I'll get dressed. We have plenty of time, Noll. No actor would kill himself without an audience."

Was Gilbert drinking heavily? Jack asked Gurney as they walked across the lawns. Yes. Having woman trouble? Yes, his third wife, Virginia Bruce, was threatening to leave him. And his first and only sound picture had been hissed at its Palo Alto premiere.

"What the hell!" Jack snorted. "Even Caruso was once hissed in Naples."

"But so many slurs have been made about Gilbert's voice," Gurney said, "that he's convinced the public thinks him some kind of a softie."

"Well," Barrymore said, "my friend Jack Dempsey has a voice like a constipated sparrow, but I'd hesitate to suggest he was anything but a lethal bull."

Gilbert was surprised to see Barrymore, but greeted him with a hollow cordiality: "Great to see you. We'll make a night of it. Drinks for everybody," he said.

"There will be no more drinks tonight for anybody," Barrymore said quietly, then added, "I hear you've been making a damned fool of yourself, all because someone says this or that. Why do actors read the papers anyway? Christ! Do you think the world turns on the importance or the unimportance of a ham? Well, it doesn't!"

Gilbert stared at the floor, stunned.

"Why should you give a damn about your voice?" Barrymore went on. "You can dig ditches, can't you? Or work for Western Union. How old are you? Shut up! Gurney here tells me you're thirty-three or thirty-four. My grandmother went broke for the tenth time when she was seventy-two. Did she bump herself off? No. She had guts, God bless her! She went out and got a job."

Above, a family group (with "Tatters").

Family matters. Top, the house in Beverly Hills; above, on vacation with Dolores and John, Jr.; at right, "The Royal Family" together: Lionel and his wife; Ethel in the center, flanked by her daughter and two sons; the John Barrymores at right.

He paused. Gilbert was sitting openmouthed, his hands clenched. He flushed.

"You've got a baby daughter. Never entered your head, did it, that you owe the *child* something? No. The ham always thinks only of himself. Get up! Where is she?"

"In the nursery," said Gilbert meekly.

"Lead the way," Jack commanded. "It'll do us all good to look at something decent in this sinkhole of culture."

In the nursery he directed Gilbert to take the child in his arms. "Just hold her close," he said. "Isn't she more important than newspaper gossip?" Gilbert was crying, and after a minute Barrymore took the baby from him and held her for a moment himself. Then he kissed her head and gently placed her back in the crib.

"You go on home, Noll," Barrymore said. "I'll stay here for a while."

At seven o'clock he left his neighbor asleep and went home to dress for the remaking of the *Counsellor-at-Law* scene.

This time, notwithstanding the experiences of the night, his own galling failure of memory, his lack of sleep, Barrymore worked expertly, unfalteringly, before the camera. He made the scene without a break, at the first trial.

Here was a champion.

IT WAS only some six weeks after Barrymore's *Counsellor-at-Law* ordeal that tests began for a screen portrayal of *Hamlet* in Technicolor. This undertaking promised an enhancement of his artistic fame as well as a significant broadening of motion-picture dimensions. Barrymore's brilliant teacher, Margaret Carrington, and her husband, Robert Edmond Jones, who was to direct the enterprise, arrived in Hollywood. John Hay ("Jock") Whitney, the young multimillionaire, had arranged to finance the project if the tests warranted the production.

The afternoon of the test found Jack ably reciting the "rogue and peasant slave" soliloquy. That evening, after dinner, he invited friends to see him do the ghost scene. He began the speech from Act I, Scene V, in which Hamlet is confronted by the specter of his dead father:

"O, all you host of heaven! O earth! What else?
And shall I couple hell? O fie! Hold, hold, my heart;
And you, my sinews, grow not instant old,
But bear me stiffly up! Remember thee?
Yea, from the table of my memory . . ."

Suddenly he broke off and put his hand to his head. He could not proceed. The reference to "memory" seemed a psychological deadlock. Mrs. Carrington prompted him but it was of no use. He tried again and again, then left the stage to sit beside Helios Hotchener, who was present.

"Are you ill?" she asked.

"No," he replied, "not ill of *body*." After a pause he said, "I've been frightened for some time by my lapses of memory. God knows I've said those lines onstage hundreds of times. Am I to be struck down as was my father? He, too, developed headaches and memory lapses onstage. I've had headaches . . ." He paused again. "But I don't want to see a doctor. I want to beat back whatever it is myself. And, by God! I will!"

Robert Jones and his wife sadly canceled their plans for *Hamlet* and went back to New York.

BARRYMORE'S homelife by now was straining at the seams. He was beset by domestic annoyances, whether real or imaginary, such as that his daughter's companionship was being denied him, and that he was unwelcome in the nursery of his young son.

When rehearsals began, in May 1934, of *Hat, Coat, and Glove*, for producer Kenneth Macgowan at RKO, he seemed listless and low in vitality, and on the first day of filming, although he had not been drinking for several days, he swayed into the scene, knew none of his lines, and kept walking in the wrong direction. When work was halted for the remainder of the day, Jack seemed unaware of what had happened.

In the morning he failed again. Macgowan, a discerning man, called Henry Hotchener aside and said: "I know he isn't drunk. His trouble is more serious than that. Please make him take a long rest. We must regretfully cancel the contract."

Dolores now advised her husband to enter the Good Samaritan Hospital, a suggestion Jack yielded to almost indifferently.

There laboratory and other tests determined beyond question that he was not a paretic, and the existence of a brain tumor as a possible cause of his memory defect was also ruled out. His doctors said, as others had before, that drink was the basic cause of his trouble, and added that he had a Korsakoff's syndrome. This is a loss of memory of recent events, presumably caused by a toxemia with a specific affinity for brain tissue, and not, in a strictly scientific sense, regarded as insanity.

In the opinion of authorities I have interviewed, Jack could have been cured of his loss of memory at this point if he could have gone on the wagon once and for all. But this was not to be. Toward the end of his life Barrymore frequently experienced a disorientation of time and place. He sometimes would forget, halfway through a recital, what subject he was discussing. Then he would enlist his great inherent dramatic art. His "ad libs" would arrest the interest of his listeners until he regained the traffic lane of his narrative. It was as if he had skidded off the road, then struggled back again to the solid pavement. He could not always get back. Then it would seem that the roadbed of memory itself had been sabotaged.

When acting in pictures, after 1934, it became necessary for him to read his speeches from a blackboard held by an athletic fellow, who dashed about the set, out of range of the camera, but always within eyeshot of the unretentive Barrymore. Jack did not even always know the story of the play; but he could give the blackboard lines such rich interpretation and inflection as to make up for their dramatic dependency upon what preceded or what followed.

CHAPTER 15

IN JUNE 1934, soon after Jack left the hospital, it was agreed that he might benefit by a nonalcoholic cruise in northern Pacific waters off the Canadian coast with his wife and children. But once aboard the *Infanta*, with alcohol denied him, Barrymore drank Dolores's perfume, downed all the mouthwash available, and even partook of a bottle of spirits of camphor.

Late in August Henry Hotchener received a telegram sent by Jack from Vancouver, stating that something serious had happened on the boat, that his family was motoring to Seattle, where they would board the train to Los Angeles, and that he would arrive alone on his yacht at Long Beach on August 24.

What actually happened the day of the "trouble" aboard the *Infanta* is not clear, but the children's nurse received a broken nose, threatened suit for damages, and sometime later was given $3,000 out of court. Meanwhile Dolores, when Hotchener discussed the matter with her, said that a "serious attack" had been made upon the nurse and herself; that Jack was far from normal, and she feared that matters were growing worse.

On the Sunday after his return from this ill-fated cruise, Barrymore, obviously disturbed, telephoned Hotchener. He asked him to come at once to the Tower Road estate and try to slip unseen into the office over the garage for a secret conference.

"I am not drinking," the actor greeted him. "There are times when a man does not *dare* drink. This is one of them."

He alleged that he had overheard on his telephone extension a conversation between Dolores and her physician, arranging for a group of specialists to examine him. This meant, in Jack's opinion, that he might be judged mentally incompetent. "It once happened to a close friend of mine," Jack said. "He was privately examined by physicians, then a few days later a petition was signed by his wife and he was put into an institution. He never came out of it."

Then he said, "I would be a damned fool not to get out of California and the jurisdiction of its courts as quickly as possible. We must get away without letting Dolores have any idea we are leaving. She'll be furious anyway, for no woman likes a man to walk out on her."

They left the Glendale Airport on Tuesday evening, traveling under fictitious names. Jack had not even packed a handbag, but he took the precaution before his departure to indicate legally that he was not "deserting" his wife. In a wire to his doctor and in a phone conversation with Dolores, he stressed that he was leaving to get radio work in order to continue supporting her and the children.

"The Great Lover" of the screen. At left, with Mary Astor in "Don Juan"; below, about to embrace Carole Lombard in "Twentieth Century."

Below, with Greta Garbo in "Grand Hotel."

Below, with Gladys Swarthout in "Romance in the Dark."

Both Dolores and the physician maintained that at no time was it planned to place Jack in an institution for the mentally unfit. Nor was any medical conference discussed "behind Jack's back." But his fears were terrifyingly real to him. It is understandable that Dolores was deeply concerned over recent events; and it is understandable that a sinister river of doubt overflowed the dikes of Jack's brilliant mind.

In New York his attorney advised that he be examined by a recognized authority on nervous and mental disorders as a precaution against possible extradition procedure. The examination was made by neurologist Dr. Lewis Stevenson, member of the faculty of the Cornell University Medical School, whose written report stated, in part, that John Barrymore's "mental status is in every way normal except that there is some slight impairment of memory for recent events, which in my opinion, is due to fatigue. . . ."

But Barrymore still felt unsafe. He announced that he would go abroad at once. "I want to put a lot of water between myself and my worries," he said. "I need a moat for my castle. The Atlantic is just the right size." Aboard the *Berengaria* he promptly locked the doors of his suite. "I'll not rest easy," he said to Hotchener, "until this damned ship passes the Statue of Liberty."

IN LONDON Barrymore signed a contract to do a picture for London Film: $60,000 for a six-week term before the English cameras. Jack suggested that his friends Ben Hecht and Charles MacArthur write the scenario. They had written the recent screen version of their own zany stage play, *Twentieth Century*, in which Barrymore's talents as a comedian had flared brilliantly. But a transatlantic telephone call to the playwrights established that they were up to their mighty chins in a dozen enterprises of their own concoction.

One evening, during a conference in Barrymore's hotel suite, Director Alexander Korda asked, "Why not film *Hamlet?*"

Barrymore agreed readily. He was pleased.

Then, after Korda's departure, he turned to Hotchener. "I wonder if I'm up to doing *Hamlet?* Thousands here remember me in it ten years ago." He examined his features in a mirror.

"Well, it would be a vintage Hamlet, but a good cameraman might be able to counteract the furrows and the dewlaps of fifty-two years."

Now he looked at his ankles. They were swollen. "That is bad for the wearing of tights," he said. "The swelling goes down when I lay off drinks. But the way I feel now . . ."

"Do you suppose you could recall the *Hamlet* lines now?" asked Hotchener.

"Sure," Jack said. He did both soliloquies without trouble, then began the ghost scene. But now Barrymore faltered at precisely the same place as during the test in Hollywood a year ago.

The actor quietly sat down near a window, stared into the night over Hyde Park, then said, "It looks as if *Hamlet* is out. What do we tell Korda?"

"If we tell him the real reason," said Hotchener, "he'll doubt your ability to do *any* picture for him. Let's think it out."

A week later Jack announced that he had "found a way out, maybe." He confided to the Hotcheners—Helios having arrived in London to join them—that he would like to go to India.

"I've just come from a luncheon with a remarkable Hindu woman," he said buoyantly, "who told me of an ancient cure for an ailing memory. Besides, she knows several maharajahs. Claims they would lend me their palaces, retinues, elephants, and other properties if I decide to make pictures in India." Then he asked Helios, "Is there such a cure?"

"Yes," she replied. "The Ayurvedic treatment."

"Do you think they'd take me on? Whom do we ask?"

"Dr. Srinivasa Murti, president of the Ayurvedic Conference. He is also a regular physician, but unless you are in earnest . . ."

A few days later Hotchener told London Film the actor wished to take a holiday in India, and *Hamlet* was postponed until the next spring.

THEY FIRST WENT to Italy, so Jack could revisit the places he had been with Edward Sheldon twenty years ago. During much of this journey he suffered from headaches and drowsiness, seemed feverishly restless, and ate hardly at all. His uncertainty was accentuated by the fact that he had heard nothing from Dolores as yet, although a letter from his caretaker was waiting at Naples and indicated much unrest at Tower Road. This put Jack into a rage, and he wrote the caretaker authorizing him to see a lawyer if necessary.

Aboard the Italian Line's *Victoria*, bound for Bombay, Jack stayed up nights, remaining most of the day in his stateroom, occasionally appearing for tea or for dinner wearing a cerise cummerbund and a smart dinner jacket. He spent his "loose" moments at the bar in the company of a Eurasian salesman from Calcutta, a person of great alcoholic capacity.

As the vessel neared Bombay, Jack frequently mentioned his father, and spoke of the times when Maurice Barrymore had described India's mysteries and beauties. He expressed a fear that he would never rejoin his wife and children on Tower Road, that he might not even return alive to the Western world.

This visit to India, Jack felt, was his "last chance"; in this time-old land of secrets he might find the miracle that would rid him of his weaknesses.

At Madras he received an undated letter from Dolores, saying his plans seemed "so indefinite" that it would be best for her to await his return to England before deciding what was "the best thing to do." She closed by saying that "the children send you their love." Jack made no reply to this letter.

He now turned his mind to the "cure."

To his surprise Dr. Srinivasa Murti was no patriarchal apostle with white beard and robes. He was a middle-aged gentleman of brisk military manner, who wore a turban, but otherwise dressed in occidental fashion. When Jack offered him a drink, he declined, but didn't seem to mind when Barrymore mixed two drinks for himself.

Then Dr. Murti explained the treatment, to last six weeks, which consisted of certain spiritual factors, internal and external medication, and a simple vegetable diet. During the first three weeks the patient would feel debilitated, but no hospitalization was required; Dr. Murti did, however, advise Barrymore to move to a quieter hotel.

"Because there is no bar there?" asked Jack.

"Not at all," replied the doctor. "There are bars almost everywhere in India. You must decide for yourself whether or not you can stay away from them."

"I've made up my mind to try," Jack said.

Tests were made in accord with modern medical practice. Then an Ayurvedic specialist and four assistants, all of whom held medical degrees, began the treatments in a room adjoining Barrymore's sleeping quarters at the hotel. They brought with them a small brass altar in which receptacles filled with sacred oils were lighted, and incense burned in a brazier.

Barrymore was asked to seat himself before the altar, and to keep in mind a desire that health be restored him. The five physicians also seated themselves near him and began to intone ancient Sanskrit chants, explaining that the purpose of the ceremony was purely psychological, intended to dissipate thoughts of ill health or depression and turn the mind into invigorating channels.

Barrymore was then undressed and placed on a broad slab of highly polished wood. Now began manipulations, each physician being assigned to a certain area of the body. The massage continued for about an hour, after which he was bathed in a brew of leaves simmered for several hours, then cooled to body temperature. Finally he was put to bed, where he lapsed at once into a deep sleep.

Massages, baths, periods of relaxation, together with herbal medication, continued for three weeks. Barrymore's memory improved. His ankles no longer were swollen, he lost his headaches and his indifference to food. He enjoyed rides around the city and along the beach of the Bay of Bengal. He asked for reading matter, listened to records of his favorite operas, and spoke infrequently of past griefs. He surely would do *Hamlet* for Korda when spring came.

But Dr. Murti admonished him not to construe his physical and mental well-being as a sign that he could return to former indulgences.

By the middle of December he seemed almost restored to good health, and he planned to tour India in a private railway car as soon as possible, staying some time in Agra, the birthplace of his father.

Then one day, while he was supposed to be napping in his room, he disappeared. The Eurasian, the Calcutta salesman who had been Jack's bar companion on shipboard, had called him at the hotel and soon afterward they left to go to a Madras club, where they had several drinks. Then they visited a bagnio, at which place Barrymore promised the madam a twelve-hundred-dollar fee to close her doors to her usual clientele.

When he returned to his hotel a week later, the doctor arrived to discuss with him the consequences of his activities. The actor apologized, and the treatments were resumed. Then two days afterward he again disappeared for several days. It now became apparent to the doctor as well as to Jack that it was futile to continue with the treatment.

Plans to visit Agra vanished; Barrymore decided to return to England to fulfill his contract for *Hamlet*. With the Hotcheners, he sailed from Bombay early in January 1935. He picked up some bar companions, a few days out of Bombay, and his headaches returned, his ankles again became swollen. By the time the ship reached Naples, he was seriously ill.

"What shall we do about *Hamlet?*" asked his manager.

"Hamlet is dead, very dead. Cable Korda that urgent business calls me to America." Then, with a smile, Jack added: "Of course, there is always King Lear . . ."

CHAPTER 16

NOW BEGAN the seven last years of a lifetime. At an ailing fifty-three Barrymore began to pay at the usurious rates demanded of a man of public name when he does not conform to the gospels of exemplary behavior. He forfeited his material belongings. He lost his health. But his spirit remained essentially young and unconquered.

He had come to Hollywood ten years before with no assets other than his talent and his fame. During the following decade he earned $2,634,500, although in 1934, the year of the flight, his gross income had shrunk to $74,264.42: the combined proceeds from one picture, *Twentieth Century*, two radio broadcasts, and the yield from bonds, but he had spent $288,497.76, and kept on spending at a maharajah's pace.

His financial position on January 31, 1935, was as follows: he had physical assets (his Tower Road home, his yacht, and a lot in Beverly Hills) in the amount of half a million dollars. He possessed negotiable securities in excess of $140,500. He had no outstanding debts. He had ready cash to pay February bills amounting to $15,108.14.

We are now about to see how a fortune melts under the high temperature of a man's caprices.

WHILE STILL in New York after his return from India, Barrymore's already depleted physical condition began further to deteriorate. News reaching him from California, where Dolores had moved the children and most of the furniture from Tower Road to a new residence in the Wilshire district, merely stimulated his reckless nature to headlong indiscretions.

Toward the end of February Jack collapsed in his hotel and was sent to New York Hospital, where he stayed until late March. It was during this time that a stagestruck young student at Hunter College, Miss Elaine Jacobs, one day entered Jack's suite, and what was left of his life. When the doctor protested his patient's reception of a stranger, Jack announced that she was his protégée, and that he was going to help her become an actress. She soon announced her new name, Elaine Barrie, and the subsequent publicity did not restore any laurel leaves to the actor's molting crown. As usual he paid no attention to the furor of print, and Miss Barrie did not seem to try to avoid public mention. She was nineteen years old, an age when a sudden emergence from prosaic privacy sometimes creates the illusion that notoriety is fame.

Jack, who seldom spent wisely, now began to spend wildly. His yacht and its crew remained idle at an East River mooring at an average expense of $3,000 a month. His bill at Saks Fifth Avenue for a month was $4,811.15. On one day he purchased gowns and coats at Milgrim's costing $1,051.31. Yet between April and September he earned only $5,000 for two radio broadcasts, an average income of $33 a day, while his expendi-

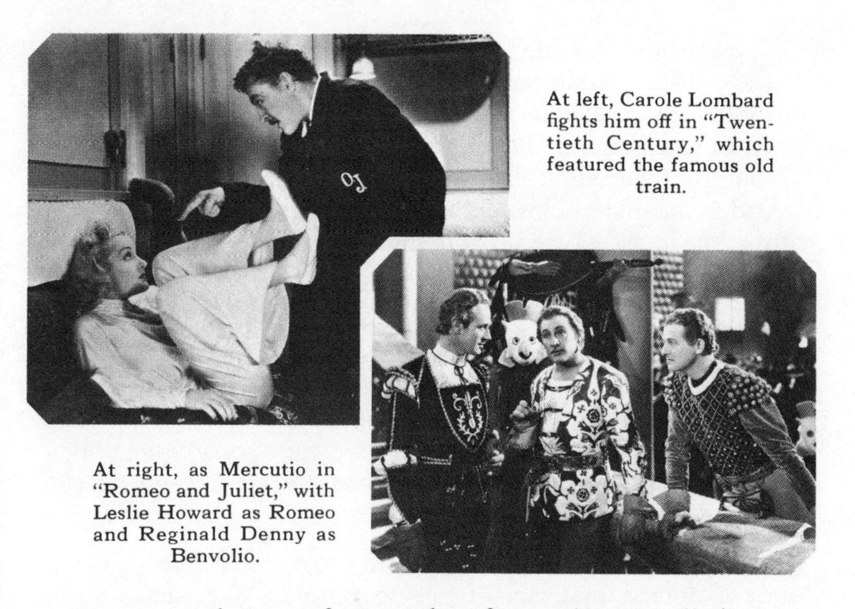

At left, Carole Lombard fights him off in "Twentieth Century," which featured the famous old train.

At right, as Mercutio in "Romeo and Juliet," with Leslie Howard as Romeo and Reginald Denny as Benvolio.

tures were at the rate of $827 a day, forcing him to sell about $125,000 in bonds.

Meantime his affairs steadily grew more muddled. Dolores's attorneys and his were conferring about divorce terms and a property settlement. The flood of publicity regarding Jack's young protégée had not put his wife in a mood to make any concessions to her hopscotching spouse, who by now was staying with Elaine and her mother at their apartment. But Jack had informed Hotchener that he was "willing to settle with Dolores on her *own* terms," as he felt he no longer could tolerate this legal obstacle to a marriage with Miss Barrie.

In early September, however, he had "a serious quarrel with Elaine," and moved to Essex House. The next day a lawyer representing Miss Barrie and Mrs. Jacobs made demands for reparations for properties Jack allegedly had brought to, then taken from the Jacobs' apartment, including a $1,800 canary diamond he had bought Elaine. The actor then moved what was left of his ready assets to a New Jersey bank, and moored his yacht beyond the reach of possible attachment.

On September 16 he received for his signature the property

agreement in his wife's suit against him, which gave custody of the children, certain stocks and bonds, and support payments to Dolores, and allowed Barrymore to retain title to the Tower Road house and the *Infanta*.

It seems incredible that on the day he received this agreement, and in the midst of his confusion, Jack, chancing to be reminded that the morrow was his wife's birthday, composed the following telegram to her:

DEAR WINKIE, HAPPY BIRTHDAY AND LOVE TO THE CHILDREN. I WOULD LOVE TO THINK THAT YOU ARE AS LONESOME AS I AM, BUT THAT IS AS IT MAY BE. ANYWAY, MY LOVE TO YOU AND THE BABIES. YOU MUST ALWAYS REMEMBER THAT ONCE WE HAD LOTS OF FUN AND DON'T LET ANYTHING EVER MAKE YOU FORGET IT. PLEASE BELIEVE I MEAN THIS, BABY, AND WE WILL BOTH FEEL BETTER. MUCH LOVE. JACK

More incredible developments were to come. With his divorce terms agreed upon and arrangements made for an out-of-court settlement of the reparations demanded by Miss Barrie and her mother, Barrymore was now free to leave New York and return to California without danger of colliding with bailiffs or psychiatrists.

He arrived in Beverly Hills on September 25, and his brother Lionel gave him sanctuary. But that same night, after Barrymore had assured his brother, as well as a delegation from the press, that his giddy interlude of young romance was done, he telephoned Miss Barrie in New York.

Dolores Barrymore obtained an uncontested divorce on October 9, 1935, and Miss Barrie and her mother soon thereafter arrived in California. Their lawyer, Aaron Sapiro, now became Jack's attorney-manager, the Hotcheners having returned to India.

New brooms began to function. The caretaker was dismissed from Tower Road; the captain was ousted from the *Infanta*, after having served for ten years as Barrymore's skipper. Some months later a mortgage of $40,000 was placed on the yacht.

During this period Jack seldom saw anyone in private other than his new mentors, although his longtime friends Ben Hecht and Charles MacArthur were trying to keep friendly eyes upon him whenever he took recess from his preoccupations with Miss Barrie. I joined them in this endeavor after returning to Los Angeles from a trip abroad early in 1936 and receiving from them a firsthand report on my friend, whom I had not seen for more than a year. The playwrights told me at this time that Barrymore, when informed by them that his romance could be seen almost daily in the headlines, seemed amazed, then splendidly detached about the whole business.

Canceled checks indicate that spending, meanwhile, continued at the rate of a Mississippi flood. Let us take, for example, the actor's bank statement for April 1936, captioned JOHN BARRYMORE (AARON SAPIRO, POWER OF ATTORNEY). It shows that on April 1 he had $22,629.17 in cash on hand, and that $17,312.84 of this sum was disbursed during the month. He or his agencies were spending his money at the average rate of $577 a day. His telephone bill was $1,691.07. Checks made out to cash, bearing the endorsement Elaine Barrie, amounted to $950. Checks drawn to and endorsed by Aaron Sapiro amounted to $4,222.27.

In India, at about this time, the Hotcheners learned that Sapiro was bringing suits against both Warner Brothers and Henry for an accounting of Barrymore's funds. The ex-manager returned to California, and, unable to get in touch with the actor, who was ill, Hotchener immediately transferred all his own financial records of Barrymore's business to his attorney, who voluntarily placed them in the custody of the court. When the case came to trial, Hotchener's testimony caused the judge to order the suit dismissed.

BARRYMORE often asked, in these later years, "What has become of all the money I've made?" He thought it strange that yammerings so often rose concerning his lack of funds. He had made $2,600,000 during his first ten years in Hollywood. He would earn another half-million dollars, $3,100,000 in all, sometimes working when half dead, with only his stout spirit to sustain him on the motion-picture set, the stage, or at the radio microphone. While he had invested in a few great luxuries, such as his yachts, his house, his hobbies, he spent comparatively little on himself. He cared nothing for clothes. He didn't own a watch. He entertained infrequently, much preferring eating in the kitchen, or in some friend's kitchen, to sitting at a costly restaurant table.

He had drunk much in his time, but he was not a connoisseur of wines. Indeed, he had a beachcomber's taste for the cheaper grades of liquor, and his tolerance for alcohol had become so slight that he drank far less than was believed of him. Many times he was accounted drunk when the fact was that he was genuinely ill.

Aside from his almost fierce desire to see that his bills were paid, he did not appear to bother much about money. He seldom had much pocket money even when affluent, and now he carried even less.

In May of 1936 he had obtained the part of Mercutio in the M-G-M production of *Romeo and Juliet*, supporting Norma Shearer as Juliet and Leslie Howard as Romeo. Returning to the screen after a year and eight months' absence, he permitted himself to be placed in residence in the private West Los Angeles sanitarium of Mrs. Louise Simar Kelley, whose husband, Jim, became Barrymore's "guard."

Jim Kelley accompanied his charge to the motion-picture sets, and watched over him during occasional social expeditions. Possibly Jack was not given money lest he wander off from the Kelley sanitarium to spend it on something more fiery than the single can of beer permitted him each day.

Jack did "wander off" frequently, to the worriment of Jim Kelley, who even became afraid to bathe, for each time that he stripped himself for the tub, the resourceful actor would flee the premises and the nude Kelley could not very well pursue him into the street. Then Hecht, MacArthur, or myself would receive the news from Kelley over the telephone: "The Monster has broke loose again!"

We had come to call Jack "The Monster." If anyone is so dull as to think this was not said with affection, and is not being recorded here with affection, then . . . but why should one explain such things?

CHAPTER 17

In November 1936 Jack suddenly decided to elope with Miss Barrie. Charlie MacArthur and Ben Hecht sought to dissuade him from this enterprise with a long list of reasons why he should not, at fifty-four, again draw on the beekeeper's veil of matrimony. He remained calm and amiable as the two playwrights harangued him, then said with finality: "Gentlemen, you are talking to a man who is about to go over Niagara Falls in a barrel!"

The next day he flew with Miss Barrie and Attorney Sapiro to Yuma, Arizona, to be married by a justice of the peace.

A separation occurred one month and twenty-three days later, after a public skirmish between husband and wife on New Year's Eve at the Trocadero, rendezvous of Hollywood's elite. There Barrymore's name-callings, directed at his young mate, rose above the happier sounds made by celebrants of the arriving year of 1937. And Elaine then went alone to the rented home in Benedict Canyon where they were residing with her mother and three servants.

Five hours after this set-to Barrymore telephoned Henry Huntington, attorney for Mrs. Kelley, in whose sanitarium he had sought temporary refuge, and asked that he come there "instantly" for a conference: his wife was contemplating filing a divorce complaint. Reluctantly the attorney, who was but slightly acquainted with Barrymore and was not, at this time, one of his admirers, went at dawn to the Kelley establishment, there to learn that Jack knew nothing of his recent business affairs, and that Aaron Sapiro still had the actor's power of attorney.

On January 2, 1937, Huntington appeared early at the courthouse to file a revocation of Sapiro's power of attorney. Things commenced to happen. Creditors began to pound for immediate payment of debts amounting to $161,503.82, including the mortgage of $40,000 on the *Infanta*. Bills for the seven weeks of Barrymore's fourth marriage added up to $10,108.90, of which $511.83 appeared to have been spent on himself. He could have undertaken ordinary bankruptcy proceedings, but he preferred to do otherwise.

"I want to owe no one," he told Huntington. "We'll pay up."

The attorney then filed a petition, under Section 74 of the Bankruptcy Act, indicating that all Barrymore sought of his creditors was time for a proper liquidation of his assets.

It was almost two years before these claims eventually reached settlement, and the bankruptcy court honorably discharged the debtor (who, in accord with his philosophy, would promptly go into debt again). At times it seemed that he could not survive the travail of ill health and harassment.

But he was never forced, now or later, to "liquidate" Tower Road. It remained a symbol to him, as the Alchemist's Corner had been, as his yachts had been. And it is important, when all else is lost, that a man of great imagination be permitted to keep the relics associated with his dreamworld.

Once, early in 1937, I called upon Jack at Kelleys' to suggest that we visit Tower Road. He brightened at once. Miss Barrie, following their marriage, had not chosen to reside at the now deserted estate, and Jack had not been there for some time.

As we walked slowly up the hill, he spoke happily of the "old days." Each landmark reminded him of some adventure: the totem pole, the aviary, the now stilled fountains, the drained pools. But Tower Road, like its master, had come to a run-down condition. He said little of the lack of life about the place, the stillness of the stripped rooms, the cobwebs in the rathskeller.

One thing, however, did disturb him. Someone had removed the John Drew Cigar band from its place of honor among other cigar bands pasted on the façade of the old Wild West bar.

"That," he said, "was worth more to me than all the rest of the things put together."

MISS BARRIE'S REPRESENTATIVES served a divorce summons the middle of February 1937, and also a temporary restraining order tying up her husband's property and possible funds. She asked for $2,500 a month alimony, listing her necessary expenses at their rented Benedict Canyon home at $2,225 a month. But Barrymore's faulty memory, unpredictable health, and un-

Visiting the set of "The Scoundrel," in which Noel Coward (right) made his film debut. With them are Martha Sleeper (left) and Julie Haydon of the cast, authors Ben Hecht (standing) and Charles MacArthur.

Above, two great hams (W. C. Fields on the left) strike a pose for posterity; above left, Clark Gable and Barrymore on the firing range; at left, in Beverly Hills with his German shepherd.

toward publicity caused producers to hesitate to employ him. How was he to meet these demands?

A number of his friends actively assisted Attorney Huntington, now a fierce admirer of the never whimpering actor, in trying to untangle his affairs. He still seemed to them a great man.

Ben Hecht made a fine effort that year to write into the scenario of *Nothing Sacred* a part for Jack, to which David O. Selznick, the producer, agreed if he would memorize but one speech of twenty lines. With only his single can of beer a day, and after a week of painstaking rehearsals at the sanitarium, Jack went to the studio. He failed this test.

"Jack didn't know a word of the speech," Hecht told me, "but he got off one of his own, ten times as good as mine; then he read like Coleridge from the script. Still David couldn't take the risk."

Trips to the desert near La Quinta were prescribed for the actor, and Kelley took him there, using a trailer he had attached to his car. A remote house was found. These holidays among the dunes seemed to benefit Jack.

Soon Edmund Goulding, who had directed him in *Grand Hotel*, agreed to give him a part in his forthcoming picture, urged to do so by Warners' executive Gordon Hollingshead, who had worked as an assistant director on many of Jack's early pictures. Here was a chance to make at least $30,000 for two weeks' work.

However, other studio officials demanded that he take a screen test before being assigned the role. Arrangements were made for such a test, and Jack now returned to the sanitarium to await the appointed day.

When he finally appeared at the studio, Goulding was reluctant, for Barrymore's own sake, to begin the test. But Hollingshead, who had recommended the part for his old friend, said, "Don't humiliate him by refusing to go through with it. And *don't* have any film in the camera to record a flop."

Goulding never let Jack know the real reason the test failed. He merely announced to one and all: "He was fine. Really fine. But he made the star a bit nervous, and the studio, you know, has to consider her wishes."

WHEN ATTORNEY HUNTINGTON took Barrymore as a client, he did so with the proviso that whenever Miss Barrie reentered the actor's life in a positive fashion, the relations between lawyer and client would automatically cease. Early in August of 1937 Jack received a telegram from Miss Barrie. She was arriving at the Glendale railway station from the East. Would he meet her?

He did meet her, with flowers. Then on August 9, 1937, the interlocutory decree of divorce was dismissed. Exit Attorney Huntington.

CHAPTER 18

AT THIS POINT the only means available to the now fifty-six-year-old man to pay his debts was the out-and-out commercialization of a great family name. Apparently no one with access at this time to the actor and his affairs reverenced the century and a half of shining tradition which had been passed on to him, and by him briefly but brilliantly enhanced. Now he permitted himself to be exploited in an array of claptrap motion pictures and a series of raffish broadcasts, which made him seem a buffoon to a new generation.

And yet, even now the man stayed peculiarly and definitely himself. Drama critic Richard Watts, Jr., a good friend of Jack's, once wrote: "In some paradoxical fashion the very manner in which Barrymore seemed almost to revel in his disintegration convinced people who had never seen him in *Hamlet* and *The Jest* that he must have been among the giants. For even when he showed signs of physical and spiritual collapse he did not enter into any kind of ordinary decline. Everything he did was in an epic way, and, even when he appeared to be making an embarrassing clown of himself, he did so on a grand and wholesale scale, coming apart with boisterous gargantuan humor and a sardonic air of self-criticism."

Or as another old friend, Ashton Stevens, once put it, when commenting on the last years of Barrymore's career: "No one can run downhill as fast as a thoroughbred."

Late in 1938 it was decided that John Barrymore would return

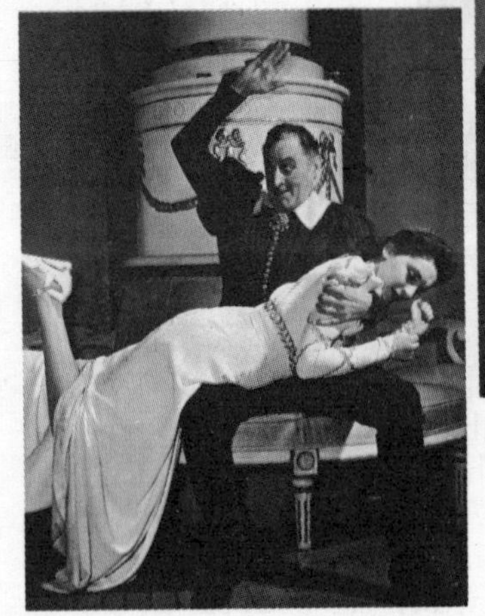

At right, Barrymore rehearses a radio script with his daughter, Diana; at left, a vigorous scene with Elaine Barrie in "My Dear Children."

to the stage with Elaine Barrie as his leading lady in a play called *My Dear Children*. His role in this crude comedy practically amounted to an autobiography of the Barrymore of first-page fiction, gossip columns, and radio self-caricature. And in playing it the shorn Samson performed a last theatrical feat, the pulling down of the pillars of the house of his art.

The play opened at the McCarter Theatre, Princeton, New Jersey, on March 24, 1939, after which a road tour began. The theatrical firm of Aldrich & Meyers produced this comic valentine and Otto L. Preminger directed it.

When the show reached St. Louis, Miss Barrie left the company after a quarrel with Barrymore. A few weeks later she notified him that she was again suing him for divorce.

"Soon I shall be unable to count these things on my fingers," Jack said. "I must rent an adding machine."

He had meanwhile telephoned Henry Hotchener in Hollywood who, in response to the actor's suggestions that they "get together on the same basis as before," flew to join him at Omaha. It had been more than three years since they had seen each other.

"This time it is final," Jack said of his troubles with his wife. "I shall never see her again."

Hotchener found Barrymore hazy about his business affairs, as always, and concerned about a home he had bought on Bellagio Road in Bel Air after his fourth marriage. He telephoned his Los Angeles lawyer, who informed Jack that the property was neither in his name nor his wife's, but in the name of a third person. After some incendiary language on Barrymore's part, there was another telephone call. The attorney now told the actor that the Bellagio Road house was in Mrs. Elaine Barrymore's name. Confused, Jack said to Hotchener: "Can't you do something about all these things?"

Hotchener asked for a statement of the play's weekly expenses and ventured an opinion that they seemed rather large. Then he learned that $500 of the weekly overhead was being paid to Mrs. Elaine Barrymore, that her contract provided for this stipend whether or not she stayed on with the troupe, and that Jack himself had approved the arrangement. Barrymore loudly denied this, but when the document was shown him, he found to his amazement that he *had* signed it.

There was an air of defeat as the company reached Des Moines on May 4. Audiences had not been large but Jack was determined to prove he could make a success of the play, particularly since Elaine had left the cast. He predicted that business would pick up in Chicago, adding, "That is a Barrymore stronghold."

When the play opened in Chicago, Jack was playing always and ever for the laugh. According to Ashton Stevens, now dean of the Chicago drama critics, he fiddled and faddled his hands, hemmed and hawed his lines, and blurted ad libs to the hoarse delight of the opening-night audience. "But what was left of the most fascinating actor of his day still held some of the old magnetism," Stevens added.

It seemed certain the show would run, so Henry Hotchener left for California three days after the Chicago opening. It was his understanding that the actor desired a restoration of their longtime business and personal relationship. But this was not to be. Whether or not Jack was influenced against Hotchener after the former manager's departure is a matter of conjecture, but the briefly renewed relationship came to a cool termination.

My Dear Children remained in Chicago for thirty-four weeks. All during that successful run of the play Ashton Stevens watched over the man who first had come to him, late on an April night in 1906, in San Francisco, with a letter of introduction from Ethel. Jack was sometimes ill, visibly and audibly, and there was a period when the show had to be temporarily closed. But Stevens said that the last performance of *My Dear Children* was the saddest of the Chicago engagement. The show was shortly to move on to New York, which meant, for Barrymore, a return to Broadway after an absence of more than fifteen years. He had been worrying about the New York critics, most of whom had been in knee pants when their predecessors acclaimed his *Hamlet*. To these brilliant young gentlemen, he would be a stranger—or worse, a picture actor, and a decayed one at that.

"Anyhow," Stevens said, "he fortified himself beyond his limited capacity, and the simple, friendly curtain speech he had intended fled his memory. He forgot this was a 'farewell'; forgot the loyal 'repeaters' out front; forgot everything but the presence in a near row of a pair of youthful nightclub performers with whom he had consorted the previous after-night. To these unknown small-timers, the grand old-timer addressed his spattering speech.

"I couldn't stay. I had grown more or less hardened to the caricatures he visited on himself—but this wasn't Jack Barrymore at all. I went out with great, gawky, sentimental tears salting my face."

BARRYMORE ARRIVED in New York in late January 1940, a few days before the play was to open at the Belasco Theatre. Ethel Barrymore stayed with her brother at Bayside, Long Island, in a place "remote from the gang," watching over him until his opening night.

The premiere proved a disappointment to the New York audience that turned out, ready for anything.

"I'm certain that the majority expected the curtain to rise on Jack removing his trousers while tossing off Oscar Wilde epigrams," wrote Spencer Merriam Berger, a longtime admirer of Barrymore. "What followed was an unbelievably baleful performance. The final curtain brought the first spontaneous reaction of the evening. Relieved that the show was over, the audience gave him a thunderous ovation, to which he responded with bows and tears."

Backstage, after the performance, Mrs. Elaine Barrymore appeared, and, ignoring his friends' protests against this reunion, Jack retired to her apartment in Fifty-ninth Street. "After all," he said, "I am not committing a statutory offense. She is still my wife."

After the third New York performance of *My Dear Children*, Barrymore's nervous depletion sent him to Mount Sinai Hospital. When he resumed his appearance in the play some days later, Miss Barrie was once again his leading lady, supplanting Miss Doris Dudley.

The play ran for four months, with its chief actor vacillating between poor health and worse. It closed toward summer, this play in which he had achieved the greatest anticlimax of his career, having earned $666,519.06. Barrymore, after long months of work, had left as his share of these proceeds $5,000. It was a check, not payable to him, but to his Japanese gardener, Nishi. Jack had thought it advisable for Nishi secretly to hold this "nest egg," so that no one might get it away from him.

"I remind myself of Grantland Rice's destitute ballplayer friend," Jack said. "That wastrel veteran of the diamond told Rice that he had enough money to last him the rest of his life—provided he drop dead on the spot!"

CHAPTER 19

SOMEHOW, BETWEEN THE TIME of his honorable discharge by the bankruptcy court in November 1939 and that summer of 1940, Barrymore had incurred another $110,000 in debts. This amount did not include the neglected payment of alimonies and child support, arrears estimated variously in court recitals at between $50,000 and $100,000.

Now in Hollywood once again, the debtor shook his head like a tired bison, then voluntarily undertook the payment of these newer liabilities. He entered, for a second time, the serfdom of a bankruptcy arrangement. And although he subsequently was to earn $241,085.18 by means of picture work and radio broadcasts, he still would be adjudged a bankrupt *after* his death.

During June and July of 1940 he made a motion picture at Twentieth Century-Fox, a celluloid delicacy instigated by his own latter-day legend. He pretended, when on public view, to be undisturbed by this cartoon, or by the radio caricatures he weekly draped about his person. But when away from all this, he sometimes seemed wilted and deeply hurt by the horseplay demands of his work. Even a tricky memory did not altogether shut out from his ears the echoes of yesterday's empty laughter.

Lionel once told me of one of his last conversations with Jack. It was on the night they did their final radio broadcast together, and Jack was near the end of everything.

"No matter what has happened of recent years," Lionel told him, "you really did climb up among the stars. You were one of the great ones."

Jack looked at him for a while, grinned, then said, "This is a hell of a time to tell me!"

THE TWO LAST YEARS of his life, notwithstanding many illnesses and the squabblings of the law, became for Barrymore a reunion with several companions who represented the gay days. The private meeting ground for these Barrymore cronies was, more often than not, the studio home of John Decker, the artist, in Bundy Drive. Actors Thomas Mitchell, Roland Young, John Carradine, Fannie Brice, and Tony Quinn were among the habitués of Decker's studio.

Decker, in his own youth, had been an art student at the Slade School in London, where Barrymore had been enrolled, and had painted scenes for Sir Herbert Tree's His Majesty's Theatre. Later, in New York, he had been the theatrical caricaturist for the *Evening World*, and as such, made Barrymore's acquaintance at the time of *The Jest*. Now the artist and his wife made Jack welcome at the studio, where his drinks would be cut

Barrymore's first wife,
Katherine Harris.

Above, with Michael Strange, his second wife; below, with Elaine Barrie.

With Dolores Costello on their wedding day, 1928.

to a small alcoholic content and he could relive his own time as a painter, sniffing the turpentine happily and watching Decker work.

"Aside from Decker's art, which I admire no end, I find him enchanting," Jack once said, "because he dislikes sunsets and his mother."

One evening early in September 1940 Decker and I received word that Barrymore was becoming increasingly unhappy at the Bellagio Road home where he was living with Elaine. We drove out there. A maid answered; then Jack, in an old bathrobe and slippers, came downstairs. His nurse, Karl Stuevers, followed him.

Jack pointed to the ceiling, then whispered, "Get me the hell out of here, quick!"

"Collect your things, Jack," I said. "We're on our way."

"I don't think I'd better go upstairs myself." Then he looked at his nurse. "Would you be so kind?"

Karl assembled an outfit, including a Tyrolean hat with a jaunty brush in the crown band, and Jack dressed hurriedly. He insisted, before we left, on inspecting the ancient olive tree from Tower Road which Nishi had transplanted to the grounds of the Bellagio place.

"Let us take this noble plant with us," Jack said. "Did you gentlemen bring derricks and spades?"

He was dissuaded from this nocturnal uprooting, but took a sprig from it for his hatband, saying that it was "an emblem of peace."

And a few hours later he was back where he belonged, at Tower Road, inspecting the grounds by flashlight and announcing plans to install a pool table in the deserted aviary. "I've wanted a pool table all my life," he said.

Jack never returned to the partner of his fourth bus accident. A divorce was granted to Mrs. Elaine Barrymore in late November 1940.

KARL STUEVERS stayed on for some months with Jack at Tower Road, and Decker and his friends in Bundy Drive also kept in close touch with Jack.

But one night, while I was visiting him, he confided that he still feared being "put out of circulation."

"What? Again? Don't be ridiculous."

"It's constantly on my mind," he said, "and besides, the creditors are planning to take Tower Road away from me for keeps."

"I think both these hurdles can be cleared," I said. "Have you known of anyone ever being committed when regularly earning big money?"

"They're always claiming people are incompetent to handle their own fortunes."

"That's an entirely different situation," I said. "If Aunt Bessie retires with a full sock and no longer earns money, she is a cinch to be put away. But never if she is making money each week. I am informed that you are making, at the moment, six thousand dollars a week—"

"Then where in hell is it?" he interrupted.

"Keep on the beam," I said. "It goes, most of it, to your creditors, though they let you have some occasionally for pin money. Now, if you keep on working, no judge is going to rule that a person smart enough to earn a thousand dollars a day is nuts. The judge himself would seem nuts to make such a ruling."

"By God!" he said. "You're right. I'll just keep on working."

"As for Tower Road, you threaten the creditors to quit work entirely . . ."

"You're reversing yourself," he said. "I must keep working to stay away from the chicken wire."

"Just a moment. You won't actually quit. You'll merely threaten to, and the creditors will be so upset at the prospect of losing a huge sum each week that they will let the golden goose stay on its nest."

"I shall burn a candle to you," Jack said, "in some great cathedral. I shall, of course, burn it at both ends."

Such creditors as had objected to maintaining Jack in the Tower Road house were persuaded by his attorney that the actor should be permitted to stay, unmolested, so that he could continue his work.

The making of the life mask, and, right, the result.

Three scenes from "The Great Profile" (1940), in which Barrymore parodied himself. The girl is Mary Beth Hughes.

BARRYMORE NOW ENTERED his final year of markedly failing health, but gamely got to his feet again and again. Nor did he complain of being ill. He *acted* the part of a well man, not the least effective of his many roles.

It became apparent to his doctor that he had cirrhosis of the liver and a kidney involvement. He caught cold frequently. He had chronic chills. But he held his chin high. Ben Hecht, at whose Hollywood house Jack spent a night, said of him:

"People are mistaken when they pity Jack. He doesn't remember his aches and pains at all the next day. Think how fine it would be for all invalids, mooning over yesterday's attacks and dreading tomorrow's, if they too could be stripped of this overshadowing fear. Jack will never die of fear. Perhaps he will never die at all."

Jack seemed equally optimistic for, when a Pennsylvania innkeeper wrote to ask if he would sell him his bed for a collection of couches of historic lovers now being assembled at the inn, he promptly answered, in part:

> I was charmed by your letter, and am devastated to have to inform you that the bed is still in use—and will continue to be, I most sincerely trust—for some years to come. When I have no further use for it, I should be most happy to consider your offer, although it is practically committed to the Smithsonian Institution. I feel sure, however, that some *blanket* arrangement might be made with them to transport the bed to your hostelry during whatever is your mating season.

CHAPTER 20

BY 1942 JACK'S MEMORY of recent events became still more loosely seated than before. He had experienced another illness, with an internal hemorrhage so severe as to warrant blood transfusions. But he stayed on at his radio work, and even appeared in a motion picture.

On the afternoon of May 19, 1942, he prepared to leave Tower Road late in the afternoon to go to the rehearsal of his weekly radio program. He dressed himself slowly, then called out for Nishi. There was no response to his summons, for now, after Pearl Harbor, Nishi no longer was at Tower Road. He had been sent weeks before to a camp for enemy aliens at Manzanar. But Jack had forgotten all about that. He had forgotten the day of leave-taking when the belongings of the gardener and his large family were piled high at the doorway. He had forgotten how he had protested when it was explained to him that, with America at war with Japan, Nishi must be interned.

Now he went out to look for his gardener in the Victory garden which Nishi himself had urged planting. When Nishi had inquired what vegetables Barrymore wished him to plant, he had replied, "Horseradish!" The obedient and literal-minded gardener had therefore planted whole beds of horseradish, and nothing else, and this pungent herb grew luxuriantly and uselessly on the estate.

Barrymore's secretary-attendant now reminded him that it was time for him to go. He settled himself in the seat of the motor car, shivering inside his camel's-hair overcoat, although the late afternoon air was not chill. He had had a bad head cold since March, but when he arrived at the broadcasting studio he said that he was fit. He had not been drinking for the last two or three days.

After the rehearsal he lost his way to his own dressing room and entered the first door that yielded to his hand, a room that had been assigned to John Carradine, who was broadcasting elsewhere in the building.

It was a curious happening, for this young actor, only two weeks before, had sought Barrymore's advice on how to play the character Louis XI in a revival of *If I Were King*. Carradine had opened in it only the night before, in Los Angeles, and now was amazed upon entering his room to find someone lying on the couch, and still further astonished to see Jack Barrymore himself slowly sit up.

"How are you, old man?" Jack asked.

"Why, hello, Jack," said Carradine. "Are you all right?"

"Never better," he said, but Carradine saw that he was gray with illness and had difficulty in breathing. Carradine was too confused for the moment to do other than mutter something about having "opened in the play last night," to which Jack said, "Of course; and I take it that you received splendid notices."

"I haven't read them yet," said the younger actor.

"Good," Jack said. "Actors should never read them. If you don't believe the bad ones, why should you pay attention to the good ones?"

Jack broke off then, dreadfully weak, and gasping. The doctor was called and Jack was half carried to his car and driven to Hollywood Hospital, where it was learned that he had bronchial pneumonia in the right lower lung. He lost consciousness.

News of his illness was withheld for a time. Lionel took his brother's place on the next radio program. Ethel, touring New England with *The Corn is Green*, kept in touch with the hospital by long-distance telephone.

The primary cause of Jack's collapse was cirrhosis of the liver. There were secondary conditions, such as the failure of kidney function, chronic gastritis, ulceration of the esophagus, which hemorrhaged, and hardening of the arteries. The pneumonia, however, was the terminal event. Still, his heart somehow beat on against all these odds for ten more days.

On the seventh day he was seemingly unconscious when I went into his room, but after I had sat there for several minutes he said, without opening his eyes, "I thought you were closer." Believing he was talking in a haze, I did not reply, but sat looking at his pale face. . . . What superb bone structure that face still owned, no matter the years or the illness.

Now he called me by name, his eyes still closed. I went and stood beside him. He opened his eyes, which seemed almost to sparkle as of other days.

"Lean over me," he said quite clearly. "I want to ask you something."

Unprepared for anything but some last request from a dying man, I did so. I should have foreseen that this mighty fellow would not surrender with a sentimental statement.

"Tell me," he asked, "is it true that you are the illegitimate son of Buffalo Bill?"

I was so jolted out of my sorrow that I laughed. That had been his purpose, I am sure, for he never wanted his friends to grieve.

"Yes," I replied, "I am told that Colonel Cody was my natural father, but we mustn't let anyone else know it."

He smiled, then said, "I have always thought so," and promptly became unconscious again. Those were the last words he ever said to me.

THREE DAYS LATER, at ten twenty o'clock the night of May 29, 1942, John Sidney Blythe Barrymore died. Shortly afterward, Dr. Hugo Kersten, his physician, made the following statement:

> "That Mr. Barrymore survived this attack for more than a few hours is more of a tribute to the patient's amazing vitality than to any medical science practiced in his behalf. Perhaps this unexplained vitality had something in common with the several other matchless qualities of this talented artist. As his physician, I became acquainted intimately with the man himself, his fine mind, his philosophies. His great personal strength and courage, even his foolhardiness, cloaked the gentlest sort of soul, tolerant, generous, without conceit, and almost childlike in honesty of thought. It is not for a medical practitioner to say that these qualities have any bearing whatsoever on a man's physical fortitude at the threshold of death. Yet, who knows?"

In writing this book, I have seen again, in rich recollection, the face of my friend; I have heard his gay, brave voice once more. I sought to fashion a green wreath, with few false leaves, and now I place it beside the crypt upon which his brother carved the words:

Good Night, Sweet Prince

QUEEN VICTORIA

A CONDENSATION OF

QUEEN VICTORIA

by

LYTTON STRACHEY

ILLUSTRATED BY ARTHUR BARBOSA

Princess Alexandrina Victoria was twelve years old when she was first informed that she would someday be Queen of England. Her immediate reply was, "I will be good."

At nineteen she did indeed become Victoria, Queen of Great Britain and Ireland, later Empress of India, and ultimately Britain's longest reigning and most beloved monarch. Her marriage to her cousin, Prince Albert of Saxe-Coburg, lasted twenty-one years and is one of the happiest of all royal love stories. By the end of her sixty-three-year reign, during which England reached the pinnacle of world power, Victoria was held in an affection and awe approaching veneration.

For many years thereafter this veil of reverence stood in the way of any attempt to view the great queen coolly as a human being. At last, in 1921, a biography appeared that did just that. Lytton Strachey's *Queen Victoria* caused a furor, and his irreverent yet strangely moving portrait has come to be regarded as a landmark in the art of biography.

CHAPTER I
Antecedents

ON NOVEMBER 6, 1817, died the Princess Charlotte, only child of the Prince Regent, and heir to the crown of England.

Her short life had hardly been a happy one. Brought up among violent family quarrels, she was by nature impulsive, capricious, and vehement; she had always longed for liberty, and never possessed it. At seventeen, she had fallen in love with Prince Augustus of Prussia, who was already married. In the end she was married, in 1816, to Prince Leopold of Saxe-Coburg.

The character of Prince Leopold contrasted strangely with that of the Princess Charlotte. The younger son of a German princeling, he was formal in manner, collected in speech, and careful in action. He was twenty-six years of age. He had served with distinction in the war against Napoleon, had shown considerable diplomatic skill at the Congress of Vienna, and was now to try his hand at the task of taming a tumultuous princess.

There was much in her, he found, of which he could not approve. She quizzed, she stamped, she roared with laughter; she had very little self-command; her manners were abominable.

There was continual friction, but he soon dominated her, and every scene ended in the same way. Standing before him like a rebellious boy in petticoats, her hands behind her back, with flaming cheeks and sparkling eyes, the Princess would say at last, "If you wish it, I will do it." "I want nothing for myself," Prince Leopold invariably answered; "when I press something on you, it is from a conviction that it is for your good."

In the household at Claremont, near Esher, where the royal pair were established, was a young German physician, Christian Friedrich Stockmar. Prince Leopold had brought him to England as his personal physician. At Claremont his position was a humble one; but the Princess took a fancy to him, called him "Stocky," and romped with him along the corridors.

Dyspeptic by constitution, melancholic by temperament, Stockmar could yet be lively on occasion, and he was known as a wit. Before long he gave proof of another quality—cautious sagacity. When, in the spring of 1817, it was known that the Princess was expecting a child, the post of one of her physicians-in-ordinary was offered to him, and he had the good sense to refuse it, perceiving that, if anything were to go wrong, it would certainly be the foreign doctor who would be blamed. Very soon, indeed, he came to the opinion that the low diet and constant bleedings to which the Princess was subjected were an error; he drew the Prince aside and told him so; but the fashionable treatment was continued for months.

On November 5, at nine p.m., after a labor of over fifty hours, the Princess was delivered of a dead boy. At midnight her exhausted strength gave way. Then, at last, Stockmar saw her; he went in, and found her obviously dying, while the doctors were plying her with wine. She seized his hand. "They have made me tipsy," she said. After a little he left, and was in the next room when he heard her call out: "Stocky! Stocky!" As he ran back the death rattle was in her throat. She tossed violently from side to side; then suddenly it was over.

The Prince, after hours of watching, had left the room for a few moments' rest; and Stockmar went now to tell him that his wife was dead. At first Leopold could not be made to realize what had happened; it was a dream; it was impossible. At last, by her bed, he knelt down and kissed the cold hands. Then rising and exclaiming, "I am desolate. Promise me never to leave me," he threw himself into Stockmar's arms.

THE TRAGEDY at Claremont was of a most upsetting kind. The succession to the throne, which had seemed so satisfactorily settled, now became a matter of urgent doubt.

King George III was still living, an aged lunatic, at Windsor Castle. Of his seven sons, the youngest was of more than middle age, and none had legitimate offspring. It seemed improbable that his oldest son, the Prince Regent, a preposterous figure of debauched obesity, could ever again become a father. The outlook for the throne, therefore, was ambiguous.

Besides the Duke of Kent, who must be noticed separately, the other sons of the King, in order of seniority, were the Dukes of York, Clarence, Cumberland, Sussex, and Cambridge; their situations and prospects require a brief description.

The Duke of York, whose escapades in times past with a Mrs. Clarke and with the army had brought him into trouble, now divided his life between London and a large, extravagantly ordered country house where he occupied himself with racing, whist, and improper stories. He had been long married to the Princess Royal of Prussia, a lady who rarely went to bed and was perpetually surrounded by vast numbers of dogs, parrots, and monkeys. They had no children.

The Duke of Clarence had lived for many years in complete obscurity with Mrs. Jordan, an actress. By her he had had a large family of sons and daughters, and had appeared, in effect, to be married to her, when he had suddenly separated from her.

The Duke of Cumberland was probably the most unpopular man in England. Hideously ugly, with a distorted eye, he was bad-tempered and vindictive, a violent reactionary in politics, and was subsequently suspected of murdering his valet and of having carried on an amorous intrigue of an extremely scandalous kind. He had lately married a German princess, but there were as yet no children by the marriage.

The Duke of Sussex had mildly literary tastes and collected books. He had married Lady Augusta Murray, by whom he had two children, but the marriage, under the Royal Marriages Act, had been declared void.

The Duke of Cambridge lived in Hanover, wore a blond wig, chattered and fidgeted a great deal, and was unmarried.

Besides his seven sons, George III had five surviving daughters. Of these, two were married and childless. The three unmarried princesses were all over forty.

THE FOURTH SON of George III was Edward, Duke of Kent. He was now fifty years of age—a tall, stout, vigorous man, highly colored, with bushy eyebrows and a bald top to his head. His dress was extremely neat, and his whole appearance was rigid. He had spent his early life in the army, and, under the influence of military training, had become at first a disciplinarian and at last a martinet. In 1802, having been sent to Gibraltar to restore order in a mutinous garrison, he was recalled for undue severity, and his active career had come to an end.

Since then he had spent his life regulating his domestic arrangements with great exactitude, and struggling to restore order to his finances, for, in spite of an income of £24,000 a year, he was hopelessly in debt. He had quarreled with most of his brothers, particularly with the Prince Regent, and it was only natural that he should have joined the political Opposition and become a pillar of the Whigs.

It has often been asserted that he was a Liberal, or even a Radical; and, if we are to believe Robert Owen, he was a Socialist. His relations with Owen—the illustrious and preposterous father of Socialism—were curious. He corresponded with him, and he even (so Owen assures us) returned, after his death, from "the sphere of spirits" to give encouragement to the Owenites on earth. Still, some uncertainty lingers over his political views. But there is no uncertainty about another circumstance: His Royal Highness borrowed from Robert Owen, on various occasions, sums of money which were never repaid and amounted in all to several hundred pounds.

After the death of the Princess Charlotte it was clearly important that the Duke of Kent should marry. From the point of view of the nation, the lack of heirs in the reigning family seemed to make the step almost obligatory. It was also likely to be expedient from the point of view of the duke. To marry as a public duty, for the sake of the royal succession, would surely deserve some recognition from a grateful country. When the Duke of York had married he had received a settlement of £25,000 a year. Why should not the Duke of Kent look forward to an equal sum? But the situation was not quite that simple; there was the Duke of Clarence; he was the elder brother, and, if *he* married, would clearly have the prior claim. On the other hand, if the Duke of Kent married, it was important to remember that he would be making a serious sacrifice: a lady was involved: namely, the duke's mistress.

The duke, reflecting upon all these matters, happened, about a month after the Princess Charlotte's death, to visit Brussels, and learned that Mr. Creevey was staying in the town. Mr. Creevey was a friend of leading Whigs and an inveterate gossip; and it occurred to the duke that there could be no better channel through which to communicate his views to political circles at home. Apparently it did not occur to him that Mr. Creevey might keep a diary. He sent for him, and a remarkable conversation ensued.

"Should the Duke of Clarence not marry," the Duke of Kent said, "the next prince in succession is myself, and although I trust I shall be at all times ready to obey any call my country may make upon me, God only knows the sacrifice it will be to make, whenever I shall think it my duty to become a married man. It is now seven-and-twenty years that Madame St. Laurent and I have lived together; we are of the same age, and have been in all climates, and in all difficulties together, and you may well imagine, Mr. Creevey, the pang it will occasion me to part with her. As for Madame St. Laurent herself, I protest I don't know what is to become of her if a marriage is to be forced upon me; her feelings are already so agitated upon the subject."

The duke then said, "My brother the Duke of Clarence is the elder brother, and has certainly the right to marry if he chooses. If he wishes to be king—to be married and have children, poor man—God help him! let him do so. For myself—I am a man of no ambition, and wish only to remain as I am. . . ." But he went on to say that if the Duke of Clarence did nothing by Eastertime, "it will become my duty, no doubt, to take some measures upon the subject myself."

Two names, the duke said, had been mentioned in this connection—those of the Princess of Baden and the Princess of Saxe-Coburg, the sister of Prince Leopold. The latter, he thought, would perhaps be the better of the two, since Prince Leopold was so popular with the nation; but before any other steps were taken, he hoped and expected to see justice done to Madame St. Laurent. "She is," he explained, "of very good family, and has never been an actress, and I am the first and only person who ever lived with her. If she is to return to live amongst her friends, it must be in such a state of independence as to command their respect."

As to his own settlement, the duke observed that he would expect the Duke of York's marriage to be considered the precedent. "That," he said, "was a marriage for the succession, and £25,000 for income was settled. I shall be contented with the same arrangement. As for the payment of my debts, I don't call them great. The nation, on the contrary, is greatly my debtor." Here a clock struck, and seemed to remind the duke that he had an appointment; he rose and Mr. Creevey left him.

Who could keep such a communication secret? Certainly not Mr. Creevey. He hurried off to tell the Duke of Wellington.

As it turned out, both the brothers decided to marry. The Duke of Kent, selecting the Princess of Saxe-Coburg, was united to her on May 29, 1818. On June 11, the Duke of Clarence followed suit with a daughter of the Duke of Saxe-Meiningen. But they were disappointed in their financial expectations; for though the government brought forward proposals to increase their allowances, the motions were defeated in the House of Commons. At this the Duke of Wellington was not surprised. "By God!" he said, "there is a great deal to be said about that. They are the damnedest millstones about the necks of any government that can be imagined." Eventually, however, Parliament increased the Duke of Kent's annuity by £6000.

The subsequent history of Madame St. Laurent has not transpired.

THE NEW DUCHESS OF KENT, Victoria Mary Louisa, sister of Prince Leopold, was a daughter of Francis, Duke of Saxe-Coburg-Saalfeld. The family was an ancient one; its principality, the duchy of Saxe-Coburg, was very small, containing about sixty thousand inhabitants, but it enjoyed independent and sovereign rights. As for Victoria Mary Louisa, in 1803, when she was seventeen years of age, she had married the Prince of Leiningen, who ruled the territory of Amorbach in Lower Franconia. Three years later her father, Duke Francis, died a ruined man. The Napoleonic harrow had passed over Saxe-Coburg; the duchy was seized by the French, and the ducal family were reduced to beggary, almost to starvation. Such was the desperate plight of the family which, a generation later, was to have gained a foothold in half the reigning houses of Europe.

In 1814 Victoria's husband died, leaving her with two children. After her brother's marriage with the Princess Charlotte, it had been proposed that she should marry the Duke of Kent; but she had declined, on the ground that the guardianship of her children and the management of her domains made other ties undesirable. The Princess Charlotte's death, however, altered the case; and when the Duke of Kent renewed his offer she accepted it. She was thirty-two years old—short, stout, with brown eyes and hair, and rosy cheeks, cheerful and voluble, and gorgeously attired in rustling silks and bright velvets.

She was certainly fortunate in her contented disposition; for she was fated, all through her life, to have much to put up with. Her second marriage, with its dubious prospects, seemed at first to be chiefly a source of difficulties. The duke, declaring that he was still too poor to live in England, moved about uneasily through Belgium and Germany, attending parades and inspecting barracks in a neat military cap. The English notabilities looked askance, and the Duke of Wellington dubbed him the Corporal. One day, at Brussels, Mr. Creevey himself had an unfortunate experience. A military school was to be inspected—before breakfast. The company assembled; everything was highly satisfactory; but the Duke of Kent continued for so long examining every detail, asking meticulous questions, that Mr. Creevey at last could bear it no longer, and whispered to his neighbor that he was damned hungry. The Duke of Wellington heard him, and was delighted. "I recommend you," he said, "whenever you start with the royal family in a morning, and particularly with *the Corporal*, always to breakfast first."

Settled down at last at Amorbach, the duke found that time hung heavily on his hands. The establishment was small, and the country was impoverished. He brooded—for the duke was not without a vein of superstition—over the prophecy of a gypsy at Gibraltar who had once told him that he was to have many losses and crosses, that he was to die in happiness, and that his only child was to be a great queen.

Before long it became clear that a child was to be expected. The duke decided that it should be born in England. Funds were lacking for the journey, but a carriage was hired, and the duke himself mounted the box. Inside were the duchess and her daughter Feodora, a girl of fourteen, with maids, nurses, lapdogs, and canaries. Off they drove—through Germany, through France; bad roads, cheap inns, were nothing to the rigorous duke and the equable, abundant duchess. The Channel was crossed, London was reached. The authorities provided a set of rooms in Kensington Palace; and there, on May 24, 1819, a female infant was born.

DUCHESS OF KENT

CHAPTER 2
Childhood

THE CHILD who, in these not very impressive circumstances, appeared in the world, received but scant attention. There was small reason to foresee her destiny. The Duchess of Clarence, two months before, had given birth to a daughter; this infant, indeed, had died almost immediately; but it seemed highly probable that the duchess would again become a mother; and so it actually fell out.

More than this, the Duchess of Kent was young, and the duke was strong; there was every likelihood that before long a brother would follow, to snatch her faint chance of the succession from the little Princess.

Nevertheless, the duke had other views: there were prophecies. . . . At any rate, he would christen the child Elizabeth, a name of happy augury. In this, however, he reckoned without the Regent, who, seeing a chance of annoying his brother, announced that he himself would be present at the baptism, and signified that one of the godfathers should be the Emperor Alexander of Russia.

And so when the ceremony took place, and the Archbishop of Canterbury asked by what name he was to baptize the child, the Regent replied "Alexandrina."

At this the duke ventured to suggest that another name might be added. "Certainly," said the Regent; "Georgina?"

"Or Elizabeth?" said the duke.

There was a pause, during which the Archbishop looked with some uneasiness from one Prince to the other. "Very well, then," said the Regent at last, "call her after her mother. But Alexandrina must come first." Thus, to the disgust of her father, the child was christened Alexandrina Victoria.

The duke had other subjects of disgust. The meager grant of the Commons had by no means put an end to his financial distresses. It was to be feared that his services were not appreciated by the nation. His debts continued to grow. For many years he had lived upon £7000 a year; but now his expenses were doubled. He could make no further reductions; as it was, there was not a single servant in his establishment who was idle for a moment from morning to night.

He poured out his griefs in a letter to Robert Owen. "I now candidly state," he wrote, "that, after viewing the subject in every possible way, I am satisfied that, to continue to live in England, even in our quiet way, *without splendour*, and *without show, nothing short of doubling the seven thousand pounds will do*, REDUCTION BEING IMPOSSIBLE." It was clear that he would be obliged to sell his house; if that failed, he would go and live on the Continent. "If my services are useful to my country, it surely becomes *those who have the power* to support me in substantiating those just claims I have for the extensive losses I experienced during the period of my professional servitude in the Colonies; and if this is not attainable, *it is a clear proof to me that my services are not appreciated;* and under that impression I shall not scruple, in *due* time, to resume my retirement abroad, when the Duchess and myself shall have fulfilled our duties in establishing the *English* birth of my child."

In the meantime, he decided to spend the winter at Sidmouth, "in order," he told Owen, "that the Duchess may have the benefit of tepid sea bathing, and our infant that of sea air, on the fine coast of Devonshire, during the months of the year that are so odious in London."

In December the move was made. With the new year, the duke remembered another prophecy. In 1820, a fortune-teller had told him, two members of the royal family would die. Who would they be? He speculated on the possibilities: the King, it was plain, could not live much longer; and the Duchess of York had been attacked by a mortal disease. Probably it would be the King and the Duchess of York; or perhaps the King and the Duke of York. He himself was one of the healthiest men in England. "My brothers," he declared, "are not so strong as I am; I have lived a regular life. I shall outlive them all. The crown will come to me and my children."

He went out for a walk, and got his feet wet. On coming home, he neglected to change his stockings. He caught cold, inflammation of the lungs set in, and on January 22 he was a dying man.

By a curious chance, young Dr. Stockmar was staying in the house at the time; two years before, he had stood by the death-bed of the Princess Charlotte; and now he watched the Duke of Kent in his agony. On Stockmar's advice, a will was hastily prepared; it was important that the guardianship of the unwitting child, whose fortunes were now so strangely changing, should be assured to the duchess. The duke was just able to understand the document and to append his signature. On the following morning he breathed his last. Six days later came the fulfillment of the second half of the gypsy's prophecy. The long, unhappy, and inglorious life of King George the Third of England was ended.

THE PRINCE REGENT, as George IV, was now King of England. Meanwhile, such was the confusion of affairs at Sidmouth that the duchess found herself without the means of returning to London.

Prince Leopold hurried down, and himself conducted his sister and her family, by slow and bitter stages, to Kensington. The widowed lady, in her voluminous blacks, needed all her equanimity to support her. Her prospects were more dubious than ever. She had £6000 a year of her own; but her husband's debts loomed before her like a mountain. Soon she learned that the Duchess of Clarence was once more expecting a child. What had she to look forward to in England? Why should she remain in a foreign country, among strangers, whose language she could not speak, whose customs she could not understand?

Surely it would be best to return to Amorbach, and there, among her own people, bring up her daughters in economical obscurity. But she was an inveterate optimist, and would not be daunted. Besides, she adored her baby. "She is my happiness, my delight," she declared; the darling should be brought up as an English princess, whatever lot awaited her. Prince Leopold came forward nobly with an offer of an additional £3000 a year; and the duchess remained at Kensington.

The child herself was extremely fat, and bore a remarkable resemblance to her grandfather. "She is the image of the mad King!" exclaimed the duchess. "It's King George in petticoats!" echoed the surrounding ladies, as the little creature waddled with difficulty from one to the other.

Before long, the world began to be slightly interested in the nursery at Kensington. When, early in 1821, the Duchess of Clarence's second child, the Princess Elizabeth, died within three months of its birth, the interest increased.

Great forces and fierce antagonisms seemed to be moving, obscurely, about the royal cradle. It was a time of faction and anger, of violent repression and profound discontent. New passions, new desires, were abroad, or rather, old passions and old desires reincarnated with a new potency: love of freedom, hatred of injustice, hope for the future of man. The mighty still sat proudly in their seats, dispensing their ancient tyranny; but a storm was gathering, and already there was lightning in the sky. But the vastest forces must needs operate through frail human instruments; and it seemed for many years as if the great cause of English liberalism hung upon the life of the little girl at Kensington; for she alone stood between the country and her terrible uncle, the Duke of Cumberland, the hideous embodiment of reaction.

Inevitably, the Duchess of Kent threw in her lot with her husband's party. Whig leaders, Radical agitators, rallied round her; and she declared in public that she put her faith in "the liberties of the People." It was certain that the young Princess would be brought up in the way that she should go; yet there, close behind the throne, waiting, sinister, was the Duke of Cumberland. Dreadful possibilities were hinted at. In the seething state of public feeling, rumors constantly leaped to the surface; and, even so late as the year before her accession, the Radical newspapers were full of suggestions that the Princess Victoria was in danger from the machinations of her wicked uncle.

But no echo of these conflicts and forebodings reached the little Drina—for so she was called in the family circle—as she played with her dolls, or scampered down the passages, or rode along the avenues of Kensington Gardens on the donkey her uncle York had given her. She was to remember, from this period, a yellow rug in one particular room at Kensington, and a watch of her father's in a tortoiseshell case ticking in her mother's bedroom. A fair-haired, blue-eyed child, she was idolized by her nurses, and her mother's ladies, and her sister Feodora; and for a few years there was danger, in spite of her mother's strictness, of her being spoiled. From time to time, she would fly into a violent passion, stamp her little foot, and set everyone at defiance; whatever they might say, she would not learn her letters—no, she *would not;* afterwards, she was very sorry, and burst into tears; but her letters remained unlearned.

When she was five years old, however, a change came, with the appearance of Fräulein Lehzen. This lady, who was the daughter of a Hanoverian clergyman, had previously been the Princess Feodora's governess. She soon succeeded in instilling a new spirit into her willful charge. At first, indeed, she was appalled by the little Princess's outbursts of temper; never in her life, she declared, had she seen such a passionate and naughty child. Then she observed something else; the child was extraordinarily truthful; whatever punishment might follow, she never told a lie.

Very firm, the new governess yet had the sense to see that all the firmness in the world would be useless, unless she could win her way into little Drina's heart. She did so, and there were no more difficulties. Drina learned her letters like an angel; and she learned other things as well. The Baroness de Späth, the duchess's lady-in-waiting, taught her how to make little boxes and decorate them with tinsel and painted flowers; her mother taught her religion. Sitting in the pew every Sunday morning, the child of six was seen listening raptly to the sermon, for she was to be examined upon it in the afternoon.

The duchess was determined that her daughter, from the earliest possible moment, should be prepared for her high station in a way that would commend itself to the most respectable; her good, plain, thrifty German mind recoiled with horror and amazement from the shameless junketings at Carlton House; Drina should never be allowed to forget for a moment the virtues of simplicity, regularity, and devotion.

The little girl, however, was really in small need of such lessons, for she was naturally simple and orderly, she was pious without difficulty, and her sense of propriety was keen. She understood very well the niceties of her own position. When, a child of six, Lady Jane Ellice was taken by her grandmother to Kensington Palace, she was put to play with the Princess Victoria, who was the same age as herself. The young visitor, ignorant of etiquette, began to make free with the toys on the floor, in a way which was a little too familiar; but "You must not touch those," she was quickly told, "they are mine; and I may call you Jane, but you must not call me Victoria."

The Princess's most constant playmate was Victoire, the daughter of Sir John Conroy, the duchess's major-domo. The two girls were very fond of one another; they would walk hand in hand together in Kensington Gardens. But little Drina was perfectly aware for which of them it was that they were followed, at a respectful distance, by a gigantic scarlet flunkey.

Warmhearted, responsive, she loved her dear Lehzen, and she loved her dear sister Feodora, and her dear friend Victoire, and her dear Madame de Späth. And her dear Mamma . . . of course, she loved her too; it was her duty; and yet—she could not tell why—she was always happier when she was staying with her uncle Leopold at Claremont.

The visits to Claremont were frequent enough; but one day, on a special occasion, she paid a visit of a rarer and more exciting kind. When she was seven years old, she and her mother and sister were asked by the King to go to Windsor Castle. George IV, who had transferred his fraternal ill temper to his sister-in-law and her family, had at last grown tired of sulking, and decided to be agreeable. The old rip, bewigged and gouty, ornate and enormous, with his jeweled mistress by his side and his flaunting court about him, received the tiny creature who was one day to hold in those same halls a very different state. "Give me your little paw," he said; and two ages touched.

Next morning, driving in his phaeton, he met the Duchess of Kent and her child in the park. "Pop her in," were his orders, which, to the terror of the mother and the delight of the daughter, were immediately obeyed. Off they dashed to Virginia Water, where there was a great barge, full of lords and ladies fishing, and another barge with a band; and the King turned to his small niece. "What is your favorite tune? The band shall play it."

" 'God Save the King,' sir," was the instant answer.

The Princess's reply has been praised as an early example of a tact which was afterwards famous. But she was a very truthful child, and perhaps it was her genuine opinion.

IN 1827 the Duke of York died. Three years later George IV also disappeared, and the Duke of Clarence reigned in his stead as William IV. The new Queen, it was now clear, would in all probability never again be a mother; the Princess Victoria, therefore, was recognized by Parliament as heir presumptive; and the Duchess of Kent was given an additional £10,000 for the maintenance of the Princess, and was appointed regent, in case

of the death of the King before the majority of her daughter.

At the same time a great convulsion took place in the constitution of the state. The power of the Tories, who had dominated England for more than forty years, suddenly began to crumble. In the tremendous struggle that followed, it seemed for a moment as if the tradition of generations might be snapped, as if revolution might be the issue. But the forces of compromise triumphed: the Reform Bill was passed. The center of gravity in the constitution was shifted towards the middle classes; the Whigs came into power; and the complexion of the government assumed a Liberal tinge.

One of the results of this new state of affairs was a change in the position of the Duchess of Kent and her daughter. From being the protégées of an opposition clique, they became assets of the official majority of the nation. The Princess Victoria was henceforward the living symbol of the victory of the middle classes. The Duke of Cumberland, on the other hand, suffered a corresponding eclipse: his claws had been pared by the Reform Act, and he grew insignificant and almost harmless.

The duchess's own liberalism was not very profound. She followed naturally in the footsteps of her husband, but she did not understand very much about the Poor Law and political economy; she hoped that she did her duty; and she ardently hoped that the same might be said of Victoria. It was her supreme duty in life, she felt, to make quite sure that her daughter should grow up into a Christian queen. To this task she bent all her energies; and, when the Princess was eleven, she desired the Bishops of London and Lincoln to submit her daughter to an examination.

"I feel the time to be now come," the duchess explained, in a letter, "that what has been done should be put to some test, that if anything has been done in error of judgment it may be corrected, and that the plan for the future should be open to consideration and revision. . . . I attend almost always myself every lesson, or a part; and as the lady about the Princess is a competent person, she assists Her in preparing Her lessons, for the various masters. The general bent of Her character," added the duchess, "is strength of intellect, capable of receiving with ease, information, and with a peculiar readiness in coming to a just decision on any point."

The bishops attended at the palace, and the result of their examination was all that could be wished. "In answering a great variety of questions proposed to her," they reported, "the Princess displayed an accurate knowledge of the most important features of Scripture history and of the leading truths and precepts of the Christian religion as taught by the Church of England, as well as an acquaintance with the chronology and principal facts of English history remarkable in so young a person. To questions in geography, the use of the globes, arithmetic, and Latin grammar, the answers which the Princess returned were equally satisfactory." They did not believe that the duchess's plan of education was susceptible of any improvement; and the Archbishop of Canterbury, who was also consulted, came to the same gratifying conclusion.

One important step, however, remained to be taken. So far, as the duchess explained to the bishops, the Princess had been kept in ignorance of the station that she was likely to fill. "She is aware of its duties, and that a Sovereign should live for others; so that when Her innocent mind receives the impression of Her future fate, she will receive it with a mind formed to be sensible of what is to be expected from Her."

In the following year it was decided that she should be enlightened on this point. A scene followed which has become well known: before a history lesson, the genealogical table of the Kings of England was slipped by her governess into the history book; finding it, the Princess, surprised, made inquiries; and finally she realized the facts. When she at last understood, she was silent for a moment, and then she spoke: "I will be good," she said.

The words were something more than a conventional protestation; they were, in their limitation and their intensity, their egotism and their humility, an instinctive summary of the dominating qualities of a life. "I cried much on learning it," Her Majesty noted long afterwards. No doubt, while others were present, even her dear Lehzen, the little girl kept up her self-command; and then crept away somewhere to ease her heart of an inward, unfamiliar agitation, with a handkerchief, out of her mother's sight.

But her mother's sight was by no means an easy thing to escape. The child grew into the girl, the girl into the young woman; but still she slept in her mother's bedroom; still she had no place where she might sit or work by herself. An extraordinary watchfulness surrounded her every step: up to the day of her accession, she never went downstairs without someone beside her holding her hand.

Plainness and regularity ruled the household. The hours, the days, the years passed slowly and methodically by. The dolls—the innumerable dolls, each one so neatly dressed, each one with its name so punctiliously entered in a catalogue—were laid aside, and a little music and a little dancing took their place. Taglioni came, to give grace and dignity to the figure, and Lablache, to train the piping treble upon his own rich bass. The Dean of Chester, the official preceptor, continued his endless instruction in Scripture history, while the Duchess of Northumberland, the official governess, presided over every lesson with becoming solemnity.

Without doubt, the Princess's main achievement during her school days was linguistic. German was naturally the first language with which she was familiar; but English and French quickly followed; and she became virtually trilingual, though her mastery of English grammar remained incomplete. At the same time, she acquired a working knowledge of Italian and some smattering of Latin. Nevertheless, she did not read very much. It was not an occupation that she cared for; partly, perhaps, because the books that were given her were all either sermons, which were dull, or poetry, which was incomprehensible. Novels were strictly forbidden.

It was her misfortune that the mental atmosphere which surrounded her during these years of adolescence was almost entirely feminine. No father, no brother, was there to break impetuously in upon the gentle monotony of the daily round. The Princess was never called by a voice that was loud and growling; never felt, as a matter of course, a hard rough cheek on her own soft one; never climbed a wall with a boy. The visits to Claremont—delicious little escapes into male society—came to an end when she was eleven years old and Prince Leopold left England to be King of the Belgians. She loved him still; he was still *"il mio secondo padre"*—"my second father"—but his fatherliness now came to her dimly, through the cold channel of correspondence.

Henceforward female duty, female elegance, hemmed her in; and her spirit was hardly reached by those two great influences without which no growing life can truly prosper—humor and imagination. The Baroness Lehzen—for she had been raised to that rank in the Hanoverian nobility by George IV before he died—was the real center of the Princess's world. When Feodora married, when Uncle Leopold went to Belgium, the baroness was left without a competitor. The Princess gave her mother her dutiful regards; but Lehzen had her heart. The girl would have gone through fire for her "*precious* Lehzen," her "best and truest friend." Her daily journal, begun when she was thirteen, bears on every page the traces of the baroness's influence. The young creature that one sees there, ingenuously self-depicted, with her sincerity, her quick affections and pious resolutions, might almost have been the daughter of a German pastor herself. Her enjoyments and admirations clothed themselves naturally in underlinings and exclamation marks. "It was a *delightful* ride. We cantered a good deal. SWEET LITTLE ROSY WENT *beautifully!!* We came home at a 1/4 past 1. . . . At 20 minutes to 7 we went out to the Opera. . . . Rubini sang *quite beautifully*. We came home at 1/2 past 11."

In Victoria's comments on her readings, the mind of the baroness is clearly revealed. One day, by some mistake, she was allowed to take up a volume of memoirs by Fanny Kemble. "One would imagine by the style that the authoress must be very pert. . . . It is a great pity that a person endowed with so much talent should publish a book which is so full of trash and nonsense." Madame de Sévigné's letters, which the baroness read aloud, met with more approval. "How truly elegant and natural her style is!" But her highest admiration was reserved for the Bishop of Chester's *Exposition of the Gospel of St. Matthew*. "It is a very fine book indeed. Just the sort of one I like; which is just plain and comprehensible and full of truth and good feeling. Lehzen gave it me on the Sunday that I took the Sacrament."

A few weeks previously she had been confirmed, and she described the event as follows: "I felt that my confirmation was one of the most solemn and important events and acts in my life. I felt deeply repentant for all what I had done which was wrong and trusted in God Almighty to strengthen my heart and mind; and to forsake all that is bad and follow all that is virtuous and right. I went with the firm determination to become a true Christian, to try and comfort my dear Mamma in all her griefs, and to become a dutiful and affectionate daughter to her. Also to be obedient to *dear* Lehzen, who has done so much for me. I was dressed in a white lace dress, with a white crape bonnet with a wreath of white roses round it. I went in the chariot with my dear Mamma and the others followed in another carriage."

In that conventional existence visits were exciting events; and when the Princess was fourteen she was delighted by the arrival of a couple of boys from Würtemberg, the Princes Alexander and Ernst, sons of her mother's sister. "They are both *extremely tall*," she noted; "Alexander is *very handsome*, and Ernst has a *very kind expression*. They are both extremely *amiable*." And their departure filled her with corresponding regrets. "We saw them get into the barge, and watched them sail away from the beach. They were so amiable and so pleasant to have in the house; *always good-humored*. Alexander took such care of me in getting out of the boat, and rode next to me; so did Ernst."

Two years later, two other cousins arrived, the Princes Ferdinand and Augustus. "Dear Ferdinand," the Princess wrote, "has elicited universal admiration from all parties. . . . He is so very unaffected, and has such a very distinguished appearance. Augustus is very amiable, too, and, when known, shows much good sense." On another occasion, "Dear Ferdinand came and sat near me and talked so dearly and sensibly. I do *so* love him. Augustus is also a dear good young man, and is very handsome." She could not quite decide which was the handsomer of the two. On the whole, she concluded, "I think Ferdinand handsomer than Augustus, his eyes are so beautiful, and he has such a lively clever expression; *both* have such a sweet expression."

Shortly afterwards, however, two more cousins arrived, who threw all the rest into the shade. These were the Princes Ernest and Albert, sons of her mother's eldest brother, the Duke of Saxe-Coburg.

This time the Princess was more particular in her observations. "Ernest," she remarked, "is as tall as Ferdinand and Augustus; he has dark hair, and fine dark eyes and eyebrows, but the nose and mouth are not good; he has a most kind, honest expression, and a very good figure. Albert, who is just as tall as Ernest but stouter, is extremely handsome; his hair is about the same color as mine; his eyes are large and blue, and he has a beautiful nose and a very sweet mouth with fine teeth; but the charm of his countenance is his expression, which is most delightful; it is full of goodness and sweetness, and very clever and intelligent."

"Both my cousins," she added, "are so kind and good; they are much more *formés* and men of the world than Augustus; they speak English well, and I speak it with them. Ernest will be 18 years old on the 21st of June, and Albert 17 on the 26th of August." A little later, "I sat between my dear cousins on the sofa and we looked at drawings. They both draw very well, particularly Albert, and are both exceedingly fond of music; they play very nicely on the piano. The more I see them the more I am delighted with them, and the more I love them."

When, after a stay of three weeks, the time came for the young men and their father to return to Germany, the moment of parting was a melancholy one. "It was our last HAPPY HAPPY breakfast, with this dear Uncle and those *dearest* beloved cousins, whom I *do* love so VERY VERY dearly. Dearly as I love Ferdinand, and also good Augustus, I love Ernest and Albert MUCH *more*. . . . They have both learnt a good deal, and are very clever, particularly Albert, who is the most reflecting of the two, and they like very much talking about serious and instructive things and yet are so *very very* gay and happy, like young people ought to be; Albert always used to have some fun and some clever witty answer at breakfast and everywhere; he used to play and fondle Dash [Victoria's spaniel] so funnily too. . . . Dearest

Albert was playing on the piano when I came down. At 11 dear Uncle, and my *dearest beloved* cousins, left us. I embraced both my cousins most warmly, as well as my Uncle. I cried bitterly, very bitterly."

The Princes shared her ecstasies and her italics between them; but it is clear enough where her secret preference lay. "Particularly Albert!" She was just seventeen; and deep was the impression left upon that budding organism by the young man's charm and goodness and accomplishments, and his large blue eyes and beautiful nose, and his sweet mouth and fine teeth.

KING WILLIAM could not abide his sister-in-law, and the duchess fully returned his antipathy. A bursting, bubbling old gentleman, with quarterdeck gestures, round rolling eyes, and a head like a pineapple, His Majesty's sudden elevation to the throne after fifty-six years of utter insignificance had almost sent him crazy. He rushed about doing preposterous things, spreading amusement and terror in every direction, and talking all the time. His speeches, made repeatedly at the most inopportune junctures, were the consternation of ministers. He was one part blackguard, people said, and three parts buffoon; but those who knew him better could not help liking him—he meant well; and he was really kindhearted, if you took him the right way.

If you took him the wrong way, however, you must look out for squalls, as the Duchess of Kent discovered.

She had no notion of how to deal with him. Occupied with her own responsibilities, she had no attention to spare for his susceptibilities. She was the mother of the heiress of England; and it was for him to recognize the fact—to put her upon a proper footing—to give her the precedence of a dowager Princess of Wales. It did not occur to her that such pretensions might be galling to a king who had no legitimate child of his own, and who yet had not altogether abandoned the hope of having one.

She pressed on, with bulky vigor; and Sir John Conroy, an Irishman with no great judgment who was her intimate counselor, egged her on. It was advisable that Victoria should become acquainted with the various districts of England, and through several summers a succession of tours—in the West, in the Midlands, in Wales—were arranged for her. The journeys, attracting enthusiastic crowds, took on the air of royal progresses. Addresses were presented by loyal citizens; the delighted Duchess of Kent, swelling in sweeping feathers and almost obliterating the diminutive Princess, read aloud, in her German accent, gracious replies prepared beforehand by Sir John Conroy; and Sir John, bustling and ridiculous, seemed to be mingling the roles of major-domo and prime minister. Naturally the King fumed over his newspaper at Windsor. "That woman is a nuisance!" he exclaimed.

Poor amiable Queen Adelaide did her best to smooth things down; but it was useless. News arrived that the Duchess of Kent, sailing in the Solent, had insisted that whenever her yacht appeared it should be received by royal salutes from all the men-of-war and the forts. The King declared that these continual poppings must cease; and the Premier and the First Lord of the Admiralty wrote privately to the duchess, begging her to waive her rights. But she would not hear of it; Sir John Conroy was adamant. "As Her Royal Highness's *confidential adviser,*" he said, "I cannot recommend her to give way on this point." Eventually the King, in a great state of excitement, issued a special order-in-council, prohibiting the firing of royal salutes to any ships except those which carried the reigning sovereign or his consort on board.

When King William quarreled with his Whig ministers the situation grew still more embittered, for now the duchess, in addition to her other shortcomings, was the political partisan of his enemies. In 1836 he made an attempt to prepare the ground for a match between the Princess Victoria and one of the sons of the Prince of Orange, and at the same time did his best to prevent the visit of the young Coburg princes to Kensington. He failed in both these objects; and the only result of his efforts was to raise the anger of the King of the Belgians, who, forgetting for a moment his royal reserve, addressed an indignant letter to his niece.

"I am really *astonished,*" he wrote, "at the conduct of your old Uncle the King; this invitation of the Prince of Orange and his sons, this forcing him on others, is very extraordinary. . . . Not later than yesterday I got a half-official communication from England, insinuating that it would be *highly* desirable that the visit of *your* relatives *should not take place this year—qu'en dites vous?*—What do you say to *that?*"

Shortly afterwards King Leopold came to England, and his reception was as cold at Windsor as it was warm at Kensington. "To hear dear Uncle speak on any subject," the Princess wrote in her diary, "is like reading a highly instructive book; his conversation is so enlightened, so clear. He is universally admitted to be one of the first politicians now extant." But her other uncle by no means shared her sentiments. He could not, he said, put up with a water drinker; and King Leopold would touch no wine. "What's that you're drinking, sir?" King William asked him one day at dinner. "Water, sir." "God damn it, sir!" was the rejoinder. "Why don't you drink wine? I never allow anybody to drink water at my table."

It was clear that there would soon be a great explosion; and in August it came. The duchess and the Princess had gone down to Windsor for the King's birthday party, and the King himself, who was in London for the day to adjourn Parliament, paid a visit at Kensington Palace in their absence. There he found that the duchess had just appropriated, against his express orders, a suite of seventeen apartments for her own use.

He was extremely angry, and when he returned to Windsor, after greeting the Princess with affection, he publicly rebuked the duchess for what she had done. But this was little to what followed. Next day was the birthday banquet; there were a hundred guests; the Duchess of Kent sat on the King's right hand, and the Princess Victoria opposite. At the end of the dinner the King rose, and, in a long, passionate speech, poured out the vials of his wrath upon the duchess. She had, he declared, insulted him—grossly and continually; she had kept the Princess away from him in the most improper manner; she was incompetent to act with propriety in the high station which she filled; and he hoped to God that his life might be spared for six months longer, so that the calamity of a regency might be avoided, and the functions of the Crown pass directly to the heiress presumptive instead of into the hands of the "person now near him."

The flood of vituperation rushed on, while the Queen blushed scarlet, the Princess burst into tears, and guests sat aghast. When the tirade was over the duchess in a tornado of rage called for her carriage. It was only with the utmost difficulty that some show of a reconciliation was patched up, and the outraged lady was prevailed upon to put off her departure till the morrow.

Her troubles, however, were not over when she had shaken the dust of Windsor from her feet. In her own household she was pursued by bitterness and vexation, for the apartments at Kensington seethed with subdued disaffection.

There was a deadly feud between her major-domo, Sir John Conroy, and Baroness Lehzen. But that was not all.

The duchess had grown too fond of Sir John Conroy. There were familiarities, and one day the Princess Victoria discovered the fact. She confided what she had seen to the baroness, and to the baroness's beloved ally, Madame de Späth. Unfortunately, Madame de Späth could not hold her tongue, and was foolish enough to reprove the duchess; whereupon she was instantly dismissed.

It was not so easy to get rid of the baroness. That lady, prudent and reserved, maintained an irreproachable demeanor. Her position was strongly entrenched; she had managed to secure the support of the King; and Sir John found that he could do nothing against her. But henceforward the household was divided. The duchess supported Sir John; but the baroness, too, had an adherent who could not be neglected. The Princess Victoria said nothing; but she adored her Lehzen.

The duchess knew only too well that in this horrid embroilment her daughter was against her. Chagrin, annoyance, tossed her to and fro. She did her best to console herself with Sir John's affectionate loquacity, or with the sharp remarks of Lady Flora Hastings. Lady Flora, one of her maids of honor, had no love for the baroness. The subject lent itself to satire; for Baroness Lehzen, the pastor's daughter, with all her airs of stiff superiority, had habits which betrayed her origin. Her passion for caraway seeds, for instance: little bags of them came to her from

Hanover, and she sprinkled them on her bread and butter, her cabbage, and even her roast beef. Lady Flora could not resist a caustic observation; it was repeated to the baroness, who pursed her lips in fury; and so the mischief grew.

THE KING had prayed that he might live till his niece was of age; and a few days before her eighteenth birthday—the date of her legal majority—a sudden attack of illness nearly carried him off. He recovered, however, and the Princess was able to go through her birthday festivities—a state ball and a drawing room—with unperturbed enjoyment.

"Count Zichy," she noted in her diary, "is very good-looking in uniform, but not in plain clothes. Count Waldstein looks remarkably well in his pretty Hungarian uniform." With the latter young gentleman she wished to dance, but there was an insurmountable difficulty. "He could not dance quadrilles, and, as in my station I unfortunately cannot valse and gallop, I could not dance with him."

Her birthday present from the King was of a pleasing nature, but it led to a painful domestic scene. In spite of the anger of her Belgian uncle, she had remained upon good terms with her English one. He had always been very kind to her, and the fact that he had quarreled with her mother did not appear to be a reason for disliking him. He was, she said, "odd, very odd," but "his intentions were often ill interpreted."

He now wrote her a letter, offering her an allowance of £10,000 a year, to be at her own disposal and independent of her mother. Lord Conyngham, the lord chamberlain, was instructed to deliver the letter into the Princess's own hands. When he arrived at Kensington, he was ushered into the presence of the duchess and the Princess, and the duchess put out her hand to take the letter. Lord Conyngham begged her pardon and repeated the King's command. Thereupon the Princess took the letter. She immediately wrote to her uncle, accepting his kind proposal. The duchess was much displeased; £4000 a year, she said, would be quite enough for Victoria; as for the remaining £6000, it would be only proper that she should have that herself.

King William had thrown off his illness, and returned to his normal life. Once more the royal circle at Windsor—Their Majesties, the elder Princesses—might be seen ranged for hours round a mahogany table, while the Queen netted a purse, and the King slept, occasionally waking to observe "Exactly so, ma'am, exactly so!" But this recovery was of short duration. The old man suddenly collapsed; he showed no power of rallying; and it was clear to everyone that his death was now close at hand.

All eyes, all thoughts, turned towards the Princess Victoria; but she still remained, shut away in the seclusion of Kensington, a small, unknown figure, lost in the shadow of her mother. The preceding year had in fact been an important one in her development. The soft tendrils of her mind had for the first time begun to stretch out towards unchildish things. In this King Leopold encouraged her. After his return to Brussels, he had resumed his correspondence in a more serious strain; he discussed details of foreign politics; he laid down the duties of kingship. "The business of the highest in a State," he wrote, "is, in my opinion, to act with great impartiality and a spirit of justice for the good of all." At the same time the Princess's tastes had been opening out. Though she was still passionately devoted to riding and dancing, she had now begun to have a genuine love of music as well, and to drink in the roulades and arias of Italian opera with high enthusiasm. She even enjoyed reading poetry—at any rate, the poetry of Sir Walter Scott.

When King Leopold learned that King William's death was approaching, he wrote several long letters of advice to his niece. In the crisis that was approaching, he said, she was not to be alarmed, but to trust in her "good natural sense and the *truth*" of her character; she was to do nothing in a hurry, and to continue her confidence in the Whig administration. Not content with letters, however, King Leopold determined that the Princess should not lack personal guidance, and sent over to her aid the trusted friend, whom, twenty years before, he had taken to his heart at Claremont. Thus, once again, as if in accordance with some preordained destiny, the figure of Stockmar is discernible—present at a momentous hour.

On June 18, the King was visibly sinking. The Archbishop of

Canterbury was by his side, with all the comforts of the church. It was the anniversary of the Battle of Waterloo, and the dying man remembered it. He should be glad to live, he said, over that day; he would never see another sunset.

"I hope Your Majesty may live to see many," said Dr. Chambers. "Oh! that's quite another thing," was the answer. One other sunset he did live to see; and he died early the following morning. It was on June 20, 1837.

When all was over, the Archbishop and the Lord Chamberlain ordered a carriage, and drove posthaste from Windsor to Kensington. They arrived at the palace at five o'clock, and it was only with difficulty that they gained admittance. At six the duchess woke up her daughter, and told her that the Archbishop of Canterbury and Lord Conyngham wished to see her. She got out of bed, put on her dressing gown, and went, alone, into the room where the messengers were standing.

Lord Conyngham and the Archbishop fell on their knees, and Lord Conyngham officially announced the death of the King; the Archbishop added some personal details. Looking at the bending, murmuring dignitaries before her, she knew that she was Queen of England. "Since it has pleased Providence," she wrote that day in her journal, "to place me in this station, I shall do my utmost to fulfill my duty; I am very young, and inexperienced, but I am sure, that very few have more real good will and more real desire to do what is fit and right than I have."

But there was scant time for resolutions and reflections. At once, affairs were thick upon her. Stockmar came to breakfast, and gave some good advice. She wrote a letter to her uncle Leopold. The Prime Minister, Lord Melbourne, came at nine and kissed her hand. She saw him alone, and repeated to him the lesson which, no doubt, the faithful Stockmar had taught her at breakfast. "It has long been my intention to retain your Lordship and the rest of the present Ministry at the head of affairs"; whereupon Lord Melbourne again kissed her hand and shortly after left her.

At eleven, Lord Melbourne came again; and at half past eleven she went downstairs into the red saloon to hold her first Council. The great assembly of lords and notables, bishops, generals, and Ministers of State saw the doors thrown open and a very short, slim girl in deep plain mourning come into the room alone and move forward to her seat with extraordinary dignity and grace; they saw a countenance not beautiful but prepossessing—fair hair, blue prominent eyes, a small curved nose, a tiny chin, a clear complexion and, over all, the strangely mingled signs of innocence, of gravity, of youth, and of composure; they heard a high unwavering voice reading aloud with perfect clarity; and then the ceremony was over. They saw the small figure rise and, with the same consummate grace, pass out from among them, as she had come in, alone.

BARONESS LEHZEN

CHAPTER 3
Lord Melbourne

THE NEW QUEEN was almost entirely unknown to her subjects. In her public appearances her mother had invariably dominated the scene. Her private life had been that of a novice in a convent; and no human being at all, except her mother and the Baroness Lehzen, had ever been alone with her in a room. Thus it was not only the public at large that was in ignorance of everything concerning her; the inner circles of statesmen and officials and highborn ladies were equally in the dark.

When she suddenly emerged from this deep obscurity, the impression that she created was profound. Her bearing at her first Council filled the whole gathering with astonishment and admiration; the Duke of Wellington, Sir Robert Peel, even the cold and caustic Charles Greville, Clerk of the Privy Council—all were completely carried away. Everything that was reported of her subsequent proceedings seemed to be of no less happy augury. Her perceptions were quick, her decisions sensible; she performed her royal duties with extraordinary facility.

Among the outside public there was a great wave of enthusiasm. Sentiment and romance were coming into fashion; and the spectacle of the little girl-queen, innocent, modest, with fair hair and pink cheeks, driving through her capital, filled the hearts of the beholders with raptures of affection. What, above all, struck everybody with overwhelming force was the contrast between Queen Victoria and her uncles. The nasty old men, debauched and pigheaded—they had vanished like the snows of winter, and here at last, crowned and radiant, was the spring. Lord John Russell, in an elaborate oration, gave voice to the general sentiment. He asked England to pray that the illustrious Princess who had just ascended the throne might see slavery abolished, crime diminished, and education improved. He trusted that her people would henceforward derive their strength from enlightened religious and moral principles, and that, so fortified, the reign of Victoria might prove celebrated to posterity and to all the nations of the earth.

Very soon, however, there were signs that the future might turn out to be not quite so simple and roseate as a delighted public dreamed. The "illustrious Princess" might perhaps, after all, have something within her which squared ill with the easy vision of a well-conducted heroine in a storybook. When, after her first Council, she had crossed the anteroom and had found her mother waiting for her, she had said, "And now, Mamma, am I really and truly Queen?"

"You see, my dear, that it is so."

"Then, dear Mamma, I hope you will grant me the first request I make to you, as Queen. Let me be by myself for an hour." For an hour she had remained in solitude. Then she had reappeared, and had given a significant order: her bed was to be moved out of her mother's room.

It was the doom of the Duchess of Kent. The long years of waiting were over at last; the moment of a lifetime had come; her daughter was Queen of England; and that very moment brought her own annihilation. She found herself, absolutely and irretrievably, shut off from every vestige of influence, of power. She was surrounded, indeed, by all the outward signs of respect; but that only made the inward truth of her position the more intolerable. Through the mingled formalities of court etiquette and filial duty, she could never penetrate to Victoria. She was unable to conceal her disappointment and her rage.

"There is no more future for me," she exclaimed to Madame de Lieven; "I have become a nothing." For eighteen years, she said, this child had been the sole object of her existence, her hopes, and now—! Sailing so gallantly through the buffeting storms of life, the stately vessel, with sails still swelling and pennons flying, had put into harbor at last; to find there nothing—a land of desolation.

Within a month of the accession, the whole royal household moved from Kensington to Buckingham Palace, and, in the new abode, the Duchess of Kent was given a suite of apartments entirely separate from the Queen's. By Victoria herself the change was welcomed, though, at the moment of departure from Kensington, she could afford to be sentimental. "Though I rejoice to *go* into Buckingham Palace for many reasons," she wrote in her diary, "it is not without feelings of regret that I shall bid adieu *for ever* to this my birthplace! I have gone through painful and disagreeable scenes here, 'tis true," she concluded, "but still I am fond of the poor old palace."

At the same time she took another decided step. She had determined that she would see no more of Sir John Conroy. She rewarded his past services with a baronetcy and a pension of £3000 a year; he remained a member of the duchess's household, but his personal intercourse with the Queen came to an abrupt conclusion.

IT WAS CLEAR that these interior changes—whatever else they might betoken—marked the triumph of one person—the Baroness Lehzen.

Discreet and victorious, she observed the ruin of her enemies, and remained in possession of the field. More closely than ever did she cleave to the side of her mistress, her pupil, and her friend; and in the recesses of the palace her mysterious figure was at once invisible and omnipresent. When the Queen's ministers came in at one door, the baroness went out by another; when they retired, she immediately returned.

Nobody knew—nobody will ever know—the precise extent and nature of her influence. She herself declared that she never discussed public affairs with the Queen, that she was concerned with private matters only—with private letters and the details of private life. Certainly her hand is everywhere discernible in Victoria's early correspondence. The journal is written in the style of a child; but the letters are not so simple; they are the work of a child, rearranged—perceptibly—by a governess.

The governess was no fool: narrow, jealous, provincial, she might be; but she was an acute and vigorous woman who had gained a peculiar ascendancy. That ascendancy she meant to keep. No doubt it was true that technically she took no part in public business; but the distinction between what is public and what is private is always subtle; and in the case of a reigning sovereign it is often imaginary. Considering all things, it was something more than a mere matter of private interest that the bedroom of Baroness Lehzen at Buckingham Palace should have been next door to the bedroom of the Queen.

But the influence wielded by the baroness, supreme as it seemed within its own sphere, was not unlimited; there were other forces at work. For one thing, the faithful Stockmar had taken up his residence in the palace. During the twenty years which had elapsed since the death of the Princess Charlotte, the unknown counselor of a princeling had gradually risen to a position of European importance. His devotion to his master had been not only wholehearted but cautious and wise. It was Stockmar's advice that had kept Prince Leopold in England during the critical years which followed his wife's death, and had thus secured to him the essential requisite of a *point d'appui* [focal point] in the country of his adoption. It was Stockmar who had induced the Prince to become the constitutional sovereign of Belgium. It was Stockmar's diplomatic skill which, through a long series of complicated negotiations, had led to the guarantee of Belgian neutrality by the great powers.

His labors had been rewarded by a German barony and by the complete confidence of King Leopold. Nor was it only in Brussels that he was listened to with respect. The statesmen who governed England—Lord Grey, Sir Robert Peel, Lord Palmerston, Lord Melbourne—had learned to put a high value upon his probity and his intelligence.

"He is one of the cleverest fellows I ever saw," said Lord

Melbourne, "the most discreet man, the most well-judging, and most cool man."

King Leopold and his counselor provide in their careers an example of the curious diversity of human ambitions. The correct mind of Leopold craved for the whole apparatus of royalty. Mere power would have held no attractions for him; he must be an actual king—crowned—recognized. The ambition of Stockmar took a form exactly complementary to his own. The sovereignty that the baron sought for was by no means obvious. The satisfaction of his being lay in obscurity, in invisibility—in passing, unobserved, through a hidden entrance, into the very central chamber of power, and in sitting there, quietly, pulling the subtle strings that set the wheels of the whole world in motion. A very few people, in very high places, knew that Baron Stockmar was a most important person: that was enough. The fortunes of the master and the servant, intimately interacting, rose together. The baron's secret skill had given Leopold his kingdom; and Leopold, in his turn, as time went on, furnished the baron with more and more keys to more and more back doors.

Stockmar took up his abode in Buckingham Palace partly as the emissary of King Leopold, but more particularly as the friend and adviser of a queen who was almost a child. For it would be a mistake to suppose that either of these two men was actuated by a vulgar selfishness. King Leopold, indeed, was well aware on which side his bread was buttered; but then, he was a constitutional monarch; and it would be highly indecorous in a constitutional monarch to have any aims that were low or personal. As for Stockmar, disinterestedness was undoubtedly a basic element in his character. The ordinary schemer is always an optimist; and Stockmar, racked by dyspepsia, was constitutionally a melancholy man. A schemer, no doubt, he was; but he schemed distrustfully, splenetically, to do good.

With Lehzen to supervise every detail of her conduct, with Stockmar in the next room, so full of wisdom, with her uncle Leopold's letters, too, pouring out so constantly their stream of encouragements, Victoria, even had she been without other guidance, would have stood in no lack of private counselors.

But these influences paled before a new star, of the first magnitude, which, rising suddenly upon her horizon, immediately dominated her life.

WILLIAM LAMB, Viscount Melbourne, was fifty-eight years of age, and had been for the last three years Prime Minister of England. In every outward respect he was one of the most fortunate of mankind. He had been born into the midst of riches, brilliance, and power. Nature had given him beauty and brains; the unexpected death of an elder brother had brought him wealth, a peerage, and the possibility of high advancement.

With little effort, he attained political eminence, and on the triumph of the Whigs he became a leading member of the government. His mind was at once supple and copious; his temperament, calm and sensitive. In society he was a notable talker, a captivating companion, a charming man. If one looked deeper, one saw at once that he was not ordinary, that the piquancies of his conversation and his manner—his free-and-easy vaguenesses, his abrupt questions, his lollings and loungings—were the outward manifestation of an individuality that was fundamental.

The precise nature of this individuality was difficult to gauge: it was complex, perhaps self-contradictory. Certainly there was an ironical discordance between the inner history of the man and his apparent fortunes. His marriage, which had seemed to be the crown of his youthful ardors, was a long, miserable, desperate failure: the incredible Lady Caroline was very nearly the destruction of his life.

When at last he emerged from the anguish and confusion of Lady Caroline's folly, he was left alone with endless memories of farce and tragedy, and an only son, who was an imbecile. But there was something else that he owed to Lady Caroline. While she had whirled with Byron in a hectic frenzy, he had stayed at home and occupied his solitude with reading. It was thus that he had acquired those habits of study which formed so unexpected a part of his mental equipment. His passion for reading never deserted him; even when he was Prime Minister he found time to master every new important book. With an incongruousness that was characteristic, his favorite study was theology; and at any odd moment he might be found turning over the pages of the Bible.

The paradox of his political career was no less curious. By temperament an aristocrat, by conviction a conservative, he came to power as the leader of the popular party, the party of change. He had profoundly disliked the Reform Bill, which he had only accepted at last as a necessary evil; and the Reform Bill lay at the root of the very existence of his government. He was far too skeptical to believe in progress of any kind. "You'd better try to do no good," was one of his dictums, "and then you'll get into no scrapes." Education at best was futile; education of the poor was positively dangerous. The ballot was nonsense; and there was no such thing as a democracy. Nevertheless, he was not a reactionary; he was simply an opportunist. The whole duty of government, he said, was "to prevent crime and to preserve contracts." All one could really hope to do was to carry on.

He himself carried on in a remarkable manner—with compromises and contradictions, and yet with shrewdness. He conducted transactions with extraordinary nonchalance. Important persons, ushered up for some grave interview, found him in a touseled bed, littered with books and papers, or vaguely shaving in a dressing room; but, when they went downstairs again, they would realize that somehow or other they had been pumped. When he had to receive a deputation, the worthy delegates of the tallow chandlers, or the Society for the Abolition of Capital Punishment, were mortified when, in the midst of their speeches, the Prime Minister became absorbed in blowing a feather, or suddenly cracked an unseemly joke. How could they have guessed that he had spent the night before diligently getting up the details of their case?

Probably, if he had been born a little earlier, he would have been a simpler and a happier man. As it was, he was a child of the eighteenth century whose lot was cast in a new, unsympathetic age. He was an autumn rose. With all his humor, his happy-go-lucky ways, a deep disquietude possessed him. He was restless and melancholy at heart. Above all, he could never harden himself; those sensitive petals shivered in every wind. Whatever else he might be, one thing was certain: Lord Melbourne was always human, supremely human—too human, perhaps.

And now, with old age upon him, his life took a sudden, extraordinary turn. He became the intimate adviser and companion of a young girl who had stepped all at once from a nursery to a throne.

His relations with women had been, like everything else about him, ambiguous. Lady Caroline had vanished; but female society of some kind or other was necessary to him, and a great part of every day was invariably spent in it. There were rumors and combustions. Lord Melbourne was twice a corespondent in a divorce action. On each occasion he won his suit. But it was clear that, with such a record, the Prime Minister's position in Buckingham Palace must be a highly delicate one.

He met the situation with consummate success. His behavior was from the first moment impeccable. His manner towards the young Queen mingled, with perfect facility, the respect of a statesman and a courtier with the tender solicitude of a parent. At the same time the habits of his life underwent a surprising change. His comfortable, unpunctual days became subject to the unaltering routine of a palace; no longer did he sprawl on sofas; not a single "damn" escaped his lips. The man of the world who had been the friend of Byron, the talker whose paradoxes had held Holland House enthralled, the lover whose soft words had captivated so much beauty, might now be seen, evening after evening, talking with infinite politeness to a schoolgirl, bolt upright, amid the silence and the rigidity of court etiquette.

ON HER SIDE, Victoria was instantly fascinated by Lord Melbourne. The good report of Stockmar had no doubt prepared the way; and the first highly favorable impression was never afterwards belied. She found him perfect; and perfect in her sight he remained.

Her absolute adoration was very natural; what innocent young creature could have resisted the charm of such a man? But, in her situation, there was a special influence which gave a peculiar glow to all she felt. After years of emptiness and dullness, she had come suddenly, in the heyday of youth, into freedom and power. She was mistress of herself, of great domains and palaces; she was Queen of England. Responsibilities and difficulties she might have; but one feeling dominated all others—the feeling of joy.

Everything pleased her. She was in high spirits from morning till night. Mr. Creevey, grown old now, catching a glimpse of her at Brighton, was much amused. "A more homely little being you never beheld, *when she is at her ease*," he wrote. "She laughs in real earnest, opening her mouth as wide as it can go, showing not very pretty gums. . . . She eats quite as heartily as she laughs, I think I may say she gobbles. . . . She blushes and laughs every instant in so natural a way as to disarm anybody."

But it was not merely when she was laughing or gobbling that she enjoyed herself; the performance of her official duties gave her intense satisfaction. "I really have immensely to do," she wrote in her journal a few days after her accession; "I receive so many communications from my Ministers, but I like it very much." And, a week later, "I *delight* in this work." Through the girl's immaturity the vigorous predestined tastes of the woman were eagerly pushing themselves into existence.

One detail of her happy situation deserves particular mention. Apart from the momentousness of her political position, she was a person of great wealth. As soon as Parliament met, an annuity of £385,000 was settled upon her. When the expenses of her household had been discharged, she was left with £68,000 a year of her own. She enjoyed besides the revenues of the duchy of Lancaster, an annual £27,000. The first use to which she put her money was characteristic: she paid off her father's debts. She had the instincts of a man of business; and she never could have borne to be in a financially unsound position.

With youth and happiness gilding every hour, the days passed merrily enough. And each day hinged upon Lord Melbourne. Her diary shows us, with clarity, the life of the young sovereign during the early months of her reign—a life full of delightful business, a life of simple pleasures, riding, eating, dancing—an easy, unsophisticated life.

If she is the heroine of the story, Lord Melbourne is the hero. Lehzen, the baron, Uncle Leopold, are unsubstantial shadows—the incidental characters of the piece. Her paradise was peopled by two persons. One sees them together still, in the artless pages of her diary, under the magical illumination of that long-ago dawn: the polished gentleman with the whitening hair and whiskers and the dark eyebrows and the mobile lips and the big expressive eyes; and beside him the tiny Queen—slim, active, in her plain girl's dress and little tippet, looking up at him earnestly, adoringly, with eyes blue and projecting, and half-open mouth. So they appear upon every page of the journal.

Their long conversations touched upon a multitude of topics. Lord M. would criticize books, throw out a remark or two on the British constitution, tell some story or make some passing reflections on human life. Then there would be business—a dispatch perhaps from Lord Durham in Canada, which Lord M. would read. But first he must explain a little.

"He said that I must know that Canada originally belonged to the French, and was only ceded to the English in 1760, when it was taken in an expedition under Wolfe: 'a very daring enterprise,' he said. Canada was then entirely French. . . . Lord M. explained this very clearly and said a good deal more about it. He then read me Durham's despatch, which took him more than 1/2 an hour to read. Lord M. read it beautifully with that fine soft voice of his, and with so much expression, so that, needless to say, I was much interested by it."

Then the talk would take a more personal turn. Lord M. would describe his boyhood, and she would learn that "he wore his hair long, as all boys then did, till he was 17 (*how* handsome he must have looked!)." Or she would find out about his queer tastes and habits—how he never carried a watch. " 'I always ask the servant what o'clock it is, and then he tells me what he likes,' said Lord M."

The day's routine, whether in London or at Windsor, was almost invariable. The morning was devoted to business and Lord M. In the afternoon the whole court went out riding. The Queen, in her velvet riding habit and a top hat with a veil about the brim, headed the cavalcade; and Lord M. rode beside her.

The lively troupe went fast and far, to the exhilaration of Her Majesty. Back in the palace again, there was still time for a little more fun before dinner—a game of battledore and shuttlecock perhaps, or a romp along the galleries with some children.

Dinner came, and the ceremonial tightened. The gentleman of highest rank sat on the right hand of the Queen; on her left—it soon became an established rule—sat Lord Melbourne. After the ladies had left the dining room, the gentlemen were not permitted to remain behind for very long; indeed, the short time allowed them for their wine drinking formed the subject—so it was rumored—of one of the very few disputes between the Queen and her Prime Minister; but her determination carried the day, and from that moment after-dinner drunkenness began to go out of fashion.

When the company was reassembled in the drawing room the etiquette was stiff. The Queen spoke in turn to each of her guests; and during these short uneasy colloquies the aridity of royalty was apt to become painfully evident. One night Mr. Greville was present; his turn soon came; the middle-aged, hard-faced *viveur* was addressed by his young hostess. "Have you been riding today, Mr. Greville?" asked the Queen.

"No, Madam, I have not," replied Mr. Greville.

"It was a fine day," continued the Queen.

"Yes, Madam, a very fine day," said Mr. Greville.

"It was rather cold, though," said the Queen.

"It *was* rather cold, Madam," said Mr. Greville. There was a pause, after which Mr. Greville ventured to take the lead, though he did not venture to change the subject. "Has Your Majesty been riding today?" asked Mr. Greville.

"Oh yes, a very long ride," answered the Queen animatedly.

"Has Your Majesty got a nice horse?" said Mr. Greville.

"Oh, a very nice horse," said the Queen.

It was over. Her Majesty gave a smile and an inclination of the head, Mr. Greville bowed, and the next conversation began with the next gentleman. When all the guests had been disposed of, the Duchess of Kent sat down to her whist, while everybody else was ranged about the round table—perhaps to discuss the contents of one of the large albums of engravings with which the round table was covered—until it was half past eleven and time to go to bed.

Occasionally, there were little diversions: the evening might be spent at the opera or at a play. Next morning the royal critic would note down her impressions. "It was Shakespeare's tragedy of *Hamlet*. . . . Mr. Charles Kean (son of old Kean) acted the part of Hamlet, and I must say beautifully." But, undoubtedly, the evenings which the young Queen most enjoyed were those on which there was dancing. She was always ready enough to seize any excuse—the arrival of cousins—a birthday—to give the command for that. Then, when the figures of the dancers swayed to the music, and she felt her own figure swaying too—then her happiness reached its height, her eyes sparkled, she must go on and on into the small hours of the morning. For a moment Lord M. himself was forgotten.

THE MONTHS flew past. The summer was over: "the pleasantest summer I EVER passed in *my life*, and I shall never forget this first summer of my reign."

With surprising rapidity, another summer was upon her. The coronation came and went—a curious dream. The antique, intricate ceremonial worked itself out like some machine of gigantic complexity which was a little out of order. The small central figure went through her gyrations. She sat; she walked; she prayed; she carried about an orb that was almost too heavy to hold; the Archbishop of Canterbury came and crushed a ring upon the wrong finger, so that she was ready to cry out with the pain; old Lord Rolle tripped in his mantle and fell down the steps as he was doing homage; she perceived Lehzen in an upper box and smiled at her as she sat, robed and crowned, on the Confessor's throne. "I shall ever remember this day as the *proudest* of my life," she noted. But the pride was soon merged once more in youth and simplicity. When she returned to Buckingham Palace at last she was not tired; she ran up to her private rooms, doffed her splendors, and gave her spaniel Dash its evening bath.

Life flowed on again with its accustomed smoothness—though, of course, the smoothness was occasionally disturbed.

For one thing, there was the distressing behavior of Uncle Leopold. The King of the Belgians had not been able to resist attempting to make use of his family position to further his diplomatic ends—to test the opportunity of bending to his wishes, by means of personal influence, the foreign policy of England. He set about the task with becoming precautions, continuing to write his usual letters of admirable advice. Within a few days of her accession, he recommended the young Queen to lay emphasis, on every possible occasion, upon her English birth; to praise the English nation and "the Established Church." And then—"before you decide on anything important I should be glad if you would consult me; this would also have the advantage of giving you time"; nothing was more injurious than to be hurried into wrong decisions unawares.

His niece replied at once with all her accustomed affection; but she wrote hurriedly—and, perhaps, a trifle vaguely. "*Your* advice is always of the *greatest importance* to me," she said.

Had he, possibly, gone too far? Well, he would be careful; he would draw back—*pour mieux sauter*—in order to jump the better—he added to himself with a smile. In his next letters he made no reference to his suggestion of consultations with himself; he merely pointed out the wisdom, in general, of refusing to decide upon important questions offhand. So far, his advice was taken; and it was noticed that the Queen, when applications were made to her, rarely gave an immediate answer.

King Leopold's counsels continued. The Princess de Lieven, he said, was a dangerous woman; there was reason to think that she would pry into what did not concern her; let Victoria beware. "A rule which I cannot sufficiently recommend is *never to permit* people to speak on subjects concerning yourself or your affairs, without you having yourself desired them to do so." Should such a thing occur, "change the conversation, and make the individual feel that he has made a mistake."

This piece of advice was also taken; for it fell out as the King had predicted. Madame de Lieven sought an audience, and appeared to be verging towards confidential topics; whereupon the Queen, becoming slightly embarrassed, talked of commonplaces. The individual felt that she had made a mistake.

The King's next warning was remarkable. Letters, he pointed out, are almost invariably read in the post. This was inconvenient, no doubt; but the fact, once grasped, was not without its advantages.

"I will give you an example: we are still plagued by Prussia concerning those fortresses; now to tell the Prussian Government many things, which we *should not like* to tell them officially, the Minister is going to write a despatch to our man at Berlin, sending it *by post;* the Prussians *are sure* to read it, and to learn in this way what we wish them to hear." Analogous circumstances might very probably occur in England. "I tell you the *trick,*" wrote His Majesty, "that you should be able to guard against it."

It seemed that the time had come for another step. The King's next letter was full of foreign politics—the situation in Spain and Portugal, the character of Louis Philippe; and he received a favorable answer. It appeared that Victoria was not unwilling to exchange observations on such matters with her uncle. So far so good. King Leopold, with a crisis impending in his diplomacy, hung back no longer. It was of the utmost importance to him that, in his maneuverings with France and Holland, he should have, or appear to have, English support. But the English government was adopting a neutral attitude; it was too bad; not to be for him was to be against him—could they not see that? Yet, perhaps, they were only wavering, and a little pressure upon them from Victoria might still save all.

"All I want from your kind Majesty," he wrote, "is, that you will *occasionally* express to your Ministers that, as far as it is *compatible* with England's interests, you do *not* wish that your government should take the lead in such measures as might bring on the *destruction* of this country, as well as that of your uncle and his family."

The result of this appeal was unexpected; there was dead silence for more than a week. When Victoria at last wrote, she was prodigal of her affection—"it would, indeed, my dearest Uncle, be *very wrong* of you, if you thought my feelings of devoted attachment to you could ever be changed—" but her references to foreign politics, though they were elaborate, were noncommittal in the extreme; they were almost cast in an official form. Her ministers, she said, entirely shared her views; she understood and sympathized with the difficulties of her beloved uncle's position; and he might rest assured "that both Lord Melbourne and Lord Palmerston are most anxious at all times for the prosperity and welfare of Belgium."

That was all. The King in his reply declared himself delighted, and reechoed the affectionate protestations of his niece. "My dearest and most beloved Victoria," he said, "you have written me a *very dear* and long letter, which has given me *great satisfaction.*" He would not admit that he had had a rebuff.

A few months later the crisis came. King Leopold determined to make a bold push, and to carry Victoria with him, this time, by a display of royal vigor and avuncular authority. In an abrupt, almost peremptory letter, he laid his case, once more, before his niece. "You know from experience," he wrote, "that I *never ask anything of you*. . . . But, as I said before, if we are not careful we may see serious consequences. . . . I remain, my dear Victoria, your affectionate uncle, Leopold R."

The Queen immediately dispatched this letter to Lord Melbourne, who replied with a carefully thought-out form of words, signifying nothing whatever, which, he suggested, she should send to her uncle. She did so, copying out the formula, with a liberal scattering of "dear Uncles" interspersed; and she concluded her letter with a message of "affectionate love to Aunt Louise and the children."

Then at last King Leopold was obliged to recognize the facts. His next letter contained no reference at all to politics. "I am glad," he wrote, "to find that you like Brighton better than last year. I think Brighton very agreeable at this time of the year, till the east winds set in. Before my marriage, it was there that I met the Regent." Like poor Madame de Lieven, His Majesty felt that he had made a mistake.

THE CORRESPONDENCE with King Leopold was significant of much that still lay partly hidden in the character of Victoria. Her attitude towards her uncle never wavered for a moment. To all his advances she had presented an unyielding front. The foreign policy of England was not his province; it was hers and her ministers'; his insinuations, his entreaties, were quite useless.

The rigidity of her position was the more striking owing to the respectfulness and the affection with which it was accompanied. From start to finish the unmoved Queen remained the devoted niece. Leopold himself must have envied such correctitude; but what may be admirable in an elderly statesman is alarming in a maiden of nineteen. And observers were not without their fears. The strange mixture of ingenuous lightheartedness and fixed determination, of frankness and reticence, of childishness and pride, augured a future full of dangers.

As time passed the less pleasant qualities in this curious composition revealed themselves more often. There were signs of an imperious temper, an egotism that was strong and hard. It was noticed that the palace etiquette, far from relaxing, grew ever more inflexible. The slightest infringements of the freezing rules of deference were invariably visited by sharp and haughty glances from the Queen. Yet Her Majesty's eyes, crushing as they could be, were less crushing than her mouth. The self-will depicted in those small projecting teeth and that small receding chin was of a more dismaying kind than that which a powerful jaw betokens; it was a self-will imperturbable, unintelligent; a self-will dangerously akin to obstinacy. And the obstinacy of monarchs is not as that of other men.

Within two years of her accession, the storm clouds which, from the first, had been dimly visible on the horizon, gathered and burst. Victoria's relations with her mother had not improved. The Duchess of Kent still remained in Buckingham Palace, a discarded figure, powerless and inconsolable. Sir John Conroy, banished from the presence of the Queen, still presided over the duchess's household, and the hostilities of Kensington continued unabated in the new surroundings. Lady Flora Hastings still cracked her malicious jokes; the animosity of the Baroness Lehzen was still unappeased.

One day, Lady Flora found the joke was turned against her. Early in 1839, traveling in the suite of the duchess, she had returned from Scotland in the same carriage with Sir John Conroy. A change in her figure became the subject of jest; tongues wagged; and the jest grew serious. It was whispered that Lady Flora [an unmarried lady of thirty-two] was with child.

The state of her health seemed to confirm the suspicion; she consulted Sir James Clark, the royal physician, and after the consultation, Sir James let his tongue wag, too. On this, the scandal flared up sky-high. Everyone was talking; the baroness was not surprised; the duchess rallied to the support of her lady; the Queen was informed. At last the extraordinary expedient of a medical examination was resorted to, during which Sir James, according to Lady Flora, behaved with brutal rudeness, while a second doctor was extremely polite.

Finally, both physicians signed a certificate entirely exculpating the lady. But this was by no means the end of the business. The Hastings family, socially a powerful one, threw itself into the fray with all the fury of outraged pride. Lord Hastings insisted upon an audience of the Queen, wrote to the papers, and demanded the dismissal of Sir James Clark. The Queen expressed her regret to Lady Flora, but Sir James Clark was not dismissed. The tide of opinion turned violently against the Queen and her advisers; and by the end of March, the popularity, so radiant and abundant, with which the young sovereign had begun her reign, had entirely disappeared.

There can be no doubt that a great lack of discretion had been shown by the court. Ill-natured tittle-tattle, which should have been instantly nipped in the bud, had been allowed to assume disgraceful proportions; and the Throne itself had become involved. A particularly awkward question had been raised by the position of Sir James Clark. The Duke of Wellington, upon whom it was customary to fall back, in cases of difficulty in high places, had been consulted, and he had given it as his opinion that, as it would be impossible to remove Sir James without a public inquiry, Sir James must certainly stay where he was. Probably the duke was right; but the fact that the peccant doctor continued in the Queen's service made the Hastings family irreconcilable and produced an unpleasant impression of unrepentant error upon the public mind.

As for Victoria, she was very young and inexperienced; and she can hardly be blamed for having failed to control an extremely difficult situation. That was clearly Lord Melbourne's task; he was a man of the world, and, with vigilance, he might have quietly put out the ugly flames while they were still smoldering. But he did not do so; he let things slide; he was lazy and easygoing; the baroness was persistent; and Victoria herself was very headstrong. Did he possess the magic bridle which would curb that fiery steed? He could not be certain. And then, suddenly, another violent crisis revealed more unmistakably than ever the nature of the mind with which he had to deal.

THE QUEEN had for long been haunted by a terror that the day might come when she would be obliged to part with her minister. The power of the Whig government was steadily declining; the general election of 1837 had left them with a very small majority in the House of Commons, and since then, they had been in constant difficulties—abroad, at home, in Ireland. The Queen watched the development of events in great anxiety. She was a Whig by upbringing, by every association; and, even if those ties had never existed, the mere fact that Lord M. was the head of the Whigs would have determined her politics. The fall of the Whigs would mean a sad upset for Lord M. But it would have a still more terrible consequence: Lord M. would have to leave her; and the daily, the hourly, presence of Lord M. had become an integral part of her life.

Of the wider significance of political questions she knew nothing; all she saw was that her friends were in office and about her, and that it would be dreadful if they ceased to be so. "I cannot say," she wrote when a critical division was impending, "(though I feel *confident* of *our success*) HOW *low*, HOW *sad* I feel, when I think of the POSSIBILITY of this excellent and truly kind man not *remaining* my Minister! Yet I trust fervently that *He* who has so wonderfully protected me through such manifold difficulties will not *now* desert me!"

Lord Melbourne realized clearly enough how undesirable was such a state of mind in a constitutional sovereign who might be called upon at any moment to receive as her ministers the leaders of the opposite party; he did what he could to cool her ardor; but in vain. With considerable lack of foresight, too, he had himself helped to bring about this unfortunate condition of affairs. From the moment of her accession, he had surrounded the Queen with ladies of his own party; the mistress of the robes and all the ladies of the bedchamber were Whigs. In the ordinary course, the Queen never saw a Tory. She disliked the whole tribe; and she particularly disliked Sir Robert Peel, who would almost certainly be the next Prime Minister. His manners were detestable, and he wanted to turn out Lord M.

But the dreaded hour was now fast approaching. Early in May the ministers were visibly tottering; on a vital point of policy they could only secure a majority of five in the House of Commons; they determined to resign. When Victoria heard the news she burst into tears. Was it possible, then, that she was about to see Lord M. for the last time?

Lord M. came; the conversation was touching and prolonged; but it could only end in one way—the Queen must send for the Duke of Wellington. When, next morning, the duke came, he advised Her Majesty to send for Sir Robert Peel. She was in "a state of dreadful grief," but she swallowed down her tears, and braced herself, with royal resolution, for the odious interview.

Peel was by nature reserved, proud, and shy. He was easily embarrassed, and, at such moments, he grew stiff and formal, while his feet mechanically performed upon the carpet a dancing master's measure. Anxious as he now was to win the Queen's good graces, his very anxiety to do so made the attainment of his object the more difficult. He made no headway whatever with the hostile girl before him. She coldly noted that he appeared to be unhappy and "put out," and, while he stood in painful fixity, with an occasional uneasy pointing of the toe, her heart sank within her at the sight of that manner—"Oh! how different, how dreadfully different, to the frank, open, most kind warm manner of Lord Melbourne."

Nevertheless, the audience passed with only one slight hint of disagreement. Peel had decided that a change would be necessary in the composition of the royal household. The Queen must no longer be entirely surrounded by Whigs, by the wives and sisters of his opponents; some, at any rate, of the ladies of the bedchamber should be friendly to his government. When this matter was touched upon, the Queen intimated that she wished her household to remain unchanged; to which Sir Robert replied that the question could be settled later, and shortly afterwards withdrew to arrange the details of his cabinet.

While he was present, Victoria had remained, as she herself said, "very collected, and betrayed no agitation"; but as soon as she was alone she broke down. Then she wrote Lord Melbourne an account of her wretchedness. Lord Melbourne replied with a very wise letter. He attempted to calm the Queen; and he had nothing but good words for the Tory leaders. As for the question of the ladies of the household, the Queen, he said, should strongly urge what she desired, as it concerned her personally, "but," he added, "if Sir Robert is unable to concede it, it will not do to refuse and to put off the negotiation upon it."

On this point there can be little doubt that Lord Melbourne was right. The question was a complicated one, and it had never arisen before; but subsequent constitutional practice has determined that a queen regnant must accede to the wishes of her prime minister as to the *personnel* of the female part of her household. Lord Melbourne's wisdom, however, was wasted. The Queen would not be soothed. It was outrageous of the Tories to want to deprive her of her ladies. She made up her mind that, whatever Sir Robert might say, she would refuse to consent to the removal of a single one of them.

Accordingly, when, next morning, Peel appeared again, she was ready for action. When he had detailed the cabinet appointments, he added "Now, Ma'am, about the ladies."

"I cannot give up *any* of my ladies," she said.

"What, Ma'am!" said Sir Robert, "does Your Majesty mean to retain them *all?*"

"All," said the Queen.

Sir Robert could not conceal his agitation. In vain he pleaded and argued; in vain he spoke of the constitution, and the public interest. Victoria was adamant; but he, too, through all his embarrassment, showed no sign of yielding; and when at last he left her nothing had been decided—the whole formation of the government was hanging in the wind.

A frenzy of excitement now seized upon Victoria. Sir Robert, she believed, had tried to outwit her, to take her friends from her; but that was not all: she had suddenly perceived the one thing that she was desperately longing for—a loophole of escape. She seized a pen and dashed off a note to Lord Melbourne.

"Sir Robert has behaved very ill," she wrote, "he insisted on my giving up my Ladies, to which I replied that I *never* would consent, and I never saw a man so frightened. . . . I think you would have been pleased to see my composure and firmness; the Queen of England will not submit to such trickery. Keep yourself in readiness, for you may soon be wanted."

Hardly had she finished when the Duke of Wellington was announced. "Well, Ma'am," he said as he entered, "I am very sorry to find there is a difficulty."

"Oh!" she replied, "*he* began it, not me." The venerable conqueror of Napoleon was outfaced by the equanimity of a girl in her teens. At last she even ventured to rally him. "Is Sir Robert so weak," she asked, "that even the Ladies must be of his opinion?" On which the duke made a brief expostulation, bowed low, and departed.

Had she won? Time would show; and in the meantime she scribbled another letter. "Lord Melbourne must not think the Queen rash in her conduct. . . . The Queen felt this was an attempt to see whether she could be led and managed like a child." The Tories were not only wicked but ridiculous.

The end of the crisis was now fast approaching. Sir Robert returned, and told her that if she insisted upon retaining all her ladies he could not form a government. She replied that she would send him her final decision in writing. Next morning the late Whig cabinet met. Lord Melbourne read to them the Queen's letters, and the group of elderly politicians were overcome by an extraordinary wave of enthusiasm. They knew very well it was doubtful whether the Queen had acted in strict accordance with the constitution; but such considerations vanished before Victoria's passionate urgency. The intensity of her determination swept them headlong down the stream of her desire. They unanimously felt that "it was impossible to abandon such a Queen and such a woman."

Forgetting that they were no longer Her Majesty's ministers, they took the unprecedented course of advising the Queen by letter to put an end to her negotiation with Sir Robert Peel. She did so; all was over; she had triumphed. That evening there was a ball at the palace. Everyone was present. "Peel and the Duke of Wellington came by looking very much put out." She was perfectly happy; Lord M. was Prime Minister once more, and he was by her side.

HAPPINESS HAD RETURNED with Lord M., but it was happiness in the midst of agitation. The domestic imbroglio continued unabated, until at last the Duke of Wellington, rejected as a minister, was called in once again in his old capacity as moral physician to the family. Something was accomplished when, at last, he induced Sir John Conroy to resign his place about the Duchess of Kent and leave the palace forever; something more when he persuaded the Queen to write an affectionate letter to her mother.

The way seemed open for a reconciliation, but the duchess was stormy still. She didn't believe that Victoria had written that letter; it was not in her handwriting; and she sent for the duke to tell him so. The duke, assuring her that the letter was genuine, begged her to forget the past.

"But what am I to do if Victoria asks me to shake hands with Lehzen?" the duchess asked.

"Do, ma'am? Why, take her in your arms and kiss her."

"What!" The duchess bristled in every feather.

"No, ma'am, no," said the duke, laughing. "I don't mean you are to take *Lehzen* in your arms and kiss *her*, but the Queen."

The duke might perhaps have succeeded, had not all attempts at conciliation been rendered hopeless by a tragical event. Lady Flora, it was discovered, had been suffering from a terrible internal malady, which now grew rapidly worse. There could be little doubt that she was dying.

The Queen's unpopularity reached an extraordinary height. More than once she was publicly insulted. "Mrs. Melbourne," was shouted at her when she appeared at her balcony; and, at Ascot, she was hissed. Lady Flora died. The whole scandal burst out again with redoubled vehemence; while, in the palace, the two parties were henceforth divided by an impassable, a Stygian, gulf.

Nevertheless, Lord M. was back, and every trouble faded under the enchantment of his presence. He, on his side, was very happy. In spite of the dullness of the court, his relationship with the Queen had come to be the dominating interest in his life; to have been deprived of it had been heartrending; he was installed once more, in a kind of triumph; let him enjoy the fleeting hours to the full! And so, cherished by the favor of a sovereign and warmed by the adoration of a girl, his life, like the autumn rose, came to a wondrous blooming. To watch, to teach, to encourage the royal young creature beside him—that was much; to feel with such a constant intimacy the impact of her quick affection, her radiant vitality—that was more. The springs of his sensibility, hidden deep within him, were overflowing. Often, as he bent over her hand and kissed it, he found himself in tears.

Upon Victoria, with all her impermeability, it was inevitable that such a companionship should have produced, eventually, an effect. She was no longer the simple schoolgirl of two years since. The change was visible even in her public demeanor. Her expression, once "ingenuous and serene," now appeared to a shrewd observer to be "bold and discontented." She had learned something of the pleasures of power and the pains of it. Lord Melbourne with his gentle instruction had sought to lead her into the paths of wisdom and moderation, but the whole unconscious movement of his character had swayed her in a very different direction. Was it possible that the secret impulses of self-expression, of self-indulgence even, were mastering her life? For a moment the child of a new age looked back, and wavered towards the eighteenth century. It was the most critical moment of her career. Had those influences lasted, the development of her character would have been completely changed.

And why should they not last? She, for one, was very anxious that they should. Let them last forever! She was surrounded by Whigs, she had Lord M. Any change would be for the worse;

and the worst change of all . . . no, she would not hear of it; it would be quite intolerable, it would upset everything, if she were to marry.

Everyone seemed to want her to—the general public, the ministers, her Saxe-Coburg relations—it was always the same story. Of course, she knew very well that there were excellent reasons for it. For one thing, if she remained childless, and were to die, her uncle Cumberland, who was now the King of Hanover, would succeed to the throne of England. That, no doubt, would be a most unpleasant event; and she entirely sympathized with everybody who wished to avoid it. But there was no hurry; naturally, she would marry in the end—but not just yet—not for three or four years. What was tiresome was that her uncle Leopold had apparently determined, not only that she ought to marry, but that her cousin Albert ought to be her husband. It was true that long ago, before her accession, she had told him that Albert possessed "every quality that could be desired to render her perfectly happy." But that had been years ago, when she was a mere child; her feelings, and all the circumstances, had now entirely changed; and Albert hardly interested her at all.

In later life the Queen declared that she had never for a moment dreamed of marrying anyone but her cousin; but her letters and diaries tell a different story. On August 26, 1837, she wrote in her journal: "Today is my *dearest* cousin Albert's 18th birthday, and I pray Heaven to pour its choicest blessings on his beloved head!" In subsequent years, however, the date passes unnoticed.

It had been arranged that Stockmar should accompany the Prince to Italy, and the baron left her side for that purpose. He wrote to her with sympathetic descriptions of his young companion; but her mind was by this time made up. She admired Albert very much, but she did not want to marry him. "At present," she told Lord Melbourne in April 1839, "*my* feeling is quite against ever marrying."

When her cousin's Italian tour came to an end, she grew nervous; she knew that, according to a long-standing engagement, his next journey would be to England. He would prob-

ably arrive in the autumn, and by July her uneasiness was intense. She wrote to her uncle to make her position clear; it must be understood, she said, that "there is *no engagement* between us." If she should like Albert, she could "make *no final promise this year*, for, at the *very earliest*, any such event could not take place till *two or three years hence*." To Lord Melbourne she was more explicit. She told him that she "had no great wish to see Albert, as the whole subject was an odious one"; she hated to have to decide about it; and she repeated once again that seeing Albert would be "a disagreeable thing."

But there was no escaping the horrid business; the visit must be made. The summer slipped by and was over; and on the evening of October 10 Albert, accompanied by his brother Ernest, arrived at Windsor.

Albert arrived; and the whole structure of her existence crumbled into nothingness like a house of cards. He was beautiful—she gasped—she knew no more. In a flash, a thousand mysteries were revealed to her; the past, the present, rushed upon her with a new significance; and an extraordinary certitude leaped into being in the light of those blue eyes, the smile of that lovely mouth.

The succeeding hours passed in a rapture. She was able to observe a few more details—the "exquisite nose," the "delicate mustachios and slight whiskers," the "beautiful figure, broad in the shoulder and a fine waist." She rode with him, danced with him, talked with him, and it was all perfection. She had no shadow of a doubt. He had come on a Thursday evening, and on the following Sunday morning she told Lord Melbourne that she had "a good deal changed her opinion as to marrying."

Next morning, she told him that she had made up her mind to marry Albert. The morning after that, she sent for her cousin. "After a few minutes I said to him that I thought he must be aware *why* I wished them to come here—and that it would make me *too happy* if he would consent to what I wished (to marry me)." Then "we embraced each other, and he was *so* kind, *so* affectionate." She said that she was quite unworthy of him, while he murmured that he would be very happy *"Das Leben mit dir zu zubringen,"*—"to spend my life with you."

They parted, and she felt "the happiest of human beings," when Lord M. came in. At first she talked of the weather and indifferent subjects. Somehow or other she felt a little nervous with her old friend. At last, summoning up her courage, she said, "I have got well through this with Albert."

"Oh! you have," said Lord M.

SIR ROBERT PEEL

CHAPTER 4
Marriage

IT WAS DECIDEDLY a family match. Prince Francis Charles Augustus Albert Emmanuel of Saxe-Coburg-Gotha—for such was his full title—had been born just three months after his cousin Victoria, and the same midwife had assisted at the two births. The children's grandmother, the Dowager Duchess of Coburg, had from the first looked forward to their marriage; as they grew up, the Duke of Saxe-Coburg, the Duchess of Kent, and King Leopold came equally to desire it. The Prince, ever since the time when, as a child of three, his nurse had told him that someday "the little English May flower" would be his wife, had never thought of marrying anyone else.

The Duke of Saxe-Coburg had one other child—Prince Ernest, Albert's senior by one year, and heir to the principality. The duchess, Ernest's and Albert's mother, was a sprightly and beautiful woman, with fair hair and blue eyes; Albert was very like her and was her declared favorite. But in his fifth year he was parted from her forever. The ducal court was not noted for the strictness of its morals; the duke was a man of gallantry, and it was rumored that the duchess followed her husband's example. There were scandals; at last there was a separation, followed by a divorce. The duchess retired to Paris, and died unhappily in 1831. Her memory was always very dear to Albert.

He grew up a pretty, clever, and high-spirited boy. Usually well-behaved, he was, however, sometimes violent. He had a will of his own; his elder brother was less passionate, less purposeful, and, in their wrangles, it was Albert who came out top. The two boys lived for the most part in one or another of the duke's country houses, among pretty hills and woods and streams. At a very early age they were put under a tutor, in whose charge they remained until they went to the university. They were brought up in a simple manner, for the duke was poor and the duchy small and insignificant.

Before long it became evident that Albert was a model lad. At the age of eleven he surprised his father by telling him that he hoped to make himself "a good and useful man." And yet he was not overserious, but full of fun—of practical jokes and mimicry. He was no milksop; he rode, shot, and fenced; above all he delighted in being out of doors. Never was he happier than in his long rambles with his brother through the wild country round his beloved Rosenau—stalking the deer, admiring the scenery, and returning laden with specimens for his natural history collection.

He was, besides, passionately fond of music. In one particular it was observed that he did not take after his father: owing either to his peculiar upbringing or to a more fundamental idiosyncrasy he had a marked distaste for the opposite sex. At the age of five, at a children's dance, he screamed with disgust when a little girl was led up to him for a partner; and though, later on, he grew more successful in disguising such feelings, the feelings remained.

The brothers were very popular in Coburg, and when the time came for them to be confirmed, the preliminary examination which, according to ancient custom, was held in public in the "Giants' Hall" of the castle, was attended by an enthusiastic crowd. "The dignified and decorous bearing of the Princes," we are told, "their strict attention to the questions, the frankness, decision, and correctness of their answers, produced a deep impression on the numerous assembly."

Albert's mental development now proceeded apace. In his seventeenth year he began a careful study of German literature and philosophy. Placed for some months under the care of King Leopold at Brussels, he came under the influence of Adolphe Quetelet, a mathematical professor, who was particularly interested in the application of the laws of probability to political and moral phenomena; this line of inquiry attracted the Prince, and the friendship thus begun continued till the end of his life.

From Brussels he went to the University of Bonn, where his energies were absorbed in metaphysics, law, political economy, music, fencing, and amateur theatricals. Thirty years later his fellow students recalled with delight the fits of laughter into which they had been sent by Prince Albert's mimicry.

After a year at Bonn, the time had come for a foreign tour, and Baron Stockmar arrived from England to accompany the Prince on the expedition to Italy. Two years previously, the baron had already been consulted by King Leopold as to his views upon the proposed marriage of Albert and Victoria. With a characteristic foresight, Stockmar had pointed out what were, in his opinion, the conditions essential to make the marriage a success. Albert, he wrote, was a fine young fellow, well grown for his age, with agreeable qualities; and it was probable that in a few years he would turn out a strong, handsome man, kindly, simple, yet dignified. "Thus, externally, he possesses all that pleases the sex." Supposing, therefore, that Victoria herself was in favor of the marriage, the further question arose as to whether Albert's mental qualities were such as to fit him for the position of husband of the Queen of England. On this point the baron preferred to reserve his opinion until he could observe Albert further. He added: "The young man ought to have not merely great ability, but a *right* ambition, and great force of will as well. To pursue for a lifetime a political career so arduous demands more than energy and inclination—it demands also that earnest frame of mind which is ready of its own accord to sacrifice mere pleasure to real usefulness."

Such were the views of Stockmar on the qualifications necessary for Victoria's husband; and he hoped, during the tour in Italy, to come to some conclusion as to how far the Prince possessed them. Albert on his side was much impressed by the baron, whom he had previously seen but rarely; he also became acquainted with a young Englishman, Lieutenant Francis Seymour, who had been engaged to accompany him, and with whom he struck up a warm friendship. He delighted in the galleries and scenery of Florence, though with Rome he was less impressed. "But for some beautiful palaces," he said, "it might just as well be any town in Germany."

On his return to Germany, Stockmar's observations, imparted to King Leopold, were still critical. Albert, he said, was intelligent, amiable, and full of the best intentions. But great exertion was repugnant to him; his good resolutions too often came to nothing. It was particularly unfortunate that he took not the slightest interest in politics, and never read a newspaper. In his manners, too, there was still room for improvement. "He will always," said the baron, "have more success with men than with women, in whose society he is too indifferent and retiring." One other feature of the case was noted by the keen eye of the old physician: the Prince's constitution was not a strong one.

On the whole, however, Stockmar was favorable to the projected marriage. But by now the chief obstacle seemed to lie in another quarter. Victoria was apparently determined to commit herself to nothing. And so it happened that when Albert went to England he himself had made up his mind to withdraw from the affair. Nothing would induce him, he confessed to a friend, to be kept vaguely waiting; he would break it all off at once. His reception at Windsor threw an entirely new light upon the situation. The wheel of fortune turned with a sudden rapidity; and he found, in the arms of Victoria, the irrevocable assurance of his overwhelming fate.

HE WAS NOT in love with her. Affection, gratitude, the natural reactions to the unqualified devotion of a lively young cousin who was also a queen—such feelings possessed him, but the ardors of passion were not his. Though he found that he liked Victoria very much, what immediately interested him in his curious position was less her than himself.

Dazzled and delighted, riding, dancing, laughing, amid the splendors of Windsor, he was aware of a new sensation—the stirrings of ambition in his breast. His place would indeed be a high, an enviable one! And then, on the instant, came another thought. The teaching of religion, the admonitions of Stockmar, his own inmost convictions, all spoke with the same utterance. He would not be there to please himself, but for a very different purpose—to do good. He must be "noble, manly, and princely in all things," he would have "to live and to sacrifice himself for the benefit of his new country."

One serious thought led on to another; after all, it was Coburg that had his heart. "While I shall be untiring," he wrote to his grandmother, "in my efforts and labors for the country to which I shall in future belong, I shall never cease *ein treuer Deutscher, Coburger, zu sein*"—"to be a true Coburg German." And now he must part from Coburg forever! Sobered and sad, he sought his brother Ernest's company; and the two young men, sitting down at the piano, would escape from the present and the future into the sweet gaiety of a Haydn duet.

They returned to Germany; and while Albert, for a few farewell months, enjoyed the happiness of home, Victoria, for the last time, resumed her old life in London and Windsor. She corresponded daily with her future husband in a mingled flow of German and English; but the accustomed routine reasserted itself; Lord M. was once more constantly beside her; and the Tories were as intolerable as ever. Indeed, they were more so. For now, in these final moments, the old feud burst out with redoubled fury.

The impetuous sovereign found, to her chagrin, that there might be disadvantages in being the enemy of one of the great parties in the state. On two occasions the Tories directly thwarted her. She wished her husband's rank to be fixed by statute, and their opposition prevented it. She wished her husband to receive a settlement from the nation of £50,000 a year; and, again owing to the Tories, who pointed out that the bulk of the population was suffering from great poverty, he was only allowed £30,000. Angrily she determined to revenge herself by omitting to invite a single Tory to her wedding. Even the Duke of Wellington she nearly refused to ask. "That old rebel! I won't have him," she was reported to have said; but eventually she was induced to send him an invitation.

Nor was it only against the Tories that her irritation rose. As the time for her wedding approached, her temper grew steadily sharper. Queen Adelaide annoyed her. King Leopold, too, was "ungracious" in his correspondence. Even Albert himself was not impeccable; he failed to appreciate the complexity of English affairs; he wanted to appoint his own private secretary. But obviously Lord M. was best qualified to make the appointment; and Lord M. had decided that the Prince should have George Anson. Albert protested, but Victoria simply announced that Anson was appointed.

And on one other matter she was insistent. Since the affair of Lady Flora Hastings, a sad fate had overtaken Sir James Clark; his practice had quite collapsed. But the Queen remained faithful, and she desired Albert to make "poor Clark" his physician in ordinary. He did as he was told; but, as it turned out, the appointment was not a happy one.

The wedding day was fixed, and it was time for Albert to tear himself away from the scenes of his childhood. With an aching heart, he revisited his beloved woods and valleys; in deep depression, he sat through farewell banquets; and then it was time to go. The streets were packed as he drove through them; for a short space his eyes were gladdened by a sea of friendly German faces. At Calais a steamboat awaited him, and, together with his father and his brother, he stepped, dejected, on board. A little later, he was more dejected still. The crossing was very rough; the duke went hurriedly below; while the two princes, we are told, lay on either side of the cabin staircase "in an almost helpless state." At Dover a large crowd was collected on the pier, and "it was by no common effort that Prince Albert, who had continued to suffer up to the last moment, got up to bow to the people." His sense of duty triumphed. It was a curious omen: his whole life in England was foreshadowed as he landed on English ground.

Meanwhile Victoria, in growing agitation, was a prey to temper and to nerves. She grew feverish, and Sir James Clark pronounced that she was going to have the measles. But, once again, Sir James's diagnosis was incorrect. Not measles but a different malady was attacking her; she was suddenly prostrated by alarm and doubt. For two years she had been her own mistress—the two happiest years of her life. And now it was all to end! She was to come under an alien domination—she would have to promise that she would honor and obey . . . someone, who might, after all, oppose her! Why had she embarked on this experiment? No doubt, she loved Albert; but she loved power too.

He reappeared, in an exquisite uniform, and her hesitations melted in his presence like mist before the sun. On February 10, 1840, the marriage took place, and the wedded pair drove down to Windsor, but they were not, of course, entirely alone. They were accompanied by their suites, and, in particular, by two persons—the Baron Stockmar and the Baroness Lehzen.

ALBERT HAD FORESEEN that his married life would not be all plain sailing; but he had by no means realized the gravity and the complication of the difficulties which he would have to face. Politically, he was a cipher. Lord Melbourne was not only Prime Minister, he was in effect the private secretary of the Queen, and thus controlled the whole of the political existence of the sovereign. A queen's husband was an entity unknown to the British constitution. In state affairs there seemed to be no place for him; nor was Victoria herself at all unwilling that this should be so. He would, she hoped, make a perfect husband; but, as for governing the country, he would see that she and Lord Melbourne could manage that very well, without his help.

But it was not only in politics that the Prince discovered that the part cut out for him was a negligible one. Even as a husband, he found, his functions were to be extremely limited. Over the whole of Victoria's private life the Baroness Lehzen reigned supreme; and she had not the slightest intention of allowing that supremacy to be diminished by one iota.

Since the accession, her power had greatly increased. Besides the enormous influence which she exercised through her management of the Queen's private correspondence, she was now the superintendent of the royal establishment and controlled the important office of Privy Purse. Albert very soon perceived that he was not master in his own house. Every detail of his own and his wife's existence was supervised by a third person: nothing could be done until the consent of Lehzen had first been obtained. And Victoria, who adored Lehzen, saw nothing in all this that was wrong.

Nor was the Prince happier in his social surroundings. A shy young foreigner, awkward in ladies' company, it was improbable that, in any circumstances, he would have been a society success. His appearance, too, was against him. Though in the eyes of Victoria he was the mirror of manly beauty, her subjects, whose eyes were of a less Teutonic cast, did not agree with her. To them what was distressingly striking in Albert's face and whole demeanor was his un-English look. His features were regular, no doubt, but there was something smooth and smug about them; he was tall, but he was clumsily put together. Really, they thought, this youth was more like some kind of foreign tenor than anything else.

These were serious disadvantages; but the line of conduct which the Prince adopted from the moment of his arrival was far from calculated to dispel them. Owing partly to a natural awkwardness, and partly to a desire to be absolutely correct, his manners were infused with an extraordinary stiffness and formality. Whenever he appeared in company, he seemed to be surrounded by a thick hedge of prickly etiquette. He never went out into ordinary society; he never walked in the streets of London; he was invariably accompanied by an equerry when he rode or drove. He wanted to be irreproachable and, if that involved friendlessness, it could not be helped. Besides, he had no very high opinion of the English; so far as he could see, they cared for nothing but fox hunting and Sunday observances. Since it was clear that with such people he could have very little in common, there was no reason whatever for relaxing in their favor the rules of etiquette. In strict privacy, he could be natural and charming; but from the support and solace of true companionship he was utterly cut off.

A friend, indeed, he had—or rather, a mentor. The baron, established once more in the royal residence, was determined to work with as wholehearted a detachment for the Prince's benefit as, more than twenty years before, he had worked for his uncle's. Albert of course was no Leopold. He had none of his uncle's ambition to be personally great; he took no interest in politics, and there were no signs that he possessed any force of character. Left to himself, he would almost certainly have subsided into a high-minded nonentity, a dilettante busy over culture, a palace appendage without influence or power. But he was not left to himself. Forever at his pupil's elbow, Stockmar pushed him forward, with tireless pressure, along the path which had been trod by Leopold so many years ago. But, this time, the goal at the end of it was something more than the mediocre royalty that Leopold had reached. The prize which Stockmar, with his disinterested devotion, had determined should be Albert's was a tremendous prize indeed.

The beginning of the undertaking proved to be the most arduous part. Albert was easily dispirited: what was the use of struggling to perform in a role which bored him and which, it was clear, nobody but the good baron had any desire that he should take up? It was simpler to let things slide. But Stockmar would not have it. Incessantly, he harped upon two strings—Albert's sense of duty and his personal pride. Had the Prince forgotten the noble aims to which his life was to be devoted? And was he going to allow himself, his wife, his family, his whole existence, to be governed by Baroness Lehzen?

The latter consideration was a potent one. Albert was constantly exasperated by the position of the baroness in the royal household. He was, he knew very well, his wife's intellectual superior, and yet he found, to his intense annoyance, that there were parts of her mind over which he exercised no influence. When, urged on by the baron, he attempted to discuss politics with Victoria, she drifted into generalities, and then began to talk of something else. When at last he protested, she replied that her conduct was merely the result of indolence; that when she was with *him* she could not bear to bother her head with anything so dull as politics. The excuse was worse than the fault: was he the wife and she the husband? The baron declared that the root of the mischief was Lehzen: that it was she who encouraged the Queen to have secrets; who did worse—induced her to give false reasons to explain away her conduct.

Minor disagreements made matters worse. The royal couple differed in their tastes. Albert, brought up in a regime of Spartan simplicity and early hours, found court functions intolerably wearisome, and was invariably observed to be nodding on the sofa at half past ten; while the Queen's favorite form of enjoyment was to dance through the night and then to watch the sun rise behind Saint Paul's. She loved London and he detested it. Only in Windsor did he feel he could really breathe; but Windsor too had its terrors: though during the day there he could paint and walk and play on the piano, after dinner black tedium descended like a pall. He would have liked to summon distinguished scientific and literary men to his presence; but unfortunately Victoria "had no fancy to encourage such people"; knowing that she was unequal to taking a part in their conversation, she insisted that the evening routine should remain unaltered; the regulation interchange of platitudes with official persons was followed as usual by the round table and the books of engravings, while the Prince, with one of his attendants, played game after game of double chess.

It was only natural that in such a situation there should have been occasionally something more than mere irritation—a struggle of angry wills. No more than Albert was Victoria in the habit of playing second fiddle. But she fought at a disadvantage; she was, in truth, no longer her own mistress; a profound preoccupation dominated her, seizing upon her inmost purposes for its own extraordinary ends. She was madly in love.

The details of their battles are unknown to us; but Prince Ernest, who remained in England with his brother for some months, noted them with a friendly and startled eye. One story, indeed, survives, ill authenticated, yet summing up, as such stories often do, the central facts of the case. When, in wrath, the Prince one day had locked himself into his room, Victoria, no less furious, knocked on the door to be admitted. "Who is there?" he asked. "The Queen of England" was the answer.

He did not move, and again there was a hail of knocks. The question and the answer were repeated many times; but at last there was a pause, and then a gentler knocking. "Who is there?" came once more the relentless question. But this time the reply was different. "Your wife, Albert." And the door was immediately opened.

Very gradually the Prince's position changed. He began to find the study of politics more interesting than he had supposed; he read Blackstone, and took lessons in English law; he was occasionally present when the Queen interviewed her ministers; and he was shown dispatches relating to foreign affairs. Sometimes he would commit his views to paper, and read them aloud to the Prime Minister. An important step was taken when, before the birth of the Princess Royal, the Prince, without any opposition in Parliament, was appointed Regent in case of the death of the Queen.

Stockmar had intervened with the Tories to bring about this happy result; now he felt himself at liberty to take a holiday with his family in Coburg; but through innumerable letters he still watched over his pupil. "Dear Prince," he wrote, "I am satisfied with the news you have sent me. Mistakes, misunderstandings, obstructions, coming in vexatious opposition to one's views, are always to be taken for just what they are—namely, natural phenomena of life, which represent one of its sides, and that the shady one. In overcoming them with dignity, your mind has to exercise, to train, to enlighten itself." The Prince had done well so far; but he must continue in the right path; above all, he was "never to relax."—"Never to relax in keeping yourself up to a high standard—in the determination, daily renewed, to be consistent, patient, courageous." It was a hard program, perhaps, for a young man of twenty-one; and yet something in it touched the depths of Albert's soul; he sighed, but he listened.

Before long, the decisive moment came. There was a general election, and it became certain that the Tories, at last, must come into power. The Queen disliked them as much as ever; but they now had a large majority in the House of Commons. They would now be in a position to insist upon their wishes being attended to. Lord Melbourne himself was the first to realize the importance of carrying out the inevitable transition with as little friction as possible; and with his consent, the Prince opened a negotiation with Sir Robert Peel. In a series of secret interviews, a complete understanding was reached upon the difficult and complex question of the bedchamber; and it was agreed that, on the formation of the Tory government, the principal Whig ladies should retire, and their places be filled by others appointed by Sir Robert. Thus, in effect, though not in form, the Crown abandoned the claims of 1839, and they have never been subsequently put forward.

The transaction was a turning point in the Prince's career. He had conducted an important negotiation with skill and tact; he had been brought into friendly relations with the new Prime Minister; it was obvious that a political future lay before him. Victoria was impressed and grateful. "My dearest Angel," she told King Leopold, "is indeed a great comfort to me." She was in need of all the comfort he could give her. Lord M. was going; and she could hardly bring herself to speak to Peel. Yes; she would discuss everything with Albert now!

Stockmar, who had returned to England, watched the departure of Lord Melbourne with satisfaction. If all went well, the Prince should now wield a supreme political influence over Victoria. But would all go well? An unexpected development frightened the baron. When the dreadful moment finally came, and the Queen, in anguish, bade adieu to her beloved minister, it was settled between them that, though it would be inadvisable to meet very often, they could continue to correspond.

Never were the inconsistencies of Lord Melbourne's character shown more clearly than in what followed. So long as he was in office, his attitude towards Peel had been irreproachable; he had done all he could to facilitate the change of government. Yet no sooner was he in opposition than his heart failed him. He could not bear the thought of surrendering altogether the privilege and the pleasure of giving counsel to Victoria. Though he had declared that he would be perfectly discreet in his letters, he could not resist taking advantage of the opening they afforded. He discussed various public questions, and, in particular, gave the Queen a great deal of advice about appointments. This advice was followed.

Stockmar was much alarmed. He wrote a memorandum, pointing out the unconstitutional nature of Lord Melbourne's proceedings and the unpleasant position in which the Queen might find herself if they were discovered by Peel; and he instructed Anson, the Prince's secretary, to take this memorandum to the ex-minister. Lord Melbourne, lounging on a sofa, read it through with compressed lips. "This is quite an apple-pie opinion," he said. When Anson ventured to expostulate further, he lost his temper. "God eternally damn it!" he exclaimed, leaping up from his sofa. "Flesh and blood cannot stand this!" And two more violent bombardments from the baron were needed before he was brought to reason. Then, gradually, his letters grew less frequent, with fewer references to public concerns; at last, they were entirely innocuous. The baron smiled; Lord M. had accepted the inevitable.

The Whig ministry resigned in September 1841; but more than a year was to elapse before another momentous change was effected—the removal of Lehzen. For, in the end, the mysterious governess was conquered.

The steps are unknown by which Victoria was at last led to accept her withdrawal with composure; but it is clear that Albert's domestic position must have been greatly strengthened by the appearance of children. The birth of the Princess Royal had been followed in November 1841 by that of the Prince of Wales; and before very long another baby was expected. The baroness, with all her affection, could have but a remote share in such family delights. She lost ground perceptibly. It was noticed as a phenomenon that, once or twice, when the court traveled, she was left behind at Windsor.

Still the Prince was cautious; but time was for him; every day his predominance grew; and at length he perceived that he need hesitate no longer—that every wish of his had only to be expressed to be at once Victoria's. He spoke, and Lehzen vanished forever. Returning to her native Hanover she established herself in a small but comfortable house, the walls of which were entirely covered by portraits of Her Majesty. The baron, in spite of his dyspepsia, smiled again: Albert was supreme.

THE EARLY DISCORDS had passed away completely—resolved into the absolute harmony of married life. Victoria had surrendered her whole soul to her husband. The beauty and the charm which so suddenly had made her his at first were, she now saw, no more than the outward manifestation of the true Albert. There was an inward beauty, an inward glory which, blind that she was, she had then but dimly apprehended, of which now she was aware in every fiber of her being—he was good—he was great!

How could she ever have dreamed of setting up her will against his wisdom, her fancies against his perfect taste? Had she really loved London and late hours and dissipation? She who now was only happy in the country, she who jumped out of bed every morning—oh, so early!—with Albert, to take a walk, before breakfast, with Albert alone! How wonderful it was to be taught by him! To be told by him which trees were which; and to learn all about the bees! And then to sit doing cross-stitch while he read aloud to her Hallam's *Constitutional History of England*! Or to listen to him playing on his new organ! And, after dinner, too—oh, how good of him! He had given up his double chess! And so there could be round games at the round table, or everyone could spend the evening in the most amusing way imaginable—spinning counters and rings.

When the babies came it was still more wonderful. Pussy was such a clever little girl ("I am not Pussy! I am the Princess Royal!" she had angrily exclaimed on one occasion); and Bertie—well, she could only pray *most* fervently that the little Prince of Wales would grow up to "resemble his angelic dearest Father in *every*, *every* respect, both in body and mind." Her dear Mamma, too, had been drawn once more into the family circle, for Albert had brought about a reconciliation. In Victoria's eyes, life had become an idyll of happiness, love and simplicity. "Albert brought in dearest little Pussy," wrote Her Majesty in her journal, "in such a smart white merino dress trimmed with blue, which Mamma had given her, and a pretty cap, and placed her on my bed, seating himself next to her, and she was very dear and good. And, as my precious, invaluable Albert sat there, and our little Love between us, I felt quite moved with happiness and gratitude to God."

Happy as she was, she wanted everyone to know it. Her letters to King Leopold are sprinkled thick with raptures. "Oh! my dearest uncle, I am sure if you knew *how* happy, how blessed I feel, and how *proud* I feel in possessing *such* a perfect being as my husband. . . ." Such ecstasies gushed from her pen unceasingly.

But this new happiness was no lotus dream. On the contrary, it was bracing, rather than relaxing. She worked more methodically than ever at the business of state; she watched over her children with untiring vigilance. She carried on a large correspondence; she was occupied with her farm—her dairy—a multitude of household avocations—from morning till night. Her active, eager little body hurrying with quick steps after the long strides of Albert down the corridors of Windsor seemed the very expression of her spirit. But amid all the softness, the deliciousness of unmixed joy, her native rigidity remained. "A vein of iron," said Lady Lyttelton, who, as royal governess, had good means of observation, "runs through her most extraordinary character."

Sometimes the delightful routine of domestic existence had to be interrupted. It was necessary to exchange Windsor for Buckingham Palace, to open Parliament, to interview official personages, or, occasionally, to entertain foreign visitors. Then the quiet court put on a sudden magnificence, and sovereigns from over the seas—Louis Philippe, or the King of Prussia, or the King of Saxony—found at Windsor an entertainment that was indeed a royal one. Few spectacles in Europe, it was agreed, produced an effect so imposing as the great Waterloo banqueting hall, crowded with guests in sparkling diamonds and blazing uniforms. But, in that wealth of splendor, the most imposing spectacle of all was the Queen. The little *hausfrau*, who had spent the day walking with her children and inspecting the livestock, suddenly shone forth, by a spontaneous transition, the very culmination of majesty. The Tsar of Russia himself was deeply impressed. Victoria on her side viewed with secret awe the tremendous Nicholas. "A great event and a great compliment *his* visit certainly is," she told her uncle. "He is certainly a *very striking* man; still very handsome. But the expression of the *eyes* is *formidable*, and unlike anything I ever saw before."

When the time came for returning some of these visits, the royal pair set forth in their yacht. "I do love a ship!" Victoria exclaimed, running up and down ladders and cracking jokes with the sailors. She and Prince Albert visited Louis Philippe at the Château d'Eu and they visited King Leopold in Brussels.

Another year, Germany was visited, and Albert displayed the beauties of his home. When Victoria crossed the frontier, she was much excited—and astonished as well. "To hear the people speak German," she noted in her diary, "and to see the German soldiers, etc., seemed to me so singular." Having recovered from this slight shock, she found the country charming. She was feted everywhere, and pretty groups of peasant children presented her with bunches of flowers. The principality of Coburg with its romantic scenery particularly delighted her; and when she woke up one morning to find herself in "dear Rosenau, my Albert's birthplace," it was "like a beautiful dream."

THE HUSBAND was not so happy as the wife. In spite of the great improvement in his situation, in spite of a growing family and the adoration of Victoria, Albert was still a stranger in a strange land, and the serenity of spiritual satisfaction was denied him.

It was something, no doubt, to have dominated his immediate environment; but it was not enough. Victoria idolized him; but it was understanding that he craved for, not idolatry; and how much did Victoria, filled to the brim though she was with him, understand him? How much does the bucket understand the well? He was lonely. He went to his organ and improvised with modulations until the sounds, swelling and subsiding, brought some solace to his heart. Then, with the elasticity of youth, he hurried off to play with the babies, or to design a new pigsty, or to read aloud the *Church History of Scotland* to Victoria, or to pirouette before her on one toe, like a ballet dancer, with a fixed smile, to show her how she ought to behave when she appeared in public places. Thus did he amuse himself; but there was one distraction in which he did not indulge. He never flirted—no, not with the prettiest ladies of the court. Throughout their married life no rival female charms ever had cause to give Victoria one moment's pang of jealousy.

What more and more absorbed him—bringing with it a comfort of its own—was his work. With the advent of Peel, he began to intervene actively in the affairs of the state. In more ways than one—in the cast of their intelligence, in their moral earnestness—the two men resembled each other; there was a sympathy between them; and thus Peel was ready enough to urge the Prince forward into public life.

A royal commission was about to be formed to inquire whether advantage might not be taken of the rebuilding of the Houses of Parliament to encourage the fine arts in the United Kingdom; and Peel, with great perspicacity, asked the Prince to preside over it. The work was of a kind which precisely suited Albert: his love of art, his love of method—it satisfied them both; and he threw himself into it *con amore*. Some of the members of the commission were somewhat alarmed when, in his opening speech, he pointed out the necessity of dividing the subjects to be considered into "categories"—the word, they thought, smacked dangerously of German metaphysics; but their confidence returned when they observed His Royal Highness's extraordinary technical acquaintance with the processes of fresco painting. When the question arose as to whether the decorations upon the walls of the new buildings should, or should not, have a moral purpose, the Prince spoke strongly for the affirmative, and the commission was convinced. The frescoes were carried out, but unfortunately before very long they became totally invisible. It seems that His Royal Highness's technical acquaintance with the processes of fresco painting was incomplete.

The next task upon which the Prince embarked was a more arduous one: he determined to reform the organization of the royal household. This reform had been long overdue. For years past the confusion and extravagance in the royal residences, and in Buckingham Palace particularly, had been scandalous; no reform had been practicable under the rule of the baroness; but her functions had now devolved upon the Prince, and in 1844, he boldly attacked the problem.

Three years earlier, Stockmar, after careful inquiry, had revealed in a memorandum an extraordinary state of affairs. The control of the household, it appeared, was divided in the strangest manner between a number of authorities, each independent of the other. Of these authorities, the most prominent

were the lord steward and the lord chamberlain—noblemen of political importance, who changed office with every administration. The distribution of their respective functions was uncertain and peculiar. In Buckingham Palace, it was believed that the lord chamberlain had charge of the whole of the rooms, with the exception of the kitchen, sculleries, and pantries, which were claimed by the lord steward. At the same time, the outside of the palace was under the control of neither of these functionaries—but of the Office of Woods and Forests; and thus, while the insides of the windows were cleaned by the department of the lord chamberlain—or possibly, in certain cases, by the department of the lord steward—the Office of Woods and Forests cleaned their outsides.

Of the servants, the housekeepers, pages, and housemaids were under the authority of the lord chamberlain; the cooks and porters were under that of the lord steward; but the footmen and underbutlers took their orders from yet another official—the master of the horse. Naturally, in these circumstances the service was extremely defective. The Queen once observed that there was never a fire in the dining room. She inquired why. The answer was, "The lord steward lays the fire, and the lord chamberlain lights it"; the underlings of those two great noblemen having failed to come to an accommodation, there was no help for it—the Queen must eat in the cold. As for Her Majesty's guests, there was nobody to show them to their rooms, and they were often left to wander helpless by the hour in the palace's complicated passages.

A surprising incident opened everyone's eyes to the confusion and negligence that reigned in the palace. A fortnight after the birth of the Princess Royal the nurse heard a suspicious noise in the room next to the Queen's bedroom. She called to one of the pages, who, looking under a large sofa, perceived there a crouching figure "with a most repulsive appearance." It was "the boy Jones." This enigmatical personage, whose escapades dominated the newspapers for several ensuing months, was an undersized lad of seventeen, the son of a tailor, who had apparently gained admittance to the palace by climbing over the garden wall. He declared that he had spent three days in the palace, hiding under various beds, that he had "helped himself to soup and other eatables," and that he had "sat upon the throne, seen the Queen, and heard the Princess Royal squall." His motives remained ambiguous, and he was sent for three months to the House of Correction. When he emerged, he immediately returned to Buckingham Palace. He was discovered, and sent back to the House of Correction for another three months. When he was found yet once again loitering round the palace, the authorities shipped him off to sea. So he passes at last out of history.

But discomfort and alarm were not the only results of the mismanagement of the household; the waste and extravagance that also flowed from it were immeasurable. There were preposterous malpractices of every kind. It was, for instance, an ancient rule that a candle that had once been lighted should never be lighted again; what happened to the old candles, nobody knew. Again, the Prince, examining accounts, was puzzled by a weekly expenditure of thirty-five shillings on "Red Room Wine."

Inquiring into the matter, he discovered that in the time of George III a room in Windsor Castle with red hangings had been used as a guardroom, and that five shillings a day had been allowed to provide wine for the officers. The guard had long since been moved elsewhere, but the payment for wine continued, the money being received by a half-pay officer who held the position of underbutler.

After much laborious investigation, and a stiff struggle with a multitude of vested interests, the Prince succeeded in effecting a complete reform. The various conflicting authorities were induced to resign their powers into the hands of a single official, the master of the household; great economies were made, and the whole crowd of venerable abuses was swept away. There were outcries and complaints; but the Prince held on his course, and before long the admirable administration of the royal household was recognized as a convincing proof of his perseverance and capacity.

At the same time his activity was increasing enormously in a more important sphere. He had become the Queen's private secretary, her confidential adviser, her second self. He was now always present at her interviews with ministers. He took, like the Queen, a special interest in foreign policy; but there was no public question in which his influence was not felt. Nobody anymore could call him a dilettante; he was a worker, a public personage. Stockmar noted the change with exultation. "The Prince," he wrote, "has improved very much lately. His mental activity is constantly on the increase, and he gives the greater part of his time to business, without complaining. . . . The relations between husband and wife," he added, "are all one could desire."

Long before Peel's ministry came to an end, there had been a complete change in Victoria's attitude towards him. Peel's appreciation of the Prince had softened her heart; she spoke now of "our worthy Peel," for whom, she said, she had "an *extreme* admiration"; and she dreaded his removal from office almost as frantically as she had once dreaded that of Lord M. It would be, she declared, a *great calamity*.

Six years before, what would she have said if a prophet had told her that the day would come when she would be horrified by the triumph of the Whigs? Yet there was no escaping it; she had to face the return of her old friends. In the ministerial crises of 1845 and 1846, the Prince played a dominating part. Everybody recognized that he was the real center of the negotiations—the actual controller of the forces and the functions of the Crown. The process by which this result was reached had been so gradual as to be almost imperceptible; but it may be said with certainty that, by the close of Peel's administration, Albert had become, in effect, the King of England.

WITH THE FINAL emergence of the Prince came the final extinction of Lord Melbourne. A year after his loss of office, he had been struck down by a paralytic seizure; he had apparently recovered, but his old elasticity had gone forever. Moody, restless, and unhappy, he wandered like a ghost about the town, bursting into soliloquies in public places, or suddenly asking odd questions. "I'll be hanged if I'll do it for you, my lord," he was heard to say in the hall at Brooks's, standing by himself, and addressing the air. Sitting at home, brooding in miserable solitude, he turned to his books—his classics and his Testaments—but they brought him no comfort. He longed for the past, for the impossible, for he knew not what; his friends had left him, and no wonder, he said in bitterness—the fire was out. His correspondence with the Queen continued, and he appeared from time to time at court; but he was a mere simulacrum of his former self; "the dream," wrote Victoria, "is *past*." She was kind to him, writing him long letters, and always remembering his birthday; but it was kindness at a distance, and he knew it. He had become "poor Lord Melbourne." The Whigs ignored him now and the leadership of the party passed to Lord John Russell. When Lord John became Prime Minister, there was much politeness, but Lord Melbourne was not asked to join the cabinet; and he understood, at last, that that was the end.

For two years or more he lingered, sinking slowly into unconsciousness and imbecility. A few days before his death, Victoria, learning that there was no hope of his recovery, turned her mind for a little towards him. "You will grieve to hear," she told King Leopold, "that our good, dear, old friend Melbourne is dying. . . . One cannot forget how good and kind he was, and it brings back so many recollections to my mind, though God knows! I never wish that time back again."

She was in little danger. The tide of circumstance was flowing now with irresistible fullness towards a very different consummation. The seriousness of Albert, the claims of her children, the movement of the whole surrounding world, combined to urge her forward along the way of public and domestic duty. Her family steadily increased. Within eighteen months of the birth of the Prince of Wales the Princess Alice appeared, and a year later the Prince Alfred, and then the Princess Helena, and, two years afterwards, the Princess Louise; and still there were signs that the pretty row of royal infants was not complete.

The parents, more and more involved in family cares and family happiness, found the pomp of Windsor galling, and longing for some more intimate retreat, they purchased the estate of Osborne, in the Isle of Wight. Their skill and economy in financial matters had enabled them to lay aside a substantial sum of money; and they could afford not merely to buy the property but to build a new house for themselves and to furnish it at a cost of £200,000.

At Osborne, by the seashore, and among the woods which Albert had carefully planted, the royal family now spent every hour that could be snatched from Windsor and London. The public looked on with approval. A few aristocrats might sniff or titter; but with the nation at large the Queen was once more extremely popular. The middle classes in particular were pleased. They liked a love match; they liked a household which combined royalty and virtue, and in which they seemed to see, reflected as in some resplendent looking glass, the ideal image of the very lives they led themselves.

It was indeed a model court. Not only were its central personages the patterns of propriety, but no breath of scandal, no shadow of indecorum, might approach it. For Victoria, with all the zeal of a convert, upheld now the standard of moral purity with an inflexibility surpassing, if that were possible, Albert's own. She had become the embodiment, the living apex of a new era in the generations of mankind. The last vestige of the eighteenth century had disappeared; cynicism and subtlety were shriveled into powder; and duty, industry, morality, and domesticity triumphed. The Victorian Age was in full swing.

ONLY ONE THING more was needed: material expression must be given to the new ideals and the new forces so that they might stand revealed, in visible glory, before the eyes of an astonished world. It was for Albert to supply this want. He mused, and was inspired: the Great Exhibition came into his head.

He thought out the details of his conception with care. There had been exhibitions before in the world, but this should surpass them all. It should contain specimens of what every country could produce in raw materials, in machinery and mechanical inventions, and in the applied and plastic arts. It should not be merely useful and ornamental; it should also be an international monument to peace, progress, and prosperity. Having matured his plans, the Prince summoned a small committee and laid an outline of his scheme before it. The committee approved, and the great undertaking was set on foot without delay.

Two years, however, passed before it was completed. The Prince labored with extraordinary energy, and at first all went smoothly. The leading manufacturers warmly took up the idea; the colonies were sympathetic; the great foreign nations were eager to send in their contributions; the support of Sir Robert Peel was obtained, and the use of a site in Hyde Park was sanctioned by the government. Out of 234 plans for the exhibition building, the Prince chose that of Joseph Paxton, famous as a designer of conservatories; and the work was on the point of being put in hand when suddenly opposition to the scheme, which had long been smoldering, burst forth.

There was an outcry, headed by *The Times*, against the use of the park for the exhibition; but, after a fierce debate in the House, the supporters of the site in the park won the day. Then it appeared that the project lacked sufficient financial backing; but this obstacle, too, was surmounted, and eventually £200,000 was subscribed as a guarantee fund. The enormous glass edifice rose higher and higher, covering acres and enclosing towering elm trees beneath its roof: and then the fury of its enemies reached a climax. It was pointed out that the exhibition would serve as a rallying point for all the ruffians in England; and that on the day of its opening there would certainly be a riot and probably a revolution. It was asserted that the glass roof was porous, and the droppings of fifty million sparrows would utterly destroy every object beneath it. Agitated nonconformists declared that the exhibition was an arrogant enterprise which would infallibly bring down God's punishment.

The Prince, with unyielding perseverance and infinite patience, pressed on to his goal. His health was seriously affected; he suffered from sleeplessness but he never relaxed. He toiled at committees, presided over meetings, and made speeches—and his efforts were rewarded. On May 1, 1851, the Great Exhibition was opened by the Queen before an enormous concourse of persons, amid scenes of dazzling brilliancy and triumphant enthusiasm.

Victoria herself was in a state of excitement which bordered on delirium. She performed her duties in a trance of joy, and, when it was all over, her feelings poured themselves out into her journal. The day had been an endless succession of glories—or rather one vast glory—one vast radiation of Albert. Her remembering pen rushed on from splendor to splendor—the huge crowds, so well behaved and loyal—flags of all the nations floating—the inside of the building, so immense, with myriads of people and the sun shining through the roof—a little side room, where we left our shawls—palm trees and machinery—dear Albert—the place so big that we could hardly hear the organ—a curious assemblage of distinguished men—God bless my dearest Albert, God bless my dearest country!—a glass fountain—Mr. Paxton, who might be justly proud, and rose from being a common gardener's boy—Sir George Grey in tears, and everybody astonished and delighted.

A striking incident occurred when, after a short prayer by the Archbishop of Canterbury, the choir of six hundred voices burst into the Hallelujah Chorus. At that moment a Chinaman, dressed in full national costume, stepped out into the nave and did obeisance to Her Majesty. The Queen, much impressed, had no doubt that he was an eminent mandarin; and, when the final procession was formed, orders were given that, as no representative of the Celestial Empire was present, he should be included in the diplomatic cortege. He subsequently disappeared, and it was rumored, among ill-natured people, that, far from being a mandarin, the fellow was a mere impostor. But nobody ever really discovered the nature of the comments that had been lurking behind that impassive yellow face.

A few days later Victoria poured out her heart to her uncle. The first of May, she said, was "the *greatest* day in our history, the most *beautiful* and *imposing* spectacle ever seen, and the triumph of my beloved Albert. . . . The triumph is *immense*."

It was. The enthusiasm was universal; even the bitterest scoffers were converted, and joined in the chorus of praise. The financial results were equally remarkable. The total profit made by the exhibition amounted to £165,000, which was employed in the purchase of land for the erection of a permanent national museum in South Kensington. During the six months of its existence in Hyde Park over six million persons visited it.

But there is an end to all things; and the time came for the

Crystal Palace to be removed to the seclusion of Sydenham. Victoria sadly paid her final visit. "It looked so beautiful," she said. "I could not believe it was the last time I was to see it. An organ, accompanied by a fine wind instrument called the sommerophone, was being played, and it nearly upset me."

When all was over, she expressed her boundless satisfaction in a dithyrambic letter to the Prime Minister. Her beloved husband's name, she said, was forever immortalized, and this to her was a source of immense happiness and gratitude. "She feels grateful to Providence," Her Majesty concluded, "to have permitted her to be united to so great, so noble, so excellent a Prince, and this year will ever remain the proudest and happiest in her life."

LORD PALMERSTON

CHAPTER 5
Lord Palmerston

IN 1851 THE PRINCE'S fortunes reached their high-water mark. The success of the Great Exhibition enormously increased his reputation. But meanwhile his unpopularity in high society had not diminished. For a moment, indeed, it had appeared as if the dislike of the upper classes was about to be converted into cordiality; for they had learned with amazement that the Prince, during a country visit, had ridden to hounds and acquitted himself remarkably well. They had always taken it for granted that his horsemanship was of some second-rate foreign quality, and here he was jumping five-barred gates and tearing after the fox as if he had been born and bred in Leicestershire. They could hardly believe it; was it possible that Albert was a good fellow after all?

Had he wished to be thought so he would certainly have seized this opportunity, purchased several hunters and used them. But hunting bored him. He continued, as before, to ride, as he himself put it, for exercise or convenience, not for amusement; and it was agreed that though the Prince, no doubt, could keep in his saddle well enough, he was no sportsman.

This was a serious matter. It was not merely that Albert was laughed at and thought unfashionable by fine ladies and gentlemen. The Prince, in a word, was un-English. What that word precisely meant it was difficult to say; but the fact was patent to every eye. Lord Palmerston, also, was not fashionable; the Whig aristocrats looked askance at him, and only tolerated him as an unpleasant necessity. But Lord Palmerston was English through and through—the very antithesis of the Prince.

By a curious chance it was to happen that this typical Englishman was to be brought into closer contact than any other of his countrymen with the alien from over the sea. Differences which, in more fortunate circumstances, might have been smoothed away, became accentuated to the highest pitch. All the mysterious forces in Albert's soul leaped out to do battle with this adversary, and, in the long violent conflict that followed, it almost seemed as if he was struggling with England herself.

Palmerston's whole life had been spent in the government of the country. His reputation had steadily grown, and when, in 1846, he became Foreign Secretary for the third time, his position in the country was almost, if not quite, on an equality with that of the Prime Minister, Lord John Russell. He was a tall man of sixty-two, with a jaunty air, a large face, dyed whiskers, and a long sardonic upper lip. Powerful, experienced, and supremely self-confident, he naturally paid very little attention to Albert. Why should he? The Prince was interested in foreign affairs? Very well, then, let the Prince pay attention to *him*, who had been a cabinet minister when Albert was in the cradle. Not that he wanted the Prince's attention—far from it: so far as he could see, Albert was merely a young foreigner whose only claim to distinction was that he had married the Queen of England.

This estimate, as he found out to his cost, was a mistaken one. Albert was by no means insignificant, and, behind Albert, there was another figure by no means insignificant either—there was Stockmar.

But Palmerston, busy, brushed all such considerations on one side; it was his favorite method of action. He lived by instinct—by a quick eye and a strong hand, a dexterous management of every crisis as it arose. He was very bold; and nothing gave him more exhilaration than to steer the ship of state in a high wind, on a rough sea, with every stitch of canvas on her that she could carry. When he saw that the case demanded it, he could go slow—very slow; but when he decided to go quick, nobody went quicker.

His immense popularity was the result partly of his diplomatic successes, partly of his extraordinary affability, but chiefly of the genuine intensity with which he responded to the feelings and supported the interests of his countrymen. The public knew that it had in Lord Palmerston not only a high-mettled master, but also a devoted servant. When he was Prime Minister, he noticed that iron hurdles had been put up on the grass in the Green Park; he immediately wrote to the minister responsible, ordering their instant removal, declaring that the purpose of the grass was "to be walked upon freely and without restraint by the people, old and young, for whose enjoyment the parks are maintained." It was in this spirit that, as Foreign Secretary, he watched over the interests of Englishmen abroad.

Nothing could be more agreeable for Englishmen; but foreign governments were less pleased. They found Lord Palmerston interfering and exasperating. In Paris they spoke of *ce terrible milord Palmerston;* and in Germany they made a little song—

Hat der Teufel einen Sohn,
So ist er sicher Palmerston.

[If the Devil had a son
Surely he'd be Palmerston.]

But their complaints were in vain; Palmerston, with his upper lip sardonically curving, braved consequences, and held on his course.

In 1848, in that year of revolutions, when, in all directions and with alarming frequency, crowns kept rolling off royal heads, Albert and Victoria were appalled to find that the policy of England was persistently directed—in Germany, in Switzerland, in Austria, in Italy, in Sicily—so as to favor the insurgent forces. The situation, indeed, was just such a one as the soul of Palmerston loved. There was danger and excitement, the opportunity for action, on every hand. He had an English gentleman's deep contempt for foreign potentates, and the spectacle of the popular uprisings, and of the oppressors bundled ignominiously out of their palaces, gave him unbounded pleasure. He was determined that there should be no doubt whatever, all over the Continent, on which side in the great struggle England stood. It was not that he had the slightest tincture in him of radicalism; he was quite content to be inconsistent—to be a Conservative at home and a Liberal abroad. There were very good reasons for keeping the Irish in their places; but when he read an account of the political prisons in Naples his gorge rose. He did not want war; but he saw that without war a skillful and determined use of England's power might do much to further the cause of the Liberals in Europe. It was a difficult and a hazardous game to play, but he set about playing it with delighted alacrity.

And then, to his intense annoyance, just as he needed all his nerve and all possible freedom of action, he found himself being hampered and distracted at every turn by . . . those people at Osborne.

He saw what it was; the opposition was systematic, and the Queen alone would have been incapable of it; the Prince was at the bottom of it. It was exceedingly vexatious; but Palmerston was in a hurry; the Prince, if he insisted upon interfering, must be brushed on one side.

Albert was very angry. He highly disapproved of Palmerston's policy. He was opposed to absolutism; but in his opinion Palmerston's proceedings were simply calculated to substitute for absolutism, all over Europe, something worse—mob violence. The dangers of this revolutionary ferment were grave; even in England Chartism* was rampant—a sinister movement, which might at any moment upset the constitution and abolish the monarchy. Surely, with such dangers at home, this was a very bad time to choose for encouraging lawlessness abroad. He naturally took a particular interest in Germany. Having considered the question of Germany's future from every point of

---

* A workingmen's reform movement (1838–1848) which advocated universal manhood suffrage and other political reforms. (Editors' note.)

view, he came to the conclusion, under Stockmar's guidance, that the great aim for every lover of Germany should be her unification under Prussia. The intricacy of the situation was extreme; yet he saw with horror that Palmerston neither understood nor cared to understand the niceties of the problem, but rushed on blindly, dealing blows to right and left, quite—so far as he could see—without system or motive—except, indeed, a totally unreasonable distrust of the Prussian state.

But his disagreement with the details of Palmerston's policy was in reality merely a symptom of the fundamental differences between the characters of the two men. In Albert's eyes Palmerston was a coarse, reckless egotist, whose combined arrogance and ignorance must inevitably have their issue in folly and disaster. Nothing could be more antipathetic to him than a mind so strangely lacking in patience, in reflection, and in the habits of ratiocination. To him it was intolerable to think in a hurry, to act on instincts; everything must be done in due order, with careful premeditation; the premises of the position must first be established, and actions must be made in strict accordance with some well-defined principle. What did Palmerston know of economics, of science, of history? How much consideration had he devoted in his life to the general amelioration of the human race? Yet it is easy to imagine what might have been Palmerston's jaunty comment. "Ah! Your Royal Highness is busy with fine schemes and beneficent calculations. Well, as for me, I must say I'm quite satisfied with my morning's work—I've had the iron hurdles taken out of the Green Park."

The exasperating man, however, preferred to make no comment, and to proceed in smiling silence on his way. The process of "brushing on one side" very soon came into operation. Important Foreign Office dispatches were either submitted to the Queen so late that there was no time to correct them, or they were not submitted to her at all; or, having been submitted, and some passage in them being objected to, they were after all sent off in their original form.

The Queen complained; the Prince complained; both complained together. It was quite useless. Palmerston was most apologetic—could not understand how it had occurred—must give the clerks a wigging, and such a thing should never happen again. But, of course, it very soon happened again.

The royal remonstrances redoubled. Victoria, thoroughly aroused, imported into her protests a personal vehemence which those of Albert lacked. Did Lord Palmerston forget that she was Queen of England? How could she tolerate a state of affairs in which dispatches written in her name were sent abroad without her approval or even her knowledge? What could be more derogatory to her position than to be obliged to receive indignant letters from the crowned heads to whom those dispatches were addressed—letters which she did not know how to answer, since she so thoroughly agreed with them?

Summoning the Prime Minister, Lord John Russell, to her presence, she poured out her indignation, and afterwards, on the advice of Albert, noted down what had passed in a memorandum: "I said that I thought that Lord Palmerston often endangered the honour of England by taking a very prejudiced and one-sided view of a question; that his writings were as bitter as gall and did great harm, which Lord John entirely assented to, and that I often felt quite ill from anxiety."

Then she turned to her uncle. "The state of Germany," she wrote in a comprehensive review of the European situation, "is dreadful, and one does feel quite ashamed about that once so peaceful and happy country. In France a crisis also seems at hand. *What* a very bad figure we are cutting! Really it is quite immoral, with Ireland quivering in our grasp and ready to throw off her allegiance at any moment, for us to force Austria to give up her lawful possessions. What shall we say if Canada, Malta, etc., begin to trouble us? It hurts me terribly."

Lord John Russell's position grew more and more irksome. He did not approve of his colleague's treatment of the Queen. When he begged him to be more careful, he was met with the reply that 28,000 dispatches passed through the Foreign Office in a year; that, if every one of these were to be subjected to the royal criticism, the delay would be most serious; that, as it was, the time involved in submitting drafts to the meticulous examination of Prince Albert was almost too much for an overworked minister. These excuses would have impressed Lord John more favorably if he had not himself had to suffer from a similar neglect. As often as not Palmerston failed to communicate even to him the most important dispatches. The Foreign Secretary was becoming an almost independent power, swaying the policy of England on his own responsibility. On one occasion, in 1847, he had actually been upon the point of threatening to break off diplomatic relations with France without consulting either the cabinet or the Prime Minister.

Such incidents were constantly recurring. When this became known to the Prince, he saw that his opportunity had come. If he could only drive in to the utmost the wedge between the two statesmen, if he could only secure the alliance of Lord John Russell, then the suppression or the removal of Lord Palmerston would be almost certain to follow.

He set about the business with all the pertinacity of his nature. Both he and the Queen put every kind of pressure upon the Prime Minister. Lord John, attacked by his sovereign and ignored by his Foreign Secretary, led a miserable life. With the advent of the dreadful Schleswig-Holstein question—the most complex in the whole diplomatic history of Europe—his position, crushed between the upper and the nether millstones, grew positively unbearable. He became anxious above all things to get Palmerston out of the Foreign Office.

But then—supposing Palmerston refused to go?

In a memorandum made by the Prince, at about this time, of an interview between himself, the Queen, and the Prime Minister, we catch a curious glimpse of the states of mind of those three high personages—the anxiety and irritation of Lord John, the vehement acrimony of Victoria, and the reasonable animosity of Albert. At one point in the conversation Lord John observed that he believed the Foreign Secretary would consent to a change of offices; Lord Palmerston, he said, realized that he had lost the Queen's confidence—though only on public, and not on personal, grounds. But on that, the Prince noted, "The Queen interrupted Lord John by remarking that she distrusted him on *personal* grounds also, but I remarked that Lord Palmerston had seen rightly; that he had become disagreeable to the Queen, not on account of his person, but of his political doings—to which the Queen assented." Then the Prince suggested that there was a danger of the cabinet breaking up, and of Lord Palmerston returning to office as Prime Minister. But on that point Lord John was reassuring: he "thought Lord Palmerston too old to do much in the future (having passed his sixty-fifth year)." Eventually it was decided that nothing could be done for the present; but that the *utmost secrecy* must be observed; and so the conclave ended.

At last, in 1850, deliverance seemed to be at hand. There were signs that the public were growing weary of the alarums and excursions of Palmerston's diplomacy; and when his support of Don Pacifico, a British subject, in a quarrel with the Greek government, seemed to be about to involve the country in a war, a heavy cloud of distrust appeared to be gathering over his head. A motion directed against him in the House of Lords was passed. The question was next to be discussed in the House of Commons, where another adverse vote was not improbable, and would seal the doom of the minister.

Palmerston received the attack with complete nonchalance, and then, at the last possible moment, he struck. In a speech lasting over four hours, a speech of consummate art, he annihilated his enemies. The hostile motion was defeated, and Palmerston was once more the hero of the hour. Simultaneously, fate itself conspired to favor him. Sir Robert Peel was thrown from his horse and killed.

By this tragic chance, Palmerston saw the one rival great enough to cope with him removed from his path. He judged—and rightly—that he was the most popular man in England; and when Lord John revived the project of his exchanging the Foreign Office for some other position in the cabinet, he absolutely refused to stir.

Great was the disappointment of Albert; great was the indignation of Victoria. The Prince, perceiving that Palmerston was more firmly fixed in the saddle than ever, decided that something drastic must be done. Five months before, the prescient baron had drawn up, in case of emergency, a memorandum, which had been carefully placed in a pigeonhole. The emergency had now arisen, and the memorandum must be used. The Queen copied out the words of Stockmar, and sent them to the Prime Minister, requesting him to show her letter to Palmerston.

"She thinks it right," she wrote, "in order *to prevent any mistake* for the *future*, to explain *what it is she expects from her Foreign Secretary*. She requires: (1) That he will distinctly state what he proposed in a given case, in order that the Queen may know as distinctly to *what* she has given her Royal sanction; (2) Having *once given* her sanction to a measure, that it be not arbitrarily altered or modified by the Minister; such an act she must consider as failing in sincerity towards the Crown, and justly to be visited by the exercise of her Constitutional right of dismissing that Minister." Lord John Russell forwarded the Queen's letter to Palmerston. This transaction, of grave constitutional significance, was entirely unknown to the outside world.

If Palmerston had been a sensitive man, he would probably have resigned on the receipt of the Queen's missive. But he was far from sensitive; he loved power, and his power was greater than ever. Nevertheless, he was seriously perturbed. He understood at last that he was struggling with a formidable adversary, whose skill and strength might do irreparable injury to his career. He therefore wrote to Lord John, acquiescing in the Queen's requirements—"I have taken a copy of this memorandum of the Queen and will not fail to attend to the directions which it contains"—and he asked for an interview with the Prince.

Albert at once summoned him to the palace, and was astonished to observe, as he noted in a memorandum, that when Palmerston entered the room "he was very much agitated, shook, and had tears in his eyes, so as quite to move me, who never under any circumstances had known him otherwise than with a bland smile on his face."

The old statesman was profuse in excuses; the young one was coldly polite. At last, after a long and inconclusive conversation, the Prince, drawing himself up, said that, in order to give Lord Palmerston "an example of what the Queen wanted," he would "ask him a question point-blank." Lord Palmerston waited in respectful silence, while the Prince proceeded to ask him what he would do if Holstein were to be attacked, as Schleswig had already been attacked by Denmark. "What will you do, if this emergency arises (provoking most likely an European war), and which will arise very probably when we shall be at Balmoral and Lord John in another part of Scotland?"

Strangely enough, to this point-blank question the Foreign Secretary appeared to be unable to reply; the whole matter, he said, was extremely complicated. For a full hour the Prince struggled to extract a categorical answer, until at length Palmerston bowed himself out of the room. Albert threw up his hands: what could one do with such a man?

What indeed? For, in spite of all his apologies, within weeks the incorrigible reprobate was at his tricks again.

The Austrian general, Baron Julius von Haynau, notorious as a suppressor of rebellion in Hungary and Italy, and in particular as a flogger of women, came to England and took it into his head to pay a visit to Messrs. Barclay and Perkins's brewery. The features of "General Hyena," as he was everywhere called —his grim thin face, his enormous pepper-and-salt mustaches— had gained a horrid celebrity; and it so happened that among the clerks at the brewery there was a refugee from Vienna, who had given his fellow workers a firsthand account of the general's characteristics. The Austrian ambassador, scenting danger, begged Haynau not to appear in public. But the general would take no advice. He went to the brewery, was recognized, surrounded by angry draymen, pushed about, shouted at, and pulled by the mustaches until, bolting down an alley with the mob at his heels, he managed to take refuge in a public house, whence he was removed, protected by several policemen.

The Austrian government was angry and demanded explanations. Palmerston, privately delighted by the incident, replied, regretting what had occurred, but adding that in his opinion the general had "evinced a want of propriety in coming to England at the present moment"; and he delivered his note to the ambassador without having previously submitted it to the Queen or to the Prime Minister. Naturally, when this was discovered, there was a serious storm. The Prince was especially indignant; the conduct of the draymen he regarded, with alarm, as "a foretaste of what an unregulated mass of illiterate people is capable"; and Palmerston was requested by Lord John to withdraw his note, and to substitute for it another omitting all censure of the general. The Foreign Secretary threatened resignation, but the Prime Minister was firm. For a moment the royal hopes rose high that Palmerston would actually resign, but they rose only to be dashed to the ground again. Palmerston, suddenly lamblike, agreed to everything; the note was withdrawn and altered, and peace was patched up once more.

It lasted for a year, and then, in October 1851, the arrival of Lajos Kossuth in England brought on another crisis. Palmerston's desire to receive the Hungarian patriot at his house in London was vetoed by Lord John; once more there was a sharp struggle; once more Palmerston yielded. But still the insubordinate man could not keep quiet. A few weeks later at the Foreign Office a deputation of Radicals from Finsbury and Islington presented him with an address, in which the emperors of Austria and Russia were stigmatized as "odious and detestable assassins." The Foreign Secretary in his reply, while mildly deprecating these words, allowed his real sentiments to appear with a most undiplomatic insouciance. There was an immediate scandal, and Victoria, in an agitated letter, urged Lord John to assert his authority. But Lord John perceived that on this matter the Foreign Secretary had the support of public opinion, and he judged it wiser to bide his time.

He had not long to wait. The culmination of the long series of conflicts came before the year was out. On December 2, Louis Napoleon's coup d'etat took place in Paris; and on the following day Palmerston, without consulting anybody, expressed in a conversation with the French ambassador his approval of Napoleon's act. Two days later, he was instructed by the Prime Minister, in accordance with a letter from the Queen, that it was the policy of the English government to maintain an attitude of strict neutrality towards the affairs of France. Nevertheless, in an official dispatch to the British ambassador in Paris, he repeated his approval of the coup d'etat. This dispatch was submitted neither to the Queen nor to the Prime Minister. Lord John's patience, as he himself said, "was drained to the last drop." He dismissed Lord Palmerston.

Victoria was in ecstasies; and Albert knew that the triumph

was his even more than Lord John's. It was his wish that Lord Granville, a young man whom he believed to be pliant to his influence, should be Palmerston's successor; and Lord Granville was appointed.

Henceforward, it seemed that the Prince would have his way in foreign affairs. After years of struggle and mortification, success greeted him on every hand. In his family, he was an adored master; in the country, the Great Exhibition had brought him respect and glory; and now in the secret seats of power he had gained a new supremacy. He had wrestled with the terrible Lord Palmerston and his redoubtable opponent had been overthrown. Was England herself at his feet? It might be so; and yet . . . it is said that the sons of England have a certain tiresome quality: they never know when they are beaten. It was odd, but Palmerston was positively still jaunty. Was it possible? Could he believe, in his arrogance, that even his ignominious dismissal from office was something that could be brushed aside?

THE PRINCE'S TRIUMPH was short-lived. A few weeks later, owing to Palmerston's influence, the government was defeated in the House, and Lord John resigned.

A coalition between the Whigs and the followers of Peel came into power, under the premiership of Lord Aberdeen. Once more, Palmerston was in the cabinet. It was true that he did not return to the Foreign Office; that was something to the good; in the Home Department it might be hoped that his activities would be less dangerous. But the Foreign Secretary was no longer the complacent Granville; and in Lord Clarendon the Prince knew that he had a minister who had a mind of his own.

These changes, however, were merely the preliminaries of a far more serious development. Events, on every side, were moving towards a catastrophe. Suddenly the nation found itself under the shadow of imminent war. For several months, amid the shifting mysteries of diplomacy, the issue grew more doubtful and more dark, while the national temper was strained to the breaking point. At the very crisis of the long and ominous negotiations, it was announced that Lord Palmerston had resigned.

The pent-up fury of the people burst forth. They had felt

that in the terrible complexity of events they were being guided by weak and embarrassed counsels; but they had been reassured by the knowledge that at the center of power there was one man with strength, with courage, whom they could trust. They now learned that that man was no longer among their leaders. The moment that Palmerston's resignation was known, there was a universal outcry, and an extraordinary tempest of anger burst, with unparalleled violence, upon the head of the Prince.

It was everywhere asserted that the Queen's husband was a traitor to the country, that he was a tool of the Russian court, that in obedience to Russian influences he had forced Palmerston out of the government, and that he was directing the foreign policy of England in the interests of England's enemies. For many weeks these accusations filled the press; repeated at public meetings, elaborated in private talk, they flew over the country, growing every moment more extreme and more improbable. The wildest rumors spread. In January it was even whispered that the Prince had been seized, that he had been found guilty of high treason, that he was to be committed to the Tower; and the Queen herself, some declared, had been arrested.

These fantastic hallucinations, the result of the fevered atmosphere of approaching war, were devoid of any basis in fact. Palmerston's resignation had been in all probability totally disconnected with foreign policy; it had been entirely spontaneous, and had surprised the Court as much as the nation. Nor had Albert's influence been used in any way to favor the interests of Russia. As often happens in such cases, the government had been swinging backwards and forwards between two incompatible policies—that of noninterference and that of threats supported by force—either of which, if consistently followed, might well have had a successful and peaceful issue, but which, mingled together, could only lead to war. Albert, with characteristic scrupulosity, attempted to thread his way through the complicated labyrinth of European diplomacy, and eventually was lost in the maze. But so was the whole of the cabinet; and, when war came, his anti-Russian feelings were quite as vehement as those of the most bellicose of Englishmen.

Nevertheless, though the charges leveled against the Prince

were without foundation, there were underlying elements in the situation which explained, if they did not justify, the popular state of mind. It was true that the Queen's husband was a foreigner, with foreign ideas and closely related to a multitude of foreign princes. The Prince's German proclivities were perpetually lamented by English ministers. But this was not all. A constitutional question of the most profound importance was raised by the position of the Prince in England. His presence gave a new prominence to an old problem—the precise definition of the functions and powers of the Crown. Those functions and powers had become, in effect, his; and what sort of use was he making of them?

His views as to the place of the Crown in the constitution are easily ascertainable, for they were Stockmar's; and it happens that we possess a detailed account of Stockmar's opinions upon the subject in a long letter addressed by him to the Prince at the time of this very crisis, just before the outbreak of the Crimean War. Constitutional monarchy, according to the baron, had suffered an eclipse since the passing of the Reform Bill. It was now "constantly in danger of becoming a pure Ministerial Government." To prevent this from happening, it was of extreme importance, said the baron, "that no opportunity should be let slip of vindicating the legitimate position of the Crown." In his opinion, the very lowest claim of the royal prerogative should include "a right on the part of the King to be the permanent President of his Ministerial Council." The sovereign ought to be "in the position of a permanent Premier, who takes rank above the temporary head of the Cabinet, and in matters of discipline exercises supreme authority."

Now it may be that this reading of the constitution is a possible one. But it is also clear that such a reading invests the Crown with more power than it possessed even under George III; it runs counter to the whole development of English public life since the Revolution. The fact that it was held by Stockmar, and instilled by him into Albert, was of serious importance. For there was good reason to believe not only that these doctrines were held by Albert in theory, but that he was making a deliberate, sustained attempt to give them practical validity. The history of the struggle between the Crown and Palmerston provided startling evidence that this was the case. That struggle reached its culmination when, in Stockmar's memorandum of 1850, the Queen asserted her "constitutional right" to dismiss the Foreign Secretary if he altered a dispatch which had received her sanction. The memorandum was, in fact, a plain declaration that the Crown intended to act independently of the Prime Minister; and Lord John Russell, anxious to strengthen himself against Palmerston, in accepting the memorandum, had implicitly allowed the claim of the Crown.

This new development in the position of the Crown, grave as it was in itself, was rendered peculiarly disquieting by the unusual circumstances which surrounded it. For the functions of the Crown were now, in effect, being exercised by a person unknown to the constitution, who wielded over the sovereign an undefined and unbounded influence. The fact that this person was the sovereign's husband, while it explained his influence, by no means diminished its strange and momentous import. An ambiguous, prepotent figure had come to disturb the ancient, subtle, and jealously guarded balance of the English constitution.

Such had been the unexpected outcome of the tentative and fainthearted opening of Albert's political life. Stockmar's pupil had assuredly gone far. Stockmar's pupil!—precisely; the public, painfully aware of Albert's predominance, had grown, too, uneasily conscious that Victoria's master had a master of his own. Deep in the darkness the baron loomed. Another foreigner! A foreign baron controlled a foreign Prince, and the foreign Prince controlled the Crown of England. And the Crown itself was creeping forward ominously; and when, from under its shadow, the baron and the Prince had frowned, a great minister, beloved of the people, had fallen. Where was all this to end?

Within a few weeks Palmerston withdrew his resignation, and the public frenzy subsided. When Parliament met, leaders in both the Houses made speeches in favor of the Prince. Immediately afterwards, the country finally plunged into the Crimean War. In the struggle that followed, Albert's patriotism was put beyond a doubt, and the animosities of the past were forgotten. But the war had another consequence, less gratifying to the royal couple: it crowned the ambition of Lord Palmerston. In 1855, the man who five years before had been pronounced by Lord John Russell to be "too old to do much in the future," became Prime Minister of England, and, with one short interval, remained in that position for ten years.

SIR JAMES CLARK

CHAPTER 6

Last Years of Prince Consort

THE WEAK-WILLED YOUTH who took no interest in politics and never read a newspaper had grown into a man of unbending determination whose energies were incessantly concentrated upon the business of government. He was busy now from morning till night. In the winter, before the dawn, he was to be seen, seated at his writing table, working by the light of the green reading lamp which he had brought over with him from Germany. Victoria was early too, but not so early as Albert; and when, in the chill darkness, she took her seat at her own writing table, placed side by side with his, she invariably found upon it a neat pile of papers arranged for her inspection and signature.

The day, thus begun, continued in unremitting industry. At breakfast, the newspapers—the once hated newspapers—appeared and the Prince would peruse them. After that there were ministers and secretaries to interview; there was correspondence to be carried on; there were memoranda to be made. Victoria, preserving every letter, was all breathless attention and eager obedience. Sometimes Albert would actually ask her advice, or consult her about his English: *"Lese recht aufmerksam, und sage wenn irgend ein Fehler ist."*—"Read this carefully and tell me if there is any mistake in it." Thus the absorbing hours passed by. Fewer and fewer grew the moments of recreation and exercise. The demands of society were narrowed down to the smallest limits. It was no longer a mere pleasure, it was a positive necessity, to go to bed early in order to be up and at work on the morrow betimes.

The exacting business of government, which became at last the dominating preoccupation for Albert, still left unimpaired his old tastes and interests; he remained devoted to art, to science, to philosophy; and a multitude of subsidiary activities showed how his energies increased as the demands upon them grew. For whenever duty called, the Prince was all alertness. With indefatigable perseverance he opened museums, laid the foundation stones of hospitals, or made speeches to the Royal Agricultural Society. The National Gallery particularly interested him; he drew up careful regulations for the arrangement of the pictures according to schools; and he attempted—though in vain—to have the whole collection transported to South Kensington.

As she watched him, her beloved Albert, Victoria, from the depth of her heart, felt certain that no other wife had ever had such a husband. His mind was apparently capable of everything, and she was hardly surprised to learn that he had made an important discovery for the conversion of sewage into agricultural manure. Filtration from below upwards, he explained, was the principle of the scheme. "All previous plans," he said, "would have cost millions; mine costs next to nothing." Unfortunately, owing to a slight miscalculation, the invention proved to be impracticable; but Albert's intelligence was unrebuffed, and he passed on, to plunge with his accustomed ardor into a prolonged study of lithography.

But naturally it was upon his children that his private interests and those of Victoria were concentrated most vigorously. The royal nurseries showed no sign of emptying. The birth of the Prince Arthur in 1850 was followed, three years later, by that of the Prince Leopold; and in 1857 the Princess Beatrice was born. A family of nine must be, in any circumstances, a grave responsibility; and the Prince realized to the full how much the high destinies of his offspring intensified the need of parental care. It was inevitable that he should believe profoundly in the importance of education; he himself had been the product of education; Stockmar had made him what he was; it was for him, in his turn, to be a Stockmar to the young creatures he had brought into the world. Victoria would assist him; a Stockmar,

no doubt, she could hardly be; but she could be perpetually vigilant, mingling strictness with her affection, and she could always set a good example.

These considerations, of course, applied preeminently to the education of the Prince of Wales, the future King of England. Albert set to work with a will. But, watching with Victoria the minutest details of the training of his children, he soon perceived, to his distress, that there was something unsatisfactory in the development of his eldest son. The Princess Royal was an extremely intelligent child; but Bertie, though he was good-humored and gentle, seemed to display a deep-seated repugnance to every form of mental exertion.

This was most regrettable, but the remedy was obvious: the parental efforts must be redoubled; instruction must be multiplied. More tutors were selected, the curriculum was revised, elaborate memoranda were drawn up. It was above all essential that there should be no slackness: "Work," said the Prince, "must be work." And work indeed it was. The boy grew up amid a ceaseless round of paradigms, syntactical exercises, dates, and genealogical tables. Constant notes flew backwards and forwards between the Prince, the Queen, and the tutors, with inquiries, reports of progress, and recommendations. It was, besides, vital that the heir to the throne should be protected from the slightest possibility of contamination from the outside world. The Prince of Wales might, occasionally, be allowed to invite sons of the nobility, boys of good character, to play with him in the garden of Buckingham Palace; but his father presided, with alarming precision, over their sports.

In short, every conceivable effort was made; yet, strange to say, the object of all this solicitude continued to be unsatisfactory—appeared, in fact, to be positively growing worse. It was certainly odd; the more lessons that Bertie had to do, the less he did them; and the more carefully he was guarded against frivolities, the more desirous of mere amusement he seemed to become. Albert was deeply grieved and Victoria was sometimes very angry; but grief and anger produced no more effect than supervision and timetables. The Prince of Wales, in spite of everything, grew up into manhood without the faintest sign of "adherence to and perseverance in the plan both of studies and life"—as one of the royal memoranda put it—which had been laid down with such extraordinary forethought by his father.

AGAINST THE INSIDIOUS worries of politics, and the boredom of society functions, Osborne had afforded a welcome refuge; but it soon appeared that even Osborne was too little removed from the world.

Ever since Victoria, together with Albert, had visited Scotland in the early years of her marriage, her heart was in the Highlands. She had returned to them a few years later, and her passion had grown. And how Albert enjoyed them too! His spirits rose quite wonderfully as soon as he found himself among the hills and conifers. "It is a happiness to see him," she wrote. "Oh! What can equal the beauties of nature!"

The Highlanders, too, were such astonishing people. "They never make difficulties," she noted, "but are cheerful, and happy, and merry, and ready to walk, and run, and do anything." She loved everything about them—their customs, their dress, even their musical instruments. "There were nine pipers at the castle," she wrote, after staying with Lord Breadalbane; "sometimes one and sometimes three played. They always played about breakfast time, again during the morning, at luncheon, and whenever we went in and out; again before dinner, and during most of dinner time. We both have become quite fond of the bagpipes."

It was quite impossible not to wish to return to such pleasures again and again; and in 1848 the Queen had taken a lease of Balmoral House, a small residence in the wilds of Aberdeenshire. Four years later she bought the place outright. Now she could be really happy every summer; now she could be simple and at ease; now she could be romantic every evening, and dote upon Albert, without a single distraction, all day long.

The diminutive scale of the house was in itself a charm. Nothing was more amusing than to find oneself living in two or three little sitting rooms, with the children crammed away upstairs, and the minister in attendance with only a tiny bedroom to do all his work in. And then to be able to run in and out of doors as one liked, and to sketch, and to walk, and to watch the red deer coming so surprisingly close!

Occasionally one could be more adventurous—one could go and stay for a night or two at the bothy at Alt-na-giuthasach—a mere couple of huts with "a wooden addition"—and only eleven people in the whole party! And there were mountains to be climbed and a cairn to be built in solemn pomp. "At last, when the cairn . . . was nearly completed, Albert climbed up to the top of it, and placed the last stone; after which three cheers were given. It was a gay, pretty, and touching sight." And in the evening there were sword dances and reels.

But Albert had determined to pull down the little old house, and to build in its place a castle of his own designing. With great ceremony a foundation stone for the new edifice was laid, and by 1855 it was habitable. Spacious, built of granite in the Scotch baronial style, with turrets, gables, and a tower a hundred feet high, the castle was skillfully arranged to command the finest views of the surrounding mountains and of the River Dee. Upon the interior decorations Albert and Victoria lavished all their care. The Balmoral tartan, in red and gray, designed by the Prince, and the Victoria tartan, with a white stripe, designed by the Queen, were to be seen in every room. Watercolor sketches by Victoria hung upon the walls, together with innumerable stags' antlers, and the head of a boar, which had been shot by Albert in Germany. In an alcove in the hall stood a life-sized statue of Albert in Highland dress.

Victoria declared that it was perfection. "Every year," she wrote, "my heart becomes more fixed in this dear paradise, and so much more so now, that *all* has become my dear Albert's *own* creation . . . and his great taste, and the impress of his dear hand, have been stamped everywhere."

And here, in very truth, her happiest days were passed. In afteryears, when she looked back upon them, a kind of glory, a radiance, seemed to glow about these golden hours. Each hallowed moment stood out clear, beautiful, eternally significant. Albert's stalkings—an evening walk when she lost her way—Vicky sitting down on a wasps' nest—with what intensity such things, and ten thousand like them, impressed themselves upon her! And how she flew to her journal to note them down! The news of the Duke of Wellington's death! What a moment—when, as she sat sketching by a loch in the hills, Lord Derby's letter had been brought to her, and she had learned that "*England's* pride, her glory, her hero, the greatest man she had ever produced, was no more!" And she filled a whole page of her diary with panegyrical regrets. "To *us* his loss is *irreparable*. . . . To Albert he showed the greatest kindness. . . . Not an eye will be dry in the whole country."

These were serious thoughts; but they were soon succeeded by others hardly less moving—by events as impossible to forget. Without doubt, the most memorable, most delightful of all the moments were the expeditions—the rare, exciting expeditions up mountains, across rivers, through strange country, and lasting several days. With only two attendants—Grant and Brown—for servants, and with assumed names . . . it was more like something in a story than real life. "We had decided to call ourselves *Lord and Lady Churchill and party!* Brown once forgot this and called me 'Your Majesty' as I was getting into the carriage, and Grant on the box once called Albert 'Your Royal Highness,' which set us off laughing, but no one observed it."

Strong, vigorous, enthusiastic, bringing, so it seemed, good fortune with her—the Highlanders declared she had "a lucky foot"—she relished everything—the scrambles and the views and the rough inns with Brown and Grant waiting at table. She could have gone on for ever and ever, absolutely happy with Albert beside her and Brown at her pony's head. But the time came for turning homewards; alas! the time came for going back to England. She could hardly bear it; she sat disconsolate in her room and watched the snow falling. The last day! Oh! If only she could be snowed up!

THE CRIMEAN WAR brought new experiences, and most of them were pleasant ones. It was pleasant to be patriotic and pugnacious, to seek out appropriate prayers to be read in the churches, to have news of glorious victories, and to know oneself, more proudly than ever, the representative of England.

With that spontaneity of feeling which was so peculiarly her own, Victoria poured out her admiration, her pity, her love, upon her "dear soldiers." When she gave them their medals her exultation knew no bounds. "Noble fellows!" she wrote to the King of the Belgians. "I feel as if these were *my own children;* my heart beats for *them* as for my *nearest and dearest.* They were so touched, so pleased; many, I hear, cried—and they won't hear of giving up their medals to have their names engraved upon them for fear they should *not* receive the *identical one* put into *their hands by me*, which is quite touching. Several came by in a sadly mutilated state." She and they were at one. They felt that she had done them a splendid honor, and she, with perfect genuineness, shared their feeling.

Albert's attitude towards such things was different; there was an austerity in him which quite prohibited such expansions of emotion. And he had other things to occupy him. He was ceaselessly at work on the tremendous task of concluding the war. State papers, dispatches, memoranda, poured from him in an overwhelming stream. Between 1853 and 1857 fifty folio volumes were filled with the comments of his pen upon the Eastern question. Weary ministers staggered under the load of his advice; nor was it advice to be ignored. Again and again the Prince's suggestions, unheeded at first, were adopted under the stress of circumstances and found to be full of value. The enrollment of a foreign legion, the establishment of a depot for troops at Malta, the institution of periodical reports as to the condition of the army at Sevastopol—such were his achievements. He went further: in a lengthy memorandum he laid down the lines for a radical reform in the entire administration of the army. This was premature, but his proposal for "a camp of evolution" for troops proved to be the germ of Aldershot.*

Meanwhile Victoria had made a new friend: she had suddenly been captivated by Napoleon III. Her dislike of him had been strong at first; she considered that he was a disreputable adventurer who had usurped the throne of poor old Louis Philippe. For a long time, although he was her ally, she was unwilling to

* The largest and most complete military training center in the United Kingdom. (Editors' note.)

meet him; but at last a visit of the Emperor and Empress to England was arranged.

Directly he appeared at Windsor her heart began to soften. She was charmed by his quiet manners, his low, soft voice. There was something deep within her which responded vehemently to natures that offered a romantic contrast with her own. From behind the vast solidity of her conventionality, she peered out with a strange delicious pleasure at that unfamiliar, darkly glittering foreign object, moving so meteorically before her. And, to her surprise, where she had dreaded antagonisms, she discovered only sympathies. He was, she said, "so quiet, so simple, *naïf* even, so gentle, so full of tact. . . . There is something fascinating, melancholy, and engaging, which draws you to him." She observed that he rode "extremely well"; he danced "with great dignity and spirit." Above all, he listened to Albert with the most respectful attention; and afterwards was heard to declare that he had never met the Prince's equal. On one occasion, indeed—but only on one—he had seemed to grow slightly restive. In a diplomatic conversation, "I expatiated a little on the Holstein question," wrote the Prince in a memorandum, "which appeared to bore the Emperor as '*très compliquée*.' "

Victoria, too, became much attached to the Empress, whose looks she admired without a touch of jealousy. Eugénie, indeed, in the plenitude of her beauty, exquisitely dressed in Parisian crinolines which set off her tall and willowy figure, might well have caused some heartburning in the breast of her short, stout hostess, in her garish middle-class garments. But to Victoria it mattered nothing that her face turned red in the heat and that her purple porkpie hat was of last year's fashion, while Eugénie, cool and modish, floated in flounces by her side. Was she not Queen of England? True majesty was hers, and she knew it. More than once, when the two were together in public, it was the woman to whom, as it seemed, nature and art had given so little, who, by the sheer force of an inherent grandeur, threw her adorned and beautiful companion into the shade.

There were tears when the moment came for the guests to leave; but before long Victoria and Albert paid a return visit to France. There everything was very delightful, and Victoria

drove incognito through the streets of Paris in a "common bonnet," saw a play at Saint-Cloud, and, one evening, at a great party given in her honor at Versailles, talked to a distinguished-looking Prussian gentleman, whose name was Bismarck. Her rooms were furnished so much to her taste that she declared they gave her quite a home feeling—that, if her little dog were there, she should really imagine herself at home. Three days later her little dog barked a welcome to her as she entered the apartments. The Emperor himself had personally arranged the charming surprise. She returned to England more enchanted than ever.

The alliance prospered, and the war drew towards a conclusion. Queen Victoria rode about on horseback reviewing the troops. At last Sevastopol was captured. The news reached Balmoral late at night, and "in a few minutes Albert and all the gentlemen in every species of attire sallied forth, followed by all the servants, and gradually by all the population of the village, up to the top of the cairn." A bonfire was lighted, pipes were played, and guns were shot off. "About three-quarters of an hour after, Albert came down and said the scene had been wild and exciting beyond everything. The people had been drinking healths in whisky and were in great ecstasy." The "great ecstasy," perhaps, would be replaced by other feelings next morning; but at any rate the war was over.

AN UNEXPECTED CONSEQUENCE of the war was a complete change in the relations between the royal pair and Palmerston. The Prince and the minister drew together over their hostility to Russia, and thus it came about that when Victoria found it necessary to summon her old enemy to form an administration she did so without reluctance. The premiership, too, had a sobering effect upon Palmerston; he grew less impatient and dictatorial; considered with attention the suggestions of the Crown, and was, besides, genuinely impressed by the Prince's ability and knowledge. Friction, no doubt, there still occasionally was—especially with regard to Italy. Albert, theoretically the friend of constitutional government, distrusted Cavour, and was horrified by Garibaldi. Palmerston, on the other hand, was eager for Italian independence. The struggle was fierce;

nevertheless Palmerston's policy was carried through, and the vigorous sympathy of England became one of the decisive factors in the final achievement of Italian unity.

Towards the other European storm center, also, the Prince's attitude continued to be very different to that of Palmerston. Albert's great wish was for a united Germany under the leadership of a constitutional and virtuous Prussia; Palmerston did not think that there was much to be said for the scheme. But he took no particular interest in German politics, and was ready enough to agree to a proposal which was warmly supported by both the Prince and the Queen—that the royal houses of England and Prussia should be united by the marriage of the Princess Royal with the Prussian Crown Prince.

Accordingly, when the Princess was not yet fifteen, the Prince, a young man of twenty-four, came over on a visit to Balmoral, and the betrothal took place. Two years later, in 1857, the marriage was celebrated. At the last moment, however, it seemed that there might be a hitch. It was pointed out in Prussia that it was customary for princes of the blood royal to be married in Berlin, and it was suggested that there was no reason why the present case should be treated as an exception. When this reached the ears of Victoria, she was speechless with indignation. In a note, emphatic even for Her Majesty, she instructed the Foreign Secretary to tell the Prussian ambassador "not to *entertain* the possibility of such a question. . . . Whatever may be the usual practice of Prussian princes, it is not *every* day that one marries the eldest daughter of the Queen of England. The question must therefore be considered as settled."

It was, and the wedding took place in St. James's Chapel. There were great festivities—illuminations, state concerts, immense crowds. At Windsor a magnificent banquet was given to the bride and bridegroom in the Waterloo room. Victoria's feelings had been growing more and more emotional, and when the time came for the young couple to depart she very nearly broke down. "Poor dear child!" she wrote afterwards. "I clasped her in my arms and blessed her, and knew not what to say. I kissed good Fritz and pressed his hand again and again. He was unable to speak and the tears were in his eyes. I embraced them both again at the carriage door . . . The band struck up. General Schreckenstein was much affected."

Albert, as well as General Schreckenstein, was much affected. He was losing his favorite child, whose opening intelligence had already begun to display a marked resemblance to his own. An ironic fate had determined that the daughter who was taken from him should be sympathetic, clever, and interested in the arts and sciences, while not a single one of these qualities could be discovered in the son who remained.

Certainly the Prince of Wales did not take after his father. Victoria's prayer had been unanswered, and with each succeeding year this became more obvious. But Bertie's parents only redoubled their efforts: it still might not be too late to incline the young branch, by careful fastenings, to grow in the proper direction.

Everything was tried. The boy was sent on a continental tour with a picked body of tutors, but the results were unsatisfactory. At his father's request he kept a diary; on his return it was found to be distressingly meager. On his seventeenth birthday a memorandum was drawn up over the names of the Queen and the Prince informing their eldest son that he was now entering manhood, and directing him henceforward to perform the duties of a Christian gentleman.

"Life is composed of duties," said the memorandum, "and in the due, punctual and cheerful performance of them the true Christian, true soldier, and true gentleman is recognised. . . . A new sphere of life will open for you in which you will have to be taught what to do and what not to do, a subject requiring study more important than any in which you have hitherto been engaged." On receipt of the memorandum Bertie burst into tears. A year later he was sent to Oxford, where the greatest care was taken that he should not mix with the undergraduates. Yes, everything had been tried—everything . . . with one single exception. The experiment had never been made of letting Bertie enjoy himself. But why should it have been? "Life is composed of duties." What possible place could there be for enjoyment in the existence of a Prince of Wales?

The same year which deprived Albert of the Princess Royal

brought him another and a still more serious loss. The Baron Stockmar had paid his last visit to England. For twenty years, as he himself said in a letter to the King of the Belgians, he had performed "the laborious office of a paternal friend and trusted adviser" to the Prince and the Queen. He was seventy; he was tired; it was time to go.

The baron returned to his home in Coburg, exchanging, once for all, the momentous secrecies of European statecraft for the tittle-tattle of a provincial capital. In his chair by the fire he nodded now over old stories—not of emperors and generals—but of neighbors and relatives and the domestic adventures of long ago. Dyspepsia and depression still attacked him; but, looking back over his life, he was not dissatisfied. He had created the Prince—an indefatigable toiler, presiding, for the highest ends, over a great nation. But had the baron no misgivings? Did he never wonder whether, perhaps, he might have accomplished not too little but too much? Albert, certainly, seemed to be everything that Stockmar could have wished—virtuous, industrious, intelligent. And yet—why was it?—all was not well with the Prince. He was sick at heart.

For in spite of everything Albert had never reached happiness. His work, which at last he came to crave with an almost morbid appetite, was a solace and not a cure; the dragon of his dissatisfaction devoured with dark relish that ever growing tribute of laborious days and nights; but it was hungry still.

The causes of his melancholy were hidden, mysterious, unanalyzable perhaps. There were contradictions in his nature, which to some made him seem an inexplicable enigma: he was severe and gentle; he longed for affection and he was cold. He was lonely, not merely with the loneliness of exile but with the loneliness of conscious and unrecognized superiority. There was something that he wanted and that he could never get. What was it? Some absolute sympathy? Some extraordinary success?

Possibly he wanted a mixture of both. To dominate and to be understood! But he could see only too clearly how faint were the responses of his actual environment. Who could appreciate him in England? The gentle virtue of an inward excellence availed all too little. Doubtless he had made some slight impression: but how very far it was from the goal of his ambitions!

How feeble and futile his efforts seemed against the enormous coagulation of dullness, of folly, that confused him! England lumbered on, impervious and self-satisfied, in her old intolerable course. He threw himself across the path of the monster with rigid purpose and set teeth, but he was brushed aside. Yes! even Palmerston was still unconquered—was still there to afflict him with his jauntiness, his muddleheadedness, his utter lack of principle.

It was too much. Neither nature nor the baron had given him a sanguine spirit; the seeds of pessimism lodged within him and flourished. He

> *questioned things, and did not find*
> *One that would answer to his mind;*
> *And all the world appeared unkind.*

He believed that he was a failure and he began to despair.

Yet Stockmar had told him that he must "never relax," and he never would. He would go on, working and striving to the bitter end. His industry grew almost maniacal. Earlier and earlier was the green lamp lighted; more vast grew the correspondence. His very recreations became duties. He enjoyed himself by timetable and went deer-stalking with meticulous gusto—it was the right thing to do. The mechanism worked with astonishing efficiency, but it never rested and it was never oiled. The Prince would not relax; he had absorbed the doctrines of Stockmar too thoroughly.

Victoria noticed that her husband sometimes seemed to be depressed and overworked. She tried to cheer him up. Realizing uneasily that he was still regarded as a foreigner, she hoped that by conferring upon him the title of Prince Consort (1857) she would improve his position in the country. But unfortunately Albert remained as foreign as before; and as the years passed his dejection deepened.

She worked with him, she watched over him, she walked with him through the woods at Osborne. When his birthday came round, she took the greatest pains to choose him presents that he would really like. In 1858, when he was thirty-nine, she gave him "a picture of Beatrice, life-size in oil, by Horsley, a complete collection of photographic views of Gotha and the country round, and a paperweight of Balmoral granite and deers' teeth, designed by Vicky." Albert was of course delighted, and his merriment at the family gathering was more pronounced than ever; and yet . . . what was there that was wrong?

No doubt it was his health. He was wearing himself out; and his constitution, as Stockmar had perceived from the first, was ill adapted to meet serious strain. He constantly suffered from minor ailments, and his appearance in itself indicated infirmity. The handsome youth of twenty years since had grown into a sallow, tired-looking man, whose body, in its stoop and its loose fleshiness, betrayed the sedentary laborer, and whose head was quite bald on top. Unkind critics, who had once compared Albert to an operatic tenor, might have remarked that there was something of the butler about him now. Beside Victoria, he presented a painful contrast. She, too, was stout, but it was with the plumpness of a vigorous matron; and an eager vitality was everywhere visible in her bearing.

Suddenly, however, Victoria was reminded that there were other perils besides those of ill health. During a visit to Coburg in 1860, the Prince was nearly killed in a carriage accident. He escaped with cuts and bruises; but Victoria's alarm was extreme, though she concealed it. "It is when the Queen feels most deeply," she wrote afterwards, "that she always appears calmest, and she dared not allow herself to speak of what might have been, or even to admit to herself (and she dare not now) the entire danger, for her head would turn!"

Shortly afterwards the Queen underwent, for the first time in her life, the actual experience of close personal loss. Early in 1861, her mother, the Duchess of Kent, was taken ill, and in March she died. The event overwhelmed Victoria. With a morbid intensity, she filled her diary for pages with minute descriptions of her mother's last hours. The horror and the mystery of death—death, present and actual—seized upon her imagination. She tried to forget, but she could not. Her lamentations continued with a strange persistency. It was almost as if, by some mysterious and unconscious precognition, she realized that for her, in an especial manner, that grisly majesty had a dreadful dart in store.

For indeed, before the year was out, a far more terrible blow was to fall upon her. Albert, who had long been suffering from sleeplessness, went, on a cold and drenching day towards the end of November, to inspect the buildings for the new Military Academy at Sandhurst. On his return it was clear that exposure had seriously affected his health. He was attacked by rheumatism, his sleeplessness continued, and he complained that he felt thoroughly unwell.

Three days later a painful duty obliged him to visit Cambridge. The Prince of Wales, who had been placed at that university in the previous year, was behaving in such a manner that a parental visit and a parental admonition had become necessary. His father, suffering in mind and body, carried through his task; but on his return journey to Windsor he caught a serious chill.

During the next week he gradually grew more miserable; yet he continued to work. It so happened that at that very moment a grave diplomatic crisis had arisen. The Civil War had broken out in America, and it seemed as if England, owing to a violent quarrel with the northern states, was upon the point of being drawn into the conflict. A severe dispatch by Lord John Russell was submitted to the Queen; and the Prince perceived that, if it was sent off unaltered, war would be the almost inevitable consequence.

At seven o'clock on the morning of December 1, he rose from his bed, and with a quavering hand wrote a series of suggestions for altering the draft, by which its language might be softened, and a way left open for a peaceful solution of the question. These changes were accepted by the government, and war was averted. It was the Prince's last memorandum.

He had always declared that he viewed the prospect of death with equanimity. "I do not cling to life," he had once said to Victoria. "You do; but I set no store by it." And he had added: "I am sure, if I had a severe illness, I should give up at once. I have no tenacity of life."

He had judged correctly. Before he had been ill many days he told a friend that he was convinced he would not recover.

He sank and sank. Nevertheless, if his case had been properly treated from the first, he might conceivably have been saved; but the doctors failed to diagnose his symptoms; and it is noteworthy that his principal physician was Sir James Clark. When it was suggested that other advice should be taken, Sir James pooh-poohed the idea. But the illness grew worse. At last, after a fierce letter from Palmerston, Dr. Watson was sent for. Dr. Watson saw at once that he had come too late. The Prince was in the grip of typhoid fever. "I think that everything so far is satisfactory," said Sir James Clark.

The restlessness and the acute suffering of the earlier days gave place to a settled torpor and a deepening gloom. Once the patient asked for music—"a fine chorale at a distance"; and, a piano having been placed in the adjoining room, Princess Alice played on it some of Luther's hymns, after which the Prince repeated "Rock of Ages." Sometimes his mind wandered; sometimes the distant past came rushing upon him; he heard the birds in the early morning, and was at Rosenau again, a boy. Or Victoria would come and read to him, and then she would bend over him, and he would murmur *"liebes Frauchen"* and *"gutes Weibchen,"* stroking her cheek.

Her distress was great, but she was not seriously frightened. Buoyed up by her own abundant energies, she would not believe that Albert's might prove unequal to the strain. Only two days before the end, which was seen now to be almost inevitable by everyone about her, she wrote, full of confidence, to the King of the Belgians: "There is nothing to cause alarm." The Princess Alice tried to tell her the truth, but her hopefulness would not be daunted.

On the morning of December 14, Albert, just as she had expected, seemed to be better; perhaps the crisis was over. But in the course of the day there was a serious relapse. Then at last she allowed herself to see that she was standing on the edge of an appalling gulf. The whole family was summoned, and, one after another, the children took a silent farewell of their father. "It was a terrible moment," Victoria wrote in her diary, "but, thank God! I was able to command myself, and remained sitting by his side."

He murmured something, but she could not hear what it was; she thought he was speaking in French. Then all at once he began to arrange his hair, "just as he used to do when well and he was dressing." *"Es ist kleines Frauchen"*—"It is your dear little wife," she whispered to him; and he seemed to understand.

For a moment, towards evening, she went into another room, but was immediately called back. She saw at a glance that a ghastly change had taken place. As she knelt by the bed, he breathed deeply, breathed gently, breathed at last no more. His features became perfectly rigid; she shrieked one long wild shriek that rang through the terror-stricken castle—and understood that she had lost him forever.

BARON STOCKMAR

CHAPTER 7
Widowhood

THE DEATH of the Prince Consort was the central turning point in the history of Queen Victoria. She herself felt that her true life had ceased with her husband's, and that the remainder of her days upon earth was of a twilight nature—an epilogue. With Albert's death a veil descends. The sudden removal of the Prince was not merely a matter of overwhelming personal concern to Victoria; it was an event of national, of European importance. He was only forty-two, and ordinarily he might have been expected to live at least thirty years longer. Had he done so it can hardly be doubted that the whole development of the English polity would have been changed. Already at the time of his death he filled a unique place in English public life; and, as time went on, his influence would certainly have enormously increased. He was permanent; while politicians came and went, he would have been perpetually installed at the center of affairs. Who can doubt that by the end of the century, such a man, grown gray in the service of the nation, would have acquired an extraordinary prestige and power? If, in his youth, he had been able to pit the Crown against the mighty Palmerston and to come off with equal honors, of what might he not have been capable in his old age? What minister, however able, could have withstood the wisdom, the authority, of the venerable Prince?

One human being alone felt the full force of what had happened. The Baron Stockmar, by his fireside at Coburg, suddenly saw the tremendous fabric of his creation crash into ruin. Albert was gone, and he had lived in vain. Even in his blackest hypochondria he had never envisioned quite so miserable a catastrophe. He looked into the fire; he murmured that he was going where Albert was—that he would not be long. He shrank into himself. His children clustered round him and did their best to comfort him, but it was useless; the baron's heart was broken. He lingered for eighteen months, and then, with his pupil, explored the shadow and the dust.

WITH APPALLING SUDDENNESS Victoria had exchanged the serene radiance of happiness for the utter darkness of woe. In the first dreadful moments those about her feared that she might lose her reason, but the iron strain within her held firm, and in the intervals between the intense paroxysms of grief it was observed that the Queen was calm.

Yet there were moments when her anguish would brook no restraints. One day she sent for the Duchess of Sutherland, and, leading her to the Prince's room, fell prostrate before his clothes, weeping, while she adjured the duchess to tell her whether the beauty of Albert's character had ever been surpassed. At other times a feeling akin to indignation swept over her. "My *life* as a *happy* one is *ended!*" she wrote to the King of the Belgians. "The world is gone for *me!* . . . Oh! to be cut off in the prime of life—to see our pure, happy life CUT OFF at forty-two—when I *had* hoped with such instinctive certainty that God never *would* part us, and would let us grow old together—is *too awful*, too cruel!" The tone of outraged majesty seems to be discernible. Did she wonder in her heart of hearts how the Diety could have dared?

But all other emotions gave way before her overmastering determination to continue, absolutely unchanged, and for the rest of her life on earth, her reverence, her obedience, her idolatry. "I am anxious to repeat *one* thing," she told her uncle, "and *that one* is *my firm* resolve, my *irrevocable decision*, viz., that *his* wishes—*his* plans—about everything, *his* views about *every* thing are to be *my law!*"

At first, in the tumult of her distresses, she declared that she could not see her ministers. The Princess Alice, assisted by the keeper of the privy purse, Sir Charles Phipps, performed, to the best of her ability, the functions of an intermediary. After a few weeks, however, the cabinet, through Lord John Russell, ventured to warn the Queen that this could not continue.

She realized that they were right: Albert would have agreed with them; and so she sent for the Prime Minister. But when Lord Palmerston arrived at Osborne, in the pink of health, brisk, with his whiskers freshly dyed, and dressed in a brown overcoat, light gray trousers, and green gloves, he did not create a very good impression.

Nevertheless, she had grown attached to her old enemy, and the thought of a political change filled her with apprehension. The government, she knew, might fall at any moment; and therefore, six months after the death of the Prince, she took the unprecedented step of sending a private message to Lord Derby, the leader of the Opposition, to tell him that she was not in a fit state to undergo the anxiety of a change of government. If he turned the present ministers out of office, she said, it would be at the risk of sacrificing her life—or her reason. When this message reached Lord Derby he was considerably surprised. "Dear me!" was his cynical comment. "I didn't think she was so fond of them as *that.*"

Though the violence of her perturbations gradually subsided, her cheerfulness did not return. For years, she continued in settled gloom. Her life became one of almost complete seclusion. Arrayed in thickest crepe, she passed dolefully from Windsor to Osborne, from Osborne to Balmoral. Refusing to take any part in the ceremonies of state, shutting herself off from the slightest intercourse with society, she became almost as unknown to her subjects as some potentate of the East. They might murmur, but she ignored them.

She was the devoted guardian of a sacred trust. Her place was in the inmost shrine of the house of mourning—where she alone had the right to enter. That, and that only was her glorious, her terrible duty.

So the years passed. Above all else, what she had to do was to make her own the master impulse of Albert's life—she must work, as he had worked, in the service of the country. That vast burden of toil which he had taken upon his shoulders it was now for her to bear.

She assumed the gigantic load; and naturally she staggered under it. While he had lived, she had worked, indeed, with conscientiousness; but it was work made easy by his care, his forethought, and his advice. The mere sound of his voice, asking her to sign a paper, had thrilled her. But now there was a hideous change.

Now there were no neat piles and docketings under the green lamp; now there were no simple explanations of difficult matters. She had her secretaries, no doubt: there were Sir Charles Phipps, and General Grey, and Sir Thomas Biddulph; and they did their best. But they were mere subordinates: the whole weight of responsibility rested upon her alone. For so it had to be. She would follow the Prince in all things. He had refused to delegate authority; he had examined into every detail with his own eyes; he had never signed a paper without having first, not merely read it, but made notes on it too. She would do the same. She sat from morning till night surrounded by huge heaps of dispatch boxes, reading and writing at her desk—at her desk, alas! which stood alone now in the room.

Within two years of Albert's death a violent disturbance in foreign politics put Victoria's faithfulness to a crucial test. The fearful Schleswig-Holstein dispute, which had been smoldering for more than a decade, showed signs of bursting out into conflagration. The complexity of the questions at issue was indescribable. "Only three people," said Palmerston, "have ever really understood the Schleswig-Holstein business—the Prince Consort, who is dead—a German professor, who has gone mad—and I, who have forgotten all about it."

But, though the Prince might be dead, had he not left a vicegerent behind him? Victoria threw herself into the seething embroilment, devoting hours daily to the study of the affair. But she had a clue through the labyrinth: whenever the question had been discussed, Albert, she recollected, had always taken the side of Prussia. Her course was clear. She became an ardent champion of the Prussian point of view.

She did not realize that the Prussia of the Prince's day was dead. A new Prussia, the Prussia of Bismarck, had been born; and Palmerston and Lord John wished to support Denmark against Prussia's claims. But opinion was sharply divided, not only in the country but in the cabinet. For eighteen months the controversy raged; while the Queen, with persistent vehemence, opposed the Prime Minister and the Foreign Secretary.

When at last the final crisis arose—when it seemed possible that England would join forces with Denmark in a war against Prussia—Victoria's agitation grew febrile in its intensity. She poured out upon her ministers a flood of appeals and protests. "The only chance of preserving peace for Europe," she wrote, "is by not assisting Denmark, who has brought this entirely upon herself. . . . The Queen suffers much, and her nerves are more and more totally shattered." In the end England did not go to war, and Denmark was left to her fate; but how far the attitude of the Queen contributed to this result it is impossible, with our present knowledge, to say. On the whole, however, it seems probable that the determining factor in the situation was the powerful peace party in the cabinet rather than the imperious pressure of Victoria.

It is, at any rate, certain that the Queen's enthusiasm for the sacred cause of peace was short-lived. Within a few months her eyes were opened to the true nature of Prussia, whose designs upon Austria were about to culminate in the Seven Weeks' War. Veering from one extreme to the other, she now urged her ministers to interfere by force of arms in support of Austria. But she urged in vain.

Her political activity, just as much as her social seclusion, was disapproved by the public. As the years passed, and the royal mourning remained as unrelieved as ever, the disapproval grew more severe. It was observed that the Queen's protracted privacy not only cast a gloom over society, and deprived the populace of its pageantry, but also exercised a highly deleterious effect upon the dressmaking, millinery, and hosiery trades. This latter consideration carried great weight.

At last, early in 1864, the rumor spread that Her Majesty was about to go out of mourning, and there was rejoicing in the newspapers; but unfortunately it turned out that the rumor was without foundation. Victoria, with her own hand, wrote a letter to *The Times* to say so. "This idea," she declared, "cannot be too explicitly contradicted. The Queen," the letter continued, "heartily appreciates the desire of her subjects to see her. . . . But there are other and higher duties than those of mere representation which are now thrown upon the Queen, alone and unassisted—duties which she cannot neglect without injury to the public service."

The justification might have been considered more cogent had it not been known that those "other and higher duties" emphasized by the Queen consisted for the most part of an attempt to counteract the foreign policy of Lord Palmerston and Lord John Russell. A large section—perhaps a majority—of the nation were violent partisans of Denmark in the Schleswig-Holstein quarrel; and Victoria's support of Prussia was widely denounced.

A wave of unpopularity, which reminded old observers of the period preceding the Queen's marriage more than twenty-five years before, was beginning to rise. The press was rude; Lord Ellenborough attacked the Queen in the House of Lords; there were curious whispers in high quarters that she had had thoughts of abdicating—whispers followed by regrets that she had not done so. Victoria, outraged and injured, felt that she was misunderstood. "Oh, how fearful it is," she herself wrote to Lord Granville, "to be suspected—uncheered—unguided and unadvised—and how alone the poor Queen feels!"

Nevertheless, suffer as she might, she was as resolute as ever. And so, when Schleswig-Holstein was forgotten, and even the image of the Prince had begun to grow dim in the fickle memories of men, as solitary watcher she remained immutably concentrated at her peculiar task. The world's hostility, steadily increasing, was confronted and outfaced by the impenetrable weeds of Victoria. It was not mere sorrow that kept her so strangely sequestered; it was devotion, self-immolation; it was the laborious legacy of love. Unceasingly the pen moved over the black-edged paper. The flesh might be weak, but that vast burden most be borne.

TO CARRY ON Albert's work—that was her first duty; but there was another, second only to that, yet nearer, if possible, to her heart—to impress the true nature of his genius and character upon the minds of her subjects. She realized that during his life he had not been properly appreciated; the full extent of his goodness had been necessarily concealed; but death had removed the need of barriers, and now her husband, in his magnificent entirety, should stand revealed to all.

She set to work methodically. She directed Sir Arthur Helps to bring out a collection of the Prince's speeches, and the weighty tome appeared in 1862. She commanded General Grey to write an account of the Prince's early years—from his birth to his marriage; General Grey obeyed, and the work was completed in 1866. But the principal part of the story was still untold, and Mr. Theodore Martin was forthwith instructed to write a complete biography of the Prince Consort. Mr. Martin labored for fourteen years. The first bulky volume was published in 1874; four others followed; and in 1880 the monumental work was finished.

Mr. Martin was rewarded by a knighthood; and yet it was sadly evident that neither Sir Theodore nor his predecessors had achieved the purpose which the Queen had in view. Sir Theodore and the others faithfully carried out the task which she had set them—faithfully put before the public the very image of Albert that filled her own mind. The fatal drawback was that the public did not find that image attractive.

Victoria's people refused, in spite of all her efforts, to rate her husband at his true worth; and Victoria herself, disappointed and chagrined, bore a grudge against them for this. She did not understand that the picture of an embodied perfection is distasteful to the majority of mankind. The cause of this is not so much an envy of the perfect being as a suspicion that he must be inhuman; and thus it happened that the public, when it saw

displayed for its admiration a figure resembling the sugary hero of a moral storybook rather than a fellow man of flesh and blood, turned away with a shrug and a flippant smile. But in this the public was the loser as well as Victoria. For in truth Albert was a far more interesting personage than the public dreamed. By a curious irony an impeccable waxwork was fixed by the Queen's love in the popular imagination, while the creature whom it represented—the real creature, so full of stress and torment, so mysterious, so unhappy and so very human—altogether disappeared.

WORDS AND BOOKS may be ambiguous memorials; but who can misinterpret the visible solidity of bronze and stone? At Frogmore, near Windsor, Victoria constructed, at the cost of £200,000, a vast mausoleum for herself and her husband. But that was a private and domestic monument, and the Queen desired that wherever her subjects might be gathered together they should be reminded of the Prince.

Her desire was gratified; all over the country—at Aberdeen, at Perth, and at Wolverhampton—statues of the Prince were erected. Nor did London lag behind. A month after the Prince's death a meeting was called together at the Mansion House to discuss schemes for honoring his memory. Opinions, however, were divided; was a statue or an institution to be preferred? Meanwhile a subscription was opened; a committee was appointed, and the Queen was consulted as to her wishes in the matter.

In the end it was agreed that a memorial hall should be erected, together with a statue of the Prince; and eminent architects were asked to prepare designs. The architect whose design was selected was Mr. George Gilbert Scott, whose industry had brought him to the head of his profession, and whose lifelong zeal for the Gothic style had given him a special prominence. "My idea in designing the memorial," he wrote, "was to erect a kind of ciborium to protect a statue of the Prince; and its special characteristic was that the ciborium was designed in some degree on the principles of the ancient shrines." At the Queen's request a site was chosen in Kensington Gardens as near as possible to that of the Great Exhibition; and in May 1864 the first sod was turned.

The work was long and complicated; a great number of workmen were employed, besides subsidiary sculptors, while at every stage sketches and models were submitted to Her Majesty, who criticized all the details with minute care and constantly suggested improvements.

After three years of toil the memorial was still far from completion, and Mr. Scott thought it advisable to give a dinner to the workmen to show "his appreciation of their skill and energy." "Two long tables," we are told, "constructed of scaffold planks, were arranged in the workshops, and covered with newspapers, for want of tablecloths. Upwards of eighty men sat down. Beef and mutton, plum pudding and cheese, and beer and gingerbeer were supplied in abundance."

Gradually the edifice approached completion. The one hundred and seventieth life-size figure in a frieze which encircled the base of the monument was chiseled, the granite pillars arose, four colossal statues representing the greater Christian virtues, and four other colossal statues representing the greater moral virtues, were hoisted into their positions; the eight bronzes representing the greater sciences—astronomy, chemistry, geology, geometry, rhetoric, medicine, philosophy, and physiology—were fixed on their glittering pinnacles, high in air; and, eight years after its inception, in July 1872, the monument was thrown open to the public.

But four more years were to elapse before the central figure was ready to be placed under its starry canopy. It was designed by Mr. John Henry Foley, though in one particular the sculptor's freedom was restricted by Mr. Scott. "I have chosen the sitting posture," Mr. Scott said, "as best conveying the idea of dignity befitting a royal personage." To identify the figure with one of the most memorable undertakings of the Prince's life—the International Exhibition of 1851—a catalogue of the works collected in that exhibition was placed in the right hand. The statue was of bronze gilt and weighed nearly ten tons. It was rightly supposed that the simple word "Albert," cast on the base, would be a sufficient means of identification.

MR. GLADSTONE

CHAPTER 8
Mr. Gladstone and Lord Beaconsfield

LORD PALMERSTON'S LAUGH—a queer metallic "Ha! ha! ha!" with reverberations in it—was heard no more in Piccadilly; Lord John Russell dwindled into senility; old Lord Derby tottered from the stage. A new scene opened; and new protagonists—Mr. Gladstone and Mr. Disraeli—struggled together in the limelight.

Victoria watched these developments with passionate and personal interest. Mr. Gladstone had been the disciple of Sir Robert Peel and had won the approval of Albert; Mr. Disraeli had hounded Sir Robert to his fall with hideous virulence, and the Prince had pronounced that Mr. Disraeli "had not one single element of a gentleman in his composition." Yet she regarded Mr. Gladstone with distrust, while upon his rival, Mr. Disraeli, she lavished confidence, esteem, and affection.

Her attitude towards Mr. Disraeli had changed when she had found that he alone among public men had divined her feelings at Albert's death. Of the others she might have said, "They pity me and not my grief"; but Mr. Disraeli's condolences had taken the form of eulogies of the departed. The Queen declared that he was "the only person who appreciated the Prince." She began to show him special favor; gave him and his wife two of the coveted seats in St. George's Chapel at the Prince of Wales's wedding, and invited him to stay a night at Windsor.

When the grant for the Albert Memorial came before the House of Commons, Disraeli, as leader of the Opposition, eloquently supported the project. He was rewarded by a copy of the Prince's speeches, bound in white morocco, with an inscription in the royal hand. In his letter of thanks he "ventured to touch upon a sacred theme," and dwelled at length upon the absolute perfection of Albert. "The Prince," he said, "is the only person whom Mr. Disraeli has ever known who realized the Ideal." As for his own acquaintance with the Prince, it had been, he said, "one of the most satisfactory incidents of his life: full of refined and beautiful memories, and exercising over his existence a soothing and exalting influence." Victoria was much affected by "the depth and delicacy of these touches," and henceforward Disraeli's place in her affections was assured.

When, in 1866, the Conservatives came into office, Disraeli's position as Chancellor of the Exchequer and leader of the House necessarily brought him into a closer relation with the sovereign. Two years later Lord Derby resigned, and Victoria, with intense delight, welcomed Disraeli as her Prime Minister.

Only for nine agitated months did he remain in power. The ministry, in a minority in the Commons, was swept out of existence by a general election. Yet by the end of that short period the ties which bound together the Queen and her Premier had grown far stronger than ever before; the relationship between them was now no longer merely that between a grateful mistress and a devoted servant: they were friends.

His official letters developed into racy records of political news and social gossip, written, as Lord Clarendon said, "in his best novel style." Victoria was delighted; she had never, she declared, had such letters in her life. In return, she sent him bunches of flowers picked by her own hands. He dispatched to her a set of his novels, for which, she said, she was "most grateful." She herself had lately published her *Leaves from the Journal of our Life in the Highlands*, and it was observed that the Prime Minister, in conversing with Her Majesty at this period, constantly used the words "we authors, Ma'am." Upon political questions, she was his staunch supporter. And when the government was defeated in the House she was "really shocked." She again dreaded the prospect of a change; a change there had to be, and Victoria tried to console herself for the loss of her favorite minister by bestowing a peerage upon Mrs. Disraeli.

Mr. Gladstone was in his shirt sleeves at Hawarden, cutting down a tree, when the royal message was brought to him. "Very significant," he remarked, when he had read the letter, and went on cutting down his tree. His secret thoughts were more explicit. "The Almighty," he wrote in his diary, "seems to sustain and spare me for some purpose of His own, deeply unworthy as I know myself to be. Glory be to His name."

The Queen, however, did not share her new minister's view of the Almighty's intentions. She could not believe that there was any divine purpose to be detected in the program of sweeping changes which Mr. Gladstone was determined to carry out. But what could she do? Mr. Gladstone, with his powerful majority in the House of Commons, was irresistible; and for five years (1869–1874) Victoria found herself condemned to live in an atmosphere of reform—reform in the Irish Church and the Irish land system, reform in education, reform in elections, reform in the organization of the army and the navy.

She disapproved, she struggled; but her protests were unavailing. The mere effort of grappling with the mass of documents which poured in upon her was terribly exhausting. When the draft of the lengthy Irish Church Bill came before her, accompanied by an explanatory letter from Mr. Gladstone covering a dozen closely written pages, she almost despaired. At last she handed the papers to Mr. Theodore Martin, who happened to be staying at Osborne, and requested him to make a précis of them. When he had done so, her disapproval of the measure was marked; but, such was the strength of the government, she actually found herself obliged to urge moderation upon the Opposition, lest worse should ensue.

In the midst of this crisis, when the future of the Irish Church was hanging in the balance, Victoria's attention was drawn to another proposed reform. It was suggested that the sailors in the navy should henceforward be allowed to wear beards. "Has Mr. Childers ascertained anything on the subject of the beards?" the Queen wrote anxiously to the First Lord of the Admiralty. On the whole, Her Majesty was in favor of the change. "Her own personal feeling," she wrote, "would be for the beards without the moustaches." After thinking over the question for another week, she wrote a final letter. She wished, she said, "to make one additional observation, viz., that on no account should moustaches be allowed without beards. That must be clearly understood."

Changes in the navy might be tolerated; to lay hands upon the army was a more serious matter. From time immemorial there had been a particularly close connection between the army and the Crown. But now Mr. Gladstone's fiat went forth, and the commander in chief was to be removed from his direct dependence upon the sovereign, and made subordinate to Parliament. Of all the liberal reforms this was the one which aroused the bitterest resentment in Victoria. But she was helpless, and the Prime Minister had his way. When she heard that the dreadful man had yet another reform in contemplation—that he was about to abolish the purchase of military commissions—she could only feel that it was just what might have been expected.

Unacceptable as were Mr. Gladstone's policies, there was something else about him which was even more displeasing to Victoria. She disliked his personal demeanor towards herself. It was not that Mr. Gladstone, in his manner towards her, was in any degree lacking in respect. On the contrary, an extraordinary reverence impregnated his manner with the sovereign. Indeed, Mr. Gladstone viewed Victoria through a haze of awe which was almost religious—as a sacrosanct embodiment of venerable traditions—a vital element in the British constitution—a Queen by Act of Parliament. But unfortunately the lady did not appreciate the compliment. The well-known complaint which Victoria is supposed to have made—"He speaks to me as if I were a public meeting"—whether authentic or no, undoubtedly expresses the essential element of her antipathy. She had no objection to being considered as an institution; she was one, and she knew it. But she was a woman too, and to be considered *only* as an institution—that was unbearable.

Thus all Mr. Gladstone's zeal and devotion, his ceremonious phrases, his low bows, were utterly wasted; and when, in the excess of his loyalty, he went further, and imputed to the object of his veneration the subtlety of intellect, the wide reading, the grave enthusiasm, which he himself possessed, the misunderstanding became complete. The discordance between the actual Victoria and this strange divinity made in Mr. Gladstone's image produced disastrous results. Her discomfort turned at last into positive animosity, and, though her manners continued to be perfect, she never for a moment unbent; while he on his side was overcome with disappointment and perplexity.

Yet his fidelity remained unshaken. When the cabinet met,

the Prime Minister would open the proceedings by reading aloud the letters which he had received from the Queen upon the questions of the hour. The assembly sat in absolute silence while, one after another, the royal missives boomed forth in all the deep solemnity of Mr. Gladstone's utterance. Not a single comment was ever hazarded; and, after a fitting pause, the cabinet proceeded with the business of the day.

LITTLE AS Victoria appreciated her Prime Minister's attitude towards her, she found that it had its uses.

The popular discontent at her uninterrupted seclusion had been gathering force for many years, and now burst out in a new and alarming shape. Republicanism was in the air. Radical opinion in England, stimulated by the fall of Napoleon III, suddenly grew more extreme than it ever had been since 1848. The monarchy was attacked. And it was attacked at a vital point: it was declared to be too expensive.

What benefits, it was asked, did the nation reap to counterbalance the enormous sums which were expended upon the sovereign? Victoria's retirement gave an unpleasant handle to the argument. It was pointed out that the ceremonial functions of the Crown had virtually lapsed; and the awkward question remained whether any of the other functions which it did perform were really worth £385,000 per annum. The royal balance sheet was examined. An anonymous pamphlet entitled *What does she do with it?* appeared, setting forth the financial position with malicious clarity. The Queen, it stated, was granted by the Civil List £60,000 a year for her private use; but the rest of her vast annuity was given, as the Act declared, to enable her "to defray the expenses of her royal household and to support the honor and dignity of the Crown." Now it was obvious that, since the death of the Prince, the expenditures for both these purposes must have been considerably diminished, and it was difficult to resist the conclusion that a large sum of money was diverted annually to swell the private fortune of Victoria.

Though it is certain that estimates of Victoria's riches were much exaggerated, it is equally certain that she was an exceedingly wealthy woman. She probably saved £20,000 a year from the Civil List, she had inherited a considerable property from the Prince Consort, and she had been left, in 1852, an estate of half a million by Mr. John Neild, an eccentric miser. In these circumstances it was not surprising that when, in 1871, Parliament was asked to vote a dowry of £30,000 to the Princess Louise on her marriage with the son of the Duke of Argyle, together with an annuity of £6000, there should have been a serious outcry.

In order to conciliate public opinion, the Queen opened Parliament in person, and the vote was passed. But a few months later another demand was made: Prince Arthur had come of age, and the nation was asked to grant him an annuity of £15,000. The outcry was redoubled.

Towards every aspect of this distasteful question, Mr. Gladstone presented an iron front. He absolutely discountenanced the extreme section of his followers. He declared that the whole of the Queen's income was justly at her personal disposal, argued that to complain of royal savings was merely to encourage royal extravagance, and successfully convoyed through Parliament the unpopular annuities, which, he pointed out, were strictly in accordance with precedent. Victoria was relieved; but she grew no fonder of Mr. Gladstone.

It was perhaps the most miserable moment of her life. The ministers, the press, the public, all conspired to vex her, to blame her, to misinterpret her actions. She was "a cruelly misunderstood woman," she told Mr. Martin, declaring to him that "the great worry and anxiety and hard work for ten years, alone, unaided, with increasing age and never very strong health" were breaking her down.

The situation was indeed deplorable. It seemed as if her whole existence had gone awry; as if an irremediable antagonism had grown up between the Queen and the nation. If Victoria had died in the early seventies, there can be little doubt that the voice of the world would have pronounced her a failure.

BUT SHE WAS RESERVED for a very different fate. The outburst of republicanism had been in fact the last flicker of an expiring cause. The liberal tide, which had been flowing steadily ever since the 1830's, had reached its height; and the inevitable ebb began. In the general election of 1874, Mr. Gladstone and the Liberals were routed; and the Tory party, for the first time in over forty years, attained an unquestioned supremacy. Their triumph was preeminently due to Disraeli. He returned to office, no longer the dubious commander of an insufficient host, but with drums beating and flags flying, a conquering hero. And as a conquering hero Victoria welcomed her new Prime Minister.

There followed six years of excitement, of enchantment, of glory, of romance. The amazing being, who now at last, at the age of seventy, after a lifetime of extraordinary struggles, had turned into reality the absurdest of his boyhood's dreams, knew well enough how to make his own, with absolute completeness, the heart of the Sovereign Lady. In women's hearts he had always read as in an open book; the more curious they were, the more intimately at home with them he seemed to be.

He surveyed Queen Victoria with the eye of a past master; and he was not for a moment at a loss. He realized everything—the interacting complexities of circumstance and character, the personal arrogance, the emotionalism, the laborious respectability shot through so incongruously by cravings for the colored and the strange, the singular intellectual limitations, and the mysteriously essential female elements impregnating every particle of the whole. A smile hovered over his impassive features, and he dubbed Victoria "the Faery." The allusion to Edmund Spenser's great poem *Faerie Queene* was very pleasant—the elegant evocations of Gloriana, Queen of Fairyland; but there was more in it than that: there was the suggestion of a diminutive creature, endowed with magical—and mythical—properties.

The Faery, he determined, should henceforward wave her wand for him alone. Bowing low with Oriental gravity, he set himself to his task. He had understood from the first that in dealing with the Faery the appropriate method of approach was the very antithesis of the Gladstonian; and such a method was naturally his. It was not his habit to harangue and exhort in official conscientiousness; he liked to scatter flowers along the path of business; to compress a weighty argument into a happy phrase, to insinuate what was in his mind with an air of friendship. He was nothing if not personal; and he had perceived that personality was the key that opened the Faery's heart.

Accordingly, he never for a moment allowed his intercourse with her to lose the personal tone; he invested all the transactions of state with the charms of familiar conversation; she was always the royal lady, the adored and revered mistress, he the devoted and respectful friend. When once the personal relation was firmly established, every difficulty disappeared. But to maintain that relation uninterruptedly in a smooth and even course a particular care was necessary: the bearings had to be most assiduously oiled. Nor was Disraeli in any doubt as to the nature of the lubricant. "You have heard me called a flatterer," he said to Matthew Arnold, "and it is true. Everyone likes flattery; and when you come to royalty you should lay it on with a trowel."

He practiced what he preached; his adulation was incessant, and he applied it in the very thickest slabs. "There is no honor and no reward," he declared, "that with him can ever equal the possession of your Majesty's kind thoughts." "In life," he told her, "one must have for one's thoughts a sacred depository, and Lord Beaconsfield* ever presumes to seek that in his Sovereign Mistress." She was not only his own solitary support; she was the one prop of the state. "If your Majesty is ill," he wrote during a grave political crisis, "he is sure he will himself break down. All, really, depends upon your Majesty." "He lives only for Her," he asseverated, "and works only for Her, and without Her all is lost."

Such tributes were delightful, but they remained in the nebulous region of words, and Disraeli had determined to give his blandishments a more significant solidity. He deliberately encouraged Victoria to hold high views of her own position. He professed to a belief that the constitution gave the sovereign a leading place in the councils of government, and he emphatically declared that there ought to be "a real Throne." His pronouncements upon the subject were indistinct; but the vagueness of his language was in itself an added stimulant to Victoria.

---

* Disraeli took the name Beaconsfield when he was granted a peerage in 1876. (Editors' note.)

Skillfully confusing the woman and the Queen, he threw, with a grandiose gesture, the government of England at her feet. In his first audience after returning to power, he assured her that "whatever she wished should be done." When the Public Worship Regulation Bill was being discussed by the cabinet, he told the Faery that his "only object" was "to further your Majesty's wishes in this matter." When he brought off his great coup of buying the controlling share of the Suez Canal for England, he used expressions which implied that the only gainer by the transaction was Victoria. "It is just settled," he wrote in triumph; "you have it, Madam!"

Nor did he limit himself to highly spiced insinuations. Writing with all the authority of his office, he advised the Queen that she had the constitutional right to dismiss a ministry which was supported by a large majority in the House of Commons. To the horror of Mr. Gladstone, he not only kept the Queen informed as to the general course of business in the cabinet, but revealed to her the part taken in its discussions by individual members of it. Lord Derby, the son of the late Prime Minister and Disraeli's Foreign Secretary, viewed these developments with grave mistrust. "Is there not," he ventured to write to his chief, "just a risk of encouraging her in too large ideas of her personal power? I only ask; it is for you to judge."

As for Victoria, she accepted everything—compliments, flatteries, prerogatives—without a single qualm. After the long gloom of her bereavement, after the chill of the Gladstonian discipline, she expanded to the rays of Disraeli's devotion like a flower in the sun. The change in her situation was indeed miraculous. No longer was she obliged to puzzle for hours over the complicated details of business, for now she had only to ask Mr. Disraeli for an explanation and he would give it her in the most concise, amusing way. He was surely the most fascinating of men. The strain of charlatanism, which had unconsciously captivated her in Napoleon III, exercised the same enchanting effect in the case of Disraeli. She became intoxicated, entranced. Believing all that he told her of herself, she completely regained the self-confidence which had been slipping away from her throughout the dark period that followed Albert's death.

Under the compelling influence, her very demeanor altered. Her short, stout figure, with its folds of black velvet, its muslin streamers, its heavy pearls at the heavy neck, assumed an almost menacing air. In her countenance, from which the charm of youth had long since vanished, and which had not yet been softened by age, the traces of grief and of displeasure were still visible, but they were overlaid by looks of arrogance and sharp lines of hauteur. But, when Mr. Disraeli appeared, the expression changed in an instant, and the forbidding visage became charged with smiles.

For him she would do anything. Yielding to his encouragements, she began to emerge from her seclusion; she appeared at hospitals and concerts; she opened Parliament; she reviewed troops. But such public signs of favor were trivial in comparison with her private attentions. During his hours of audience, she could hardly restrain her delight. "I can only describe my reception," he wrote to a friend on one occasion, "by telling you that I really thought she was going to embrace me. She was wreathed with smiles, and, as she tattled, glided about the room like a bird."

In his absence, she talked of him perpetually, and there was a note of unusual vehemence in her solicitude for his health. She often sent him presents; an illustrated album arrived for him regularly from Windsor on Christmas Day. But her most valued gifts were the bunches of spring flowers which were gathered by herself and her ladies in the woods at Osborne. Among these it was, he declared, the primroses that he loved best. "They show," he told her, "that your Majesty's sceptre has touched the enchanted Isle." He sat at dinner with heaped-up bowls of them on every side and told his guests that "they were all sent to me this morning by the Queen from Osborne, as she knows it is my favorite flower."

As time went on, and as it became clearer and clearer that the Faery's thralldom was complete, his protestations grew steadily more highly colored and more unabashed. At last he ventured to import into his blandishments a strain of adoration that was almost romantic. He addressed her as "the most loved and illustrous being," as the "Sovereign whom he adores."

Did he smile as he uttered such words? Perhaps; and yet it would be rash to conclude that his declarations were altogether without sincerity. Detachment he possessed in a supreme degree. Nonetheless, actor and spectator both, the two characters were so intimately blended together in him that they formed an inseparable unity, and it was impossible to say that one of them was less genuine than the other. When he wrote to a lady about the court, "I love the Queen—perhaps the only person in this world left to me that I do love," was he not creating for himself an enchanted palace out of the Arabian Nights, in which he actually believed? Victoria's state of mind was far more simple; untroubled by imaginative yearnings, she never confused feeling and fancy. Her emotions, with all their exaggeration, retained the prosaic texture of everyday life. She was, she told her Prime Minister, at the end of an official letter, "yours aff'ly V.R. and I." In such a phrase the deep reality of her feeling is instantly manifest. The Faery's feet were on the solid earth; it was the artful cynic who was in the air.

He had taught her, however, a lesson, which she had learned with alarming rapidity. In May 1874 the Tsar was in London following the marriage of his daughter to Victoria's second son. By an unfortunate error, it had been arranged that his departure should not take place until two days after the date on which his royal hostess had previously decided to go to Balmoral. Her Majesty refused to modify her plans. It was pointed out to her that the Tsar would certainly be offended, that the most serious consequences might follow, but the Faery was unconcerned; she had settled to go to Balmoral on the 18th, and on the 18th she would go.

At last Disraeli, exercising all his influence, induced her to agree to stay in London for two days more. "My head is still on my shoulders," he told Lady Bradford. "The great lady has postponed her departure! Everybody had failed, even the Prince of Wales; . . . Salisbury says I have saved an Afghan War."

But before very long, on another issue, the triumph was the Faery's. Disraeli, who had suddenly veered towards a new imperialism, had thrown out the suggestion that the Queen of England ought to become the Empress of India. Victoria seized upon the idea with avidity, and pressed it upon her Prime Minister. He demurred; but she was not to be balked; and in 1876, in spite of his unwillingness, he found himself obliged to add to the troubles of a stormy session by introducing a bill for the alteration of the royal title. His compliance, however, finally conquered the Faery's heart. The measure was angrily attacked in both Houses, and Victoria was deeply touched by the untiring energy with which Disraeli defended it.

At last the affair was successfully concluded, Victoria was proclaimed Empress of India, and the triumph was celebrated in a suitable manner. On the day of the Delhi proclamation, the Prime Minister went to Windsor to dine with the new Empress of India. That night the Faery, usually so homely in her attire, appeared in a glittering panoply of enormous uncut jewels, which had been presented to her by the reigning Princes of her *raj*. At the end of the meal Disraeli, breaking through the rules of etiquette, arose, and in a flowery oration proposed the health of the Queen-Empress. His audacity was well received, and his speech was rewarded by a smiling curtsy.

These were significant episodes; but a still more serious manifestation of Victoria's temper occurred in the following year during the crowning crisis of Disraeli's life. His growing imperialism, his desire to magnify the power and prestige of England, had brought him into collision with Russia. The terrible Eastern Question loomed up, and when war broke out between Russia and Turkey, the gravity of the situation became extreme.

The Prime Minister's policy was fraught with difficulty. Realizing perfectly the appalling implications of an Anglo-Russian war, he was yet prepared to face even that eventuality if he could obtain his ends; but he believed that Russia in reality was still less desirous of a rupture, and that, if he played his game with sufficient adroitness, she would yield all that he required without a blow.

It was clear that the course he had marked out for himself was full of hazard, and demanded an extraordinary nerve. But nerve he had never lacked. He began his diplomatic egg dance with high assurance. And then he discovered that, besides the

Russian government, besides the Liberals and Mr. Gladstone, there were two additional sources of perilous embarrassment with which he would have to reckon. In the first place there was a strong party in the cabinet, headed by Lord Derby, the Foreign Secretary, which was unwilling to take the risk of war; but his culminating anxiety was the Faery.

From the first, her attitude was uncompromising. The old hatred of Russia surged up within her; she remembered Albert's prolonged animosity; she felt the prickings of her own greatness; and she flung herself into the turmoil with passionate heat.

Her indignation with the Opposition—with anyone who ventured to sympathize with the Russians in their quarrel with the Turks—was unbounded. When anti-Turkish meetings were held in London, she considered that "the Attorney General ought to be set at these men. . . . It can't," she exclaimed, "be constitutional." Never in her life, not even in the crisis over the ladies of the bedchamber, did she show herself a more furious partisan. But her displeasure was not reserved for the Radicals; the backsliding Conservatives equally felt its force. She was even discontented with Disraeli himself. Failing entirely to appreciate the delicate complexity of his policy, she constantly assailed him with demands for vigorous action, interpreted each finesse as a sign of weakness, and was ready at every juncture to let slip the dogs of war.

As the situation developed, her anxiety grew feverish. "The Faery," Disraeli told Lady Bradford, "writes every day and telegraphs every hour; this is almost literally the case."

"The Queen," Victoria wrote, "is feeling terribly anxious lest delay should cause us to be too late and lose our prestige for ever!" She raged loudly against the Russians. "The language," she cried, "the insulting language—used by the Russians against us! It makes the Queen's blood boil!" "Oh," she wrote later, "if the Queen were a man, she would like to go and give those Russians, whose word one cannot believe, such a beating!"

The unfortunate Prime Minister, urged on to violence by Victoria on one side, had to deal, on the other, with a Foreign Secretary who was fundamentally opposed to any policy of interference at all. Between the Queen and Lord Derby he held

a harassed course. He gained, indeed, some slight satisfaction in playing off the one against the other—in stimulating each to attack the other. But this only gave a temporary relief; and it soon became evident that Victoria's martial ardor was not to be sidetracked by hostilities against Lord Derby; hostilities against Russia were what she wanted. Casting aside the last relics of moderation, she began to attack her friend with a series of extraordinary threats. Not once but many times she held over his head the formidable menace of her abdication. "If England," she wrote to Disraeli, "is to kiss Russia's feet, she will not be a party to the humiliation of England and would lay down her crown." When the Russians advanced to the outskirts of Constantinople she fired off three letters in a day demanding war; and when she learned that the cabinet had only decided to send the fleet to Gallipoli she declared that "her first impulse" was "to lay down the thorny crown, which she feels little satisfaction in retaining if the position of this country is to remain as it is now."

It is easy to imagine the agitating effect of such a correspondence upon Disraeli. This was no longer the Faery; it was a genie whom he had rashly called out of her bottle, and who was now intent upon showing her supernal power. More than once, dispirited, shattered by illness, he had thoughts of withdrawing altogether from the game.

He held on, however, to emerge victorious at last. The Queen was pacified; Lord Derby was replaced by Lord Salisbury; and at the Congress of Berlin he carried all before him. But soon there was an unexpected reverse. At the general election of 1880 the country, mistrustful of the forward policy of the Conservatives, returned the Liberals to power.

Victoria was horrified, but within a year she was to be yet more nearly hit. The grand romance had come to its conclusion. Disraeli, worn out with age and maladies, but moving still, an assiduous mummy, from dinner party to dinner party, suddenly moved no longer.

When she knew that the end was inevitable, she seemed, by a pathetic instinct, to divest herself of her royalty, and to shrink, with hushed gentleness, beside him, a woman and nothing more. "I send some Osborne primroses," she wrote to him with touching simplicity, "and I meant to pay you a little visit this week, but I thought it better you should be quite quiet. And I beg you will be very good and obey the doctors." She would see him, she said, "when we come back from Osborne, which won't be long." "Everyone is so distressed at your not being well," she added; and she was, "Ever yours very aff'ly, V.R.I."

When the royal letter was given him, the strange old comedian, stretched on his bed of death, poised it in his hand, appeared to consider deeply, and then whispered to those about him, "This ought to be read to me by a privy councillor."

JOHN BROWN

CHAPTER 9
Old Age

MEANWHILE IN Victoria's private life many changes had taken place. With the marriages of her elder children her family circle widened; grandchildren appeared; and a multitude of new interests sprang up.

The death of King Leopold in 1865 had removed the predominant figure of the older generation, and the functions he had performed as the center of a large group of relatives in Germany and in England devolved upon Victoria. These functions she discharged with industry, carrying on an enormous correspondence and following every detail in the lives of the ever-ramifying cousinhood. She also took a particular delight in her grandchildren, though she could be, when the occasion demanded it, severe. The eldest of them, little Prince Wilhelm of Prussia, was a remarkably headstrong child. Once, when she told him to bow to a visitor, he disobeyed her outright. The order was repeated, and the naughty boy, noticing that his grandmama had suddenly turned into a most terrifying lady, submitted, and bowed very low indeed.

It would have been well if all the Queen's domestic troubles could have been got over as easily. Among her more serious distresses was the conduct of the Prince of Wales, who was now independent and married; and beginning to do as he liked.

Victoria's worst fears seemed to be justified when in 1870 he appeared as a witness in a society divorce case. Clearly the heir to the throne had been mixing with people of whom she did not approve. What was to be done? She saw that it was not only her son that was to blame—that it was the whole system of society; and so she dispatched a letter to Mr. Delane, the editor of *The Times*, asking him if he would "frequently *write* articles pointing out the *immense* danger and evil of the wretched frivolity and levity of the views and lives of the Higher Classes."

More and more did she find refreshment in her Highland domain; and twice yearly, in spring and in autumn, she set her face northwards, in spite of the protests of ministers, who murmured vainly in the royal ears that to transact the affairs of state over an interval of six hundred miles added considerably to the cares of government. Her ladies, too, felt occasionally a slight reluctance to set out, for the pilgrimage was not without its drawbacks. The royal railway train remained for long immune from modern conveniences, and when it drew up, on some moorland, far from any platform, the high-bred dames were obliged to descend to earth by the perilous footboard.

But Victoria cared for none of these things. She was only intent upon regaining, with the utmost swiftness, her enchanted castle. And it was not only the place that she loved; she was equally attached to "the simple mountaineers," from whom, she said, "she learned many a lesson of resignation and faith." Smith and Grant and Ross and Thompson—she was devoted to them all; but, beyond the rest, she was devoted to John Brown.

Brown, the Prince's attendant, had now become the Queen's personal attendant—a body servant from whom she was never parted, who accompanied her on her drives, waited on her during the day, and slept in a neighboring chamber at night. She liked his strength, his solidity, the sense he gave her of physical security; she even liked his rugged manners and speech. She allowed him to take liberties with her which would have been unthinkable from anybody else. To bully the Queen, to order her about, to reprimand her—who could dream of venturing upon such audacities? And yet, when she received such treatment from John Brown, she positively seemed to enjoy it.

The eccentricity appeared to be extraordinary; but, after all, it is no uncommon thing for an autocratic dowager to allow some trusted servant to adopt towards her an attitude of authority. When Victoria meekly obeyed the abrupt commands of her henchman to get off her pony or put on her shawl, people might wonder. She could not help that; this was the manner in which it pleased her to act.

John Brown had, too, in her mind, a special connection with Albert. In their expeditions the Prince had always trusted him more than anyone; the gruff, kind, hairy Scotsman was, she felt, in some mysterious way, a legacy from the dead. She came to believe at last—or so it appeared—that the spirit of Albert was nearer when Brown was near. Often, when seeking inspiration over some complicated political question, she would gaze with deep concentration at her late husband's bust. But it was also noticed that sometimes in such moments of doubt Her Majesty's looks would fix themselves upon John Brown.

Eventually, the "simple mountaineer" became almost a state personage. The influence which he wielded was not to be overlooked. Disraeli himself was careful, from time to time, to send courteous messages to "Mr. Brown" in his letters to the Queen, and the French government took particular pains to provide for his comfort during the visits of the English sovereign to France. It was only natural that among the elder members of the royal family he should not have been popular, and that his failings—for failings he had, including too acute an appreciation of Scotch whisky—should have been the subject of comment at court. But he served his mistress faithfully, and to ignore him would be a sign of disrespect in her biographer.

The Queen herself, far from making a secret of her affectionate friendship, took care to publish it to the world. By her orders two gold medals were struck in Brown's honor; and on his death, in 1883, a long and eulogistic obituary notice of him appeared in the *Court Circular*. In the second series of extracts from the Queen's *Highland Journal*, published in 1884, her "devoted personal attendant and faithful friend" appears upon almost every page, and is in effect the hero of the book. With a remarkable absence of reticence, Victoria seemed to demand, in this private matter, the sympathy of the whole nation; and yet—such is the world!—there were those who actually treated the relations between their sovereign and her servant as a theme for ribald jests.

THE BUSY YEARS hastened away; and old age, approaching, laid a gentle hold upon Victoria. The gray hair whitened; the mature features mellowed; the short firm figure amplified and moved more slowly, supported by a stick. And, simultaneously, in the whole tenor of the Queen's existence an extraordinary transformation came to pass. The nation's attitude towards her, critical and even hostile as it had been for so many years, altogether changed; and there was a corresponding alteration in the temper of Victoria's own mind.

Many causes led to this result. Among them were the repeated strokes of personal misfortune which befell the Queen during a cruelly short space of years. In 1878 her daughter Alice, who had married in 1862 the Prince Louis of Hesse-Darmstadt, died [of diphtheria]. In the following year the Prince Imperial, the only son of the Empress Eugénie, to whom Victoria had become devotedly attached, was killed in the Zulu War. Two years later, in 1881, she lost Disraeli, and, in 1883, John Brown. In 1884 her son Leopold, who had been an invalid from birth, also died. Victoria's cup of sorrows was indeed overflowing; and the public, as it watched the widowed mother weeping for her children and her friends, displayed a constantly increasing sympathy.

An event which occurred in 1882 revealed and accentuated the feelings of the nation. As the Queen, at Windsor, was walking from the train to her carriage, a youth named Roderick Maclean fired a pistol at her from a few yards away. An Eton boy struck up Maclean's arm before the pistol went off; no damage was done, and the culprit was at once arrested.

This was the last of a series of seven attempts upon the Queen—attempts which, taking place over a period of forty years, resembled one another in a curious manner. All, with a single exception, were perpetrated by adolescents, none of whose pistols was loaded. In 1842 an Act had been passed making any attempt to hurt the Queen a misdemeanor, punishable by transportation for seven years, or imprisonment for three years. Subsequent attempts were all dealt with under this new law; but Roderick Maclean's attempt in 1882 was treated differently. On this occasion the pistol was found to have been loaded; public indignation, emphasized as it was by Victoria's growing popularity, was great.

But it was not only through the feelings—commiserating or indignant—of personal sympathy that the Queen and her people were being drawn more nearly together; they were beginning, at last, to come to a close agreement upon the conduct of public affairs. Mr. Gladstone's second administration (1880–1885) was a succession of failures, ending in disaster and disgrace; liberalism fell into discredit, and Victoria perceived with joy that her distrust of her ministers was shared by an ever-increasing number of her subjects.

During the crisis in the Sudan, the popular temper was her own. She had been among the first to urge the necessity of an expedition to Khartoum, and, when the news came of the catastrophic death of General Gordon, her voice led the chorus of denunciation against the government. It was even rumored that she had sent for Lord Hartington, the Secretary of State for War, and vehemently upbraided him. "She rated me," he was reported to have told a friend, "as if I'd been a footman." "Why didn't she send for the butler?" asked his friend. "Oh," was the reply, "the butler generally manages to keep out of the way on such occasions."

But the day came when it was impossible for the butler to keep out of the way any longer. Mr. Gladstone was defeated, and resigned. Victoria, at a final interview, received him with her usual amenity, but, besides the formalities demanded by the occasion, the only remark she made to him was to the effect that she supposed he would now require some rest.

Such was Mr. Gladstone's exit; and then, in the general election of 1886, the majority of the nation showed decisively that Victoria's politics were now identical with theirs. Casting the contrivers of Home Rule into outer darkness, they placed Lord Salisbury in power. Victoria's satisfaction was profound.

A flood of new hopefulness swept over her, stimulating her vital spirits with a surprising force, and she threw herself vigorously into a multitude of public activities. She appeared at drawing rooms, at concerts, at reviews; she laid foundation stones; she went to Liverpool to open an exhibition, driving in her open carriage in heavy rain amid vast applauding crowds. Delighted by the welcome which met her everywhere, she warmed to her work; she visited Edinburgh, where the ovation of Liverpool was repeated and surpassed; and in London, seated on a gorgeous throne of hammered gold, she opened in high state the Colonial and Indian Exhibition.

Next year was the fiftieth of her reign, and in June the anniversary was celebrated in solemn pomp. Victoria, surrounded by the highest dignitaries of her realm, escorted by a glittering galaxy of kings and princes, drove through the crowded enthusiasm of the capital to render thanks to God in Westminster Abbey. In that triumphant hour the last remaining traces of past antipathies and disagreements were altogether swept away. The Queen was hailed at once as the mother of her people and as the embodied symbol of their imperial greatness; and she responded to the double sentiment with all the ardor of her spirit. At last, after so long, happiness had returned to her. The unaccustomed feeling filled and warmed her consciousness. When, at Buckingham Palace again, the long ceremony over, she was asked how she was, "I am very tired, but very happy," she said.

AND SO, after the toils and tempests of the day, a long evening followed—mild, serene, and lighted with a golden glory. For an atmosphere of success and adoration invested the last period of Victoria's life. The solid splendor of the decade between Victoria's two jubilees can hardly be paralleled in the annals of England; the country seemed to settle down, with calm assurance, to the enjoyment of an established grandeur. And—it was only natural—Victoria settled down too.

Her own existence came to harmonize more and more with what was around her. Gradually, the image of Albert receded. It was not that he was forgotten—that would have been impossible—but that the void created by his absence grew less agonizing, and even, at last, less obvious. And, as Albert's figure slowly faded, its place was taken, inevitably, by Victoria's own. Her egotism proclaimed its rights; and her force of character, emerging at length in all its plenitude, imposed itself absolutely upon its environment by conscious effort.

It was in her family that Victoria's ascendency reached its highest point. All her offspring were married; the number of her descendants rapidly increased; there were many marriages in the third generation; and no fewer than thirty-seven of her great-grandchildren were living at the time of her death. Over all of this family she ruled with a most potent sway. The small concerns of the youngest aroused her passionate interest; and the oldest she treated as if they were children still. The Prince of Wales, in particular, stood in tremendous awe of his mother. It could not be denied that he enjoyed himself—out of her sight; but, in that redoubtable presence, his abounding manhood suffered a miserable eclipse. Once, at Osborne, when he was late for a dinner party, he was observed standing behind a pillar, wiping the sweat from his forehead, trying to nerve himself to go up to the Queen. When at last he did so, she gave him a stiff nod, whereupon he vanished immediately behind another pillar, and remained there until the party broke up. At the time of this incident the Prince of Wales was over fifty years of age.

With no Albert to guide her, with no Disraeli to inflame her, Victoria at last grew willing to abandon the dangerous questions of diplomacy to the wisdom of her Prime Minister, Lord Salisbury. She concentrated her energies upon objects which touched her more nearly. Her home—her court—the monuments at Balmoral—the livestock at Windsor—such matters played now an even greater part in her existence than before. Every moment of her day was mapped out beforehand; the dates of her journeys —to Osborne, to Balmoral, to the South of France—were hardly altered from year to year. She demanded from those who surrounded her a rigid precision in details. Unpunctuality was one of the most heinous of sins. But sometimes somebody was unpunctual; then her dreadful displeasure became all too visible. At such moments there seemed nothing surprising in her having been the daughter of a martinet.

But these storms, unnerving as they were while they lasted, were quickly over, and they grew more and more exceptional. With the return of happiness a gentle benignity flowed from the aged Queen. Her smile, once so rare, flitted over her features with an easy alacrity; the blue eyes beamed; the whole face brightened and softened and cast an unforgettable charm over those who watched it. For in her last years there was a fascination in Victoria's amiability which had been lacking even from the vivid impulse of her youth. Over all who approached her—or nearly all—she threw a peculiar spell. Her grandchildren adored her; her ladies waited upon her with a reverential love. The honor of serving her obliterated a thousand inconveniences.

What, above all, seemed to make such service delightful was the detailed interest which the Queen took in those around her. She became the confidante of the household affairs of her ladies; her sympathies reached out to the palace domestics; even the housemaids and scullions—so it appeared—were the objects of her searching inquiries, and of her heartfelt solicitude when their lovers were ordered to a foreign station, or their aunts suffered from an attack of rheumatism.

Nevertheless the due distinctions of rank were preserved. Every evening after dinner the Queen's guests were still led up to her one after the other, and, while duologue followed duologue, the rest of the assembly stood still, without a word. Only in one particular was the severity of the etiquette allowed to lapse. Throughout the greater part of the reign the rule had been absolute that ministers must stand during their audiences with the Queen. When Lord Derby, as Prime Minister, had had an audience with Her Majesty after a serious illness, he mentioned afterwards, as a proof of the royal favor, that the Queen had remarked "How sorry she was she could not ask him to be seated." Once Disraeli, after an attack of gout, had been offered a chair; but he had thought it wise humbly to decline the privilege. In her later years, however, the Queen invariably asked Mr. Gladstone and Lord Salisbury to sit down.

Sometimes the solemnity of the evening was diversified by a concert, an opera, or even a play, for now Victoria resumed—after an interval of thirty years—her old custom of commanding dramatic companies from London to perform before the court at Windsor. On such occasions her spirits rose high. She loved acting; she loved a good plot; above all, she loved a farce. Engrossed by everything that passed upon the stage she would follow, with childlike innocence, the unwinding of the story. Her sense of humor was of a vigorous though primitive kind. She could roar with laughter, in the privacy of her household, over some small piece of fun—some oddity of an ambassador, or some ignorant minister's faux pas. When the jest grew subtle she was less pleased; but, if it approached the confines of the indecorous, the danger was serious. To say something improper called down at once Her Majesty's most crushing disapprobation. Then the royal lips sank down at the corners, the royal eyes stared in astonished protrusion. The transgressor shuddered into silence, while the awful "We are not amused" annihilated the dinner table.

In general, her aesthetic tastes had remained unchanged since the days of Mendelssohn and Sir Edwin Landseer. She still delighted in the roulades of Italian opera; she still demanded a high standard in the execution of a pianoforte duet. Her views on painting were decided; Sir Edwin, she declared, was perfect. As for literature, she was devoted to Lord Tennyson.

But as a rule the leisure hours of that active life were occupied with recreations more tangible than the study of literature or art. Victoria was a woman not only of vast property but of innumerable possessions. She had inherited an immense quantity of furniture, of ornaments, of china; her purchases, throughout a long life, made a formidable addition to these stores; and there flowed in upon her, besides, from every quarter of the globe, a constant stream of gifts. Over this enormous mass she exercised an unceasing supervision, and the contemplation of it, in all its details, filled her with an intimate satisfaction.

When she considered the multitudinous objects which belonged to her, she saw herself reflected from a million facets, and was well pleased. But then came the dismaying thought—everything slips away, crumbles, vanishes; Sèvres dinner services get broken; golden basins go unaccountably astray; even one's self, with all the recollections and experiences that make up one's being, fluctuates, perishes, dissolves. . . . But no! It could not, should not be so! There should be no changes, no losses! Nothing should ever move—neither the past nor the present—and she herself least of all! And so the tenacious woman, hoarding her valuables, decreed their immortality. She would not lose one memory or one pin.

She gave orders that nothing should be thrown away—and nothing was. There, in drawer after drawer, in wardrobe after wardrobe, reposed the dresses of seventy years. But not only the dresses—the furs, the muffs, the parasols, and the bonnets—all were ranged in chronological order, dated and complete. A great cupboard was devoted to the dolls; in the china room at Windsor a special table held the mugs of her childhood, and her children's mugs as well. Mementos of the past surrounded her in serried accumulations. In every room the tables were powdered thick with the photographs of relatives; their figures, in solid marble, rose up from pedestals, or gleamed from brackets in the form of statuettes. The dead, in every shape—in miniatures, in porcelain, in oil paintings—were perpetually about her. John Brown stood upon her writing table in solid gold. Her favorite horses and dogs, endowed with a new durability, crowded round her in silver and in bronze. And it was not enough that each particle of the past should be given the stability of metal or of marble: the whole collection, in its arrangement, was immutably fixed. There might be additions, but there might never be alterations. To ensure this, every article in the Queen's possession was photographed from several points of view. These photographs were placed in a series of albums. Then, opposite each photograph, an entry was made, indicating the number of the article, the room in which it was kept, and its exact position in the room. The fate of every object which had undergone this process was henceforth irrevocably sealed. And Victoria, with a gigantic volume or two of the endless catalogue always beside her, to look through, to ponder upon, could feel, with contentment, that the transitoriness of this world had been arrested by the amplitude of her might.

Thus the collection, ever multiplying, became one of the dominating influences of her existence. And it was a collection not merely of things but also of thoughts, of states of mind. The celebration of anniversaries grew to be an important branch of it—of birthdays and marriage days and death days. Especially around the circumstance of death commemorative cravings clustered thickly. On a certain day, for instance, flowers must be strewn on John Brown's monument at Balmoral.

Every bed in which Victoria slept had attached to it, at the back, on the right-hand side, above the pillow, a photograph of the head and shoulders of Albert as he lay dead, surmounted by a wreath of immortelles. And the suite of rooms which Albert had occupied in Windsor Castle was kept for ever shut away. Within those precincts everything remained as it had been at the Prince's death. Victoria had also commanded that her husband's clothing should be laid afresh, each evening, upon the bed, and that, each evening, the water should be set ready in the basin, as if he were still alive; and this incredible rite was performed with scrupulous regularity for nearly forty years.

Such was the inner worship; and still the daily hours of labor proclaimed Victoria's consecration to duty and to the ideal of the dead. Yet, with the years, the sense of self-sacrifice faded; the natural energies of that ardent being discharged themselves with satisfaction into the channel of public work. In her old age, to have been cut off from her papers would have been, not a relief, but an agony to Victoria.

Thus the whole process of government continued, till the very end, to pass before her. Nor was that all; ancient precedent had made the validity of an enormous number of official transactions dependent upon the application of the royal signature; and a great proportion of the Queen's working hours was spent in this mechanical task. At last, when the increasing pressure of business made the delays of the antiquated system intolerable, she consented that, for certain documents, her oral sanction should be sufficient. Each paper was read aloud to her, and she said at the end, "Approved." Often, for hours at a time, she would sit, with Albert's bust in front of her, while the word "Approved" issued at intervals from her lips. The word came forth with a majestic sonority; for her voice now—how changed from the silvery treble of her girlhood!—was a contralto, full and strong.

THE FINAL YEARS WERE YEARS OF apotheosis. Criticism fell dumb; deficiencies were ignored; and in the dazzled imagination of her subjects Victoria soared aloft towards the regions of divinity through a nimbus of purest glory.

That the nation's idol was a very incomplete representative of the nation was hardly noticed, and yet it was conspicuously true. For the vast changes which, out of the England of 1837, had produced the England of 1897, seemed scarcely to have touched the Queen. The immense industrial and scientific development of the period, the significance of which had been so thoroughly understood by Albert, meant little indeed to Victoria. Her conception of the universe, and of man's place in it remained, throughout her life, entirely unchanged. Her religion was the religion which she had learned from the Baroness Lehzen and the Duchess of Kent. She seemed to feel most at home in the simple faith of the Presbyterian Church of Scotland. For many years Dr. Norman Macleod, an innocent Scotch minister, was her principal spiritual adviser; and, when he was taken from her, she drew much comfort from quiet chats about life and death with the cottagers at Balmoral.

From the social movements of her time Victoria was equally remote. Towards the smallest no less than towards the greatest changes she remained inflexible. During her youth and middle age smoking had been forbidden in polite society, and so long as she lived she would not withdraw her anathema against it. Kings might protest; bishops and ambassadors, invited to Windsor, might be reduced, in the privacy of their bedrooms, to lie full-length upon the floor and smoke up the chimney—the interdict continued.

It might have been supposed that a female sovereign would have lent her countenance to one of the most vital of all the reforms to which her epoch gave birth—the emancipation of women—but, on the contrary, the mere mention of such a proposal sent the blood rushing to her head. In 1870, her eye having fallen upon the report of a meeting in favor of Women's Suffrage, she wrote to Mr. Theodore Martin in royal rage—"The Queen is most anxious to enlist everyone who can speak or write to join in checking this mad, wicked folly of 'Woman's

Rights.' Lady——ought to get a *good whipping*. It is a subject which makes the Queen so furious that she cannot contain herself. . . . The Queen is sure that Mrs. Martin agrees with her." The argument was irrefutable; Mrs. Martin agreed; and yet the canker spread.

In another direction Victoria's comprehension of the spirit of her age has been constantly asserted. It was for long the custom for polite historians to compliment the Queen upon the correctness of her attitude towards the constitution. But such praises seem hardly justified by the facts. In her later years Victoria alluded with regret to her conduct during the bedchamber crisis and let it be understood that she had grown wiser since. Yet in truth it is difficult to trace any fundamental change either in her theory or her practice in constitutional matters throughout her life.

The same despotic spirit which led her to break off the negotiations with Peel is equally visible in her animosity towards Palmerston and in her threats of abdication to Disraeli. The complex and delicate principles of the constitution cannot be said to have come within the compass of her mental faculties; and in the actual developments which it underwent during her reign she played a passive part. From 1840 to 1861 the power of the Crown steadily increased in England; from 1861 to 1901 it steadily declined. The first process was due to the influence of Prince Albert, the second to that of a series of great ministers. Perhaps, difficult as Victoria found it to distinguish clearly between the trivial and the essential, she was only dimly aware of what was happening. At the end of her reign, the Crown was weaker than at any other time in English history. Paradoxically enough, Victoria received the highest eulogies for assenting to this political evolution; yet, had she completely realized its import, the evolution would have filled her with supreme displeasure.

But if, in all these ways, the Queen and her epoch were profoundly separated, the points of contact between them also were not few. Victoria understood very well the meaning and the attraction of power and property, and in such learning the English nation, too, had grown to be more and more proficient.

During the last fifteen years of the reign imperialism was the dominant creed of the country. It was Victoria's as well.

Under Disraeli's tutelage the British dominions over the seas had come to mean much more to her, and, in particular, she had grown enamored of the East. India fascinated her; she learned a little Hindustani; she engaged some Indian servants who became her inseparable attendants, and one—Munshi Abdul Karim—eventually almost succeeded to the position which had once been John Brown's.

At the same time, the imperialist temper of the nation invested her office with a new significance. For imperialism is a faith as well as a business; as it grew, the mysticism in English public life grew with it; and simultaneously a new importance began to attach to the Crown. The need for a symbol—a symbol of England's might, of England's extraordinary destiny—became felt more urgently. The Crown was that symbol: and the Crown rested upon the head of Victoria. Thus it happened that while by the end of the reign the power of the sovereign had appreciably diminished, the prestige of the sovereign had enormously grown.

Yet this prestige was not merely the outcome of public changes; it was an intensely personal matter, too. Victoria was the Queen of England, the Empress of India—but how much more besides! For one thing, she was of a great age—an almost indispensable qualification for popularity in England. She had given proof of persistent vitality—she had reigned for sixty years, and she was not out. And then, she was a character. The outlines of her nature were firmly drawn. The great majority of the nation prized goodness above every other human quality; and Victoria, who had said that she would be good at the age of twelve, had kept her word.

Such qualities were obvious and important; but, in the impact of a personality, it is something deeper, something fundamental and common to all its qualities, that really tells. In Victoria, it is easy to discern the nature of this underlying element: it was a peculiar sincerity. Her truthfulness, her single-mindedness, the vividness of her emotions and her unrestrained expression of them, were the varied forms which this central characteristic assumed. "She talks all out," Lady Lyttelton, the royal governess, once said, "just as it is, no more and no less." She talked all out, without reserve; and she wrote all out, too. Undoubtedly it was through this kind of writing that she touched the heart of the public. Not only in her *Highland Journals*, where the mild chronicle of her private proceedings was laid bare without a trace of affectation or of embarrassment, but also in those remarkable messages to the nation which, from time to time, she published in the newspapers, her people found her very close to them indeed. They felt instinctively Victoria's irresistible sincerity, and they responded.

The little old lady, with her white hair and her plain mourning clothes, in her wheeled chair or her donkey carriage—one saw her so; and then—close behind—with their immediate suggestion of mystery, and of power—the Indian servants.

That was the familiar vision, and it was admirable; but, at chosen moments, it was right that the widow of Windsor should step forth apparent Queen. The last and the most glorious of such occasions was the Jubilee of 1897. Then, as the splendid procession escorted Victoria through the thronged reechoing streets of London, the greatness of her realm and the adoration of her subjects blazed out together. The tears welled to her eyes, and, while the multitude roared round her, "How kind they are to me! How kind they are!" she repeated over and over again. That night her message flew over the Empire: "From my heart I thank my beloved people. May God bless them!"

The long journey was nearly done. But the traveler, who had come so far, and through such strange experiences, moved on with the old unfaltering step. The girl, the wife, the aged woman, were the same: vitality, conscientiousness, pride, and simplicity were hers to the latest hour.

THE EVENING had been golden; but, after all, the day was to close in cloud and tempest. Imperial needs, imperial ambitions, involved the country in the South African War. There were checks, reverses, bloody disasters; for a moment the nation was shaken. But the Queen's spirit was high, and neither her courage nor her confidence wavered for a moment. Throwing herself heart and soul into the struggle, she interested herself in every detail of the hostilities, and sought by every means in her power to render service to the national cause.

In April 1900, when she was in her eighty-first year, she made the extraordinary decision to abandon her annual visit to the South of France, and to go instead to Ireland, which had provided a large number of recruits to the armies in the field. She stayed for three weeks in Dublin, driving through the streets, in spite of the warnings of her advisers, without an armed escort; and the visit was a complete success. But, in the course of it, she began, for the first time, to show signs of the fatigue of age.

Though in periods of depression she had sometimes supposed herself an invalid, Victoria had in reality throughout her life enjoyed remarkably good health. In her old age, she had suffered from a rheumatic stiffness of the joints, which had necessitated the use of a stick, and, eventually, a wheeled chair; but no other ailments attacked her, until, in 1898, her eyesight began to be affected by incipient cataract. In the summer of 1900, however, more serious symptoms appeared. Her memory now sometimes deserted her; there was a tendency towards aphasia.

While no specific disease declared itself, by the autumn there were signs of a general physical decay. Yet, even in these last months, the strain of iron held firm; the daily work continued. By midwinter, however, the last remains of her ebbing strength had almost deserted her. On January 14, she had at Osborne an hour's interview with Lord Roberts, the victorious general who had just returned from South Africa. She inquired into all the details of the war; she appeared to sustain the exertion successfully; but, when the audience was over, there was a collapse.

On the following day her medical attendants recognized that her state was hopeless; and yet, for two days more, the indomitable spirit fought on; for two days more she discharged the duties of a Queen of England. But after that there was an end of working. The brain was failing, and life was gently slipping away. Her family gathered round her; for a little more she lingered, speechless and apparently insensible; and, on January 22, 1901, she died.

When, two days previously, the news of the approaching end had been made public, astonished grief had swept over the country. The vast majority of her subjects had never known a time when Queen Victoria had not reigned over them. She had become an indissoluble part of their whole scheme of things, and that they were about to lose her appeared a scarcely possible thought.

She herself, as she lay blind and silent, seemed to those who watched her to be divested of all thinking—to have glided already, unawares, into oblivion. Yet, perhaps, in the secret chambers of consciousness, she had her thoughts, too. Perhaps her fading mind called up once more the shadows of the past to float before it, and retraced, for the last time, the vanished visions of that long history—passing back and back, through the cloud of years, to older and ever older memories—to the spring woods at Osborne, so full of primroses for Mr. Disraeli—to Lord Palmerston's queer clothes and high demeanor, and Albert's face under the green lamp, and Albert's first stag at Balmoral, and Albert in his blue and silver uniform, and the baron coming in through a doorway, and Lord Melbourne dreaming at Windsor with the rooks cawing in the elm trees, and the Archbishop of Canterbury on his knees in the dawn, and Uncle Leopold's soft voice at Claremont, and Lehzen with the globes, and her mother's feathers sweeping down towards her, and a great old repeater watch of her father's in its tortoiseshell case, and a yellow rug, and some friendly flounces of sprigged muslin, and the trees and the grass at Kensington.

ILLUSTRATION CREDITS

LIFE OF CHRIST: *Photographs of the Holy Land: Pages 6, 51:* Countryside outside Jerusalem, John Bryson, Rapho Guillumette Pictures. *13:* Bethlehem, Charles Harbutt, Magnum Photos, Inc. *19:* Ancient Nazareth, Dr. Glauboch, Photo Researchers, Inc. *30:* Negev, Dr. Georg Gerster, Rapho Guillumette Pictures. *38:* Galilee, P. Larsen, Photo Researchers, Inc. *59:* Storm on Sea of Galilee, Israel Sun from Pix. *83:* Sheep grazing at Nazareth, Charles Harbutt, Magnum Photos, Inc. *122:* Garden of Gethsemane. *146:* Jerusalem, Israel Sun from Pix. *171:* Ascension, Louis Goldman, Rapho Guillumette Pictures. *Works of art: Page 7:* "Nativity of Christ" (carved oak panel, Franco-Flemish, early 16th century), The Metropolitan Museum of Art, The Cloisters Collection, 1950. *9 front view, 172 rear view:* Bury St. Edmunds Cross (12th-century English), The Metropolitan Museum of Art, The Cloisters Collection, 1963. *11:* "Holy Family at Work," M. 917, *The Book of Hours of Catherine of Cleves*, M-p. 149, The Pierpont Morgan Library. *23:* Adam and Eve Laboring (stone relief, Wiligelmo, 12th century) façade of the Cathedral, Modena. *28:* "Baptism of Christ" (enamel plaque, 12th-century Mosan), The Metropolitan Museum of Art, Gift of J. Pierpont Morgan, 1917. *34:* "The Temptation of Christ" (woodcut, Christoffel Jegher, after Rubens), The Metropolitan Museum of Art, Rogers Fund, 1917. *43:* Christ (11th-century medallion, cloisonné enamel on gold, part of a set from the ikon of San Gabriel Monastery at Jumati in Georgia, U.S.S.R.), The Metropolitan Museum of Art, Gift of J. Pierpont Morgan, 1917. *54:* "The Healing of the Blind Man and the Raising of Lazarus" (fresco, 12th-century Spanish), The Metropolitan Museum of Art, The Cloisters Collection, Gift of the Clowes Fund, Inc., and Elijah B. Martindale, 1959. *62:* "The Samaritan at the Well" (mosaic), San Apollinare Nuovo, Ravenna; photo: European Art Color, Peter Adelberg, N.Y.C. *73:* Architrave of the doorway from San Leonardo al Frigido (circa 1175), The Metropolitan Museum of Art, The Cloisters Collection, 1962. *80:* Christ teaching (carved stone relief, 12th-century French), façade of the Abbey Sainte Madeleine, Vézelay. *87:* Washing of feet (woodcut, 15th century), reproduced from an 1859 facsimile version of *Biblia pauperum*, 1465 block book in the British Museum, Rare Book Division, The New York Public Library, Astor, Lenox and Tilden Foundations. *95:* "Entry into Jerusalem" (carved oak panel, Franco-Flemish, early 16th century), The Metropolitan Museum of Art, The Cloisters Collection, 1950. *108:* "The Kiss of Judas" (woodcut from the *Small Passion*, 1509–1511, by Albrecht Dürer). *121:* "Christ Receiving Cup on Mount of Olives" (scene from back of altarpiece "Maesta," by Duccio di Buoninsegna), Museo dell'Opera del Duomo, Siena; photo: European Art Color, Peter Adelberg, N.Y.C. *133:* Pilate Washing His Hands (carved wood panel, Franco-Flemish, from Jumièges), The Metropolitan Museum of Art, The Cloisters Collection, 1950. *145:* Crucifix (12th-century Spanish), The Metropolitan Museum of Art, The Cloisters Collection, Samuel D. Lee Fund, 1935. *155:* "The Chalice of Antioch" (early Christian, 4th or 5th century), The Metropolitan Museum of Art, The Cloisters Collection, 1950. *161:* "Supper at Emmaus" (mosiac), Monreale Cathedral, Sicily; photo: European Art Color, Peter Adelberg, N.Y.C. *170:* Emperor Otto I offering a model of Magdeburg Cathedral to Christ in Majesty (carved ivory, 10th century), The Metropolitan Museum of Art, Gift of George Blumenthal, 1941.

THE HOUSE OF EXILE: *Pages 230–231, 242, 256, 267, 292, 317, 324:* Tony Chen. *233, 241, 250, 257, 269, 288, 300, 313:* Maggie Linn. *234, 236, 245, 254, 261, 272, 275, 278, 283, 286, 297, 309, 319, 331:* Lin Chia Li. *247, 248, 259, 262, 270, 284, 310, 314, 326, 332:* Harry McNaught. *264, 276, 280, 290, 298, 303, 306, 320:* Joseph Giordano.

Good Night, Sweet Prince: *Pages 345* top left and right, bottom right; *358* top right, bottom right; *372* top left, bottom left and right; *381* top center and right, bottom left; *389; 397; 400; 404; 407* right; *413* center left and right, bottom; *418* bottom right; *425* right; *431* top right; *434, 439:* Culver Pictures, Inc. *345* bottom left: Free Library of Philadelphia Theatre Collection. *358* top left: Jane Parlan. *358* bottom left: Museum of the City of New York. *372* top right; *381* center right (MGM), bottom right (Columbia Pictures); *418* top left (Warner Bros.) and right (Columbia Pictures), bottom left (MGM); *425* left (Columbia Pictures); *431* top left, bottom left and right; *442* (Twentieth Century Fox): From the collection of Penguin Photo. *381* top left: The Bettmann Archive. *407* left; *413* top: Wide World Photos.